CORE CONCEPTS IN CRIMINAL LAW AND CRIMINAL JUSTICE

Volume I

Attempts at trans-jurisdictional debate and agreement are often beset by mutual misunderstanding. Professionals and academics engaged in comparative criminal law sometimes use the same terms with different meanings or different terms which mean the same thing. Although English is the new lingua franca in international and comparative criminal law, there are many ambiguities and uncertainties with regard to foundational criminal law and criminal justice concepts.

However, significant commonalities exist among diverse systems of criminal law and justice. This book explores the foundational principles and concepts that underpin different domestic systems. It focuses on Germany and several Anglo-American jurisdictions, which serve as examples of the common law and civil law systems.

Kai Ambos has a Chair for Criminal Law, Criminal Procedure, Comparative Law and International Criminal Law at the University of Göttingen, Germany and is acting director of the Institute of Criminal Law and Justice. He is Judge at the Kosovo Specialist Chambers in The Hague; Advisor (amicus curiae) of the Colombian Special Jurisdiction for Peace; Director of the Centro de Estudios de Derecho Penal y Procesal Penal Latinoamericano (CEDPAL); editor-in-chief Criminal Law Forum, Life Member Clare Hall College, University of Cambridge. He has been visiting professor in several universities in Italy, Portugal, Spain and Latin America and research fellow in Oxford and Cambridge. His main research lies in criminal law and procedure, comparative law, and international criminal law with a regional focus on Latin America, Portugal, Spain and Eastern Europe.

Antony Duff is Professor Emeritus at the University of Stirling, where he taught from 1970 to 2009. From 2010 to 2015 he held a half-time chair in the University of Minnesota Law School, where he was a founding co-director of the Robina Institute of Criminal Law and Criminal Justice. He is a Fellow of the British Academy and of the Royal Society of Edinburgh, and holds honorary doctorates from the Universities of Oslo and Edinburgh.

Julian Roberts is a professor of Criminal Justice at the Centre of Criminology, University of Oxford and Executive Director of the Sentencing Academy of England and Wales. He has been a Visiting Professor at the University of Haifa; University of Minnesota; Cambridge University; Kings College School of Law, London; Université Libre de Bruxelles; Dipartimento di Giurisprudenza, L'Universita di Ferrara, and the Catholic University of Leuven.

Thomas Weigend (Dr jur, University of Freiburg, Germany) until 2016 served as a professor of criminal law and criminal procedure at the University of Cologne (Germany). He taught as a visiting professor at several universities including the University of Tokyo, New York University, Peking University and the University of Bologna. Most of his research has been dedicated to basic questions of criminal justice and policy, (comparative) criminal procedure and international criminal law.

Alexander Heinze is an Assistant Professor at the University of Göttingen School of Law. He holds a PhD in International Criminal Law, was awarded the Trinity College Alumni scholarship and received his Magister in Utroque Jure (LLM) from Trinity College, Dublin with distinction. His research and publications (in English and German) deal with various aspects of comparative law, media law, international criminal procedure, legal theory, philosophy and sociology of law. Alexander Heinze is an elected member of the International Law Association Committee on Complementarity in International Criminal Law, co-editor of the *German Law Journal* and book review editor of the *Criminal Law Forum*.

CORE CONCEPTS IN CRIMINAL LAW AND CRIMINAL JUSTICE

Anglo-German Dialogues
Volume I

General Editor

KAI AMBOS

Georg-August University, Göttingen, Germany

Editors

ANTONY DUFF (CRIMINAL LAW)

University of Stirling, Scotland

JULIAN ROBERTS (CRIMINAL JUSTICE)

University of Oxford, England

THOMAS WEIGEND (CRIMINAL PROCEDURE)

University of Cologne, Germany

Assistant Editor

ALEXANDER HEINZE

Georg-August University, Göttingen, Germany

CAMBRIDGE
UNIVERSITY PRESS

CAMBRIDGE
UNIVERSITY PRESS

University Printing House, Cambridge CB2 8BS, United Kingdom

One Liberty Plaza, 20th Floor, New York, NY 10006, USA

477 Williamstown Road, Port Melbourne, VIC 3207, Australia

314–321, 3rd Floor, Plot 3, Splendor Forum, Jasola District Centre, New Delhi - 110025, India

79 Anson Road, #06–04/06, Singapore 079906

Cambridge University Press is part of the University of Cambridge.

It furthers the University's mission by disseminating knowledge in the pursuit of education, learning, and research at the highest international levels of excellence.

www.cambridge.org
Information on this title: www.cambridge.org/9781108483391
DOI: 10.1017/9781108649742

First published 2020

A catalogue record for this publication is available from the British Library.

ISBN 978-1-108-48339-1 Hardback

CONTENTS

PREFACE

This volume is the first of three (for now) to emerge from the *Anglo-German Dialogue project* (which is described in the Introduction). The chapters are based on drafts that were discussed at a series of biannual workshops (see https://www.department-ambos.uni-goettingen.de/index.php/anglo-german-dialogue). We are very grateful to all the participants in those workshops, both for their helpful comments on the draft papers and for their central role in defining and developing the project. We are also indebted to Alexander Heinze whose coordination and editorial work was indispensable for the preparation of this volume. We are also very grateful to the Göttingen Association for Comparative and International Criminal Law and Criminal Justice, the Fritz Thyssen Foundation, and the Universities of Cambridge, Göttingen, Oxford, Frankfurt a. M., Edinburgh, Zurich and Rutgers for the funding that made these workshops and future meetings possible. Finally, we express our thanks to the staff of Cambridge University Press, particularly Finola O'Sullivan, for their help and encouragement over the course of the project.

ABBREVIATIONS

A2d	Atlantic Reporter, Second Series
ABA	American Bar Association
Abs.	Absatz (paragraph)
AC	Appeals Chamber/Law Reports Appeal Cases/Appeal Cases
ACLU	American Civil Liberties Union
AG	Amtsgericht
All ER	All England Law Reports
BayObLG	Bayerisches Oberstes Landesgericht (Highest Regional Court of Bavaria)
BGBl	Bundesgesetzblatt (Federal Law Gazette)
BGH	Bundesgerichtshof (German Federal Supreme Court)
BGHR StGB	BGH-Rechtsprechung in Strafsachen
BGHSt	Entscheidungen des Bundesgerichtshofes in Strafsachen (Decisions of German Federal Court of Justice, Official Collection)
BT-Drs	Bundestags-Drucksache
BVerfG	Bundesverfassungsgericht (German Constitutional Court)
BVerfGE	Entscheidungen des Bundesverfassungsgerichts (Decisions of the Constitutional Court, Official Collection)
BvR	Bundesverfassungsgericht, Verfahren über Verfassungsbeschwerden nach Art. 93 Abs. 1 Nr. 4a sowie über Kommunalverfassungsbeschwerden nach Art. 93 Abs. 1 Nr. 4b GG (Federal and Regional Constitutional Complaints according to Article 93(1) No. 4a and 4b of the German Constitutional Court Act)
CC	Criminal Code
CCP	Code of Criminal Procedure
CP	Code Pénal, Código Penal, Codice Penale (French, Spanish, Portuguese, and Italian Criminal Code)
CPS	Crown Prosecution Service
Cr. App. R.	Criminal Appeal Reports
Crim. LR	Criminal Law Review

DPP	Director of Public Prosecutions
ECHR	European Convention on Human Rights
ECtHR	European Court of Human Rights
EWCA Crim.	England & Wales Court of Appeal Criminal Division
F2d	Federal Reporter, Second Series
F3d	Federal Reporter, Third Series
Fed. R. Crim. P.	Federal Rules of Criminal Procedure
FJP	Fair and Just Prosecution
GG	Grundgesetz (German Basic Law, Constitution)
GVG	Gerichtsverfassungsgesetz (Court Organisation Act)
HC col.	House of Commons, Column (Hansard citation)
HCJAC	High Court of Justiciary Appeal Court
ICC	International Criminal Court
ICTR	International Criminal Tribunal for Rwanda
ICTY	International Criminal Tribunal for the Former Yugoslavia
IPBPR	Internationaler Pakt über bürgerliche und politische Rechte (International Covenant on Civil and Political Rights, ICCPR)
JCCP	Japanese Code of Criminal Procedure
JCE	joint criminal enterprise
KB	King's Bench
KG	Kammergericht (Berlin High Regional Court)
LECrim	Ley de Enjuiciamiento Criminal (Spanish Criminal Procedure Code)
LG	Landgericht (District Court)
LK-StGB	Leipziger Kommentar zum Strafgesetzbuch
mn.	margin number
MPC	Model Penal Code (American Law Institute)
MRK	Menschenrechtskonvention (ECHR)
NICA	Northern Ireland Court of Appeal
NIQB	Northern Ireland Queen's Bench Division
NJW	Neue Juristische Wochenschrift (Journal)
NStZ	Neue Zeitschrift für Strafrecht (Journal)
NStZ-RR	Neue Zeitschrift für Strafrecht - Rechtsprechungsreport (Journal)
OLG	Oberlandesgericht (Higher Regional Court)
PACE	Police and Criminal Evidence Act 1984
PAL	parasitic accessorial liability
POA	Prosecution of Offences Act
QB	Law Reports Queen's Bench
RGSt	Entscheidungen des Reichsgericht in Strafsachen (Decisions of the Supreme Court of the German Reich, Official Collection)

RiStBV	Richtlinien für das Strafverfahren und das Bußgeldverfahren (Guidelines for Criminal and Administrative Proceedings)
RStPO	Reichsstrafprozessordnung (Criminal Procedure Code of the Reich)
SCA	Serious Crime Act
SCR	Supreme Court Reports (Canada)
SK-StGB	Systematischer Kommentar zum Strafgesetzbuch
StA	Staatsanwaltschaft (German Prosecution Service)
StGB	Strafgesetzbuch (German Criminal Law Code)
StPO	Strafprozessordnung (German Criminal Procedure Code)
StV	Strafverteidiger (Journal)
UKHL	United Kingdom House of Lords
UKSC	United Kingdom Supreme Court
USAM	United States Attorneys' Manual
USC	United States Code
USSC	US Supreme Court
VereinsG	Gesetz zur Regelung des öffentlichen Vereinsrechts (German Law on Associations)
WLR	Weekly Law Reports

CONTRIBUTORS

Kai Ambos has a Chair for Criminal Law, Criminal Procedure, Comparative Law and International Criminal Law at the University of Göttingen, Germany and is acting director of the Institute of Criminal Law and Justice. He is Judge at the Kosovo Specialist Chambers in The Hague; Advisor (amicus curiae) of the Colombian Special Jurisdiction for Peace; Director of the Centro de Estudios de Derecho Penal y Procesal Penal Latinoamericano (CEDPAL); editor-in-chief Criminal Law Forum, Life Member Clare Hall College, University of Cambridge. He has been visiting professor in several universities in Italy, Portugal, Spain and Latin America and research fellow in Oxford and Cambridge. His main research lies in criminal law and procedure, comparative law, and international criminal law with a regional focus on Latin America, Portugal, Spain and Eastern Europe.

Stefanie Bock is a Professor of Criminal Law, Criminal Procedure, International Criminal Law and Comparative Law at the Philipps University, Marburg, Germany, and the Acting Director of the International Research and Documentation Centre for War Crimes Trials. Her main fields of research are international criminal law, European criminal law, comparative law and victims' rights.

Dominik Brodowski is Junior Professor of Criminal Law and Criminal Procedure at Saarland University, Saarbrücken. His main fields of research are Criminal Justice and Digitalisation, European Criminal Justice, and the Foundations and Frontiers of Criminal Justice. He is a Senior Fellow at the Carol and Lawrence Zicklin Center for Business Ethics Research, The Wharton School, University of Pennsylvania, and was Visiting Professor at the University of São Paulo Law School, Campus Ribeirão Preto.

Andrew Cornford is a Lecturer in Law at the University of Edinburgh. His research interests lie within criminal law and legal theory. His work to date has mostly focused on the substantive criminal law, especially questions of criminalisation. He previously studied at the Universities of Warwick, Oxford and Southampton.

Antje du Bois-Pedain is Reader in Criminal Law and Philosophy in the Faculty of Law and Deputy Director of the Centre for Penal Theory and Penal Ethics in the Institute of Criminology, University of Cambridge. Following earlier work on transitional justice, published inter alia in a monograph, *Transitional Amnesty in South Africa* (Cambridge University Press, 2007) and an edited collection on *Justice and Reconciliation in Post-Apartheid South Africa* (Cambridge University Press, 2008), her research has concentrated on the justification of criminal justice practices, where recent publications include co-edited volumes on *Criminal Law and the Authority of the State* (Hart, 2017) and on *Penal Censure: Engagements within and Beyond Desert Theory* (Hart, 2019).

Antony Duff is Professor Emeritus at the University of Stirling, where he taught from 1970 to 2009. From 2010 to 2015 he held a half-time chair in the University of Minnesota Law School, where he was a founding co-director of the Robina Institute of Criminal Law and Criminal Justice. He is a Fellow of the British Academy and of the Royal Society of Edinburgh, and holds honorary doctorates from the Universities of Oslo and Edinburgh.

Richard Frase is the Benjamin Berger Professor of Criminal Law at the University of Minnesota. He has also taught in French and German law schools under Minnesota's international exchange programmes. His principal research interests are Minnesota and other state sentencing guidelines, punishment and proportionality theories, comparative criminal procedure, cross-national comparative sentencing, and comparative sentencing within the United States (between states).

Shannon Fyfe is an Assistant Professor of Philosophy at George Mason University, where she is also a Fellow in the Institute for Philosophy and Public Policy, and an Adjunct Professor at the Antonin Scalia Law School. She holds both a PhD in philosophy and a JD from Vanderbilt University. She recently published *International Criminal Tribunals: A Normative Defense* (with Larry May) (Cambridge University Press, 2017).

Stefan Harrendorf is Professor of Criminology, Criminal Law, Criminal Procedure and Comparative Criminal Law and Justice at the University of Greifswald. His research interests lie in the fields of crime and criminal justice systems in international comparison, minor offences, criminal careers, reconviction, violent crime, preventive detention, sanctioning, pre-trial detention and penology. Stefan Harrendorf is a founding member of the European Sourcebook of Criminal Justice e.V. and member of the European Sourcebook of Crime and Criminal Justice Statistics experts group. He is co-editor of the *Criminal Law Forum* and the *European Journal on Criminal Policy and Research.*

Alexander Heinze is an Assistant Professor at the University of Göttingen School of Law. He holds a PhD in International Criminal Law, was awarded the Trinity College Alumni scholarship and received his Magister in Utroque Jure (LLM) from Trinity College, Dublin with distinction. His research and publications (in English and German) deal with various aspects of comparative law, media law, international criminal procedure, legal theory, philosophy and sociology of law. Alexander Heinze is an elected member of the International Law Association Committee on Complementarity in International Criminal Law, co-editor of the *German Law Journal* and book review editor of the *Criminal Law Forum.*

Elisa Hoven is a Professor of Criminal Law and Criminal Procedure Law at the University of Leipzig. She worked as Visiting Professional at the International Criminal Court in The Hague and for the Civil Parties at the Extraordinary Chambers in the Courts of Cambodia. She was a Visiting Scholar at Pannasastra University in Phnom Penh, at the Lauterpacht Centre for International Law at the University of Cambridge, at the War Crimes Studies Center at the University of California, Berkeley, at Harvard University and at the University of California, Los Angeles. Her main research interests are in the fields of national and international criminal law and criminal policy.

Carsten Momsen is Professor of Criminal Law, Criminal Procedure, Corporate and Environmental Criminal Law at the Freie University, Berlin. His research focuses on (comparative) criminal procedure (Germany, USA/Canada), criminal justice reform, white-collar crimes, substantive criminal law, criminal law in sports, digital evidence and cybercrimes. He is Permanent Member of the Program Committee of the International Conference on Systematic Approaches on Digital Forensic Engineering and Director of the 'FU Law Clinic – Practice of Criminal Defense'.

Tom O'Malley is a Senior Lecturer in Law at NUI Galway, Ireland, a practising barrister and a member of the Irish Law Reform Commission. His main research interests are in the fields of criminal law, sentencing and constitutional law. He is the author of ten books including *Sentencing Law and Practice*, 3rd edn (Dublin, 2016); *Sexual Offences*, 2nd edn (Dublin, 2013); *Sentencing: Towards a Coherent Approach* (Dublin, 2011); and *The Criminal Process* (Dublin, 2009). He is currently chairing a government-appointed Review Group on the investigation, prosecution and trial of sexual offences.

Anneke Petzsche is a Senior Research Fellow and Lecturer at Humboldt University, Berlin. Her research interests lie in criminal law, criminal procedural law and European criminal law. Her PhD thesis, published in 2013, focused on German, English and Spanish anti-terrorism law and she has published various articles on the subject of terrorism. She holds a law degree from Humboldt University and a Master of Criminology and Criminal Justice from Oxford University.

Julian Roberts is a professor of Criminal Justice at the Centre of Criminology, University of Oxford and Executive Director of the Sentencing Academy of England and Wales. He has been a Visiting Professor at the University of Haifa; University of Minnesota; Cambridge University; Kings College School of Law, London; Université Libre de Bruxelles; Dipartimento di Giurisprudenza, L'Universita di Ferrara, and the Catholic University of Leuven.

Findlay Stark is a University Senior Lecturer in the Faculty of Law, University of Cambridge, and a Fellow of Jesus College, Cambridge. His publications include *Culpable Carelessness: Recklessness and Negligence in the Criminal Law* (Cambridge University Press, 2016) and (with Simester et al.), *Simester and Sullivan's Criminal Law: Theory and Doctrine*, 7th edn (Hart/Bloomsbury, 2019).

Carl-Friedrich Stuckenberg is Professor of German and International Criminal Law and Criminal Procedure, Comparative Criminal Law and Criminal Law History, Rheinische Friedrich Wilhelms University, Bonn.

Stephen C. Thaman (J.D., University of California, Berkeley; Dr. iur, University of Freiburg, Germany) is Professor of Law Emeritus at Saint Louis University, USA. He is the author of *Comparative Criminal Procedure: A Casebook Approach* (2nd edn 2008), editor of *World Plea Bargaining* (Carolina Acad. Press, 2010) and *Exclusionary Rules in Comparative Perspective* (Springer, 2013), and co-editor of *Comparative Criminal Procedure* (Elgar, 2016). He was an Assistant Public Defender in Alameda County, California, from 1976 to 1987.

Jenia Turner is the Amy Abboud Ware Centennial Professor in Criminal Law at SMU Dedman School of Law, where she teaches and writes about US and comparative criminal procedure, international criminal law and international law. She is the author of *Plea Bargaining across Borders* (Wolters Kluwer, 2009) and a co-editor of *The Oxford Handbook of Criminal Process* (Oxford University Press, 2019) and *Criminal Procedures: Cases, Statutes, and Executive Materials* (Wolters Kluwer, 2019).

Sarah Lisa Washington is a public defense attorney with the Bronx Defenders in New York City. Her LLM studies at Columbia Law School were focused on criminal law and racial justice. Sarah earned her first law degree from Humboldt University in Berlin where she was awarded a full scholarship. She is a senior research assistant and PhD candidate at the Free University. Her research focuses on racial justice, comparative criminal law and procedure (USA/Germany).

Thomas Weigend (Dr jur, University of Freiburg, Germany) until 2016 served as a professor of criminal law and criminal procedure at the University of Cologne (Germany). He taught as a visiting professor at several universities including the University of Tokyo, New York University, Peking University and the University of Bologna. Most of his research has been dedicated to basic questions of criminal justice and policy, (comparative) criminal procedure and international criminal law.

Lucia Zedner is Senior Research Fellow at All Souls College and Professor in the Law Faculty, University of Oxford. She is also Conjoint Professor, Law Faculty, University of New South Wales, Sydney since 2007. She was elected a Fellow of The British Academy in 2012, as an Overseas Fellow of the Australian Academy of Law in 2015 and presently serves on the Fachbeirat of the Max Planck Institute for Foreign and International Criminal Law, Freiburg.

PART I

Introduction

1

Introductory Remarks

KAI AMBOS, ANTONY DUFF, JULIAN ROBERTS AND THOMAS WEIGEND

I The Need for a Comparative Conceptual Analysis

Criminal law and criminal justice are becoming increasingly globalised. In open societies, the era in which individual jurisdictions developed their own codes, statutes and systems of justice with no regard to other systems and countries is long over. There is a growing desire to develop common approaches to common problems and to learn from the diversity of current practice in different countries. This development has been reinforced by the internationalisation of criminal justice in international and mixed criminal tribunals. However, attempts at trans-jurisdictional discourse are often hampered by mutual misunderstanding. Some problems are linguistic: although English is the new *lingua franca* in international and comparative criminal law, not all foundational concepts of criminal law and justice originate in the English-speaking world; some of them are rooted in civil law jurisdictions, such as France, Germany and Italy. The translation of these concepts into English is thus subject to ambiguity and potential error: the same term may have different meanings in different legal contexts. As a consequence, critical and theoretical discussions too often take place within the different legal traditions rather than between them: Anglo-American scholars talk to each other, as do those taught in Continental European criminal law traditions; too rarely do they engage seriously with each other across these jurisdictional borders.

If we are to overcome these obstacles, we need to engage in a multi-jurisdictional comparative conceptual analysis of a kind that has not been provided by existing comparative projects, which typically focus on specific topics or issues. The aim of such an analysis is to see whether it is possible to articulate a common grammar or set of foundational concepts that could provide the basis for productive trans-jurisdictional discussion and progress. Such an articulation need not result in uncovering or excavating some already existent 'universal grammar' of criminal law – although, on the basis of prior comparative projects, we have good reason to believe that there exists greater unity among diverse systems of criminal law and justice than is commonly assumed.[1] It might instead involve an attempt to construct a shared grammar from the diverse and sometimes conflicting materials that the comparative analysis reveals. Nor should we assume in advance that either such an excavation or such a (re)construction of a shared grammar will be possible: perhaps it will turn out that the most we can achieve, in trying to develop principles, doctrines and procedures for international and transnational criminal processes, is a set of compromises between conflicting structures of legal thought. But equally we should not rule out in advance the possibility of such a shared grammar; and the attempt to unveil or to construct it will be illuminating whether it succeeds or fails.

This enterprise requires us to delve beneath the surface details and the linguistic variations of various criminal codes, statutes and procedures, to explore their normative foundations and underlying conceptual and logical structures. On the face of it, there are striking differences in the structures of different systems. To give just two examples, German criminal procedure, like that in other civil law systems, assumes an 'inquisitorial' structure, whereas English and American criminal procedure, like that in other common law systems, is 'adversarial' in nature. However, the ways in which 'adversarial' systems are being reformed in 'inquisitorial' directions, and vice-versa, suggest that there are real prospects, if not for uncovering some already existing common foundations, at least for establishing commonalities of both means and ends. Secondly, criminal liability in German law is structured by a three-part schema, of *Tatbestand*, *Rechtswidrigkeit* and *Schuld*; the *Tatbestand* includes both subjective and objective dimensions of the offence, and the subjective dimension is analysed in terms of just two basic concepts – those of *Vorsatz* and *Fahrlässigkeit*. By contrast, English criminal law (like other common law systems) does not draw a firm distinction between offences and defences; but traditional theory distinguishes *actus reus* from *mens rea* as the two elements of an offence, and distinguishes no fewer than four general types of *mens rea* or 'fault' – intention (or purpose), knowledge, recklessness and negligence (though there is not even agreement

[1] See G. P. Fletcher, *Basic Concepts of Criminal Law*, Oxford University Press (1998); also, as an example of previous explorations of this topic, A. Eser, G. P. Fletcher and K. Cornils (eds.), *Justification and Excuse: Comparative Perspectives*, vols 1 and 2 Max Planck Institute for Foreign and International Criminal Law (1987).

about the relationship between intention and knowledge, or about the status of negligence as a species of fault). To determine whether these surface differences reflect deeper, foundational differences in the understanding of criminal law and its proper aims and values, we must engage in a more theoretical discussion that transcends particular legal cultures – and that might reveal deeper connections, similarities or commonalities between the different systems.

II The Aims and Scope of the Project

This book is the first published volume of the project 'Core Concepts in Criminal Law and Criminal Justice' which is part of a broader Anglo-German Dialogue (see https://www.department-ambos.uni-goettingen.de/index.php/anglo-german-dialogue). The aim of the project is to explore the foundational principles and concepts that underpin the different domestic systems and local rules. Of course, many issues will remain unexplored, but we intend to cover the principal ones and are confident that the (first) three volumes will constitute a key collection of comparative essays for individuals and institutions around the world.

The three volumes focus on the Germanic (Germany, Austria, Switzerland) and principal Anglo-American (England and Wales, Scotland, USA, Canada) jurisdictions. The Germanic and Anglo-American systems are employed as examples of the civil law and the common law worlds. The project is thus, at this stage, far from universal in its scope: it pays no attention to a number of significant jurisdictions and legal traditions which certainly cannot be regarded as mere subsets of the German and Anglo-American types. Such a limitation is unavoidable: any attempt at a universal comparative study would inevitably produce a set of comparisons too superficial to reveal the deeper connections and differences in which we are interested. Further serious work will then be needed to discover the extent to which our findings can also be applied to other jurisdictions.

The contributors to these three volumes reflect a diversity of jurisdictional and disciplinary backgrounds. Some have a more empirical focus, the interests of others are more theoretical or normative, but all are committed to methodological pluralism within the framework of the following principles, which were agreed at the start of the project:

(a) Chapters are comparative, comparing concepts, doctrines, principles and structures. They employ, as a rule, a 'tandem approach' (explained below) and engage in a discourse encompassing both legal systems.

(b) Chapters are conceptual. They do not attempt a comprehensive doctrinal survey of the respective countries' laws relating to their topic; instead they dig beneath the superficial similarities or differences between legal rules to identify and compare the underlying concepts, values, principles, and structures of thought.

To ensure that the chapters are appropriately comparative and coherent, most are co-authored, with one author from a civil law system and one from a common law system. These 'tandem' chapters are either fully integrated comparative discussions, or take the form of a dialogue or exchange. Exceptionally, a few chapters are single-authored by a scholar who possesses sufficient familiarity with both legal traditions.

This dialogical tandem approach has characterised the project from its outset. The enterprise began its life with a 'scoping meeting' held in Cambridge in July 2016. The General Editor's initial aim was to form a discussion group consisting of like-minded colleagues who would meet to discuss their joint interests in legal comparison and would present papers on topics in criminal law and criminal justice. During the first meeting, it was agreed that the individual contributions should eventually complement each other to form a broad overview over the most relevant topics in criminal law and procedure. As a result, the initial meeting was followed by meetings in Göttingen (March 2017), Oxford (September 2017), Frankfurt am Main (April 2018), Edinburgh (September 2018) and Zürich (April 2019). These intensive meetings were devoted to the critical discussion of draft papers, from which the chapters of the present volume have emerged. Future meetings will take place at Rutgers University, USA (September 2019), in Berlin (spring 2020), Sussex (autumn 2020), and Marburg (spring 2021).

Given the broad range of research interests of the group's members, and the fact that topics in the criminal justice field tend to be closely interrelated, we decided to publish volumes which cover a panoply of themes rather than being devoted to a single area of the criminal justice universe. Putting discussions of general legal theory, substantive law, criminal justice and procedure together also demonstrates the richness of the comparative approach and the multiple ways in which authors from different countries and different spheres of criminal law can fruitfully interact.

III Volume I

The present volume contains eleven chapters discussing general theory as well as substantive criminal law and criminal procedure. Each chapter provides an original, critical and accessible account of its topic as it is dealt with in the two traditions of criminal law thought; each aims to uncover underlying commonalities and differences, and to explore the scope for constructive agreement or reform.

The first five chapters examine selected topics in substantive criminal law.

In his descriptive and normative chapter on 'Omissions', Kai Ambos takes a closer look at the duties to act which form the basis of omission liability in both civil and common law jurisdictions. On the doctrinal and descriptive level, the central distinction in the chapter is between two types of omission offence: 'commission by omission' ('improper offences of omission'), and 'failure to rescue' (the paradigmatic example of 'genuine offences of omission', grounded in a statutory duty to act). The bulk of the doctrinal discussion in the chapter concerns possible bases for obligations to act in cases of commission by omission. As Ambos explains, in the civil law approach, there are two sorts of obligation and two corresponding sorts of duty holder (these are non-exclusive categories): supervisor guarantors, with a special duty to secure and supervise particular sources of danger (e.g. owners of dangerous animals), and protector guarantors, with a special duty to protect certain people from harm (e.g. parents' duties to care for their children). In the common law tradition, there has been an attempt to categorise various sources of the duty to act. The canonical list includes: statute, contract, special relationship, voluntary assumption of care and having caused the danger. Comparing these, Ambos finds that there are great similarities: in terms of the duties to act, the rationales for these duties and uncertainties about the extent of the duties. Also, the underlying normative arguments for or against a failure to rescue offence are largely identical in both civil and common law debates.

Findlay Stark and Stefanie Bock discuss the very current topic of 'Preparatory Offences'. They first provide a definition of 'preparatory offences', which is not a formal category in English or in German criminal law. At the most general level, preparatory offences – as the authors identify them – criminalise conduct perceived to carry with it the risk that, at a later time, a completed crime will be committed (whether by the person(s) who perpetrate the preparatory offence, or by another person). Preparatory offences move criminal responsibility from the actual occurrence of harmful conduct forward to the planning and preparation stage of a crime. Bock and Stark contend that the main justification for such offences is the management of the risk of completed offences, namely actual harm/violation of legal goods protected by means of the criminal law. They then move on to defend a number of constraints on the criminalisation of preparatory offences. In their view, both English and German law (to some extent) fall short of respecting these limiting principles. The last part of the chapter deals with the punishment of preparatory offences.

In the next chapter, on 'Participation in Crime', Antje du Bois-Pedain focuses on the principles that govern the ascription of criminal responsibility to different parties involved in the commission of a crime. Her chapter has the twofold objective of introducing readers to the main doctrinal frameworks for the regulation of participation in crime in two well-known jurisdictions (England and Germany) as well as the theoretical foundations proposed for them, and of making the case for a reworked differentiated system based on separate doctrines of criminal participation formulated for three different participatory paradigms: acting through another, acting with another and acting alongside another. She argues that the main flaws in existing doctrines of participation arise from a failure to recognise that it is inappropriate to apply them across the entire range of multi-party scenarios to which they are currently applied. However, the counsel of some defenders of unitary perpetrator systems – that we should give up on the very project of distinguishing between different modes of liability-ascription for parties to crime on account of the practical difficulties to which they all give rise – is a counsel of despair. Once the areas of application for the different participatory paradigms are appropriately demarcated, distinct sets of rules and principles for each of these paradigms enable the resolution of various disputed issues and seemingly intractable difficulties that beset this area of law.

'Consent in the Law Relating Sexual Offences', the topic addressed by Tom O'Malley and Elisa Hoven, is currently a matter of some controversy in many jurisdictions. The authors argue that consent in this context is closely connected with the right to personal autonomy and the concept of human dignity. Children and persons with severe mental disability are generally treated as legally incapable of consenting to sexual activity. However, all mentally competent adults should have a right to choose to engage in consensual sexual acts and, equally importantly, the right to refuse to engage in any such act. Adopting this as their guiding principle, the authors critically examine the laws in the United Kingdom, Ireland and Germany with a view to assessing the extent to which they reflect respect for personal autonomy. They note that some vestiges of legal conservatism remain, as in the English and German laws that deny the right to consent to conduct that may inflict serious injury upon oneself, and the continued criminalisation of sexual activity between family members, even where the parties are consenting adults. The authors devote most of their attention to the meaning of consent in the context of rape, sexual assault and similar offences. The common law was traditionally reluctant to find absence of consent to a sexual act unless there was evidence of force, fear or fraud. Today, the emphasis is more on the simple question of whether the complainant consented. The same change of focus has taken place in Germany. But some problems remain, especially in relation to the validity of consent where a person engages in sexual activity while unaware of some significant circumstantial factor or as a result of pressure other than a threat of physical violence.

In their chapter on 'Terrorism Offences', Andrew Cornford and Anneke Petzsche address the question of how the criminal law should respond to the threat of terrorism. The authors provide two possible answers: one answer would be that no special response is needed, as legal systems around the world already criminalise such things as killing, maiming and causing explosions, as well as attempting, inciting or conspiring to do any of these things. Another answer would be that the criminal law has a role to play in pre-empting terrorist attacks. Since these attacks can cause such severe and extensive harm, the criminal law is justified in intervening at an earlier stage than usual, in order to ensure that they are not carried out. After addressing the problem of a definition of terrorism and the procedural, 'door opener' function of terrorism offences, Cornford and Petzsche examine this pre-emptive use of the criminal law in the context of terrorism through a comparative analysis of the laws in the UK and Germany. From this pre-emptive approach, it follows in both jurisdictions that not just the terrorist act itself but also much conduct preparatory to it is criminalised. The authors focus on four groups of offences: offences of preparing terrorist acts, offences of encouraging terrorism, offences related to terrorist organisations, and terrorism-related possession offences. They examine how these offences have expanded the scope of criminal liability in relation to terrorism, highlighting differences between the jurisdictions in the extent to which they have done so. They conclude that, in the context of terrorism, both jurisdictions have departed significantly from the traditional principles of inchoate criminal liability, which has led in both jurisdictions to similar concerns. However, the UK offences are in almost every respect broader than their German counterparts.

The next six chapters focus upon issues of criminal procedure and criminal justice, including sentencing.

Richard Frase, Carsten Momsen, Sarah Lisa Washington and Tom O'Malley explore the topic 'Proportionality of Punishment in Common Law Jurisdictions and in Germany'. This is the only chapter in this volume that has four authors from three different jurisdictions. After describing the relationship between the principles of sentencing and punishment and a jurisdiction's historical and philosophical roots, the four authors stress that the German concept of proportionality is not congruent with the same principle in a common law understanding. In German law, the relation between the principles of guilt and of constitutional proportionality is still unclear, as is their relevance for concrete sentencing purposes. According to the different traditions, the basis for sentencing in Germany is the offender, whereas in common law it is the offence. Both systems ultimately match offence- and offender-based criteria, but the perspective is different. Frase, Momsen, Washington and O'Malley examine which elements of proportionality in a common law understanding have equivalents in the German theory of sentencing – if there is such an equivalent – and where ideas of retributive and consequentialist proportionality should be incorporated. In their conclusion, they summarise how far the German system has incorporated proportionality principles and give a stimulus for further comparative discussion, asking whether the principles of guilt, *ultima ratio*, suitability, necessity, adequacy, prevention and proportionality can be recognised in a single punishment model.

In their chapter 'Criminal History Enhancements at Sentencing' Julian Roberts and Stefan Harrendorf compare and contrast the use of prior convictions at sentencing in Anglo-Saxon countries and in Germany. Previous convictions are central to decision-making regarding a new conviction for the following reasons. First, an offender's past – whether law abiding or including previous crimes – is perceived by many practitioners to be relevant to culpability and/or the offender's risk of reoffending. If this is true, a criminal record may justify harsher sentencing for recidivists and/or less punitive treatment for first offenders. As the authors demonstrate, retributive theories take conflicting positions on whether and to what extent prior crimes should affect current sentencing. Preventive justifications also vary in their approach to prior offending. Secondly, most offenders appearing for sentencing have previous adjudications of one kind or another. As an aggravating factor, prior convictions therefore affect a large proportion of the caseload of the courts, up to 80 per cent of defendants in England and Wales. Thirdly, statutory sentencing provisions in many countries identify prior crimes as an important aggravating circumstance at sentencing, suggesting that legislators ascribe considerable importance to this factor. Fourthly, empirical research into sentencing practices demonstrates that in many jurisdictions, criminal history is the second most powerful predictor of sentencing outcomes (after the seriousness of the current crime). In some US jurisdictions an offender's prior crimes carry more weight at sentencing than his current crime. Finally, lay or public theories of punishment incorporate an offender's past as a factor: research into public views suggests that most people favour harsher treatment for recidivists and support significantly mitigated punishments for people who have led a law-abiding life. Roberts and Harrendorf contrast the German and the common law approaches to criminal history, paying particular attention within the common law systems to England and Wales and to representative US jurisdictions.

Lucia Zedner and Carl-Friedrich Stuckenberg explore 'Due Process', a concept whose history dates back to the English Magna Carta of 1215. Due process lies at the core of criminal justice in the common law world but is much less familiar in Germany, where analogous concepts of *schützende Formen, Justizförmigkeit* and *faires, rechtsstaatliches Verfahren* prevail. The chapter explores the history of due process in both England and Germany in order to understand the historical origins of its present form and character. It examines the role that due process, and its German equivalents, play in structuring the relationship between state and citizens by acting simultaneously as a declaration of the rights of citizens, as a limit on the exercise of state power over those subject to the criminal process, and as an articulation of the values, principles and forms that should structure and guide that process. In both countries, the importance of procedural protections has been secured by Article 6 of the European Convention on Human Rights, which sets out the right 'to a fair and public hearing within a reasonable time by an independent and impartial tribunal established by law'. The chapter examines how the fundamental right to a fair trial has been further elaborated, and vigorously defended, in the jurisprudence of the Strasbourg Court, and it explores the implications not only for defendants but for all those who participate in the trial process. How the right to a fair trial plays out in practice varies significantly between adversarial and inquisitorial systems, and the chapter explores how the form, structure and goals of the criminal process in England and in Germany privilege different conceptions of truth and of due process. Whereas the defence of due process in England lies, above all, in the articulation of core criminal justice values and principles, in Germany it derives from the foundational concept of the *Rechtsstaat*, a constitutional principle that encompasses important guarantees upheld by the German Federal Constitutional Court. The chapter critically considers how due process has been theorised by scholars in different jurisdictions and calls for a thicker, substantive conception of due process that engages not only with procedural but also with doctrinal criminal law, the better to recognise the indivisibility of law and process. The chapter also calls for better recognition of erosions and abuses of due process, including miscarriages of justice, that render the provision of mechanisms for review, rectification, and redress no less a vital part of due process than the articulation of its core values.

Alexander Heinze's and Shannon Fyfe's chapter 'The Role of the Prosecutor' provides a twofold approach to the role(s) of the prosecutor: a descriptive one and an analytical/explanatory one. The authors provide both an analysis of prosecutors' roles and examples of how prosecutors carry out their purported roles. Heinze and Fyfe show that prosecutorial work is influenced by two role-related factors: role duality and role ambiguity. They start with the common conception of US prosecutors as partisan lawyers tasked with obtaining and preserving convictions, even though prosecutors in the United States are not supposed to be mere adversaries but also have a special duty to seek justice and the truth. German prosecutors – Heinze and Fyfe show – are committed to objectivity, which in the 1980s offered instructive lessons for an American system beset by claims of prosecutorial overreaching. While comparative scholars have condemned American prosecutors for their 'conviction mentality', they commended German prosecutors for their dedication to objectivity. Yet, fiscal constraints, combined with the emergence of new types of economic crime, put pressure on the ability of the prosecution service to fulfil the ambitious fact-finding function mandated by the German Code of Criminal Procedure (StPO). Today, the StPO contains many elements that will seem all too familiar to a US prosecutor and are reminiscent of an adversarial setting. Heinze and Fyfe show that the different roles of the prosecutor mirror different models of procedure. Beyond the common adversarial–inquisitorial dichotomy, they employ Damaška's concepts of coordinate vs hierarchical officialdom and reactive vs activist state with conflict-solving vs policy-implementing types of proceedings. The prosecutorial roles in these systems are in conflict with one another. Adversarial/conflict-solving lawyering requires acting strategically to win litigation, howsoever the client defines victory, regardless of the lawyer's own personal commitments or beliefs. Seeking justice/ truth etc., however, requires choosing what substantive values to pursue. And so, these two roles push prosecutors in different directions. Alas, role duality does not always unfold as cogently as we might want it to in order to perfectly assign prosecutorial roles to the conflict-solving or policy-implementing ideals. Heinze and Fyfe show that more often than not, prosecutorial roles that seem clear cut prima facie are, upon closer consideration, blurred. The distinction between prosecutors as elected officials, directly accountable to the public, and as appointed officials, indirectly accountable to the public, reveals the limitations of a role duality analysis.

Jenia Turner and Thomas Weigend examine 'Negotiated Case Dispositions in Germany, England and the United States'. They explain that the phenomenon of 'bargained criminal justice' has spread from the United States, where it originated in the early twentieth century, to many jurisdictions around the world. Its common feature is the exchange of leniency in sentencing for the defendant's cooperation in the criminal process, which permits the court to dispense with or radically shorten the process of taking evidence. In common law jurisdictions, the guilty plea is the perfect tool for this exchange. Continental 'inquisitorial' systems, emphasising the trial court's independent obligation to search for the truth, have greater difficulty with integrating elements of bargaining into their criminal process. In Germany, it took the legislature until 2009 to recognise and legitimise a practice which had existed for decades. German law attempts to reconcile the systemic interest in shortening the trial with the need to establish the 'truth', relying on the defendant's confession as a device for reducing or eliminating the court's duty to examine all relevant evidence at the trial. The authors maintain that the US and the German systems are faced with similar problems, especially the pressure on the defendant to cooperate brought about by the threat of a very severe sentence if he refuses. Similar problems also need to be resolved if an intended 'bargain' fails to be carried out. The authors suggest that these and other difficulties cannot be resolved completely but favour an open approach where the relevant facts are accessible to all parties and the judge is actively involved in the process.

Stephen C. Thaman and Dominik Brodowski, in their chapter on 'Exclusion or Non-Use of Illegally Gathered Evidence in the Criminal Process: Focus on Common Law and German Approaches', inquire what consequences wrongdoing by state agents in the course of gathering evidence in a criminal investigation should have on the subsequent trial:

to what extent should such evidence be admissible or excluded in the criminal trial? Answering this question sheds much light on the core features of criminal justice and its theoretical as well as constitutional underpinnings. The authors put particular focus on the development of balancing tests and the factors which may or may not be taken into account. To exemplify the theoretical framework, they address the admissibility of evidence obtained in violation of the right to privacy as it relates to the inviolability of the home and the confidentiality of communications, and in violation of the rules on interrogations.

We hope that this collection, representing various aspects of criminal justice, serves to demonstrate the value and richness of the comparative approach we have taken. In collaborating to put together the chapters of this volume, the editors and authors have enjoyed learning from each other – not only about foreign legal systems but also, by responding to the view from outside, about their own system, and about the deeper connections, and differences, between the systems. We hope that our readers find in these pages many ideas to whet their appetite for comparative thinking. The chapters in this volume have certainly not yet uncovered a universal grammar of criminal law; but they do show how fruitful this kind of deep comparative work and a true dialogue can be in identifying connections and tensions that point the way towards further mutually illuminating investigations.

PART II

Criminal Law

2

Omissions

KAI AMBOS*

I The Basic Distinction between Act and Omission: Towards a Normative Approach

From a naturalistic perspective, omission is the opposite of action – it is non-action (not-doing), absence of action. From this perspective, an act or active conduct can be easily identified because of the expenditure of energy it generates, for example, through a bodily movement causing a certain result in the empirical world. In contrast, an omission lacks a physical reality; it does not display any (causal) energy; it is, in this sense, simply non-existent.[1] As a consequence of such a naturalistic approach, it has been argued that omissions cannot actually cause any result and thus cannot have any legal relevance, let alone create criminal liability.[2]

This argument is inherently flawed, however. It comes close to a naturalistic fallacy in that it draws an erroneous inference from the mere empirical existence of things (the 'is') to the moral world of goals and values (the 'ought').[3] But the naturalistic fact that an omission lacks a

* I thank Antony Duff, Matt Dyson, Findlay Stark, Carl-Friedrich Stuckenberg, Alec Walen and Thomas Weigend for critical comments.

1 For this so-called 'ontological' position, based on Radbruch's naturalistic distinction between active conduct and passivity in terms of the generation or not of (causal) energy see: Roxin, *Strafrecht* (2003), § 31 mn. 70; Weigend, '§ 13' (2007), mn. 2 with relevant references. See also Kirchheimer, 'Criminal Omissions' (1942), 617–19; Gómez-Aller, 'Omissions' (2008), 431. For the early common law debate see Bentham, *Principles* (2000), 72 ('motion or exertion' versus 'keeping at rest'); Husak, *Philosophy* (1987), 173 ff.; Moore, *Act* (1993), 28 ff.; crit. Fletcher, 'Irrelevance' (1994), 1443–54; Simester, *Theory* (1995), 313 ff.

2 Cf. Moore, *Act* (1993), 267–78. On the variety of causal idioms in this area, especially 'causing as making to happen', see Feinberg, *Harm* (1984), 180–1.

3 The *locus classicus* of the 'Is–Ought' problem is Hume's *Treatise of Human Nature* (1739), at 469. Kant formulated it more clearly in 1781, in his *Critique of Pure Reason*, 199: 'For as regards nature, experience presents us with rules and is the source of truth, but in relation to ethical laws experience (alas!) is the parent of illusion, and it is in the highest degree reprehensible to limit or to deduce the laws which dictate what I *ought* to do, from what *is*

physical reality does not answer the normative question of whether the omitter should incur criminal liability for the harmful outcome of her omission. In other words, the naturalistic distinction between act and omission – more precisely, the existence or absence of bodily movement (not-doing) – has no moral, normative relevance with a view to the establishment of criminal responsibility.[4] In fact, the recognition of criminal liability for 'commission by omission', as so aptly expressed in the French concept *commission par omission*,[5] makes clear that the issue is not about bodily movements but about the normative question of whether and when we can expect someone to act,[6] so that her omission – understood in a legal sense as opposed to a mere naturalistic not-doing[7] – amounts to a commission of a crime. This is the reason why the German doctrine – followed by the Spanish and Portuguese doctrines – speaks in this type of case of an 'improper' (*unechte*) omission: it is not really an omission, but rather a form of commission, namely one by omission.[8] Take the protection of human life by the universally recognised offence of homicide or murder: can it make a legally (normatively) relevant difference whether someone is killed by action or by omission with regard to the violation of the respective legal interest/the causation of the respective harm? Whether *A* kills *B* by shooting at her (an action) or by (only) letting her drown in the sea despite being able to save her (an omission), the life of *B* has been taken in both cases by a conduct imputable to *A*, notwithstanding the naturalistic distinction between act and omission (and further conditions of *A's* criminal responsibility).

Thus, *with regard to the legal interest violated or the harm caused*,[9] it is irrelevant whether the result was brought about by action or omission, so

done.' (Emphasis added.) Common law writers have tried to clarify Hume's thesis, often ignoring Kant: see e.g. Malec, 'Is–Ought' (2007), 11–12; Greene, 'Implications' (2003), 847.

4 The point has most forcefully been made by Fletcher, 'Irrelevance' (1994), 1445, 1448, 1453 (what matters is not the presence or absence of 'voluntary acts'; instead, the question is one of human agency, 1444). See also Gómez-Aller, 'Omissions' (2008), 431–4, 437, 444; Husak, 'Act' (2011), 107 ff. (for a general critique of the act requirement).

5 See e.g. Bouzat and Pinatel, *Criminologie* (1963), 121 ff.; and see in more detail below at n. 44 with main text.

6 On this underlying, pre-existing normative expectation cf. Roxin, *Strafrecht* (2003), § 31 mn. 6–7; Simester, *Theory* (1995), 320; Duff, *Answering* (2007), 108.

7 On this juxtaposition see also Duff, *Answering* (2007), 108; Ashworth, *Obligations* (2013), 31.

8 See e.g. Gómez-Aller, 'Omissions' (2008), 444. For explanation of the proper/improper omission distinction, see below Section II.

9 On the concepts of harm and Rechtsgut from a comparative perspective cf. Ambos, 'Function' (2015), 301–29.

long as it was – in a normative sense – 'caused' or 'committed';[10] and this is the case if the omitter had the material possibility to intervene[11] and she took a conscious decision not to do so, thereby accepting the possibility of a harmful outcome.[12] In other words, from a normative perspective, there are results that can be seen as the product of omissions, namely, if the non-performance of an act produces harm to legal interests.[13] As a consequence, criminal liability is not predicated on an act but on a view of conduct encompassing both acts and omissions.[14] The relevance of the distinction is thus limited to the question of whether we focus on the act or omission limb of the respective conduct when we conceptualise the agent's responsibility;[15] at any rate, in both cases criminal responsibility may ensue.

The perspective may change if we attend to the *responsible agent* rather than to the harmful outcome. We normally do not treat action as equivalent to non-action. Our moral intuition distinguishes between them.[16]

[10] We will not deal here with the complex issue of hypothetical or negative causation in cases of omission according to which the failure to act (non-performance of the relevant duty to act) can be said to have 'caused' the harmful result since the active intervention (performance of this duty) would have avoided it (i.e. the result would not have ensued but for that omission). In fact, the underlying naturalistic concept of causation had already been displaced by a normative one at the end of the nineteenth century (Jescheck, 'Unterlassungsdelikte' (1965), 115–16). From a normative perspective, it must be inquired – in line with the theory of objective (fair) imputation – whether the harmful result was produced by the omitter's failure to act and thus can be imputed to her. See further Duff, *Answering* (2007), 111; Simester et al., *Criminal Law* (2016), 82–3, 111–12; Horder, *Principles* (2016), 129–30; for a stricter test, see Law Commission, *Criminal Code* (1989), 51, cl. 17(1)(b) (causing a result as omission 'to do an act which *might* prevent its occurrence'; emphasis added); crit. insofar Ormerod and Laird, *Criminal Law* (2018), 57; against any 'true' causation but instead in favour of 'double' objective imputation, see Luzón Peña, 'Kausalität' (2018), 520 ff.; for a normative approach also Gómez-Aller, 'Omissions' (2008), 429–30, 444; from an international perspective Kolb, 'Droit' (2012), 195, 202–3 ('considérations normatives').

[11] Cf. Roxin, *Strafrecht* (2003), § 31 mn. 8–15; Weigend, '§ 13' (2007), mn. 4, 65; for a 'defence of impossibility' Simester et al., *Criminal Law* (2016), 122–4.

[12] Cf. Roxin, *Strafrecht* (2003), § 31 mn. 3 (arguing that the agent's decision to violate a certain legal interest, independent of the nature of the conduct, is decisive).

[13] Cf. Ashworth, *Principles* (2013), 111–12; Horder, *Principles* (2016), 129–30.

[14] See also the MPC's definition in § 2.01(1) MPC: 'conduct' encompassing both 'act' and 'omission'.

[15] Cf. Roxin, *Strafrecht* (2003), § 31 mn. 69 ff.; Weigend, '§ 13' (2007), mn. 5 ff.; Ormerod and Laird, *Criminal Law* (2018), 57–61; also Horder, *Principles* (2016), 117–8; Simester et al., *Criminal Law* (2016), 83–4.

[16] See for a critical discussion Simester, *Theory* (1995), 311, 321 ff.; against equivalence also Duff, *Answering* (2007), 113–14; Ashworth, *Obligations* (2013), 31, 78.

Thus, a person who actively commits a wrong – for example, kills another by shooting – generally seems to be more to blame than a person who just lets the death happen – for example, does not intervene to prevent the other from drowning. I have already expressed this imbalance above when adding the word 'only' in brackets: in the second alternative of our example, *A* 'only' omitted to act. Yet, a closer look at the prima facie, intuitively convincing act/omission distinction reveals that many of its apparent implications are flawed. Take, for example, the argument that acts and omissions are different already critically discussed above: while this is, from a naturalistic perspective, indeed true, it does not entail the normative conclusion that omissions are never morally wrong per se, or are less wrong than actions.[17] It is, of course, true that letting someone die is a worse wrong than slapping someone's face. What grounds this normative judgement of the two kinds of conduct, however, is not their form, as act or omission, but the seriousness of the harm that flows from them. If the harm was the same – compare fatally shooting someone with letting him drown – and if the omitter was under an obligation to prevent the relevant harm, our normative judgement of the wrongfulness of each kind of conduct should be the same. In other words, the important difference does not lie in the naturalistic act/omission distinction, but in the normative status of the kind of conduct at stake,[18] and in the seriousness of the harm produced by it.[19] Also, even if one holds that the omitter is less responsible/culpable than the active agent, he/she may still be responsible/culpable, albeit to a lesser, 'secondary' extent,[20] especially in the mere failure-to-rescue cases (to be looked at more closely below).

II Two Forms of Omission: Pure Omission and Commission by Omission

It follows from the above considerations that crimes of omission can appear in two different forms: as an offence of the special part of criminal law (a special, statutory offence) that makes certain omissions punishable; or as a commission by omission based on a rule in the general part.[21] In

[17] Against the 'moral significance claim', see Feinberg, *Harm* (1984), 166–72, 186.
[18] Tadros, *Responsibility* (2005), 188–90, 208.
[19] Feinberg, *Harm* (1984), 140.
[20] Tadros, *Responsibility* (2005), 196 ('secondarily rather than primarily responsible').
[21] On that basis especially Kaufmann, 'Gleichstellung' (1961), 173–5 has argued that statutory omission offences are always written (codified in the special part) while

the former case a proper (genuine, authentic or separate) offence of a pure omission (*délit de pure omission*;[22] *echtes Unterlassungsdelikt*) is created; the classical failure to rescue offence – the failure to assist other citizens in need under certain circumstances – is perhaps the most important example of such a pure omission,[23] although by no means the only one.[24]

In the case of a commission by omission a general (part) provision[25] defines the requirements under which crimes of active conduct can be committed by an omission causing a result – that is, by omitting to prevent a result ('improper' or 'inauthentic offence of omission', *délit de commission par omission, unechtes Unterlassungsdelikt*). This kind of omission can be understood as the flip side of the active conduct (e.g. killing, assaulting etc. by an act or omission).[26] In essence, beyond the formal distinction between these two forms of omission, the difference concerns the object of attribution (*imputatio*): while in the case of an improper offence of omission the agent is held responsible for the non-prevented result (e.g. for the death of her child, which she did not

commission by omission offences are unwritten ones, albeit not as (reverse/negative) forms of commission but *delicta sui generis*.

[22] Sometimes also called *délit d'omission simple* or *vraies infractions d'omission*, see e.g. Pradel, *Comparé* (2016), 76.

[23] See e.g. Arts. 223–6 French Code Pénal ('Quiconque pouvant empêcher par son action immédiate, sans risque pour lui ou pour les tiers, soit un crime, soit un délit contre l'intégrité corporelle de la personne s'abstient volontairement de le faire est puni. . . . Sera puni . . . quiconque s'abstient volontairement de porter à une personne en péril l'assistance que, sans risque pour lui ou pour les tiers, il pouvait lui prêter soit par son action personnelle, soit en provoquant un secours.') and § 323c German Criminal Code (CC) ('Whosoever does not render assistance during accidents or a common danger or emergency although it is necessary and can be expected of him under the circumstances, particularly if it is possible without substantial danger to himself and without violation of other important duties shall be liable to imprisonment not exceeding one year or a fine.' Translation Bohlander, *English Translation* (2008)). See also Art. 195 Spanish CC (*De la omisión del deber de socorro*), Art. 593 Italian CC (*Omissione di soccorso*) and Art. 162 § 1 Polish CC. For overviews see Maihold, 'Nothilfepflicht' (2013), 137–8; Wittmann, 'Hilfeleistung' (2017), 367–9.

[24] See e.g. § 123 alt. 2 ('remains therein without authorisation') and § 138 ('omission to bring planned offences to the attention of the authorities') German CC; all translations from Bohlander, *English Translation* (2008); see also Gómez-Aller, 'Omissions' (2008), 426–9.

[25] Note that there are also special part provisions criminalising results brought about by an omission, e.g. § 225(1) StGB (harming a person by neglecting one's special protective duty).

[26] For this reverse-theory see e.g. Stuckenberg, 'Causation' (2014), 479; previously Schmitt, 'Unterlassungsdelikte' (1959), 432–3; Jescheck, 'Probleme' (1993), 120–1; but see crit. Kaufmann, *Dogmatik* (1959), 241 ff.

prevent), in the former case (proper offence of omission) the agent is held responsible for the failure to carry out the socially expected and legally codified conduct (e.g. helping a person in need),[27] on the basis of her failure to conform to socially expected levels of care or diligence.[28]

While this twofold distinction prevails, notwithstanding certain controversies[29] in civil law jurisdictions,[30] it is at best acknowledged,[31] but not fully embraced, in common law jurisdictions. Indeed, many common law writers do not clearly distinguish between improper and proper omission offences as set out above[32] – which may have to do with the conspicuous absence of the latter, especially failure-to-rescue offences.[33] At any rate, from the traditional common law perspective, the discussion

[27] See e.g. Kaufmann, 'Gleichstellung' (1961), 173; Harzer, *Situation* (1999), 84, 88, 192 ff. ('duty/tendency to prevent the ensuing danger' [*Gefährdungsabwendungspflicht-/tendenz*]); Kühl, 'Solidaritätsbegriff' (2013), 96.

[28] For the classical distinction between a duty to prevent the harmful result and a duty to perform a certain conduct cf. Jescheck, 'Unterlassungsdelikte' (1965), 122; 'Probleme' (1993), 118–9; for critical discussion of the different theories of delimitation cf. Herzberg, *Unterlassung* (1972), 21 ff.; Kahlo, *Pflichtwidrigkeitszusammenhang* (1990), 26 ff.

[29] Thus e.g. the German juxtaposition 'echt-unecht' has been criticised (cf. Schmidhäuser, 'Unterlassensbegriffe' (2001), 761; Harzer, *Situation* (1999), 83–4; Weigend, '§ 13' (2007), mn. 16; Freund, '§ 13' (2016), mn. 60; crit. also Fletcher, *Rethinking* (1978), 422, n. 8) but at least the qualifier 'unecht' can be reasonably understood as a *commission par omission* within the ambit of application of § 13 CC (insofar conc. Weigend, '§ 13' (2007), mn. 60 *in fine*).

[30] For the German-speaking jurisdictions, see Roxin, *Strafrecht* (2003), § 31 mn. 16 ff.; Jescheck and Weigend, *Strafrecht* (1996), 605–8; for France, see Pradel, *Général* (2016), 346–7 (but note that liability for *commission par omission* is not recognised; see below at n. 47); for the Spanish-speaking jurisdictions, see Muñoz Conde and García Arán, *Derecho* (2015), 255 ff.; Mir Puig, *Derecho* (2016), 321 ff.; for Portuguese-speaking jurisdictions, see Figueiredo Dias, *Direito* (2007), 913; for Italy, see Pulitanò, *Diritto* (2017), 205 ff. From a comparative perspective, see Pradel, *Comparé* (2016), 76–8; from an ICL perspective, see Duttwiler, 'Liability' (2006), 4 ff. For a third category of 'omissions of medium gravity' or 'pure omissions of a special duty to act', Sánchez, 'Omisión' (2000), 153 ff.; 'Dreiteilung' (2011), 641 ff.; conc. Gómez-Aller, 'Omissions' (2008), 421–2, 446–51.

[31] See Fletcher, 'Irrelevance' (1994), 1447 ff.; *Rethinking* (1978), 422; *Concepts* (1998), 46; Duff, *Answering* (2007), 108; Allen, *Textbook* (2017), 40; Ormerod and Laird, *Criminal Law* (2015), 73 ff.; Robinson, 'Liability' (1984), 101–2, and Ashworth, 'Liability' (1989), 433 introducing as a third, middle category, 'hybrid act-omission offences' (e.g. driving without licence).

[32] See e.g. Kadish, Schulhofer and Steiker, *Criminal Law* (2012), 227 (discussing whether the defendant in *Pope* could 'be convicted of criminal homicide' on the basis of a Bad Samaritan provision and thereby equating a mere failure-to-rescue offence with commission by omission), but in favor of a "Good Samaritan" Rule now Kadish, Schulhofer and Steiker, *Criminal Law* (2017), 243–4; Klotter and Pollock, *Criminal Law* (2013), 51 (discussing both under statutory duties).

[33] See below at n. 43.

revolves around the establishment of a duty to act which seems to be seen as an exception to the general 'no duty' rule, rejecting any general failure-to-act liability.[34] At best, a distinction in wrongfulness and blameworthiness may entail different levels of punishment, with a mere failure to rescue receiving the lowest punishment.[35]

In the case of a *proper omission* offence, the agent is held responsible for having fulfilled the conduct as defined in the relevant offence. The broadest liability in this regard is created by the already mentioned general failure to rescue offence.[36] This offence is well known in modern civil law jurisdictions,[37] but has traditionally been rejected by common law jurisdictions,[38] especially in England,[39] and also, somewhat surprisingly given the great German influence there, in China and Japan.[40] The recourse to the parable of the Good Samaritan[41] shows the religious and moralistic undertones of the debate: While the priest and the Levite fail to assist another in need, the Samaritan complies with the moral and, perhaps, legal (pursuant to statute or case law) obligation to help.[42] At any rate, the exceptional codification of 'bad Samaritan' statutes in some

[34] See for the traditional rule-exception view Stewart, 'Failure' (1998), 393–4; Simester et al., *Criminal Law* (2016), 73–4.

[35] See Ashworth, *Obligations* (2013), 37, 69–73, distinguishing between five levels of criminalisation.

[36] For other proper omission offences in Germany, see Bosch, Vorbemerkung' (2019), mn. 134; for France, see Leroy, *Général* (2010), 185–6 (mentioning six such offences in the CP, namely Arts. 223-6(1), (2) and 223-7, 227-5, 434-1, 434-11; others, e.g. Bouloc and Matsopoulou, *Droit* (2016), 103, list more, e.g. Art. 434-3); for England/Wales, see Allen, *Textbook* (2017), 238–45; for the USA, see Stewart, 'Failure' (1998), 406 ff.

[37] See Maihold, 'Nothilfepflicht' (2013), 137–8; Wittmann, 'Hilfeleistung' (2017), 367–9.

[38] Cf. Feldbrugge, 'Samaritans' (1965), 630 ff.; Stewart, 'Failure' (1998), 387–8, 392–4, 407; Schiff, 'Samaritans' (2005), 77 ff. (with a comparative analysis); also Kadish, Schulhofer and Steiker, *Criminal Law* (2012), 222–8; Kaplan, Weisberg and Binder, *Criminal Law* (2017), 128.

[39] Cf. Ashworth, *Obligations* (2013), 39–40; 'Liability' (1989), 424–30; 'Rettungspflicht' (2013), 115 ff.

[40] Cf. Wittmann, 'Hilfeleistung' (2017), 363–5.

[41] The term goes back to the parable of the *Good* Samaritan in Luke 10:25, 30–4.

[42] Interestingly, the general failure to rescue offences are sometimes labelled 'bad Samaritan' and sometimes 'good Samaritan' provisions (for the former see e.g. Feinberg, *Harm* (1984), 185; for the latter see e.g. Gómez-Aller, 'Omissions' (2008), 421). I prefer the former term since these criminal provisions punish the person who does not live up to the standard of the good Samaritan – i.e. the bad Samaritan. Moreover, the term 'bad Samaritan provision' is less ambiguous since good Samaritan laws can also be provisions which exclude or limit the liability for civil damages caused while administering emergency care, see e.g. § 2305.23 Ohio Good Samaritan Law or s. 2 Ontario's Good Samaritan Act (2001).

US jurisdictions[43] on the one hand, and the principled critique against such criminal responsibility by academic writers in civil law jurisdictions on the other, show that the discussion is by no means concluded. In fact, as we will see in the final section of this chapter, the underlying normative assumptions of both positions have much in common, and this commonality traverses jurisdictional lines.

In contrast, liability for *improper offences* of omission, based on a general omission definition,[44] is derived from active result crimes – as their reverse – and is thus best captured by the above-mentioned concept of *commission par omission.* These offences can rightly be termed 'improper offences of omission' for, as already explained above, they are punished as commissions rather than omissions; that is, as the flip side of the active offence. The agent is held liable for the harmful result that he/she did not prevent. A classic example is the one discussed above: *A* lets *B* drown and would be liable for homicide by omission if he was the father of *B* – that is, has the position of a (protector) guarantor vis-à-vis *B's* life (and the other conditions of liability, especially the reasonable possibility of saving *B's* life, were met).

It is important to point out, however, that this kind of omission liability is not uncontroversial. In common law jurisdictions it is – due to the moral distinction between acts and omissions[45] – essentially confined to the classic result crimes against life and bodily integrity

[43] According to Schiff, 'Samaritans' (2005), 92 ff. five US jurisdictions have 'bad Samaritan' statutes: see e.g. § 940.34 Wisconsin Statute & Annotations, § 604A.01 Minnesota Statute & Annotations. Kadish, Schulhofer and Steiker, *Criminal Law* (2017), 242–3 speak of six jurisdictions with misdemeanour offences; see also Klotter and Pollock, *Criminal Law* (2013), 51–2. In Canada there are no 'bad Samaritan' provisions in the (federal) Criminal Code; however, s. 2 of the Quebec Charter of Human Rights and Freedoms establishes a 'right to assistance'. Also, the Law Reform Commission recommended an 'easy rescue' offence, either in the General Part or as a Special Part offence (*Omissions* (1985), 19–20). In Australia, only s. 155 of the Criminal Code Act of the Northern Territory provides for a 'bad Samaritan' rule.

[44] § 13(1) German CC: 'Whosoever fails to avert a result which is an element of a criminal provision shall only be liable under this law if he is responsible under law to ensure that the result does not occur, and if the omission is equivalent to the realisation of the statutory elements of the offence through a positive act.' (Translation Bohlander, *English Translation* (2008)). Corresponding provisions are Arts. 11 Spanish CC, 40(2) Italian CC, 2 Austrian CC, 2 Polish CC, 10(2) Portuguese CC and 18 Korean CC (for further examples see Duttwiler, 'Liability' (2006), 39–41, 43–5, including Islamic Sharia law at 42). However, in some civil law countries these cases are covered by liability for negligent conduct, e.g. in Chile (Art. 492 CC, see Politoff, Koopmans and Ramírez, 'Chile' (1999), 78 f., probably due to French influence, see below n. 61).

[45] See above at n. 16 with main text.

(causing a specially serious harm), namely murder, manslaughter and causing (serious) injury.[46] In civil law jurisdictions, such liability does not enjoy unreserved support, with French law invoking a relatively strict understanding of the legality principle, in particular of its *lex certa* and *stricta* (prohibition of analogy) components (which are difficult to reconcile with a general omission definition) to limit liability for offences of commission by omission.[47] This position is also adopted in Belgium,[48] some former French and Belgian African colonies[49] and even by important German scholars.[50] Interestingly, though, in French customary law (*Ancien Droit*) general omissions liability was recognised, albeit religiously inspired, if someone had an opportunity to prevent the occurrence of a harmful result ('Qui peut et n'empêche, pèche');[51] in other words, the non-prevention of the harmful result – within the meaning of an improper omission offence – was the basis of criminal responsibility. Yet, the Code Pénal of 1810 did not adopt the rule,[52] and this remains the state of the law today. While *commission par omission* in the case of serious harm is, probably since the famous case of the 'locked up woman of Poitiers',[53] widely recognised to merit *moral* reproach, at the same time there is general agreement that *criminal* responsibility can only arise if the legislator precisely determines the conduct to be taken into account for omissions liability.[54] This seems to point in the direction of proper omission offences precluding any offences of commission by omission.

[46] Cf. Ormerod and Laird, *Criminal Law* (2018), 48–51; on the controversy surrounding assault/battery by omission *ibid.*, 77; also Smith, 'Liability' (1984), 98–100; Simester et al., *Criminal Law* (2016), 81.

[47] Cf. Pradel, *Général* (2016), 346 (*interprétation stricte*, Arts. 111–14 Code Pénal); Jescheck, 'Unterlassungsdelikte' (1965), 130–1; Schrägle, *Unterlassungsdelikt* (2017), 41 ff.

[48] Cf. Hennau and Verhaegen, *Droit* (2003), 156; previously Jescheck, 'Unterlassungsdelikte' (1965), 130 ff.

[49] Cf. Duttwiler, 'Liability' (2006), 41.

[50] Kaufmann, 'Gleichstellung' (1961), 175–6.

[51] 'Who is able but does not prevent commits a sin', as stated by Antoine Loysel (1536–1617), see Bouloc and Matsopoulou, *Droit* (2016), 212, mn. 231.

[52] Bouzat and Pinatel, *Criminologie* (1963), 122.

[53] In this case of 1901 a mother had locked up her daughter for twenty-four years in a room. The brother, who frequently visited the house, was charged with bodily injury for not stopping his mother ill-treating his sister. He could not be convicted for *commision par omission* due to the absence of a general rule on omission liability (see Schmidt-Künzel, *Unterlassungsdelikte* (1971), 136 ff.; Bell, Boyron and Whittaker, *Principles* (2008), 215; for a novelistic account, see Gide, *Séquestrée* (1930)).

[54] Cf. e.g. Mayaud, *Droit* (2018), 207.

At any rate, the French approach has something to it, given the uncertainty generated by a general improper omission rule like § 13 of the German CC, in particular with regard to the precise scope of the guarantor duties (to be treated in more detail below).[55] Thus, Bouzat and Pinatel stress the difference between a moral judgement and the criminal responsibility of the omitter and argue in particular that proof of the necessary *intention mauvaise* would often be very *délicate* – that is, it would be too difficult to prove.[56] In a more philosophical vein, Desportes and le Gunehec argue that the French approach is based on a *conception individualiste*, according to which the decision to intervene for rescue is a highly personal question of conscience, which cannot be subject to legal regulation.[57] In the same vein, Bouloc and Matsopoulou warn that punishing every voluntary and culpable failure to intervene would endanger the *liberté individuelle*, since a strict line between lawful and unlawful inaction could not be easily drawn.[58] This brings us right back to the 'conventional view' in traditional common law (rejecting a general failure-to-rescue liability),[59] but it provokes the question of why French law then contains a bad Samaritan provision in Article 223-6 CP at all.[60] Also, while the individualist and legalist conception in French law leads to the result that (intentional) commission by omission is, as such, not punishable, the relevant conduct is often covered by a general negligence[61] (result) liability or by one of the various proper omission offences of the CP.[62] Thus, for example,

55 For a summary of the critique Gómez-Aller, 'Omissions' (2008), 426–9.
56 Bouzat and Pinatel, *Criminologie* (1963), 122.
57 Desportes and le Gunehec, *Droit* (2009), 398.
58 Bouloc and Matsopoulou, *Droit* (2016), 103–4.
59 See above n. 39 and main text.
60 Art. 223-6 CP contains two paragraphs distinguishing between the failure to prevent a crime against the bodily integrity of a person (para. 1) and the failure to assist a person in danger (para. 2). See also Art. 223-5 (hindering help to a person in danger), Art. 223-7 (failing to take measures against a natural disaster putting people in danger); see also Rebut, *Omissions* (2017), mn. 16.
61 In case of negligent conduct, act and omission are treated alike and only the harmful result counts: cf. Véron, *Droit* (2015), 96; Mayaud, *Droit* (2018), 207–8; see also Duttwiler, 'Liability' (2006), 38. This corresponds with Canadian law, see below at n. 90.
62 Cf. Pradel, *Général* (2017), 345–7; Debove and Falletti, *Précis* (2016), 115–16; see also Elliot, *French* (2001), 61; Jescheck, 'Unterlassungsdelikte' (1965), 144–6; 'Probleme' (1993), 116; Schrägle, *Unterlassungsdelikt* (2017), 151–2 (demonstrating that the failure-to-rescue liability in part assumes the function of improper omission liability).

our case of homicide by omission would fall under the general failure-to-rescue offence.[63]

III *Commission par Omission*: The Duty to Act and Its Foundation

The alleged moral difference between action and omission is the reason why omission liability always depends on a legal duty to act which, in turn, is predicated on a pre-legal normative expectation. In other words, a pre-existing normative expectation is turned into a legal obligation. This is, in principle, true for both proper omission offences and improper ones (*commission par omission*), but in the latter case the equivalence with the respective active conduct and the imputation of the non-prevented harmful result calls for an especially demanding (legal) duty to act, expressed as *Garantenpflicht, deber de garante* or *obbligo di garanzia* in relevant non-English-speaking jurisdictions.[64] The person owing such a duty may be called a 'guarantor' (*Garant* in German, *garante* in Italian/Spanish); he/she holds the relevant position (*Garantenstellung, posición de garante, posizione di garanzia*), which, in a way, is the flip side of the respective duty.

While the philosophical or theoretical foundation of such a duty to act is arguably the most difficult and controversial issue of the so-called general part of criminal law,[65] it is widely accepted that this special duty must exist in order to compensate for the act/omission distinction in cases of improper omission – that is, liability for the non-prevented harmful result. Only then can the normative equivalence between the

[63] Arts. 223–6 CP, see above n. 36; cf. Pradel and Danti-Juan, *Droit* (2017), 52. This provision, however, provides for a much lower sentence than the analogous improper omission offence, for example §§ 212, 13 StGB.

[64] The duty requirement was apparently first mentioned by the German scholar Paul Johann Anselm von Feuerbach: see von Feuerbach, *Lehrbuch* (1803), § 24, 24–5, with reference to Winkler, *Dissertation* (1776): 'If another subject is entitled to a certain action performed by another subject, there exists a crime of omission (*del. omissionis*, in contrast to *del. commissionis*). As, however, the original obligation of the citizen is only aimed at omissions; a crime of omission always requires a special legal reason (statute or contract) which establishes an obligation to act. Without the latter, no one can become a criminal by omission.' (Translation and emphasis by K. A.)

[65] Roxin, *Strafrecht* (2003), § 32 mn. 2; Jakobs, *Strafrecht* (1993), 799. In a similar vein, see de la Torre and Arroyo Zapatero, *Derecho* (2016), 268, Demetrio Crespo, 'Tipo omisivo' (2015), 179. For the less elaborated Anglo-American theory, see Husak, *Philosophy* (1987), 83 ('[o]missions' as 'most puzzling tests of the *actus reus* requirement'). For an early discussion, see Kirchheimer, 'Criminal Omissions' (1942), 621–36.

active causation of harm and the failure to prevent this very harm be justified and the latter result be imputed to the agent as a *punishable* omission. Otherwise, mere inaction may at best constitute the basis of proper omission liability.[66]

1 *Guarantor Duties under Civil Law*

The modern doctrine in civil law jurisdictions refers to two different sets of obligations as bases for such a duty: on the one hand, it is imposed upon persons with a special responsibility over certain sources of danger – for example, dangerous products or industrial plants, which entails a *duty to secure and supervise* them (*Überwachungs-/Sicherungspflicht*); they are 'supervisor guarantors'. On the other hand, a duty is imposed on persons who, because of their special protective position with regard to certain legal interests, for example parents with regard to their children or the bank manager with regard to the assets of the bank's clients, have a *protective duty* towards them (*Schutz-/Obhutspflicht*); they are 'protector guarantors'.[67] The same twofold distinction is made in other civil law jurisdictions.[68] It may be graphically presented as set out in Figure 2.1.

This dualist approach has an important classificatory and systematising function, but it does not account for the underlying foundations of guarantor duties. For example, while a father undoubtedly has a legal duty to protect his child (as a protector guarantor), the deeper reason underlying this duty is the special relationship of care which is typical in this kind of family relationship. These deeper reasons justifying guarantor duties have been the concern of German doctrine since the beginning of the nineteenth century with Anselm von Feuerbach's call for a specific legal duty (based on statute or contract),[69] complemented about 100 years

[66] Feinberg, *Harm* (1984), 161–2; Ashworth, 'Liability' (1989), 434; also Cassese, 'Liability' (2013), 180; Berster, *Unterlassungverantwortlichkeit* (2008), 113; Roxin, *Strafrecht* (2003), § 31 mn. 5 ff.

[67] This twofold approach goes back to Kaufmann, *Dogmatik* (1959), 283–4; conc. Roxin, *Strafrecht* (2003), § 32 mn. 17 ff.; Jescheck, 'Probleme' (1993), 124–5, 128; critically Schrägle, *Unterlassungsdelikt* (2017), 62 ff.

[68] For Italy, see Romano, *Commentario* (2004), Art. 40 mn. 58 ff.; Pulitanò, *Diritto* (2017), 210 ff.; for Portugal, see Dias, *Direito* (2007), 938 ff.; for Spain, see Muñoz Conde and García Arán, *Derecho* (2015), 260 ff.; Mir Puig, *Derecho* (2016), 328 ff.; for a different, more normative approach, see Sánchez, *Estudios* (2004), 231–2, 247 ff.

[69] Von Feuerbach, *Lehrbuch* (1803), § 24, 24–5; on the history of the German doctrine cf. Schrägle, *Unterlassungsdelikt* (2017), 13 ff.

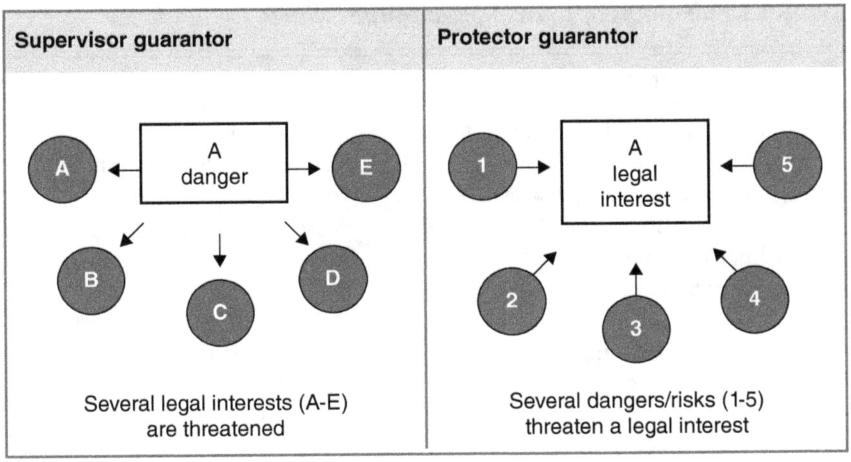

Figure 2.1 Dualist foundation of guarantor status and duties

later with the discovery of the guarantor position by Johannes Nagler.[70] Since then, a series of theories has been produced by German scholars.[71] According to the most plausible domination/control theories (*Herrschaftslehren*) all guarantor duties have as a common starting point that the criminal result brought about by the relevant omission is imputed to the guarantor because of her control over the relevant dangerous event or the protected interest – that is, because of her *Kontrollherrschaft*.[72]

[70] Nagler, 'Begehung' (1938), 59–63 (explicitly referring to the omitter as 'guarantor for the non-entry of the result who is therefore obliged to eliminate energies hostile to the legal order' (translation by K. A.)).

[71] See e.g. Jakobs, *Strafrecht* (1993), 800 ff. (duties pursuant to organisational or institutional competence) and Weigend, '§ 13' (2007), mn. 24 (threefold approach: assumption of responsibility, creation of danger and control over certain risks). For a profound historical account, Schrägle, *Unterlassungsdelikt* (2017), 13 ff., 51 ff. (himself developing a typology of five forms of guarantor duties: assumption/assignation of certain tasks, certain areas of legal traffic, responsibility for dangers/risks, care and supervision and certain close communities, 272 ff.); for a review, see Ambos, 'Review' (2017).

[72] This theory has originally been developed by Schünemann, *Unterlassungsdelikte* (1971), 231 ff. (control 'over the reason of the result') and, more specifically, 294–5, 323–33 (control over the source of danger, e.g. persons, as a relevant cause for the harmful result) and 334–58 (control over the helplessness of the legal interest/victim); also 'Garantenstellung' (2009), 313–15; essentially conc. Roxin, *Strafrecht* (2003), § 32 mn. 17 ff. (19: *Schutzherrschaft* versus *Sicherungsherrschaft*); in a similar vein, focusing on the control

Table 2.1 *Subgroups of sources of guarantor duties*

Supervisor guarantor	Protector guarantor
(1) Control/supervision of sources of danger within own ambit of organisation (e.g. company owner)	(1) Family or other close relations (e.g. parents/children; husband/wife)
(2) Responsibility for unlawful conduct of third persons (parents/child, employer/employee)	(2) Close community/relationship in situations of emergency/danger (e.g. mountain climbers)
(3) Previous (unlawful) conduct (*Ingerenz*, e.g. causing accident)	(3) Voluntary assumption of duty of care (e.g. babysitting)
	(4) Official duties on the basis of official status (e.g. police)

However, the concept of control only operates as a guiding principle,[73] and thus needs a more precise determination.[74] This, unavoidably, entails a casuistic approach by which groups of cases, belonging to either protective or supervisory duties, are developed. We cannot go into details here, but only summarise the recognised subgroups in Table 2.1.[75]

2 *Special Duties under Common Law*

English law has recognised, at least since the beginning of the nineteenth century, that an omission can be punishable if there was a legal (statutory or contractual) duty to prevent a possible harmful result.[76] James Stephen

over the sources of danger, see Gómez-Aller, 'Omissions' (2008), 434–43; for a critique see e.g. Brammsen, *Garantenpflichten* (1986), 74–6.

[73] This has always been acknowledged by Roxin (*Strafrecht* (2003), § 25 mn. 17, § 32 mn. 21), but it is often ignored by the critics, e.g. Maiwald, 'Unterlassungsdelikte' (1981), 480–1; Brammsen, *Garantenpflichten* (1986), 75–6; Pawlik, *Unrecht* (2012), 182.

[74] For an attempt at a more precise determination Schünemann, 'Garantenstellung' (2009), 292–302.

[75] See for a detailed treatment Roxin, *Strafrecht* (2003), § 32 mn. 33 ff.; Weigend, '§ 13' (2007), mn. 25 ff.; Schrägle, *Unterlassungsdelikt* (2017), 51 ff.

[76] Cf. '*Rex* v. *John*' (1825), 20–2 (failure to provide sufficient food, bedding etc. to infant apprentice received in the house with serious consequences for health as an 'indictable offence' if the receiving person was 'bound by duty or contract to provide for, if such child … be of tender years and unable to provide for itself.'). See for the historical development Schrägle, *Unterlassungsdelikt* (2017), 33 ff.

reaffirmed the legal duty concept at the end of the nineteenth century,[77] and developed a series of life-protecting duties.[78] In the case of statutory duties, English courts often take a linguistic approach, inquiring whether the wording of the conduct verb can be construed as encompassing omissions.[79] However, the restrictive potential of this approach has largely been watered down by a case law that generally interprets conduct verbs such as 'destroy', 'damage', 'falsify' or 'deceive' to encompass both act and omission;[80] in some instances even the term 'act' has been interpreted to include an omission.[81] In line with this approach, the Law Commission has proposed a broad definition of an 'act ... as including references to the omission'.[82] It also recommended the redrafting of some offences in terms of 'causing' a result, in order 'to leave fully open to the courts the possibility of so construing the relevant (statutory) provisions as to impose liability for omissions'[83] (and thereby employing a use of the term 'causing' which is incompatible with the naturalistic concept of causation rejected above). As to murder and manslaughter by omission, the Law Commission proposed the replacement of 'kill' in these offence definitions (considered as being linguistically inappropriate to encompass omission) with the term 'causing death'.[84] Thus, one can recognise 'a principle that criminal statutes should be interpreted so as to apply to omissions as well as to acts, where a relevant duty can be established, unless the context indicates

[77] Stephen, *History* (1883), 10 ('killing by omission is in no case criminal, unless' there is 'a legal duty' to prevent death); also Hughes (1857), as quoted by Smith, 'Liability' (1984), 97 (killing – murder or manslaughter – 'as the direct consequence of the ... omission of the performance of a duty').

[78] Stephen, *History* (1883), 10–11.

[79] The point has been made by Williams, 'Excuses' (1982), 773 (demanding that verbs 'implying active conduct should not be stretched by interpretation to include omissions.').

[80] See Smith, 'Liability' (1984), 95 ff. referring, inter alia, to 'destroy' and 'damage' as including commission by omission; Ormerod and Laird, *Criminal Law* (2018), 48; Ashworth, *Principles* (2013), 99; Horder, *Principles* (2016), 116.

[81] See Ormerod and Laird, *Criminal Law* (2018), 48 with n. 188.

[82] Law Commission, *Criminal Code* (1989), 51, cl. 16. On the Law Commission's discussions, see Landes and Poser, 'Good Samaritans' (1978), 92 ff.; Ashworth, 'Liability' (1989), 436.

[83] Law Commission, *Criminal Code* (1989), 188, para. 7.13. Note that some offences are already drafted that way, e.g. s. 18 Offences Against the Person Act 1861 ('cause any grievous bodily harm').

[84] Law Commission, *Criminal Code* (1989), 188, para. 7.13.

otherwise'.[85] In other words, the mere recourse to linguistic limitations cannot exclude omission liability if there are valid normative reasons, as reflected in a duty to act, to require it.[86]

In the United States, § 2.01(1) Model Penal Code (MPC) defines 'conduct' as encompassing both 'act' and 'omission'. Omissions liability is predicated on an explicit provision to that effect, or a legal duty to act,[87] and the corresponding capacity.[88] This approach has been adopted by various states.[89] Other common law jurisdictions understand commission as incorporating omission.[90] The Canadian CC punishes negligently causing death by omission by including in its definition of criminal negligence an omission in the case of a duty to act (s. 219),[91] and explicitly providing for (criminally) negligent caused death (s. 220) as 'culpable homicide' ('manslaughter by omission').[92]

What are the recognised sources of duties to act?[93] First of all, it does not come as a surprise that one of their primary sources is the common law – that is, old common law doctrines which may be invoked by the

85 Ashworth, 'Liability' (1989), 438.

86 In a similar vein Simester et al., *Criminal Law* (2016), 82 ('linguistic conventions ... should normally not pre-empt the possibility of liability for omissions'). But see *R* v. *Lowe* [1973] QB 702 Court of Appeal according to which manslaughter by unlawful act cannot be committed by omission.

87 § 2.01(3) MPC refers to (a) 'the omission expressly made sufficient by the law defining the offense; or (b) a duty to perform the omitted act'.

88 Cf. Duttwiler, 'Liability' (2006), 34.

89 See e.g. §§ 18–109 Idaho Code (defining as a crime 'an act committed or *omitted* in violation of a law forbidding or commanding it' (emphasis added)) or § 702(203) Hawaii Revised Statutes (repeating § 2.01(3) MPC). For further examples and discussion, see Robinson, 'Liability' (1984), 101 with n. 1 and 103–5; also Duttwiler, 'Liability' (2006), 33–4.

90 See e.g. for Canada s. 21 CC (party to an offence 'everyone who ... (b) does or *omits* to do anything' (emphasis added)) and s. 24 (regarding attempt including the intent to omit anything); for Nigeria similarly Chapter 77, Part 1, Chapter 2, s. 7 CC with regard to party to an offence. For further examples, see Duttwiler, 'Liability' (2006), 34–5.

91 'Duty' here means a duty imposed by law.

92 s. 222(5) in combination with s. 234: '[C]ulpable homicide ... is manslaughter' (murder requires a higher *mens rea*, ss. 229, 230).

93 For a good summary of the English law, see Ashworth, 'Liability' (1989), 439 ff.; slightly different, Ashworth, *Positive Obligations* (2013), 42 ff.; also Ormerod and Laird, *Criminal Law* (2018), 51–6; Allen, *Textbook* (2017), 42–7; Simester et al., *Criminal Law* (2016), 75 ff.; for the USA, see Robinson, 'Liability' (1984), 111–18; Stewart, 'Failure' (1998), 393 ff.; Kadish, Schulhofer and Steiker, *Criminal Law* (2017), 245–51; for Canada, see Manning, Mewett and Sankoff, *Criminal Law* (2009), 116 ff.; briefly Roach, *Criminal Law* (2018), 128–30; Colvin and Anand, *Principles* (2007), 141–6.

courts to come to certain results. Thus, in the English case of *Dytham*,[94] a police constable was convicted of the offence of misconduct of an officer of justice for failing to intervene to protect the Queen's peace and, more concretely, to prevent a person from being killed by a 'bouncer'. The relevant duty was imposed by the common law on any police officer.[95] Of course, such unwritten, judge-made duties are difficult to foresee for citizens, and are therefore criticised in light of the legality principle;[96] at any rate, this criticism can also be levelled against the many vague and uncertain duties recognised in both civil and common law jurisdictions.[97]

Going beyond such unwritten sources, the original approach in the US case of *Jones* was rather formalistic: it invoked four sources (statute, contract, special relationship and voluntary assumption of care),[98] which all have a statutory or contractual basis, partly originating in common law; this approach reminds us of the old (German) theory of the formal legal duties (*formelle Rechtspflichtslehre*) that governed the ('germanised') civil law debate at the beginning of the twentieth century.[99] In a later development the above list was expanded to include a duty to act if a person sets in motion a chain of events which imperils relevant legal interests such as life, bodily integrity and property (prior dangerous act/creation of peril);[100] this comes close to the civil law *Ingerenz* mentioned

94 *R* v. *Dytham* [1979] QB 722 Court of Appeal.

95 Allen, *Textbook* (2017), 40; see also on common law doctrines as sources of a duty to act Kadish, Schulhofer and Steiker, *Criminal Law* (2017), 235.

96 Cf. with regard to s. 9(a) Canadian Criminal Code Stuart, Delisle and Coughlan, *Criminal Law* (2018), 280.

97 For a principled critique regarding the English law cf. Ashworth, *Obligations* (2013), 66–8.

98 *Jones* v. *US*, US Court of Appeals for the District of Columbia Circuit, 308 F2d 307 (1962); essentially followed by Husak, *Philosophy* (1987), 157 and the mainstream American literature, cf. Kaplan, Weisberg and Binder, *Criminal Law* (2017), 124–6; Kadish, Schulhofer and Steiker, *Criminal Law* (2017), 234–5 Klotter and Pollock, *Criminal Law* (2013), 50 ff.

99 Cf. Roxin, *Strafrecht* (2003), § 32 mn. 4; for a parallel to the common law approach, see Gómez-Aller, 'Omissions' (2008), 426 with n. 12.

100 This goes back to the case of *R* v. *Miller* [1983] 2 AC 161 House of Lords; cf. Smith, 'Liability' (1984), 91–2 (suggesting, at 94–5, pursuant to *Miller*, as a 'general principle' a person's duty to prevent a harm if this person, even without knowledge, 'imperils' by an act another person or 'any other interest protected by the criminal law' and 'becomes aware of the events creating the peril'); for a good discussion see Ormerod and Laird, *Criminal Law* (2018), 50, 54–6; also Stewart, 'Failure' (1998), 396; Allen, *Textbook* (2017), 46–7; Kadish, Schulhofer and Steiker, *Criminal Law* (2017), 249–51; Horder, *Principles* (2016), 116; Simester et al., *Criminal Law* (2016), 78–9; for relevant extracts

above,[101] although the later case of *Evans* seems to go beyond this by requiring only a contribution 'to the creation of a state of affairs' together with reasonable foreseeability of the danger associated with that state of affairs.[102] In perhaps the most systematic account, Andrew Ashworth[103] identifies four broad groups of sources of duties – family obligations, voluntarily incurred obligations, obligations arising from personal (causal) responsibility and civic obligations – which themselves are divided into two to four subgroups amounting to a total of twelve sources of duties to act.[104] In general, to impose liability for commission by omission, 'the ascription of stringent responsibilities', based on 'tight normative bonds', is required.[105]

3 *The Civil and Common Law Approaches Combined*

A closer look at the duties to act which form the basis of omission liability in both civil and common law jurisdictions reveals great similarities both in terms of the rationale of the guarantor's responsibility and in terms of the individual duties recognised, at least if one compares the systematising efforts of criminal law theorists. Of course, the approaches to solve the equivalence problem have been different in historical terms and for reasons of principle, with the German law pursuing a marked abstract-theoretical approach and the English law basically leaving it to the judges to develop relevant classes of legal duties.[106] At any rate, when it comes to the rationale of criminalisation, the twofold civil law approach – supervisory vs. protective duties – ultimately rests on the assumption that the omitting guarantor exercises, in principle, *sufficient control* (*Kontrollherrschaft*) over matters to prevent any harm caused by the respective source of danger, or inflicted upon his object of protection.

see Stuart, Delisle and Coughlan, *Criminal Law* (2018), 265–8; discussing a fictional case Alexander, 'Omissions' (2002), 123 ff.

101 See also Ormerod and Laird, *Criminal Law* (2018), 54, n. 209.

102 *R* v. *Evans* [2009] EWCA Crim. 650, para. 31; for a principled critique Simester et al., *Criminal Law* (2016), 79–80 (yet, the question is not what 'kind of non-causal contribution to the danger is required' (at 80) – the defendant's contribution was causal anyway – but how to deal with the autonomy of the later victim or third persons; see further below).

103 Ashworth, *Obligations* (2013), 42–65.

104 For a summary see Ashworth, *Obligations* (2013), 42–3.

105 Duff, *Answering* (2007), 112.

106 Cf. Schrägle, *Unterlassungsdelikt* (2017), 13 ff., 51 ff.; previously on the historical development Jescheck, 'Unterlassungsdelikte' (1965), 111 ff.

The key requirement of 'control' – as a basis of criminal liability in general, independent of action or omission – has also been recognised by common law theorists in our context. It allows, in the words of Duff, 'responsibility for involuntary movements, conditions and states of affairs if they were within the agent's control'.[107] The exact contours of the control requirement, including of its qualifier 'sufficient', are of course open to debate but that is only a consequence of the – already mentioned[108] – concept's mere function of a general guidance which is in need of a more precise, casuistic determination.

As to the *sources of duties to act*, one finds first of all a historic coincidence in that both civil and common law systems originally relied on the formal sources of statute and contract.[109] While the *formelle Rechtspflichtslehre* was soon overtaken by theoretical developments in Germany, the English case law and statutory development has never been fully emancipated from it. Apart from that, it is fair to say that many of the duties and cases discussed in English law correspond to the ones recognised in civil law jurisdictions. To give but a few examples: under *special relationships* – 'family obligations' in Ashworth's terms – there is the classic parental duty to protect their children which may turn into a children's duty once they are grown up and the parents need their help.[110] Of course, both the children's and parents' autonomy may operate here as a bulwark against paternalistic overreach.[111] On a more general level, the problem is how far this special relationship duty reaches beyond close family members, generating tricky issues with regard to the quality (intensity, duration) of the relationship – covering for example short-term (vulnerable) guests of the household – and the quality (intensity) of the duty.[112] The '*voluntary assumption of care*' category of

[107] Cf. Duff, *Answering* (2007), 106–7; conc. Husak, 'Act' (2011), 116 ff. (121); previously, Husak, *Philosophy* (1987), 170–1 ('control principle' as 'preferable alternative' to causality requirement).

[108] Roxin, *Strafrecht* (2003), § 25 mn. 27.

[109] See also Schrägle, *Unterlassungsdelikt* (2017), 50 (historical comparison between England, Germany and France).

[110] Ormerod and Laird, *Criminal Law* (2018), 51–2; crit. Ashworth, *Obligations* (2013), 45.

[111] Cf. e.g. Roxin, *Strafrecht* (2003), § 32 mn. 35–6, 42; in the same vein Stuart, Delisle and Coughlan, *Criminal Law* (2018), 294–6 (autonomy of the elderly towards children as protective guarantors).

[112] Cf. on the one hand Ashworth, *Obligations* (2013), 46–9, on the other hand Roxin, *Strafrecht* (2003), § 32 mn. 51–2, 53 ff.; Weigend, '§ 13' (2007), mn. 39 *in fine* (temporary accommodation of acquaintance as assumption of – limited – responsibility).

common law jurisdictions has been broadened to 'voluntarily incurred obligations', including the joint execution of a hazardous activity,[113] which corresponds to the *Gefahrengemeinschaft* under German law.[114] This is surprising, given the common law's traditional critical stance towards omission liability without clear statutory requirements (or clear common law authority) pointing to the existence of a duty; under German law, too, the boundaries of a duty to act when part of a group jointly carrying out a hazardous activity are highly controversial.

At any rate, it seems to go too far to hold a person (a good Samaritan) who helps another in need without any legal obligation (given the absence of a failure-to-rescue offence) *generally* responsible for the omission to continue offering assistance, arguing that the initial help entails a continuing duty to assist since 'abandoning one's effort would leave the victim in a worse condition than before'.[115] For this is only true if the assister has created a new or additional (not purely hypothetical)[116] risk that will materialise if he discontinues his assistance.[117] Take the case of helping an old lady over a street but then leaving her alone mid-way – that is, bringing her into a more dangerous situation than she was before, when standing on the pavement. In such cases of goal-oriented assistance, the benefit to the recipient accrues only if/when the goal is reached, and thus the recipient of the assistance might indeed be worse off if the assister stops trying to reach the relevant goal before that.[118] This is, however, not true in cases of continuing/incremental assistance when at each stage the recipient has benefited, and the further stages just add further benefit. Discontinuing the assistance would then not leave the recipient of the assistance worse off than she would have been without the intervention, but would only fail to further better the recipient's position. Thus, to hold the assister criminally liable in the latter scenario would be to

[113] Ormerod and Laird, *Criminal Law* (2018), 52–3.

[114] Roxin, *Strafrecht* (2003), § 32 mn. 54; Weigend, '§ 13' (2007), mn. 40.

[115] Klotter and Pollock, *Criminal Law* (2013), 54.

[116] The risk created must be real (see example in the text), not purely hypothetical like, for example, the possibility that others refrain from assisting because they see that someone is already assisting.

[117] I am indebted to Antony Duff for bringing the following distinction to my attention.

[118] The liability of this assister, of course, also depends on the reason for her discontinuing the assistance. If she gives up because of impossibility or ineptitude she can only be blamed if she did not try *her* best to complete the assistance.

'punish' her – who intervenes without any legal obligation – for her good deed; it would take this deed, something worthy and positive, as a basis for criminalisation instead of rewarding her for the (aborted) act of assistance.

As to cases of *prior creation of a risk* (*Ingerenz*, mentioned above), both common and civil law theorists discuss the classic hit-and-run case where a driver negligently hits a pedestrian and drives on instead of helping the victim, grounding his duty to rescue on the prior (active) causation of the accident.[119] Yet, while in this case there is little controversy as to the omitter's duty to act – after all, on the basis of his negligent driving, he initially committed a criminal act – matters are more complicated if the danger-creating act does not amount to an offence or even to a violation of a non-criminal norm of care. Imagine that the driver is complying with all the rules of careful driving, but accidentally hits a pedestrian who crosses on a red light.[120] Or take the often discussed case of accidentally locking a colleague in a store-room, which might amount to an unlawful imprisonment by omission if the prior act – the locking of the colleague – is considered sufficient to trigger a duty to act (to unlock the door and liberate the colleague). These cases point to one of the major problems of the *Ingerenz*-doctrine, namely the quality of the previous dangerous act, which leaves us with three options: the most liberal view would require a prior criminal act, a stricter view merely demands an act violatory of a non-criminal norm of conduct (e.g. the general duty of care), and for the strictest view any dangerous act would suffice. Each of these views is defended in the German discussion,[121] while the few common law authors who accept the *Ingerenz*-doctrine as a basis of omission liability at all adopt the strictest view.[122] In fact, common law theorists merely demand, on an objective level, causal responsibility,[123] and the

[119] Cf. on the one hand Smith, 'Liability' (1984), at 96 and on the other hand Roxin, *Strafrecht* (2003), § 32 mn. 143, 145.

[120] Rejecting in this case a position of a guarantor with the respective duty to act BGHSt 25, 218; contra Freund, '§ 13' (2016), mn. 123.

[121] Cf. Roxin, *Strafrecht* (2003), § 32 mn. 160 ff.; Weigend, '§ 13' (2007), mn. 43–7; also Schrägle, *Unterlassungsdelikt* (2017), 142, 222 ff., 288 ff.

[122] Smith, 'Liability' (1984), at 94–5 (any act entailing a dangerous sequence of events suffices, so long as there is an offence 'capable of being committed by omission' and the omitter possessed the required fault element of the respective crime).

[123] Cf. Ashworth, *Obligations* (2013), 53–4 ('causal responsibility', accidental creation of danger).

case law has even considered that a contribution 'to the creation of a state of affairs' is sufficient to hold the contributor responsible if he fails to prevent the ensuing harmful result. In *R* v. *Evans*,[124] the defendant bought drugs for the victim, who freely took, and died as a result; the court upheld her conviction for manslaughter, because she had 'contributed to' the creation of the risk to the victim's life, and failed to help her when the risk was actualised. Thus, what is at stake here is not so much the quality of the prior act – the supply of illegal drugs is a criminal offence – but the victim's autonomous decision to take these drugs: this should turn the supplier's responsibility into a secondary one at most, similar to that of a mere accomplice. At any rate, if one reduces the quality of the prior act to the naturalist causation of any danger, only subjective limitations can bring about the necessary restriction of criminal responsibility, requiring, as is indeed done by common law theorists, knowledge or intention with regard to the creation of the danger;[125] in turn, that means that the existence of the respective mental requirement triggers criminal responsibility with regard to the main act. Yet, this kind of subjective requirement/limitation not only creates often insurmountable evidentiary problems but also fails to comply with rules of fair imputation: if I lend my flat or my car to someone and this person commits a crime in the flat or with the car, I cannot be held responsible for my failure to intervene even if I was aware of the criminal activity, for it is not my business to interfere when the fully autonomous person's acts become criminal; I can only be held responsible for dangers arising out of the specific characteristics of my property.[126] In the terminology of the theory of objective (fair) imputation: the autonomous acts of third persons are supervening events which fully set aside my initial causal responsibility (i.e. arguably, by the loan of my apartment or car). I am not responsible for a risk created by the subsequent acts of fully autonomous agents.[127]

[124] *R* v. *Evans* [2009] EWCA Crim. 650, para. 31; see Simester et al., *Criminal Law* (2016), 79–80.

[125] Ashworth, *Obligations* (2013), 54.

[126] Cf. Roxin, *Strafrecht* (2003), § 32 mn. 112–23, 125–6; Freund, '§ 13' (2016), mn. 156–7; Ashworth, *Obligations* (2013), 54–5; Schrägle, *Unterlassungsdelikt* (2017), 238–40, 263.

[127] Roxin, *Strafrecht* (2003), § 32 mn. 125 ff.

IV Failure to Rescue Liability: The Underlying Normative Assumptions

1 *Towards a Convergence of the Common and Civil Law Approach*

As already seen above, general offences that impose liability on bystanders for failures to rescue ('Bad Samaritan laws')[128] – the paradigmatic form of a proper omission offence – are generally rejected in common law jurisdictions,[129] but well entrenched in modern day civil law jurisdictions.[130] Yet, a closer look reveals that the underlying normative assumptions in favour of or against liability for failure to rescue are similar if not identical in both systems.[131] In fact, in France, Article 475 no. 12 of the 1810 CP punished (albeit only as a *contravention*) the failure to assist in case of fire, flooding or other disasters if the assistance was requested by a public authority.[132] It also criminalised the non-reporting of the crimes of treason and counterfeiting.[133] In Germany, the failure to assist was only part of police law, which made the (administrative) sanction dependent on a police order for assistance.[134] The German failure to rescue offence was only introduced in its original form on 28 June 1935 by the Nazi government, which invoked the infamous *gesunde Volksempfinden* ('healthy sentiment of the people') as triggering the duty to assist, especially but not exclusively pursuant to a police order.[135] § 330c of the *Strafgesetzbuch* (StGB) of the Reich was only amended in 1953,[136] to be replaced

[128] On the term see above n. 41.

[129] This can be traced back to Lord Macaulay's concerns as to how to draw the line between punishable and non-punishable omissions (cf. Feinberg, *Harm* (1984), 150–9; Allen, *Textbook* (2017), 40 and was afterwards most clearly expressed by Phillimore LJ in *R* v. *Lowe* [1973] QB 702 Court of Appeal. See also Honoré, *Responsibility* (1999), 41–54, 60–6; Smith, 'Liability' (1984), 90 ff.; Vranken, 'Duty' (1998), 935–6; on Macaulay's influence in Canada see Stuart, Delisle and Coughlan, *Criminal Law* (2018), 259–60.

[130] See Section II herein.

[131] For a historic account starting with the religiously inspired 'early phase of uncritical codification' in the Ancient World and Middle Ages cf. Harzer, *Situation* (1999), 33 ff.

[132] On the influence of this provision in Europe cf. Huschens, *Hilfeleistung* (1938), 17 ff.; also Schrägle, *Unterlassungsdelikt* (2017), 42 according to whom the provision was derogated in 1832. It is overlooked by Vranken, 'Duty' (1998), 937.

[133] Rebut, *Omissions* (2017), mn. 2 (who, however, seems to overlook Art. 475 no. 12 CP).

[134] Harzer, *Situation* (1999), 37–9, 45, 49–52; Kühnbach, *Solidaritätspflichten* (2007), 96 ff.

[135] Reichsgesetzblatt I 1935, 839. On the foundations of Nazi criminal law see Ambos, *National Socialist* (2019), 36 ff.

[136] BGBl 1953 (4 Aug.) I 735. Recently, a second paragraph was added punishing hindering a person who assists another (BGBl 2017, 23 May, I 1226; thereto in favour Schöch, 'Strafbarkeit' (2018), 510 ff.). This corresponds to Art. 223-5 CP, n. 60 above.

by the current § 323c, which removed the reference to the 'gesunde Volksempfinden' and the relic of the police order.[137]

From a normative perspective, it is important to note that the groundwork for this offence was laid by the steady suppression of the liberal, enlightment-based theory of rights violations and its replacement by the theory of duty violations[138] as a sufficient ground for criminalisation.[139] The already mentioned von Feuerbach, liberal-minded and heavily inspired by the Kantian focus on the reason of the person as the starting point of any responsibility, defended the separation between law and morals. As a consequence, he rejected the idea of enforcing moral duties through the criminal law, distinguished between police infractions and criminal offences,[140] and did not include a proper failure to rescue offence in his 1813 Bavarian CC.[141] Similarly, nineteenth-century French doctrine rejected such an offence, given its impact on individual liberty and on the basis of a strict separation of morality and law.[142] As we have seen above, this individualistic approach still informs current French doctrine.[143] In contrast, advocates of the duty violation view consider a violation of a (collective) duty – instead of an (individual) right or concrete interest – usually towards the 'people's community' (*Volksgemeinschaft*) as a whole, as sufficient ground for criminalisation. Given the imprecise boundaries of the duty concept, its unclear direction and the lack of any requirement of a tangible harm, it has rightly been

137 On the Nazi-background of § 323c in detail Harzer, *Situation* (1999), 57 ff.; briefly also Wittmann, 'Hilfeleistung' (2017), 366–7; from a Swiss perspective Maihold, 'Nothilfepflicht' (2013), 136–7.

138 Cf. Schaffstein, '*Pflichtverletzung*' (1935), 108–42 developing his theory of a duty violation in opposition to the 'individualistic disintegration of the past decades' (108) as represented by the liberal theory of the Rechtsgut or Rechtsverletzung (rights violation). The aim was to give more weight to 'criminal attacks against the people's community' and thus to overcome the individualism of the post-enlighment period (109). The person would no longer be seen as an individual but as a 'people's comrade' with intrinsic duties towards the community. The concepts of honour, loyalty and duty take centre stage, preparing the ground for a 'unity of criminal law and the people's moral order' (translations by K. A.).

139 Cf. Harzer, *Situation* (1999), 44 ff.

140 Cf. *ibid.*, 42 ff.; but see also Jakobs, 'Verbrechensbegriff' (2014), 210, 211 ff. (though *Feuerbach* rejected the protection of morals by criminal law, he used police law for this very purpose).

141 Art. 78 Bavarian CC only criminalised the failure to report an offence and to assist in case of harm to others in one common provision, as (secondary) participation of third degree; cf. Harzer, *Situation* (1999), 47.

142 Cf. Rebut, *Omissions* (2017), mn. 4–5.

143 See above Section II *in fine*.

characterised as 'the most expansive conception of crime'.[144] In the case of § 330c StGB (mentioned above), this duty was predicated on the infamous conception of society as the 'people's community' in which the 'people's comrades' (*Volksgenossen*) had to assist each other: a duty of loyalty (*Treuepflicht*) existed towards the people's community – excluding from this community, of course, all non-Aryan persons and those opposing the Nazi-regime.[145] This community-based approach was by no means limited to (Nazi) Germany. In 1911, the Swiss author Ernst Pedotti justified the duty to assist with the duty towards the community that one belongs to and that would not be able to exist without this assistance from all its members.[146]

The traditional common law reluctance 'to impose liability for omissions except in clear and serious cases'[147] is, normatively speaking,[148] rooted in a liberal, rights-focused view which comes close to the Kantian-inspired rejection of such liability by post-enlightenment civil law theorists (like Feuerbach). Both approaches share a strict and formal understanding of personal autonomy and liberty. However, the 'conventional' or 'orthodox' view of the common law has recently been challenged with powerful arguments by criminal law theorists. Thus, Joel Feinberg[149] defends a general failure to rescue offence on the basis of an expanded harm principle,[150] believing such offences to be acceptable as long as the harm is serious enough and no third person with a special duty is likely to assist.[151] In this case, there is a moral/social duty to assist if the agent is able to do so without unreasonable risk to herself,[152] so that the harm sought to be prevented is considerably greater than the harm

[144] Fletcher, *Grammar* (2007), 37.

[145] Cf. BGHSt. 6, 147, 149 ff. (150) explaining the former § 330c StGB ('duty of the individual towards the people's community' (translation by K.A.)). See also the (national socialist) doctoral thesis by Huschens, *Hilfeleistung* (1938), 1, 22 ff.; for further details Ambos, *National Socialist* (2019), 130 ff.

[146] Pedotti, *Nothilfe* (1911), 1–4; thereto Maihold, 'Nothilfepflicht' (2013), 133.

[147] Ashworth, 'Liability' (1989), 424–5; in a similar vein, see Husak, 'Act' (2011), 116.

[148] Some opponents also argue that such a general failure-to-rescue-offence will have no positive effect on people's disposition to assist others in need but may rather 'have a chilling effect on altruistic behaviour', cf. Stewart, 'Failure' (1998), 434.

[149] Feinberg, *Harm* (1984), 126–8; crit. Kühnbach, *Solidaritätspflichten* (2007), 105–6.

[150] Feinberg, *Harm* (1984), 128, 166 and 186 (arguing, at 128, that the harm principle can be understood in the sense of 'harm prevention', thereby approving 'statutes that require people to prevent harm to others' or 'from allowing harm to others that they could prevent').

[151] *Ibid.*, 162, 168, 186.

[152] *Ibid.*, 162–3.

that will be caused by this invasion of the bystander's liberty.[153] In sum, Feinberg, albeit acknowledging the dangers of unchecked police or prosecutorial powers directed 'against decent but unheroic samaritans',[154] advocates a balancing test which rests on the 'plausibility of the moral claim' of an endangered individual 'to be saved . . . without unreasonable risk'.[155]

There are further important voices.[156] Ashworth rejects the 'conventional view', based on an extreme understanding of autonomy with no room for social solidarity, and replaces it with a 'social responsibility view', which points to 'co-operative elements in social life' on the basis of which 'it may be fair to place citizens under obligations to render assistance to other individuals in certain situations'.[157] Fletcher argues that the rejection of a general failure to rescue offence has more to do with 'casual attitudes towards the principle of legality' than with a less-developed communitarian attitude;[158] the degree or quality of any intrusion on liberty depends on the 'content of that which is demanded or prohibited' (the 'substance'), not the 'form (active or passive) of the duty'.[159] The real problem with affirmative duties is not that they ask us to act but 'that they fall due at a time and place over which we have no control'.[160]

153 *Ibid.*, 129–50, 163–5.

154 *Ibid.*, 157: however, he overlooks the even greater dangers in – mainly civil law – criminal justice systems that espouse the principle of mandatory prosecution.

155 *Ibid.*, 185. Similarly, for a reasonableness test, Vranken, 'Duty' (1998), 942.

156 Apart from the ones mentioned in the following cf. Duff, *Answering* (2007), 110, 113; Ormerod and Laird, *Criminal Law* (2018), 61–2 (narrow Bad Samaritan provision can outweigh the objections; high mental threshold applying the callousness standard of Northern Territory in Australia); Chiesa, 'Comparative' (2014), 1092–3 (absence of failure to rescue offence as a disconnect between law and morality).

157 Ashworth, 'Liability' (1989), 425, 430–1; also Ashworth, 'Rettungspflicht' (2013), 116–9. Against Ashworth, Williams, 'Criminal Omissions' (1991), 86, 89–90 arguing that the former misrepresents the 'conventional view'. Essentially following and complementing Ashworth with moral considerations Tadros, *Responsibility* (2005), 182–211 (arguing that an omission is often 'disvaluable' to the relationship among citizens (207 with n. 51) and concluding that the role for the criminal law regarding omissions 'ought to depend upon where we ought to draw the line between what is morally required, one's moral obligations, and what one merely *ought* to do, what would be *for the best*' (208, emphasis in original)).

158 Fletcher, 'Irrelevance' (1994), 1449–50 ('loose, duty-generating canon').

159 *Ibid.*, 1450.

160 *Ibid.*, 1451.

2 *From an Ethical Duty to a Legal Obligation: Solidarity and Conditions of Effective Liberty*

Any morality-based argumentation is, of course, predicated on the assumption that moral duties can be translated directly into legal obligations without further ado, in line with a sort of legal moralism 'as the new orthodoxy in English-language criminal law theory'.[161] This is difficult to reconcile with the separation of law and morals as one of the cornerstones of a liberal and secular criminal law, product of the post-enlightment period.[162] Such a view can admit, at best, a modest legal moralism where criminalisation always requires more than a mere moral wrong, namely a public wrong.[163] At any rate, the turn from a religiously inspired community with failure to rescue offences being justified by reference to the biblical narrative of the good Samaritan, to a liberal, secular, post-enlightenment society based on reason and science entails that a moral, ethical or religious duty to assist does not automatically translate into a legal obligation, never mind a duty demanded by the criminal law.[164] On the contrary, the modern liberal society is characterised by a high degree of individualism and atomisation, which largely displaces communitarian tendencies and assigns to the state responsibility for acting as a substitute for the lack of communitarian solidarity.[165] Thus, while mutual duties to assist can plausibly be justified for ethical reasons in a society based on mutual solidarity[166] – after all, who would not prefer to live in a society where a minimum solidarity exists instead of one where citizens must stand for themselves against all others ('dog eat dog')[167] – it is a different matter whether such ethical reasons trigger a legal duty, let alone one that can be enforced by the criminal

[161] Thorburn, 'Constitutionalism' (2011), 86; for an overview of the varieties of legal moralism see Duff, 'Moralism' (2014), 217 ff.

[162] Cf. Hörnle, 'Rights' (2014), 176–8, 183–4; see in our context of the failure-to-rescue-offence Kargl, 'Hilfeleistung' (1994), 247–8, 261; Seelmann, 'Hilfeleistung' (1995), 282–3 (discussing the classical argument against *legal* duties of solidarity, namely, the argument of the protection of liberty of the assister and her margin of appreciation as well as the argument of the (limited) generalisation of such a duty); Kühl, 'Solidaritätsbegriff' (2013), 98.

[163] Duff, 'Moralism' (2014), 217. Crit of the concept of the 'public' wrong, however, Edwards and Simester, 'Crime' (2017), 105.

[164] Against any recourse to 'moralism' altogether Hörnle, 'Rights' (2014), 178.

[165] Cf. Pawlik, 'Zuständigkeitsbegründung' (1995), 361–3.

[166] Seelmann, 'Hilfeleistung' (1995), 282–3; Kühl, 'Solidaritätsbegriff' (2013), 100.

[167] Wittmann, 'Hilfeleistung' (2017), 370.

law.[168] The concept of solidarity, often invoked to justify criminalisation of a failure to rescue,[169] is not a legal concept proper,[170] and, more importantly, is too vague to be acceptable as a ground for criminalisation.[171] It describes, at best, a preliminary way of identifying putative legal duties,[172] and may merely serve as a general guideline for our behaviour.[173]

At any rate, in order to justify criminalisation on the basis of solidarity, such a concept must be compatible with autonomy and liberty as the building blocks of any liberal society.[174] The key issue then is how to resolve the tension between solidarity and liberty, inherent to any failure to rescue offence. While a formal concept of liberty does not tolerate any infringement upon one's liberty caused by duties to act in a certain way, a material concept of liberty (*effective liberty*) focuses on the actual (material) conditions of the exercise of one's liberty in a liberal society and conceives the duty to assist in certain, exceptional emergency situations as a prerequisite for the fulfilment of this liberty. In other words, our liberty as members of a society can only be fully realised if we can rely on the assistance of fellow citizens in existential emergency situations. The protection of our basic existential freedom is the prerequisite of the exercise of freedom-based rights.[175] On that basis, a limited failure to rescue offence – limiting the duty to assist to dangers to life and limb – can be justified in general terms.[176]

[168] See for this twofold distinction also Seelmann, 'Hilfeleistung' (1995), 283; von der Pfordten, 'Hilfeleistungspflichten' (2013), 106.

[169] Cf. Kühnbach, *Solidaritätspflichten* (2007), 104 (with n. 370), 117. For Kargl, 'Hilfeleistung' (1994), 263 the disposition to assist (*Hilfsbereitschaft*) – which is an expression of solidarity – is a positive value.

[170] Cf. Kühl, 'Solidaritätsbegriff' (2013), 100. For a thorough analysis see Kühnbach, *Solidaritätspflichten* (2007), 149 ff. (221–2): she derives a duty of solidarity from the idea of the social state (*Sozialstaatlichkeit*) and sees it as the other side of the coin of the (negative) duty of *neminem laedere* which is based on the rule of law (*Rechtsstaatlichkeit*); on that basis she tries to develop solidarity as a legal concept (223 ff.) that complements *neminem laedere* as a further principle that justifies the limitation of liberty (225). On the parallel to the idea of the social state see also Seelmann, 'Hilfeleistung' (1995), 282.

[171] Crit. also Pawlik, *Notstand* (2002), 58 ff.; *Unrecht* (2012), 190; Maihold, 'Nothilfepflicht' (2013), 143.

[172] Cf. Harzer, *Situation* (1999), 190–1.

[173] Cf. Kühnbach, *Solidaritätspflichten* (2007), 234–9.

[174] Kühl, 'Solidaritätsbegriff' (2013), 101.

[175] Kühnbach, *Solidaritätspflichten* (2007), 117–8.

[176] Kühl, 'Solidaritätsbegriff' (2013), 101.

3 *The Responsibility of the Concrete Assister*

Yet, this approach – as similar approaches focusing on the legal interests of the person in need[177] – begs the question of why it is the responsibility of the individual assister to protect the material liberty of the person in danger (i.e. the question why *this* very assister is under a duty to assist remains unanswered). An answer can only be found if one focuses on the *situational relationship* between the assister and the person in need. More concretely speaking, to justify the assister's obligation to intervene one must focus on her relationship with the receiver of the assistance, and ask whether a duty to assist can be derived from this relationship, notwithstanding the societal context or framework in which the relationship exists. Thus, the duty to assist is predicated on an interpersonal/intersubjective relationship between the person in need and the assister – drawing on Hegel's relationship of mutual recognition between citizens – which in turn justifies the situational competence of the assister.[178] Only this context of situation *and* legal relationship can trigger legal duties to rescue.[179] The interpersonal relationship can only be protected, in case of a threat to one citizen,[180] by the intervention of another citizen who is competent to assist and part of this intersubjective relationship.[181] However, the assister's competence is limited to the factual basis of the legal relationship and the securing of the victim's autonomy, thus to situations where life, bodily integrity or liberty are endangered.[182] In sum, criminal responsibility is predicated on the trichotomy of situation, legal relationship and competence.[183]

Against this background § 323c StGB seems too broad, and could only be justified by the classic theory of the *contrat social*, where the (moral) duty to assist turns into a legal duty pursuant to the agreement between the citizens (including this duty). Yet, while the contractual idea can be defended in light of modern society's lack of a communitarian or

[177] Cf. regarding the Rechtsguts-approach Maihold, 'Nothilfepflicht' (2013), 142.

[178] Cf. Harzer, *Situation* (1999), 105, 108, 187–219; crit. Maihold, 'Nothilfepflicht' (2013), 152–3.

[179] Harzer, *Situation* (1999), 197.

[180] 'Citizen' needs to be understood broadly here, including persons with temporary residence or just being visitors.

[181] Harzer, *Situation* (1999), 202; on the justification of the competence of the assister cf. 203 ff.

[182] *Ibid.*, 216.

[183] *Ibid.*, 215, 218, 241, 298 (norm proposal).

institutional basis,[184] it is difficult to reconcile with the intersubjective, pre-state relationship of the citizens explained above,[185] unless the underlying contract is also prior to the state (consisting of the very intersubjective relationship of citizens). Apart from that, the fact that the modern social state of Continental Europe imposes a rescue duty on its citizens (and criminalises the failure to intervene) shows that the state needs its citizens – as its administrative agents to whom original state functions are delegated in emergency situations – to fully comply with its protective duties.[186]

A further important theoretical justification for a limited failure-to-rescue offence on the basis of the close relationship between assister and person in need has been offered by von der Pfordten.[187] He advocates the ethical theory of normative individualism according to which – in contrast to communitarian approaches – a justification can only flow directly from the individuals concerned, and not from any collective entity. Any duty towards another person is predicated on an additional and specific relationship, the intensity and duration of which determines the strength of the duty imposed on a citizen. At its highest, such a relationship may be the basis of guarantor duties as discussed above in the context of improper offences of omission; at its lowest, it may arise from ordinary social conduct, for example being part of a group or community (a collective entity), or the realisation of common projects, for example as a member of a collective of farmers. Positive duties of assistance may ensue in such relationships taking into account the interests of the respective individuals and their adequate balancing. Yet, there is no duty to enforce these duties by criminalising non-compliance; at most, such criminalisation is permitted only if the interests at stake are important enough (i.e. life or limb of the person in need of assistance): for only then does the (naturalistic) difference between act and omission lose relevance; and the assister may legitimately be asked to tolerate a minor infringement upon his interests when the endangered interests are of fundamental importance and thus incomparably higher.

If one sums up these different justifications of a duty to assist, it is easy to see that their common ground is the *interpersonal relationship between*

[184] Pawlik, 'Zuständigkeitsbegründung' (1995), 363–4.

[185] Harzer, *Situation* (1999), 221–38 (dismissing Fichte's social contract approach at 229 ff.).

[186] Pawlik, 'Zuständigkeitsbegründung' (1995), 364–5; *Unrecht* (2012), 190–2; crit. Maihold, 'Nothilfepflicht' (2013), 145–8.

[187] Von der Pfordten, 'Hilfeleistungspflichten' (2013), 107–13.

the assister and the person in need. The limitation of the assister's freedom by asking her to intervene can be justified by reference to the grave danger to the freedom of the person in need, a danger which can only be prevented by the assistant. Solidarity operates in this relationship not so much as a duty towards the community but towards the concrete fellow citizen in need – that is, as an interpersonal, guiding principle.[188] So understood, solidarity complements and reinforces liberty and autonomy in the sense of the material concept of liberty defended above; it guarantees the material conditions of liberty and thus the exercise of a real, material liberty.[189]

Of course, a liberal justification of a legal duty to intervene, based on the interpersonal relationship between the assister and the person in need, both acting as autonomous agents, entails, as already pointed out above, the justification of a narrowly defined failure-to-rescue offence, limiting the duty to cases of dangers to life and limb – for only then can the ensuing interference with the liberty of the innocent assister be justified, and her solidarity be demanded.[190] Further, the duty to assist is subsidiary – that is, it is only triggered if the person in need cannot prevent the grave danger to herself, and it cannot be prevented by the state.[191] Last but not least, the duty to intervene must reasonably be expected from the assister; this idea is captured in the normative concept of 'Zumutbarkeit'.[192]

Bibliography

Alexander L., 'Criminal Liability for Omissions: An Inventory of Issues', in Simester A. and Shute S. (eds.), *Criminal Law Theory: Doctrines of the General Part*, Oxford University Press (2002), 121–42.

Allen M., *Textbook on Criminal Law*, 14th edn, Oxford University Press (2017).

188 Kühnbach, *Solidaritätspflichten* (2007), 225–6.

189 See also Kühnbach, *Solidaritätspflichten* (2007), 227–9.

190 Seelmann, 'Hilfeleistung' (1995), 282–3; Kühl, 'Solidaritätsbegriff' (2013), 101; Maihold, 'Nothilfepflicht' (2013), 154; Kühnbach, *Solidaritätspflichten* (2007), 118; more broadly Harzer, *Situation* (1999), 105 ('highly personal legal interests'), 216–7; Pawlik, *Unrecht* (2012), 192.

191 Maihold, 'Nothilfepflicht' (2013), 154; Kühnbach, *Solidaritätspflichten* (2007), 228–9.

192 Maihold, 'Nothilfepflicht' (2013), 154; Pawlik, 'Zuständigkeitsbegründung' (1995), 370–2.

Ambos K., 'The Overall Function of International Criminal Law: Striking the Right Balance between the Rechtsgut and the Harm Principles', *Criminal Law and Philosophy*, 9 (2015), 301–29.

'Book Review "Schrägle, Unterlassungsdelikt (2017)"', *Criminal Law Forum*, 28 (2017), 777–81.

National Socialist Criminal Law, Baden-Baden and Oxford, Nomos and Hart, (2019).

Ashworth A., 'The Scope of Criminal Liability for Omissions', *Law Quarterly Review*, 105 (1989), 424–59.

'Die Rettungspflicht im englischen Recht. Sinnvolle Einschränkungen oder "Island Mentality"?', in Hirsch A. von, Neumann U. and Seelmann K. (eds.), *Solidarität im Strafrecht: zur Funktion und Legitimation strafrechtlicher Solidaritätspflichten*, Baden-Baden, Nomos (2013), 115–31.

Positive Obligations in Criminal Law, Oxford, Hart (2013).

Principles of Criminal Law, 7th edn, Oxford University Press (2013).

Bachmaier L. and del Moral García A., 'Spain', in Verbruggen F. (ed.), *Int. Encyclopaedia: Criminal Law*, 4 vols. Alphen aan den Rijn, Kluwer (2010), IV.

Bohlander M., *The German Criminal Code: A Modern English Translation*, Oxford, Hart (2008).

Bell J., Boyron S. and Whittaker S., *Principles of French Law*, Oxford University Press (2008).

Bentham J. D., *An Introduction to the Principles of Morals and Legislation*, Kitchener, Batoche Books (2000 [1781]).

Berster L. C., *Die völkerstrafrechtliche Unterlassungverantwortlichkeit*, Munich, Utz (2008).

Bosch N., (and Eisele J.) 'Vorbemerkung zu §§ 13 ff.', in Schönke A. and Schröder H. (eds.), *StGB Kommentar*, 30th edn, Munich, C. H. Beck (2019), mn. 1–161.

Bouloc B. and Matsopoulou H., *Droit pénal général et procédure pénale*, 20th edn, Paris, Dalloz (2016).

Bouzat P. and Pinatel J., *Traité de droit pénal et de criminologie*, Paris, Dalloz (1963).

Brammsen J., *Die Entstehungsvoraussetzungen der Garantenpflichten*, Berlin, Duncker & Humblot (1986).

Cassese A., 'Omission Liability and Superior Responsibility', in Cassese A. (ed.), *International Criminal Law*, 3rd edn, Oxford University Press (2013), 180–92.

Chiesa L. E., 'Comparative Criminal Law', in Dubber M. and Hörnle T. (eds.), *The Oxford Handbook of Criminal Law*, Oxford University Press (2014), 1089–114.

Colvin E. and Anand S. S., *Principles of Criminal Law*, 3rd edn, Toronto, Thomson Carswell (2007).

Debove F. and Falletti F., *Précis de droit pénal et de procédure pénale*, 6th edn, Paris, Puf (2016).

Demetrio Crespo E., 'Lección 8: El tipo omisivo', in Crespo D. (ed.), *Lecciones y materiales para el estudio del Derecho Penal*, 7 vols., 2nd edn, Madrid, Iustel (2015), II, 173–93.

Desportes F. and le Gunehec F., *Droit pénal général*, 16th edn, Paris, Economica (2009).

Dias F., *Direito Penal: Parte Especial*, 2nd edn, Lissabon, AAFDL (2007).

Duff R. A., *Answering for Crime: Responsibility and Liability in the Criminal Law*, Oxford, Hart (2007).

'Towards a Modest Legal Moralism', *Criminal Law and Philosophy*, 8 (2014), 217–35.

Duttwiler M., 'Liability for Omission in International Criminal Law', *International Criminal Law Review*, 6 (2006), 1–61.

Edwards J. and Simester A., 'What's Public about Crime?', *Oxford Journal of Legal Studies*, 37 (2017), 105–33

Elliot C., *French Criminal Law*, Uffculme, Willan Publication (2001).

Feinberg J., *Harm to Others*, Oxford University Press (1984).

Feldbrugge F. J. M., 'Good and Bad Samaritans', *The American Journal of Comparative Law*, 14 (1965), 630–57.

Feuerbach P. J. A., *Lehrbuch des gemeinen in Deutschland gültigen peinlichen Rechts*, 2nd edn, Giessen, Heyer (1803).

Fletcher G. P., *Rethinking Criminal Law*, 2nd edn, Boston, Little Brown (1978) [reprint 2002].

'On the Moral Irrelevance of Bodily Movements', *University of Pennsylvania Law Review*, 142 (1994), 1443–54.

Basic Concepts of Criminal Law, Oxford University Press (1998).

The Grammar of Criminal Law, Oxford University Press (2007).

Freund G., '§ 13', in Heintschel-Heinegg B. von (ed.), *Münchener Kommentar StGB*, 8 vols., 3rd edn, Munich, C. H. Beck (2017), I.

Gide A., *La Séquestrée de Poitiers*, Paris, Éditions Gallimard (1930).

Gómez-Aller J. D., 'Criminal Omissions: A European Perspective', *New Criminal Law Review*, 11 (2008) 419–51.

Greene J., 'From Neural "Is" to Moral "Ought": What Are the Moral Implications of Neuroscientific Moral Psychology?', *Nature Reviews Neuroscience*, 4 (2003), 846–50.

Harzer R., *Die tatbestandsmäßige Situation der unterlassenen Hilfeleistung*, Frankfurt a.M., Klostermann (1999).

Hennau C. and Verhaegen J., *Droit pénal général*, Brussels, Bruylant (2003).

Herzberg R. D., *Die Unterlassung im Strafrecht und das Garantenprinzip*, Berlin, De Gruyter (1972).

Honoré T., *Responsibility and Fault*, Oxford, Hart (1999).

Horder J., *Ashworth's Principles of Criminal Law*, Oxford University Press (2016).

Hörnle T., 'Rights of Others in Criminalisation Theory', in Simester A. P., du Bois-Pedain A. and Neumann U. (eds.), *Liberal Criminal Theory: Essays for Andreas von Hirsch*, Oxford, Hart (2014), 169–85.

Hume D., *Treatise of Human Nature*, Books I-III (1739), https://oll.libertyfund.org/titles/hume-a-treatise-of-human-nature.

Husak D. N., *Philosophy*, Totowa, Rowman & Littlefield (1987).

'The Alleged Act Requirement in Criminal Law', in Deigh J. and Dolinko D. (eds.), *The Oxford Handbook of Philosophy and Criminal Law*, Oxford University Press (2011), 107–24.

Huschens W., *Die Unterlassene Hilfeleistung im nationalsozialistischen Strafrecht*, Speyer am Rhein, Pilger (1938).

Jakobs G., *Strafrecht Allgemeiner Teil*, 2nd edn, Berlin, De Gruyter (1993).

'Feuerbachs Verbrechensbegriff: Rechtsverletzung', in Koch A., Kubiciel M., Löhning M. and Pawlik M. (eds.), *Feuerbachs Bayerisches Strafgesetzbuch*, Tübingen, Mohr Siebeck (2014), 209–26.

Jescheck H.-H., 'Die Behandlung der unechten Unterlassungsdelikte im deutschen und ausländischen Strafrecht' *Zeitschrift für die gesamte Strafrechtswissenschaft*, 77 (1965), 109–48.

'Probleme des unechten Unterlassungsdelikts in rechtsvergleichender Sicht', in Wolter J. (ed.), *140 Jahre GA*, Heidelberg, Decker's (1993), 115–29.

Kadish S. H., Schulhofer S. J. and Steiker C. S., *Criminal Law and its Processes*, 9th edn, New York, Aspen Publishers (2012).

Criminal Law and its Processes, 10th edn, New York, Aspen Publishers (2017).

Kahlo M., *Das Problem des Pflichtwidrigkeitszusammenhangs bei den unechten Unterlassungsdelikten*, Berlin, Duncker & Humblot (1990).

Kant I., 'Kritik der reinen Vernunft', in Preussische Akademie der Wissenschaften (ed.), *Gesammelte Schriften*, Berlin, Reimer (1903 [1781]), 3-252, www.korpora.org/kant/aa04/Inhalt4.html; English translation by Meiklejohn, J. M. D., Generic NL Freebook Publisher (1855).

Kargl W., 'Unterlassene Hilfeleistung (§ 323c StGB): Zum Verhältnis von Recht und Moral', *Goltdammer's Archiv für Strafrecht*, 141 (1994), 247–63.

Kaplan J., Weisberg R. and Binder G., *Criminal Law: Cases and Materials*, 8th edn, New York, Aspen Publishers (2017).

Kaufmann A., 'Methodische Probleme der Gleichstellung des Unterlassens mit der Begehung', *Juristische Schulung*, 1 (1961), 173–5.

Die Dogmatik der Unterlassungsdelikte, Göttingen, Otto Schwartz (1988 [1959]).

Kirchheimer O., 'Criminal Omissions', *Harvard Law Review*, 55 (1942), 617–19.

Klotter J. C. and Pollock J. M., *Criminal Law*, 10th edn, Waltham, Elsevier (2013).

Kolb R., 'Droit international pénal', in Kolb R. and Scalia D. (eds.), *Droit international pénal: Précis*, 2nd edn, Bâle, Helbing Lichtenhahn (2012), 195–203

Kühl K., 'Zur Anwendung des Solidaritätsbegriffs auf die unterlassene Hilfeleistung nach § 323c StGB', in Hirsch A. von, Neumann U. and Seelmann K. (eds.), *Solidarität im Strafrecht*, Baden-Baden, Nomos (2013), 93–102.

Kühnbach L., *Solidaritätspflichten Unbeteiligter*, Baden-Baden, Nomos (2007).

Landes W. M. and Poser R. A., 'Salvors, Finders, Good Samaritans, and Other Rescuers: An Economic Study of Law and Altruism', *Journal of Legal Studies*, 7 (1978), 83–128.

Law Commission, *Criminal Law: A Criminal Code for England and Wales*, London, Her Majesty's Stationery Office (1989).

Leroy J., *Droit pénal général*, 3rd edn, Paris, LGDJ (2010).

Liszt F. von, *Der Zweckgedanke im Strafrecht*, 3rd edn, Frankfurt/Main, Vitorio Klostermann (1968 [1883]).

Luzón Peña D.-M., 'Kausalität beim unechten Unterlassungsdelikt?', *Goltdammer's Archiv für Strafrecht* 165 (2018), 520–8.

Maihold H., 'Jenseits weltanschaulicher Ideologien? – Zur Einführung und Begründung der allgemeinen Nothilfepflicht im Schweizerischen Strafrecht', in Hirsch A. von, Neumann U. and Seelmann K. (eds.), *Solidarität im Strafrecht*, Baden-Baden, Nomos (2013), 131–54.

Maiwald M., 'Grundlagenprobleme der Unterlassungsdelikte', *Juristische Schulung*, 21 (1981), 473–83.

Malec A., 'The Is–Ought Problem and Legal Rationality', *Studies in Logic, Grammar and Rhetoric*, 24 (2007), 7–13.

Manning M., Mewett A. W. and Sankoff P., *Criminal Law*, 4th edn, Markham, Lexis Nexis (2009).

Mayaud Y., *Droit pénal général*, 6th edn, Paris, PUF (2018).

Mir Puig S., *Derecho Penal: Parte General*, 10th edn, Barcelona, Editorial Reppertor (2016).

Moore M. S., *Act and Crime*, Oxford University Press (1993).

Muñoz Conde F. and García Arán M., *Derecho Penal: Parte General*, 9th edn, Valencia, Tirant lo Blanch (2015).

Nagler J., 'Die Problematik der Begehung durch Unterlassung', *Der Gerichtssaal*, 111 (1938), 1–63.

Oldnall Russell W. and Ryan E. (eds.), 'Rex v. John Friend and Anne his Wife', in Oldnall Russell W. and Ryan E., *Crown Cases Reserved for Consideration and Decided by the Twelve Judges of England from the Year 1799 to the Year 1824*, London, Butterworth (1825), 20–2.

Ormerod D. C. and Laird K., *Smith, Hogan, and Ormerod's Criminal Law*, Oxford University Press (2018).

Pawlik M., 'Unterlassene Hilfeleistung: Zuständigkeitsbegründung und systematische Struktur', *Goltdammer's Archiv für Strafrecht*, 142 (1995), 363–4.

Der rechtfertigende Notstand, Berlin, De Gruyter (2002).

Das Unrecht des Bürgers, Tübingen, Mohr Siebeck (2012).

Pedotti E., *Die Unterlassung der Nothilfe mit besonderer Berücksichtigung des geltenden und künftigen schweizerischen Rechtes*, Aarau, Sauerländer (1911).

Pfordten D. von der, 'Zur Rechtfertigung von Hilfeleistungspflichten', in Hirsch A. von, Neumann U. and Seelmann K. (eds.), *Solidarität im Strafrecht*, Baden-Baden, Nomos (2013), 103–15.

Politoff I., Koopmans E. and Ramírez J. B., 'Chile', in *International Encyclopaedia of Laws: Criminal Law*, Alphen aan den Rijn, Kluwer Law International (1999), 79.

Pradel J., *Droit pénal général*, 20th edn, Paris, Dalloz (2016).

Droit pénal comparé, 4th edn, Paris, Dalloz (2016).

Pradel J. and Danti-Juan M., *Droit pénal spécial*, 7th edn, Paris, Éditions Cujas (2017).

Pulitanò D., *Diritto Penale*, 7th edn, Torino, Giappichelli (2017).

Rebut D., 'Omissions de porter secours – entrave aux mesures d'assistance', *Répertoire de droit pénal et de procédure pénale* (2017 [2003]).

Roach K., *Criminal Law*, 7th edn, Toronto, Irvin Law (2018).

Robinson P. H., 'Criminal Liability for Omissions: A Brief Summary and Critique of the Law in the United States', *New York Law School Law Review* 29 (1984), 101–27.

Romano M., *Commentario sistematico del Codice penale*, 3 vols. Milan, Giuffré (2004), I.

Roxin C., *Strafrecht Allgemeiner Teil II*, Munich, C. H. Beck (2003).

Sánchez S., 'Entre la omisión de socorro y la comisión por omisión', *Derechos Procesales Fundamentales (Consejo General del Poder Judicial)* 4 (1999), 153–72.

Estudios sobre los delitos de omisión, Lima, Grijley (2004).

'Zur Dreiteilung der Unterlassungsdelikte', in von Schünemann B., Achenbach H., Bottke W., Haffke B. and Rudolphi H.-J. (eds.), *Festschrift für Claus Roxin zum 70. Geburtstag am 15. Mai 2001*, Berlin, De Gruyter (2011), 641–50.

Schaffstein F., '*Das Verbrechen als Pflichtverletzung*', in Dahm G. (ed.), *Grundlagen der neuen Rechtswissenschaft*, Berlin, Junker & Dünnhaupt (1935), 108–42.

Schiff D., 'Samaritans: Good, Bad and Ugly', *Roger Williams University Law Review*, 11 (2005), 77–141.

Schmidhäuser E., 'Über Unterlassensbegriffe – Terminologie und Begriffe', in Britz G. and Müller-Dietz H. (eds.), *Grundfragen staatlichen Strafens: Festschrift für Heinz Müller-Dietz*, Munich, C. H. Beck (2001), 761–82.

Schmidt-Künzel B., *Die Unterlassungsdelikte im französischen Code Penal unter besonderen Berücksichtigungen der unechten Unterlassensdelikte*, Freiburg, Dissertation (1971).

Schmitt R., 'Zur Systematik der Unterlassungsdelikte', *JuristenZeitung*, 14 (1959) 432–4.

Schöch H., 'Zur Strafbarkeit der Behinderung von hilfeleistenden Personen', *Goltdammer's Archiv für Strafrecht*, 165 (2018), 510–19.

Schrägle H., *Das begehungsgleiche Unterlassungsdelikt: eine rechtsgeschichtliche, rechtsdogmatische und rechtsvergleichende Untersuchung und die Entwicklung eines Systems der Garantietypen*, Berlin, Duncker & Humblot (2017).

Schünemann B., *Grund und Grenzen der unechten Unterlassungsdelikte: zugleich ein Beitrag zur strafrechtlichen Methodenlehre*, Göttingen, Schwartz (1971).

'Zur Garantenstellung beim unechten Unterlassungsdelikt', in Böse M. and Sternberg-Lieben D. (eds.), *Grundlagen des Straf- und Strafverfahrensrechts. Festschrift für Knut Amelung*, Berlin, Duncker & Humblot (2010), 303–24.

Seelmann K., '"Unterlassene Hilfeleistung"oder: Was darf das Strafrecht?', *Juristische Schulung*, 35 (1995), 281–6.

Simester A. P., *Legal Theory*, Cambridge University Press (1995).

Simester A. P., Spencer J. R., Sullivan G. R. and Virgo G. J., *Simester and Sullivan's Criminal Law*, 5th edn, Oxford, Hart (2016).

Smith J. C., 'Liability for Omissions in the Criminal Law', *Legal Studies*, 14 (1984) 88–101.

Stephen J. F., *A History of the Criminal Law of England*, 3 vols. London, Macmillan (1883), III.

Stewart M. J., 'How Making the Failure to Assist Illegal Fails to Assist', *The American Journal of Comparative Law*, 25 (1998) 385–436.

Stuart D., Delisle R. J. and Coughlan S., *Learning Canadian Criminal Law*, 14th edn, Toronto, Carswell (2018).

Stuckenberg C.-F., 'Causation', in Dubber M. and Hörnle T. (eds.), *The Oxford Handbook of Criminal Law*, Oxford University Press (2014), 468–89.

Tadros V., *Criminal Responsibility*, Oxford University Press (2005).

Thorburn M., 'Constitutionalism and the limits of the Criminal Law', in Duff R. A., Farmer L., Marshall S. E., Renzo M. and Tadros V. (eds.), *The Structures of Criminal Law*, Oxford University Press (2011), 85–105.

Torre I. B. G. de la and Arroyo Zapatero L., *Curso de Derecho Penal: Parte General*, 3rd edn, Barcelona, Ediciones Experiencia (2016).

Véron M., *Droit Pénal Spécial*, 15th edn, Paris, Dalloz (2015).

Vranken M., 'Duty to Rescue in Civil Law and Common Law: Les extrêmes se touchent?', *International and Comparative Law Quarterly*, 47 (1998), 934–42.

Weigend T., '§ 13', in Laufhütte H. W., Tiedemann K. and Rissing-van Saan R. (eds.), *Leipziger Kommentar Strafgesetzbuch*, 13 vols., 12th edn, Berlin, De Gruyter (2007).

Williams G., 'The Theory of Excuses', *Criminal Law Review*, 1 (1982), 732–73.

'Criminal Omissions: The Conventional View', *Law Quarterly Review*, 107 (1991), 86–98.

Winkler C. W., *Dissertation de Crimine Omissionis*, Leipzig, Breitkopf (1776).

Wittmann R., 'Die unterlassene Hilfeleistung aus rechtsvergleichender und rechtsethischer Sicht', in Joerden J. and Schmoller K. (eds.), *Rechtsstaatliches Strafen. Festschrift Yamanaka*, Berlin, Duncker & Humblot (2017), 363–70.

3

Preparatory Offences

STEFANIE BOCK AND FINDLAY STARK

I 'Preparatory Offences': Definition and Importance

To establish the importance of 'preparatory offences' to a book of this sort, it is necessary to define that concept. 'Preparatory offences' is not a formal category in English or German criminal law.[1] At the most general level, preparatory offences criminalise conduct perceived to carry the risk that, in the future, a 'completed' crime will be committed.[2] Preparatory offences move criminal responsibility back from the actual occurrence of harmful[3] conduct to the planning and preparation stage[4] – conduct that 'pre-dates' the completed offence, and is often quite remote from the threatened harm.

Formally, preparatory offences exist beyond the limit of the *actus reus* of attempts:[5] in English law, 'an act . . . more than merely preparatory to

[1] Cf. the discussion of *Vorfeldstrafrecht* (law on preparatory offences) in Puschke, *Legitimation* (2017), 12–9. The (English and Welsh) Law Commission once proposed an offence of 'criminal preparation'. The proposed offence would have covered much of the ground presently occupied by criminal attempts, rather than expand the scope of liability greatly. See Law Commission, *Conspiracy and Attempts (Consultation)* (2007), pt 16; Rogers, 'The Codification of Attempts' (2008), 937. The idea was abandoned in Law Commission, *Conspiracy and Attempts (Report)* (2009), pt 15.

[2] Puschke, *Legitimation* (2017), 10; Simester, 'Prophylactic Crimes' (2012), 70. The *completed* offence can be another inchoate offence (e.g. intentionally encouraging the commission of an attempt), but we refer to 'completed offences' on the basis that they are more often at issue.

[3] We leave to the side completed offences that are defined in the 'inchoate mode' (that is, not in terms of harm). See, however, n. 52 below.

[4] Murmann, *Grundkurs Strafrecht* (2017), § 28 mn. 4; Wörner, 'Predating Criminal Responsibility' (2012), 1038.

[5] Bein, 'Preparatory Offences' (1993), 186. Cf. Murmann, *Grundkurs Strafrecht* (2017), § 28 mn. 1; Wörner, 'Die deutsche Versuchsdogmatik' (2011) 136. Note, however, that even attempts liability may be regarded as preparatory liability, because it does not presuppose fulfilment of all elements of the completed offence: Puschke, *Legitimation* (2017), 18. Moreover, the reference to the law of attempt runs the risk of oversimplifying the matter as it lays an emphasis on the (formal) incompletion of the offence.

the commission of an offence';[6] in German law, the taking of 'steps which will immediately lead to the completion of the offence as envisaged by' the defendant (*D*).[7] Roughly stated, attempts liability presupposes that *D* has taken 'a significant step towards' committing a substantive crime.[8] Punishing attempts is typically[9] legitimate because (as German theory recognises well) such significant steps, taken in the light of *D's* beliefs about what those steps will lead to, pose a sufficiently concrete danger to a legally protected interest (or at least would do so were *D's* beliefs about what those steps would lead to true). Through taking those steps, *D* has shown clearly his hostile attitude towards the law; an attitude that (as English theorists tend to emphasise) is just as bad as that demonstrated by a 'successful' attempter.[10] Attempts may thus (as German theory tends to emphasise) shatter society's trust in the legal order and can legitimately be punished to reinforce the broken norm, and stabilise the population's legal loyalty (*Rechtstreue*),[11] as well as reflecting (as Anglo-American theory emphasises) *D's* culpability. Our view is that any successful justification of attempts liability must fuse these types of arguments together.

Preparatory offences, by contrast, cover conduct that is less proximate to a completed offence.[12] They shift the focus further from tangible harm-doing, into more tangential risk creation, expanding the boundaries of traditional criminal law.[13] In this chapter, we assume that the

[6] Criminal Attempts Act 1981, s. 1(1). Whether an act is more than merely preparatory is a question of fact (s. 4(3)), making it difficult to derive lessons from the case law. See, however, Clarkson, 'Attempt' (2009), 25.

[7] German Criminal Code, § 22 (*Strafgesetzbuch* (StGB)). This test has been interpreted to mean that *D* must take a step which, in his eyes, means that the completed crime will occur without any further substantial intermediate steps: BGHSt 26, 201, 203–4.

[8] International Law Commission, *Draft Code* (1966), 22.

[9] Special circumstances – such as attempts that would, to any person of ordinary intelligence, appear doomed to fail – are distinct. See Section IV.4 below.

[10] As we note below in Section IV, English law (and the law of many Anglo-American systems) and theory can *over*emphasise the importance of culpability in discussions regarding preparatory offences. It is important that, even in attempts, such culpability is attached to sufficiently threatening conduct.

[11] See Roxin, *Strafrecht II* (2003), § 29 mn. 9; Ambos, *International Criminal Law I* (2013), 234–5, Kühl, *Strafrecht* (2017), § 15 mn. 5. For comprehensive treatment of issues around attempt in Anglo-American criminal law, see Duff, *Attempts* (1996).

[12] Concerns that English and German criminal law might assess proximity differently are left aside, though the German test appears (perhaps far) narrower than Anglo-American equivalents.

[13] The term 'traditional criminal law' is used here to describe criminal norms which – in line with the *Rechtsgutslehre* (criminal law as a means to protect fundamental legal goods), or

further away from the commission of a completed offence Φ-ing is, the more difficult it should be to argue that criminalising Φ-ing is a *proportionate* response.[14] We call this the 'Proportionality Principle'.[15] The Proportionality Principle is closely linked to traditional[16] ideas of justice and state self-restraint. In a nutshell, it forbids the state to go beyond what is necessary and appropriate to achieve a certain (legitimate) objective. By requiring a careful balancing of competing values, the Proportionality Principle restrains government action and prevents the state from excessive interventions into the personal freedoms of its citizens.[17] The Proportionality Principle may thus be regarded as a cardinal principle[18] for any state action. It does not, however, reveal clear and definite limits on particular types of state conduct such as the criminalisation of preparatory offences – rather, the details have to be developed within the framework of a comprehensive balancing exercise taking into account in particular the aims of the criminal law and the rights enjoyed by citizens. In other words, proportionality provides a 'thin', rather than a 'thick', principle.[19]

What the Proportionality Principle readily *does*, however, is challenge the implicit assumption in English and German law that matters should always be resolved in the same way in relation to attempts and to more remote (at least in terms of their conduct elements) preparatory offences.

the harm principle – criminalise only conduct that violates important interests/causes tangible harm. For comparison between these concepts, see Ambos, *International Criminal Law I* (2013), 62–5. It is possible to conceive of there being a *range* of harm principles, some allowing the *risk* of harm to be a potential ground of criminalisation, thus meeting the argument that preparatory offences must be exceptions to the harm principle (e.g. Ashworth, 'Criminal Attempts' (1988), 733–4). See Edwards, 'Harm Principles' (2014), 253. See, also: Carvalho, *Preventive Turn* (2017); Prittwitz, *Strafrecht und Risiko* (1993).

[14] Cf. Simester's requirement of a 'nexus' between the preparatory offence and the anticipated completed offence: Simester, 'Prophylactic Crimes' (2012).

[15] At least some formulations of Ashworth's 'remoteness principle' are similar to the proportionality principle (e.g. the invocation of remoteness throughout Ashworth, 'Criminal Attempts' (1988), 725), but often Ashworth's principle is presented as being solely about *mens rea*, hence the different label.

[16] The Proportionality Principle can be traced back to Greek practical philosophy, Merten, 'Verhältnismäßigkeit' (2009), 521–2.

[17] See the sources cited *ibid.*, 518–21. See, further, Kasper, *Verhältnismäßigkeit und Grundrechtsschutz* (2014), 100–3, 340–52.

[18] See German Federal Constitutional Court (BVerfGE) 23, 127, 133 ('übergreifende Leitregel allen staatlichen Handelns').

[19] Cf. Duff, *Realm of Criminal Law* (2018), 253–5.

In addition, the Proportionality Principle reminds legislatures that the criminalisation of preparatory acts requires careful justification if illegitimate state intervention is to be avoided. The potential for over-criminalisation in this area means that preparatory offences merit consideration in a collection such as this one.

We cannot, however, consider *all* preparatory offences here. That would be unmanageable in one chapter. (Preparatory offences concerned specifically with terrorism are dealt with in another chapter.[20]) Additionally, our arguments are concerned only with the *criminalisation* of preparatory conduct. The infliction of criminal punishment is the severest intrusion into citizens' rights available to a state bound by the rule of law, and carries with it a message of condemnation.[21] Criminalisation is accordingly the last resort – the *ultima ratio* – and should be employed only when all other means are considered ineffective.[22] If we conclude that certain conduct should not be criminalised, then, this does not exclude the use of other, typically less intrusive, means of management by the state (e.g. police warnings or preventive detention of potentially dangerous persons). We cannot, however, address those matters further here.[23]

The definition of preparatory offences offered so far remains a sketch. Section II fleshes it out by reference to a number of examples from English and German criminal law. Section III contends that the main justification for preparatory offences is the management of the risk of the commission of completed offences. Section IV defends a number of constraints on the criminalisation of preparatory offences that stem from a concern with proportionality. Finally, Section V considers the punishment of preparatory offences.

20 See Cornford and Petzsche, Ch. 6, 'Terrorism Offences' (in this volume).

21 See e.g. BVerfGE 90, 145. 172; BVerfGE 120, 224, 240; also European Commission, *EU Criminal Policy*, 11 (criminal law sanctions express 'strong disapproval'). Condemnation here is juxtaposed with the disapproval that may attend an 'administrative' sanction in Germany.

22 This principle is recognised with great force in Germany. See: Roxin, *Strafrecht I* (2006), § 2 mn. 97; Hassemer and Neumann, 'Vorbemerkung zu § 1' (2017), mn. 72; Kasper, *Verhältnismäßigkeit und Grundrechtsschutz* (2014), 243. See, also, BVerfGE 39, 1, 47; Jareborg, 'Last Resort' (2005). Cf. Husak, 'Last Resort' (2004).

23 Difficult questions arise regarding what 'less intrusive' means here (including the types of procedure utilised). See generally Ashworth et al., *Prevention*, and the sources cited in Bock and Harrendorf, 'Strafbarkeit und Strafwürdigkeit' (2014), 374.

II Some Examples of Preparatory Offences

Before discussing examples of preparatory offences from England and Wales, and Germany, it should be noted that the *practical* boundaries of preparatory offences are set in two distinct ways. The focus here is on the limits of offence definitions, which – in Germany[24] – should (as a rule) mean the range of prosecution. In contrast, English law makes use of prosecutorial discretion in the 'public interest'.[25] The 'substantive' criminalisation of preparatory conduct will thus depend to varying extents on police and prosecutorial discretion. What is said below concerns the 'formal' criminalisation of preparatory conduct – 'the law in the books'.[26]

English law has two general offences of preparation: encouraging or assisting crime (a tag for three 'disturbingly wide'[27] offences under the Serious Crime Act 2007 (SCA 2007)) and statutory conspiracy.[28] The SCA 2007 offences replaced the general offence of incitement.[29] They cover *D's* act (or omission to perform a legal duty)[30] where it is *capable* of encouraging or assisting the commission of an offence (or offences) by a principal offender (*P*),[31] and: (i) it is *D's purpose* to encourage or assist *P* to commit an offence (the s. 44 offence);[32] or (ii) *D* believes that his conduct *will* encourage or assist *P* to commit an offence, and believes that *P will* commit that offence (the s. 45 offence); or (iii) *D* believes that *P will* be encouraged or assisted to commit a number of offences, and believes that *P will* commit at least one of those offences, even if *D* is not sure which one(s) *P* will choose (the s. 46 offence).[33] This simplified account

[24] German criminal procedure is based on the principle of mandatory prosecution ('legality'). The prosecutor is – as a rule – obliged to investigate and prosecute all crimes that come to his knowledge; cf. §§ 160, 170 of the German Code of Criminal Procedure (*Strafprozessordnung*).

[25] See CPS, 'Code for Crown Prosecutors', available at www.cps.gov.uk/publication/code-crown-prosecutors.

[26] See Lacey, 'Historicising Criminalisation' (2009), 936.

[27] Ormerod and Fortson, 'Serious Crime Act 2007' (2009), 397.

[28] Under s. 1 of the Criminal Law Act 1977. Other forms of conspiracy in English criminal law are ignored here.

[29] Sometimes known as 'solicitation' in other Anglo-American jurisdictions. Some specific English offences of incitement continue to exist, e.g. Misuse of Drugs Act 1971, s. 19.

[30] SCA 2007, s. 47(8)(a).

[31] *Ibid.*, ss. 44(1)(a), 45(a), 46(1)(a).

[32] This purpose-based understanding of intention is (probably) what Parliament intended: Stark, 'Only Words' (2013), 157; *Hansard*, HC col. 211 (3 Jul. 2007).

[33] It will be noted that, with even this minor level of doctrinal detail, the distinction between attacks and endangerments no longer tracks the distinction between inchoate offences (*in English law*, at least) and offences of endangerment.

will suffice for present purposes, but matters can become more complicated, reducing the fault required to be proved with regard to certain elements of the anticipated offence to recklessness, and making the reach of these offences more controversial.[34] The SCA 2007 covers situations of putative complicity. Were *P* to proceed to commit the encouraged/assisted offence, *D* would be liable as an accessory.[35]

The second general preparatory offence in English law is conspiracy. The *actus reus* is complete once the parties[36] have agreed 'that a course of conduct shall be pursued which, if the agreement is carried out in accordance with their intentions . . . will necessarily amount to or involve the commission of any offence or offences by one or more of the parties to the agreement'.[37] The gist of the *mens rea* of this offence is the parties' common intention that the agreed offence(s) be committed.[38] Although the English courts have at times confused this simple picture,[39] conspiracy *should* require an intention that the relevant agreed conduct be performed and agreed consequences occur, and at least knowledge of (a settled belief in the existence of) any relevant circumstances needed for the commission of the agreed offence.[40] The intention (and agreement) can be conditional, if the ultimate aim of the plan is unequivocally criminal.[41] There is no requirement that such conditions are *likely* to be satisfied,[42] although the more unlikely it is that the conditions will be satisfied, the less secure a finding of the relevant intention to go through

34 See, further, Child, 'Assisting and Encouraging Offences' (2012).

35 *Jogee and Ruddock* [2017] AC 387; *DPP* v. *Maxwell* [1978] 1 WLR 1363.

36 There is no liability for conspiracy where the *only* parties to the agreement are married or in a civil partnership, where one of the two parties to an agreement is under the age of criminal responsibility (10), or where one of the parties is the intended victim of the agreed crime: Criminal Law Act 1977, s. 2(2). On the 'victim rule', see *Gnango* [2012] 1 AC 827, [49]; cf. SCA 2007, s. 51.

37 Criminal Law Act 1977, s. 1(1). 'Course of conduct' ought to be read to refer to conduct and consequences necessary for the completed crime. Cf. *Nock* [1978] AC 979.

38 See Ormerod, 'Statutory Conspiracies' (2006), 389.

39 On occasion, courts have held that the parties need not intend for the ultimate crime to be committed, so long as they intend to 'play their part': e.g. *Anderson* [1986] AC 27. Cf. *Yip Chiu-Cheung* [1995] 1 AC 111; *Edwards* [1991] Crim. LR 45; *Saik* [2007] 1 AC 18, [3].

40 Criminal Law Act 1977, s. 1(2). See, also, *Saik* [2007] 1 AC 18.

41 Cf. *O'Hadhmaill* [1996] Crim. LR 509 and *Reed* [1982] Crim. LR 819. Cf. *Saik* [2007] 1 AC 18, [99]. For criticism of the law on this point, see: Horder, *Ashworth's Principles* (2016), 492; Simester et al., *Criminal Law* (2016), 318; Ormerod and Laird, *Criminal Law* (2018), 449–50. See, further, Child, 'Ulterior *Mens Rea*' (2017), 311.

42 Cf. the proposal in Broderick, 'Conditional Objectives' (1985), 905.

with the agreement may be.[43] Conspiracy thus criminalises a wide range of preparatory conduct between parties (and, it ought to be noted, some conduct that falls short of being even 'preparatory').[44] The offence could – in the wrong hands – become a 'dragnet'.[45]

German law's preparatory offences are ostensibly narrower than those of English law. § 30 StGB is a general provision on conspiracy (or 'attempted participation'),[46] and captures four offences: (i) attempted instigation of a felony;[47] (ii) declaring one's willingness to commit a felony; (iii) accepting another's offer that she will commit a felony; (iv) agreeing with another person to commit a felony or to induce the commission of a felony.

Another general German preparatory offence is § 111 StGB, which criminalises (unsuccessful) *public* incitement to commit crime.[48] This offence exists because of concern that *public* incitement may prompt a large number of persons to engage in criminal activities and cause widespread crime.[49] In contrast to § 30, § 111 is thus aimed not only at the protection of those legal goods of which the instigator invites the violation, but also at the maintenance of public peace[50] – a highly questionable and contested legal concept, which essentially refers to the inviolability of, and society's trust in, the legal order.[51]

Both English and German criminal law also contain a wealth of *specific* preparatory offences. The focus here will be on the general structure of these offences, and the extent to which differing approaches raise different questions of justification and scope.[52]

43 *Saik* [2007] 1 AC 18, [5].

44 See, famously, Johnson, 'Unnecessary Crime' (1973), 1137.

45 American Law Institute, *Model Penal Code* (1985), 387.

46 The German title (*Versuch der Beteiligung*) is perhaps better translated as 'attempted participation'.

47 This provision can cover attempts to induce another person to induce a third person to commit a crime ('chain inducing').

48 Criminal liability arises irrespective of whether or not the incitement is successful: § 111 (2) StGB.

49 BayObLG, *NJW*, 47 (1994), 396; OLG Karlsruhe, *NStZ*, 13 (1993), 398, 390.

50 BGHSt 29, 258, 267; BayObLG, *NJW*, 47 (1994), 396, 397; OLG Karlsruhe, *NStZ*, 13 (1993), 398, 390.

51 Cf. Bock and Harrendorf, 'Strafbarkeit und Strafwürdigkeit' (2014), 369–73.

52 Another issue that may be thought to arise in this context is offences defined in the 'inchoate mode' – that is, without reference to concrete harm/results (this concept was first noted, it appears, in Ashworth, 'Defining Criminal Offences' (1987), 8). For instance, fraud under English law requires an *intention* to make a gain or cause another a loss (or a risk of loss), but no such gain, loss or risk of loss need be proved: Fraud Act 2006, s. 2.

One approach is to criminalise the commission of offence *x* with intent to commit offence *y*. For instance, in English law, it is criminal to commit an offence (e.g. battery) with the intent to thereby[53] commit one or more of a number of sexual offences.[54] German law has few such offences, but an example is aggravated arson – that is, arson committed with the intention of facilitating or covering up another offence.[55] The best view of such offences is that the defendant's ulterior purpose *aggravates* offence *x*.[56]

A second approach is to create preparatory offences that combine *civil* wrongs and the intention to commit an ulterior criminal offence. One form of burglary in English law, for example, requires that *D* enters a building as a trespasser (a civil wrong)[57] with the intention to commit theft, cause grievous bodily harm or cause criminal damage.[58] Trespass with intent to commit a sexual offence is also criminalised.[59] These offences aggravate civil wrongs, transforming them into criminal offences, demonstrating the importance of 'ulterior' intentions in creating preparatory offences.

A third approach is to make preparatory offences dependent on an intention to commit an ulterior offence, even if the base conduct engaged in by *D* is perfectly legal and, 'objectively' unobjectionable. An example is the English offence of 'going equipped to steal'.[60] The items that could be used to steal need not, in themselves, be (civilly or criminally) illegal to possess – such as a crowbar. What makes such possession criminal is *D's* nefarious intention. A German example is

Such conduct is not 'preparatory' in the sense meant here, because it does not anticipate further 'complete' crimes (there is no distinct crime, for example, of 'successful fraud'). Furthermore, the *conduct* caught by these offences will often appear similar to that involved in an attempt.

53 Presumably there must be a close enough link between commission of offence *x* and commission of the relevant sexual offence(s). Driving without insurance would, presumably, not satisfy the requirements of s. 62 if *D* was simply driving to a place where he could find somebody to abuse sexually: Rook and Ward, *Sexual Offences* (2016), para. 14.05. Cf. Ormerod and Laird, *Criminal Law* (2018), 818.

54 Sexual Offences Act 2003, s. 62(1).

55 § 306b(2) no. 2 StGB.

56 See, further, BGH, *NJW*, 53 (2000), 3581, 3582.

57 Note, however, that German criminal law generally considers trespassing a criminal wrong, see § 123 StGB.

58 Theft Act 1968, s. 9(1)(a).

59 Sexual Offences Act 2003, s. 63.

60 Theft Act 1968, s. 25.

§ 89a(2a) StGB, which criminalises the preparation of a serious violent offence endangering the (German) state. This offence requires proof of (i) an attempt to leave Germany, in order to (ii) go to a state where people are trained in the use of firearms, or other skills, that can (iii) be used for the commission of a serious offence[61] against the German state, with (iv) the intention of receiving such training, and (v) the intention to commit an offence of serious violence that endangers the security of the state.[62]

Fourthly, preparatory offences may rely on interactions with other persons. Apart from the general offences mentioned above (the SCA 2007 offences, conspiracy and § 30 StGB), some special preparatory offences are premised on inciting others to engage in *specific* criminal conduct. An example is incitement to racial hatred,[63] or incitement to exploit children sexually.[64] Such offences do not require any practical result. As with the SCA 2007 offences, such crimes combat putative complicity.

The above categories of offence explain explicitly[65] – or at least as a matter of fairly obvious implication[66] – what threatened harm the preparatory offence is aimed at reducing the risk of. Typically, because they are based on a particular ulterior intention, they may be regarded as (what some authors refer to as) attacks,[67] as opposed to endangerments,[68] and are hopefully uncontroversially 'preparatory'.

[61] The following offences are 'serious' for these purposes: intentional killing, abduction for the purpose of blackmail and taking hostages, provided that the offence is intended to impair, and capable of impairing, the existence or security of a state, or of an international organisation, or to abolish, deprive of legal effect or undermine German constitutional principles: § 89a(1) StGB.

[62] See, further, BGH, *NJW*, 70 (2017), 2928, 2929, 2931.

[63] § 130(1) StGB; Public Order Act 1986, pt 3.

[64] Protection of Children Act 1978, s. 1. Cf. §§ 176(2), 176(5) StGB.

[65] For the 'explicit'/'implicit' endangerment distinction, see Duff, 'Criminalizing Endangerment' (2005), 59.

[66] Consider incitement to racial hatred. Presumably *part* of the reason for criminalising such activity is to reduce incidences of racially aggravated violence and property damage. Yet there could be *other* ends that such offences pursue, such as ensuring assured citizenship for citizens who are of a minority racial or ethnic group. To that extent there remains a *slight* lack of clarity over exactly what end is being pursued (and there need not simply be one end). See Duff, *Answering for Crime* (2007), 145.

[67] This depends on whether attacks have an in-built '*actus reus*' requirement that stretches beyond preparation (e.g. an act demonstrating 'practical hostility' towards its target: *ibid.*, 149–50). We cannot resolve that question here.

[68] See Duff and Hörnle, 'Crimes of Endangerment' (forthcoming).

More controversially, it is possible to conceive of a wider class of preparatory offences, which criminalise: (i) dangerous conduct, but do not include the ultimate threatened harm/completed offence in the offence definition; or (ii) the simple possession, acquisition or display of articles, or of knowledge and skills, on the basis that they could be used in the commission of a completed offence.[69] Here, *D's* intentions are (legally) irrelevant,[70] and such intentions may be thought (in terms of ordinary language) as integral to the idea of *preparation*. Perhaps a nefarious purpose may be inferred from the nature of the prohibited item itself,[71] but the object of that purpose is not spelt out in the offence definition.[72] Guesswork is involved. Criminal offences relating to the possession of certain weapons are a classic example;[73] but this final category might also include the 'dissemination of certain written materials' as a more subtle way of influencing the behaviour of others.[74] According to § 184a StGB, for example, it is a criminal offence to disseminate child pornography. The legislature argued that such distribution may create the impression that engaging in sexual activity with children is normal and trivialise the consequences of child abuse. This in turn might – so the legislator feared – encourage child abuse.[75]

We cannot hope to give a full account here of *all* of these varieties of preparatory offences, but note them in order to make clear how broad a field of conduct is conceivably covered by this label, and how such offences push the boundaries of the criminal law far beyond the traditional model of responsibility for *choate* wrongs.

We now consider the general justification for such offences.

[69] Ashworth, 'Possession Offences' (2011), 237: 'risk-based possession offences'. See, further, Husak, *Overcriminalization* (2007), 159–77.

[70] See, also, Puschke, *Legitimation* (2017), 339. Puschke does not consider these offences as preparatory offences. See, also, Dubber, 'The Possession Paradigm' (2005), 101.

[71] Cf. Ashworth, 'Possession Offences' (2011), 237.

[72] See Duff, 'Risks, Culpability and Criminal Liability' (2012), 125.

[73] It is more controversial to conceive of offences of possession of proscribed substances as being preparatory offences. The offence of drug possession *could* be aimed at ensuring that drugs are removed from the streets, reducing the risk of future supply to others, but this justification appears weak in the majority of cases. The more compelling case for criminalisation is possession of drugs *with intent to supply* (a distinct offence). See, further: Puschke, *Legitimation* (2017), 340; Husak, 'Nonconsummate offences' (1995), 179–81.

[74] See, further, Bock and Harrendorf, 'Strafbarkeit und Strafwürdigkeit' (2012), 353–5.

[75] Deutscher Bundestag, *Kinderpornographie* (1992), 6.

III Why Criminalise Preparatory Offences?

By far the most common justification for criminalising preparatory conduct is that doing so reduces the risk[76] that completed crimes will be committed by allowing early state intervention.[77] It is important to state this justification clearly. The availability of early state intervention *in itself* is not a reason to criminalise preparatory conduct.[78] Similarly, arguments based on procedural advantages relating to conspiracy that are found in most Anglo-American systems[79] are not justifications for *having* an offence of conspiracy.[80] These points are not uncontroversial. For instance, potential liability for a preparatory offence might enable the police to put pressure on a suspect to reveal the internal workings of a criminal organisation or to legitimatise procedural measures like property searches or telecommunications surveillance.[81] On this view, the criminal law is a tool to seek cooperation from suspects or to otherwise further criminal investigations.

This is, for us, an illegitimate view of what criminalisation decisions *ought* to involve. On our view, for Φ-ing to be criminalised legitimately on the grounds of controlling a risk of harm, Φ-ing must itself be wrongful in a way that warrants the deployment of the criminal justice system, with its burdens and ultimate message of condemnation.[82] This stems from our conception of the expressive consequences of criminal liability: a criminal conviction announces, loudly, that *D* is a (culpable) wrongdoer.[83] It does not announce that *D* performed non-wrongful

[76] We do not have space to elaborate on the nature of risk. See, however: Stark, *Culpable Carelessness* (2016), 18–20; Oberdiek, *Imposing Risk* (2017), chs. 1 and 2.

[77] See the sources cited in Puschke, *Legitimation* (2017), 30–1.

[78] See, e.g., Law Commission, *Conspiracy (Consultation)* (2007), paras. 2.4–2.10; Dennis, 'Criminal Conspiracy' (1977), 41–3.

[79] Such as the ease of joining defendants in a conspiracy on one indictment and exceptions to the hearsay rule for conspiracies (e.g. Criminal Justice Act 2003, s. 118, rule 7). The US literature tends to emphasise another practical advantage of having an offence of conspiracy: the (Federal) rule ('*Pinkerton* doctrine') that parties to a conspiracy will be parties to offences committed in furtherance of it. See *Pinkerton* v. *US*, 328 US 640 (1946). English law has no such doctrine.

[80] Cf. Law Commission, *Conspiracy (Consultation)* (2007), paras. 2.20–2.21.

[81] See, further, Schäfer, 'Bildung krimineller Vereinigungen' (2017), mn. 8, 172.

[82] See Puschke, *Legitimation* (2017), 437.

[83] This view is common in the English language literature. See, also: BVerfGE 90, 145, 172; BVerfGE 120, 224, 240. If this approach is rejected, then a very different view of the legitimate limits of the criminal law in terms of pursuing consequential ends such as harm-reduction will be arrived at.

conduct that we worry may give rise to wrongdoing (by *D*, or by someone else) at a later date. Nor does it announce that *D* engaged in conduct that, although not wrongful, is of a sort that, if not criminalised, will conduce to wrongful harms (whether perpetrated by *D*, or by *P*). To countenance, through criminalisation, the deployment of the criminal sanction without regard to this message of condemnation is to countenance the moral defamation of the defendant.[84] On our view, then, that Φ-ing is wrongful in a way that warrants condemnation is a necessary (but not sufficient) condition of its being a legitimate candidate for criminalisation.[85]

A preferable version of the harm- and risk-based justification for criminalising preparatory conduct is based on the idea of endangerment of legally protected interests. Preparatory offences combat the *wrongful* risk that the defendant's conduct poses to society generally,[86] or to certain protected goods. In order to guarantee effective protection of legal goods, state intervention at a stage before a criminal attempt should be permitted.[87] Yet, as will be seen, this does not mean that the state may intervene (at least with criminal law measures) whenever there is *any* risk of a completed crime ultimately being committed.

IV The Legitimate Boundaries of Preparatory Offences

Identifying risks worthy of punishment is crucial to ensuring the legitimacy of preparatory offences. The next sections develop principled limitations on the criminalisation of preparatory offences, in line with the Proportionality Principle.

1 *Which Completed Offences?*

In English law, liability for encouraging or assisting crime under section 44 is relatively unlimited in terms of completed offences, and liability for conspiracy can extend to any criminal offence (although the consent of

84 Simester, 'Prophylactic Crimes' (2012), 67.

85 We do not have space here to explore the details of the wrongfulness constraint, but see Simester and von Hirsch, *Crimes, Harms and Wrongs* (2011), ch. 2. Cf. Cornford, 'The Wrongfulness Constraint' (2017); Jescheck and Weigend, *Lehrbuch des Strafrechts* (1996), 50–2; Frisch, 'Grenzen des Strafrechts' (1993), 90–106.

86 E.g. Law Commission, *Assisting or Encouraging Crime* (2006), paras. 4.8, 4.21.

87 Cf. Schünemann, 'Kritische Anmerkungen' (1995), 221; Wohlers, *Deliktstypen des Präventionsstrafrechts* (2000), 281; Ashworth and Zedner, *Preventive Justice* (2014), 95; Puschke, *Legitimation* (2017), 83–125.

the Director of Public Prosecutions is required to prosecute a conspiracy to commit a summary – typically minor – offence).[88] Sections 45 and 46 are slightly more limited, and cannot be committed in relation to attempts, conspiracy, or another section 44, 45 or 46 offence, together with more discrete exceptions.[89]

Liability under § 30 StGB is, by contrast, limited to felonies – offences with a minimum sentence of one year's imprisonment.[90] § 30 is thus far narrower, in terms of relevant completed offences, than English law's general preparatory offences.[91] In this regard, § 30 seems to pay due regard to the Proportionality Principle. Even if it is accepted that *D's* conduct endangers a certain interest through running the risk of the commission of a certain completed crime, it will only be proportionate to criminalise *D's* conduct where the interest is particularly important, or (if not) the defendant has got closer to committing the completed offence by reaching the stage of an attempt.[92] Although *violations* of less important interests are (rightly) captured by the criminal law, the arguments in favour of criminalising *risks* to such interests through preparatory offences are insufficient in the light of concerns regarding proportionality.

One proposal for English law, which would guarantee legal coherence with attempts,[93] would be to decriminalise preparatory offences connected with summary-only offences. This would, however, leave potential liability for a wide range of relatively minor completed offences. A focus on indictable offences would not come close to matching the principled narrowness and proportionality of the German model. This is a shortcoming of English law's approach to categorising offences procedurally.

[88] Criminal Law Act 1977, s. 4(1). A summary offence is one that can be tried only by lay magistrates, as opposed to a judge and jury. Cf. SCA 2007, s. 51A (s. 44 does not apply to the offence of encouraging or assisting suicide).

[89] SCA 2007, s. 49(4), sch. 3.

[90] § 12(1) StGB.

[91] It is difficult to compare German felonies with English crimes, because it is unusual in English law for even the most serious – 'indictable' – crimes (those triable only before a judge and jury in the Crown Court: Interpretation Act 1978, sch. 1) to have minimum sentences.

[92] See, further: Thalheimer, *Vorfeldstrafbarkeit* (2008), 18–21; Bock and Harrendorf, 'Strafbarkeit und Strafwürdigkeit' (2014), 379. Cf. the view that attempts are conceptually distinct from offences based on managing the risk of completed offences in Yaffe, *Attempts* (2012), ch. 1.

[93] Attempts can only be committed in relation to indictable offences: Criminal Attempts Act 1981, s. 1(1).

One potential remedy (short of reflecting offence seriousness more fully in the distinction between summary-only and indictable offences) would be to focus on the sentencing ranges utilised by the Sentencing Council in passing its guidelines. The helpfulness of this suggested solution depends, however, on such guidance being both internally coherent (within each 'type' of offence) and externally coherent (with the sentencing ranges for other 'types' of offence). That is a matter that we cannot probe further here.[94]

2 *Which Risks?*

To minimise the risk of over-criminalisation, pre-dating criminal responsibility is legitimate only if *D* creates an *unacceptable* risk of the completed offence's occurrence.[95] This is not only a question of the value of the threatened interest, but also of how substantial the risk to this interest must be before criminalisation is proportionate.

In English law, this concern is not taken seriously. Encouraging or assisting crime, for example, requires only that the defendant's conduct was *capable* of encouraging or assisting an offence.[96] German law is again more restrictive. As a general rule, it does not criminalise attempted aiding and abetting.[97] § 30(2) StGB applies only to agreements to commit crimes *jointly*, criminalising putative liability as joint principals under § 25(2) StGB.[98] For instance, if *D* supplies *P* with plans to *V's* bank vault, intending thereby to assist *P* in the burglary, *D* will be an accessory to the completed burglary if *P* commits it. If, however, the burglary is not attempted by *P*, *D* is not liable under § 30. Yet *D* would be liable for

94 The Sentencing Council's guidance aims at making existing sentencing practice consistent and tracking existing trends (typically upwards in terms of severity over time), rather than rethinking sentences from the ground up.

95 With regard to preparatory offences/offences of abstract endangerment, see Schünemann, 'Kritische Anmerkungen' (1995), 211. Cf. Bock and Harrendorf, 'Strafbarkeit und Strafwürdigkeit' (2014), 378; Puschke, *Legitimation* (2017), 417–8.

96 For criticism, see Ormerod and Fortson, 'Serious Crime Act' (2009), 394–5.

97 Thalheimer, *Vorfeldstrafbarkeit* (2008), 130; Rackow, Bock and Harrendorf, 'Überlegungen zur Strafwürdigkeit' (2014), 693.

98 Joint commission is characterised by a functional division of the criminal tasks between co-perpetrators, linked together by a common agreed plan. Every co-perpetrator fulfils a certain task which contributes substantially to the commission of the crime (in the sense that, without it, the commission of the offence would be impossible). See, further: Ambos and Bock, 'Germany' (2013), 330–2.

encouraging or assisting burglary under s. 44 of the SCA 2007 as soon as he supplied the plans.[99]

The German view is based on the notion that, when compared to instigating conduct, acts of putative assistance constitute a lesser concern,[100] and thus do not reach the threshold level of risk necessary to justify the pre-dating of criminal responsibility.[101]

(Such an argument could, incidentally, have explained English law's pre-2007 position, which covered urging *P* to commit a crime (even if unsuccessfully), but not trying to help *P* to commit a crime.[102])

Additionally, under German law, any plan to commit an offence must be sufficiently 'concrete' to incur liability under § 30 StGB.[103] A conviction for agreeing to commit murder, for example, does not require the defendants to have decided on the time and place that they will kill *V*. Agreement has to be reached, however, on the offence (e.g. murder), means of killing (e.g. poison), the victim (e.g. one of the parties' wives),[104] and – more controversially – the parties' motive (e.g. to allow the parties to have a future together without *V*).[105]

99 This broader approach is thought necessary to avoid impunity gaps. With more restrictive preparatory offences, the argument runs, the state could be powerless to punish criminal 'bosses' who plan crimes on a large scale, with no intention of getting their hands dirty, at least until completed offences have been attempted. By contrast, heads of criminal organisations are regarded as co-perpetrators if they play a suitably dominant role in the planning stage. Cf. BGHSt 33, 50, 53; BGHSt 37, 289, 292; Ambos and Bock, 'Germany' (2013), 331 and the sources cited there. Accordingly, their involvement in conspiratorial agreements would be covered by § 30(2) StGB, even if the agreement is not put into action.

100 This is not merely an empirical claim in the sense that acts of putative assistance do less to increase the likelihood that the anticipated crime will be committed. It also (and primarily) reflects different levels of normative involvement. If *D* wants to persuade *P* to kill *V*, he tries to exercise direct influence and aligns himself fully with the later crime. If *D* merely agrees to supply *P* with a weapon so that *P* can shoot *V*, *D's* influence is more subtle; he subordinates himself and his contribution to *P's* plans. For this reason, German law grants aiders and abettors a mandatory statutory discount in sentencing (§§ 27, 49 StGB) while instigators are sentenced as if they were principals (§ 26 StGB).

101 Cf. Eisele, 'Teilnahme' (2016) mn. 177, 93; Murmann, *Grundkurs Strafrecht* (2017), § 28 mn 14.

102 An approach criticised, influentially, in Spencer, 'Trying to Help' (1987), 148.

103 BGHSt 44, 97, 101; BGHSt 50, 142; Heine and Weißer, 'Versuch der Beteiligung' (2019), mn. 5. See, further, Schünemann, 'Versuch der Beteiligung' (2014), mn. 24–30, mn. 67–8 and the sources cited there.

104 The courts have been less restrictive with regard to agreements to commit robbery: BayOBL, *NJW*, 7 (1954), 1257.

105 BGH, *NStZ*, 27 (2007), 697. The position in English law regarding the details that must be agreed in order to form a conspiracy is vague: see Simester et al., *Criminal Law* (2016), 317.

A requirement that criminal plans be suitably developed conduces to proportionality.[106] Pre-dating criminal responsibility necessarily restricts citizens' sphere of individual freedom.[107] In order to avoid undue interference with liberty, preparatory offences should thus exclude cases where *D* has a legitimate interest in engaging in the relevant conduct.[108] The legislature – even when driven by the idea of risk management and harm prevention – must respect the right to free development of one's personality.[109] The state has no right to criminalise purely 'internal' matters like thoughts and ideas (or, for that matter, character traits),[110] unless and until they become manifest in 'external' (socially threatening) behaviour.[111] To criminalise such matters is incompatible with the respect for autonomy that the criminal law should show citizens,[112] and constitutes a disproportionate intervention into privacy.

The same is true, we suggest, of intentions that are not yet deployed in an action that sufficiently threatens to bring about a completed offence. Walen has argued that 'illicit' intentions, which cause 'an agent to be, in a certain way, disposed to perform actions that can independently be determined to be impermissible'[113] are distinct from other intentions. He suggests that 'the choice to form and act on an illicit intention itself' is impermissible (presumably in a way that the criminal law could respond to).[114] We disagree. Leaving aside the unclear line between desire and intent in such cases,[115] defendants should have the opportunity to change their minds, and show due respect to the criminal law's commands, even if they form 'illicit' intentions.[116] Although this does not rule out the legitimacy of *any* intervention at a stage before the 'last act' of a criminal

[106] See, similarly, Puschke, *Legitimation* (2017), 364.

[107] See Cornford, 'Indirect Crimes' (2013), 497–505; Ashworth and Zedner, *Preventive Justice* (2014), 109.

[108] Schünemann, 'Kritische Anmerkungen' (1995), 212–13.

[109] Puschke, *Legitimation* (2017), 404.

[110] Cf. Husak, 'Preventive Detention' (2013).

[111] Jakobs, 'Kriminalisierung' (1985), 756; Ashworth and Zedner, *Preventive Justice* (2014), 110; Puschke, *Legitimation* (2017), 404.

[112] See Duff, *Answering for Crime* (2007), 104–5.

[113] Walen, 'Illicit Intentions' (2006), 39.

[114] *Ibid.*, 46. Walen's paper is about *permissibility* of conduct in general, rather than the criminal law. He has nevertheless pushed us, in correspondence, to consider its implications for the criminalisation of preparatory offences.

[115] Alexander and Ferzan with Morse, *Crime and Culpability* (2009), 202–3; Duff, 'Risks, Culpability and Criminal Liability' (2012), 122, 133.

[116] For further difficulties, see: Alexander and Ferzan, 'Pre-Emptive Action' (2012), 647–57; Simester, 'Prophylactic Crimes' (2012), 70.

attempt, it should make us nervous about *very early* interventions (and sympathetic to a defence of withdrawal in preparatory offences, as discussed below).[117] It is instructive, in this regard, that Walen discusses such intentions when tied to conduct that approaches the upper limit of preparatory offences (i.e. attempts), but not much more preliminary conduct.[118] We think that Walen's position is closer to ours than it may initially seem.

Even when behaviour that risks the commission of a completed crime has been engaged in, the state – in accordance with the Proportionality Principle – must consider *D's* conduct and the possible impact on individual rights of its criminalisation.[119] For example, offences of hate speech must not unduly constrain freedom of expression.[120] Also problematic is the criminalisation of acquiring knowledge and skills that can be used to commit certain offences.[121] Learning is a key element of human betterment and thus should only rarely be subjected to criminal punishment, if at all.[122] Again, until such learning is deployed in a sufficiently threatening action, the criminal law should be not capable of deployment. Finally, one must consider the impact on privacy of a criminal law that probes into 'illicit intentions' (when not actualised in externally threatening conduct) and the risks of 'false positives'.[123]

Implicit English acceptance that preparatory liability may intrude disproportionately into citizens' liberty is provided in section 50 SCA 2007, which provides a defence to encouraging/assisting crimes concerned with 'acting reasonably'. This defence requires consideration of '(a) the seriousness of the anticipated offence[(s)]; (b) any purpose for which [*D*] claims to have been acting; [and] (c) any authority by which

[117] See Section IV.6 below.

[118] See e.g. Walen, 'Illicit Intentions' (2006), 65–7.

[119] This is the consequence of the Proportionality Principle requiring a careful balancing of competing values. A measure is disproportionate if the claimed benefit (a reduction in the risk that completed offences are committed) exceeds the costs (restrictions on liberty rights etc.).

[120] The case-by-case approach adopted by the German Constitutional Court is visible in e.g. BVerfG, *NJW*, 6 (2003), 660. Cf. the US Supreme Court's jurisprudence on the need for a 'clear and present danger … [of] the substantive evils that the United States Congress has a right to prevent': see *Schenck* v. *US*, 249 US 47 (1919).

[121] See e.g. § 89a(2) no. 1 StGB: receiving instruction in the use of firearms or other skills that can be of use for the commission of a serious offence endangering the state.

[122] See Puschke, *Legitimation* (2017), 406. See, also, Chou, *Legitimität von Vorbereitungsdelikten* (2011), 196.

[123] See, similarly, Simester, 'Prophylactic Crimes' (2012), 65.

[*D*] claims to have been acting'. There is no case law on this defence.[124] The defendant shoulders the burden of proving this defence on the balance of probabilities.[125] The 'acting reasonably' defence is a shameful definitional cop-out. Rather than identify properly the preparatory *conduct* that merits criminalisation, when balanced against citizens' interests in liberty etc., the legislature has left it to *D* to prove that his conduct did not unjustifiably threaten some legal good. Not even this indulgence is extended to those charged with conspiracy.[126]

3 *Preparatory Offences and Imputation*

With preparatory offences, the criminal law is deployed before anyone's choice to commit an offence solidifies into the execution of a criminal plan. This is particularly problematic for preparatory offences that rely on *D's* interactions with others.[127] Even if *D* and *P* agree that *P* should murder *V*, it is still *P's* choice whether to keep to his word. Even if *D* will almost always contribute to the *risk* of *P's* offending (the general justification of criminalising preparatory conduct) in such scenarios,[128] the significance of *P's* choice remains.

An extreme argument is that actions like the planning, attempted instigating etc. of a crime do not themselves endanger a protected legal good, because of *P's* freedom of choice. They are thus *never* criminalisable wrongs.[129] This view links the assessment of preparatory conduct to more general ideas of causation and imputation[130] and might offer

124 The Law Commission provided some examples (Law Commission, *Assisting or Encouraging Crime* (2006), para. 6.23). These are not binding on the courts.

125 *Carr-Briant* [1943] KB 607. The compatibility of this provision with Art. 6(2) ECHR's guarantee of the presumption of innocence has not yet been challenged. For English law's approach to such matters, see *Sheldrake* v. *DPP; Attorney-General's Reference (No. 4 of 2002)* [2005] 1 AC 264.

126 The Law Commission has, however, suggested that a similar reasonableness defence should be available there: Law Commission, *Conspiracy (Report)* (2009), pt 6.

127 This is sometimes referred to as an offence involving 'remote harm' (e.g. Simester and von Hirsch, *Crimes, Harms and Wrongs* (2011), chs. 4–5), but can also be referred to as an 'indirect crime' (e.g. Cornford, 'Indirect Crimes' (2013), 485).

128 Cornford, 'Indirect Crimes' (2013), 493–4.

129 Köhler, *Strafrecht* (1997), 32, 545. See, similarly, Jakobs, 'Kriminalisierung' (1985), 765; Chou, *Legitimität von Vorbereitungsdelikten* (2011), 187.

130 As a matter of principle, on this view, free, deliberate and informed human inventions break the chain between the defendant's conduct and its result(s). See: Bohlander, *German Criminal Law* (2009), 48; Kühl, *Strafrecht* (2017), § 4 Rn. 83–96; Simester, 'Causation in (Criminal) Law' (2017), 434–5.

another explanation for Germany's reluctance to criminalise attempted aiding and abetting. This extreme view should, however, be rejected.[131] At least *sometimes D's* conduct properly marks him out as a criminal, even if *P* would have to choose (in)appropriately in order for the completed offence to come about. The difficulty lies in identifying such situations.[132]

One view holds that *D's* preparatory conduct is appropriately criminalised where he is 'normatively involved' with *P's* potential choice.[133] Often, this sense of involvement is one of *D's* allying herself with *P's* probable choices in a way that makes imputing those choices to *D* through the medium of criminalisation legitimate. Simester and von Hirsch argue that such alliances are present in situations of advocacy (incitement).[134] Their ultimate thesis is that assistance can ally *D* with *P's* choices when what *D* provides has a 'core use' consistent with *P's* wrongful choice: for instance, the supply of a handgun (in a system where handgun possession is generally prohibited) allies *D* with *P's* plan to shoot *V*; the supply of a crowbar to *P* does not ally *D* with *P's* choice to break into *V's* house.[135] This distinction is sometimes difficult to draw, but it emphasises the importance of the fact that the commission of the completed offence is dependent largely on *P's* voluntary decision(s).

This concern about normative involvement may illuminate German law's approach to preparatory offences. § 30 StGB's criminalisation of attempted participation is often justified on the assumption that planning a crime is more dangerous if done by several people rather than a person

[131] We do not have room here to deal with the question of whether causation is necessarily problematic where there is a voluntary choice by *P* following *D's* original contribution. We merely note that this matter is contested in theory. See e.g. Moore, *Causation and Responsibility* (2009), chs. 11–13.

[132] For a recent attempt to do so, albeit in a different framework from ours, see Alexander and Ferzan, *Reflections* (2018), ch. 2. There, it is argued (inter alia) that the interest in not having other people's choices restrict one's options is to be taken into the balance when asking whether *D* took an unjustified risk that, as a result of her actions, *P* would be in a position to choose to bring about criminal harm.

[133] Simester and von Hirsch, *Crimes, Harms and Wrongs* (2011), 81. Simester and von Hirsch are clear that this is a broad concept, which leaves much normative work to be done by specific arguments in specific contexts (81–5).

[134] *Ibid.*, 82.

[135] *Ibid.*, 84–5. See, also, Simester, 'Prophylactic Crimes' (2012), 75. It may be thought that this example points in favour of criminalising attempted aid. The 'core use' thesis is, however, almost always deployed in relation to inherently dangerous or illicit items, and the supply of such a dangerous item almost necessarily suggests that *D* is accepting of *P* using the item in a criminal manner.

acting alone. On one view, this is because of economies of scale, which can be regarded as increasing the risk that the completed crime will be committed.[136]

A connected point concerns group dynamics. The lone plotter need not explain or defend a decision to abort the criminal plan to others. When two or more people are acting together, however, peer pressure and felt obligations towards others may reduce the chances of *P* turning back.[137] The parties may have entered into 'quasi-contractual' obligations,[138] where the common planning of a completed crime increases the risk that it will be committed.[139] It could be argued that it is this 'quasi-contractual' element that makes imputation of *P's* anticipated choices to *D* less objectionable; it 'normatively involves' the group in *P's* putative choice to continue.

Consider the prominent (German) case where *D1* and *D2* 'met' under pseudonyms in an internet chat-room and agreed to abduct, abuse and finally kill a schoolboy during the next school holiday. The *Bundesgerichtshof* held that the defendants were not accountable for agreeing to commit a crime, because they had not revealed their true identities to each other and thus were not able to hold one another 'to their word' – that is, the agreement was not 'enforceable' in the relevant sense.[140] English law would have no difficulty in convicting these defendants of either encouraging or assisting crime(s) or conspiracy. Indeed, a defendant who attempted to incite another internet user to kidnap a child would be liable for a section 44 offence as soon as the message was posted

[136] See: Katyal, 'Conspiracy Theory' (2003), 1307; Bock and Harrendorf, 'Strafbarkeit und Strafwürdigkeit' (2014), 338–47; BGHSt 10, 388, 389; BGHSt 44, 91, 95; Law Commission, *Assisting or Encouraging Crime* (2006), para. 5.27; Law Commission, *Conspiracy (Consultation)* (2007), paras. 2.11–2.19; *Callanan* v. *United States*, 364 US 587, 593–4 (1961); *Hamilton* [2005] SCR 432, [25]–[26]. This argument depends on predictions about *general* dangerousness. Some individual offenders must be more determined/ capable than some inept conspirators.

[137] See Katyal, 'Conspiracy Theory' (2003), 1307.

[138] This is arguably not the case in an attempted aiding and abetting scenario. Even if *P* accepts the plans to the bank given to him by *D*, this does entail the (felt) obligation to rob the bank.

[139] BGHSt 10, 388, 389; BGHSt 44, 91, 95; Roxin, *Strafrecht II* (2003), § 28 mn. 5; Schünemann, 'Versuch der Beteiligung' (2007), mn. 3; Murmann, *Grundkurs Strafrecht* (2017), § 28 mn. 6; Kühl, *Strafrecht* (2017), § 20 mn. 245; Bock and Harrendorf, 'Strafbarkeit und Strafwürdigkeit' (2012), 361 and the sources cited there. Cf. American Law Institute, *Model Penal Code* (1985), 388; Letzgus, *Vorstufen der Beteiligung* (1972), 130–1.

[140] BGH, *NStZ*, 21 (2011), 570.

online,[141] even if nobody read it.[142] Such early liability cannot easily be justified, because *D1* could legitimately claim not to be sufficiently involved with spurring on *D2's* choices through the operation of group dynamics/peer pressure. Even if one may *feel* encouraged by the words of strangers, there is no real sense in which one is *bound* by them. The anonymous case is, however, a borderline example. Although it is true that the 'quasi-contractual' element is not fully fulfilled, anonymous internet communication might be regarded as particularly dangerous. The exchange with people with similar (socially and legally marginalised) ideas in a secure environment, such as a closed chat-room, may reinforce a person's deviant disposition and thus ally the parties to their criminal plans to a much higher degree than non-virtual, face-to-face communication would.[143]

Not all examples of the operation of § 30 can be explained by the idea of quasi-contractual agreements. A person who asks another to commit a crime is in no way obliged to that person. Another reason for punishing the (attempted) *instigator* (as compared with the attempted aider or abettor) might be that he cannot fully control how the other person will act in the future. A risk is unleashed by the communication itself,[144] and one with which the instigator has allied himself sufficiently, through *seeking* to create a crime that otherwise would not have been contemplated.

This idea is nevertheless employed too broadly in both the English and German systems. If *D* writes a letter to *P*, inciting *P* to murder *V*, but the letter is lost in the post, *D* is liable, respectively, for encouraging or assisting murder (her conduct in sending the letter was *capable* of encouraging or assisting *P* to commit murder) and for attempted instigation (§ 30(1) StGB).[145] As in the case of attempted aiding and abetting, the principle of personal responsibility and self-determination calls for a narrow(er) approach here. Arguably, the risk unleashed by *D* becomes

[141] When *D* posts the message, he has done an act *capable* of encouraging the kidnapping, and *intended* that his conduct would in fact encourage the kidnapping.

[142] It is not always clear, in English cases, to whom *precisely* encouragement to commit a crime was addressed. It does not matter for liability. See e.g. *Blackshaw* [2012] 1 WLR 1126.

[143] See, further, Bock and Harrendorf, 'Strafbarkeit und Strafwürdigkeit' (2012), 337.

[144] Schünemann, 'Versuch der Beteiligung' (2007), mn. 3; Roxin, *Strafrecht II* (2003), § 28 mn. 5; Bock and Harrendorf, 'Strafbarkeit und Strafwürdigkeit' (2012), 361; Puschke, *Legitimation* (2017), 400.

[145] Cf. BGH, *NJW*, 9 (1956), 299; Schünemann, 'Versuch der Beteiligung' (2007), mn. 17.

concrete enough to justify punishment *only* if *P* reads the letter. Only then does it seem legitimate to punish *D*.[146]

Indeed, one might go further. *D's* conduct remains remote from the ultimate crime (*V's* murder) even when *P* reads the letter. The risk of a completed offence increases markedly only if *P* is persuaded to commit murder (which will be a matter to be ascertained from *P's* subsequent conduct). It would, however, be a radical restriction (but not an unjustifiable one) to require such persuasion of *P* to be proved before criminal liability could be imposed on *D*.

4 *Objectively Non-Dangerous Conduct*

If preparatory offences are justified because they manage the risk of completed crime, does this require it to be 'objectively' possible for the completed crime to be committed?[147] Consider if *D* agrees with *P* that *P* should murder *V*. Unbeknownst to *D* and *P*, *V* had died earlier that day. From an 'objective'[148] point of view (assuming that this would be based on the knowledge that *D* and *P* lack), the conspiracy between *D* and *P* does not threaten a protected interest; they cannot risk *V's* life. Nevertheless, both contemporary[149] English[150] and German[151] law reject such 'factual impossibility' as a bar to liability for preparatory offences. *D* and *P* would be liable for conspiracy to/attempted participation in murder.

There are two explanations for this approach. First, in *this* example, the specific target (*V*) cannot be threatened, and the assumption is that this fact removes the danger to the relevant protected interest (life). If, however, *D* and *P* are plotting a crime against *V1*, but *V1's* absence means they will simply move on to *V2*, there is still a risk to the relevant protected interest *in the long run*. This does not appear to be an

146 See Zaczyk, 'Strafbarkeit des Versuchs' (2017), mn. 12; Letzgus, *Vorstufen der Beteiligung* (1972), 175; Puschke, *Legitimation* (2017), 400.

147 We assume that *legal* impossibility (e.g. an agreement to commit non-criminal conduct that *D* and *P* believe to be criminal) should operate as a 'defence'.

148 See generally Fletcher, *Rethinking Criminal Law* (1978), ch. 3.

149 At common law, 'factual impossibility' was a defence to conspiracy and incitement: *Nock* [1978] AC 979; *Fitzmaurice* [1983] QB 1083.

150 On conspiracies, see Criminal Law Act 1971, s. 1(1)(b). Although the SCA 2007 is silent on this matter, it is *assumed* that 'factual impossibility' is no bar to liability for encouraging or assisting crime. See Ormerod and Laird, *Criminal Law* (2018), 500.

151 Cf. BGHSt 4, 254; Schünemann, 'Versuch der Beteiligung' (2007), mn. 30, 32, 69; Zaczyk, 'Strafbarkeit des Versuchs' (2017), mn. 61.

argument for not allowing a factual impossibility defence. Rather, it is an argument for doubting that factual impossibility with regard to the risk of the commission of a completed offence exists. There will always be more potential victims to target.

Furthermore, this 'next time . . .' argument is only plausible in some situations, such as a group of thieves agreeing to victimise a general class of persons (say, patrons at a particular nightclub), rather than specific individuals. It is true that the factual impossibility of stealing from *V1* (who has no money), if recognised as a 'defence', would leave the defendants free to try again against *V2* and *V3* on different nights.[152] Although this is – in the end – an empirical question, it is highly doubtful that many murderers would be similarly indiscriminate. In such cases, it is plausible that *V's* absence would remove any realistic risk of a completed murder; and in cases of more complexity (e.g. where the defendants are caught long before it is apparent whether there was any possibility of success) the issue of whether such a risk remained would have to be decided by a court.

A focus on the culpability of the plotters better explains why factual impossibility is deemed irrelevant even in cases where there is no 'objective' risk of a completed crime being committed. Indeed, this is the dominant reason why Anglo-American criminal law rejects 'factual' impossibility in contexts such as criminal attempts.[153] *D* and *P*, in the example above, have an intention to commit murder that is just as culpable (given their ignorance of *V's* death) as that held by defendants who *could* realistically threaten another person's life. Epistemic issues aside, it would (the argument goes) be 'unacceptable' to allow *V's* (premature!) death – a matter of luck – to determine liability here.[154] A similar approach could be taken towards encouraging/assisting crime and other preparatory offences.

Focusing on culpability/*mens rea* alone, however, risks over-criminalisation. Holding persons liable although they have not created an objective risk may be appropriate (at least most of the time) in the law of attempt. Here, *D* has come considerably closer to the actual violation of a protected interest by taking steps proximate to the commission of the crime. His action – in combination with his subjectively culpable

[152] Law Commission, *Attempt and Impossibility* (1980), paras. 2.85–2.100.

[153] E.g. Criminal Attempts Act 1981, ss. 1(2), 1(3); Model Penal Code, § 5.01(1) (cf. § 5.05(2)).

[154] *Dynar* v. *United States* [1997] 2 SCR 462, [106].

attitude – is capable of seriously threatening society's trust in the legal order,[155] and thus arguably deserves punishment, even if the attempt will necessarily fail.[156] This argument, however, is less persuasive with regard to preparatory offences.[157] As the Proportionality Principle suggests, as *D's* conduct moves further away from the commission of a completed offence, its possible social impact is less obvious, which makes justifying punishing *D's* behaviour more difficult. Where it was factually impossible for the completed crime to come about, justifying criminalisation becomes even harder.

We nevertheless think it is possible to justify the criminalisation of preparatory offences related to 'impossible' ends. Consider if *D1* and *P1* formulate a detailed plan to kill *V1*, intend to carry it out, etc. and are then arrested. *D2* and *P2* formulate an identical plan to kill *V2*, with an identical intention, etc. and are arrested at the same stage. Unbeknownst to *D1* and *P1*, *V1* has died. *V2* has not. If this simple fact were to make the difference between liability and non-liability, one may argue that this over-privileges factors that do not redound to *D1* and *P1's* credit and therefore reject a *general* defence of factual impossibility for preparatory conduct.[158]

This approach to factual impossibility is subject to one mandatory exception, in our view: where it was obvious, when the preparatory conduct was carried out, that there was no substantial risk that it would culminate in the commission of the threatened offence. If nobody of ordinary intelligence[159] would have feared the eventual commission of the threatened completed offence, then the defendants should be

155 Our view is that it is enough to criminalise Φ-ing that Φ-ing is the *type* of action that threatens trust in the social order. We are not persuaded that the fact that individual tokens of Φ-ing might not actually threaten trust in the social order (e.g. where the only person who ever discovers the preparatory conduct is a police officer) necessitates a different approach.

156 Cf. Köhler, *Strafrecht* (1997), 458–9; Zaczyk, *Unrecht der versuchten Tat* (1989), 128. See, also, Duff, *Attempts* (1996), 219–33.

157 Cf. *Nock* [1978] AC 979, 997 (where it was contended that all inchoate offences must adopt the same position on factual impossibility).

158 This does not mean, however, that a more restrictive approach could not be justified. Given that the actual conduct is so remote from harm-doing, the legislator may also decide to recognise factual impossibility as a general defence for preparatory offences and take the fact that *D1's* and *P1's* conspiracy does not objectively endanger *V1's* life as a sufficient ground to treat them differently from (and to privilege them over) *D2* and *P2* (who engaged in objectively dangerous conduct).

159 Difficult questions inevitably arise when defining 'ordinary' for these purposes, but we do not see this as being fatal to our proposal.

acquitted, even if – from their misguided perspective – the chances of the completed crime's completion were high.[160] To hold otherwise would be to over-privilege the defendants' culpability, and get too far from the justifying aim of preparatory offences – namely the management of the risk of completed offences being committed.[161] If the preparatory conduct is obviously doomed to 'failure', it cannot threaten the type of social volatility with which the criminal law ought to be concerned in this context.[162] Such situations are likely to be rare (examples of similar approaches in relation to criminal attempts are almost always hypothetical). It is nevertheless important that the law recognises them, especially in a system like Germany, where prosecutorial discretion is (as a rule) unavailable as a convenient mechanism for avoiding real doctrinal thought about such scenarios.

Similar concerns apply to the penalisation of fake offers; for instance, *D* promises that he will supply to *P* a child for the purposes of sexual abuse,[163] but has no intention of actually doing so. *D* does not unleash any risk for the sexual autonomy of a child.[164] Nor does he intend to. To punish *D* would be to deploy the criminal law disproportionately.[165] What of *P*? It is a contested matter whether *P* would be liable under § 30 StGB if he accepted *D's* offer,[166] whilst it is assumed that liability for encouraging or assisting crime (on the basis that *P's* acceptance is *capable* of encouraging *D* to go ahead, and is intended to do so) would be available in English law. Our view is that *P* can only be held liable for a preparatory offence if *D's* offer was *not so obviously fake* that no person of ordinary intelligence would have thought it was serious.

5 *Culpability and the 'Remoteness Principle'*

As has been seen already at various points, a risk-based understanding of preparatory offences means that more justificatory work is done by *D's*

[160] For a broadly similar approach to factual impossibility in attempts, see Duff, *Attempts* (1996), 380–4.

[161] Letzgus, *Vorstufen der Beteiligung* (1972), 186–7.

[162] See, similarly, Weigend, 'Attempting the Impossible' (1978).

[163] An offence under § 176(5) StGB. See Deutscher Bundestag, *Sexualverbrechen* (2002), 13.

[164] Renzikowski, 'Sexueller Missbrauch von Kindern' (2017), mn. 61; Bock and Harrendorf, 'Strafbarkeit und Strafwürdigkeit' (2014), 360.

[165] Notably, criminal responsibility under § 30 StGB is to a large extent limited to genuine offers/declarations: Schünemann, 'Versuch der Beteiligung' (2007), mn. 20, 63, 87 and the sources cited there. Cf. Letzgus, *Vorstufen der Beteiligung* (1972), 186.

[166] Schünemann, 'Versuch der Beteiligung' (2007), mn. 97.

mens rea than in completed offences. Accordingly, preparatory offences ought to require *D* to be *more* culpable than the equivalent completed offence requires, to make up for the deficit in harm that is present in preparatory offences.[167] This is sometimes referred to as the 'remoteness principle',[168] which flows from the Proportionality Principle.[169]

In English law, most (but not all)[170] preparatory offences are premised on an intention that a completed crime be committed.[171] A focus on intention is somewhat unusual in English criminal law, which often allows lower forms of fault – most prominently recklessness (typically understood as the advertent taking of an unjustified risk)[172] – to be sufficient for criminal liability in completed offences. At first blush, then, the remoteness principle, an offshoot of the Proportionality Principle, is respected in English law.

In German law, *dolus eventualis* will in most cases satisfy the fault element of the preparatory and complete offences.[173] The relationship

[167] BGH, *NJW*, 67 (2014), 3459; Puschke, *Legitimation* (2017), 363; see also BGH, *NJW*, 70 (2017), 2928, 2931. The remoteness principle cannot answer, abstractly, the question of *how* culpable a risk-taker must be to legitimately be held liable: Husak, *Overcriminalization* (2007), 174–5.

[168] See: Horder, *Ashworth's Principles* (2016), 492; Ormerod, 'Statutory Conspiracies' (2006), 187; Law Commission, *Assisting or Encouraging Crime* (2006), para. 4.61. Cf. Husak's 'high culpability' requirement in Husak, 'Nonconsummate Offenses' (1995), 171–2. Remoteness becomes even more of an issue with 'double inchoate' liability (e.g. encouraging or assisting the formation of a conspiracy): Wade, 'Prevention of Harm' (2008), 247.

[169] This does not necessarily mean that *attempts* ought to require intention as to all elements of the completed offence. For the English debate on this issue, see Ormerod and Laird, *Criminal Law* (2018), 414–20.

[170] E.g. the offences under SCA 2007 can be committed without intention (so long as there is belief, or in some cases recklessness – see the text accompanying n. 176 below). Basic possession-based offences do not require proof of a relevant 'ulterior' intention.

[171] Intention may not always be understood in the same way in relation to each crime: Stark, 'Only Words' (2013), 155. In English law, intention is also not always synonymous with purpose. In a range of contexts, intention *may* be found where *D* realised that it was virtually certain that a certain circumstance or consequence would come to pass, e.g. in murder (*Woollin* [1999] 1 AC 82). In encouraging/assisting crime, the focus in s. 44 is on purpose exclusively, with foresight of virtual certainty falling under the requirement of *belief* in ss. 45/46 (see n. 32 above). This makes no explicit difference to the potential sentence, but in practice might do so. In conspiracy, it is possible that foresight of virtual certainty may result in a finding of the relevant intention(s): see Simester et al., *Criminal Law* (2016), 325–6. The same approach may be taken in other forms of preparatory offence (typically, there is no case law available).

[172] See *G and Another* [2004] 1 AC 1034. See, also, Stark, *Culpable Carelessness* (2016), ch. 2.

[173] With regard to attempted instigation, see: BGHSt 44, 97, 101; Heine and Weißer, 'Versuch der Beteiligung' (2019), mn. 28; cf. Puschke, *Legitimation* (2017), 375. With

between *dolus eventualis* and English law's fault elements (particularly recklessness) is not straightforward, but *dolus eventualis* is certainly wider than English law's understanding of intention.[174] This slight narrowing in culpability cannot, however, compensate for English law's extremely wide *actus reus* elements in the preparatory offences.[175]

In any event, matters become more complicated in English law because, although the SCA 2007 offences require an intention to encourage or assist the commission of an offence, or a belief that a crime will be encouraged or assisted (and committed), this rule applies only to *conduct* elements of *P's* crime. For circumstance and consequence elements, and *P's mens rea*, *recklessness* on *D's* part will suffice. For instance, for a section 45 offence of encouraging or assisting murder, it would be enough to prove that: (i) *D* committed an act *capable* of encouraging or assisting *P* to commit murder, *believing* that it *would* encourage or assist *P*; whilst (ii) believing that *P* would perform whatever conduct element kills *V* (e.g. hit *V* repeatedly); and (iii) foreseeing a risk (and taking it without adequate justification) that *P* would cause *V's* death; and (iv) foreseeing a risk (and taking it without adequate justification) that *P* would mean to cause *V* at least serious bodily harm.[176] These culpability requirements are extremely low, given how far removed from murder *D's* conduct

regard to public incitement, see: OLG Frankfurt, *Neue Zeitschrift für Strafrecht – Rechtsprechungs-Report* NStZ-RR, 8 (2003), 327. Notably, the requirement that the plan to commit an offence must be sufficiently 'concrete' to incur liability under § 30 StGB can in practice rarely be met by a person acting with *dolus eventualis*.

174 According to the German Supreme Court, *D* acts with *dolus eventualis* (and thus with intention), 'when he recognizes the occurrence of the result in the definition of the crime as possible and not entirely unlikely, and therefore agrees with it in such a way that he accepts and condones the realization of the definition or at least comes to terms with it for the sake of the objective which he seeks, even if the occurrence of the result is in itself not desired', BGHSt 36, 1, 9 – English translation by Dubber and Hörnle, *Criminal Law* (2014), 569. See, further, Taylor, 'Concepts of Intention' (2004), 99.

175 To illustrate this point by (further) examples: § 30(1) StGB's conception of instigation presupposes some form of communication (mental contact) between instigator and perpetrator, which means that the creation of a situation which may cause another person to commit a crime is not sufficient: Schünemann, 'Versuch der Beteiligung' (2007), mn. 14; Heine and Weißer, 'Versuch der Beteiligung' (2019), mn. 17. See, further, Ambos and Bock, 'Germany' (2013), 333. Thus, it would be insufficient for *D* to leave a knife out, desiring that *P* will use it to murder *V*. This would (in theory) be sufficient for liability for encouraging/assisting murder under s. 44 of the SCA 2007. A general announcement of willingness to commit a felony on Facebook would also be insufficient to incur liability under § 30 StGB: Rackow, Bock and Harrendorf, 'Überlegungen zur Strafwürdigkeit' (2012), 693, but could be a s. 44 offence of encouraging or assisting the formation of a conspiracy (assuming *mens rea* could be proved).

176 This is the result of reading s. 44 in line with s. 47 of the SCA 2007.

may be.[177] The remoteness principle (and thus the Proportionality Principle, from which it stems) is violated in this abstract sense, but also in the more concrete sense that conspiracies, carrying an ostensibly higher risk of completed crime (because of group dynamics and the nature of agreements), generally require *higher* fault elements (intention as to conduct and consequences, and knowledge/intention as to circumstances).[178]

Moreover, even relatively high *mens rea* requirements may not themselves be sufficient to justify punishment. Consider the German offence that is committed once *D* attempts to leave Germany and go to a state where people are trained in skills that can be of use for the commission of serious violent offences endangering the (German) state, with the intention of receiving such training.[179] This offence requires three intentions: the intention to leave Germany, the intention to receive terrorist training in another state, and the intention to commit a serious violent offence endangering the (German) state. This is doubly preparatory liability:[180] § 89(2a) criminalises the preparation (leaving Germany) for the preparation (receiving terrorist training) of a crime (a violent offence endangering the state). *D's* conduct is 'objectively' neutral and far removed from the ultimate feared harm. § 89(2a) comes very close to the criminalisation of purely 'internal' matters and is, in our view, unjustifiable.[181]

6 *Withdrawal*

English law does not recognise a 'defence' of withdrawal[182] in preparatory offences.[183] The act capable of encouraging or assisting crime, or the

[177] The Law Commission had proposed originally that *belief* would be the lowest form of fault, but – peculiarly – defined it with regard to *D's* 'not caring' whether a foreseen circumstance existed or consequence occurred: Law Commission, *Assisting or Encouraging Crime* (2006), para. 5.118. There is no real space between this conception of belief and the standard understanding of recklessness in English criminal law.

[178] Criminal Law Act 1977, s. 1(1)–(2).

[179] § 89a(2a) StGB.

[180] BGH, *NJW*, 70 (2017), 2928, 2931.

[181] See, also, Paeffgen, 'Vorbereitung' (2017), mn. 58. The BGH has nevertheless deemed it to be compatible with the German Constitution, BGH, *NJW*, 70 (2017), 2928, 2931.

[182] There is not space to consider this matter here, but it is in theory possible to distinguish amongst abandonment (desistance), withdrawal (notifying confederates of an intention to not proceed with the plan) and renunciation (active rejection of the plan/intervention): Robinson, *Criminal Law Defenses* (1984), 347.

[183] It should be noted that this harsh approach towards withdrawal is found in other Anglo-American jurisdictions (see e.g. Stuart, *Criminal Law* (2011), 734–5), though certainly not all (see e.g. Model Penal Code, §§ 5.02(3), 5.03(6)).

agreement,[184] will be enough to found liability (even if, in practice, some cases will never come to the attention of the authorities and/or be prosecuted). Subsequent steps to prevent the encouraged/assisted/agreed crime can, strictly, only mitigate sentence, even if successful.[185] The best that a defendant can hope for is to secure an arrangement whereby he is not prosecuted (perhaps in return for giving evidence against other persons).[186]

§ 31 StGB, by contrast, provides a specific rule on withdrawal in relation to § 30. *D* is not liable if he voluntarily[187] gives up the further execution of the criminal endeavour and – if necessary – averts any existing danger that the completed crime will be committed.[188] The effort required by *D* depends on the concrete circumstances of the case – that is, how far any plan has advanced. If, for example, *D* has declared to *X* that he is willing to kill *V*, he can withdraw simply by giving up his plans, that is, by changing his mind. It is not necessary that he informs *X* accordingly, or in any other way openly revokes his declaration.[189] The reason for this broad approach is that *D* – as would-be direct perpetrator – fully controls the future course of action. If he gives up the criminal purpose, he eliminates any risk to the legal interest threatened by the suggested crime.[190] Imagine on the contrary that *D* managed to persuade *P* to kill *V*. *D* is exempted from punishment, under existing German law (as a rule) only if he successfully annihilates the risk caused by his instigating conduct, for example by convincing *P* to give up his plan, or

[184] *Hussain* [2002] Crim. LR 407. Cf. withdrawals *before* an agreement has been concluded: *Walker* [1962] Crim. LR 458.

[185] Law Commission, *Conspiracy (Report)* (2009), para. 2.37.

[186] What used to be known as 'turning Queen's evidence' is now regulated by a statutory framework found in the Serious Organised Crime and Police Act 2005.

[187] The prevailing German view understands 'voluntarily' in a strict psychological sense. *D* must be driven by autonomous motives and capable of deciding of his own free will to carry on or abandon his plans. Cf. Bohlander, *German Criminal Law* (2009), 149, Roxin, *Strafrecht II* (2003), § 30 mn. 354–8; Dubber and Hörnle, *Criminal Law* (2014), 384–5. Notably (and correctly), 'voluntariness' is excluded in particular when the matter is taken out of *D's* hands (e.g. *D* is arrested) or where the circumstances overwhelm the freedom of *D's* choice to desist (e.g. an unexpectedly high police presence in a certain area). See the overview on the German case law in Hoffmann-Holland 'Rücktritt' (2017), mn. 106–8. See, also, Duff, *Attempts* (1996), 395–7.

[188] Cf. Heine and Weißer, 'Rücktritt vom Versuch' (2019), mn. 3, 8, 9; Schünemann, 'Rücktritt vom Versuch' (2007), mn. 4, 15, 19.

[189] Cf. Heine and Weißer, 'Rücktritt vom Versuch' (2019), mn. 8; Schünemann, 'Rücktritt vom Versuch' (2007), mn. 15.

[190] Schünemann, 'Rücktritt vom Versuch' (2007), mn. 15.

informing the police of the intended crime, who then prevent its commission.[191]

Satisfying the elements of § 31 results in a full acquittal. The rationale behind this exemption is controversial.[192] The most convincing account[193] links withdrawal provisions to the purposes of punishment. By his (late, yet voluntary) turning back, the actor can show that he again embraces and respects the legal order, even if he had, previously, acted wrongfully and culpably.[194] This of course depends on what it means to withdraw (which will, in turn, depend on how much *D* has done, and to what extent the relevant risk of a completed crime has begun to materialise).[195] He has also compensated adequately for unleashing a risk on the putative victim(s).[196] As the legal order was ultimately upheld, punishment appears unnecessary to prevent him from future crimes (special prevention), to deter others (negative general prevention), or to restore public confidence in law's integrity (positive general prevention).[197]

191 Heine and Weißer, 'Rücktritt vom Versuch' (2019), mn. 5. See, similarly, Robinson, *Criminal Law Defenses* (1984), 362. Cf. Model Penal Code (1985), § 5.03(6) (requiring that the defendant 'thwarted the success of the conspiracy'). In some cases it seems questionable to require *D's* efforts to be successful. It would be unduly harsh, for example, to hold *D* liable on the basis of an unexpectedly ambivalent/negligent police response. Contrast a situation where *D* becomes involved in preparatory conduct with a particularly stubborn *P*.

192 See: Lilie and Albrecht, 'Rücktritt' (2007), mn. 5–45; Ambos, 'Rücktritt' (2017), mn. 1 and the sources cited there.

193 For different approaches see: RGSt 73, 53, 60; American Law Institute, *Model Penal Code* (1985), 359, 458; Hoffmann-Holland, 'Rücktritt' (2017), mn. 21–4. Cf. Ambos, 'Rücktritt (2017), mn. 1; Fletcher, *Rethinking Criminal Law* (1978), 186. The state may also be urged to balance the probability that *D* will respond to the law's reasons (by withdrawing) against the potential harm that may result from advanced preparatory conduct: Ohana, 'Desert and Punishment' (2007), 123–4. Indeed, there is a risk that *D*'s cooperation with the authorities may speed up *P's* criminal plans: Law Commission, *Conspiracy (Report)* (2009), paras. 2.38–2.45.

194 Revocation does not make the previous conduct non-wrongful or non-culpable: Duff, 'Risks, Culpability and Criminal Liability' (2012), 135.

195 A similar proportionality-based test is accepted in the English law of complicity: *O'Flaherty* [2004] 2 Cr. App. R. 20. Cf. the narrow test of renunciation in the Model Penal Code (noted in n. 191 above).

196 See, similarly, with regard to withdrawal from attempts, Roxin, 'Rücktritt vom unbeendeten Versuch' (1972), 270.

197 BGHSt 9, 48, 52; English translation by Dubber and Hörnle, *Criminal Law* (2014), 382. See, further: Ambos, 'Rücktritt' (2017), mn. 1; Roxin, 'Rücktritt vom unbeendeten Versuch' (1972), 270. Cf. Duff 'Risks, Culpability and Criminal Liability' (2012), 139–41.

Despite this, it has been contended that prosecutors need to be able to induce suspects to cooperate in order to catch more serious offenders, and the threat of liability for conspiracy is one such incentive.[198] As we have already suggested, this is an unsound basis for the *creation* or *maintenance* of criminal offences. It (once again) confuses the consequences of having a criminal offence in place (and its functional benefits) with the question of whether that offence justifiably criminalises the defendant's conduct.

Overall, the withdrawal defence is a necessary safeguard against over-criminalisation,[199] ensuring the proportionality and legitimacy of preparatory offences.[200] Notably, this holds true not only for general preparatory offences like conspiracy and encouraging/assisting crime but also for specific, risk-based offences which criminalise certain preparatory acts as such. In the latter case, withdrawal provisions are disposable only if the prohibited conduct itself represents a violation of another (e.g. lesser) legal good worthy of criminal protection.[201] It is thus striking that withdrawal defences are often omitted in *specific* preparatory offences, even in those Anglo-American systems where (something like) withdrawal can negate liability for general preparatory offences.[202]

V How Should Preparatory Offences Be Punished?

A final (brief)[203] point, again related to the issue of proportionality, concerns the sentencing of preparatory offences.

198 E.g. Law Commission, *Conspiracy (Report)* (2009), para. 2.37.

199 This point has been noted by some English authors. For support of a 'defence' of withdrawal for encouraging/assisting crime and conspiracy, see: Spencer, 'Trying to Help' (1987), 160; Simester et al., *Criminal Law* (2016) 307, 318–9. Cf. Horder, *Ashworth's Principles* (2016), 485, 502.

200 Puschke, *Legitimation* (2017), 412–15.

201 Take, for example, the dissemination of child pornography. The legislative aim is stated to be the prevention of copycat crimes. However, the dissemination and viewing of pornographic material also violates the personal rights and dignity of the child (cf. Hörnle, 'Verbreitung, Erwerb und Besitz' (2017), mn. 4). This is a discrete legal interest so that it is not necessary (nor meaningful) to back up this offence with a withdrawal provision.

202 See Husak, 'Nonconsummate Offenses' (1995), 174, 178. 'Something like' is necessary because there is a potential debate about whether renunciation of a criminal purpose is identical to withdrawal. See n. 182 above.

203 We cannot deal here with a number of deeper points about the purpose(s) of punishment, and what punishment is imposed for (the preparatory offence itself, the

In German Law, the basis for sentencing (guilt)[204] is determined by the gravity of the crime, its overall significance for the legal order and the personal blameworthiness of the defendant.[205] This means that sentences must match the 'wrongfulness of the act' (*Handlungsunrecht*) and the 'wrongfulness of the result' (*Erfolgsunrecht*).[206] Preparatory offences are generally characterised by a lesser Erfolgsunrecht than completed offences, because the defendant has neither violated a protected legal good, nor caused tangible harm. He has merely created a risk. Preparatory offences are thus less serious and the defendant's guilt is accordingly lessened.[207]

This idea is reflected in the sentencing regime relating to § 30 StGB. The sentencing range for attempted participation/conspiracy depends on the sentencing range for the intended offence, but a mandatory statutory discount is applied (via §§ 30(1) and 49(1)).[208] This structured approach is not applicable to specific preparatory offences. Here, it is up to the legislature to avoid over-punishment by determining the sentencing range in a way which duly reflects the risk-based nature of the crime.[209]

English law's approach to sentencing preparatory offences is, predictably, less determinate. The maximum sentence for conspiracy or section 44 or 45 offences is the maximum penalty for the intended/envisaged

preparatory offence *and* any conduct carried out in pursuit of moving to the next stage of commission?). Nor can we deal with issues around the 'merging' of offences.

204 § 46 StGB.

205 The seminal case is BGHSt 20, 264, 266.

206 Cf. Miebach and Maier, 'Grundsätze der Strafzumessung' (2016), mn. 29–31.

207 Cf. in the context of attempted offences: Zaczyk, 'Strafbarkeit des Versuchs' (2017), mn. 4; Ashworth and Zedner, *Preventive Justice* (2014), 95. The German approach could, ultimately, result in *no* punishment being imposed, but the conviction standing: § 59 StGB.

208 In the case of intentional killings, for example, principals are liable to imprisonment for between five and fifteen years (§§ 212, 38 StGB), unless the law provides for life imprisonment. For preparatory offences relating to the commission of an intentional killing under § 30 StGB, sentences range from two years to eleven years and three months' imprisonment.

209 Consider public incitement to crime (§ 111 StGB). If the completed offence is carried out, the defendant is sentenced as if he were a principal. Otherwise, the penalty is reduced to imprisonment not exceeding five years, or a fine. In other cases, however, it is highly questionable whether the statutory sentencing ranges are proportionate. A person preparing a terrorist offence by leaving Germany in order to receive arms training in another state is liable to imprisonment from six months to ten years. This is harsh considering that the conduct – departing the Federal Republic of Germany – is very remote from the ultimate harm. See Paeffgen, 'Vorbereitung' (2017), mn. 60.

offence.[210] The maximum penalty for a section 46 offence is the maximum penalty available for the most serious of the offences *D* believes *P* may commit.[211] The Law Commission said nothing in the relevant reports to justify this approach to sentencing. As no sentencing guidelines exist for preparatory offences,[212] it is left to the discretion of the judge to assess the seriousness of the crime. While this flexible approach allows responsiveness to the particularities of each case, it offers no effective safeguards against disproportionate punishment as a result of, for example, an overestimation of the dangerousness of *D* or his conduct. In order to avoid arbitrary (non-)gradation of punishments, it would be preferable to have some sort of normative guidelines on how to weigh the inchoate nature of *D's* conduct and culpability. This would also be effective in sending out a firm message that committing a completed crime usually *is* worse (because harm has occurred) than preparing to commit one.[213]

The little relevant guidance that does exist in England and Wales could be clearer in this regard. For instance, the Definitive Guideline regarding fraud (which is defined in the 'inchoate mode' in English law)[214] suggests that actual harm to the victim's interests matters.[215] Although part of the 'harm' component of the Guideline treats intended harm as being the same as actual harm, the impact on the victim allows adjustments to be made to the starting point for the sentence. It is, however, more difficult to assess the approach to fraud-related preparatory offences. Consider the guidance on possessing an article for use in fraud (a preparatory

[210] Criminal Law Act 1977, s. 3; SCA 2007, s. 58(3). The maximum penalty for encouraging/assisting/conspiracy to murder is a discretionary life sentence, rather than a mandatory life sentence (the penalty for murder): Criminal Law Act 1977, s. 3(2); SCA 2007, s. 58(2).

[211] SCA 2007, s. 58(3). This approach has resulted in some unsatisfactory case law: see. Stark, 'Encouraging or Assisting' (2013), 497.

[212] Any sentencing guidelines and scales for relevant intended/envisaged offences are considered, but it is not clear how much weight they hold. See e.g. *Watling* [2013] 2 Cr. App. R. (S.) 37, [13]; *Hall* [2014] 2 Cr. App. R. (S.) 20. The Sentencing Council has produced guidance on *some* preparatory offences relating to terrorism: *Terrorism Offences: Definitive Guideline* (2018).

[213] The English approach is no doubt premised on the fear that an exceptional case of preparatory conduct may merit a sentence in line with the sentences for completed offences. Exceptional cases should not be allowed to rule the approach to ordinary cases to *this* extent.

[214] See Fraud Act 2006, ss. 1–4.

[215] Sentencing Council, *Fraud, Bribery and Money Laundering Offences: Definitive Guideline* (2016).

offence),[216] where 'harm' is calculated by 'weighing up all the factors of the case to determine the harm that would be caused if the article(s) were used to commit a substantive offence'. In short, the relevant 'harm', for sentencing purposes, is that which *would* have occurred had *D* carried out her plan. It is not plain, from the guidelines, what difference should occur in sentences where the harm does, and does not, occur. This lack of certainty is indefensible and unsustainable in a context where more and more sentencing discretion is being mediated by formal guidelines.

VI Conclusion

This chapter has sketched an account of constraints, flowing from the Proportionality Principle, that could stem the rampant use of preparatory offences – particularly in England and Wales, but also to an extent in Germany. The reasons why Germany is slightly more reluctant in pre-dating criminal liability are probably to a great extent linked to cultural differences that reflect different preconceptions about the legitimate deployment of the criminal sanction. In particular, the Proportionality Principle is a basic idea in German constitutional law and, as such, plays a crucial role in the (political and academic) discourse on the criminal law. In addition, in a system based on the principle of mandatory prosecution, it is vital strictly to limit offence definitions to acts truly worthy of punishment. In a system that grants broad discretionary powers to the prosecution, who can filter out cases which do not deserve or require a criminal law response, more latitude in offence definitions can exist without injustice *necessarily* following. These are explanations, and not justifications, for the differing approaches in German and English criminal law. In order to avoid criminal offences that pre-date completed criminality to an unjustified extent, preparatory offences should be deployed only: (i) in relation to sufficiently serious interests; (ii) in relation to unacceptable risks of the completed crimes coming to pass; (iii) in relation to situations where *D* has contributed meaningfully to *P's* potential decision to commit a completed crime; (iv) where it is plausible, at the time of the preparatory conduct and from the perspective of a person of ordinary intelligence, that the completed offence may be committed; (v) where *D* is significantly at fault with regard to the ultimate harm relevant to the completed offence; and (vi) where *D* fails to

[216] Fraud Act 2006, s. 6.

prevent the completed crime's occurrence. Additionally, preparatory offences should (obviously)[217] be punished less severely than completed crimes, but a more structured approach to such sentences would (perhaps equally obviously) better reflect relative harm and culpability than a looser, discretionary model.

Bibliography

Alexander L. and Ferzan K. K., 'Danger: The Ethics of Pre-Emptive Action', *Ohio State Journal of Criminal Law*, 9 (2012), 647–67.

Reflections on Crime and Culpability: Problems and Puzzles, Cambridge University Press (2018).

Alexander L. and Ferzan K. K. with Morse, S. J., *Crime and Culpability: A Theory of Criminal Law*, Cambridge University Press (2009).

Ambos K., *Treatise on International Criminal Law, I: Foundations and General Part*, Oxford University Press (2013).

'§ 24 – Rücktritt', in Dölling D., Duttge G., König S. and Dieter R. (eds.), *Gesamtes Strafrecht – Handkommentar*, 4th edn, Baden-Baden, Nomos Verlag (2017), 301–16.

Ambos K. and Bock S., 'Germany', in Reed A. and Bohlander M. (eds.), *Participation in Crime: Domestic and Comparative Perspectives*, Farnham, Ashgate (2013), 322–39.

American Law Institute, *Model Penal Code and Commentaries, Part I*, Philadelphia, The American Law Institute (1985).

Ashworth A., 'Defining Criminal Offences without Harm', in Smith P. (ed.), *Criminal Law: Essays in Honour of J. C. Smith*. London, Butterworths (1987), 7–23.

'Criminal Attempts and the Role of Resulting Harm under the Code, and in the Common Law', *Rutgers Law Journal*, 19 (1988), 725–72.

'The Unfairness of Risk-Based Possession Offences', *Criminal Law and Philosophy*, 5 (2011), 237–57.

Ashworth A. and Zedner L., *Preventive Justice*, Oxford University Press (2014).

Ashworth A., Zedner L. and Tomlin P. (eds.), *Prevention and the Limits of the Criminal Law*, Oxford University Press (2013).

Bein D., 'Preparatory Offences', *Israel Law Review*, 27 (1993), 185–212.

Bock S. and Harrendorf S., 'Strafbarkeit und Strafwürdigkeit tatvorbereitender computervermittelter Kommunikation', *Zeitschrift für die gesamte Strafrechtswissenschaft*, 126 (2014), 337–81.

[217] This point is less obvious in so-called completed attempts cases, but it is undeniable in the context of the preparatory offences discussed in this chapter, given their remoteness from the completed crime.

Bohlander M., *Principles of German Criminal Law*, Oxford, Hart (2009).

Broderick P. A., 'Conditional Objectives of Conspiracies', *Yale Law Journal*, 94 (1985), 895–908.

Carvalho H., *The Preventive Turn in Criminal Law*, Oxford University Press (2017).

Child J. J., 'Exploring the Mens Rea Requirements of the Serious Crime Act 2007 Assisting and Encouraging Offences', *Journal of Criminal Law*, 76 (2012), 220–31.

'Understanding Ulterior Mens Rea: Future Conduct Intention is Conditional Intention', *Cambridge Law Journal*, 76 (2017), 311–36.

Chou Y.-Y., *Zur Legitimität von Vorbereitungsdelikten*, Baden-Baden, Nomos Verlag (2011).

Clarkson C. M. V., 'Attempt: The Conduct Requirement', *Oxford Journal of Legal Studies*, 29 (2009), 25–41.

Cornford A., 'Indirect Crimes', *Law and Philosophy* 32 (2013), 485–514.

'Rethinking the Wrongfulness Constraint on Criminalisation', *Law and Philosophy*, 36 (2017), 615–49.

Dennis I. H., 'The Rationale of Criminal Conspiracy', *Law Quarterly Review*, 93 (1977), 39–64.

Deutscher Bundestag, *Entwurf eines [. . .] Strafrechtsänderungsgesetzes – Kinderpornographie*, Bundestagsdrucksache 12/3001 (1992).

Entwurf eines Gesetzes zur Verbesserung des Schutzes der Bevölkerung vor Sexualverbrechen und anderen schweren Straftaten, Bundestagsdrucksache 15/29 (2002).

Dubber M. D., 'The Possession Paradigm: The Special Part and the Police Power Model of the Criminal Process', in Duff R. A. and Green S. (eds.), *Defining Crimes: Essays on the Special Part of the Criminal Law*, Oxford University Press, (2005) 91–118.

Dubber M. D. and Hörnle T., *Criminal Law: A Comparative Approach*, Oxford University Press (2014).

Duff R. A., *Criminal Attempts*, Oxford University Press (1996).

'Criminalizing Endangerment', in Duff R. A. and Green S. (eds.), *Defining Crimes: Essays on the Special Part of the Criminal Law*, Oxford University Press (2005), 43–64.

Answering for Crime, Oxford University Press (2007).

'Risks, Culpability and Criminal Liability', in Sullivan G. R. and Dennis I. (eds.), *Seeking Security: Pre-Empting the Commission of Criminal Harms*, Oxford, Hart (2012), 121–42.

The Realm of Criminal Law, Oxford University Press (2018).

Duff R. A. and Hörnle T., 'Crimes of Endangerment', in Ambos K. et al. (eds.), *Core Concepts in Criminal Law and Justice*, II, Cambridge University Press (forthcoming).

Edwards J., 'Harm Principles', *Legal Theory*, 20 (2014), 253–85.

Eisele J., '§ 26 – Teilnahme', in Baumann J., Weber U., Mitsch W. and Eisele K. (eds.), *Strafrecht Allgemeiner Teil – Lehrbuch'*, 12 edn, Bielefeld, Gieseking Verlag (2016), 797–860.

European Commission, *Towards an EU Criminal Policy: 'Ensuring the Effective Implementation of EU Policies through Criminal Law'*, COM(2011) 573 final (2011).

Fletcher G. P., *Rethinking Criminal Law*, Boston, Little & Brown (1978).

Frisch W., 'An den Grenzen des Strafrechts', in Dencker F., Marxen K., Schneider H.-J., Schumann H., Struensee E. and Vormbaum T. (eds.), *Beträge zur Rechtswissenschaft. Festschrift für Walter Stree und Johannes Wessels*, Heidelberg, C. F. Müller (1993), 69–106.

Hassemer W. and Neumann U., 'Vorbemerkung zu § 1', in Kindhäuser U., Neumann U. and Paeffgen H.-U. (eds.), *Kommentar zum Strafgesetzbuch*, 5th edn, Baden-Baden, Nomos Verlag (2017), 79–191.

Heine G. and Weißer B., '§ 30 – Versuch der Beteiligung', in Schönke A. and Schröder H. (eds.), *Strafgesetzbuch – Kommentar*, 30th edn, Munich, C. H. Beck (2019), 560–8.

'§ 31 – Rücktritt vom Versuch der Beteiligung', in Schönke A. and Schröder H. (eds.), *Strafgesetzbuch – Kommentar*, 30th edn, Munich, C. H. Beck (2019), 568–71.

Hoffmann-Holland K., '§ 24 – Rücktritt', in Joecks W. and Heintschel-Heinegg B. von (eds.), *Münchener Kommentar zum Strafgesetzbuch*, I: *§§ 1–37*, 3rd edn, Munich, C. H. Beck (2017), 1139–219.

Horder J., *Ashworth's Principles of Criminal Law*, 8th edn, Oxford University Press (2016).

Hörnle T., '§ 184b – Verbreitung, Erwerb und Besitz kinderpornographischer Schriften', in Joecks W. and Heintschel-Heinegg B. von (eds.), *Münchener Kommentar zum Strafgesetzbuch*, III, *§§ 80–184j*, 3rd edn, Munich, C. H. Beck (2017), 1723–47.

Husak D. N., 'The Nature and Justifiability of Nonconsummate Offenses', *Arizona Law Review*, 37 (1995), 151–83.

'The Criminal Law as Last Resort', *Oxford Journal of Legal Studies*, 24 (2004), 207–35.

Overcriminalization: The Limits of the Criminal Law, Oxford University Press (2007).

'Preventive Detention as Punishment? Some Potential Obstacles', in Ashworth A., Zedner L. and Tomlin P. (eds.), *Prevention and the Limits of the Criminal Law*, Oxford University Press (2013), 178–93.

International Law Commission, *Draft Code of Crimes against the Peace and Security of Mankind with Commentaries* (1996).

Jakobs G., 'Kriminalisierung im Vorfeld einer Rechtsgutsverletzung', *Zeitschrift für die gesamte Strafrechtswissenschaft*, 97 (1985), 751–85.

Jareborg N., 'Criminalization as Last Resort (Ultima Ratio)', *Ohio State Journal of Criminal Law*, 2 (2005), 521–34.

Jescheck H. H. and Weigend T., *Lehrbuch des Strafrechts – Allgemeiner Teil*, 5th edn, Berlin, Duncker & Humblot (1996).

Johnson P. E., 'The Unnecessary Crime of Conspiracy', *California Law Review*, 61 (1973), 1137–88.

Kaspar J., *Verhältnismäßigkeit und Grundrechtsschutz im Präventionsstrafrecht*, Baden-Baden, Nomos (2014).

Katyal N. K., 'Conspiracy Theory', *Yale Law Journal*, 112 (2003), 1307–98.

Köhler M., *Strafrecht – Allgemeiner Teil*, Heidelberg, Springer (1997).

Kühl K., *Strafrecht Allgemeiner Teil*, 8th edn, Munich, Franz Vahlen (2017).

Lacey N., 'Historicising Criminalisation: Conceptual and Empirical Issues', *Modern Law Review*, 72 (2009), 936–60.

Law Commission, *Attempt and Impossibility in Relation to Attempt*, Conspiracy and Incitement, Law Com. No. 102 (1980).

Inchoate Liability for Assisting or Encouraging Crime, Law Com. No. 300 (2006).

Conspiracy and Attempts: Consultation Paper, Law Com. CP No. 183 (2007).

Conspiracy and Attempts: Report, Law Com. No. 318 (2009).

Letzgus K., *Vorstufen der Beteiligung*, Berlin, Duncker & Humblot (1972).

Lilie H. and Albrecht D., '§ 24 – Rücktritt', in Laufhütte H. W., Rissing-van Saan R. and Tiedemann K. (eds.), *Strafgesetzbuch – Leipziger Kommentar*, I: *Einleitung, §§ 1 bis 31*, 12th edn, Berlin, De Gruyter (2007), 1649–811.

Merten D., '§ 68 Verhältnismäßigkeit', in Merten D. and Papier H. J. (eds.), *Handbuch der Grundrechte in Deutschland und Europa*, III: *Grundrechte in Deutschland: Allgemeine Lehren II*, Heidelberg, C. F. Müller (2009), 517–68.

Miebach K. and Maier S., '§ 46 – Grundsätze der Strafzumessung', in Joecks W. and Heintschel-Heinegg B. von (eds.), *Münchener Kommentar zum Strafgesetzbuch*, II: *§§ 38–79b*, 3rd edn, Munich, C. H. Beck (2016), 181–337.

Moore M. S., *Causation and Responsibility: An Essay in Law, Morals, and Metaphysics*, Oxford University Press (2009).

Murmann U., *Grundkurs Strafrecht*, 4th edn, Munich, C. H. Beck (2017).

Oberdiek J., *Imposing Risk: A Philosophical Analysis*, Oxford University Press (2017).

Ohana D., 'Desert and Punishment for Acts Preparatory to the Commission of a Crime', *Canadian Journal of Law and Jurisprudence*, 20 (2007), 113–42.

Ormerod D., 'Making Sense of Mens Rea in Statutory Conspiracies', *Current Legal Problems*, 59 (2006), 185–230.

Ormerod D. and Fortson R., 'Serious Crime Act 2007: The Part 2 Offences', *Criminal Law Review* (2009), 389–414.

Ormerod D. and Laird K., *Smith, Hogan and Ormerod's Criminal Law*, 15th edn, Oxford University Press (2018).

Paeffgen H.-U., '§ 89a – Vorbereitung einer schweren staatsgefährdenden Gewalttat', in Kindhäuser U., Neumann U. and Paeffgen H.-U. (eds.), *Kommentar zum Strafgesetzbuch*, 5th edn, Baden-Baden, Nomos (2017), 225–67.

Prittwitz C., *Strafrecht und Risiko*, Frankfurt, Vittorio Klostermann (1993).

Puschke J., *Legitimation, Grenzen und Dogmatik von Vorbereitungstatbeständen*, Tübingen, Mohr Siebeck (2017).

Rackow P., Bock S. and Harrendorf S., 'Überlegungen zur Strafwürdigkeit tatvorbereitender computervermittelter Kommunikation im Internet', *Strafverteidiger*, 32 (2012), 687–95.

Renzikowski J., '§ 176 – Sexueller Missbrauch von Kindern', in Joecks W. and Heintschel-Heinegg B. von (eds.), *Münchener Kommentar zum Strafgesetzbuch*, III: *§§ 80–184j*, 3rd edn, Munich, C. H. Beck (2017), 1386–414.

Robinson P. H., *Criminal Law Defenses*, 2 vols., St Paul, West (1984).

Rogers J., 'The Codification of Attempts and the Case for "Preparation"', *Criminal Law Review* (2008), 937–54.

Rook P. and Robert W., *Rook and Ward on Sexual Offences*, 5th edn, London, Sweet & Maxwell (2016).

Roxin C., 'Über den Rücktritt vom unbeendeten Versuch', in Lüttger H. (ed.), *Festschrift für Ernst Heinitz*, Berlin, De Gruyter (1972), 251–76.

Strafrecht Allgemeiner Teil, II: *Besondere Erscheinungsformen der Straftat*, Munich, C. H. Beck (2003).

Strafrecht Allgemeiner Teil, I: *Grundlagen. Der Aufbau der Verbrechenslehre*, 4th edn, Munich, C. H. Beck (2006).

Schäfer J., '§ 129 StGB – Bildung krimineller Vereinigungen', in Miebach K. (ed.), *Münchener Kommentar zum Strafgesetzbuch*, II: *§§ 80–184j*, 3rd edn, Munich, C. H. Beck (2017), 613–64.

Schünemann B., 'Kritische Anmerkungen zur geistigen Situation der deutschen Strafrechtswissenschaft', *Goltdammer's Archiv für Strafrecht*, 142 (1995), 201–29.

'§ 30 – Versuch der Beteiligung', in Laufhütte H. W., Rissing-van Saan R. and Tiedemann K. (eds.), *Strafgesetzbuch – Leipziger Kommentar*, I: *Einleitung, §§ 1 bis 31*, 12th edn, Berlin, De Gruyter (2007), 2109–156.

'§ 31 – Rücktritt vom Versuch der Beteiligung', in Laufhütte H. W., Rissing-van Saan R. and Tiedemann K. (eds.), *Strafgesetzbuch – Leipziger Kommentar*, I: *Einleitung, §§ 1 bis 31*, 12th edn, Berlin, De Gruyter (2007), 2157–169.

Simester A. P., 'Prophylactic Crimes', in Sullivan G. R. and Dennis I. (eds.), *Seeking Security: Pre-Empting the Commission of Criminal Harms*, Oxford, Hart (2012), 59–78.

'Causation in (Criminal) Law', *Law Quarterly Review*, 133 (2017), 416–41.

Simester A. P. and Hirsch A. von, *Crimes, Harms and Wrongs: On the Principles of Criminalisation*, Oxford, Hart (2011).

Simester A. P., Spencer J. R., Stark F., Sullivan G. R. and Virgo G. J., *Simester and Sullivan's Criminal Law: Theory and Doctrine*, 6th edn, Oxford, Hart/Bloomsbury (2016).

Spencer J. R., 'Trying to Help Another Person Commit a Crime', in Smith P (ed.), *Essays in Honour of J.C. Smith*, London, Butterworths (1987), 148–69.

Stark F., 'Encouraging or Assisting Clarity?', *Cambridge Law Journal*, 72 (2013), 497–501.

'It's Only Words: On Meaning and Mens Rea', *Cambridge Law Journal*, 72 (2013), 155–77.

Culpable Carelessness: Recklessness and Negligence in the Criminal Law, Cambridge University Press (2016).

Stuart D., *Canadian Criminal Law: A Treatise* (Student Edition), 6th edn, Scarborough, Carswell (2011).

Taylor G., 'Concepts of Intention in German Criminal Law', *Oxford Journal of Legal Studies*, 24 (2004), 99–127.

Thalheimer K., *Die Vorfeldstrafbarkeit nach §§ 30, 31 StGB*, Frankfurt, Peter Lang (2008).

Wade C., 'Prevention of Harm: Legislative Strategies for Law Reform', *Journal of Criminal Law*, 72 (2008), 236–50.

Walen A., 'The Doctrine of Illicit Intentions', *Philosophy and Public Affairs*, 34 (2006), 39–67.

Weigend T., 'Why Lady Eldon Should Be Acquitted: The Social Harm in Attempting the Impossible', *DePaul Law Review*, 27 (1978), 231–73.

Wohlers W., *Deliktstypen des Präventionsstrafrechts – zur Dogmatik 'moderner' Gefährdungsdelikte*, Berlin, Duncker & Humblot (2000).

Wörner L., 'Die deutsche Versuchsdogmatik – eine Frage der Vorverlagerung des Strafrechts', in Sinn A., Gropp W. and Ferene N. (eds.), *Grenzen der Vorverlagerung in einem Tatstrafrecht*, Osnabrück: Universitätsverlag Osnabrück (2011), 135–54.

'Expanding Criminal Laws by Predating Criminal Responsibility: Punishing Planning and Organizing Terrorist Attacks as a Means to Optimize Effectiveness of Fighting against Terrorism', *German Law Journal*, 13 (2012), 1037–55.

Yaffe G., *Attempts: In the Philosophy of Action and the Criminal Law*, Oxford University Press (2012).

Zaczyk R., *Das Unrecht der versuchten Tat*, Berlin, Duncker & Humblot (1989).

'§ 23 – Strafbarkeit des Versuchs', in Kindhäuser U., Neumann U. and Paeffgen H.-U. (eds.), *Kommentar zum Strafgesetzbuch*, 5th edn, Baden-Baden, Nomos (2017), 1078–84.

4

Participation in Crime

ANTJE DU BOIS-PEDAIN

I Introduction

Questions of criminal participation arise when more than one person is in some way involved in the commission of a crime. In some cases, there may be no single individual who, in his own person, fulfils all the definitional elements of the criminal offence. Even where there is one such individual, the criminal law may want to tie other persons to the commission of the offence as well, on the basis that these other persons are complicit in and therefore share responsibility for its commission. What rules and principles do – and which ones should – govern the ascription of criminal responsibility to different agents in multi-party settings is the theme of this chapter. The answer to the should-question is approached with a view to the general aims of the criminal law regarding parties to crime. These are understood to be the following: (i) to guide judges and other decision-makers towards fair responsibility-attributions for criminal norm-violations and their outcomes; (ii) to ensure that the conviction offence fairly reflects the gravamen of the accused's criminal conduct; and (iii) to facilitate accurate reflection of different degrees of responsibility in sentencing decisions.

In service of these aims, practically all legal systems distinguish at some stage between different kinds of party to crime – specifically, between primary and secondary parties. Some do so at the liability-incurring stage, others do so (exclusively or additionally) at the sentencing stage. Where the distinctions are drawn at the liability-incurring stage, they are usually understood to serve both a liability-extending and a liability-limiting function. The liability-extending function lies in the manner in which the provisions on secondary liability hold participants who have influenced the commission of the offence without meeting all the requirements of the offence definition responsible for the commission of that offence. This extension of liability is particularly important where the offence prohibition uses colourful activity-describing words that in group scenarios considerably limit the range of those who can plausibly be said to meet the offence description, and where liability requires a particular status, role or duty. Conversely, the liability-limiting function rests in the fact that (whatever definition of the preconditions of secondary liability is chosen) there will be some behaviours of persons which have somehow had a bearing on the commission of a criminal offence that fall outside it (e.g. the novelist who describes a particularly gruesome killing that inspires one of his readers to 'enact' the imaginary event described in the book).

The necessity and desirability for legal systems to differentiate at the liability-incurring stage between different parties to crime is nevertheless hotly disputed, as are the reasons for which the distinctions are drawn. The more expansive the definition of perpetratorship, the more provisions of secondary liability function as modifications of a responsibility that is in any event incurred – thereby introducing complications into an initially straightforward responsibility-ascription that may appear more trouble than they're worth. Indeed, some legal systems refuse to draw any distinction between primary and secondary parties at the liability-incurring stage, leaving such distinctions as should be drawn to the sentencing stage. Note, however, that this choice has important and potentially troublesome liability-limiting effects in precisely the cases where secondary liability was described in the preceding paragraph as liability-extending.

This chapter has the twofold objective of introducing readers to the main doctrinal frameworks for the regulation of participation in crime, as well as the theoretical foundations proposed for them, and of making the case for a reworked differentiated system based on separate doctrines of criminal participation formulated for three different participatory paradigms: acting through another, acting with another and acting alongside another. It argues that the main flaws in existing doctrines of participation arise from a failure to recognise that it is inappropriate to apply them across the entire range of multi-party scenarios to which they are currently applied. However, the counsel of some defenders of unitary perpetrator systems – that we should give up on the very project of distinguishing between different modes of liability-ascription for parties to crime on account of the practical difficulties to which they all give rise – is a counsel of despair. Once the areas of application for the different participatory paradigms are appropriately demarcated, distinct sets of rules and principles for each of these paradigms enable the resolution of various disputed issues and seemingly intractable difficulties that beset this area of law.

To situate the discussion, Section I of this chapter explains the terminology used and provides a brief historical-comparative introduction to different theoretical approaches to the liability of participants in crime. This discussion points to the historical affinity between certain approaches to causation and preferences for unitary or differentiated systems but argues that causation is not decisive: rather, how the practical objectives of this area of law identified above can be met should govern the design of the system. Section II turns to two well-known systems – those of England and Germany – to explore the liability regimes applicable under each to participants in crime. The differences between these systems are suggestive of a degree of inherent instability, as is the fact that neither system offers fully convincing practical solutions – let alone persuasive theorisations – for a number of classic problems in the law of secondary liability, including the in practice very important treatment of escalating violence cases. That neither of these systems is able to offer stable and convincing solutions to these problems suggests that their theorisation of secondary participation is at fault. Accordingly, in Section III, I turn to the basic outlines of an improved differentiated system. Such a system should distinguish between three paradigms, which I will refer to as the mediated action paradigm ('acting through another'), the concerted action paradigm ('acting with another'), and the parallel actions paradigm ('acting alongside another'). I will set out these paradigms and highlight how a liability regime that uses this threefold distinction overcomes the problems of existing models. In conclusion, I offer some further reflections on what questions must be resolved at the liability-incurring stage and what issues can be left to the sentencing stage in order to meet the objectives set out in the opening paragraph.

1 Terminology: Primary and Secondary Parties; Unitary and Differentiated Systems

I will follow the widespread convention of designating as the *perpetrator* or *principal* (*P*) the person who satisfies all the definitional elements of an offence (in what follows I will use 'perpetrator' and 'principal' interchangeably), and as *secondary parties* (*S*) those who are connected to the crime without satisfying all the definitional elements in their own person.[1] By using this terminology, I do not mean to prejudge any

[1] See e.g. Horder, *Ashworth's Principles* (2016), 433 (also pointing out that the terms 'accomplice' and 'accessory' are used as alternatives to 'secondary parties').

questions about the nature of the secondary party's contribution and the structure of her liability. In particular, I want to keep it open whether secondary liability is in all instances, or necessarily, structurally 'accessorial' and 'derivative' in nature. It should also be recalled that, where 'secondary participation' is used in a wide sense in the existing literature, it can encompass forms of participation (particularly in so-called joint enterprises) that in some legal systems would be conceptualised as a type of (co-)perpetratorship. Moreover, where *S* acts through an innocent agent, *S* is also frequently categorised as a perpetrator or principal[2] – although I will later argue that cases of innocent agency (which in German law are conceptualised as indirect perpetratorship) are best grouped with traditional 'assisting and encouraging' cases under the same participatory paradigm.

While the focus of this chapter is on secondary participation in this wide sense, no discussion of this topic can proceed without at least a rough understanding of who, in a multi-party setting, counts as a perpetrator or principal. The core case of perpetratorship is constituted by an agent who performs the *actus reus* of the criminal offence with *mens rea* ('direct perpetrator'). Peripheral cases arise (i) in the context of innocent agency (the person who performs the conduct element of the offence lacks criminal capacity, is labouring under a mistake of fact that leads to an absence of *mens rea*, or has an excusatory supervening defence); (ii) in respect of status offences where the direct agent may lack the required status; and (iii) in respect of joint action (which some but not all systems conceptualise as a distinct form of co-perpetratorship). What may also be disputed is whether perpetratorship is in principle limited to someone who performs the conduct element of the crime either individually or with others, or whether someone who does not carry out the conduct element of the offence (even with others) may also be classed as a perpetrator.[3]

[2] See e.g. Law Commission for England and Wales, *Draft Criminal Code* (1989), cl. 26. This convention is now followed by numerous writers (e.g. Wilson, *Criminal Law* (2014), 562, with further references). That there is no necessity to this terminological convention is illustrated by the case of *Bourne* (1952) 36 CAR 125, where a husband compelled his wife to commit bestiality with a dog. The decision to convict the husband as aider and abettor was upheld notwithstanding the fact that the wife was not liable for any criminal offence. For discussion, see Williams, *Textbook* (1983), 372.

[3] While there are some interesting theoretical issues here, I merely note in the present context of clarifying the meaning of terms used in this chapter, that to the extent that a legal system includes the peripheral cases of perpetratorship in that notion, my statement

The preceding paragraph assumed that the classification of someone as a perpetrator as opposed to a secondary party carries some normative significance within the relevant system. This is, however, not necessarily so. Not all legal systems draw a conceptual distinction between principals and secondary parties. Some systems treat everyone who in some way contributes to the commission of the crime as someone who commits the offence. Legal systems which follow this approach are sometimes described as 'unitary perpetrator systems' (*Einheitstätersysteme*).[4] They are to be contrasted with systems which draw at least a basic distinction between primary and secondary parties. These 'differentiated participation systems' (*Teilnahmesysteme*) are quite varied. They may recognise further distinctions and sub-divisions beyond the basic distinction between principals and secondary parties (e.g. they may place common purpose-based liability alongside, and treat it as separate from, accessorial liability), and they may also draw the conceptual boundaries of perpetratorship and secondary participation differently (e.g. placing common purpose-based crimes into the category of co-perpetratorship, or alternatively treating such crimes as a special form of secondary liability). Indeed, as we shall see in Section III below, the real question is how many different paradigms of involvement an ideal differentiated system should work with.

There is some variation in how writers use the notion of a unitary system. All include within that notion systems which define perpetrators in terms broad enough to encompass any sort of contribution made to the crime (e.g. a perpetrator is 'anyone who made a contribution to the commission of an offence').[5] Many writers also count as 'functionally unitary' systems where the relevant legal provisions do set out a range of different behaviours (including such behaviours as 'helping' or 'commanding'), provided these behaviours are understood to matter legally for the same reasons, and in the same way as the behaviour of the person

above that those who do not fulfil all the definitional elements of a crime are referred to as secondary parties, would have to be qualified. As Stewart, 'Complicity' (2014), 537, remarks: 'the idea that "all actors whose conduct does not satisfy the definition of the offence are accessories" is conceptually unsafe'.

4 See e.g. Schöberl, *Einheitstäterschaft als europäisches Modell* (2006) (distinguishing between the three varieties of unitary theories of perpetration described in the text). See also Kienapfel, *Einheitstäter* (1971); Rotsch, *Einheitstäterschaft statt Tatherrschaft* (2009).

5 Samson, *SK-StGB* (1993), § 25 mn. 2, applies the designation 'unitary' only to systems of this kind. Writers such as Schöberl, *Einheitstäterschaft als europäisches Modell* (2006), who also accept other types of unitary systems refer to these systems as 'pure unitary systems'.

carrying out the conduct element of the offence (i.e. as causal and individually culpable contributions to the commission of the offence). Such systems are unitary in that they do not recognise the existence of distinctive 'accessorial' wrongs. Each party's responsibility is ultimately still assessed on the same evaluative tracks.[6]

Some authors also apply the classification 'unitary' to legal systems which instantiate conceptually different liability-incurring routes for principals and accessories but make all participants liable to the same punishment. I find this extension unhelpful. How the system approaches sentencing decisions is a separate question. Even where everyone involved in the crime is liable to be sentenced 'as/like a perpetrator', differentiations are likely to develop according to the type and degree of involvement shown. The important question is whether such types and degrees of involvement are formalised and stabilised through different paradigms of responsibility-ascription at the liability-incurring stage – a step which has not only a guiding but also a liability-limiting effect. In contrast to authors who base the application of the term 'unitary system' on a lack of differentiation between participants at the sentencing stage, I therefore classify as differentiated systems all systems that set out different liability-incurring routes for primary and secondary parties, whether or not they also provide for different punishments or punishment ranges depending on the classification of each party.[7]

It is important to note that even differentiated systems may contain particular offences where the *actus reus* requirement is defined so broadly that any kind of contributory conduct directly fulfils the definitional requirement.[8] In respect of these offences, anyone who contributes to the commission of the offence will count as a perpetrator. Note also that, in practice, some differentiated participation systems will apply the differentiated model of liability only in relation to crimes of intent; for instance, the German system is in reality a 'mixed system' since it follows a unitary model (based on making a negligent causal contribution) when

[6] See especially Bloy, *Beteiligungsform* (1985), 318. For discussion of five different legal systems classified as unitary according to the pure or functional variants, see Stewart, 'History' (2016).

[7] For a similar classificatory approch, see Weißer, *Täterschaft in Europa* (2011), 61–5. Stewart likewise questions whether 'the sentence-based account is properly classified as unitary at all'; see Stewart, 'History' (2016), 6 at n. 11.

[8] Cf. s. 4(2)(b) of the Misuse of Drugs Act 1971 (England and Wales) ('being concerned' in the production of controlled drugs).

it comes to crimes of negligence (and also for the non-criminal *Ordnungswidrigkeiten*).

Finally, I should point out that I will not address the liability of secondary parties in international criminal law. The literature and, to an extent, the principles themselves (especially those governing command responsibility and 'joint criminal enterprises' or JCEs) are by now so different that participation in crime under international criminal law cannot be appropriately covered as an adjunct to a discussion of solutions found in domestic criminal law.[9]

2 *Unitary or Differentiated Systems: A Matter of Choice or Structural Necessity?*

Before proceeding further, we should briefly address the question whether there is a knock-down argument from structural or logical necessity (*sachlogische Strukturen*)[10] for the adoption of either a unitary or a differentiated model of participant liability. Danish scholar Carl Torp claimed in 1905 that:

> [T]he true reference point for criminal punishment is not the external conduct, but the criminal will of which the conduct is only the external manifestation that the criminal law requires; hence it follows naturally that every participant is punished only for *his own* deed, with the conduct of others with whom he may have cooperated of relevance only to the extent that, like other circumstantial factors which had an effect on his deed, it can be taken into account when evaluating the character of his deed.[11]

Torp concluded from this that the liability model of criminal participation must be a unitary one: each person involved in a criminal incident is judged according to his or her criminal will manifested in her conduct.[12]

[9] For a comprehensive survey and discussion of that literature, see Ambos, *Treatise I* (2013), chs. 4 and 5 (especially 160–3; 172–6 on JCEs and 197–232 on command responsibility).

[10] Küpper, *Strafrechtsdogmatik* (1990), 138, draws on the notion of 'sachlogische Strukturen' when arguing that differentiated systems are inevitable due to the deeper structures of human agency that need to be reflected by law.

[11] Torp, *Strafferets* (1905), 581 quoted in Hamdorf, *Beteiligungsmodelle* (2002), 51, who provides the German translation on which my English translation is based.

[12] See further Hamdorf, *Beteiligungsmodelle* (2002).

A will-based understanding, this time not only of criminal liability as such but also of causation, has, however, led other scholars to insist that a distinction between principals and secondary parties must be drawn. Sanford Kadish for instance has argued that the principal is directly causal whereas the secondary party cannot be a 'cause' of the results of the principal's actions – the influence the secondary party exerted over the principal was an influence on the formation of the latter's criminal will, and that influence must be recognised as a distinct liability-basis that is unlike the causal responsibility of the principal.[13]

But causation analysis can just as well be used to support the opposite conclusion. Michael Moore has defended a unitary model based on an ontological view of causation where criminal liability in each and every case flows from a person's causal effectiveness in the world. On the ontological grounds Moore defends – Moore sees influencing another person's decision-making processes as having a causal influence on that person's later actions – participatory acts can be and must be causal, and liability for them can be explained through their being causal.[14]

Even if the ontological disagreements between these writers are, in principle, capable of resolution, the above discussion also raises doubts about whether the choice between unitary and differentiated systems of participation is indeed best approached as a question whose answer follows with logical necessity from the deeper structures of human agency. While such analyses may help us to understand the specific issues that arise when more than one person is involved in the commission of a crime, these insights arguably do not determine the choice between unitary and differentiated models of liability. Rather, the choice between these models depends on which model is better suited to achieving the general aims of the criminal law in dealing with parties to crime that were identified above, that is to say: whether they assist courts in arriving at fair responsibility-attributions at the liability stage and fair responsibility-differentiations at the sentencing stage.[15]

Arguments in favour of unitary systems tend to combine a wide understanding of causation (which treats all factual causes of an event, including causes that have their effect by influencing the decisions of

[13] Kadish, 'Complicity, Cause and Blame' (1985).

[14] Moore, 'Superfluity' (2007). For a sustained critique of the specifics of Moore's position, see Duff, 'Accomplice Liability' (2008) and Gardner, 'Moore on Complicity' (2008).

[15] For such an argument, see Husak, 'Abetting' (2014), who also stresses the importance of fair labelling in this context.

other agents, as 'equivalent', and resists the notion that free, deliberate and informed choices made by intervening agents break the causal connection between an earlier human act and a later outcome) with a theoretical and a pragmatic claim. Theorists such as Moore claim that the wrong of each party concerned in the commission of an offence is the wrong of making a causal contribution to its commission, albeit in different ways, and that it is for this wrong that each party is therefore held responsible.[16] The pragmatic claim is that distinctions made between primary and secondary parties at the liability-incurring stage prove unwieldy in practice and do not help decision-makers in allocating degrees of responsibility accurately for the purpose of sentencing. The traditional distinctions between primary and secondary parties are, it is claimed, unhelpful in tracking gradations of responsibility and guilt between different parties.[17]

Theorists who argue in favour of differentiated systems are not necessarily committed to any particular theory of causation, although they often develop restrictive understandings of perpetratorship in their quest for a boundary line between primary and secondary participation. Of course, if one is (like Kadish) committed to an understanding of human agency that does not accept that a human agent's willed act can be caused, in the relevant sense, by another human agent, one must also be committed to a dual-track theory of responsibility-incurring behaviour: one track on which an agent is effective in the world through causally-determined processes, and a second track on which an agent influences events in the world by exerting an influence over the will of another agent. These tracks are then followed to map out a basic distinction between (causal) perpetration and (non-causal, will-influencing) participation. But it is important to realise that arguments for differentiated systems are also put forward by theorists who subscribe to broad theories of causation.[18]

16 Moore's argument is, more precisely, that: 'Aiding another to cause some bad result is not an independent desert basis. It is a mere stand-in for one of the four general bases on which we are rightly blamed.' See Moore, 'Superfluity' (2007–8), 395. Stewart sums up Moore's approach as 'subsum[ing] [accomplice liability] within generic principles of attribution' ('Complicity' (2014), 543). Note that the same is true for Torp's position (quoted above at n. 11).

17 The pragmatic argument is developed e.g. by Stewart, 'History' (2016). It also finds support among scholars concerned to develop appropriate modes of liability for large-scale organised crime. For further discussion, see Hamdorf, *Beteiligungsmodelle* (2002), ch. 5.

18 See e.g. Lord Toulson, writing extrajudicially (Toulson, 'Complicity in Murder' (2013), 238–40) and citing his judgments in *Mendez* [2011] 3 WLR 1 and *Stringer* [2011] EWCA Crim. 1396. Gardner's challenge to Moore in 'Moore on Complicity' (2008) is based on

There is greater variety here than among theorists who build their arguments on their theories of causation, but in essence these promoters of differentiated systems claim that (while it may well be true that all participants make some kind of causal contribution) the distinction between primary and secondary parties picks up on morally important differences inherent in different modes of contribution to a crime, such that drawing the distinction is both theoretically warranted and practically desirable as an aid to good decision-making.[19]

My own sympathies lie with a wider, Feinbergian rather than Hart-Honoréian conception of causation.[20] From such a perspective, the participatory paradigms I develop in this chapter depend on considerations that should take priority over the causal connection because they register and react to distinctive differences between various multi-party scenarios in respect of the nature and quality of the participant's wrong. Even for those who are happy to describe (responsible) actions of human beings as caused by certain (responsible) actions of other human beings, it matters *how* this effect is brought about. At least, this is my claim, and the basis on which I hope to persuade readers of this chapter that allocating liability to multiple participants in crime by developing separate sets of principles that apply to cases of acting through another, acting with another, and acting alongside another, makes good moral and legal sense – whatever the theory of causation one endorses.

II Differentiated Liability Systems Compared

This section aims to provide an overview of the main liability systems used in different jurisdictions in order to lay the ground for their subsequent evaluation. It focuses on the English and German approaches as alternative versions of differentiated systems, but also draws on examples from other jurisdictions in the context of clarifying distinctive elements of the two main systems under discussion.

what Gardner refers to as a commitment to causal pluralism, which involves drawing causal distinctions between different modes of causation, in particular between indirect and direct causal contributions.

[19] Husak, 'Abetting' (2014), 68 observes with characteristic bluntness: 'It is a huge advantage of any approach to complicity that it does not depend on a particular theory of causation.'

[20] For the classic statements of these divergent approaches, see Hart and Honoré, *Causation* (1985) and Feinberg, 'Causing Voluntary Actions' (1970).

1 *England and Wales*

The criminal law of England and Wales today provides an example of a simple bifurcated system which only recognises the basic distinction between principals and secondary parties and channels the liability of everyone who is not a direct perpetrator through the accessorial route. The accessorial route thus includes not just standard secondary parties (those who aid, encourage or instigate the principal's offence), but also those who acted with a common purpose but did not in their own person commit the *actus reus* of the offence in whole or in part.[21] It is important to note that the common law of secondary participation has for some time developed in a different direction in England and Wales as compared to other common law jurisdictions such as Australia; some of these differences will be highlighted in what follows.

England and Wales's differentiated liability system derives, as mentioned, from the common law. The only pertinent legislative provision is section 8 of the Accessories and Abettors Act 1861 (as amended), which reads:

> Whosoever shall aid, abet, counsel, or procure the commission of any indictable offence . . . shall be liable to be tried, indicted, and punished as a principal offender.

At first blush, this provision could be taken to instantiate a unitary system (and, indeed, if one were to follow the view I rejected earlier, that systems which make accessories and principals liable to the same punishment are unitary systems, this would undoubtedly be so).

On the preferable functional criterion for the classification of systems as 'unitary' adopted above, however, systems only count as unitary if they, in substance, 'subsume [accomplice liability] within generic principles of attribution'.[22] This English common law has never done. Accessorial liability developed as a distinct avenue of responsibility-ascription with its own distinctive *actus reus* and *mens rea* requirements that differed from the grounds on which perpetrators were held liable. Historically the distinction also had important procedural implications. These procedural implications were removed by section 8 of the Accessories and Abettors Act 1861 (which originally only applied to

[21] See further n. 62 below on when participants qualify as co-principals in the English system.

[22] This is the felicitous phrase with which Stewart described Moore's approach to complicity (Stewart, 'Complicity' (2014), 543).

misdemeanours but became applicable to all indictable offences after the distinction between felonies and misdemeanours was abolished in 1967). The provision thus presupposes, but does not amend or prescribe the future application of, the substantive liability of parties to crime as governed by the common law.[23] Its procedural effect is twofold: first, both principal and secondary party will be charged with, and eventually be convicted of (say) 'burglary' (instead of charging and convicting the principal for 'burglary', and the secondary party for 'assisting burglary'). Secondly, the sentencing range of the conviction offence applies to the secondary party without modification merely by reason of the fact that S is a secondary party and not a principal. Despite these elements of uniform treatment, the English system thus constitutes in substance a differentiated model of participant liability, in view of the fact that distinct liability-incurring avenues for principals and for secondary parties have developed under the common law.[24]

While English law differentiates between primary and secondary liability (that is, between principals and secondary parties), it uses a broad and fairly undifferentiated notion of secondary liability. Specifically, in the English legal context the 'common purpose' doctrine was never fully differentiated from secondary liability doctrine.[25] It originally emerged to hold all rioters who were still continuing to riot after the Riot Act had been read to them (imposing an obligation to disperse within one hour) liable for any act of rioting or of resistance against officials trying to curb the riot that was performed afterwards by any of their number.[26] But in the context of more quotidian crime the function of the doctrine was not to instantiate a distinct liability paradigm.[27] It is therefore unsurprising that, in an exchange in the late 1990s between Jonathan Burchell and J. C. Smith, Smith insisted that there was no separate 'doctrine of joint

[23] This interpretation of the historical development is, as far as I can see, uncontroversial. See Williams, *Textbook* (1983), 329–32 and Dyson, 'Principals' (2018), 298–9.

[24] The same conclusion is reached by Weißer, *Täterschaft in Europa* (2011), 61 and 65 (who also adopts a functional definition of unitary systems).

[25] For a summary of the historical development, see e.g. Toulson, 'Complicity in Murder' (2013), 235–8.

[26] See Dyson, 'Principals' (2018), 303–4.

[27] Dyson, *ibid.*, 301–2, states that common purpose 'made all participants in a common criminal venture into principals' by 'attributing the physical elements of the offence to each participant', but (as this was done for certain procedural reasons) he also suggests that it is unclear whether 'common purpose had normative content' since '[t]here was no deeper explanation for common purpose, beyond this procedural work needing to be done' (303).

enterprise' in English criminal law. Participants in a common venture were liable either qua principals or qua accessories, depending on the type of their contribution.[28]

This question mattered in practical terms because of a trend in the case law that had expanded the liability of participants for crimes committed by the principal, from crimes that they had intended or known the principal would commit, to crimes that they had foreseen the principal might commit in the course of the joint venture.[29] Despite Smith's insistence to the contrary, it was widely thought that this expansion of liability – for which Smith had coined the term 'parasitic accessorial liability (PAL)'[30] – only applied to participants in a 'joint enterprise' (a term that had come to be used to designate what common law systems traditionally described as liability based on a 'common purpose').[31] However, in a key 2016 judgment in the conjoined cases of *Jogee* and *Ruddock*,[32] the UK Supreme Court rejected not only the liability-expansion that had occurred in respect of incidental crimes whose commission by the principal was merely foreseen as a possibility by another participant, but also insisted that there was no separate *legal* liability paradigm of 'joint enterprise'.[33] The post-*Jogee* orthodoxy therefore holds that the concept of joint enterprise-based liability as such has

[28] See Burchell, 'Joint Enterprise and Common Purpose' (1997) and Smith, 'Joint Enterprise and Accessory Liability' (1998).

[29] *Chan Wing-Siu* [1985] AC 168; *Maxwell* [1978] 1 WLR 1350; *R* v. *Powell and English* [1999] 1 AC 1.

[30] Smith, 'Criminal Liability of Accessories' (1997).

[31] Glanville Williams put forward this interpretation of the case law in an article published in 1990, when he argued that 'the only acceptable way to reconcile the decisions [which hold the secondary party liable for crimes he realised may be committed in pursuit of the venture] is to point to a distinctive feature . . . setting them apart from the other cases . . . Both of these decisions . . . establishing the wider measure of liability were cases of a joint criminal purpose.' (Glanville Williams, 'Complicity, Purpose – 2' (1990), 102). It was also persuasively advanced by Simester in an influential article: see Simester, 'Mental Element' (2006).

[32] *R* v. *Jogee; Ruddock* v. *The Queen* [2016] UKSC 8, [2016] UKPC 7 (hereafter: *Jogee*).

[33] In doing so, the court fell in line with a position argued for by Smith but not accepted by many other scholars, who viewed joint enterprise as a separate doctrine with its own distinct liability rules. For Smith's view, see Smith, 'Criminal Liability of Accessories' (1997), 462: 'if [*S*] and *P* set out together to . . . murder, how does [*S*] "participate" in *P's* . . . pulling of the trigger and shooting *V* . . . except by assisting him or encouraging him (i.e. aiding, abetting, counselling or procuring him) to do the act? It is submitted that there is no other way.' For the opposing view, see Simester, 'Mental Element' (2006) and Simester 'Accessory Liability' (2017).

partaken in PAL's demise and that only the standard kind of secondary liability remains.

The practically more important aspect of the judgment is undoubtedly its rejection of 'parasitic accessorial liability', as it affects the high-stakes question of the basis on which a secondary party can be held liable for (further) crimes committed by the principal offender. From the perspective of the optimal design of a legal system, however, the effects of denying 'joint enterprise' recognition as a separate doctrine are of considerable significance in their own right. I will address these effects in my discussion of the *actus reus* of secondary participation, to which I turn next, before considering doctrinal-theoretical and practical implications of the *Jogee* judgment specifically in cases where (further) crimes were committed in situations of escalating or spontaneously erupting violence.

According to *Jogee*, standard secondary liability arises when *S* encourages or assists *P* to commit the main offence,[34] intending (at least conditionally) such assistance or encouragement and *P's* commission of the main offence, while knowing the main elements of *P's* envisaged offence.[35] The *mens rea* requirement has recently attracted renewed attention due to the reference made in *Jogee* to conditional intent.[36] While there are some interesting issues here, my analysis in this section will concentrate on the *actus reus* of secondary participation. It is important to note the breadth of the *actus reus* of secondary participation. If we think of the 'headings' of secondary liability explicitly mentioned in section 8 of the Accessories and Abettors Act 1861, we find counselling, procuring, aiding and abetting. The central linguistic meaning of procuring is the commissioning or instigating of a crime. That notion has been widened in the case law to include 'procuring by endeavour', in order to capture innocent and semi-innocent agent cases.[37] While this is linguistically somewhat counterintuitive it is in practice unproblematic, as it is confined to an easily recognisable subset

[34] *P's* crime must reach at least the stage of a criminal attempt, but it need not be a completed offence.

[35] *Jogee* at [90]–[95].

[36] See e.g. Child, 'Ulterior Mens Rea' (2017). In some ways, the focus on what conditional intent means is a distraction from the older – and arguably more relevant – debate on whether certain or all forms of secondary participation should require purpose. For this earlier discussion, see Williams, 'Complicity, Purpose – 1' (1990). This question is connected to the question concerning the nature of the accessory's wrongful act, a question addressed in Section III.1 below.

[37] See *Attorney-General's Reference (No. 1 of 1975)* [1975] QB 773.

of cases with very distinctive fact patterns. Counselling the commission of the crime means advising or advocating its commission.[38] Aiding and abetting both connect to the notion that the principal is assisted in the commission of the crime in some concrete way – including by psychological encouragement. Causal potency is a requirement in these cases.[39]

For some considerable time, however, the view has been taken that the *actus reus* of secondary liability is accurately captured through the notion of 'assisting or encouraging' the principal's crime. Encouraging, in turn, has been given a very wide reading, which includes the possibility of encouraging the principal's crime through one's supportive presence alone. The case which is taken to have recognised this expansive notion of participation by encouraging presence is *Coney*.[40] In *Coney*, it was held that attending an illegal prize fight could constitute secondary participation in that offence. Now, it is true that the prize fight was arranged before any spectators came to attend it, so their attendance cannot have procured the fight. It is also true that, merely by attending it, the spectators signalled that they wanted the fight to take place. Every member of the audience at an event that is put on to attract an audience (even if it is a free performance) is understood to have come to watch the performance, so (unless she clarifies that her presence is for a different reason altogether) her attendance communicates that she wants the performance to take place. Hence one can without stretching language or logic say that, by being quietly present, she 'counsels' the occurrence of the event.[41] The case has, however, been taken to support a much wider principle: that anyone who encourages the principal's actions through his presence alone at the scene of the crime (without the need for any words of support to be spoken) fulfils the *actus reus* requirement of

[38] Some writers prefer to regard all cases where there is a meeting of the minds between principal and accessory as 'counselling', including cases where the accessory hires the principal as a hit-man, from a sense that encouragement is easier to prove than the stronger (causal) relationship required for 'procuring', that 'the principal acts in consequence of the accomplice's conduct'. See Horder, *Ashworth's Principles* (2016), 443.

[39] There is some dispute regarding the existence and stringency of this causal requirement. See Horder, *Ashworth's Principles* (2016), 443–4.

[40] *Coney* (1882) 8 QBD 534. Coney and his co-accused were acquitted on appeal because it was possible that they had merely walked up to the crowd surrounding the fighters out of curiosity, in order to find out what was attracting the crowd. The wider principle decided in *Coney* was applied in *Wilcox* v. *Jeffrey* [1951] 1 All ER 464 to a music critic attending a jazz concert he knew was given by a musician without a work permit.

[41] Williams, *Textbook* (1983), 350–1 nevertheless rejects the *Coney* judgment as extending liability unreasonably far.

secondary participation. The *Jogee* court emphatically underwrites this wide reading of the *actus reus* requirement, and it is this move that enables the court to insist that all cases of group action – even cases of spontaneous multi-handed violence – can pass through the liability channel of standard secondary participation.[42] More problematically, it is this same wide reading that turns the notion of secondary liability into an amorphous catch-all with respect to participants in incidents of spontaneous or escalating violence.

Of course, doctrinal clarification in its own right was not the main objective of the *Jogee* court: its main objective was to limit the availability of murder convictions for participants in deadly fights. Before the emergence of the doctrine of 'parasitic accessorial liability' in the 1990s, the legal position in cases where violent escalations beyond the initial scope of an attack arise organically out of its commission was captured, inter alia, by Lord Parker in a hypothetical example, in the following terms:

> If two men attack a third without any intention of killing in the mind of either of them, and, as the fight develops, one . . . conceives in his mind an intention to kill and does kill, . . . [the fact that the other did not intend or foresee this development] does not absolve the other man from facing a charge of manslaughter. It is true that death resulted . . . from the intentional act of the one, but it was as a result of something that resulted and grew out of the initial attack in which two men were engaged.[43]

Writing extrajudicially in 2013 Lord Toulson clarified that this type of manslaughter verdict would constitute a form of unlawful act manslaughter.[44] When Toulson was writing, the judgment of the House of Lords in *Powell and English* had effectively removed the possibility of a manslaughter verdict in cases of this kind, and 'those who would formerly have been convicted of that offence [were] either convicted of murder or acquitted of both murder and manslaughter'[45] (the latter if the principal was held to have done something that the other participant had not even foreseen as a possibility). The significant increase in convictions for murder that had resulted from this facilitation of murder convictions, and a widespread view that those convictions were unfair,[46] provided the

42 See *Jogee*, at [78]: '[T]he giving of intentional support by words or deeds, including by supportive presence, is sufficient to attract secondary liability on ordinary principles.'

43 *Betty* (1963) 48 Cr. App. R. 6.

44 Toulson, 'Complicity in Murder' (2013), 244.

45 *Ibid.*

46 Traced in Crewe et al., 'Joint Enterprise' (2015).

main practical impetus behind the judgment in *Jogee* (where Lord Toulson was a member of the court).[47] The doctrinal path the judgment took – which had largely been foreshadowed in Toulson's 2013 publication – was embarked upon to reach the practical result of limiting the availability of murder convictions in cases of group violence, while restoring the option of a manslaughter conviction. The *Jogee* court is at pains to stress that in cases where *S* is part of a violent incident where death is caused but lacks any conditional intent for *P* to inflict grievous bodily harm or death, a manslaughter conviction should ordinarily result.[48]

Secondary liability thus now covers:

(a) The 'classic' cases of accessorial liability, where *S* becomes liable in respect of *P's* offence because *S* intentionally aids, abets, counsels or procures *P* to commit the offence (knowing the essential matters that make *P's* conduct into the offence it is). Viewed from *S's* perspective, these situations are about *S's* agency becoming effective 'through' *P*. In cases of procuring, *S's* interest in the commission of the crime by *P* is at least as strong as *P's*, such that the crime is just as much (or even more) *S's* project as it is *P's*; in cases of aiding, abetting and counselling, *S* may simply view himself as helping *P* to pursue *P's* project.

(b) Cases where the participants (in different roles) implement a common plan by coordinated action. Many Continental and some common law systems pack these cases under notions of co-perpetratorship.[49] Common law systems refer to these cases as 'common purpose' or 'joint enterprise'-based liability. In English law, as described above, they have come to rest under secondary liability and have in this context contributed to a looser notion of 'assisting and encouraging' as being the modes of secondary participation recognised by the common law.

[47] Cf. *Jogee* at [74]: 'There was no consideration in *Chan Wing-Siu*, or in *Powell and English*, of the fundamental policy question whether and why it was necessary and appropriate to reclassify such conduct as murder rather than manslaughter. Such a discussion would have involved, among other things, questions about fair labelling and fair discrimination in sentencing.'

[48] *Jogee* at [96]. For sustained discussion, see Krebs, 'Joint Enterprise Manslaughter' (forthcoming).

[49] In South Africa, which is in some respects closer to Continental systems, common purpose-based liability is (as in the German system, see below) placed under the umbrella of perpetratorship. See Burchell, 'Joint Enterprise and Common Purpose' (1997).

(c) Cases of escalating violence where one participant goes further than the others do, and the question arises whether the others are liable for the principal's 'further crime'. In English law, as explained above, these cases are, after the decision in *Jogee*, no longer separated from standard secondary liability. On the one hand, this means that, in terms of *mens rea*, *S's* liability now depends on whether he at least conditionally intended to encourage or assist that further crime. On the other hand, given that standard secondary liability also requires proof of an *actus reus* in respect of the further crime, post-*Jogee* case law may further widen the already problematically loose notion of 'participation by encouragement', with mere intentional participation in the base crime arguably sufficing as encouragement of the further crime. In other common law systems, by contrast, such cases are seen as falling under a subset of 'common purpose'-based rules, called 'extended common purpose', where liability for the further crime is ascribed according to principles based on foresight, very much on the lines that the English courts followed for a period of time between the decisions of *Chan Wing-Siu* and *Jogee*.[50]

(d) Cases of spontaneous multi-handed violence where 'the evidence may be too nebulous for the jury to find that there was some form of agreement, express or tacit'.[51] This is said not to matter because 'liability as an aider or abettor does not ... depend on there being some form of agreement between the [parties], it depends on proof of intentional assistance or encouragement'.[52] A fairly typical occurrence in such cases is that one participant goes further than the others in his use of violence, yet (since the original crime was never clearly defined) the 'further crime' analysis addressed in (c) does not apply. This difference notwithstanding, English courts had, prior to

[50] For details, see Simester, 'Accessory Liability' (2017) and Dyer, 'Australian Position' (2018). In most US states, the courts still apply an extreme version of such a doctrine based on notions of 'common design' or of 'natural and probable consequences', where the secondary party is held liable for all further offences whose commission was (objectively) a natural and probable consequence of the crime originally encouraged. This doctrine raises all the familiar objections to objective liability in criminal law, and some more. I will not analyse it separately in this chapter, except to say that it would follow from the rejection of the extended common purpose doctrine embraced by the Australian courts that a 'natural and probable further crime' doctrine would be even more unsupportable. On US criminal law, see Dressler, *Criminal Law* (2012), 475–6, and Heyman, 'Losing All Sense' (2013).

[51] *Jogee* at [95].

[52] *Ibid.*

> *Jogee*, applied the foresight rule to fact patterns of this kind.[53] Thus, one may expect that after *Jogee* participants will now be viewed as having encouraged each other in the commission of a range of fairly broadly defined violent crimes (again, conditional intent would now need to be shown in relation to *S* encouraging *P* to commit the crime *P* commits). Other common law jurisdictions have long diverged from English criminal law on this point. Australia, for example, has never included scenario (d) among the cases to which its (extended) common purpose rules apply. It has instead held participants in such cases liable only for their own contribution, plus any involvement in another's acts covered by narrowly conceived secondary liability rules.[54]

Before critiquing the English model, I will set out the German approach.

2 *Germany*

German criminal law may on the face of it appear to follow a simple bifurcated approach which operates only with a distinction between principals and secondary parties. On closer analysis, however, it emerges that it is best thought of as a three-tiered system, since a third liability paradigm is nested under the primary liability strand of perpetratorship. This third paradigm consists of a notion of co-perpetration that shares much with the common law's doctrine of common purpose liability, when that latter concept is viewed as a separate head of (secondary) liability in a common law system.

The legislative scheme is extremely terse. It defines as principals: (1) anyone who commits the offence himself or through another (direct and indirect perpetrators); and (2) anyone who commits the offence jointly with others (co-perpetrators) (see § 25 *Strafgesetzbuch* (StGB)). It then recognises standard secondary parties of two kinds: (1) instigators, who intentionally induce the principal to commit a crime of intent (§ 26 StGB: *Anstiftung*), and (2) aiders and abettors, who intentionally

[53] See e.g. *R* v. *O'Flaherty, Ryan and Touissant* [2004] EWCA Crim. 526, extensively analysed in du Bois-Pedain, 'Violent Dynamics' (2016).

[54] See *Miller* v. *The Queen* [2016] HCA 30 (Judgment of 24 Aug. 2016) (High Court of Australia). For Hong Kong, see *HKSAR* v. *Chan Kam Shing* [2016] HKCFA 87 (Judgment of 16 Dec. 2016) (Court of Final Appeal of the Hong Kong Special Administrative Region).

help the principal commit a crime of intent (§ 27: *Beihilfe*). Further explication of these concepts has been left to case law and doctrinal scholarship. This approach has given rise to a very rich and complex literature, and the German scheme can only be understood with some reference to this literature.[55]

German scholarship has devoted much attention to the notion of perpetratorship, and it is here that the most deep-seated disagreements can be found.[56] Historically, an influential view insisted that only a person who had performed the behaviour that meets the description of the offence definition could be recognised as a perpetrator (*formal-objektive Theorie*). This approach lost ground after the legislator explicitly recognised the possibility that a person who acts 'through another' can be a principal. The discredited formalistic approach always competed with different 'substantive' approaches to perpetratorship, all of which are still supported by some writers. One type of theory (*materiell-objektive Theorie*) focuses on external criteria, such as causation, dominance, or control over the performance of the *actus reus* of the main offence. Another type of theory (*subjektive Theorie*) puts the emphasis on the mindset/attitude of the persons involved in the commission of the crime and regards as a perpetrator someone who wills the crime as his own. The most protracted theoretical dispute over the last fifty years or so in this area of law has pitted the subjective approach favoured in many post-World War II trial judgments[57] against a version of an objective theory fully developed by Claus Roxin in the 1960s. The latter, called *Tatherrschaftslehre* or 'doctrine of control over the criminal act', holds that a perpetrator is the person who controls whether the offence is committed or not. In ordinary cases, this is the direct perpetrator. The theory however recognises that someone who is not the direct criminal agent can have control over the direct agent for structural reasons – particularly, such control can be exerted through organisational/institutional authority structures and lines of command. The theory thus makes it possible to apply the notion of 'indirect perpetratorship' to cases

[55] A good English-language exposition of the German scheme with illustrative examples from decided cases can be found in Ambos and Bock, 'Germany' (2013).

[56] For overviews of the debate, see e.g. Samson, *SK-StGB* (1993), '§ 25', mn. 6–32; Roxin, *LK-StGB* (2003), 'Vor § 25', mn. 3–12, 16 and '§ 25', mn. 3–46. The larger commentaries also always include extensive lists of relevant publications, going back to the late nineteenth century and often running into hundreds of entries.

[57] From the extensive literature, see e.g. Nehmer, 'Täter als Gehilfen' (1998); Klug, 'Rechtsprechung' (1987).

where the direct agent is not an innocent or semi-innocent agent but a criminally fully responsible individual. At the same time, it insists that a fully responsible individual who directly carries out the offence is a perpetrator, given that this individual could have stopped herself from performing the criminal act.[58] The latter position is what brings the Tatherrschaftslehre in conflict with the subjective approach, since that approach is prepared to treat the fully responsible direct agent as someone who merely considered himself an instrument of another's will (and consequently as a secondary party). This disagreement was of particular relevance in trials of concentration camp guards and other Nazi officials for murder.[59] As a doctrine that appears tailor-made for crimes committed by persons in large institutional structures, the Tatherrschaftslehre has also more recently been influential in international criminal law.[60]

As regards the domestic system and the comparative perspective, another important area of German doctrine concerns the notion of co-perpetratorship or *Mittäterschaft*. Courts and scholars traditionally require two elements: a common plan (*gemeinsamer Tatplan*), and its cooperatively shared execution (*arbeitsteilige Tatausführung*).[61] Provided these two elements are in place, a person can be a co-perpetrator even if she is not at the scene of the crime (but does something that furthers the commission of the crime in its planning or its success-securing stages) or even if their own conduct, viewed in isolation, does not constitute any of

58 For the canonical statement of the theory, see Roxin, *Tatherrschaft* (2015 [1963]). Most commentators (and even some more recent court judgments) subscribe to this theory. But it also has some serious critics (see especially Haas, *Theorie der Tatherrschaft* (2008) and Rotsch, *Einheitstäterschaft statt Tatherrschaft* (2009)) and competitors (such as the extensive notion of perpetratorship grounded in 'the implementation of an individual's plan of action' developed by Schild, *NK-StGB* (2005), '§ 25').

59 For exposition, critique and historical appraisal of court judgments adopting the subjective theory, which could turn almost anyone involved in mass killings, including those who directly carried out the murders, into mere accessories, see e.g. Eichmüller, *Keine Generalamnestie* (2012), 251–3 (with further references); Greve, *Umgang mit NS-Gewaltverbrechern* (2001), 151 ff.; Just-Dahlmann and Just, *Gehilfen* (1988), 206 ff.; Perels, *Das juristische Erbe* (1999), 171 ff.

60 For details and discussion, see Ambos, *Treatise I* (2013), 149–60 and 177 ff.

61 For detailed exposition, see Samson, *SK-StGB* (1993), '§ 25', mn. 116–31; Roxin, *LK-StGB* (2003), '§ 25', mn. 153–200; Lackner, *StGB-Kommentar* (1997), '§ 25', mn. 9–19; and other leading commentaries. On the protracted historical development of the modern notion of Mittäterschaft through a gradual merging and reshaping of the Continental common law's conceptions of 'authorship' of a crime (*Urheberschaft*), and its special provision addressing conspiracies to kill (referred to as *Komplott* or *Verschwörung*), see Kriegsmann, *Mittäterschaft und Raufhandel* (1907), 7–99.

the *actus reus* elements of the offence.[62] This conceptualisation of co-perpetratorship is very close to Christopher Kutz's theoretical analysis of joint action. Kutz's criteria for joint action are: strategic responsiveness, shared goals, mutual openness and a sort of horizontal intention that all the participants have 'to do his or her part of promoting the group activity or outcome' which, according to Kutz, is a 'further intentional component, by which agents conceive of their actions as standing in a certain instrumental relation to the group act'.[63]

The doctrine of joint perpetration was developed in order to provide a liability regime for actors whose actions only constitute a criminal offence when they are viewed in aggregate and taken together, whereas their respective individual actions viewed in isolation would not amount to that offence. Joint perpetration is a doctrine of mutual agency/act-attribution (as opposed to a doctrine of derivative responsibility-attribution).[64] Perhaps surprisingly from a common law perspective, where one of the main practical functions of common purpose doctrines is to serve as a launching pad for extended liability attributions for further crimes, this has not been a function of the – more individualistic – doctrine of co-perpetration. What is not part of the plan falls outside the plan, and the other co-perpetrators are not liable if one of their number exceeds the scope of the plan with her actions and thereby commits a further or more serious crime than was agreed in the common plan

[62] By contrast, English law's notion of co-principals appears much narrower, treating as co-principals multiple parties who 'together … satisfy the definition of the substantive offence and each of them engaged in some part of the external element of the offence with the required fault', as well as those who 'each of them by his own act contributes to the commission of the offence, if all their acts together fulfil all the conduct elements, and if each of them has the required mental element' (Horder, *Ashworth's Principles* (2016), 433). This excludes treating the person who drives the getaway car, or the mastermind who planned the crime but was not on the scene during its commission, as a co-principal (cf. Wilson, *Criminal Law* (2014), 562).

[63] Kutz, *Complicity* (2000), 78. On the proximity to the German conception of co-perpetration, see further Hamdorf, 'Concept of a Joint Criminal Enterprise' (2007).

[64] This was first clearly seen by those writers who offered a trenchant critique of Feuerbach's early proposal to construe Mittäterschaft as a relationship of 'mutual instigation' between the participants (see Feuerbach, *Lehrbuch* (1808), § 46 – this 4th edn is the earliest edition in which Feuerbach put forward this view). Feuerbach's concern had been to identify a ground on which those joined together in a criminal conspiracy constituted authors (*Urheber*) of the crime once it was committed, and instigation was then one of the recognised forms of authorship. His view came to be rejected because it excluded treating as co-perpetrators those who were brought together by coincidence and spontaneously cooperated in the execution of a crime. For a summary of the debate that followed Feuerbach's proposal, see Kriegsmann, *Mittäterschaft und Raufhandel* (1907), 13–51.

(*Mittäterexzeß*).[65] It is worth observing that, in escalating violence cases, this position is qualified in that, where the escalation and thus the exceeding of the plan was predictable, the courts can hold others than the direct agent liable for negligence/recklessness-based qualifications of the basic intention-based crime of violence.[66] The practical result is rather similar to a conviction of a secondary party post-*Jogee* under the manslaughter route.

While instigation was historically grouped with forms of direct commission under the general concept of 'authorship' of a crime,[67] secondary liability incurred through instigation or help is nowadays seen as fundamentally different from perpetratorship. The difference is both conceptual and normative. Conceptually, secondary liability involves ways for *S* to become effective in the world through the agency of another person (the principal). Normatively, *S's* responsibility depends on *S* having the right kind of connection to *P's* crime. This is the reason why secondary liability is standardly conceptualised as 'derivative' – if *P* never acts as *S* intended for *P* to act, there is no (at least attempted) main offence by *P* to which *S's* liability could attach.[68] Comparably to orthodox secondary liability in English criminal law, the secondary party's *actus reus* requires conduct that amounts to instigating or helping *P* commit an offence. In German criminal law, according to express legislative stipulation this offence has to be a crime requiring intention on the part of the perpetrator. The *mens rea* is twofold, requiring (1) an intention to

[65] This is the accepted view of all leading commentators, see only Lackner and Kühl, *StGB-Kommentar* (2018), '§ 25', mn. 17.

[66] See Stuckenberg, 'Exzeß des Mittäters' (2007). When death resulted from the intentional commission of bodily injury and the participant foresaw or should have foreseen that death might result, the conviction offence is § 227 StGB ('intentional bodily injury resulting in death', with a sentence range of between three years' and fifteen years' imprisonment). When certain particularly serious and lasting injuries or disfigurements were caused and the participant foresaw or should have foreseen these as possible consequences, the conviction offence is § 226 ('grave bodily injury', covering intentional bodily injury resulting in loss of limb, sight, hearing, speech, procreative function, lasting disfigurement, permanent ailing health, paralysis, mental illness or disability, with a sentence range of between one year's and ten years' imprisonment).

[67] The then orthodox position is set out in the 1st edn of Feuerbach's *Lehrbuch* (1801), § 52. See also Kriegsmann, *Mittäterschaft und Raufhandel* (1907), 13–14, 19–20. For the further historical development of the notion of 'offence authorship' in conjunction with broad theories of causation, see Haas, *Theorie der Tatherrschaft* (2008), 69–78.

[68] It is a different question whether the term 'derivative' is the most apt to capture this relationship. *Kadish* contends that 'dependent' would be preferable. Kadish, 'Complicity, Cause and Blame' (1985), 337.

perform the *actus reus* of secondary participation, and (2) an intention that *P* commit the target crime. Beyond that common structure, however, German law draws a sharp line between these two modes of secondary participation, subjecting them to rather different liability outcomes. Instigators are liable to the same punishment as principal offenders, whereas mere aiders and abettors benefit from a compulsory reduction of the penalty scale. (It is also only in respect of 'would be'-instigators that pre-inchoate liability for attempted instigation of a serious crime arises.[69])

These modes of liability are accessorial in a narrow, technical sense. Viewed from the perspective of the principal, the secondary party is an add-on. The principal's behaviour is criminal in its own right; the existence of the accessory does not in any way affect the legal classification of his action. By contrast, the accessory's liability *is* affected by what the principal does. Even where the secondary party's conduct is criminalised under some other offence description in its own right, the accessory incurs some further liability for the principal's offence the moment the principal commits (or at least attempts the commission of) the main offence. This does not detract from the fact that *S's* liability as a secondary party is, of course, based on *S's* own, autonomous choice. The subsequent commission of the crime by *P* is simply the particular manner in which *S* succeeds in affecting the state of the world through his, *S's*, own conduct that consisted in the instigation or facilitation of *P's* crime. The peculiarities of what it means to 'act through another', fully responsible, agent notwithstanding, *P's* crime thus stands in relation to *S's* actions in much the same moral position as other consequences of *S's* actions do.

3 *Particular Issues and Their Resolution*

(a) Can Principal and Secondary Party Be Liable for Different Offences?

It is sometimes assumed that, because of the accessorial structure of standard secondary liability, the accessory must of necessity be liable for the same offence as the principal. In both systems, this is, however, not necessarily the case, although the reasons why modifications are possible differ, and the theoretical justifications given for these modifications differ as well.

69 For details, see Bock and Stark, Ch. 3, 'Preparatory Offences' (in this volume).

Unproblematic examples of divergence in both systems concern situations where the divergence arises on the basis of *P* having a full capacity-based or other non-justificatory personal defence. Both systems apply special rules when *P's* personal characteristics (being under-age, insane or under duress) mean that *P* has a defence personal to him that explains why *P* cannot incur criminal liability, or why his liability is reduced. Here, the difference in liability between *P*, who has the defence, and *S*, who does not in his own person have the defence, arises under the principles governing the availability of defences: certain defences are personal and thus do not reach across to other parties.[70]

We now turn to cases of fully responsible primary and secondary parties who nevertheless incur liability for different crimes.

In the German system, the accessorial principle is explicitly qualified and restricted by a second principle: the principle that each party's liability must reflect that party's own guilt (§ 29 StGB). This principle is supplemented by a special rule regarding 'personal characteristics' of a party which influence the party's criminal liability (§ 28 StGB). This provision is, for instance, relevant in respect of homicide offences where one party may be liable for murder due to the presence of a certain personal characteristic (say, that the party acts in order to gratify a sexual desire) whereas the other party, who lacks this characteristic, will only be liable for intentional homicide.[71]

In England, as Keating et al. point out, 'it has long been possible to convict [secondary parties] present at the scene of the crime of a more serious offence than the principal',[72] and the case of *Howe*[73] extended this rule to accessories not present on the scene.[74] As Glanville Williams reports, leading seventeenth- and eighteenth-century commentators such as Sir Matthew Hale and Sir Edward Hyde East had already accepted the rule that '[o]ne who kills without malice aforethought ... may be guilty

[70] In German law, some of these cases are resolved by holding the participant with capacity or without defence responsible as an indirect perpetrator. Others fall under the application of the special provision regarding 'personal characteristics' explained in the next paragraph. Due to debated conceptualisations of perpetratorship, the German system is more troubled by semi-innocent agents than the English one. It has, however, also come to accept this possibility.

[71] On the structure of German homicide law, see du Bois-Pedain, 'Intentional Killings' (2007).

[72] Keating et al., *Criminal Law* (2014), 587.

[73] [1987] 1 AC 417.

[74] Keating et al., *Criminal Law* (2014), 586.

of manslaughter, while an abettor or instigator, having malice aforethought, may be guilty of murder'.[75] He also mentions the direction in *Conroy*[76] where a woman was accused of infanticide for killing her newborn baby while her husband, who was alleged to have abetted her, was charged with murder. The inverse situation – that the secondary party is guilty of a less serious offence than the principal – is also viewed as possible, when the personal factors affecting liability in the examples given above are inverted.[77] England thus reaches the same outcomes in particular cases as are generated by application of the rule that German law has formulated in general terms.

(b) Escalating Violence Cases

As we have seen, both systems operate with certain expansions to the liability of secondary parties in escalating violence scenarios. The issue in such cases is the in-between nature of how *P's* further/collateral crime comes about. From the perspective of *S*, it is neither within the goal-defined venture nor unconnected. Rather it is connected to the venture but not connected to the intentions of *S* in the same way as *P's* other acts taken 'in execution of the common plan'. K. J. M. Smith describes *P's* (often fatal) acts in such cases as 'overzealous principal actions which, although outside the common design, were carried out in its pursuance and were objectively foreseeable'.[78]

English and German law are now aligned in that such extended liability of the secondary party arises *not* for the further crime of intent that the primary party committed (e.g. murder) but for a different crime which (in substance) processes the secondary party's connection to the risk of escalation. This is made explicit in German law, where such liability-extensions come about through the application of provisions that combine the intentional commission of a 'base crime' (such as criminal injury) with the occurrence of particularly serious unintended consequences in respect of which the defendant was at least negligent.[79] That responsibility is ascribed on the basis of *S's* connection to the risk of escalation provides the best explanation of English law's position, too, although this is less obvious from the conviction offence, which as

75 Williams, *The General Part* (1961), 390–1.
76 [1954] Crim. LR 143.
77 Williams, *The General Part* (1961), 390.
78 Smith, *Modern Treatise* (1991), 211.
79 See the discussion at n. 66 above and Gössel, 'Dogmatische Überlegungen' (1976), 230–1.

regards non-fatal offences remains identical to the offence committed by *P* (due to the wide *mens rea* of these offences). In cases where *P* commits murder by his further act, the conviction offence for the secondary party post-*Jogee* will, however, be different (namely, manslaughter – which, however, provided it is conceptualised as unlawful act manslaughter, does not require demonstrating that *S* was negligent in respect of *V's* death).

By contrast, common law jurisdictions such as Australia that still recognise an extended common purpose rule ascribe responsibility to *S* for *P's* 'further crime' on what is perhaps best thought of as a 'modified' secondary liability paradigm, where (to put it simply) it is held sufficient that *S* foresaw the possibility that *P* might commit the relevant further crime, even if *S* did not intend that *P* commit it.[80] The conviction offence for *S* is then the same as *P's* further crime – in homicide cases, murder, even when *S* did not intend for *P* to commit murder but merely foresaw that possibility.[81] The moral justification for this move is doubtful. As the *Jogee* court clarified, secondary liability gives out at this point. At the very least, therefore, the rule is not justified by the same considerations that justify secondary liability as such. It must be justified by a separate principle, and no principle that could conceivably justify conviction for a crime of intent when the structural basis for the extension is that *S* took a conscious risk in respect of what (else) *P* might do, has been forthcoming.[82]

(c) Recklessness/Negligence and Secondary Liability

This gets us to another fundamental issue that the law on secondary liability needs to resolve: can *S* be a secondary party to the principal's crime if *S's* contribution to that crime is based on recklessness/negligence rather than on intention?[83] This issue can sometimes arise in respect of (negligent) mistakes of fact by *P*/*S*, and more generally: Can *S* 'aid and abet' *P's* burglary by negligently or recklessly leaving the front door wide

[80] See Simester, 'Accessory Liability' (2017).

[81] See text at n. 50 above.

[82] See Dennis Baker's critique (in Baker, 'Reinterpreting the Mental Element' (2016)) of Simester's reliance (in Simester, 'The Mental Element' (2006)) on the normative gateway through which *S* has allegedly passed. Even if *S* has done that, it is a gateway which connects *S* to the risk of further crime, and no more.

[83] Further complicated issues that I cannot go into here, but which affect the location of the boundary lines between liability and non-liability drawn in each system, arise from the different conceptions of intention in both systems.

open at night, or 'procure by endeavour' *P's* offence of battery by telling *P* untruthfully that *V* sexually assaulted her (not with a view to getting *P* to assault *V*, but with a view to getting *P's* sympathy, negligently failing to realise that given *P's* aggressive nature a physical attack on *V* is *P's* far likelier reaction)? German law excludes this explicitly by requiring *S's* *actus reus* to be performed with the intention of instigating or assisting *P* in the commission of his crime. English common law requires such an intention as well (see e.g. *Jogee*).

The inverse problem is whether *S* can, by performing an act intended to encourage or assist *P* in the commission of some criminal act, become a secondary party to *P's* offence if *P's* offence is not a crime of intent but based on recklessness or negligence. In the German system, the answer is no, and is provided for by statutory fiat: instigation and aiding/abetting both require that *S* instigates or aids/abets *P's* 'intended and unjustified criminalised act'. In English law, there appears to be no reason in principle why *P's* main offence shouldn't be a crime of negligence/recklessness or even of strict liability, so long as *S* possesses the secondary party's two-pronged (conditional or unconditional) intention to (1) provide her contribution (aid, abet, counsel, procure) and (2) for *P* to carry out the target offence. Of course, some forms of contribution must run through *P's* conscious will (and hence his crime must be one of intent for that avenue to work). But other forms of influence over another person's actions are more subtle, and in respect of those there is no reason why the offending behaviour thus influenced should require any intention at all.[84]

In German law, the position is less clear in respect of co-perpetration, since the law here merely speaks of 'the offence' being committed jointly. The majority position holds that true joint perpetration of a negligence-based crime is impossible, since a joint criminal plan will of necessity be absent where a crime is not intended. A (preferable) minority view argues that joint perpetration is possible in respect of reckless/negligent crimes, and covers cases where the parties engage jointly and cooperatively in a project or activity that each of them does, or ought to, realise gives rise to unjustified risk of harm.[85]

This is an appropriate juncture at which to raise the principled question of how the liability of participants in multi-party cases ought

[84] For sustained discussion of recklessness/negligence and accessorial liability, see Kadish, 'Reckless Complicity' (1997) and Williams, 'Complicity, Purpose – 2' (1990).

[85] See Renzikowski, 'Fahrlässige Mittäterschaft' (2007), 431, 433, 439.

to be structured. It is to the principles underlying this area of law, and to the development of an ideal model, that the next section turns.

III Developing a Sufficiently Differentiated Liability Model

A theory of participation in crime must engage with the social reality of participatory conduct, in that it must capture the social significance and reflect the social meaning of the various contributory acts.[86] Its liability-paradigms must capture the gravamen of the secondary party's wrong. The English model has caused difficulties in practice because the simple distinction between primary and secondary parties is too crude to permit the system to operate with the same set of sub-principles in all cases falling within the broad camp of secondary participation. Liability under this model is too wide (a person can be convicted of an offence even though he has done extremely little by way of contribution). Moreover, in many cases the English liability regime, in claiming that *S* is held responsible for aiding, abetting, counselling or procuring *P's* crime, appears to misdescribe why we want to attribute responsibility for *P's* offence to *S*. Take the example of young men involved in unplanned group violence, where all participants have made a spontaneous choice to attack *V* but one participant out-aggresses the others from the start. In situations of this kind, the others do not join in because they want the prime aggressor to feel supported but because they themselves want to join the fight. They have their own ideas of what sort of fight it is. Neither notions of 'common purpose' nor of 'derivative liability' capture this.

Looking at the types of multi-party case that arise in the case law and ordering these according to the gravamen of the wrong, I argue that we ought to distinguish three paradigms, which I have defined in the introduction as the mediated action paradigm ('acting through another'), the concerted action paradigm ('acting with another'), and the parallel actions paradigm ('acting alongside another').[87] I will now set out these

[86] See e.g. Otto, 'Teilnahme' (1976), 204.

[87] When I first proposed this three-fold distinction (in 'Violent Dynamics' (2016)) I referred to these paradigms as 'the secondary participation paradigm', 'the collective action or "group act" paradigm' and 'the independent assessment paradigm'. I believe that the labels I give here capture the paradigms more accurately. I also then believed that the 'independent assessment paradigm' was coextensive in its application with all escalating violence scenarios. I now believe that the boundaries of the concept need to be drawn slightly differently.

paradigms and then highlight how a liability regime that uses this threefold distinction can overcome the problems of existing models.

1 *The Mediated Action Paradigm ('Acting through Another')*

The classic secondary participation model attributes responsibility to *S* for a crime *P* commits by focusing on the influence that *S* exerted over *P's* actions. To be a secondary party to *P's* crime, *S* must (in the standard form of this model) do something that encourages or assists *P* in the commission of his crime, intending (i) for *P* to commit the crime, and (ii) for his action to support or influence *P* in doing so. In these cases of standard accessorial involvement, *S's* liability *derives* from *P's* commission of the crime with *S's* supportive contribution. Were it not for the connection to *P's* crime, what *S* does would be harmless to *V*. *S's* contribution brings evil into the world 'through *P*' – and *S* is held responsible for that evil, along with *P*, because he intends for his, *S's*, agency to be effective in precisely this way, through *P*.

The mediated action paradigm serves us well in cases where the wrong that *S* commits is essentially the wrong of bringing harm into the world through *P*. What ordinary accessorial liability recognises is that *P's* actions are sufficiently influenced by *S*, such that *P*, in doing what he, *P*, chooses to do, also does what *S* wants *P* to do, and does so (at least in part) as a result of the influence that *S* exerted on *P* with the aim of assisting or encouraging *P's* act.

If one centres this paradigm on what one might call the phenomenology of acting through another person, then the common element lies in the particular manner in which *S* is connected to the violation of *V's* legally protected interests. *S's* connection to the harm *V* suffers is not direct, but indirect. It runs through the specific connection *S* has to the violation that is directly carried out by *P*. This mediated action structure is present in all cases where the violation of *V's* legally protected interest is brought about by *S* influencing the actions of another direct human agent (whether this is a responsible or a non-responsible agent, so long as phenomenologically action is present). *S's* activity takes effect through *P's* actions and thus *S's* effectiveness is entirely dependent on *P's* choices – whether these choices are responsible or irresponsible, informed or uninformed, pressurised, manipulated or self-motivated ones.

This means that the mediated action paradigm encompasses standard cases of 'assisting and encouraging' as well as cases of innocent agency or what German law classifies as indirect perpetration.[88] This suggestion is less radical than it may seem, though, because different sub-principles of attribution are appropriate for the different kinds of cases that are broadly cases of acting through another. It is revisionist only in its insistence that (structurally) accessorial liability on the part of *S* can arise in respect of acts by *P* that constitute objective violations of interests protected by criminal provisions, irrespective of the question whether *P* himself is criminally liable for that violation (including in cases where *P* lacks *mens rea* due to a mistake of fact). The notion in play here was captured by Lord Justice Lawton, who gave the judgment of the English Court of Appeal in *Cogan and Leak*, when he upheld the conviction of a husband for procuring the rape of his wife when the direct agent, persuaded by the husband that the wife would welcome the sexual interaction, had had intercourse with the wife against her will but without the *mens rea* for rape: 'No one outside a court of law would say that [the woman] had not been [raped].'[89] That 'popular or sociological' conception of rape[90] reflects the fact that the rights-violation against which the law of rape seeks to protect the victim had occurred. It is this unlawful act, the conduct element of the *actus reus* of a criminal offence, to which *S* must stand in a structurally accessorial relation.[91]

The special way in which *S* does so in cases where *P* is his innocent agent is best reflected in a special legal provision catering for these

[88] German law's misallocation of these cases to a separate category of indirect perpetration arises in part from a widespread misconception that the irresponsible agent does not 'act' in the criminal law sense, combined with an assumption that it is therefore the responsible (indirect) agent whose will controls the act, and who therefore possesses *Tatherrschaft*. Unless one reduces both Tatherrschaft and agency to purely normative notions, one however has to acknowledge that non-responsible humans are influenced by communication and direct their own behaviour by exercising their admittedly constrained capacities of will and reason, and that this being so, another person can no more effectively have complete control over what a non-responsible human does than over what a responsible human does.

[89] *Cogan and Leak* [1976] QB 217.

[90] The description is from Williams, in his *Textbook* (1983), 372.

[91] The same conclusion regarding Leak, that he should be liable as an accessory to rape because the 'wrongful act' (the *actus reus* of the offence) is in place is reached by Alldridge, 'Innocent Agency' (1990), 52. Before the relevant legal provisions in the StGB were reworded to require an 'intentional unlawful act' by *P* to which liability as a secondary party could attach, some German authors also defended the position that accessorial liability could attach to an act for which the direct perpetrator lacked legal responsibility due to lack of capacity or mistake.

scenarios.[92] Glanville Williams proposes the formulation that accessorial liability should in such cases arise if '[*S*] causes [*P*] to do an act (or make an omission) that would have been an offence if [*P*] had lacked an excuse, but [*P*] had an excuse, and [*S*] would have been an accomplice in the offence if it had been committed by [*P*]' (the notion of an excuse covers cases where *P* lacks the fault element as well as cases where *P* lacks capacity or has a non-justificatory personal defence).[93] Williams suggested wording is serviceable, provided that the expression '*S* causes *P*' is replaced with '*S* directs, encourages or assists *P*' in order to take account of the basic accessorial structure of *S's* conduct.

This last point, concerning the 'basic accessorial structure of *S's* conduct', needs to be grounded further in a discussion of the nature or character of *S's* wrongful act. Constraints of space prevent me from expanding my discussion of the basic accessorial structure in a way that could do justice to the rich and varied literature that exists on this point.[94] All I can do here is outline my own position. I agree with Buxton's observation that:

> [T]he central point in complicity is the relation of the accessory to the will or intention of the perpetrator to do those things which constitute the principal crime, rather than his relation to the principal crime as such, since the accessory differs from the perpetrator in that he interposes between himself and the legally-prohibited harm the volition of another party.[95]

The distinction Buxton draws between the accessory's relation 'to the will or intention of the perpetrator', on the one hand, and to 'the principal crime as such', on the other hand, is of central importance. The accessory's relation to the latter is usually seen to consist in causation (although it could also reside in risk-creation). Buxton's remark makes it clear that *this relation* (albeit that it may well be present) is not the decisive one. Rather, the specific character of accessorial wrongdoing resides in the accessory's relation to 'the will or intention of the perpetrator to do those things which constitute the principal crime'. This is the

[92] In the English context this was apparently first proposed by Buxton, 'Complicity' (1969), 272.
[93] For this suggested formulation, see Williams, 'Excuses' (1982), 737–8, who builds his draft upon a provision in the Model Penal Code.
[94] In the German discussion, this is addressed under the heading 'Strafgrund der Teilnahme'.
[95] Buxton, 'Complicity' (1969), 270.

kernel of truth in the views that see the wrong of participation in the corruption by *S* of *P* and/or in *S's* showing solidarity with *P's* wrongdoing. The accessory's wrong is the combined wrong of leading or supporting *P* on the path to crime, *and* of thereby conducting an indirect attack (via *P*) on the interest protected by the principal offence in question. Two important implications follow:

(a) The mere creation of a tempting opportunity, or provocative behaviour, by *S* is not enough to make *S* liable under this paradigm when *P* goes on to commit an offence – these behaviours merely create a broadly causal connection between *S's* action and *P's* crime, which by itself is not enough.
(b) The inherently goal-directed quality of an action properly conceived of as helping or instigating the commission of *P's* unlawful act gives the accessory's conduct a purposive dimension. This affects the appropriate *mens rea* of the accessory. It must be such that *S* intends for *P* to carry out the act which amounts to the external element of the principal offence, and (arguably) also such that *S* directly intends his own act to provide encouragement or assistance.[96]

Beyond these commonalities between all cases within the remit of the mediated action paradigm, there are certain important differences between instigators and helpers that need to be recognised. In the main, these differences pertain to the more subordinate role played by a helper compared to the influence exerted by an instigator – and, connected to this, the fact that the instigator tends to have greater personal 'investment' in *P's* commission of the principal offence than the typical assister. These differences explain the long-prevailing separation in Continental criminal law of instigators from assisters/encouragers and their placement along with direct perpetrators in the category of 'offence authorship', and continue to account for the mandatory sentence reduction for helpers (as opposed to instigators) in German law. A full exploration of the ways in which these differences should be reflected in the criminal law must be left to another occasion. All that should be noted in the present context is that these differences should be recognised within the overall framework of the mediated action paradigm.

[96] On what it means to intend to assist another's crime, see Duff, 'Can I Help You' (1990). For further distinctions to be drawn between the kind of intention required (requiring 'direct intention' for instigation but settling for certain knowledge in respect of assistance), see Williams, 'Complicity, Purpose – 1' (1990).

2 *The Concerted Action Paradigm ('Acting with Another')*

At the heart of Mittäterschaft lies the idea of concerted action taken in the execution of a common plan. Kutz identifies as a 'common structural feature' of a group act (which he calls a 'collective action') that 'individual members of a group intentionally do their parts in promoting a joint outcome'.[97] For this structural feature to be present, the participants must (at a minimum) (i) have a particular outcome in mind, which is broadly the same outcome intended by them all; (ii) have the notion that they will bring about this outcome by acting together (rather than by each of them trying to bring about the outcome on his or her own); and (iii) this notion of acting together also usually requires some plan or shared idea about how they will collaborate and coordinate their activities in order to bring the outcome about.[98]

Kutz maintains that 'what makes a set of individual acts a case of jointly intentional action is the content of the intentions with which the individuals act', and, specifically, that 'jointly intentional action is primarily a function of the way in which individual agents regard their own actions as contributing to a collective outcome'.[99] What is special about collaborating actors, according to Kutz, is that '[j]ointly acting individuals do not merely act in parallel: Each responds to what the others do and plan to do.'[100] Kutz's final and most important criterion is a sort of horizontal intention that all the participants have 'to do his or her part of promoting the group activity or outcome' which, according to Kutz, is a 'further intentional component, by which agents conceive of their actions as standing in a certain instrumental relation to the group act'.[101] For this criterion to be made out, each participant must at least know what his or her 'part' is and how it serves the collective aim. Absent this special contributory intent behind my actions I cannot be said to intend to participate in a 'group act' by doing what I do.

The concerted action paradigm serves us well when the gravamen of the wrong lies in doing the criminal or harmful thing together. The paradigm allows us to treat the actions of each of the participants as an action performed by all. This seems appropriate because of the special

[97] Kutz, *Complicity* (2000), 69.
[98] For the equivalent requirements of German doctrine, see Küpper, 'Der gemeinsame Tatentschluß' (1993), 301 ff.
[99] Kutz, *Complicity* (2000), 74 (referred to by Kutz as 'participatory intention').
[100] *Ibid.*, 76.
[101] *Ibid.*, 78. See also, from the German jurisprudence, BGH StV 1992, 160.

participatory intent that holds the actions of group members together. Where such participatory intent is lacking, it would be unjust to hold me responsible for anything other than my own actions.[102]

3 *The Parallel Actions Paradigm ('Acting alongside Another')*

For the just-mentioned reason it is important to distinguish the concerted action paradigm from the parallel actions paradigm. Spontaneous, unplanned violent fights typically do not meet the criteria developed above for a joint act. Their goal is too undefined to allow participants in the fight to relate to each other with the nuanced participatory intentions of doing their bit towards a shared goal. Spontaneously erupting violent fights may be instances of group offending in the sense that offences are committed during an incident involving more than one participant, but the interrelation between these participants is not ordinarily governed by the interwoven intentions that mark an act out as an act of a group.[103] This is why it is unsatisfactory for the law to treat spontaneous, unplanned violent fights as cases of Mittäterschaft. As one German commentator puts the point with admirable clarity: 'joint enterprises involve the deliberate and intentional cooperative behaviour of a multitude of individuals (not merely that people act from within a group)'.[104]

Nor does *S's* contribution to such an incident fit under the mediated action paradigm. The distinctive feature of *S's* joining-in is not that *S* wants to make a difference in the world by exerting an influence over the other fighters. Even if he had an awareness that others who fight on his side might feel comforted and supported by the knowledge that *S* has joined in, this is not the point of *S's* joining-in. *S* intends for his agency to be effective in the world through the things he himself does after joining. What *S* does is not about exerting an influence on another through encouragement or assistance: it is about doing his own thing by taking part.

We therefore need to jettison both the mediated and the concerted action paradigms in favour of a different basis for responsibility-ascription in such cases. While participants in spontaneous violent encounters that turn nasty and lead to fatalities do see themselves as

[102] See e.g. Küpper, 'Der gemeinsame Tatentschluß' (1993), 301 ff.
[103] Cf. Kutz, *Complicity* (2000), 82–3.
[104] Lackner and Kühl, *StGB-Kommentar* (2018), '§ 25', mn. 9.

potentially implicated in the outcome through their involvement in the incident more broadly,[105] it is clear that the relation in which they stand to the direct agent's fatal act is not mediated through anything like an influence they have exerted on the direct agent at that very moment. The decisive question in instances of loose, spontaneous, disorganised group action is simply this: how do the actions of each protagonist implicate him or her in the result? Once we have decided that, due to its distinctive features, a set of facts is best addressed under the parallel actions paradigm, we need to abandon the search for some distinct link that each protagonist has to the direct agent's act/crime and focus instead on the protagonist's connection (including through his or her early-stage behaviour) to the harmful outcome.

In situations where *S* was not the one to strike the fatal blow, *S's* own acts are linked to this fatal outcome only to the extent that *S's* contribution created a risk that has manifested itself in *V's* death. That *P's* action is not just his free, informed and voluntary act but also the realisation of such a risk is why *S* is linked to this act and its outcome – as a manifestation of a risk that he created. The fact that the harm was brought about through the culpable agency of *P* does not block responsibility-attribution to *S* when *P's* act, however much it may go beyond the common plan or the initial goal, is still a 'predictable' result that organically develops out of the heat of the fighting situation. Where *S* is or should have been aware of a risk of death, conviction for a homicide offence of some kind may be appropriate. Where such actual or potential awareness was lacking, the most appropriate legal solution is to create a specific offence for those who participate in a fight during which very serious injury or death is caused to another person (as German law has done in § 231 StGB ('participation in a fight where serious injury or death are caused')).[106]

IV Conclusion

I have argued that appropriate distinctions between different modes of participation in crime need to be drawn at the liability-incurring stage because of structural differences in the wrongdoing the law seeks to

[105] See the interviews with prisoners reported in Crewe et al., 'Joint Enterprise' (2015), 266–7.

[106] Using affray would be an alternative charge in the English system. For details, see du Bois-Pedain, 'Violent Dynamics' (2016), 1068 f.

respond to. As a first filtering step, three paradigms of participation should be distinguished – these paradigms pick up on pre-legal phenomenological differences in the type of relationship participants bear to the violation of rights/interests protected by the criminal law. Principles of responsibility-ascription cannot be general across the three paradigms. Instead, each paradigm requires its own, appropriate, subset of principles. Questions such as whether secondary liability is causal or non-causal, whether it is centrally about act-imputation or about responsibility-ascription, whether it is risk-based or intention-based, and the like, thus cannot be answered in the abstract, but can only be posed and answered separately for each of the different liability paradigms, where the answers will differ. For this reason, English law's strategy of extending standard principles of accessorial liability across the full range of the participatory paradigms must be rejected. German law fares better in this regard, but still misallocates indirect perpetration cases, which are properly placed with standard 'assisting and encouraging' cases in the same participatory paradigm. English law's failure to reflect modes of participation in the conviction offence runs counter to the aim of fair labelling. The sentencing stage is the appropriate stage at which actual differences in the extent of the involvement of secondary parties can be appropriately reflected, but the foundations for this need to be laid by a clear understanding of the basis on which each party is held liable under the different paradigms.

Bibliography

Alldridge P., 'The Doctrine of Innocent Agency', *Criminal Law Forum*, 2 (1990), 45–83.

Ambos K., *Treatise on International Criminal Law*, I: *Foundations and General Part*, Oxford University Press (2013).

Ambos K. and Bock S., 'Germany', in Reed A. and Bohlander M. (eds.), *Participation in Crime: Domestic and Comparative Perspectives*, Aldershot, Ashgate (2013), 323–39.

Baker D. J., 'Reinterpreting the Mental Element in Criminal Complicity: Change of Normative Position Theory Cannot Rationalize the Current Law', *Law & Psychology Review*, 40 (2016), 119–296.

Bloy R., *Die Beteiligungsform als Zurechnungstypus im Strafrecht*, Berlin, Duncker & Humblot (1985).

Du Bois-Pedain A., 'Intentional Killings: the German Law', in Horder J. (ed.), *Homicide Law in Comparative Perspective*, Oxford, Hart (2007), 55–81.

'Violent Dynamics: Exploring Responsibility-Attribution for Harms Inflicted during Spontaneous Group Violence', *Oñati Socio-legal Series*, 6(4) (2016), 1053–78.

Burchell J., 'Joint Enterprise and Common Purpose: Perspectives on English and South African Criminal Law', *South African Journal of Criminal Justice*, 10 (1997), 125–40.

Buxton R., 'Complicity in the Criminal Code', *Law Quarterly Review*, 85 (1969), 252–74.

Child J., 'Understanding Ulterior Mens Rea: Future Conduct Intention is Conditional Intention', *Cambridge Law Journal*, 76 (2017), 311–36.

Crewe B., Liebling A., Padfield, N. and Virgo G., 'Joint Enterprise: The Implications of an Unfair and Unclear Law', *Criminal Law Review* (2015), 252–69.

Dressler J., *Understanding Criminal Law*, 6th edn, New Providence, NJ, LexisNexis (2012).

Duff R. A., 'Can I Help You? Accessorial Liability and the Intention to Assist', *Legal Studies*, 10 (1990), 165–81.

'Is Accomplice Liability Superfluous?', *University of Pennsylvania Law Review PENNumbra*, 156 (2008), 444–51.

Dyer A., 'The "Australian Position" Concerning Criminal Complicity: Principle, Policy or Politics?', *Sydney Law Review*, 40 (2018), 289–318.

Dyson M., 'Principals without Distinction', *Criminal Law Review* (2018), 296–320.

Eichmüller A., *Keine Generalamnestie. Die strafrechtliche Verfolgung von NS-Verbrechen in der frühen Bundesrepublik*, Munich, Oldenbourg Wissenschaftsverlag (2012).

Feinberg J., 'Causing Voluntary Actions', in Feinberg J., *Doing and Deserving: Essays in the Theory of Responsibility*, Princeton University Press (1970) 152–86.

Feuerbach P. J. A., *Lehrbuch des gemeinen in Deutschland gültigen peinlichen Rechts*, 4th edn, Gießen, Heyer (1808 [1801]).

Gardner J., 'Moore on Complicity and Causality', *University of Pennsylvania Law Review PENNumbra*, 156 (2008), 432–43.

Gössel K. H., 'Dogmatische Überlegungen zur Teilnahme am erfolgsqualifizierten Delikt nach § 18 StGB', in Warda G., Waider H., Hippel R. von and Meurer D. (eds.), *Festschrift für Richard Lange zum 70. Geburtstag*, Berlin, De Gruyter (1976), 219–40.

Greve M., *Der justitielle und rechtspolitische Umgang mit den NS-Gewaltverbrechern in den sechziger Jahren*, Frankfurt, Peter Lang (2001).

Haas V., *Die Theorie der Tatherrschaft und ihre Grundlagen*, Berlin, Duncker & Humblot (2008).

Hamdorf K., *Beteiligungsmodelle im Strafrecht. Ein Vergleich von Teilnahme- und Einheitstätersystemen in Skandinavien, Österreich und Deutschland*, Freiburg, edition iuscrim (2002).

'The Concept of a Joint Criminal Enterprise and Domestic Modes of Liability for Parties to a Crime: A Comparison of German and English Law', *Journal of International Criminal Justice*, 5 (2007), 208–26.

Hart H. L. A. and Honoré, T., *Causation in the Law*, 2nd edn, Oxford University Press (1985).

Heyman M. G., 'Losing All Sense of Just Proportion: The Peculiar Law of Accomplice Liability', *St John's Law Review*, 87 (2013), 129–70.

Horder J., *Ashworth's Principles of Criminal Law*, 8th edn, Oxford University Press (2016).

Husak D., 'Abetting a Crime', *Law & Philosophy*, 33 (2014), 41–73.

Just-Dahlmann B. and Just, H., *Die Gehilfen. NS-Verbrechen und Justiz nach 1945*, Frankfurt/Main, Athenäum (1988).

Kadish S. H., 'Complicity, Cause and Blame: A Study in the Interpretation of Doctrine', *California Law Review*, 73 (1985), 323–410.

'Reckless Complicity', *Journal of Criminal Law and Criminology*, 87 (1997), 369–94.

Keating, H., Cunningham, S., Walters, M. and Elliot, T., *Criminal Law: Text and Materials*, London, Sweet & Maxwell (2014).

Kienapfel D., *Der Einheitstäter im Strafrecht*, Frankfurt/Main: Klostermann (1971).

Klug U., 'Die Rechtsprechung des Bundesgerichtshofes in NS-Prozessen', in Schoeps H. J. and Hillermann H. (eds.), *Justiz und Nationalsozialismus. Bewältigt – Verdrängt – Vergessen*, Stuttgart/Bonn: Burg-Verlag (1987), 92–117.

Krebs B., 'Joint Enterprise Murder Is Dead – Long Live Joint Enterprise Manslaughter?', in Krebs B. (ed.), *Accessorial Liability after Jogee*, Oxford, Hart/Bloomsbury (forthcoming).

Kriegsmann H., *Mittäterschaft und Raufhandel seit Feuerbach*, Breslau, Schlettersche Buchhandlung (1907).

Küpper G., *Grenzen der normativierenden Strafrechtsdogmatik*, Berlin, Duncker & Humblot (1990).

'Der gemeinsame Tatentschluß als unverzichtbares Moment der Mittäterschaft', *Zeitschrift für die gesamte Strafrechtswissenschaft*, 105 (1993), 295–305.

Kutz C., *Complicity: Ethics and Law for a Collective Age*, Cambridge University Press (2000).

Lackner K. and Kühl K., *Strafgesetzbuch mit Erläuterungen*, 29th edn, Munich, C. H. Beck (2018).

Law Commission for England and Wales, *A Criminal Code for England and Wales* (LAW COM. No. 177), London, Her Majesty's Stationary Office (1989).

Moore M., 'Causing, Aiding and the Superfluity of Accomplice Liability', *University of Pennsylvania Law Review*, 156 (2007), 395–452.

Nehmer B., 'Täter als Gehilfen? Zur Ahndung der Einsatzgruppenverbrechen', in Redaktion Kritische Justiz (eds.), *Die juristische Aufarbeitung des Unrechtsstaats*, Baden-Baden, Nomos (1998), 635–68.

Otto H., 'Straflose Teilnahme?', in Warda G., Waider H., von Hippel R. and Meurer D. (eds.), *Festschrift für Richard Lange zum 70. Geburtstag*, Berlin, De Gruyter (1976), 197–217.

Perels J., *Das juristische Erbe des 'Dritten Reichs'. Beschädigung der demokratischen Rechtsordnung*, Frankfurt/New York, Campus Verlag (1999).

Renzikowski J., 'Die fahrlässige Mittäterschaft', in Dannecker G., Langer W., Ranft O., Schmitz R. and Brammsen J. (eds.), *Festschrift für Harro Otto zum 70. Geburtstag*, Cologne, Heymanns (2007), 423–39.

Rotsch T., *'Einheitstäterschaft' statt Tatherrschaft: Zur Abkehr von einem differenzierenden Beteiligungsformensystem in einer normativ-funktionalen Straftatlehre*, Tübingen, Mohr Siebeck (2009).

Roxin C., *Täterschaft und Tatherrschaft*, 9th edn, Berlin, De Gruyter (2015 [1963]).

'§ 25', in Jähnke B., Laufhütte H. W. and Odersky W. (eds.), *Strafgesetzbuch: Leipziger Kommentar*, 11th edn, Berlin, De Gruyter (2003), I.

Samson E., '§ 25', in Rudolphi H.-J. and Horn E. (eds.), *Systematischer Kommentar zum Strafgesetzbuch*, loose-leaf edn, 22nd instalment, 5th edn, Neuwied, Luchterhand (September 1993).

Schild W., '§ 25', in Kindhäuser U., Neumann U. and Paeffgen H.-U. (eds.), *Nomos-Kommentar zum Strafgesetzbuch*, 2nd edn, Baden-Baden, Nomos (2005).

Schöberl W., *Die Einheitstäterschaft als europäisches Modell: Die strafrechtliche Beteiligungsregelung in Österreich und den nordischen Ländern*, Vienna, Neuer Wissenschaftlicher Verlag (2006).

Simester A. P., 'The Mental Element in Complicity', *Law Quarterly Review*, 122 (2006), 578–601.

'Accessory Liability and Common Unlawful Purpose', *Law Quarterly Review*, 133 (2017), 73–90.

Smith J. C., 'Criminal Liability of Accessories: Law and Law Reform', *Law Quarterly Review*, 113 (1997), 453–67.

'Joint Enterprise and Accessory Liability', *South African Journal of Criminal Justice*, 11 (1998), 337–49.

Smith K. J. M., *A Modern Treatise on the Law of Criminal Complicity*, Oxford, Clarendon Press (1991).

Stewart J. G., 'Complicity', in Dubber M. D. and Hörnle T. (eds.), *The Oxford Handbook of Criminal Law*, Oxford University Press (2014), 534–59.

'The Strangely Familiar History of the Unitary Theory of Perpetration', in Ackerman B., Ambos K. and Sikirić H. (eds.), *Visions of Justice. Liber Amicorum Mirjan Damaška*, Berlin, Duncker & Humblot (2016), 327–52.

Stuckenberg C. F., 'Körperverletzung mit Todesfolge bei Exzeß des Mittäters', in Pawlik M. and Zaczyk R. (eds.), *Festschrift für Günther Jakobs zum 70. Geburtstag am 26. Juli 2007*, Cologne, Heymanns (2007), 693–713.

Torp C., *Den danske Strafferets almindelige Del*, Copenhagen, G. E. C. Gads Forlag (1905).

Toulson R., 'Sir Michael Foster, Professor Williams and Complicity in Murder', in Baker D. J. and Horder J. (eds.), *The Sanctity of Life and the Criminal Law: The Legacy of Glanville Williams*, Cambridge University Press (2013), 230–46.

Weißer B., *Täterschaft in Europa. Ein Diskussionsvorschlag für ein europäisches Tätermodell auf der Basis einer rechtsvergleichenden Untersuchung der Beteiligungssysteme Deutschlands, Englands, Frankreichs, Italiens und Österreichs*, Tübingen, Mohr Siebeck (2011).

Williams G., 'The Theory of Excuses', *Criminal Law Review* (1982), 732–42.

Textbook of Criminal Law, 2nd edn, London, Stevens & Sons (1983).

'Complicity, Purpose and the Draft Code – 1', *Criminal Law Review* (1990), 4–21.

'Complicity, Purpose and the Draft Code – 2', *Criminal Law Review* (1990), 98–108.

Wilson W., *Criminal Law*, 5th edn, Harlow, Pearson (2014).

5

Consent in the Law Relating to Sexual Offences

TOM O'MALLEY AND ELISA HOVEN

I Introduction

It seems obvious that the presence or absence of consent can make all the difference between, on the one hand, a meaningful and loving sexual act between two people and, on the other, a serious violation of the human dignity and personal autonomy of one of those people. Yet, there is a surprising degree of uncertainty as to the precise circumstances in which a person can genuinely be treated as consenting. This is scarcely a satisfactory state of affairs in an era where there is a growing and welcome emphasis internationally on the importance of the right to sexual autonomy. The comparative analysis we undertake in this chapter will reveal parallels between the British and Irish jurisdictions and Germany insofar as the meaning and scope of consent are concerned. It will also show that certain situations are evaluated quite differently, with the English-speaking jurisdictions tending to be more restrictive when it comes to accepting the presence of valid consent. Recent developments in German criminal law may, however, point in the direction of a rapprochement between the two sets of jurisdictions. It may well be that global tendencies toward stronger protection of the interests of women in particular overshadow the formerly more 'liberal' instincts of German law.[1]

Within the available space, we cannot offer a comprehensive account of the laws governing rape and other sexual offences in our chosen jurisdictions. However, our concentration on the issue of consent is probably justified because, as a result of reforms to German law in 2016, the general structure of the offences of rape and other sexual assaults are quite similar in all of those jurisdictions. These offences are

[1] The Council of Europe Convention on Preventing and Combating Violence against Women and Domestic Violence (the Istanbul Convention), adopted in 2011, obliges Member States to ensure that 'non-consensual' sexual acts are criminalised.

now essentially defined as the performance of a sexual act without the valid consent of one or other party. We therefore focus on this issue of consent and discuss other elements of offence definitions only to the extent that they bear upon the question of consent.

II The Role of Consent

Consent has been described as 'moral magic' because of its capacity to transform the moral quality of an act.[2] To hit another person, unless it is done in self-defence, is ordinarily illegal and indeed immoral. Yet, if a blow is struck during a properly regulated boxing match, it is quite lawful because the participants will have consented, expressly or otherwise, to being struck by their opponents. Opinions may vary about the morality of boxing but, from a legal perspective at least, the consent of one participant transforms the moral quality of the blows inflicted on him or her by another.[3] Consent in such circumstances is therefore morally transformative. Sexual relations are often viewed from the same perspective. An act of heterosexual intercourse may be a crime or an expression of mutual love, depending on whether both parties freely consent to the act. It may therefore seem axiomatic that there should be legal certainty as to the circumstances in which consent is deemed to be present or absent. There is, to be sure, a fair degree of certainty in this regard, but there also exists a penumbra of doubt surrounding the extent to which certain kinds of fraud, deception or pressure may vitiate consent.

Legal and moral conceptions of consent are by no means co-extensive. The law, both in English-speaking jurisdictions and in Germany, was traditionally prepared to assume the existence of consent to a sexual act save where submission was obtained by force, fear or – under limited circumstances – fraud. Until 2016, a conviction for sexual coercion in Germany required proof that the perpetrator performed a sexual act by means of violence or threats to the health or life of the victim, or by exploiting the victim's helpless situation.[4] In 2016, a new version of the relevant provision was adopted, which makes it a criminal offence to

[2] Hurd, 'Moral Magic' (1996); Miller and Wertheimer, *Ethics of Consent* (2010), esp. chs. 1, 8 and 9.

[3] The legality of boxing and similar activities such as prize fighting was subject to an insightful analysis in *Pallante* v. *Stadiums Pty Ltd* [1976] VR 331. See also *R* v. *Coney* (1882) 8 QBD 534; and Brayne, Sergeant and Brayne, 'Could Boxing Be Banned?' (1998).

[4] Former version of § 177(1) of the German Penal Code (*Strafgesetzbuch* (StGB)).

perform sexual acts upon or before another person against the recognisable will of that person (§ 177(1) German Penal Code). Similarly, courts and legislatures in common law jurisdictions have adopted wider definitions of consent, using formulae such as 'free and voluntary agreement' (as discussed further below).

But this development has generally failed to resolve the difficulties posed by various kinds of deception and threats, not to mention the problem of the intoxicated complainant. This, in turn, calls for a close examination of the concept of consent and its relationship with allied concepts such as assent, acquiescence, agreement and submission. Certain provisions in the New Zealand Crimes Act 1961 illustrate the problem under discussion. Section 128A lists a range of circumstances in which 'allowing sexual activity does not amount to consent'. Those circumstances include, quite predictably, the actual or threatened use of force, mistake on the part of the complainant as to the identity of the other party, mistake about the nature or quality of the act, and so forth. 'Allows' is defined as 'acquiesces in, submits to, participates in, or undertakes'. However, under s. 129A it is an offence to have sexual connection with another person 'knowing that the other person has been induced to consent to the connection by threat'. The latter offence is committed where, for example, the defendant threatens to make improper use, to the detriment of the complainant, of 'a power or authority arising out of (i) an occupational or vocational position held by the [defendant]; or (ii) a commercial relationship between the person making the threat and the person consenting'. The clear implication is that a person may be held to consent as a result of being threatened in certain ways (such as where an employer threatens to dismiss an employee unless she has sexual intercourse with him). Yet there remains the question of whether consent can exist in any meaningful way when it has been obtained through the abuse of a power relationship or by deception. This, in turn, brings the potential conflict between law and morality into sharp focus. Few would say that an employer acts morally if he persuades an employee to have sexual intercourse with him by promising her promotion to which she would otherwise have no claim. But the law may not regard him as guilty of rape or, indeed, of any other offence if consent is as narrowly defined as it has traditionally been.

Legal requirements of consent, whether in relation to sexual offences, other offences against the person, or indeed in civil law contexts involving, for example, the assumption of contractual obligations or entry into a valid marriage, are grounded on respect for individual autonomy. They reflect the Kantian imperative that persons should be treated as ends in themselves and never as means.[5] In the context of sexual offences, autonomy should mean that persons of full age and capacity are free to engage in sexual activity with willing partners of their own choosing (provided any such partner is also of full age and capacity).[6] It further means that everyone has an absolute right to refuse to engage in sexual activity, either generally or with a particular individual or in particular circumstances. Sexual autonomy therefore entails two complementary freedoms: the freedom to engage and the freedom to refuse. Or, in more conventional rights language, it guarantees in equal measure the rights to associate and not to associate. Many sexual offences are designed to protect persons who, on account of youth or disability, are vulnerable to abuse or exploitation.[7] Measures of this kind are quite compatible with the autonomy principle, since they are based on the assumption that those being protected do not (as yet, in the case of children) have the capacity to exercise a genuinely free choice when it comes to participating in sexual activity.

What this chapter essentially seeks to investigate is the extent to which the laws of England and Wales (and of closely related jurisdictions such as Ireland) and of Germany reflect this twofold ideal of personal autonomy. We shall begin by considering circumstances in which consent provides no defence to conduct which, according to judicial opinion, should be outlawed in the public interest, irrespective of the wishes of individual participants. The remainder of the chapter will concentrate on the range of factors that may vitiate consent, particularly in respect of rape.

At the outset, however, something must be said about how consent operates within the overall structure of the criminal law. Consent may provide a defence to a criminal charge although, as we shall see, it will not excuse all conduct that inflicts serious injury on another. Some offences, of which rape has traditionally been a notable example, are so defined as to make the absence of consent a definitional element of the offence, rather than allowing its presence to operate as a defence (in common law

[5] Kant, *Metaphysische Anfangsgründe der Rechtslehre* (1999). See also Kant, *Practical Philosophy* (1996); Murphy, *Retribution* (1979); and Byrd, 'Kant's Theory of Punishment' (1989).

[6] Munro, 'Sexual Autonomy' (2014).

[7] See e.g. § 176 StGB (Sexual abuse of children), § 177(2) subsec. 1, (4) (Sexual assault of persons unable to form or express their will).

systems) or as a ground of justification (in German law).[8] Absence of consent remains a definitional element of rape in many jurisdictions, including England and Wales, Scotland and Ireland.[9] This arrangement makes sense if we accept that an act of sexual intercourse or some other expression of sexual intimacy is not presumptively wrong.[10] Provided both parties are of full capacity and genuinely consenting, it is entirely legal. What makes it wrong is the absence of consent on the part of one participant. The legal and moral norm being violated is not engagement in a sexual act per se, but rather the failure of one person to respect the personal autonomy and bodily integrity of the other.

One consequence of this arrangement is that the presence of consent legally exonerates a defendant even if he or she believed it was absent. *A* may have had sexual intercourse with *B* while firmly believing that *B* was not consenting to it. Yet, if it transpires that *B* was, in fact, consenting at the time, *A* cannot be convicted of rape. An essential element of the offence, absence of consent, is missing. The moral judgement we pass on *A* in these circumstances might be quite severe, but he is legally innocent of the crime. German law comes to the same conclusion with respect to the completed offence of rape. However, *A* could well be convicted of attempted rape based on his mistaken belief that he had intercourse with a person without her consent.[11] The same might apply under English law under the Criminal Attempts Act 1981 (s. 1).

Another significant consequence of this arrangement is that the prosecution in common law jurisdictions bears the burden of proving the absence of consent while, formally at least, the accused is relieved of any obligation to demonstrate its presence.[12]

[8] On the conceptual issues connected with the distinction between offences and defences, see Williams, 'Offences and Defences' (1982): Fletcher, *Rethinking Criminal Law* (2000) 963–6; Duff, *Answering for Crime* (2007), ch. 9.

[9] Sexual Offences Act 2003, s. 1 (England and Wales); Sexual Offences (Scotland) Act 2009, s. 1; Criminal Law (Rape) Act 1981, s. 2 (Ireland). See Horder, *Ashworth's Principles* (2016), ch. 9; Simester et al., *Simester and Sullivan* (2018), ch. 12; Herring, *Criminal Law* (2018), ch. 7; Ormerod and Laird, *Criminal Law* (2018), ch. 17; O'Malley, *Sexual Offences* (2013), ch. 3.

[10] Duff, *Answering for Crime* (2007), ch. 9.

[11] This would be regarded as a case of 'impossible attempt' which is punishable according to § 23(3) StGB. For a case in point, see Federal Court of Justice (BGH), Judgment of 24 Jun. 1993 – 4 StR 33/93, BGHSt 39, 244.

[12] In Germany's inquisitorial system, neither the prosecution nor the defendant bears a burden of proof. The defendant will be convicted only if the court, on the basis of the proof presented at trial, is convinced that the defendant performed a sexual act without

Consent is not normally an issue in offences involving sexual relations with children under the prescribed age of consent or persons with mental disabilities. A person accused of committing a sexual act with a child may have a defence if he or she was honestly or reasonably mistaken as to the child's age. Nowadays, the tendency in common law jurisdictions is to make this a matter of defence rather than require the prosecution to prove that the accused was aware of the child's age.[13] By contrast, in Germany a defendant can be convicted of sexual child abuse only if the court is convinced, at the end of the trial, that the defendant was aware that the other person was below the legal age of consent (which is generally 14 years). The defendant does not have to prove that he was unaware of the other person's young age. However, under the German concept of *dolus eventualis* the defendant can be convicted of an intentional crime even if he only regarded it as possible that the victim was below the age of consent, and accepted that possibility.[14]

The law governing consent and its meaning must, of course, be viewed against the backdrop of prevailing constitutional and human rights norms. To force or pressurise another person to engage in a sexual act without his or her consent is to violate that person's rights to bodily integrity, personal autonomy and human dignity. Significantly, in this regard, the German Constitution (*Grundgesetz* (GG)) opens with a ringing declaration of the right to human dignity: 'die Würde des

the other person's valid consent. If the issue of consent remains in doubt, the defendant will be acquitted.

13 The English Sexual Offences Act 2003 (ss. 5 and 9) imposes strict liability for the rape of a child under 13 years, whereas in the case of sexual activity, including sexual intercourse, with a child between the ages of 13 and 16 years, the defendant is guilty if he did not reasonably believe that the child is 16 years or older. The strict liability element of the first of these offences was, perhaps surprisingly, found to be compatible with the European Convention on Human Rights by both the House of Lords in *R* v. *G* [2008] UKHL 37, [2009] 1 AC 92 and the European Court of Human Rights in *G* v. *United Kingdom* (2011) 53 EHRR SE 25. See Ashworth, 'Comment on *R* v. *G*' (2008). The Irish Criminal Law (Sexual Offences) Act 2006, s. 2(3), as substituted by the Criminal Law (Sexual Offences) Act 2017, s. 16 provides: 'It shall be a defence to proceedings for an offence under this section for the defendant to prove that he or she was reasonably mistaken that at the time of the alleged commission of the offence, the child against whom the offence is alleged to have been committed had attained the age of 15 years.' The standard of proof required for this purpose is that applicable in civil proceedings. See O'Malley, 'The New Law on Sexual Offences' (2017).

14 *Dolus eventualis* bears some resemblance to the common law concept of recklessness but is regarded as one type of intent under German law. For a discussion from a comparative perspective, see Dubber and Hörnle, *Criminal Law* (2014), 241–2.

Menschen ist unantastbar' ('the dignity of the human person is inviolable').[15] In Ireland, the preamble to the Constitution refers to the 'dignity and freedom of the individual'. The Irish Supreme Court has recognised an implied constitutional right to bodily integrity,[16] and it has accepted human dignity and personal autonomy as fundamental constitutional values.[17] The United Kingdom has no written constitution similar to Ireland's, but it is party to the European Convention on Human Rights which, through Articles 8 and 3 in particular, demands that all persons within the jurisdiction of a state party be given effective legal protection from physical (including sexual) abuse and exploitation.

III The Limits of Consent

Within a liberal theory of criminal law that privileges individual autonomy, subject to safeguards for the young and the mentally disabled, a person should be free to consent to any act or omission even if it inflicts harm on him/herself.[18] Only activity causing harm to others may legitimately be outlawed. By contrast, a system of criminal law informed by a philosophy of moral conservatism or paternalism is more likely to restrict the freedom of individuals to inflict harm, including moral harm, on themselves, whether in order to preserve a certain social ethos (in the case of moral conservatism) or simply to protect people from themselves (in the case of paternalism).[19] The criminalisation of consensual sexual acts between adult males, while it lasted, was a classic example of moral conservatism at work, since there was no credible evidence that such acts caused harm to any of the participants. In fact, the criminal prohibition

15 Art. 2(2) GG also protects the bodily integrity (*körperliche Unversehrtheit*) of every person. Sexual autonomy is not mentioned explicitly in the German Constitution but is regarded as one aspect of human dignity; see Hörnig and Wolff (eds.), *Grundgesetz* (2018), Art. 1 mn. 12.

16 *Ryan* v. *Attorney General* [1965] IR 294.

17 *Fleming* v. *Ireland* [2013] 2 IR 417.

18 The harm principle is most closely associated with Mill, *On Liberty* (1859), and Hart, *Law, Liberty and Morality* (1963). Feinberg's formulation is probably more relevant in the present context, since it permits interference in freedom of action solely for the purpose of preventing wrongful harm to others: given the *volenti non fit iniuria* principle, what I consent to cannot wrongfully harm me: Feinberg, *Harm to Self* (1986).

19 For a discussion of these three philosophical approaches to the criminal law, see Law Commission, *Consent in the Criminal Law* (1995), Appendix C, 'Consent and the Criminal Law: Philosophical Foundations', based on a paper prepared by Paul Roberts, University of Nottingham. See also Shute, 'The Second Law Commission Consultation Paper' (1996).

itself probably caused considerable psychological harm to many gay men. (Same-sex relations between adult women were never criminalised, in Britain, Ireland or Germany at least.) There are few traces of explicit moral conservatism in the criminal laws of most liberal democracies today. The harm principle has triumphed although, as Bernard Harcourt has persuasively argued, it has also become of a victim of its own success.[20] During the heyday of that principle, as formulated by Mill and Hart, activities such as prostitution and the consumption of adult pornography were widely regarded as harmless (to others), but there is no such consensus today. Some countries, including most recently Ireland, have adopted the 'Swedish model' of regulating prostitution.[21] Persons offering their services as prostitutes are no longer breaking the law by doing so, but anyone who pays or offers any reward to another to engage in sexual activity commits an offence. This is based on the assumption, which has not gone uncontested, that prostitution inevitably causes harm to those (predominantly women) who engage in it, even where, to all appearances, they are doing so voluntarily. Many feminist scholars and activists have argued that the production and consumption of adult pornography causes harm to women, if only by objectifying them.[22]

Germany has so far withstood this challenge to traditional liberalism in sexual criminal law. Germany legalised prostitution in 2001 within certain limits.[23] Prostitutes, the argument went, are adult women who have freely chosen to sell sex to consenting customers. Although the state may regulate their business, the harm principle stands in the way of imposing criminal penalties on prostitutes and their customers. However, persons exploiting prostitutes (§§ 180a, 181a StGB) as well as those engaging in human trafficking for sexual purposes (§ 232a StGB) are subject to punishment. Customers will not be punished unless they pay for sexual services from a person who is under 18 (§ 182(2) StGB) or who has been the victim of human trafficking (§ 232a(6) StGB). In either case,

20 Harcourt, 'The Collapse of the Harm Principle' (1999) and Harcourt, 'The Collapse of the Harm Principle Redux' (2013).

21 Current Irish law on the matter is set out in the Criminal Law (Sexual Offences) Act 2017, s. 25 (amending earlier legislation).

22 See e.g. MacKinnon, *Only Words* (1993).

23 See Prostitution Act (*Prostitutionsgesetz* (ProstG)) of 20 Dec. 2001, Bundesgesetzblatt (2001 Teil I Nr. 74, 3983 f.). Communities may designate certain areas where prostitution is illegal, and a person obstinately violating such regulations is punishable under §§ 184 f. StGB.

the offender must at least have been aware of the possibility that the other person was under 18 or had been brought to Germany through human trafficking. (English law, by contrast, is rather stricter: under s. 14 of the Policing and Crime Act 2009, someone who pays for sexual services from someone who is in fact a victim of sexual exploitation is guilty of an offence whether or not he 'is, or ought to be, aware' of the exploitation.) With regard to pornography, a general prohibition exists only with regard to pornographic materials depicting sexual acts involving children, juveniles or animals, or which depict acts of violence (§§ 184a, 184b, 184c StGB).

In common law jurisdictions, public policy is the other major justification called in aid, particularly by courts, to justify legal restrictions on certain consensual activities that result in tangible personal injury. In so doing, courts seldom, if ever, pin their colours to any philosophical mast, whether it be liberal, conservative or paternalist. Historical precedent is often their main justification, though usually coupled with some assertion that society as a whole may suffer, economically or otherwise, if the conduct in question is allowed to go unchecked. This approach is particularly evident in cases where courts must decide if consent provides a defence to conduct that inflicts serious personal injury on a willing participant.

The well-known case of *R* v. *Brown*[24] concerned consensual sado-masochistic activities among adult males. These activities involved the infliction of severe genital and other injuries upon one another. Incidentally, some of the parties were still teenagers when they were first introduced to these activities by some of the older men, a point occasionally ignored in commentary on the case. The defendants were charged with assault occasioning actual bodily harm, and unlawfully and maliciously wounding or inflicting grievous bodily harm. They pleaded guilty once the trial court held that consent was not a defence. A majority of the House of Lords, in upholding the convictions, held that consent provided no defence in these circumstances. It was not in the public interest, absent a valid reason, that people should inflict such injuries upon each other. Satisfying sado-masochistic desires was not a valid reason for this purpose. Consent could provide a defence to conduct constituting a basic assault offence but not to conduct coming within the definition of more serious offences such as those charged.

[24] [1994] 1 AC 212. See Kell, 'Social Disutility' (1994).

The appellants fared no better before the European Court of Human Rights.[25] While expressing some doubt as to whether activities of this nature were protected by Article 8 of the European Convention on Human Rights in the first place, the Court held that on the assumption that the criminal convictions in this case amounted to an interference with the applicants' private lives, that interference was justified as necessary in a democratic society under the terms of Article 8(2). The Court held that a Member State is unquestionably entitled to regulate, by means of the criminal law, activities involving the infliction of physical harm. The level of harm to be tolerated is primarily a matter for Member States to decide. The reasons advanced by the United Kingdom were sufficiently relevant and proportionate to bring this case within the terms of Article 8(2) where the protection of health is listed as a legitimate reason for restricting the right to privacy.

A recent decision of the English Court of Appeal has confirmed *Brown*. The appellant in *R* v. *B.M.*[26] was a tattooist and body piercer who had diversified into body modification. The charges he faced resulted from certain procedures (for want of a better term) he had performed on three customers at their own request. He had removed one customer's ear, split the tongue of another to make it resemble that of a reptile and removed the nipple of a third. All three procedures were carried out without anaesthetic. The prosecution accepted that all the customers had given their informed consent. The appellant was charged with offences of grievous bodily harm under sections 18 and 20 of the Offences Against the Person Act 1861. The Court of Appeal upheld the trial judge's ruling that consent provided no defence to those charges. In so doing, it relied heavily on the majority judgment of the House of Lords in *R* v. *Brown*.[27] Problematically, *Brown* and the earlier Court of Appeal decision in *Attorney General's Reference (No. 6 of 1980)*[28] which it effectively approved, had acknowledged the existence of exceptions to this rule. Properly conducted sports, reasonable surgical interference, lawful chastisement of children, ritual (male) circumcision, tattooing and ear-piercing were all listed as 'lawful activities'. This is clearly an unsatisfactory arrangement because it is difficult to identify any

[25] *Laskey* v. *United Kingdom* (1997) 24 EHRR 39. See Moran, '*Laskey* v. *United Kingdom*' (1998).

[26] [2018] EWCA Crim. 560, [2018] 3 WLR 883.

[27] [1994] 1 AC 212.

[28] [1981] QB 715.

underlying rationale or value system which helps to identify the precise range of exceptions. In *B.M.*, the Court of Appeal rather candidly acknowledged this problem and held that new exceptions should not be recognised on a case-by-case basis, save perhaps where there is a close analogy with an existing exception. It said:

> The recognition of an entirely new exception would involve a value judgement which is policy laden, and on which there may be powerful conflicting views in society. The criminal trial process is inapt to enable a wide-ranging inquiry into the underlying policy issues, and which are much better explored in the political environment.[29]

This may well be true, but it is equally true that the fundamental rule as set out in *Brown* and applied in *B.M.* itself is also policy laden. The Court in *B.M.* concluded that '[t]he personal autonomy of his customers does not provide the appellant with a justification for removing body modification from the ambit of the law of assault'.[30]

The law relating to the infliction of serious personal injury, as reflected in *R* v. *Brown*,[31] may seem to depart from the harm principle. Yet, we also see in the relevant judicial decisions a distinct effort to bring these rules within the ambit of the harm principle. For instance, in *R* v. *Brown* we find Lord Templeman, one of the majority, writing:

> Although the law is often broken, the criminal law restrains a practice which is regarded as dangerous and injurious to individuals and which if allowed and extended is harmful to society generally.[32]

The Court of Appeal in *R* v. *B.M*,[33] without expressly invoking the harm principle, also placed great emphasis on public protection. Certainly, it did not attempt to rely on any moral grounds to justify its decision.

In Germany, consent is generally regarded as a ground of justification for bodily injury. The most common explanation is respect for individual autonomy: if a person, capable of making a choice, regards it as preferable to have his body injured, the state is not to interfere with this decision.[34]

29 [2018] EWCA Crim. 560, [2018] 3 WLR 883, para. 41.
30 [2018] EWCA Crim. 560, [2018] 3 WLR 883, para. 44.
31 [1994] 1 AC 212.
32 [1994] 1 AC 212 at 235.
33 [2018] EWCA Crim. 560, [2018] 3 WLR 883.
34 Roxin, *Allgemeiner Teil I* (2004), 546; Lenckner and Sternberg-Lieben, in Schönke and Schröder (eds.), *StGB* (2014), Vorbem. §§ 32 ff. mn. 33.

But, as in the common law world, there exists a strong paternalistic counter-current. A social interest in keeping individuals alive, for example, has led to the introduction of criminal prohibitions on killing a person with his or her consent (§ 216 StGB) and, in 2016, on commercially offering opportunities for committing suicide (§ 217 StGB). With respect to bodily integrity, the German Penal Code contains a curious provision. § 228 reads: 'Whoever inflicts bodily injury with the consent of the injured person acts unlawfully only if the act, in spite of the consent, violates the rules of proper behaviour [*gute Sitten*].' The meaning of 'rules of proper behaviour' has been interpreted in different ways by different courts and writers.[35] In a landmark case of 2004,[36] the Federal Court of Justice had to deal with a couple's consensual sexual play that turned fatal: the male defendant had, in the context of mutually agreed sexual practices, used an iron bar to exert strong pressure on the throat of the female victim to make her gasp for air; unfortunately the woman died as a consequence. In its judgment, the Federal Court of Justice joined what had until then been a minority position: the violation of 'gute Sitten' was held not to depend on the moral or immoral purpose of the activity, but only on its objective risk to life. Only if, as in the instant case, the consensual infliction of pain and injury leads to a concrete danger of death does it violate the rules of proper behaviour. In later cases, the Federal Court of Justice broadened this narrow definition to include situations where a risk of death was not imminent but the actors – groups of football hooligans who had arranged 'battles' against each other – had failed to establish enforceable rules to avoid the risk of an escalation of the (consensual) mutual violence.[37]

Incest, insofar as it outlaws consensual sexual acts between closely related adults, must also be considered under this heading. The justification for retaining a separate offence of incest remains debatable, though much depends on the range of conduct covered by its legal definition and the extent to which it overlaps with other offences, particularly those dealing with child sexual abuse. Some countries may no longer have an offence called 'incest' (if they ever did), but they may well have offences that are so defined as to capture behaviour that constituted incest, as traditionally defined in English law. Under England's Punishment of

[35] For an overview, see Joecks and Miebach (eds.), *Münchener Kommentar* (2017), § 228 mn. s 16–33.

[36] BGH, Judgment of 26 May 2004 – 2 StR 505/03, BGHSt 49, 166.

[37] BGH, Judgment of 20 Feb. 2013 – 1 StR 585/12, BGHSt 58, 140; Judgment of 22 Jan. 2015, BGHSt 60, 166.

Incest Act 1908, which remains in force in Ireland with some minor modifications, it was an offence for a male to have sexual intercourse with his mother, sister, daughter or granddaughter, and for a female aged 16 years[38] or over to permit her father, grandfather, brother or son to have sexual intercourse with her. The conduct element of this offence was strictly confined to heterosexual intercourse, but the offence could be committed by persons of any age (subject to the exemption for females under 16 years) provided they were related in one of the specified ways, even if there was no realistic prospect of pregnancy resulting from the act of intercourse. This in turn raises questions about the true purpose of the offence, and that has been a matter of debate for some time.[39]

In England and Wales, the Sexual Offences Act 2003 replaced 'incest' with a number of familial sex offences. One set of provisions (ss. 25 and 26) deals with sexual relations with a child who is related to the defendant in the specified ways, while another (ss. 64 and 65) prohibits certain sexual acts by a person aged 16 years or more with a person who is aged 18 years or more, where the parties are within certain prohibited degrees of relationship – namely, parent, grandparent, child, grandchild, brother, sister, half-brother, half-sister, aunt, uncle, nephew, niece. The conduct element of this offence consists solely of sexual penetration, though it is not confined to penile-vaginal penetration.[40] Eugenic considerations clearly cannot provide a justification for such a widely defined offence. Indeed, they were regarded as secondary at best by the Home Office Report on which much of the 2003 Act was based.[41] The authors of the Report were more influenced by what they described as a large body of research showing that incestuous relationships between adult family members often began when one of the parties was a child and continued as a long-term abuse of power. They concluded that:

> [I]t would not be right to seem to legitimise sexual relationships between adult family members. The dynamics and balance of power within a family require special recognition, and we were concerned to ensure that patterns of abuse established in childhood were not allowed to continue in adulthood. Our new offence of familial abuse contains as its first limb an

[38] In Ireland, the age is 17 years.

[39] On the original motivation, see Bailey and Blackburn, 'The Punishment of Incest' (1979) (arguing that eugenic considerations were by no means crucial to the passage of the Act); Bowsher, 'Incest' (2015).

[40] For a critical analysis of these provisions, see Spencer, 'The Sexual Offences Act 2003 (2)' (2004).

[41] Home Office, *Setting the Boundaries* (2000), ch. 5 ('Abuse within the Family').

> offence comparable to incest – sexual penetration between blood relatives and also between adoptive parents and their children. We thought that there was clear justification in terms of the protection of the family unit that such behaviour should continue to be illegal.[42]

The argument has therefore shifted from moral to empirical grounds, but with distinctly less emphasis, if any, on eugenics. The justification for continuing to criminalise sexual relations between adult relatives, irrespective of consent, therefore depends on the reliability of the empirical evidence.

In Germany, the definition of incest is limited to sexual penetration of the vagina by the penis (*Beischlaf*). Under § 173 StGB this act is punishable if committed with a (natural) parent or grandparent, with a child or grandchild, or with a brother or sister. Children and siblings are not punishable if they were younger than 18 years at the time when the act was committed. Since non-consensual penetration is sanctioned more severely under other headings, the crime of incest concerns exclusively consensual sexual intercourse. It is difficult to find a plausible rationale for criminalisation that is consistent with the narrow definition of the offence. It can hardly be argued that one (or both?) of the participants is especially vulnerable and therefore needs protection. Nor is it convincing to base criminal liability on the risk that offspring may be genetically affected, because that rationale would have to lead to the incrimination of any sexual intercourse by persons with (possible) genetic defects; the offence definition would, moreover, be overly broad in that it extends to situations where conception is excluded, for example because one of the partners has been sterilised.

The Federal Constitutional Court, in a 2008 judgment,[43] has nevertheless held the statute to be constitutional. The defendant and his sister had grown up in separate foster homes. They got acquainted only when the defendant was 24 and his sister was 16 years of age. They began to live together and had four children. After having been sentenced to 14 months' imprisonment for incest, the defendant submitted the case to the Federal Constitutional Court, claiming that the relevant provision of § 173(2) StGB violated, among others, his right to privacy. The Court rejected his appeal with a majority of 7:1. The majority cited a number of social interests such as the protection of family coherence, the woman's

42 *Ibid.*, ch. 5 ('Abuse within the Family'), para. 5.8.3.

43 Federal Constitutional Court (BVerfG), Judgment of 26 Feb. 2008 – 2 BvR 392/07, BVerfGE 120, 224.

self-determination and public health; but in the last resort the Court based its decision on the argument that society 'was convinced' that incest deserved punishment.[44] The Court's decision was strongly criticised by German scholars,[45] since it smacks of 1950s-style incrimination of anything that appears in bad taste, without concern for the harm principle and the protection of privacy.

Surprisingly, the European Court of Human Rights found no violation of Article 8 of the European Convention on Human Rights.[46] The judges held that the criminalisation of incest, even between consenting adults, was within the margin of appreciation of Member States. That is hardly convincing. The best one can say of the German statute is that its narrow definition does less harm than the broader stroke of the comparable English statute.

IV Lack of Capacity to Consent

Children below a certain age (which varies across jurisdictions) and persons who, due to mental disability, lack certain cognitive capacities, are generally treated as legally incapable of consenting to sexual acts. All chronological age limits are to some degree arbitrary. Ideally, perhaps, the question of whether a person genuinely consented to an act would be determined by assessing that person's actual capacity at the relevant time. This, however, might present serious practical difficulties and differences of opinion, and would be largely pointless in the case of very young children. There is no universally valid age at which people make the transition to full maturity for all purposes. As Feinberg says:

> Childhood, of course, is not all of a piece. There is no sharp line between the capacities of childhood and adulthood; they are only useful abstractions from a continuous development every phase of which differs only in degree from that preceding it . . . Such boundary lines as the eighteenth and twenty-first birthdays are simply approximations (plausible guesses) for the point where all the person's decision-making capacities are fully matured.[47]

44 'The provision of the Penal Code under attack here can be justified as being grounded on plausible purposes of punishment against the background of a social conviction that the act of incest deserves punishment, which is still effective and can also be found abroad' (our translation)), Judgment of 26 Feb. 2008 – 2 BvR 392/07, BVerfGE 120, 224 at 248 f.

45 See e.g. Duttge, 'Strafbarkeit des Geschwisterinzestes' aufgrund 'eugenischer Gesichtspunkte'?' (2011); Hörnle, 'Das Verbot des Geschwisterinzests' (2008); Roxin, 'Zur Strafbarkeit des Geschwisterinzests' (2009).

46 Case 43547/08, *Stübing* v. *Germany* [2012], 55 EHRR 24.

47 Feinberg, *Harm to Self* (1986), 326.

In light of this reality, legislators must make what Thomist philosophers call a *determinatio*, meaning that they must have regard to the relevant overarching principle – in this case that children must be protected from sexual exploitation – and then use their judgement to decide how best to give effect to this principle in positive law.[48] In England and Wales, the general age of consent is 16 years, although there are special and more stringent provisions relating to sexual activity with a child under the age of 13 years.[49] The same is broadly true in Scotland.[50] In Ireland, the general age of consent is 17 years, although a person, on reaching the age of 15 years, may consent to an act that does not involve vaginal or anal intercourse. Under recent legislation, the age of consent in Ireland has been raised to 18 years in the very particular circumstances of where the sexual act is committed by a person in authority such as a parent, guardian or teacher.[51] In Germany, sexual acts concerning children under 14 years are prohibited without exception (§ 176 StGB). It is punishable even to make contact, in writing or through telecommunication, with a child with the intent that he or she perform or take part in a sexual act (§ 176(4) no. 3 StGB). Children younger than 16 years are protected by criminal law against the abuse of a relationship of education or training for sexual purposes (§ 174(1) no. 1 StGB), and against the exploitation of their lack of autonomy in sexual matters by a person older than 21 years (§ 182(3) StGB). With respect to young persons under 18 years, sexual acts are punishable when the person is in a legally defined relationship of dependency with the perpetrator, for example, as his pupil or apprentice (§ 174(1) no. 2 StGB), as a factual member of his family, even if there is no natural relationship between perpetrator and victim (§ 174(1) no. 3 StGB), or as an inmate in an institution where the perpetrator has a professional role as an educator or supervisor (§ 174(2)).

Criminal laws regulating sexual activity with or between persons with mental disabilities, mental illness or learning difficulties must attempt to strike a delicate balance between protection and autonomy. On the one hand, we want to protect such persons from being abused or exploited; on the other, we do not want to deprive them unnecessarily of their right to sexual freedom and fulfilment. This has always proved to be a difficult

48 On the concept of *determinatio*, see Finnis, *Natural Law* (2004), 284–9.

49 Sexual Offences Act 2003, ss. 5–15.

50 Sexual Offences (Scotland) Act 2009, ss. 18–41.

51 Criminal Law (Sexual Offences) Act 2017, ss. 15–19; see also, for England and Wales, Sexual Offences Act 2003, ss. 16–24.

area for law reformers. Indeed, it is not just a problem for the criminal law. Individuals and organisations caring for persons with intellectual disabilities are often unsure and understandably concerned about the extent of their potential civil liability if a person in their care engages in a sexual relationship with another person (who may also have limited mental capacity). Until recently, the criminal law tended to adopt a categorical approach by providing, for example, that persons with certain levels of mental disability were incapable of consenting to sexual acts (though some of the earlier English and Irish laws in this area were confined to outlawing heterosexual intercourse with females with certain kinds of mental illness or disability).[52]

Today, criminal laws in this area adopt a more functional approach. The question now is whether the protected person was capable of consenting to the particular sexual act involved. Incapacity to consent will generally be found where the person is unable to understand the nature and consequences of the act, evaluate relevant information for the purpose of deciding whether or not to engage in the act, or communicate consent in an effective way.[53] In the same vein, German law makes it a criminal offence for the perpetrator to abuse the fact that another person is incapable of forming or expressing his or her will opposing sexual acts (§ 177(2) no. 1 StGB). If the other person's capacity is merely limited, as opposed to being entirely lacking, sexual acts are permissible, but the actor must first have made certain that the other person agrees with each act (§ 177(2) no. 2 StGB). This arrangement seeks to strike a reasonable balance between the right to sexual fulfilment and the need to protect against sexual exploitation.

V Factors Vitiating Consent

Courts are seldom confronted with cases involving conduct such as that in *R* v. *Brown* or (apparently consensual) sexual acts between closely related adults. What they are more commonly called upon to decide is

[52] In Ireland, for example, the Criminal Law Amendment Act 1935 (s. 4) made it an offence to have vaginal intercourse with a female who was 'an idiot, an imbecile or feebleminded'. There was a similar provision in the Criminal Law Amendment Act 1885 (s. 5(2)) which applied at the time to the entire United Kingdom. See O'Malley, *Sexual Offences* (2013), 151.

[53] See e.g. Sexual Offences Act 2003, ss. 30–3 (England and Wales); Criminal Law (Sexual Offences) Act 2017, ss. 20–2 (Ireland). The analysis and recommendations in the Home Office Report, *Setting the Boundaries* (2000), ch. 4 had a strong influence on these reforms.

whether a complainant consented to an act that would, in the absence of consent, constitute rape or sexual assault. This in turn may raise the question of when exactly a person may be said to consent to such an act. The law provides some answers, but there remains the more normative question of whether certain kinds of fraud and deception (to be described later in more detail) should vitiate consent to sexual acts. Under the law as it now stands in many jurisdictions, a person who has sexual relations with another as a result of fraud or deception may be guilty of some other offence such as assault. But some would argue that consent, properly understood, should entail an understanding of all the surrounding circumstances and not just an awareness and understanding of the physical act itself. If indeed consent is to be viewed as 'moral magic', it should undoubtedly be as genuine and well-informed as possible, rather than being based upon or induced by a mistake as to some significant circumstantial factor. We shall begin therefore by reviewing some current definitions of consent and then consider the desirability of broadening the concept of consent in the manner just adumbrated.

1 *Statutory and Common Law Definitions of Consent*

During the past twenty years or so, several common law jurisdictions have adopted statutory definitions of consent in relation to rape and other sexual offences. Their general thrust is that consent consists in agreement that is freely and voluntarily given. For instance, the English Sexual Offences Act 2003 (s. 74) provides that 'a person consents if he agrees by choice, and has the freedom and capacity to make that choice'.[54] Ireland's Criminal Law (Sexual Offences) Act 2017 (s. 48) provides that '[a] person consents to a sexual act if he or she freely and voluntarily agrees to engage in that act'. Similar formulations are found elsewhere.[55] The same statutes typically include lists of situations in which consent is presumed or deemed to be absent, such as where the

[54] For a detailed description and analysis of the case law developed under all sections of the 2003 Act, see Rook and Ward, *Sexual Offences* (2016). For further analysis of the consent issue in particular, see Temkin and Ashworth, 'The Sexual Offences Act 2003' (2004) and the general texts on English criminal law listed in n. 9 above.

[55] Under the Canadian Criminal Code (s. 153.1(2)) consent, for the purpose of certain offences means 'the voluntary agreement of the complainant to engage in the sexual activity in question'; Sexual Offences (Scotland) Act 2009 (s. 12), consent means 'free agreement'; New South Wales Crimes Act 1900 (s. 61HA(2)), a person consents to a sexual intercourse 'if the person freely and voluntarily agrees to sexual intercourse'.

complainant submits to a sexual act as a result of the use or threat of force, or where he or she is asleep or unconscious. The English Act of 2003 (ss. 75–6) lists several such factors that will result in either a conclusive or an evidential presumption that consent was absent. The Irish Act of 2017 (s. 48) contains a list of circumstances in which it is simply stated that a person does not consent to a sexual act. All of them are quite standard and are found in similar legislation elsewhere – for instance, that the person is asleep or unconscious, is unable to consent because of the effect of alcohol or some other drug, is mistaken as to the nature and purpose of the act and so forth. Proof of the presence of any of these factors at the time of sexual act will not, of course, automatically result in the defendant being convicted. The prosecution must also prove beyond a reasonable doubt the requisite mental element which varies across jurisdictions. In England and Wales, for example, it must prove that the defendant did not reasonably believe that the complainant was consenting, whereas in Ireland the test remains subjective. There the prosecution must prove that the defendant did not actually believe that the complainant was consenting or that he was reckless in that regard.[56]

Significantly, however, modern legislation enumerating factors that are deemed, conclusively or otherwise, to vitiate consent often includes a further provision stating (in the words of the aforementioned Irish Act) that the list 'does not limit the circumstances in which it may be established that a person did not consent to a sexual act'. This, in turn, is consistent with modern case law, notably *R* v. *Ojugboja*,[57] where the English Court of Appeal said:

> [A jury should be directed] that consent, or the absence of it, is to be given its ordinary meaning and if need be, by way of example, that there is a difference between consent and submission; every consent involves a submission, but it by no means follows that a mere submission involves consent ... Where intercourse takes place after threats not involving violence or the fear of it, ... [the jury] should be directed to concentrate on the state of mind of the victim immediately before the act of intercourse having regard to all the relevant circumstances, and in particular, the events leading up to the act and her reaction to them showing their impact on her mind.

[56] Sexual Offences Act 2003, s. 1 (England and Wales); Criminal Law (Rape) Act 1981, s. 2 (Ireland). This aspect of Irish law is currently under review by the Law Reform Commission.

[57] [1982] 1 QB 320 at 332.

In a similar vein, the Irish Court of Criminal Appeal said:

> Consent means voluntary agreement or acquiescence to sexual intercourse by a person of the age of consent with the requisite mental capacity. Knowledge or understanding of facts material to the act being consented to is essential for the consent to be voluntary or constitute acquiescence.[58]

All of this suggests that the notion of consent should be (or may be) interpreted in a dynamic rather than a static manner; it should not be assumed that there is a limited and immutable set of factors that will operate to destroy it. Courts may well be empowered to extend the range of conduct that will vitiate consent, at least in the context of sexual offences.

The German definition of sexual abuse (*sexueller Übergriff*, § 177(1) StGB) refers to sexual acts performed against the other person's recognisable will. This definition implies that the victim's lack of actual consent is a necessary element of the offence. But it is not sufficient that the victim secretly disagrees with the actor's sexual advances; the lack of consent must also be 'recognisable' by a hypothetical observer.[59] It is unclear to what extent this observer is construed to know about the victim's way of expressing himself or herself; but the legislature seems to have envisaged that only acts commonly understood to express disagreement (shaking one's head, pushing away the actor) are 'recognisable' non-verbal ways of informing the actor of the victim's will. Of course, 'consent' given under threat of force or even of any other serious harm is not valid. Sexual acts brought about by such threats are indeed punishable under § 177(5) no. 2 StGB (threat of risk for life or health) and § 177(2) no. 5 (threat of any serious harm). The latter provision covers situations where the actor lets the victim know that he will bring about a loss or disadvantage that is regarded as serious by a person in the victim's position, such as the loss of the victim's job or the filing of a criminal complaint against the victim.[60]

[58] *People (DPP)* v. *C* [2001] 3 IR 345 at 360.

[59] Hörnle, 'Das Gesetz zur Verbesserung des Schutzes sexueller Selbstbestimmung' (2017); Renzikowski, 'Nein! – Das neue Sexualstrafrecht' (2016).

[60] See BGH, Judgment of 25 Feb. 1993 – 1 StR 652/92, BGH, *NJW* 1993, 1807; BGH, Judgment of 13 Mar. 1997, BGH *NStZ* 1997, 494 (threat of not supervising victim's doctoral dissertation); Laufhütte et al. (eds.), *Leipziger Kommentar* (2014), § 240 mn. s 80–2.

2 *Fraud and Deception*

As already noted, a strong cross-jurisdictional consensus now exists to the effect that consent should be interpreted as free and voluntary agreement, or in terms to that effect. This immediately raises the question: free and voluntary agreement to what? The conventional answer is: the sexual act involved, typically intercourse of some kind, with this particular person.[61] Suppose, however, we were to adopt Onora O'Neill's argument that 'we need an account of genuine, morally significant consent, and to distinguish this from spurious or morally trivial consent'.[62] That might force us to reconsider the notion of an act and to think of it not only in terms of its physical manifestation but also in terms of its meaning for the parties involved. After all, a given physical gesture may have radically different meanings depending on the context in which it is performed, the intention of the performer and the message it communicates to another.[63] In the context of sexual relations, can a person be truly said to have consented if she agreed to participate because she had no reason to believe that, say, the other party was HIV positive, or because the other party pretended to be of a different gender than he or she actually was (as in *R* v. *McNally*, discussed below), or because he promised to do something which she desired (such as marrying her) although he had no intention of fulfilling that promise?[64]

Some of these examples, such as the one involving a promise to marry, raise the question of whether the law should insist on informed consent. The English Law Commission expressed reservations about incorporating such a requirement into the law relating to consent in offences such

[61] This was clearly the view of the High Court of Australia in *R* v. *Papadimitropoulos* (1957) 98 CLR 249, which involved a false representation that the parties were validly married. The court said that for the purpose of rape, 'it is consent to [the] physical act of penetration which is in question … Such a consent demands a perception as to what is about to take place, as to the identity of the man and the character of what he is doing. Once the consent is comprehending and actual, the inducing causes cannot destroy its reality and leave the man guilty of rape.' This, of course, was consistent with *R* v. *Clarence* (1888) 22 QBD 23 at 44, where it was said: 'the only sorts of fraud which so far destroy the effect of a woman's consent as to convert a connection consented to in fact into a rape are frauds as to the nature of the act itself, or as to the identity of the person who does the act'.

[62] O'Neill, 'Between Consenting Adults' (1985), 258.

[63] Herring, 'Mistaken Sex' [2005] Crim. LR 511.

[64] For an extended discussion of these issues from a philosophical perspective, see Feinberg, *Harm to Self* (1986), particularly his discussion of 'coercive offers' in ch. 24). See also Laird, 'Rapist or Rogue' (2014).

as rape. It did, however, provisionally recommend the introduction of an offence of procuring consent by deception. It proposed that deception should mean 'any deception (whether deliberate or reckless) by words or conduct as to fact or as to law, including deception as to the present intentions of the person using the deception or any other person'.[65] If we accept that women and men have an absolute right to sexual autonomy in terms of being able to choose when and with whom they will engage in sexual relations, then for the choice to be genuine, it cannot be made as a result of a mistake arising from deception as to a significant matter on someone else's part. Again, it bears repeating that here we are solely concerned with the question of whether a person can genuinely be said to consent to a sexual act while under a misapprehension or mistake as to some important circumstantial factor, other than the identity of the other party or the nature of the act. The defendant's knowledge or recklessness as to the absence of consent for any of these reasons, the *mens rea* of the offence under English and Irish law, must be considered separately although, in the examples just given. the defendant would almost certainly be aware that the complainant was agreeing to participate in the sexual act on account of his (the defendant's) own deception.

Historically, a mistake as to the nature of the sexual act vitiated consent. For example, a person who was deceived into believing that an act of sexual intercourse was, in fact, a medical procedure was held not to have consented.[66] The common law went further by holding that there was no consent where a person was mistaken as to the nature and quality of the act. In *R* v. *Tabassum*[67] three women allowed a man to feel their breasts at a time when they believed that he was medically qualified although, in fact, he was not. The Court of Appeal upheld his conviction for indecent assault, holding that there had been consent to the nature of the act, but not as to its quality.[68] Likewise, a woman who believed that a man having intercourse with her was her husband was deemed at common law not to have consented. This remains the law save that it has been extended to cover mistake as to the identity of any other person with whom the complainant would have been willing to have sexual relations. The present English legislation refers to mistake as to 'the

[65] Law Commission, *Consent in the Criminal Law* (1995), Part VI.

[66] *R* v. *Flattery* (1877) 2 QBD 410; *R* v. *Williams* [1923] 1 KB 340; *R* v. *Case* (1850) 4 Cox CC 220; *R* v. *Harms* (1944) 2 DLR 61 (Canada).

[67] [2002] 2 Cr. App. R. 328.

[68] See also *R* v. *Clarence* (1888) 22 QB 23; *R* v. *Linekar* [1995] QB 250.

nature or purpose of the act', and similar provisions are now found in Irish and Scottish law.[69] Whether the reference to purpose can plausibly be interpreted to cover a broader range of fraudulent or deceptive conduct than has traditionally been accepted as vitiating consent remains to be seen. What is now certain, under English law at least, is that mistake as to the gender of the other party can vitiate consent. In *R* v. *McNally*[70] the female defendant, while pretending to be male, had engaged in sexual acts with a young woman, including penetration of the young woman's vagina. Although she pleaded guilty to charges of assault by sexual penetration, she later appealed against conviction on the basis that deception as to gender did not vitiate consent.[71] The Court of Appeal, in upholding the conviction, rejected this argument. It accepted that the physical nature of the acts remained the same irrespective of whether they were perpetrated by a male or a female, but their sexual nature differed where the complainant was deceived into believing that the perpetrator was a man when she was in fact a woman. This decision certainly shows that the court is no longer preoccupied with the physical manifestation of the offending conduct. It is much more concerned to protect the complainant's right to sexual autonomy.

Should a man be convicted of rape if he knows that he is HIV positive and has unprotected sexual intercourse with a woman who is either unaware of his HIV status or who is misled by him into thinking that he is HIV negative, and who would not have had unprotected, or perhaps, any sexual intercourse with him if she was aware of the true situation? In other words, does mistake or lack of knowledge as to her partner being HIV positive mean that the woman is not consenting to sexual intercourse in these circumstances? It is difficult to argue that she is mistaken as to the purpose of the act, but it could be argued that she is mistaken as to the nature of the act. If the lack of medical qualifications on the part of the defendant in *Tabassum* created a mistake as to the nature of the act, surely a mistake as to a factor that could result in far more serious consequences (the communication of a life-threatening

[69] Sexual Offences Act 2003, s. 76. The same applies in Scotland under the Sexual Offences (Scotland) Act 2009, s. 13. In Ireland, the Criminal Law (Sexual Offences) Act 2017 (s. 48) refers to the 'nature and purpose of the act'.

[70] [2013] EWCA Crim. 1051, [2014] QB 593. For critical comment see Sharpe, 'Expanding Liability for Sexual Fraud' (2016); and Sharpe, 'Queering Judgment' (2017).

[71] It is an essential element of this offence under s. 2 of the Sexual Offences Act 2003 that the complainant must not have consented to the penetration. See Card, *Sexual Offences* (2004),

disease) should have a similar effect.[72] Granted, the man in our hypothetical example will not be treated with impunity. On the basis of authorities such as *R* v. *Dica*[73] and *R* v. *Konzani*[74] he will be convicted of a serious assault offence, such as inflicting grievous bodily harm contrary to s. 20 of the Offences Against the Person Act 1861. However, a rape conviction carries a particular stigma and, more significantly for present purposes, it would amount to an affirmation that the victim has suffered a serious violation of her rights to personal autonomy, bodily integrity and human dignity. It is arguably the proper verdict where there has been no morally significant consent.[75]

The availability of an alternative charge, such as inflicting grievous bodily harm, mitigates the injustice that might seem to flow from failing to treat mistake about a partner's HIV positive status as negativing consent to sexual intercourse. The same could hold true of various kinds of deception. The Criminal Law Amendment Act 1885 (s. 2) provided in part that any person who 'by false pretences or false representations procures or attempts to procure any woman or girl . . . to have any unlawful connection' was guilty of an offence punishable with a maximum of two years' imprisonment. This section, to the extent just quoted, remains in force in Ireland, though it is rarely, if ever, prosecuted. There was a similar provision in the English Sexual Offences Act 1956 (s. 3). Strangely enough, there is nothing to this effect in the Sexual Offences Act 2003.

In *R* v. *Linekar*,[76] a leading English authority pre-dating the 2003 Act, the appellant had sexual intercourse with a prostitute to whom he had promised to pay £25 but, once they had intercourse, he made off without paying. He was initially convicted of rape, but the Court of Appeal quashed that conviction, stating that the reality of the complainant's consent to intercourse was 'not destroyed by being induced by the

[72] As McLachlan J. said in *R* v. *Cuerrier* [1998] 2 SCR 371, para. 72: 'The complainant does not consent to the transmission of diseased fluid into her body. This deception in a very real sense goes to the nature of the sexual act, changing it from an act that has certain natural consequences (whether pleasure, pain or pregnancy) to a potential sentence of disease or death.'

[73] [2004] QB 1257.

[74] [2005] EWCA Crim. 706.

[75] It seems that prior to *R* v. *Clarence* (1888) 22 QBD 23, the common law accepted that deception as to a venereal disease carrying a high risk of infection amounted to fraud which vitiated consent to sexual intercourse. The early authorities are reviewed by McLachlan J. in *R* v. *Cuerrier* [1998] 2 SCR 371.

[76] [1995] QB 250.

appellant's false pretence' that he intended to pay the agreed amount. The court said that, if anything, the appellant was guilty of an offence under s. 3 of the 1956 Act (procurement of unlawful sexual intercourse by false pretences or false representations). It may well be that this is the policy that the law should continue to pursue and develop, as it would obviate some, though not all, of the difficulties associated with deception or misrepresentation as to matters other than the nature of the act itself. Yet because sexual intercourse or, for that matter, any sexual act, unless performed with genuine consent, is such an intrusion on the human dignity and personal autonomy of one or other party, there is a strong argument to be made that consent may be vitiated by mistake, however induced, as to an important circumstantial factor.

The deeper and more difficult question is whether any kind of deception that may have 'induced', in the words of English and Australian courts,[77] a complainant to have sexual intercourse should operate to vitiate consent. Courts and scholars alike have accepted that deception has always played a role in sexual encounters. For instance, in *R* v. *Cuerrier*[78] McLachlan J., as she then was, remarked:

> Deceptions, small and sometimes large, have from time immemorial been the by-product of romance and social encounters. They often carry the risk of harm to the deceived party. Thus far in the history of civilization, these deceptions, however sad, have been left to the domain of song, verse and social censure.

This may well be true as a matter of history, but Western society has moved on, as indeed the Canadian Supreme Court itself has often recognised, not least in *Cuerrier* where it held that Cuerrier's failure to disclose his HIV status amounted to a fraud vitiating consent and that he would therefore be tried for aggravated assault. In contrast to the position in common law jurisdictions, the German Penal Code does not mention fraud as an element vitiating the validity of expressed consent. Nor, curiously, does there appear to be any case law directly on point. The principle of legality precludes any extension of the definitions of rape and sexual coercion to situations not expressly covered by the wording of the statute. Therefore, a man who actively misleads his sexual partner about the fact that he is HIV positive, and thus makes the partner agree to have

[77] The expression was used in both *R* v. *Linekar* [1995] QB 250 and *R* v. *Papadimitopoulos* (1957) 98 CLR 249.

[78] [1998] 2 SCR 371, para. 47.

unprotected sex, can be convicted of (attempted, as the case may be) infliction of aggravated bodily harm (§ 224(1) no. 5 or § 227 StGB),[79] but cannot be convicted of rape or sexual abuse.[80] However, where the victim is led to believe that the sexual act is part of a necessary medical examination or therapy, there is no consent to any 'sexual' act, so it can be argued that a sexual act is performed against the victim's 'recognisable' will, and is thus punishable under § 177(1) StGB.[81]

3 *Strong Inducements and Non-Violent Threats*

A person may be persuaded to engage in a sexual act as a result of being promised something which he or she desires or of being promised that he or she will be spared some unpleasant experience that would otherwise materialise. We are not concerned here with prostitution type situations where, for example, a woman agrees to have sexual intercourse with a man in return for a monetary reward. Rather we are concerned with circumstances where there is a distinct power imbalance between the parties. The weaker party could refuse to engage in the sexual act but at the expense of being deprived of something to which he or she is entitled or really needs for career or other reasons. To illustrate the difference between the common law and German law in this regard, let us consider these three examples:

(1) A professor tells a student that he will fail her in her examination (irrespective of whether she deserves to fail or not) unless she has sexual intercourse with him. She has intercourse with him solely because she fears failing the examination.
(2) A professor tells a student that he will award her a first-class honours grade in her examination (although she deserved only an upper second) if she has sexual intercourse with him. She agrees to intercourse solely in order to achieve the higher grade.
(3) Peter approaches a neighbour Jane who has a young child in urgent need of medical treatment but who will have to wait for a long time to get it under the public health system. Peter offers to pay for the treatment to be given privately and immediately if Jane will have sexual intercourse with him. She agrees to do so, solely for that reason.

79 See BGH, Judgment of 13 Jan. 1993 – 1 StR 737/81, BGHSt 36, 1.
80 Hoven and Weigend, 'Zur Strafbarkeit von Täuschungen im Sexualstrafrecht' (2018).
81 According to § 174c StGB, a physician who abuses the therapeutic relationship in order to perform a sexual act, is independently punishable.

Can the woman in any of these examples be said to have genuinely consented to sexual intercourse? The professor in case (1) is certainly engaging in a gross abuse of power, but since intercourse was not induced by the use or threat of force, in a common law jurisdiction he would probably not be guilty of rape under the law as it now stands unless the courts were to give a more dynamic interpretation than hitherto to the rule that consent means free and voluntary agreement. In Germany, by contrast, the professor would be guilty of sexual coercion (§ 177(2) no. 5 StGB) because he coerced the student into having sex with him by threatening her with a serious harm (i.e. that she would not pass the examination).

Cases (2) and (3), however, are more difficult to answer, under German law at least. The Federal Court of Justice has ruled that withholding benefits can amount to a serious harm (*empfindliches Übel*).[82] This view has been subjected to substantial criticism. In our cases, the 'perpetrator' does not threaten the 'victim' with depriving her of something to which she has a rightful claim; instead he offers her a benefit which she may or may not desire to obtain in exchange for her sexual cooperation.[83] Since the student in case (2) and Jane in case (3) can accept or refuse the (immoral) offer, there is no coercion involved. In common law jurisdictions, the male party in cases (2) and (3) would not be guilty of rape. He did not engage in any force or threat of force, nor did he put the woman in any fear (of physical harm at least) and there was no ambiguity as to the nature of the contemplated act. In fact, it is doubtful if he would be guilty of any offence. One could envisage an offence of exercising coercion through abuse of power, but it would probably be difficulty to define and keep within manageable limits, especially at a time when we are rightly concerned about over-criminalisation.[84]

VI Impact of Intoxication

In common law jurisdictions, the relationship between intoxication and consent has become a highly contentious issue in recent years. Many allegations of rape and sexual assault arise from sexual activity that

82 BGH, Judgment of 13 Jan 2004 – 1 StR 737/81, BGHSt 31, 195.

83 Hoven, 'Bestechlichkeit als Nötigung?' (2016); Kuhlen L, 'Drohungen und Versprechungen' (2014).

84 Husak, *Overcriminalization* (2008); Farmer, *Making the Modern Criminal Law* (2016).

occurred while one or both parties were to some extent under the influence of alcohol or drugs.[85] High levels of alcohol consumption seem particularly prevalent in acquaintance rape.[86] Sexual intercourse with a person who is so intoxicated as to be unable to give or withhold consent will amount to rape provided the accused has the necessary *mens rea* which, depending on the jurisdiction, means that he was actually aware of at least a real risk that the person was thus incapacitated, or did not reasonably believe that the other party was consenting. Lack of capacity to consent or lack of awareness of what is happening as a result of alcohol or drug consumption means that one essential element of the *actus reus* of rape, absence of consent, is present.[87] A defendant will, of course, be guilty of rape if, through the administration of alcohol or some other psychoactive substance, he deliberately rendered the complainant incapable of refusing consent. For the purpose of deciding if a complainant consented, the manner in which the intoxication arose is, for all practical purposes, irrelevant. The question is simply whether she or he was, at the relevant time, capable of giving or refusing consent.[88] As already noted, a defendant's knowledge or belief as to whether the complainant was consenting is a different matter. The law does not specify any particular degree of intoxication that should be regarded as negativing consent, nor could it realistically do so. Instead, a court must have regard to the decision-making capacity of the complainant at the particular time. As the English Court of Appeal said in *R* v. *Bree*:

> If, through drink (or for any other reason) the complainant has temporarily lost her capacity to choose whether to have sexual intercourse on the relevant occasion, she is not consenting, and subject to questions about the defendant's state of mind, if intercourse takes place this would be rape. However, even where the complainant has consumed even substantial quantities of alcohol, but nevertheless remains capable of choosing whether or not to have intercourse, and in drink agrees to do so, this would not be rape. We should perhaps underline that, as a matter of

[85] Research studies in the United States have shown that a significant percentage of both perpetrators and victims of sexual assault had consumed alcohol in advance of the act constituting the offence. Depending on the samples studied, the percentages ranged from 34 to 74% of perpetrators and 30 to 79% of victims: Abbey et al., 'Alcohol and Sexual Assault' (2001) (the authors conclude that at least half of all violent crimes involve alcohol consumption by the perpetrator, the victim or both, and that sexual assaults fit into this pattern).

[86] Ryan, 'Intoxicating Encounters' (2004), 411.

[87] *R* v. *Malone* [1998] 2 Cr. App. R. 447 at 457–8; *R* v. *Camplin* (1845) 1 Cox CC 220.

[88] *R* v. *Lang* (1976) 62 Cr. App. R. 50.

> practical reality, capacity to consent may evaporate well before a complainant becomes unconscious. Whether this is so or not, however, is fact specific or, more accurately, depends on the actual state of mind of the individuals involved on the particular occasion.[89]

Bree was decided under the Sexual Offences Act 2003, s. 74 of which provides that a person consents 'if he agrees by choice, and has the freedom and capacity to make that choice'; many other jurisdictions now have similar statutory provisions. In *R* v. *Nightingale*[90] the appellant was convicted of raping a woman who seems to have been comatose as a result of alcohol consumption.

The most difficult cases are those where the complainant, as a result of having been intoxicated when the alleged sexual activity occurred, cannot recall what exactly happened or what her state of mind was at the time. This, to say the least, can create a doubt as to whether consent was absent. Yet to exclude such evidence, as some have advocated, could be unfair to the accused. The complainant may, in fact, have been consenting at the time (assuming she was still conscious and retained some degree of decision-making capacity) and the defendant may have believed, honestly or reasonably, depending on the prevailing test, that she was consenting. A jury is entitled to hear all the evidence in order to make informed decisions on these crucial questions. When a question of identification arises, as it sometimes will in so-called stranger rape, evidence of intoxication on the complainant's part may be particularly relevant. In one Irish case, though one in which a conviction for rape was upheld on appeal, the complainant admitted to being quite intoxicated when intercourse took place and could describe the suspect only as 'small, black and from Africa'.[91] Granted, a sober complainant might not, in similar circumstances, be able to give a better description, but particular care is needed when there is evidence of intoxication.

89 [2008] QB 131, para. 34. The Court took the opportunity to comment on a much-publicised case, *R* v. *McDougal*, heard at Swansea Crown Court in Nov. 2005. It resulted in a directed acquittal after the prosecution decided to offer no evidence on learning that the complainant was intoxicated at the time. The controversy arose mainly from prosecuting counsel having told the jury: 'a drunken consent is still a consent'. The judge had indicated his agreement with the course taken by the prosecution. Commenting on this, the Court of Appeal in *Bree* said that it was unexceptionable that where a person who has had a lot to drink consents to sexual intercourse, that is precisely what she or he is doing: consenting. But if, after taking drink, the person is not consenting, the intercourse is obviously non-consensual.

90 [2010] 2 Cr. App. R. (S.) 59.

91 *R* v. *Mekonnen* [2012] 1 IR 210.

So-called date-rape drugs, especially flunitrazepam, better known as Rohnypol, have become a major cause of concern, but research in both Britain and the United States has shown that surreptitious drugging is a factor in very few rape cases.[92] We should not allow preoccupation with covert drugging to detract attention from the much greater problem of sexual violence and exploitation committed against persons who have become voluntarily intoxicated.

German law does not have any special rules regarding intoxication and its impact on capacity to consent. Intoxication can, however, be so debilitating as to make it impossible for a person to form or express his or her disagreement with sexual acts performed by the actor. If that is the case, and the actor intentionally profits from this state of affairs, he is punishable for sexual coercion (§ 177(2) no. 1 StGB). In that case, it makes no difference whether the actor had brought about the intoxication of the other person or abused his or her existing drunkenness. If an intoxicated person's ability to form or express his or her will is severely reduced (but the person still retains some ability to make a determination and to express his or her will), the actor may enter into sexual relations with that person only if he or she has positively ascertained that the person consents to the sexual acts proposed (§ 177(2) no. 2 StGB). This provision, which incorporates the 'Only Yes means Yes' rule, has been adopted in order to make it possible for mentally impaired persons to have sexual relations, but also applies to drunken or drugged persons. Despite the well-meaning protective purpose behind the rule, it seems impractical to expect that a partially disabled person would give positive and specified consent to particular sexual acts. Moreover, the requirements for the actor's *mens rea* are problematic in this situation: he or she must have realised that the other person is (not totally but) partially unable to understand the situation and/or the meaning of consent, and have understood that the other person withheld consent to those sexual acts that the actor actually performed.[93]

If the perpetrator (as well) was intoxicated, German law treats him or her as acting without culpability if the degree of the intoxication was such that it rendered him or her unable to realise the unlawfulness of his or

[92] Hindmarch and Brinkmann, 'Trends in the Use of Alcohol' (1999); Benyon et al., 'Involvement of Drugs and Alcohol' (2008). The latter is a British study based on one primary study which showed that covert drugging accounted for only 2% of drug-facilitated sexual assault.

[93] Hoven and Weigend, 'Nein heißt Nein' (2017).

her conduct, or to act in accordance with that realisation (§ 20 StGB). However, the perpetrator may be punished for the crime of voluntary intoxication if he, by using alcohol or drugs, caused himself to be in a state of lack of culpability, and unlawfully committed the *actus reus* of a criminal offence while in this state (§ 323a StGB).

VII Temporal Aspects of Consent

Sometimes one partner to an initially consensual sexual encounter changes his or her mind and wishes to refrain from particular sexual acts or to terminate the sexual interchange altogether. The question then arises whether that person may withdraw his or her original consent, with the consequence that any continuation on the part of the other sexual partner turns into sexual coercion.

It appears to be beyond doubt that consent may be revoked before sexual activity takes place. The key question is whether consent existed at the moment at which the relevant sexual activity began.[94] A person who had previously indicated a willingness to engage in a sexual act is always entitled to change his or her mind in that regard.[95] The Supreme Court of Canada had to deal with a more difficult issue in *R* v. *J.A.*,[96]where the complainant had agreed to be choked by her partner until she lost consciousness. When she regained consciousness, she found him performing a sexual act upon her. They then had sexual intercourse. Some months later, she complained to the police that, while she had consented to losing consciousness, she had not consented to the particular sexual act her partner performed upon her. She later withdrew that allegation, claiming that she had made it because her partner was trying to get sole custody of their child. He was convicted of assault but that conviction was quashed on appeal. However, a majority of the Supreme Court reinstated the conviction, holding that under the Criminal Code, the concept of consent does not cover advance consent to sexual acts performed while a person is unconscious. What is required is ongoing conscious consent so that a person engaging in sexual activity can ask his or her partner to stop at any time. A dissent by three members of the Court is, in many ways, more compelling. They argued that a person in the position of this complainant is exercising autonomy by freely

[94] *R* v. *Olugboja* [1982] QB 320 at 332.
[95] See e.g. *Tyson* v. *Trigg*, 50 F3d 436 at 448 (7th Cir. 1995).
[96] [2011] 2 SCR 440.

agreeing to lose consciousness for a short period during which sexual activity is to take place. While admitting that an unconscious person cannot withdraw consent, the minority reasoned that it scarcely followed from this that a person could not freely and voluntarily put him/herself in a position of being physically unable, for a short interval, of withdrawing previously granted consent. Both the majority and the minority proclaimed fidelity to the principle of personal autonomy, but they differed as to its implications where a person had freely put him/herself in a position of being unable to grant or withhold consent at the moment when the sexual act occurred.

With regard to withdrawal of consent while sexual relations are en route, for the common law world, the decision of the Privy Council in *Kaitamaki* v. *The Queen*[97] has proved to be enormously influential. The decision hinged on the proper interpretation of a New Zealand law which provided, first, that for the purpose of rape sexual intercourse is complete upon penetration and, secondly, that rape is the act of a male person having sexual intercourse with a female without her consent.[98] Broadly similar statutory provisions existed in many other countries at the time. The Privy Council agreed with a majority of the New Zealand Court of Appeal that 'complete' means having come into existence and not having come to an end. Sexual intercourse was therefore a continuing act so that if, at any time while it was taking place, the woman withdrew her consent and the man was aware that she had done so, he was guilty of rape. The *Kaitamaki* principle has now been incorporated into modern rape legislation in several jurisdictions, including England and Wales, Scotland and Ireland.[99]

The appellant in *Kaitamaki* would have attracted little sympathy in any court. He had broken into a house in the early hours of the morning and, according to the prosecution, twice raped a young woman who lived there. He claimed that she had consented or, alternatively, that he had honestly believed she was consenting. Eventually he conceded that while he was having intercourse with her for the second time, he became aware that she was not consenting, but he still did not desist. Most courts would be instinctively disinclined to acquit him in these circumstances. Neither

97 [1985] AC 147.

98 Crimes Act 1961, ss. 127 and 128.

99 Sexual Offences Act 2003, s. 79(2); Sexual Offences (Scotland) Act 2009, s. 15(3); Criminal Law (Rape) (Amendment) Act 1990, s. 9 as substituted by Criminal Law (Sexual Offences) Act 2017 (s. 48) (Ireland).

Kaitamaki itself nor any of the cases in which it seems to have been applied subjects the notion of continuing consent to any close scrutiny.[100] It seems to have been adopted without question by the Irish Court of Criminal Appeal in *People (DPP)* v. *Keogh*[101] in which a prostitute agreed to have sex with a man provided he paid her a specified sum of money and provided he wore a condom. While intercourse was taking place, he became aggressive and removed the condom, and she apparently then withdrew her consent. He was convicted, and appealed unsuccessfully against conviction, but the consent issue under discussion here did not feature among the grounds of appeal. Nor was it mentioned by the appeal court.[102] While courts apply the principle for the purpose of establishing criminal responsibility, they tend to be lenient when it comes to sentencing. In *R* v. *Greaves*,[103] the sentence for rape was reduced from forty-two months to eighteen months. In *Ibbs* v. *The Queen*[104] the High Court of Australia considered six months' imprisonment appropriate for a rape committed in similar circumstances, though the facts of that case were highly unusual. The charge resulted from a statutory provision in Western Australia which defined rape as capable of being committed by continuing penetration following the withdrawal of consent. Most American states have also adopted the *Kaitamaki* principle, either by way of case law or legislation, although a few have refused to do so.[105]

German authors emphasise that any partner in a sexual encounter is free to withdraw his or her consent both before the actual performance of and in the course of sexual acts. That also applies to acts other than heterosexual intercourse, such as oral or anal intercourse. If withdrawal has been communicated to the other partner (in a 'recognisable' manner), the activity must stop or must be limited to sexual acts that are still welcome to the other person. Otherwise, the perpetrator is punishable (at least) under § 177(1) StGB.

VIII Conclusion

Our comparative study has shown remarkable similarities between the common law and the German systems. They all regard sexual

[100] *R* v. *Cooper and Schaub* [1994] Crim. LR 531; *R* v. *Greaves* [1999] 1 Cr. App. R.(S.) 319; *R* v. *Leaver* [2006] EWCA Crim. 2988; *R* v. *Tarmohammed* [1997] Crim. LR 458.

[101] [2009] IECCA 93.

[102] *Ibid.*

[103] [1999] 1 Cr. App. R. (S.) 319.

[104] (1987) 163 CLR 447.

[105] Ryan, 'No Means No?' (2004).

autonomy – that is, the ability to determine when and with whom one wishes to have sexual relations of what kind – as an important value that is directly connected with human dignity. Criminal law is an indispensable instrument for protecting that value. Since 2016, German law has also fallen in line with the common law approach that does not require, for a conviction for rape or sexual coercion, the use of force or threat of force. Criminality now hinges only on whether the perpetrator has acted in spite of the other person's (recognisable) lack of consent.

Legislation and case law in common law jurisdictions is gradually displaying more sensitivity to factors that may impede 'true' consent even where the person affected has not objected to sexual acts. This concerns cases where the affected partner was intoxicated as well as those where he or she withdrew the original consent in the course of a sexual encounter. While there exist only slight differences between the legal systems in these cases, they are more pronounced with regard to fraud. It is here that at least some tendencies in common law jurisdictions point toward an extensive understanding of sexual autonomy, whereas German law tends not to scrutinise too closely the motives that may have influenced the complainant's consent. It is in these areas that the dialogue between the legal systems will continue.

Bibliography

Abbey A., Zawacki T., Buck P. O., Clinton A. M. and McAuslan P., 'Alcohol and Sexual Assault', *Alcohol Research and Health*, 25 (2001), 43–51.

Ashworth A., 'Comment on *R* v. *G* [2008] UKHL', 37, *Criminal Law Review* (2008), 818–20.

Bailey V. and Blackburn S., 'The Punishment of Incest Act 1908: A Case Study of Law Creation', *Criminal Law Review* (1979), 708–18.

Benyon C. M., McVeigh C., McVeigh L., Leavey C. and Bellis M. A., 'The Involvement of Drugs and Alcohol in Drug-Facilitated Sexual Assault: A Systematic Review of the Evidence', *Trauma, Violence and Abuse*, 9 (2008), 178–88.

Bowsher P., 'Incest – Should Incest between Consenting Adults Be a Crime?', *Criminal Law Review* (2015), 208–18.

Brayne H., Sergeant L. and Brayne L., 'Could Boxing Be Banned? A Legal and Epistemological Perspective', *British Medical Journal*, 316 (1998), 1813.

Byrd B. S., 'Kant's Theory of Punishment: Deterrence in its Threat, Retribution in Its Execution', *Law and Philosophy*, 8 (1989), 151–200.

Card R., *Sexual Offences: The New Law*, Bristol, Jordans (2004).

Clough A., 'Conditional Consent and Purposeful Deception', *The Journal of Criminal Law*, 82 (2018), 178–90.

Dubber M. D. and Hörnle T., *Criminal Law: A Comparative Approach*, Oxford University Press (2014).

Duff R. A., *Answering for Crime: Responsibility and Liability in the Criminal Law*, Oxford, Hart (2007).

Duttge G., 'Strafbarkeit des Geschwisterinzestes aufgrund 'eugenischer Gesicht-spunkte?', in Heinrich M., Jäger C. and Schünemann B. (eds.), *Strafrecht als Scientia Universalis – Festschrift für Claus Roxin zum 80. Geburtstag am 15. Mai 2011*, Berlin, De Gruyter (2011), 227–44.

Eser A., Perron W., Sternberg-Lieben D., Eisele J., Hecker B., Kinzig J., Bosch N., Schuster F., Weißer B. and Schittenhelm U., in Schönke A. and Schröder H. (eds.), *Strafgesetzbuch Kommentar*, 29th edn, Munich, C. H. Beck (2014).

Farmer L., *Making the Modern Criminal Law: Criminalisation and Civil Order*, Oxford University Press (2016).

Feinberg J., *Harm to Self*, Oxford University Press (1986).

Finnis J., *Natural Law and Natural Rights*, Oxford, Clarendon Press (2004).

Fletcher, G. P., *Rethinking Criminal Law*, Oxford University Press (2000).

Harcourt B., 'The Collapse of the Harm Principle', *Journal of Criminal Law and Criminology*, 90 (1999), 109–94.

'The Collapse of the Harm Principle Redux: On Same-Sex Marriage, the Supreme Court's Opinion in *United States* v. *Windsor*, John Stuart Mill's Essay *On Liberty* (1859) and H. L. A. Hart's *Modern Harm Principle*', University of Chicago Law School Public Law and Legal Theory Working Paper (2013).

Hart H. L. A., *Law, Liberty and Morality*, Oxford University Press (1963).

Herring J, 'Mistaken Sex', *Criminal Law Review* (2005), 511–24.

Criminal Law: Text, Cases and Materials, 8th edn, Oxford University Press (2018).

Hindmarch I. and Brinkman R., 'Trends in the Use of Alcohol and Other Drugs in Cases of Sexual Assault', *Human Psychopharmacology: Clinical and Experimental*, 14 (1999), 225–31.

Home Office, *Setting the Boundaries: Reforming the Law on Sexual Offences*, Home Office, London (2000).

Horder J, *Ashworth's Principles of Criminal Law*, 8th edn, Oxford University Press (2016).

Hörnig D. and Wolff H. A. (eds.), *Grundgesetz für die Bundesrepublik Deutschland Handkommentar*, 12th edn, Baden-Baden, Nomos (2018).

Hörnle T., 'Das Verbot des Geschwisterinzests – Verfassungsgerichtliche Bestätigung und verfassungsrechtliche Kritik', *Neue Juristische Wochenschrift*, 61 (2008), 2085–8.

'Das Gesetz zur Verbesserung sexueller Selbstbestimmung', *Neue Zeitschrift für Strafrecht*, 13 (2017), 13–21.

Hoven E., 'Bestechlichkeit als Nötigung?', *Zeitschrift für die gesamte Strafrechtswissenschaft*, 128 (2016), 173–93.

Hoven E. and Weigend T., 'Nein heißt Nein' – und viele Fragen offen. Zur Neugestaltung der Strafbarkeit sexueller Übergriffe', *Juristenzeitung*, 18 (2017), 182–91.

'Zur Strafbarkeit von Täuschungen im Sexualstrafrecht', *Kriminalpolitische Zeitschrift*, 3 (2018), 156–61.

Hurd H. M., 'The Moral Magic of Consent', *Legal Theory* 2 (1996), 121–46.

Husak D., *Overcriminalization: The Limits of the Criminal Law*, Oxford University Press (2008).

Joecks W. and Miebach K. (eds.), *Münchener Kommentar zum Strafgesetzbuch*, IV: *§§ 185–262*, 4 vols. 3rd edn, Munich, C. H. Beck (2017).

Kant I., *Practical Philosophy*, ed. and trans. McGregor M. J., Cambridge University Press (1996).

'Metaphysische Anfangsgründe der Rechtslehre', in Höffe O. (ed.), *Metaphysische Anfangsgründe der Rechtslehre*, Berlin, De Gruyter (1999).

Kell D., 'Social Disutility and the Law on Consent', *Oxford Journal of Legal Studies*, 14 (1994) 121–35.

Kuhlen L., 'Drohungen und Versprechungen', in Hefendehl R., Hörnle T. and Greco L. (eds.), *Streitbare Strafrechtwissenschaft – Festschrift für Bernd Schünemann zum 70. Geburtstag am 1. November 2014*, Berlin, De Gruyter (2014), 611–30.

Laird K., 'Rapist or Rogue? Deception, Consent and the Sexual Offences Act 2003', *Criminal Law Review* (2014), 492–510.

Laufhütte H. R., Rissing-van Saan R. and Tiedemann K. (eds.), *Strafgesetzbuch Leipziger Kommentar – Großkommentar*, 12th edn, Berlin, De Gruyter (2014).

Law Commission of England and Wales, *Consent in the Criminal Law*, Consultation Paper 139, London, Her Majesty's Stationery Office (1995).

Lyon M. R., 'No Means No? Withdrawal of Consent during Intercourse and the Continuing Evolution of the Definition of Rape', *J. Crim. L. and Criminology*, 95 (2004), 277–314.

Mackinnon C., *Only Words*, Harvard University Press (1993).

Mill J. S., *On Liberty* (1859), London, Penguin Books (1982).

Miller F. G. and Wertheimer A. (eds.), *The Ethics of Consent: Theory and Practice* Oxford University Press (2010).

Moran L. J., 'Laskey v. The United Kingdom: Learning the Limits of Privacy', *Modern Law Review*, 61 (1988), 77–84.

Munro V., 'Sexual Autonomy', in Dubber M. D. and Hörnle T. (eds.), *The Oxford Handbook of Criminal Law*, Oxford University Press (2014).

Murphy J. G., *Retribution, Justice and Therapy: Essays in the Philosophy of Law*, Dordrecht, D. Reidel Publishing Co. (1979).

'Does Kant Have a Theory of Punishment?', *Columbia Law Review*, 87 (1987), 509–32.

O'Malley T., *Sexual Offences*, 2nd edn, Dublin, Round Hall (2013).

'The New Law on Sexual Offences', *Irish Criminal Law Journal*, 27 (2017), 78–89.

O'Neill O. 'Between Consenting Adults', *Philosophy and Public Affairs*, 14 (1985), 252–77.

Ormerod D. and Laird K., *Smith, Hogan, and Ormerod's Criminal Law*, 15th edn, Oxford University Press (2018).

Renzikowski J., 'Nein! – Das neue Sexualstrafrecht', *Neue Juristische Wochenschrift*, 49 (2016), 3553–8.

Rook P. and Ward R., *Sexual Offences: Law and Practice*, 5th edn, London, Sweet and Maxwell (2016).

Roxin C., *Strafrecht Allgemeiner Teil Grundlagen. Der Aufbau der Verbrechenslehre*, 4th edn, Munich, C. H. Beck (2006).

'Zur Strafbarkeit des Geschwisterinzests', *Strafverteidiger*, 29 (2009), 544–50.

Ryan V. M., 'Intoxicating Encounters: Allocating Responsibility in the Law of Rape', *California Western Law Review*, 40 (2004), 407–29.

Sharpe A., 'Expanding Liability for Sexual Fraud through the Concept of "Active Deception": A Flawed Approach', *The Journal of Criminal Law*, 80 (2016), 28–44.

'Queering Judgment: The Case of Gender Identity Fraud', *The Journal of Criminal Law*, 81 (2017), 417–35.

Shute S., 'The Second Law Commission Consultation Paper on Consent', *Criminal Law Review* (1996), 684–93.

Simester A. P., Spencer J. R., Stark F., Sullivan G. R. and Virgo G. J., *Simester and Sullivan's Criminal Law: Theory and Doctrine*, 6th edn, Oxford, Hart (2018).

Spencer J. R., 'The Sexual Offences Act 2003 (2): Child and Family Offences', *Criminal Law Review* (2004), 347–60.

Temkin J. and Ashworth A., 'The Sexual Offences Act 2003: (1) Rape, Sexual Assaults and the Problem of Consent', *Criminal Law Review* (2004), 348–6.

Wertheimer A., 'Consent and Sexual Relations', in Miller F. G. and Wertheimer A., *The Ethics of Consent*, Oxford University Press (2010).

Williams G., 'Offences and Defences', *Legal Studies*, 2 (1992), 233–56.

Williams R., 'Deception, Mistake and Vitiation of the Victim's Consent', *Law Quarterly Review*, 124 (2008), 132–59.

6

Terrorism Offences

ANDREW CORNFORD AND ANNEKE PETZSCHE

I Introduction

How should the criminal law respond to the threat of terrorism? One possible answer is that no special response is needed. Legal systems around the world already criminalise such acts as killing, maiming and causing explosions, as well as attempting, inciting or conspiring to do any of these things. Another possible answer is that the criminal law has a role to play in pre-empting terrorist attacks. Since these attacks can cause such severe and extensive harm, the criminal law is justified in intervening at an earlier stage than usual, in order to ensure that they are not carried out. This second answer has recently proved the more popular among legislators in many jurisdictions, including Germany and the UK.[1]

The question of how the criminal law should deal with terrorism is worthy of comparative study for several reasons. In recent decades, terrorism and the fight against it have (again) taken centre stage in Europe; consequently, all European countries are grappling with this challenge. In doing so, they are tested on the importance that they afford to both substantive and procedural protections for suspected offenders. Terrorists are an 'easy target' when it comes to weakening such protections: it is comparatively easy for legislators to justify curtailing their rights. Besides the inherent problems with weakening legal protections in this context, there is a risk that, once this has been done, they become more easily weakened in other areas of the law. Additionally, while criticism of counter-terrorism law has focused mostly on the weakening of procedural safeguards, the expansion of substantive criminal liability

[1] This reflects a more general development in the role of the criminal law from punishing crimes to preventing them. The discourse focuses on concepts such as the securitisation of criminal law (Naucke, 'Sicherheitsstrafrecht' (2010), 129, with further references) and enemy criminal law (see Hörnle, 'Dimensionen des Begriffs "Feindstrafrecht"' (2006), 80, with further references).

also gives us cause for concern. Our aim in this chapter is to examine this expansion, through a comparative analysis of UK and German law.

We focus on four groups of offences: offences of preparing terrorist acts, offences of encouraging terrorism, offences related to terrorist organisations, and terrorism-related possession offences. We examine how these offences have expanded the scope of criminal liability in relation to terrorism, highlighting differences between the jurisdictions in the extent to which they have done so. We should note that these are not the only terrorism offences to have been enacted in either jurisdiction. We have excluded offences that do not play a straightforwardly pre-emptive role,[2] and even some that do:[3] we focus on those pre-emptive offences that are most important and most frequently prosecuted. We hope thereby to enable a deeper analysis of the offences that we examine.

We conclude that, in the context of terrorism, both jurisdictions have departed significantly from the traditional principles of inchoate criminal liability.[4] This has led to similar concerns about both sets of offences: for example, their breadth and their criminalisation of apparently neutral or innocent conduct. However, the UK offences have been interpreted and applied in a particularly expansive way, and they are broader than the German offences in almost every material respect. The UK especially has come worryingly close to criminalising fantasy, obsession and the expression of dissent.

Before commencing our analysis, we discuss two preliminary points. The first is the definition of terrorism and its importance to the provisions that we examine.[5] In UK law, there is a statutory definition of acts of terrorism, to which all the UK offences refer.[6] Roughly speaking, this definition requires (i) one of a list of specific types of conduct, such as serious violence or endangerment of life; (ii) that is designed to influence a government or to intimidate the public; and (iii) that has the purpose of advancing a political, religious, racial or ideological cause. References

[2] E.g. offences relating to the provision of information. In UK law, see e.g. Terrorism Act 2000, ss. 19, 38B and 39; in German law, see e.g. § 138(2) *Strafgesetzbuch* (StGB).

[3] E.g. offences relating to financing of terrorism. In UK law, see e.g. Terrorism Act 2000, ss. 15–18; in German law, see e.g. § 89c StGB.

[4] On the function of such offences from a German and Spanish viewpoint, see Cancio Meliá and Petzsche, 'Precursor Crimes' (2015), 194.

[5] On the problems of a definition of terrorism at the international level, see Saul, 'Attempts to Define Terrorism' (2005), 57, 76–82; Cassese, 'The Multifaceted Criminal Notion of Terrorism' (2006), 933, 936–7; Ambos, 'Judicial Creativity' (2011), 655.

[6] Terrorism Act 2000, s. 1.

below to 'terrorism' or 'acts of terrorism' in the context of UK law must be understood in accordance with this definition.

By contrast, German criminal law does not contain a definition of terrorism,[7] and many of the relevant offences do not refer to terrorism directly. For example, §§ 89a, 89b and 91 StGB, which were introduced in order to criminalise certain acts preparatory to terrorism, only refer to the planning of 'a serious violent offence endangering the state', without ever mentioning the words 'terrorist' or 'terrorism'. Only three provisions explicitly mention terrorism in their title: § 89c StGB (financing of terrorism) and §§ 129a and 129b StGB (forming terrorist organisations and terrorist organisations abroad). None of these provisions contains a definition of terrorism, but their wording suggests that a central difference between terrorism offences and 'normal' crimes lies in an additional subjective element, requiring that the act 'is intended to impair and capable of impairing the existence or security of a state or of an international organisation, or to abolish, rob of legal effect or undermine constitutional principles of the Federal Republic of Germany'.[8]

In both jurisdictions, the question has arisen of whether terrorism offences apply equally to actions directed against undemocratic or otherwise illegitimate regimes. UK courts have consistently held that they do – an approach that has now been confirmed by the UK Supreme Court, albeit with evident discomfort.[9] In Germany, the Federal Court of Justice also showed considerable reluctance to accept this, but felt bound by the clear wording of the law ('a state'). It therefore held that § 89a StGB is applicable even where the prepared act is intended and suitable to affect the existence or security of a dictatorial state or an otherwise unjust regime.[10]

[7] However, the definition included in the European Directive 2017/541 on combating terrorism is binding in the interpretation of any relevant provision of domestic law.

[8] § 89a (1) cl. 2 StGB, official translation by Bohlander. This official translation is used throughout this chapter, except where we indicate otherwise. See also § 89c(1) cl. 2 StGB, with a similar, but slightly different wording: 'is intended to substantially intimidate the population, to unlawfully coerce an authority or an international organisation by force or the threat of force, or to eliminate or significantly impair the political, constitutional, economic or social structures of a State or an international organisation, and by the nature of its commission or its effects may cause considerable damage to a State or an international organisation' (translation by the authors).

[9] The leading case is *R* v. *Gul* [2013] UKSC 64, [2014] AC 1260. See also *R* v. *F* [2007] EWCA Crim. 243, [2007] QB 960; *R* v. *Sarwar* [2015] EWCA Crim. 1886, [2016] 1 Cr. App. R. (S) 54.

[10] BGH 3 StR 326/16 [2017] BGHSt 62, 102; critical with regard to the breadth of the provision, see Ambos, 'Anmerkung' (2017), 655; Gazeas and Grosse-Wilde, 'Anmerkung' (2009), 84.

However, it showed its discomfort in stressing that restraint should be exercised in the prosecution of such cases.[11] This point should be borne in mind as we explain the breadth of both sets of offences: they apply equally to the early stages of freedom-fighting action that many would sympathise with or even support.

A second preliminary issue that we should highlight is a key function of these offences that we do not discuss below: their procedural 'door opener' function. By expanding the scope of criminal liability in relation to terrorism, not only do these offences expand the conduct for which one may be convicted and punished; they expand the powers of enforcement officials to investigate and restrict the liberties of terrorist suspects. Indeed, making it easier for officials to stop, search, surveil, arrest and detain suspected terrorists is perhaps the main way in which these offences perform their pre-emptive task. Although we focus below on the substantive scope of these offences, we therefore acknowledge that there is a certain artificiality in this focus. We highlight the significant ways in which these offences have expanded the scope of criminal liability; we leave it to readers to imagine the even more significant ways in which they have expanded investigative and enforcement powers.

II Preparation of Terrorism

The UK offence of preparation of terrorist acts is simply defined. One commits the offence if one intends either to commit or to assist an act of terrorism, and one 'engages in any conduct in preparation for giving effect to' that intention.[12] The required *mens rea* is thus an intention to commit or assist an act of terrorism, in the general sense explained above; one need not intend to commit or assist a specific terrorist act.[13] The *actus reus* is any conduct – literally any – in preparation for giving effect to such an intention. The offence carries a maximum sentence of life imprisonment,[14] and is the most frequently prosecuted terrorism offence in UK law.[15]

[11] BGH 3 StR 218/15 [2015] BGHSt 61, 36 at [14]. Restraint is possible because the 'legality principle' of mandatory prosecution is not applicable in cases which occur outside of Germany; instead, the so-called 'opportunity principle' (*Opportunitätsprinzip*) applies, which leaves the decision to prosecute to the discretion of the prosecutor: § 153c(1) no. 1 German Code of Criminal Procedure (StPO).

[12] Terrorism Act 2006, s. 5(1).

[13] *Ibid.*, s. 5(2).

[14] *Ibid.*, s. 5(3).

[15] Home Office, *Operation of Police Powers under the Terrorism Act 2000*, Table A.05a.

The comparable German offences covering specific acts of preparation – §§ 89a and 89b StGB – were mainly introduced in 2009.[16] Whereas, in the beginning, these new provisions were rarely used, the number of prosecutions under § 89a StGB has substantially increased in recent years.[17] Under § 89a StGB, a person who prepares a serious violent offence[18] – that is, an offence against life[19] or personal freedom[20] – with the distinguishing subjective element mentioned above (an intention to endanger the existence or security of a state etc.), is punishable by imprisonment of between six months and ten years. § 89a(2) StGB clarifies that, unlike the UK provision, only specific acts of preparation fall within the offence. It gives an exhaustive list of such acts, such as instructing another person or receiving instruction in the production or use of firearms, explosives, explosive or incendiary devices, nuclear fission material, or other radioactive substances; and producing, obtaining for oneself or another, storing or supplying to another such weapons, substances or devices. A clear example is training in a terrorist training camp in Syria in order to later participate in the fighting there. In addition, in 2015, a travelling provision was introduced (§ 89a(2a) StGB), which criminalises whoever undertakes to leave the country with a certain terrorist purpose.

Not only are the objective requirements of the offence complex; the subjective requirements are multiple. The *mens rea* element has three points of reference: intent is required regarding (i) the preparatory act, (ii) the later commission of the serious offence against life or personal freedom, and (iii) the suitability of the later offence to impair state security ('is intended to impair').[21] While the wording of the provision only requires contingent intent (*dolus eventualis*),[22] the highest federal

[16] The 'Gesetz zur Verfolgung der Vorbereitung von schweren staatsgefährdenden Gewalttaten' introduced §§ 89a, 89b and 91 into the German Criminal Code (StGB); in 2015, § 89a StGB was expanded, adding a new subsection 2a. Also covering certain preparatory acts are §§ 129a(5) and 91(1) no. 2 StGB; these will be considered below, as part of the offences related to terrorist organisations and possession offences respectively.

[17] In absolute numbers, there are still few convictions, but the numbers are rising: see Tabelle 2.1, Fachserie 10 (Rechtspflege) Reihe 3 der Strafverfolgungsstatistik.

[18] Under the conditions listed in § 89a(2) StGB.

[19] §§ 211, 212 StGB: murder and manslaughter

[20] §§ 239a, 239b StGB: abduction for the purpose of blackmail and taking hostages.

[21] Petzsche, 'The European Influence' (2012), 1056, 1063.

[22] German criminal law differentiates between three forms of intentional conduct (*Vorsatz*). The strongest form is purpose (*Absicht* or *dolus directus ersten Grades*), which means that the offender commits a crime while knowing and intending to realise the elements of the

court has interpreted the provision as requiring that the offender is firmly determined (*fest entschlossen*) to commit a serious violent offence endangering a state – so as to fulfil constitutional requirements.[23]

Additionally, § 89b StGB creates an offence of establishing contacts with the intention of receiving instruction for the purpose of the commission of a serious violent offence endangering the state, with a maximum punishment of three years' imprisonment or a fine. There is no offence if the act exclusively serves the fulfilment of lawful professional or official duties.[24] Despite what the section's heading suggests ('Establishing contacts for the purpose of committing a serious violent offence endangering the state'), the defendant's intent need not include committing a terrorist act, but only the prior step of receiving instructions – thereby criminalising the 'preparation of preparations'. Since its introduction, there have been barely any prosecutions for this offence.[25]

Both the UK and the German provisions aim to increase legal protection from terrorism by broadening the scope of criminal liability to encompass the preliminary stages of attacks. They expand liability beyond the traditional scope of the general inchoate offences in both jurisdictions: most importantly, those of attempt and conspiracy.[26] Attempt encompasses some preparatory conduct, but only a narrow range: roughly, conduct that comes very close to the actual perpetration of the crime,[27] or by which the offender is trying to commit that crime.[28] Thus, in UK jurisdictions, prospective robbers are guilty of an attempt when they enter the bank, even though they have not yet demanded money from the cashier; but they are not guilty of an attempt when they

crime. The second degree is certain knowledge (*dolus directus zweiten Grades*), which means that the offender is certain that his action will fulfil the elements of a crime. The lowest degree is so-called *dolus eventualis* (*Eventualvorsatz*), which means that the offender realises that his actions could fulfil the elements of a crime and knowingly accepts this while acting.

23 BGH 3 StR 243/13 [2014] BGHSt 59, 218.

24 § 89b(2) StGB.

25 The official statistics show one conviction in 2016: see Tabelle 2.1, Fachserie 10 (Rechtspflege) Reihe 3 der Strafverfolgungsstatistik.

26 This was actually one of the reasons given by the German legislator for creating these offences and thus expanding the substantive German criminal law: Bundestag-Drucksache 16/12428, 1–2, 14.

27 Hoffmann-Holland, '§ 22 StGB' (2017), mn. 102 ff.

28 In English law, see Criminal Attempts Act 1981 s. 1, and the interpreting case law discussed in Simester et al., *Simester and Sullivan's Criminal Law* (2016), 340–3. In Scots law, see Gane, Stoddart and Chalmers, *A Casebook on Scottish Criminal Law* (2009), 190–6.

arrive outside the bank, even though they have finished planning their crime. In German law, meanwhile, even entering the bank would often not suffice for attempt liability, especially if the robber has not yet threatened anyone or demanded money.[29] As we will see below, the terrorist preparation offences catch conduct at much earlier stages of criminal plans than this.

The preparation offences also expand on the general offences of conspiracy. In UK jurisdictions, any agreement to commit an offence, with the intention that this offence be committed, amounts to a criminal conspiracy.[30] The German conspiracy offence (*Verbrechensverabredung*) covers only serious crimes (felonies, *Verbrechen*).[31] A sufficient specificity to the plan is required, and as in UK jurisdictions, at least two persons need to be involved.[32] Clearly, these definitions overlap significantly with those of the preparation offences. This raises important questions about how the two systems deal with such overlap:[33] it should be noted, for example, that UK prosecutors have typically preferred conspiracy charges in the most serious cases that the preparation offence catches.[34] For our purposes, however, the important point is that these definitions clearly also exclude some relevant preparatory conduct. For example, they exclude the preparation of 'lone wolf' attacks, as well as the early stages of joint plots, when these are still too vague to count as agreements to commit an offence.

29 Though this depends on the specific circumstances of the case.

30 The definition is similar in England and Scotland. In English law, see Criminal Law Act 1977, s. 1. In Scots law, conspiracy is still a common law offence: see Gane, Stoddart and Chalmers, *A Casebook on Scottish Criminal Law* (2009), 177–90.

31 See Bock and Stark, Ch. 3, 'Preparatory Offences' (in this volume).

32 Joecks, '§ 30 StGB' (2017), mn. 54–66; though with the restrictive interpretation of the *mens rea* element requiring a firm determination, the difference regarding the specificity of the planned acts should be less pronounced.

33 These questions are especially significant in UK jurisdictions, where they must be solved through the exercise of prosecutorial discretion. German law, in contrast, goes some way towards solving problems of overlap through *concursus delictorium:* the general rules governing sentencing for multiple offences. These rules specify how courts have to deal with cases where an act violates multiple laws or the same law more than once, or where multiple offences are committed by multiple acts: §§ 52 and 53 StGB.

34 See the discussion in *R* v. *Kahar* [2016] EWCA Crim. 568, [2016] 1 WLR 3156 at [30]–[31]. This reflects a more general point about conspiracy in UK law: it catches little conduct, if any, that other offences do not also catch. As one leading work puts it: 'It is habit of mind and long-standing practice that favours recourse to conspiracy rather than any unique advantage that the charge brings': Simester et al., *Simester and Sullivan's Criminal Law* (2016), 338.

These departures from the ordinary principles of inchoate liability have led to similar criticisms of both sets of provisions. Both UK and German scholars have questioned not only the design of such offences but also their basic legitimacy.[35] In particular, these offences have been criticised for their criminalisation of otherwise innocent or 'neutral' conduct: conduct that is not wrongful apart from the required harmful intention, and from which such harmful intention is not easily inferred. Since the general legitimacy of preparatory offences is considered elsewhere in this volume, we will not consider such criticisms in detail here.[36] Instead, we focus on two more specific aspects of these offences that have led to doubts about their legitimacy: first, the breadth of their *actus reus* elements, and secondly, the resulting significance of their *mens rea* elements, and the evidentiary problems to which this gives rise. As we will see, the offences are strikingly similar in these respects, although the doubts apply especially forcefully to UK law.

Beginning with the *actus reus*, the breadth of the conduct covered is striking in both jurisdictions. Consider § 89b StGB as an example: this provision considerably expands German criminal law, since purely neutral acts of communication become punishable by up to three years' imprisonment. There may exist a connection to a terrorist organisation, as one of its members has to be the respondent of the relevant communication. But that alone should not be enough: German doctrine requires the criminalised behaviour to constitute a wrong in itself, to which the legislature can legitimately react through criminalisation.[37] Although contact with a terrorist organisation may represent a first step towards radicalisation, countless other steps are required before the person seeking contact comes close to threatening a legal interest or causing any harm. Here, the only suggestion of a wrong is in the subjective *mens rea* requirement that there be 'the intention of receiving instruction for the purpose of the commission of a serious violent offence endangering the state'. Some therefore argue that § 89b StGB – along with other such

[35] On the German offences, see e.g. Backes, 'Der Kampf des Strafrechts' (2008) 654; Deckers and Heusel, 'Strafbarkeit terroristischer Vorbereitungshandlungen' (2008), 169; Gierhake, 'Vorbereitung terroristischer Straftaten' (2008), 397; Sieber, 'Gefährdungsdelikten im Vorfeld von terroristischer Gewalt' (2009), 353; Weißer, 'Terroristischen Bedrohungslagen' (2009), 131; Petzsche, *Strafrecht und Terrorismusbekämpfung* (2013), 168–86, 195–9. On the UK offence, see e.g. Ashworth and Zedner, *Preventive Justice* (2014), 109–13; Ramsay, 'Preparation Offences' (2011); Simester, 'Prophylactic Crimes' (2012).

[36] Bock and Stark, Ch. 3, 'Preparatory Offences' (in this volume).

[37] Bock and Stark, Ch. 3, 'Preparatory Offences' (in this volume).

preparatory offences – fails to fulfil constitutional requirements for criminalisation in German law.[38]

However, while both the UK and German offences cover a wide range of conduct, herein also lies the most notable difference between the two jurisdictions. Whereas the German provisions give an exhaustive list of specific conduct that is covered, the UK offence catches any preparatory conduct. Thus, in the UK, prospective terrorists are guilty of this offence when they eat their morning porridge in preparation for a day's combat training, even though their plans for their terrorist acts remain undeveloped and vague. Eating porridge with terrorist intent has not (yet) been the subject of a prosecution for this offence. However, a wide range of other conduct has been. Although most prosecutions involve conduct of the specific types caught by German law – for example, giving or receiving terrorist training, or obtaining and supplying weapons and other useful materials – some have gone significantly beyond this.[39] Most notably, merely discussing any of these things, or contacting or meeting others for the purpose of discussing them, clearly also counts as relevant preparatory conduct. In cases involving large groups of prospective terrorists, both core and marginal participants can thus be charged with this offence.[40]

Because these offences catch such a broad range of conduct, they also catch conduct of greatly varying seriousness.[41] At their most serious, they catch highly developed and firmly intended conspiracies that have almost become attempted terrorist attacks. A good illustration is the English case of *Khan*.[42] This case involved a large network of prospective terrorists from across the country, whose meetings and communications were

[38] On the discussion in the context of terrorism offences specifically, see Zöller, *Terrorismusstrafrecht* (2009), 585–7, with further references.

[39] See e.g. *R* v. *Tabbakh* [2009] EWCA Crim. 464, [2010] Crim. LR 79; *R* v. *Roddis* [2009] EWCA Crim. 585; *R* v. *Khan* [2009] EWCA Crim. 1085, [2010] 1 Cr. App. R. (S) 35; *Re Coney's Application for Bail* [2012] NIQB 110; *R* v. *Khan* [2013] EWCA Crim. 468; *R* v. *Dart* [2014] EWCA Crim. 2158; *Sarwar* [2015] EWCA Crim. 1886. While mere possession of such materials might not count as 'conduct', acquiring them or choosing to retain them will do so: see *Roddis* at [9].

[40] For vivid illustrations, see e.g. the cases of *Khan* [2009] EWCA Crim. 1085 and *Khan* [2013] EWCA Crim. 468.

[41] This has raised a further question that we cannot explore here: how courts should approach sentencing for these offences. Again, the problem has afflicted UK courts in particular, since the maximum sentence for the UK offence is imprisonment for life. A sentencing guideline has now been produced in response to these problems: see Sentencing Council, *Terrorism Offences: Definitive Guideline*.

[42] *Khan* [2013] EWCA Crim. 468.

covertly surveilled for around two months. The group began by discussing jihadist violence in general terms, before turning to possible attacks in the UK. They discussed the necessary supplies, training and recruitment for such an attack. The discussions gradually became more specific, considering who would be involved in the attacks, and when and where they would take place (the London Stock Exchange was provisionally chosen as a target). Finally, they discussed bombing methods, and some of them experimented with building a pipe bomb. Only at this point were the defendants arrested.

At their least serious, by contrast, these offences catch those who have taken some steps towards their terrorist goals, but whose plans remain vague and preliminary. Again, this is true of both jurisdictions, but especially the UK: as just noted, discussing terrorism with others can suffice for the *actus reus* of the UK offence, even if this never leads to a more serious plan for an attack. A good illustration is the case of *Ulhaq*.[43] The defendant in this case had online conversations with extremists, during which he expressed a desire to go to Syria to join the Islamic State. He contacted a British Islamic State fighter, who gave him practical advice on how to fulfil this desire. However, he did not act on this advice or actually travel to Syria – let alone join the Islamic State or become involved in concrete terrorist plots. Again, it was enough that he intended to commit acts of terrorism, generally defined, and that he had taken some preparatory steps towards this goal.

This brings us to the *mens rea* elements of the offences: the intention to commit or assist an act of terrorism (in UK law) and the firm determination to later commit a serious offence against life or personal freedom (in German law). Since the *actus reus* elements of these offences cover such a broad range of conduct, liability here turns almost entirely on whether the defendant has the required terrorist intention – or perhaps more accurately, on whether such an intention can be proved. This problem is less apparent in more serious cases, involving advanced terrorist plots. In such cases, the principal evidence typically comes from long and intensive covert surveillance, and so defendants are often caught expressing their intentions clearly and repeatedly.[44] Rather, it is in less

[43] *R* v. *Ulhaq* [2016] EWCA Crim. 2209.

[44] See e.g. *Khan* [2009] EWCA Crim. 1085; *Khan* [2013] EWCA Crim. 468; *Dart* [2014] EWCA Crim. 2158. Alternatively, investigators uncover such expressions when acting on information from others, such as concerned family members: see e.g. *Sarwar* [2015] EWCA Crim. 1886.

serious cases, in which such clear evidence is unavailable, that intention tends to become the main issue at trial. The question then becomes crucial of how we can prove the key element of intention at the early stages of (alleged) terrorist plots.

While UK and German law have both had to confront this question, they have answered it in different ways. In particular, UK courts have been readier to accept circumstantial evidence to establish terrorist intent in less serious cases. Two types of such evidence have proved especially important. One is evidence of association with known terrorists, who have often themselves been targets of covert surveillance.[45] The other is evidence of what the defendant possessed. UK prosecutors have invited inferences of terrorist intent from a wide range of possessions, including weapons, explosive materials, and instructions on their use; videos of beheadings and terrorist attacks; other 'extremist material', such as jihadist songs, photos of terrorists, and documents about combat; and even, in more than one case, balaclavas.[46] While the higher courts in the UK have rarely explicitly considered the admissibility of such evidence, the quantity and content of material found can presumably help to justify its use.[47]

Indeed, in some prosecutions for the UK preparation offence, the prosecution case has been based almost entirely on such circumstantial evidence. A good example is the case of *Tabbakh*,[48] in which the defendant, who had assembled some explosive materials, was charged with preparing a terrorist bombing. The evidence of his alleged terrorist intent consisted entirely of other materials found in his possession, such as songs and videos, and his failure to give evidence to explain these materials away. The defendant, who was mentally ill, chose not to give evidence: he feared that, due to his illness, he would appear forgetful and unconvincing. Nevertheless, the trial judge was prepared to allow an adverse inference from his choice to remain silent, given the significance of his testimony in the circumstances of the case. The appellate court agreed and upheld his conviction.

[45] See e.g. *Ulhaq* [2016] EWCA Crim. 2209; *Re Coney's Application for Bail* [2012] NIQB 110.

[46] See e.g. *Tabbakh* [2009] EWCA Crim. 464; *Roddis* [2009] EWCA Crim. 585; *Iqbal* [2010] EWCA Crim. 3215; *Re Coney's Application for Bail* [2012] NIQB 110; *Ulhaq* [2016] EWCA Crim. 2209.

[47] See e.g. the discussion of the videos found in the defendant's possession in *Roddis* [2009] EWCA Crim. 585; *Iqbal* [2010] EWCA Crim. 3215.

[48] *Tabbakh* [2009] EWCA Crim. 464.

Such cases raise the question of whether, in less serious cases, UK law satisfactorily distinguishes terrorist intent from fantasy or obsession. One might worry that it does not: the substantive law requires only intention, rather than firm determination, and this intention need only relate to terrorism in general, rather than any specific terrorist act. Moreover, the evidence from which such intention is typically inferred, such as possession of terrorism-related materials, could equally be evidence of obsession or fantasism – neither of which entails an intention to act. Indeed, this line of defence is often put forward by defendants in less serious cases.[49] The juries who convict these defendants are presumably convinced, having heard all the evidence, that their claims are false. However, based on the substantive law and the evidence as presented in the reports, there seems to be scope for reasonable doubt.

German law, on the other hand, provides a higher threshold in requiring a firm determination to later commit a serious offence against life or personal freedom. In practice, this prevents courts from inferring intent from general evidence of radical beliefs, as has sufficed in many UK cases. The following case illustrates the problems in proving the necessary intention.[50] During a search of the flat of a suspected Islamic terrorist, inter alia a bottle of hydrochloric acid was found and seized. This chemical substance can be used to build explosive devices, but also for cleaning. During the search, the accused's wife had spontaneously declared to the police officers that she herself had bought this bottle for the purpose of cleaning the bathroom. Her husband chose to remain silent. The court found the wife's statement not entirely unbelievable. And even though the accused was found to be in contact with other suspected terrorists, and in possession of a substantial amount of terrorist propaganda material including instructions on how to build explosive devices, it held that sufficient evidence for a terrorist purpose was lacking.

This case illustrates how difficult it can be to secure convictions in German courts in cases where the accused refuses to admit any wrongdoing or chooses to remain silent. Another good illustration is a Frankfurt case, in which the accused was suspected of planning to bomb a bike race taking place in Frankfurt city centre. A pipe bomb, weapons, ammunition and chemicals suitable for building an explosive device

[49] See e.g. *Roddis* [2009] EWCA Crim. 585; *Iqbal* [2010] EWCA Crim. 3215. Some also argue that they engaged in the conduct charged for some other, legitimate purpose: see e.g. *Re Coney's Application for Bail* [2012] NIQB 110; *Tabbakh* [2009] EWCA Crim. 464.

[50] KG Berlin 4 Ws 92/11 [2011] StV 2012, 345.

were found in his cellar. Though he was charged with preparation of terrorism under § 89a StGB, he was (only) convicted of violations of the Weapons Act (*WaffenG*) and Explosives Act (*SprengstoffG*) and of falsification of documents, because the necessary terrorist intent could not be proven beyond a reasonable doubt.[51]

In analysing both the UK and the German offences of preparation of terrorist acts, we can therefore see some striking similarities. Both criminalise a significantly wider range of preparatory conduct than the traditional, general inchoate offences of attempt and conspiracy: in particular, conduct at the early stages of terrorist plots that are still vague in their details. This has led to similar problems and potential criticisms: for example, the criminalisation of neutral conduct, and the consequent problems of proving terrorist intent. However, these problems are significantly more concerning in relation to the UK preparation offence. This offence criminalises any preparatory conduct, rather than conduct of specific types, and requires only a general terrorist intention, rather than a firm determination to commit a relevant offence. The risk of criminalising those who are not truly prospective terrorists therefore seems significantly higher in UK law.

III Encouraging Terrorism

UK law contains two offences that specifically target encouragement of terrorism.[52] The first is the offence called encouragement of terrorism.[53] The *actus reus* of this offence is (i) publishing a statement; (ii) that is likely to be understood as a 'direct or indirect encouragement or other inducement' to commit or prepare acts of terrorism. The required *mens rea* is intention or recklessness as to such encouragement. In cases of reckless encouragement, it is a defence that the statement neither expressed the defendant's views nor had his or her endorsement, and that this was clear in the circumstances. The prosecution need not show that anyone was actually encouraged by the defendant's conduct, or that there was any connection to a particular terrorist act.

[51] LG Frankfurt/Main 5/27 KLs 26/15, 6140 Js 214340/15 [2016].

[52] There are also offences of inciting terrorism overseas: Terrorism Act 2000, ss. 59–61. However, since these do not substantively expand the scope of criminal liability, we do not examine them here.

[53] Terrorism Act 2006, s. 1.

The second and more frequently prosecuted offence is dissemination of terrorist publications.[54] The *actus reus* of this offence encompasses several forms of dissemination, as well as conduct preparatory to dissemination (we say more about this below). What is disseminated must be a 'terrorist publication'. This means a publication that either encourages terrorism (as defined in relation to encouragement of terrorism, above) or the purpose of which is, wholly or primarily, to be useful to prospective terrorists. The *mens rea* is intention or recklessness as to the potential encouragement or assistance, as relevant. For cases of reckless encouragement, the same defence exists as for the previous offence. Again, the prosecution need not prove any connection to a particular terrorist act, or that anyone was actually encouraged or assisted. The maximum penalty for both offences is seven years' imprisonment.

In contrast, German law contains only a single, narrowly defined offence that specifically targets encouragement of terrorism: the offence of encouraging the commission of a serious violent offence endangering the state.[55] The required conduct is displaying or supplying written material that by its content is capable of serving as an instruction to the commission of a serious violent offence endangering the state. The circumstances of dissemination must also be conducive to awakening or encouraging the preparedness of others to commit such an offence. Intention is required as to all these elements of the offence, for which *dolus eventualis* is sufficient. There is no offence (*Tatbestandsausschluss*) if the act serves certain purposes, such as citizenship education, defence against anti-constitutional movements, arts and sciences, research or teaching, or reporting about current or historical events; or if it exclusively serves the fulfilment of lawful professional or official duties. The maximum penalty is three years' imprisonment or a fine.

There are also further special part offences in German criminal law that could catch encouragement of terrorism, but that are not specifically aimed at doing so. While detailed examination of these offences lies beyond the scope of this chapter,[56] it will be helpful briefly to mention the conduct that they target. This includes attempting to cause certain

[54] Terrorism Act 2006, s. 2. The definition of this offence is complex; we present it in a somewhat simplified form here, to aid understanding.

[55] § 91(1) no. 1 StGB.

[56] Although see below for detailed examination of one further such offence: the offence of supporting a terrorist organisation.

offences by means of publishing instructional materials;[57] approving publicly of certain offences, in a manner capable of disturbing the public peace;[58] and disseminating depictions of violence that violate human dignity, in a manner that expresses glorification.[59] For present purposes, the important point to note is that these offences are all limited in their scope: they criminalise only specific forms of encouraging conduct, under specific conditions, in contrast to the general criminalisation of both direct and indirect encouragement in UK law.[60]

These groups of offences have a common function: they expand inchoate liability for assisting and encouraging crime.[61] In both Germany and the constituent jurisdictions of the UK, there are general inchoate offences that target such conduct, but the scope of these offences is limited.[62] For example, they require some connection to a specific prospective crime; they require intentional or at least knowing encouragement; and they require specific types of encouraging conduct, most often direct incitement.[63] The offences described above dispense with some or all of these limitations. However, they vary in the extent to which they do so, and overall, the UK offences have expanded liability in this area to a significantly greater degree. We will highlight three respects in particular in which the UK offences are broader than their German counterparts.

First, UK law criminalises a broader range of encouraging conduct than German law does. In particular, it generally criminalises 'indirect' forms of encouragement: that is, encouragement that does not involve direct instruction or incitement to commit acts of terrorism. The German offence of encouraging a serious violent offence etc. is limited to

57 § 130a StGB.

58 § 140 StGB.

59 § 131 StGB.

60 For more detailed discussion, see Petzsche, 'The Penalization of Public Provocation' (2017), 250–4.

61 Questioning the legitimacy of broadly defined terrorist speech offences, see Petzsche and Cancio Meliá, 'Speaking of Terrorism and Terrorist Speech' (2018), 151.

62 In German law, the relevant general offence is conspiracy, which includes attempted inducement: § 30(1) StGB. In UK jurisdictions, the relevant offence was traditionally the common law offence of incitement, which still applies in Scotland: see e.g. Gane, Stoddart and Chalmers, *A Casebook on Scottish Criminal Law* (2009), 175–7. In English law, however, incitement has been replaced by a complex statutory scheme of inchoate liability for assisting and encouraging crime: Serious Crime Act 2007, ss. 44–6.

63 This is, of course, to oversimplify somewhat. In particular, the new English offences mentioned in the previous note are significantly broader than the old common law in these respects: see Ormerod and Fortson, 'Serious Crime Act 2007' (2009). Still, they remain significantly narrower than the terrorist encouragement offences considered here.

instructional materials that directly encourage terrorism. And although the other provisions mentioned above catch some forms of indirect encouragement, their scope is limited:[64] there is no general offence that catches (say) terrorist propaganda or glorification of terrorist acts.[65] By contrast, the UK offences catch anything that is likely to be understood as encouragement or inducement to commit such acts, including their glorification.[66] To illustrate this difference between the two jurisdictions, it will help to consider some examples.

The most obvious cases of indirect encouragement are materials that explicitly praise or justify acts of terrorism. A common example is videos of terrorist acts that are accompanied by praise for the attackers and their conduct. The dissemination of such material is clearly criminal in the UK,[67] but could be criminal in Germany only if the violence depicted violates human dignity,[68] or if the publication actually provided a tangible benefit for a specific terrorist organisation.[69] A related example is apologia for terrorism. Tracts that aim to justify past acts of terrorism, or acts of terrorism in the abstract, also seem like clear cases of indirect encouragement – so long, at least, as others might realistically apply these justifications to their own current circumstances. Again, dissemination of such material is clearly criminal in the UK,[70] but will be criminal in Germany only if further conditions are satisfied: for example, that the dissemination is also capable of disturbing the public peace.[71]

The differences become even clearer when we consider more marginal cases of indirect encouragement: for example, materials that feature terrorists or terrorist acts, but that do not explicitly praise or justify them. UK courts have been worryingly ready to count such materials

[64] See Petzsche, 'The Penalization of Public Provocation' (2017), 249–54.

[65] Whether this remains the case will have to be seen, since the new EU Terrorism Directive 2017/541 now explicitly specifies 'glorification' as an example of indirect incitement, as part of the offence 'public provocation to commit a terrorist offence'.

[66] 'Glorification' suffices if others 'could reasonably be expected to infer that what is being glorified is being glorified as conduct that should be emulated by them in existing circumstances': Terrorism Act 2006, ss. 1(3) and 2(4).

[67] See e.g. *R* v. *Gul* [2013] UKSC 64, [2014] AC 1260.

[68] An example is videos depicting the beheading of hostages: BGH 3 StR 314/12 [2012] BGHR StGB §129a Abs 5 Unterstützen 4.

[69] BGH 3 StR 314/12 [2012] at [11]. Such conduct would fall under § 129a(5) StGB, the supporting of a terrorist organisation: see below.

[70] See e.g. some of the material discussed in *R* v. *Faraz* [2012] EWCA Crim. 2820, [2013] 1 WLR 2615.

[71] § 140 StGB.

as terrorist publications – presumably because they normalise terrorism or portray it in a positive light, although from the reported cases, it is hard to be sure. Examples include interviews with terrorists, historical and biographical materials, home videos made by terrorists, and even photos of terrorists.[72] In one case, a personal letter from a known terrorist – which appears simply to have described his experiences fighting alongside other terrorists in Pakistan – was deemed, seemingly without controversy, to be a terrorist publication.[73] Since such materials do not serve as instruction, depict violent terrorist acts or express approval of them in a manner that is capable of disturbing the public peace, their dissemination would not be criminal under German law.

Interpretations of the UK offences have been suggested that would narrow their scope towards that of the German law. For example, the English Court of Appeal endorsed one such interpretation in the case of *Faraz*,[74] although their remarks on the point were probably obiter. The court approved of the directions of the trial judge, who had said that 'encouraging' here means encouraging 'directly or by necessary implication'. This interpretation would exclude the marginal cases of indirect encouragement just mentioned, and would thus significantly narrow the gap between the UK and German offences. However, the legal basis of this interpretation is unclear, and it excludes much of the material that has in fact been the basis of prosecutions for these offences – including in *Faraz* itself. Thus, although UK courts might have some scope to limit 'indirect encouragement' through further interpretation, the concept probably remains broad.[75]

A second way in which the UK offences are broader than their German counterparts is that they extend to reckless encouragement. Whereas the applicable German offences require intention as to encouragement, or as to the relevant encouraging conduct, the UK offences can be committed even in the proven absence of any terrorist intent. Although intent in this context includes *dolus eventualis*, this concept remains significantly narrower than recklessness. To be reckless

[72] See e.g. *Faraz* [2012] EWCA Crim. 2820; *R* v. *Iqbal* [2010] EWCA Crim. 3215; *R* v. *Rahman* [2008] EWCA Crim. 1465, [2008] 4 All ER 661.

[73] *R* v. *Rahman* [2008] EWCA Crim. 1465, [2008] 4 All ER 661.

[74] *Faraz* [2012] EWCA Crim. 2820 at [52]–[54].

[75] Part of the problem here is that Parliament rejected a sensible definition of indirect encouragement: i.e. making clear that the relevant acts should be emulated. It is therefore hard to understand what they thought this term should encompass. See Hunt, 'Criminal Prohibitions on Direct and Indirect Encouragement of Terrorism' (2007), 448–51.

as to encouragement in English law, one need only be aware of an unjustifiable risk that one's conduct would assist or encourage terrorism;[76] one need not endorse or otherwise accept this risk. The offences therefore catch (potential) encouragement that is an unwelcome side-effect of the pursuit of some other purpose, such as the expression of moral, political or religious opinion.

To illustrate this difference between the two sets of offences, consider the case of *Bilal Mohammed*.[77] The defendant in this case sold Islamic literature at book stalls, most of which was legal – indeed, all of which was legal before the introduction of the UK offences – but some of which was deemed to glorify terrorism. The prosecution accepted that the defendant himself did not intend to encourage terrorism, but alleged that he was reckless: he knew that this material might fall into the hands of people whom it would encourage. On this basis, he chose to plead guilty, and was sentenced to two years' imprisonment on appeal. By contrast, had the case occurred in Germany, the defendant could not have been prosecuted at all, due to his agreed lack of any terrorist intent.

The scope of liability for recklessly encouraging terrorism might also be even broader in practice than it appears to be on paper, for a couple of reasons. First, English courts notoriously focus on the 'awareness' element of recklessness, to the exclusion of the 'unjustifiability' element.[78] In cases like *Bilal Mohammed*, it seems crucial to know when a risk of encouragement is unjustifiable, but the courts did not address this issue: it was enough that the defendant was aware of the risk, the unjustifiability of which was simply assumed.[79] Secondly, in some encouragement cases, there is worrying evidence that courts have ignored the definition of recklessness altogether. For example, in the case of *Brown*, the court seemingly accepted a pre-sentence report, according to which the defendant did not consider the publication he sold to be dangerous, did not

[76] This is the generally accepted definition of recklessness in English law: see *R* v. *G* [2003] UKHL 50, [2004] 1 AC 1034. In Scots law, however, the mental element of the offence will be even broader than this: while it is hard to be sure, the appropriate test is probably that the accused disregarded or was indifferent to the relevant risk. For the definitive account of recklessness in Scots law, see Stark, 'Rethinking Recklessness' (2011).

[77] Reported in *Rahman* [2008] EWCA Crim. 1465.

[78] Stark, *Culpable Carelessness* (2016), 11. Stark speculates that this neglect is due to the role of prosecutorial discretion in filtering out justified risk-taking in Anglo-American systems, and to the lack of appeals from any jury acquittals due to the justifiability of a risk.

[79] *Rahman* [2008] EWCA Crim. 1465 at [36].

think that it would interest actual terrorists, and did not realise until the trial how his behaviour might be viewed. Nevertheless, he was convicted, and the mental element of the offence was not even considered on appeal.[80]

In response to these concerns, one might point to the defence that is available in cases of reckless encouragement: that the relevant statement or publication did not express the defendant's views or have his or her endorsement, and that this was clear in the circumstances. This defence seems to have been designed for defendants like Bilal Mohammed, who was agreed not to have endorsed the views expressed in the materials that he sold. Yet he did not use the defence, and nor did the defendants in any of the other reported cases of reckless encouragement. We can only speculate as to the reason for this, but perhaps it lies in the second element of the defence: the requirement for the non-endorsement to have been clear. The statute also requires defendants to show that this was clear, which may be interpreted as shifting the burden of proof onto them.[81] Because it is difficult to prove that one clearly did not endorse a given view, the defence is perhaps less attractive in practice than it appears at first glance. The German approach, of explicitly excluding certain legitimate purposes from the scope of the offence, would perhaps also prove more effective in limiting liability for reckless encouragement.[82]

Finally, the UK offences are broader than the German offences in that they catch not only encouragement itself, but also certain conduct preparatory to encouragement. In particular, the dissemination offence catches not only actual dissemination of terrorist publications, but also offering them for sale, hosting them on the internet and even possessing them 'with a view to' their dissemination.[83] While most prosecutions have targeted the actual publication or sale of terrorist materials, some have targeted only such preparatory conduct. For example, in one case, the mere possession of a letter, which the defendant intended to circulate

[80] *R* v. *Brown (Terence Roy)* [2011] EWCA Crim. 2751, [2012] 2 Cr. App. R. (S) 10.

[81] UK courts' approach to interpreting such provisions is less clear than it might be. In relation to the encouragement provisions, higher courts would probably find that the burden on the defendant is evidential only, although it is hard to be certain. See e.g. Ashworth, 'Four Threats to the Presumption of Innocence' (2006), 257–70; Dennis, 'Reverse Onuses and the Presumption of Innocence' (2005).

[82] Arguably, this would also be normatively preferable: see Cornford, 'Indirect Crimes' (2013), 502–5.

[83] Terrorism Act 2006, s. 2(2).

to six other people, was sufficient for the conduct element of the dissemination offence.[84] Once again, such a case would not have been caught by any of the relevant German provisions.

The UK offences of encouraging terrorism, then, are broader than the relevant German offences in several significant respects. However, it is the combination of these that is perhaps the most concerning thing about the UK law in this area. The breadth of 'indirect encouragement' and the lack of a requirement for intention, combined with the apparently relaxed approach of courts and prosecutors to both issues, raise concerns about the impact of these offences on freedom of expression. UK courts have so far been dismissive of challenges on this ground,[85] but further challenges may well be possible. The German approach, which criminalises only those specific types of encouragement that are deemed the most concerning, seems more likely to be judged proportionate as an interference with this right.[86]

IV Offences Related to Terrorist Organisations

The central provision of the German terrorism offences is § 129a StGB.[87] It covers specific conduct in the context of a terrorist organisation, such as the formation of such an organisation, participation as a member[88] and supporting the organisation or recruiting members or supporters.[89] It is necessary to distinguish among these different types of conduct within the *actus reus* element. However, all require as a reference point the existence of a terrorist organisation. This raises the question of what requirements need to be fulfilled in order for a group of people to be a terrorist organisation, within the meaning of § 129a StGB. The provision does not contain a singular definition of a terrorist organisation, but subsections 1, 2 and 3 describe the basis on which a group would be considered as such.[90] This structure is quite complicated: broadly

84 *Rahman* [2008] EWCA Crim. 1465.

85 *Brown* [2011] EWCA Crim. 2751 at [20]–[21]; *Faraz* [2012] EWCA Crim. 2820 at [49]–[57].

86 Petzsche, 'The Penalization of Public Provocation' (2017), 254–6.

87 While there have never been high absolute numbers of convictions, the number has risen in recent years and is expected to rise further due to returnees from Syria: see Tabelle 2.1, Fachserie 10 (Rechtspflege) Reihe 3 der Strafverfolgungsstatistik.

88 § 129a(1) StGB; with a higher penalty for 'ringleaders or hintermen': § 129a(4) StGB.

89 § 129a(5) StGB.

90 To be read in conjunction with § 129(2) StGB.

speaking, the group must have a certain organisational structure,[91] and its aims or activities must be directed at the commission of certain offences.[92]

In order to fall under this provision, an organisation does not need to be proscribed. Rather, the courts will consider in each individual case whether the relevant group fulfils the requirements for being a terrorist organisation, as was recognised e.g. for the Red Army Faction (RAF).[93] Foreign terrorist organisations such as Jabhat al-Nusra and the Islamic State[94] are also covered.[95]

For both § 129a(1) and (5), the required *mens rea* is the lowest form of intent (*dolus eventualis*). The offender needs to know that the aim of the terrorist organisation is directed at the commission of the listed crimes and must knowingly accept this.[96]

Again, the German provision is quite extensive and broadens the scope of inchoate liability by encompassing many preparatory acts. It is especially notable that no terrorist crime need ever be committed (by the organisation) for the members etc. to face a penalty of up to ten years' imprisonment; it is enough for the organisation to be aimed at the commission of crimes. In addition, as we will examine further below, the *actus reus* covers a wide range of conduct that goes beyond active participation as a member.

91 Detailed in § 129(2) StGB.

92 To give a more detailed overview of the structure of the offence: § 129a StGB contains additional requirements covering organisations whose aims or activities are directed at the commission of certain serious crimes such as genocide (§ 129a(1) StGB); at the commission of certain less serious offences such as offences against the environment or violations of the Weapons of War (Control) Act, combined with an additional intent requirement (§ 129a(2) StGB); or even at threatening the commission of one of the offences listed in § 129a(1) or (2) StGB (§ 129a(3) StGB).

93 There have been numerous cases dealing with its main, sub- and subsequent bodies: BGH 3 StR 28/82 [1982] BGHSt 31, 16; 3 StR 526/83 [1984] BGHSt 32, 243; 3 StR 62/84 [1984] BGHSt 33, 16; I BGs 151/89 [1989] BGHSt 36, 205; 3 StR 284/05 [2006] NStZ-RR 2006, 232.

94 BGH AK 61, AK 62/17 [2017] NStZ-RR 2018, 44.

95 §§ 129a, 129b StGB.

96 For organisations within the meaning of § 129a(2) StGB, an additional and stronger intent is necessary: the offender needs to intend the (planned) criminal acts to seriously intimidate a population; to unduly compel a government or international organisation to perform or abstain from performing any act; or to seriously destabilise or destroy the fundamental political, constitutional, economic or social structures of a country or an international organisation.

The UK offences relating to terrorist organisations are set out in the Terrorism Act 2000. They apply only to specific 'proscribed organisations' that are listed in a schedule to the Act,[97] to which the Home Secretary has the power to add.[98] The Home Secretary may proscribe an organisation only if he or she believes that it is 'concerned in terrorism', which includes the commission, preparation and encouragement of terrorist acts.[99] The offences relate to membership of, inviting support for, and wearing the uniform of a proscribed organisation.[100] While these offences are not as central in the UK regime as they are in Germany, they are still important: following the offences of preparation and possession, they are the most frequently used as a principal charge in terrorism prosecutions in the UK.[101]

As Liat Levanon has argued, such offences function as further extensions of inchoate liability for preparing, assisting, encouraging and conspiring to commit crimes.[102] In one respect, they are narrower than the offences considered so far: they apply only in relation to terrorist organisations – in the UK, organisations that have been explicitly proscribed[103] – rather than terrorist activity in general. In other respects, however, they are broader. By itself, membership of a terrorist organisation need not involve preparation for, assistance or encouragement of, or even agreement to participate in any act of terrorism. Moreover, both the UK and German offences extend significantly beyond

[97] Terrorism Act 2000, sch. 2.

[98] Similarly, the German Law on Associations (*VereinsG*) allows in s 3 for an association to be prohibited by either the Home Secretary (*Bundesminister des Innern*) or certain designated governmental bodies of the *Länder* if its purposes or activities are in conflict with criminal law, or are contrary to the constitutional order or the idea of international cooperation.

[99] Terrorism Act 2000, s. 3.

[100] Terrorism Act 2000, ss. 11–13. We will not discuss the last of these offences here, as it is relatively non-serious and has led to few reported cases. German law knows a similar offence in § 20(1) no. 5 VereinsG, which criminalises wearing the insignia of a proscribed association as a summary offence, with imprisonment up to a year or a fine. However, § 20 VereinsG is subsidiary to the criminal offence in § 129a StGB, meaning it is only applicable if the same conduct is not covered by § 129a StGB. Therefore, this section has (so far) gained little importance in the context of terrorist organisations.

[101] Home Office, *Operation of Police Powers under the Terrorism Act 2000* (2018), Table A.05a.

[102] Levanon, 'Criminal Prohibitions on Membership in Terrorist Organisations' (2012)

[103] This limitation is not without its problems, given the sometimes diffuse and/or splintered nature of terrorist organisations. See e.g. *R* v. *Z* [2005] UKHL 35, [2005] 2 AC 645.

active membership of such organisations. To illustrate how, let us consider the provisions in turn.

Consider first the membership provisions. § 129a(1) StGB criminalises the forming of a terrorist organisation[104] and participation as a member with imprisonment from one to ten years. Participating as a member requires that the person, by integration into the organisation, submits to its will and carries out an activity aimed at promoting its criminal objectives.[105] For this purpose, it is necessary for participation in the life of the organisation to be planned for a relatively long period of time, though it is sufficient if the offender later only actually takes action once.[106] Mere activities for the organisation without integration, however intensive they may be, are not sufficient, for an outsider does not become a member by the promotion of the organisation alone. Rather, membership by its very nature presupposes a relationship that cannot be imposed on the organisation, but that requires its approval. Participation as a member is therefore excluded if these actions are not supported by a shared intention that the defendant continue to participate in the organisation.[107] Examples of participating as a member are seeking funds for the purchase of military equipment or calling to travel to the Syrian civil war zone and fight there.[108] However, participation is possible even through legal conduct: for example, through participation in demonstrations and cultural activities.[109]

The UK membership provision makes it an offence simply to belong to, or to profess to belong to, a proscribed organisation.[110] Unlike the German provision, the offence requires no *mens rea* as to the nature of the organisation: the defendant need not know or suspect that the relevant organisation was proscribed, or even that it was concerned in

[104] Forming a terrorist organisation means playing a leading and guiding role in its creation. See BGH 3 StR 427/77, 21.12.1977, BGHSt 27, 325 (327); Schäfer, '§ 129 StGB' (2017), mn. 77; Heger, '§ 129 StGB' (2018), mn. 4.

[105] See BGH 3 StR 5/63 [1963] BGHSt 18, 296, 299 f.; 3 StR 552/08 [2009] BGHSt 54, 69, 111; Schäfer, '§ 129 StGB' (2017), mn. 82.

[106] BGH StB 52/79, 22.10.1979, BGHSt 29, 114 (122); 3 StR 9/80, 11.6.1980, BGHSt 29, 288 (294); 3 StR 552/08, 14.8.2009, BGHSt 54, 69 (111); Schäfer, '§ 129 StGB' (2017) mn. 82; Fischer, '§ 129 StGB' (2018), mn. 24.

[107] BGH StB 12/11 [2011] NStZ-RR 2011, 372. This prerequisite definitely raises questions of proof.

[108] BGH AK 54/17 [2017] NStZ-RR 2018, 42 at [28].

[109] BGH StB 23/16 [2016] BGHR StGB § 129a Abs 1 Mitgliedschaft 3.

[110] Terrorism Act 2000, s. 11(1).

terrorism.[111] However, it is a defence that the organisation was not proscribed when the defendant first became or professed to be a member, and that he or she has not been involved in its activities since its proscription.[112] The maximum sentence for the membership offence is ten years' imprisonment.

This offence catches a broader range of conduct than the equivalent German offence. On the one hand, the concept of 'membership' is probably limited in similar ways in both jurisdictions. The English Court of Appeal has indicated (albeit *obiter*) that unilateral alignment with an organisation, or even active promotion of its aims, is not enough; membership requires an additional 'element of acceptance or reciprocity'.[113] On the other hand, whereas the German offence requires at least active participation as a member, the UK offence simply requires membership. Passive or nominal membership of a terrorist organisation will therefore suffice for criminal liability in the UK.[114]

Moreover, the UK provision catches not only actual membership but also professed membership of proscribed organisations. Exactly what 'professed membership' means is unclear; in the leading case, the House of Lords (then the UK's highest court) was divided on this point.[115] In one judge's opinion, given the aims of the offence, it should be interpreted as catching only believable declarations of membership.[116] In another's opinion, it seems to catch all declarations of membership, no matter how unbelievable.[117] On either view, the offence clearly extends to at least some people who are not actual members of a proscribed organisation. Again, the law here criminalises fantasists as well as actual prospective terrorists – a risk that, in this instance, the courts themselves have acknowledged.[118]

111 See e.g. *R* v. *Hundal* [2004] EWCA Crim. 389, [2004] 2 Cr. App. R. 19.

112 Terrorism Act 2000, s. 11(2). The defendant bears only an evidential burden in relation to this defence: see *Attorney-General's Reference (No. 4 of 2002)* [2004] UKHL 43, [2005] 1 AC 264.

113 *R* v. *Ahmed* [2011] EWCA Crim. 184, [2011] Crim. LR 734 at [89].

114 Thus, it does not matter if (for example) the defendant's joining the organisation and participation in its activities occurred in another jurisdiction; he or she needs simply to have been a member whilst in the UK: see *Hundal* [2004] EWCA Crim. 389.

115 *Attorney-General's Reference (No. 4 of 2002)* [2004] UKHL 43.

116 Lord Rodger, *ibid.*, [64].

117 Lord Bingham, *ibid.*, [48].

118 *Ibid.*, per Lord Bingham. In fact, Lord Bingham observed that the defendant in the instant case might well have come into this category.

Consider next the offence of supporting a terrorist or proscribed organisation. In German law, support of a terrorist organisation and recruitment of members or supporters for a terrorist organisation are penalised with imprisonment from six months to ten years. Support[119] encompasses certain forms of aiding and abetting by non-members. Though the wording encompasses a wide range of activities, its scope is narrowed by the requirements that such acts be effective in promoting, enhancing or securing the specific potential threat that the organisation poses, and in benefiting the organisation. It is sufficient if the organisation is promoted in its endeavours and its activity, such as by procuring military equipment and handing it over to the organisation, so that it is at their disposal.[120] However, it is not enough for the accused to try to send money – unsuccessfully. Nor did the handing over of clothes, food and deodorant, as well as €275, to a foreign terrorist fighter fulfil the *actus reus* requirement, because the necessary link to the organisation was missing, and no positive effect on the organisation could be proven: the benefit remained exclusively with the member and did not benefit the organisation as a supra-individual entity.[121]

Mere endorsements of organisations like Al-Qaeda, justification of their aims or glorification of their criminal acts do not constitute the offence of supporting terrorism in German law.[122] For example, the highest federal court held that it was not enough to provide a link to a video of 'Al-Qaeda in the Land of the Two Rivers', which showed the beheading of an American hostage by the leader of the group, Abu Musab Al Zarkawi, in 2004.[123] The execution was preceded by a message in which Al Zarkawi referred to the events in Abu Ghraib and called on all Muslims to fight and take revenge on America. In his speech, which was translated in subtitles, the leader said, inter alia: 'Kill the polytheists, wherever you find them!' The court found that posting the link did not provide a tangible benefit for the terrorist organisation.[124] It is commendable that this section is construed narrowly by German courts.

[119] § 129a(5) cl. 1 StGB.

[120] BGH AK 10/15 [2015] NStZ-RR 2015, 242. It is not relevant if it is then stolen from the organisation.

[121] BGH StB 18/17, [2017] NStZ-RR 2018, 72 at [20].

[122] BGH 3 StR 314/12 [2015] BGHR StGB § 129a Abs 5 Unterstützen 4; von Heintschel-Heinegg, '§ 129a StGB' (2016), mn. 17.

[123] BGH 3 StR 314/12 [2015] BGHR StGB § 129a Abs 5 Unterstützen 4.

[124] *Ibid.*, [11]. However, this did not mean that the defendant was acquitted. Even though the court had quashed the conviction under § 129a(5) StGB, it stressed that other

Recruitment[125] must be directed towards the group's organisational preservation or enhancement, through recruiting new members or third-party supporters. It encompasses propaganda activities that are beneficial to the organisation and that are directed at individuals or the public. The penalty is imprisonment from six months to five years.[126] The recruitment must be undertaken in favour of a specific terrorist organisation: a general call to participate in terrorist acts or in the 'Jihad' does not suffice.[127] German courts have been strict in requiring this threshold to be met: the mere posting of propaganda is not sufficient by itself; posts are examined to determine whether they actually solicit new members or supporters. An example in which the court considered the acts to be recruitment was the following message in a video: participation in the violent 'Jihad' under the leadership of Al-Qaeda and Osama bin Laden is the legitimate continuation of a defensive fight by Muslims against aggressions of the Western world that has been going on since the Crusades, and is thus the duty of every believer. This message showed not only that the perpetrator clearly embraced Osama Bin Laden's appeal to participate in the 'Jihad', and thus to undertake violent actions on the side of Al-Qaeda, but also that he approached the addressees with the request to support the 'brothers' with funds and to risk their lives in support.[128]

The UK offence of supporting a proscribed organisation[129] encompasses three types of conduct: (i) inviting support for a proscribed organisation; (ii) arranging a meeting, knowing that the meeting is to support or further the aims of such an organisation;[130] and (iii) addressing a meeting oneself, for the same purpose. While the 'inviting support' branch of the offence appears to lack a *mens rea* element, courts have found that the word 'invite' implies a requirement of intention: there can

criminal offences were indeed applicable, mainly § 131 StGB – the dissemination of depictions of violence.

125 § 129a(5) cl. 2 StGB.

126 In cases under subsections (1) and (2), and to imprisonment not exceeding five years or a fine in cases under subsection (3).

127 Von Heintschel-Heinegg, '§ 129a StGB' (2016), mn. 15a.

128 BGH 3 StR 197/14 [2015] BGHR StGB § 129a Abs 5 Werben 4.

129 Terrorism Act 2000, s. 12.

130 This branch of the offence also encompasses meetings that are to be addressed by a member of a proscribed organisation; in such cases, it is a defence that the defendant had no reasonable cause to believe that the address would support the organisation or further its activities: Terrorism Act 2000, s. 11(2).

be no such thing as an unintentional 'invitation' of support.[131] Again, the maximum penalty for this offence is ten years' imprisonment.

This offence is also broader in scope than its German counterpart. In one important respect, the two offences are similar: like the German support provision, this offence does not catch mere endorsement of proscribed organisations or mere expression of support for them.[132] However, unlike the German provision, it does not require the defendant to succeed in benefiting the organisation or its activities. Indeed, people have been convicted under this section where it was accepted that their conduct did not actually encourage anyone to support the relevant organisation.[133] Courts have also confirmed that 'support' here extends beyond practical support: it also includes encouragement and advocacy.[134] Thus, while it is not criminal in UK law merely to express support for a proscribed organisation, it is criminal to invite others, even unsuccessfully, to advocate for such an organisation.

Also notable is that defendants need only invite support for the proscribed organisation; they need not invite support for its commission or preparation of terrorist acts.[135] Again, there have been convictions under this section where this is all that was proved. For example, in one case, the defendants had posted talks online that did not encourage violence or terrorism, but that did encourage support for the Islamic State.[136] In another, the defendants were recorded at meetings making speeches that had similar content.[137] For prosecutors, this is perhaps the most attractive feature of this offence. As we have seen, other UK offences already catch involvement in an organisation's terrorist activities, as well as many ways of encouraging these activities; a charge of supporting the organisation will be tempting because it requires neither of these.

131 *R* v. *Choudary* [2016] EWCA Crim. 61, [2018] 1 WLR 695 at [42].

132 *Ibid.*, [70]. The English Court of Appeal relied on this point in holding that the interference of s. 12 with the defendants' right to free expression was proportionate.

133 See e.g. *R* v. *Alamgir* [2018] EWCA Crim. 21.

134 *Choudary* [2016] EWCA Crim. 61 at [52]–[60].

135 How significant this point is will depend on the character of the organisation concerned. If an organisation is exclusively or constitutively directed towards the commission of terrorist acts, then support for the organisation might arguably entail support for such acts. However, as mentioned above, proscribed organisations need only be concerned in terrorism; this need not be their sole or defining aim.

136 *Choudary* [2016] EWCA Crim. 61.

137 *Alamgir* [2018] EWCA Crim. 21.

Again, then, there are notable similarities between the approaches taken in the two jurisdictions to the criminalisation of terrorist organisations. Both have criminalised types of involvement with such organisations that go beyond the actual preparation, assistance or encouragement of specific terrorist activities. But UK law goes significantly further in the types of involvement that it criminalises. In particular, it criminalises membership and invitation of support even when these yield no benefit for the organisation's activities. Its membership offence also extends beyond active membership to passive, nominal and even merely professed membership of proscribed organisations. While both sets of offences have thus significantly expanded criminal liability in this area, the UK offences have again done so to a greater degree.

V Terrorism-Related Possession Offences

Finally, both the UK and Germany have expanded the scope of inchoate criminal liability in relation to terrorism by creating new offences of possession.[138] This is not an unusual strategy: in both jurisdictions, the general inchoate offences are already supplemented by offences that criminalise, for example, the unlawful possession of nuclear, biological, chemical[139] and other weapons.[140] However, what is unusual in these new offences is their criminalisation of less ostensibly dangerous articles, because of their potential connection to terrorism. Once again, UK law has gone significantly further than German law in this respect, both in the relevant legislation and in practice: the possession offences are the second most frequently prosecuted terrorism offences in UK law, following the preparation offence.[141] Indeed, it should be emphasised that these UK statistics refer to prosecution as a principal charge. In a significant proportion of UK terrorism prosecutions, possession has thus been the most serious conduct alleged against the defendant.

The main German possession offence that is specifically relevant to the context of terrorism is that contained in § 91(1) no. 2 StGB. This

[138] On the principled concerns regarding possession offences, see Ambos, 'Possession' (2015), 391, with further references.

[139] In German law, see §§ 19 ff. Weapons of War (Control) Act (*KriegswaffenKontrollG*). In UK law, see Chemical Weapons Act 1996, s. 2; Terrorism Act 2006, s. 9.

[140] In German law, see § 51 WaffenG. In UK law, see Firearms Act 1968, ss. 1, 2 and 5; and in English law, Criminal Justice Act 1988, ss. 139 and 141.

[141] Home Office, *Operation of Police Powers under the Terrorism Act 2000* (2018), Table A.05a.

criminalises whosoever obtains written material which by its content is capable of serving as an instruction to the commission of a serious violent offence endangering the state, for the purpose of committing such an offence. Again, possession for certain purposes is explicitly excluded from the scope of the offence: for example, citizenship education, defence against anti-constitutional movements, arts and sciences, research or teaching, or reporting about current or historical events. Possession is also excluded if it exclusively serves the fulfilment of lawful professional or official duties. However, the *actus reus* covers having at one's disposal material that can include not only 'dangerous' material, such as instructions on how to build a bomb, but also neutral material,[142] such as a textbook on flying or operating instructions for a cell phone.[143] In these cases, it remains unclear where the objective wrong of the act lies, of the kind required to legitimise criminal sanctions according to German doctrine. Consequently, questions regarding its constitutionality have been raised.[144]

UK law, by contrast, contains two terrorist possession offences. The first is the offence of possession for terrorist purposes. The *actus reus* of this offence is possessing an article 'in circumstances which give rise to a reasonable suspicion that [the] possession is for a purpose connected with the commission, preparation or instigation of an act of terrorism'.[145] Courts have interpreted this to mean a purpose of using the article for the commission etc. of an act of terrorism.[146] The offence has no further *mens rea* element, but it is a defence that the defendant's possession of

142 The German legislator stressed that such material is covered: BT-Drs. 16/12428, 18. This view is mostly supported in the literature: see Schäfer, '§ 91 StGB' (2017) mn. 11; Fischer, '§ 91 StGB' (2018) mn. 7; Sieber, 'Legitimation und Grenzen von Gefährdungsdelikten' (2009), 353, 363; Gazeas, Grosse-Wilde and Kießling, 'Die neuen Tatbestände im Staatsschutzstrafrecht' (2009), 593, 602; Petzsche, *Strafrecht und Terrorismusbekämpfung* (2013), 207.

143 Cases in the highest federal court dealing with this section were decisions on pre-trial custody. They mostly dealt with explosive devices (such as explosive belts: BGH AK 56/17 [2017] StV 2018, 103; a tweet on how to build a bomb: AG München 1117 Ds 111 Js 206538/14 [2016]) or weapons (a Kalashnikov: BGH AK 56/17 [2017] StV 2018, 103). Though in one decision, a tunnel drilling machine manual – together with instructions on explosives – was found to be covered by § 91(1) no. 2 StGB (BGH AK 42/17 [2017] NStZ-RR 2018, 10).

144 Gierhake, 'Zur geplanten Einführung' (2008), 397; Radtke and Steinsiek, 'Bekämpfung des internationalen Terrorismus' (2008), 383; Weißer, 'Über den Umgang des Strafrechts' (2009), 131; Zöller, *Terrorismusstrafrecht* (2009), 214–9.

145 Terrorism Act 2000, s. 57(1).

146 *R* v. *Zafar* [2008] EWCA Crim. 184, [2008] QB 810.

the article was not actually for a terrorist purpose.[147] If the defendant offers some evidence that he or she had a non-terrorist purpose, then the prosecution must disprove this claimed purpose beyond a reasonable doubt.[148] This is the more serious of the two offences, carrying a maximum sentence of fifteen years' imprisonment.[149]

This offence is broader than the offence under § 91(1) no. 2 StGB in two respects. First, it encompasses possession of any article, rather than just written materials that provide instruction. While such materials are certainly caught by the offence,[150] it is primarily used to prosecute those who are found in possession of bomb-making ingredients: articles that may have legitimate everyday uses, but that can also be used in making or detonating explosives.[151] The offence has also been used to target propaganda materials,[152] as well as a range of 'legitimate' articles recovered in suspicious circumstances. Its breadth is well-illustrated by this list of articles targeted in just one case: 'two steel batons, two sleeping bags, a portable computer hard drive, a compact disc, night vision binoculars, medical clothing, three rucksacks, two British passports, a number of mobile telephones and nearly £9,000 in cash'.[153]

Secondly, terrorist intent plays a different role within this offence than it does within § 91(1) no. 2. Under the German provision, intention to commit a serious violent offence endangering the state is a required *mens rea* element of the offence. By contrast, under the UK provision, what is required is a circumstantial element of reasonable suspicion of a terrorist purpose. It is for defendants to raise their lack of terrorist purpose as a defence. In theory, one can thus be convicted of the UK offence in the

[147] Terrorism Act 2000, s. 57(2).

[148] *Ibid.*, s. 118; *R* v. *G* [2009] UKHL 13, [2010] 1 AC 43 at [67]–[68].

[149] Terrorism Act 2000, s. 57(4).

[150] This means that there is a substantial overlap between this offence and the second UK possession offence, discussed below: confirmed in *R* v. *Rowe* [2007] EWCA Crim. 635, [2007] QB 975. Examples of prosecutions under this section involving instructional materials include *R* v. *Worrell* [2009] EWCA Crim. 1431, [2010] 1 Cr. App. R. (S) 27; *R* v. *Muhammed* [2009] EWCA Crim. 2653, [2010] 1 Cr. App. R. 103; *Siddique* v. *HM Advocate* [2010] HCJAC 7, 2010 JC 110; *R* v. *Lusha* [2010] EWCA Crim. 1761.

[151] See e.g. *Worrell* [2009] EWCA Crim. 1431, [2010] 1 Cr. App. R. (S) 27; *R* v. *Lusha* [2010] EWCA Crim. 1761; *R* v. *Khyam* [2008] EWCA Crim. 1612; *R* v. *Wong* [2012] NICA 54. Though, as described above, in German law the possession of such ingredients can be prosecuted under § 89a StGB, if the necessary terrorist intent is proven.

[152] Although only in restricted circumstances: as mentioned above, such materials must be possessed for the purpose of instigating terrorism. See *Zafar* [2008] EWCA Crim. 184 at [29]–[31].

[153] *Attorney-General's Reference (No. 7 of 2008)* [2008] EWCA Crim. 1054 at [3].

absence of a proven terrorist purpose.[154] In practice, however, this might not be a significant difference. The reported cases suggest that only very modest evidence of a non-terrorist purpose is required before the defence must be left to the jury; in none of these cases did the courts doubt that a terrorist purpose had been proved.[155] Rather, the greater concern is what courts accept as proof of a terrorist purpose in the first place. As with the UK preparation offence, examined above, it is questionable whether terrorist intention is adequately distinguished here from fantasy.[156]

The second terrorism-related possession offence in UK law is the offence of collecting or possessing information 'of a kind likely to be useful to a person committing or preparing an act of terrorism'.[157] This means information that provides 'practical assistance' to terrorists and that 'would typically be of use to terrorists, as opposed to ordinary members of the population'.[158] The courts have read into this offence a *mens rea* element of knowledge of the nature of the material possessed.[159] However, unlike both the German offence and the previous UK offence, this offence does not require any terrorist purpose or intent. It is a defence that the defendant had a 'reasonable excuse' for his or her possession;[160] however, lack of a terrorist purpose is not a reasonable excuse, in and of itself.[161] While this is the less serious of the two possession offences, it nevertheless carries a maximum sentence of ten years' imprisonment.[162]

The complete irrelevance of terrorist intent to this offence is the main difference between it and § 91(1) no. 2. To understand why this

[154] It is therefore difficult to see this offence as anything other than a blatant attempt to circumvent the presumption of innocence: see e.g. Duff, *Answering for Crime* (2007), 10.2–10.3; Tadros and Tierney, 'The Presumption of Innocence and the Human Rights Act' (2004), 406–16.

[155] Indeed, in the only case in which there was any doubt, the accused's conviction was quashed, as the jury had not been properly directed on the relevance of his claims about his purpose: *Siddique* [2010] HCJAC 7.

[156] See e.g. *Attorney-General's Reference (No. 7 of 2008)* [2008] EWCA Crim. 1054. The defendant in this case was described as a 'Walter Mitty character'; both the sentencing and appellate courts recognised a substantial chance that his statements of terrorist intent were mere exaggeration or play-acting. Nevertheless, he was convicted, and on appeal, he did not even raise the issue of what his purpose had been.

[157] Terrorism Act 2000, s. 58(1).

[158] *G* [2009] UKHL 13 at [43].

[159] *G* [2009] UKHL 13 at [47].

[160] Terrorism Act 2000, s. 58(3).

[161] *G* [2009] UKHL 13 at [71]–[85].

[162] Terrorism Act 2000, s. 58(4).

difference is significant, however, we must first understand what constitutes information 'likely to be useful to' a prospective terrorist. As with the German offence, this definition seems to catch entirely neutral material: favourite examples in the UK include train timetables and city maps.[163] This is why, as noted above, the courts have insisted that the offence be limited to material that is practically useful to prospective terrorists, rather than ordinary people. However, while this interpretation has genuinely narrowed the scope of the offence,[164] it still catches much neutral information. Seemingly, to fall within the offence, information need only be useful to prospective terrorists and not useful to ordinary people. It is therefore irrelevant that the information has other uses besides terrorist uses, or even that its practical value for terrorists is limited.[165]

Two recent decisions of the English Court of Appeal illustrate this point powerfully. The first concerned an electronic document entitled 'Draft ideas', which two of the defendants had written. This contained practical tips in bullet-point form, mostly concerning how to avoid detection by the authorities. It would admittedly have been useful to anyone with such a purpose, such as ordinary criminals. The appellate court concluded without hesitation that, on the interpretive approach just mentioned, the document contained information likely to be useful to a terrorist.[166] The second case concerned a physical fitness regime, comprising a hand-written list of exercises under the heading 'Mujahid minimum training'. Again, the appellate court concluded unhesitatingly that this document fell within the scope of the offence: crucial here was its striking similarity to materials written by known terrorists, which suggested that it was designed for terrorist rather than innocent uses.[167]

Because this offence catches such a wide range of information, the 'reasonable excuse' defence becomes crucial in limiting its scope. Yet as we noted above, a non-terrorist purpose is not a reasonable excuse, in and of itself. Rather, a reasonable excuse seems to require an objectively reasonable explanation: the defendant must provide good reasons for his

[163] See e.g. *G* [2009] UKHL 13 at [42].

[164] E.g. it will no longer catch documents containing propaganda or glorification, which had been the subject of some earlier prosecutions: see e.g. *R* v. *Malik* [2008] EWCA Crim. 1450.

[165] See e.g. Hodgson and Tadros, 'How to Make a Terrorist Out of Nothing' (2009), 987–90; Cornford, 'Narrowing the Scope of Absurdly Broad Offences' (2017), 293.

[166] *R* v. *Muhammed* [2010] EWCA Crim. 227, [2010] 3 All ER 759.

[167] *R* v. *Amjad* [2016] EWCA Crim. 1618, [2017] 1 Cr. App. R. 22.

or her possession of the relevant information. Innocent purposes for possession – research, professional interest, idle curiosity, personal amusement, freedom of expression; purposes that are mostly explicitly excluded from the German offence – might or might not be good enough reasons; it will be for the jury to decide.[168] The result is that the criticism of the German offence – that it does not require an objective wrong that legitimises criminal sanctions – applies even more forcefully to the second UK offence. For this offence does not even require any subjective culpability that might legitimise punishment. If wrongdoing and/or culpability should indeed be required for this purpose, then it is hard to see any plausible justification for the collection of information offence.

VI Conclusion

In both the UK and Germany, there has been a general development to broaden the scope of criminal liability in the context of terrorism. On this pre-emptive approach, not only terrorist acts themselves but also much conduct preparatory to them are criminalised. These pre-emptive offences can be grouped into different categories, including offences of preparing terrorist acts, offences of encouraging terrorism, offences related to terrorist organisations and terrorism-related possession offences. In all these cases, both jurisdictions have departed significantly from the traditional principles of inchoate criminal liability. Although there are differences in the make-up of these offences, the resulting problems are similar: the breadth of their *actus reus* elements, the resulting importance of *mens rea* (and the evidential problems that this creates), the fact that neutral or innocent conduct is covered, the legitimacy and proportionality of the offences and their interference with individuals' rights. Both countries have thus witnessed worrisome developments in this area of law. However, the UK offences are, in almost every aspect, broader than their German counterparts.

All of this raises the question of why the UK has consistently gone further than Germany in this context. The question is worth asking, since both countries – being subject to the same international and European

[168] See e.g. *G* [2009] UKHL 13 at [71]–[85]; *R* v. *Y* [2010] EWCA Crim. 762, [2010] 1 WLR 2644; *Brown* [2011] EWCA Crim. 2751 at [22]. A claimed reasonable excuse need not be left to the jury if it is not capable of being reasonable in this objective sense: examples are unlawful purposes or the defendant's severe mental illness. See further *R* v. *F* [2007] EWCA Crim. 243, [2007] QB 960.

obligations – have expanded their criminal laws in similar ways and for similar reasons. A large part of the answer doubtless lies in differing political dynamics and processes. However, to assess these would mostly be speculation on our part, as few answers can be found even in the respective legislative histories: both German and UK legislators have shared little information on why they created the offences examined here, or why they defined them exactly as they did.

Another part of the answer might lie in legal factors that differ between the two systems, which might make such expansion of the criminal law more difficult in Germany than it is in the UK. Here, the above analysis allows us to make some tentative observations, although again, we can ultimately only speculate. For example, consider the differing *actus reus* elements of the preparation offences: for the UK offence, any preparatory conduct; and for § 89a StGB, a comprehensive list of criminalised conduct. This difference might be explained partly by the German constitutional principle of certainty (*Bestimmtheitsgebot*), which obliges the legislature to describe the preconditions of criminal liability in a concrete way, such that the scope of the offence and its application result from the wording of the provision – or at least, can be determined by interpretation.[169] While a comparable principle exists in UK law, especially since the incorporation of the European Convention on Human Rights, it excludes only offences framed in impossibly vague language.[170] The UK preparation offence would almost certainly be held compatible with this principle.[171]

A further example is the requirement of German doctrine that criminalised behaviour constitute a wrong in itself, to which the legislature can legitimately react through criminalisation. As we have seen, this requirement seemingly serves to halt the expansion of German criminal law, and generates potential challenges to some of the offences examined

[169] BVerfGE 92, 1 (11 ff.). This obligation serves a dual purpose. On the one hand, it is intended to ensure that the norm addressees can foresee which conduct is prohibited and punishable. On the other hand, it is intended to ensure that the decision on punishable conduct is taken in advance by the legislature and not subsequently by the executive or judicial authorities.

[170] See e.g. the discussion in Simester et al., *Simester and Sullivan's Criminal Law* (2016), 21–32.

[171] It is worth noting here that the second possession offence examined above – an offence framed in language far more vague than that of the preparation offence – was found to be compatible with this minimal requirement of certainty. See *Jobe* v. *UK* (2011) 53 EHRR SE17.

above. By contrast, there is no such requirement in UK law, and thus no similar doctrinal discussion. Although criminal law theorists might accept the absence of wrongfulness as a valid criticism of criminal legislation, such criticisms do not amount to potential legal challenges.

Ultimately, however, the limiting effect of such principles is difficult to prove. For example, in relation to offences of encouraging terrorism, one would expect human rights concerns – especially respect for freedom of expression – to have played a pivotal role in the definition of these offences. Since UK law criminalises a broader range of encouraging conduct than German law does – and since UK courts have displayed a dismissive attitude towards the few challenges brought on grounds of freedom of expression – one might argue that German law shows greater respect for this fundamental right. But while this might be a result of the German approach, it remains unclear whether it was intended: again, the German legislator did not explicitly address this question in the legislative history. Therefore, it is difficult to conclude with any certainty that such concerns have had a stronger influence on German than on UK criminal law.

Bibliography

Ambos K., 'Judicial Creativity at the Special Tribunal for Lebanon: Is There a Crime of Terrorism under International Law?', *Leiden Journal of International Law*, 24 (2011), 655–75.

'Possession as a Criminal Offence and the Function of the Mental Element: Reflections from a Comparative Perspective', in Linton S., Simpson G. and Schabas W. A. (eds.), *For the Sake of Present and Future Generations: Essays on International Law, Crime and Justice in Honour of Roger S. Clark*, Leiden, Boston: Brill Nijhoff. (2015), 391–408.

'Anmerkung zu einer Entscheidung des BGH, Beschluss vom 06.04.2017 (3 StR 326/16) – Zur Vorbereitung einer schweren staatsgefährdenden Straftat durch die Ausreise aus der Bundesrepublik Deutschland', *Juristische Rundschau*, 12 (2017), 655–60.

Ashworth A., 'Four Threats to the Presumption of Innocence', *International Journal of Evidence and Proof*, 10 (2006), 241–79.

Ashworth A. and Zender L., *Preventive Justice*, Oxford University Press (2014).

Backes O., 'Der Kampf des Strafrechts gegen nicht-organisierten Terror – Anmerkungen zum Referentenentwurf eines Gesetzes zur Verfolgung der Vorbereitung von schweren Gewalttaten', *Strafverteidiger* (2008), 654–60.

Cancio Meliá M. and Petzsche A., 'Precursor Crimes of Terrorism', in Lennon G. and Walker C. (eds.), *Routledge Handbook of Law and Terrorism*, London and New York: Routledge (2015), 194–205.

Cassese A., 'The Multifaceted Criminal Notion of Terrorism in International Law', *Journal of International Criminal Justice*, 4 (2006), 933–58.

Cornford A., 'Indirect Crimes', *Law and Philosophy*, 32 (2013), 485–514.

'Narrowing the Scope of Absurdly Broad Offences: The Case of Terrorist Possession', *Statute Law Review*, 38 (2017), 286–97.

Deckers R. and Heusel J., 'Strafbarkeit terroristischer Vorbereitungshandlungen rechtsstaatlich nicht tragbar', *Zeitschrift für Rechtspolitik*, 6 (2008), 169–73.

Dennis I., 'Reverse Onuses and the Presumption of Innocence: In Search of Principle', *Criminal Law Review* (2005), 901–36.

Duff R. A., *Answering for Crime: Responsibility and Liability in the Criminal Law*, Oxford: Hart (2007).

Fischer T. (ed.), *Strafgesetzbuch mit Nebengesetzen*, 65th edn, Munich, C. H. Beck (2018).

Gane C. H. W., Stoddart C. N. and Chalmers J., *A Casebook on Scottish Criminal Law*, 4th edn, Edinburgh: W. Green (2009).

Gazeas N. and Grosse-Wilde T., 'Anmerkung zu einer Entscheidung des BGH, Beschluss vom 06.04.2017 (3 StR 326/16) – Zur Vorbereitung einer schweren staatsgefährdenden Straftat durch die Ausreise aus der Bundesrepublik Deutschland', *Strafverteidiger*, 2 (2018), 84–8.

Gazeas N., Grosse-Wilde T. and Kießling A., 'Die neuen Tatbestände im Staatsschutzstrafrecht – Versuch einer ersten Auslegung der §§ 89a, 89b und 91 StGB', *Neue Zeitschrift für Strafrecht*, 11 (2009), 593–604.

Gierhake K., 'Zur geplanten Einführung neuer Straftatbestände wegen der Vorbereitung terroristischer Straftaten', *Zeitschrift für internationale Strafrechtsdogmatik*, 9 (2008), 397–405.

Heintschel-Heinegg B. von (ed.), *Beck'scher Online Kommentar StGB*, 39rd edn, Munich, C. H. Beck (2018).

Hodgson J. and Tadros V., 'How to Make a Terrorist out of Nothing', *Modern Law Review*, 72 (2009), 984–98.

Home Office, *Operation of Police Powers under the Terrorism Act 2000: Quarterly Update to June 2018: Annual Data Tables* (2018).

Hörnle T., 'Deskriptive und normative Dimensionen des Begriffs "Feindstrafrecht"', *Goltdammer's Archiv für Strafrecht* (2006), 80–95.

Hunt A., 'Criminal Prohibitions on Direct and Indirect Encouragement of Terrorism', *Criminal Law Review* (2007), 441–58.

Joecks W. and Miebach K. (eds.), *Münchener Kommentar Strafgesetzbuch*, 8. vols., 3rd edn, Munich, C. H. Beck (2017), I and III.

Lackner K. and Kühl K. (eds.), *Strafgesetzbuch Kommentar*, 29th edn, Munich, C. H. Beck (2018).

Levanon L., 'Criminal Prohibitions on Membership in Terrorist Organisations', *New Criminal Law Review*, 15 (2012), 224–76.

Naucke W., 'Die robuste Tradition des Sicherheitsstrafrechts', *Kritische Vierteljahresschrift für Gesetzgebung und Rechtswissenschaft*, 2 (2010), 129–36.

Ormerod D. and Fortson R., 'Serious Crime Act 2007: The Part 2 Offences', *Criminal Law Review* (2009), 389–414.

Petzsche A., 'The European Influence on German Anti-Terrorism Law', 13 *German Law Journal*, 9 (2012), 1056–65.

Strafrecht und Terrorismusbekämpfung – Eine vergleichende Untersuchung der Bekämpfung terroristischer Vorbereitungshandlungen in Deutschland, Großbritannien und Spanien, Baden-Baden: Nomos (2013).

'The Penalization of Public Provocation to Commit a Terrorist Offence', *European Criminal Law Review*, 7 (2017), 241–57.

Petzsche A. and Cancio Meliá M., 'Speaking of Terrorism and Terrorist Speech: Defining the Limits of Terrorist Speech Offences', in Lennon G., King C. and McCartney C. (eds.), *Counter-terrorism, Constitutionalism and Miscarriages of Justice – A Festschrift for Professor Clive Walker*, Oxford, Hart (2018), 151–66.

Radtke H. and Steinsiek M., 'Bekämpfung des internationalen Terrorismus durch Kriminalisierung von Vorbereitungshandlungen? – Zum Entwurf eines Gesetzes zur Verfolgung der Vorbereitung von schweren Gewalttaten (Referentenentwurf des BMJ vom 21.4.2008)', *Zeitschrift für internationale Strafrechtsdogmatik*, 9 (2008), 383–96.

Ramsay P., 'Preparation Offences, Security Interests, Political Freedom', in Duff R. A., Farmer L., Marshall S. E., Renzo M. and Tadros V. (eds.), *The Structures of Criminal Law*, Oxford University Press (2011), 203–28.

Saul B., 'Attempts to Define Terrorism in International Law', *Netherlands International Law Review*, 52 (2005), 57–83.

Sentencing Council, *Terrorism Offences: Definitive Guideline* (2018), available at www.sentencingcouncil.org.uk.

Sieber U., 'Legitimation und Grenzen von Gefährdungsdelikten im Vorfeld von terroristischer Gewalt – eine Analyse der Vorfeldtatbestände im 'Entwurf eines Gesetzes zur Verfolgung der Vorbereitung von schweren staatsgefährdenden Gewalttaten', *Neue Zeitschrift für Strafrecht*, 7 (2009), 353–64.

Simester A. P., 'Prophylactic Crimes', in Sullivan G. R. and Dennis I. (eds.), *Seeking Security: Pre-Empting the Commission of Criminal Harms*, Oxford, Hart (2012). 59–78.

et al., *Simester and Sullivan's Criminal Law: Theory and Doctrine*, 6th edn, Oxford, Hart (2016).

Stark F., 'Rethinking Recklessness', *Juridical Review* (2011), 163–203.

Culpable Carelessness: Recklessness and Negligence in the Criminal Law, Cambridge University Press (2016).

Tadros V. and Tierney S., 'The Presumption of Innocence and the Human Rights Act', *Modern Law Review*, 67 (2004), 402–34.

Weißer B., 'Über den Umgang des Strafrechts mit terroristischen Bedrohungslagen', *Zeitschrift für die gesamte Strafrechtswissenschaft*, 121 (2009), 131–61.

Zöller M. A., *Terrorismusstrafrecht - Ein Handbuch*, Heidelberg, C. F. Müller (2009).

PART III

Criminal Justice and Procedure

7

Proportionality of Punishment in Common Law Jurisdictions and in Germany

RICHARD S. FRASE, CARSTEN MOMSEN, TOM O'MALLEY AND SARAH LISA WASHINGTON

I Introduction

One of the most broadly accepted principles of punishment is that the severity of criminal sanctions should be proportional to the seriousness of the offence being punished. But proportionality requires a normative frame of reference – proportional relative to what underlying legal or normative values? Retributivists believe that punishment should be proportional to the offender's degree of blameworthiness for the act(s) being punished. There are also several consequentialist (utilitarian) principles, which assess the proportionality of a penal measure relative to the expected benefits to be achieved by applying that measure. This chapter examines each of these meanings of proportionality in punishment, identifying the key elements of each concept, their similarities and differences, the ways in which common law legal systems and the German system have applied them and the possibilities for accommodating all of these principles in a single punishment model.

As noted, retributive proportionality seeks to match punishment severity to the offender's degree of blameworthiness for the crime being punished, or at least, to ensure that punishment severity is not clearly too severe or too lenient relative to the offender's blameworthiness (a concept often referred to as limiting retributivism). Under either retributive approach, proportionality of punishment is viewed as a good thing in itself, without regard to the desirable effects which the punishment will have on the offender or other would-be offenders, the undesirable effects or the costs.

In contrast, non-retributive proportionality concepts focus entirely on the costs, good effects and bad effects of a penalty; proportionate punishment (or at least, the avoidance of disproportionate punishment) is viewed as good thing only if and to the extent that three requirements are met: (1) such punishment has desirable effects on the offender and/or other would-be offenders (in particular: making future crimes less frequent and/or less serious); (2) such good effects outweigh the undesired effects and costs of the punishment; and (3) the good effects cannot be achieved with less severe punishment. The second and third of these requirements correspond to what we will refer to, respectively, as 'ends–benefits' proportionality and 'alternative-means' proportionality.

Despite these core differences, however, retributive and non-retributive proportionality principles have some important elements in common, in particular: both sets of principles give substantial emphasis to the individual and social harms caused or risked by the offence; it is therefore necessary, under both sets of principles, to ask: what makes one crime more 'serious' than another? We will also argue that both sets of principles recognise, or ought to recognise, the 'parsimony' principle – that punishment should be no more severe than necessary to achieve its intended purpose(s). We also suggest that both sets of principles should recognise an important corollary of parsimony: whatever the underlying punishment purposes, penalties can err in either of two directions – too lenient, or too severe – but these two kinds of errors are not equally serious; as a normative matter, it is better to err on the side of too little punishment rather than too much.

The remainder of this chapter is organised as follows. Section II first examines the constituent elements of retributive proportionality in common law systems, and notes important distinctions between relative and absolute proportionality measures, and between positive and negative retributive goals and limitations. This section then considers the role of retributive values in German sentencing. Section III elaborates and gives examples of the two common law consequentialist proportionality principles referred to above, and shows how consequentialist goals and limitations have been viewed by German writers. Section IV briefly examines the most important similarities and differences between retributive and non-retributive proportionality principles. Section V provides some examples of the operation of each of these principles in common law systems.[1] Section VI shows how the German system has incorporated various proportionality principles. Section VII considers the ways in which a legal system could harmonise and combine all of

[1] For further discussion, and numerous examples of proportionality principles in US law as well as some examples from foreign laws (especially, German law), European Union law, and the law of war, see Sullivan and Frase, *Proportionality Principles* (2009).

these proportionality principles into a single model. Section VIII examines several potential challenges to adoption of such a model. The Conclusion strikes a more optimistic tone, emphasising the underlying similarities between common law and German proportionality principles.

II Retributive Proportionality Principles

This part of the chapter examines the basic elements of a retributive account of proportionality as proposed by writers in common law systems, while also noting important distinctions between relative and absolute proportionality and between proportionality as a positive (determining) versus only a negative (limiting) principle. The remainder of this part considers retributive elements in German sentencing.

1 Constituent Elements of Common Law Retributive Theory

Retributive theory focuses on the actor's degree of blameworthiness for his or her past actions, which is generally thought to depend on two elements: (1) the nature and seriousness of the harm(s) foreseeably caused or threatened by the crime, and (2) the offender's degree of culpability in committing the crime – his or her intent (*mens rea*), motive, role in the offence (if there are multiple parties), possible diminished capacity to obey the law and so forth.[2]

2 Relative (Ordinal) versus Absolute (Cardinal) Retributive Proportionality Principles

A critical distinction, in applying retributive proportionality principles, is between relative and absolute assessments – what Andrew von Hirsch calls ordinal and cardinal proportionality.[3] The first of these deals with the rank-order and spacing of severity increments of penalties, for offences of increasing seriousness – penalties given to crime A, versus penalties given to crime B. Cardinal proportionality evaluates the degree of a penalty's severity in absolute terms – is five years in prison undeservedly lenient or severe, for this offence? Von Hirsch believes that

[2] For further discussion of these retributive punishment principles, by one of the best-known proponents of this rationale, see von Hirsch, *Past or Future Crimes* (1985), 64–74.

[3] See e.g. *ibid.*, 39–46.

at least two important issues of cardinal proportionality must be addressed in any punishment system. The first issue relates to the definition of the upper and lower extremes ('anchoring points') of the punishment scale – the top of the scale would be the death penalty or, if that is not authorised, the maximum prison term allowed for any offence; the bottom of the scale is marked by suspended sentence, or some other least-severe authorised penalty. A second kind of cardinal proportionality issue involves the exact placement of lines dividing different zones or types of punishment (e.g. the point at which incarceration is the appropriate disposition rather than some relatively severe non-custodial penalty).[4] Von Hirsch views the requirements of cardinal desert as much less constraining than those of ordinal desert. Like some proponents of 'limiting' (or 'negative') retributivism, discussed below, von Hirsch concedes that it is difficult to say exactly what absolute degree or type of severity each offender deserves; but he believes that we can and should at least say that some penalty scales are clearly too severe or too lenient in the type or degree of sanctions. Given this greater degree of uncertainty, von Hirsch would allow the legislature to consider non-retributive punishment goals – including crime-control, parsimony (discussed below), and available resources – when deciding issues of cardinal proportionality.

3 *Determining (Positive) versus Limiting (Negative) Retributive Principles*

Another critical distinction, in applying retributive proportionality principles, is between positive and negative retributive theories. Under the former, punishing offenders in proportion to their degree of blameworthiness is deemed to be a right or even a duty of the state, and the degree of blame should determine the exact degree of punishment severity. Proponents of negative retributivism assert that blameworthiness only sets outer (upper and lower) limits on sanction severity, within

[4] A third issue is treated by von Hirsch in a manner somewhat similar to questions of cardinal desert. That issue is whether 'hard treatment' such as prison is the required means with which to express retributive censure, or whether symbolic, verbal denunciation is sufficient. Von Hirsch believes that this choice is not determined by the logic of desert, and (like the two 'cardinal' desert issues noted in text) depends instead on crime-prevention needs. See von Hirsch, 'Proportionality' (1992), 73–4. For further discussion of the issue of hard treatment, and the value of symbolic denunciation via suspended-execution custodial terms, see Frase, *Just Sentencing* (2013), 31–2, 52–7.

which other punishment goals and principles may be applied. The most widely recognised non-retributive goal is crime control, and an important principle applied within outer desert limits is parsimony – penalties should be no more severe than necessary to achieve the intended goal(s). Here too, Andrew von Hirsch has been a prominent theorist, advocating the former (positive/determining) view.[5] The most prominent American advocate of negative/limiting retributivism is Norval Morris, who argued that assessments of blameworthiness or just deserts (even relative/ordinal desert) are too imprecise and contestable to permit this criterion to precisely define the proper degree of punishment; we can only say that some penalties are clearly undeservedly severe, that other penalties are clearly undeservedly lenient, and that in between those outer limits any penalty is 'not undeserved' and therefore permissible.[6]

An alternative version of negative/limiting retributivism agrees with the positive/determining retributivists that ordinal desert can be assessed with some precision (or at least, with as much precision as any other quantifiable assessment commonly made by public officials and agents). But this theory posits that while government is not permitted to punish in excess of desert, it is also not obligated to impose the full measure of deserved punishment – desert is an asymmetric principle, setting firm upper limits on punishment severity, but looser lower limits and sometimes none at all. (However, lower limits on sanction severity will often be set by other punishment goals, including crime control, expressive functions such as norm reinforcement, and the desire to avoid imposing extremely unequal penalties on similar criminal conduct.[7])

4 *The Elements of Retribution and Retributive Proportionality in German Sentencing*

Having substantially influenced the concept of punishment as understood by the German Constitutional Court (*Bundesverfassungsgericht*

[5] See e.g. von Hirsch, *Deserved Criminal Sentences* (2017). See also von Hirsch, *Past or Future Crimes* (1985); von Hirsch, 'Proportionality' (1992); and von Hirsch, *Censure and Sanctions* (1993).

[6] See e.g. Morris, *Future of Imprisonment* (1974); Morris, *Madness and the Criminal Law* (1982); Morris and Tonry, *Between Prison and Probation* (1990). For further discussion, elaborating and expanding Morris's theory of Limiting Retributivism, see Frase, 'Sentencing Principles' (1997). See also Frase, 'Limiting Retributivism' (2004).

[7] See e.g. Frase, *Just Sentencing* (2013), 25–31, 88–94 (citing many writers who have endorsed either Norval Morris's imprecise-desert version of limiting retributivism, or the alternative, precise-but-asymmetric view).

(BVerfGE))[8] today, an understanding of the principles set out in the philosophical movement of 'German idealism' is indispensable. The term 'German idealism' refers particularly to the works of the philosophers Fichte, Schelling and Hegel. With respect to the philosophy of Kant, however, there is debate about whether it marks the beginning of idealism or whether idealism constitutes a 'post-Kantian' movement.[9] The works of Kant, Fichte, Schelling and Hegel share the proposition that 'ultimate reality is mental or spiritual, or at least not physical'.[10]

Concepts of punishment based on the ideas of German idealism are often referred to as 'absolute'. Meaning that they disregard empirically measurable social effects of punishment. Whereas concepts of punishment based on deterrence or reformation, are referred to as 'relative'.[11]

(a) Kant

In his work 'The Metaphysics of Morals', Kant states that 'the punishment of a judge . . . must never be merely a means to promote the good for the criminal or the society itself but must be imposed at all times *only because he has committed the crime*'.[12] Although there is debate about the interpretation of this passage – some say that Kant intended only to refuse concepts of punishments that are *purely* based on considerations of usefulness[13] – the most common interpretation is that it introduces a retributive concept of punishment. Kant understood criminal law as a categorical imperative.[14] In regard to the proportionality of punishment, Kant favoured a retaliation approach (*ius talionis*). By contrast, the proportional punishment would be to also violate the honour of the perpetrator by making him apologise publicly and 'kiss the hand of the victim'. Consequently, Kant is very strict in regard to the proportional punishment for homicide: 'If one has murdered one must die.'[15]

8 BVerfG NJW 1977, 1525, 1531.

9 See e.g. Pinkard, 'How Kantian Was Hegel?' (1990).

10 Honderich, 'Idealism' (2005), 413.

11 Today, this differenciation is being questioned increasingly, see Stübinger, *Das idealisierte Strafrecht* (2008), 291; also sceptical: Hörnle, 'Gegenwartige Strafbegrundungstheorien' (2011), 12; and Weigend, 'Kommentar zu Tatjana Hornle' (2011), 31.

12 Kant, *Die Metaphysik der Sitten* (1990), 192.

13 Hörnle, *Straftheorien* (2011), 19 with further references.

14 Jakobs, *Strafrecht* (1991), s. 1 mn. 19.

15 Kant, *Die Metaphysik der Sitten* (1990), 194.

(b) Hegel

Hegel described retribution through punishment as a communicational process. According to Hegel, an offender has a split will: the real and implicit will to obey the law (his own ethical substance), and an actual will which is manifested in the crime.[16] In committing the crime, the offender therefore acts self-contradictory.[17] By punishing the offender, her particular will is being violated. This 'constitutes the neutralisation of the crime and therefore the recovery of the law'. Punishment, therefore, is the 'negation of the negation'[18] as it 'corrects' the negation of the law expressed in the crime. Hegel's concept of punishment can be regarded as 'forward-looking' and preventative.[19] With regard to proportionality, Hegel did not stick to the inflexible *ius talionis* shaped by Kant. Hegel states that equality of offence and punishment required for retribution does not have to be equality in the specific sense but is defined by the 'value of the violation'.[20] This represents an offence-oriented approach and may be of use for a retributive proportionality principle. He further stipulates that the necessary degree of punishment can differ according to the level of 'consolidation' of a society,[21] thereby considering general preventive aspects.

(c) Fichte

Elements of Kant's and Hegel's thoughts can be found in Fichte's 'Principles of Natural Law' (*Grundlage des Naturrechts*). Fichte is arguing with the idea of a sphere of liberty belonging to every individual by natural law. In his paradigm, an offence is the violation of somebody else's sphere. Fichte grounds sentencing on a very clear idea of retribution: 'Everyone must necessarily risk as much of their own rights and freedoms as they are tempted to violate the rights and freedoms of others.' In this expiatory treaty (*Abbüßungsvertrag*), however, the 'theory of counterweight' is only a part of the justification for punishment. Otherwise the offender 'would have done nothing more than merely

[16] Tunick, *Hegel's Political Philosophy* (2014), 29.

[17] *Ibid.*, 32; Hegel, *Grundlinien* (1970), § 199.

[18] Hegel, *Grundlinien* (1970), § 99.

[19] 'The difference between Hegel's concept and "positive general prevention" is marginal' states Jakobs in *Strafrecht* (1991), s. 1 mn. 21; similar Streng, 'Schuld ohne Freiheit?' (1980), 101.

[20] Hegel, *Grundlinien* (1970), § 101.

[21] Cf. Jakobs, *Strafrecht* (1991), 21; Hegel, *Grundlinien* (1970), § 218.

attempting in vain'. In punishment, the 'evil will' must also be taken into account. In addition, an adequate punishment prevents the 'exclusion of the criminal from society'. Therefore, the criminal must voluntarily submit to the punishment, otherwise there is the threat of exclusion. The purpose of non-exclusive punishment is not merely to obtain a counterweight and compensation for the evil will. For the assessment of the penalty, the possible improvement of the offender must also be taken into account. This can only take place outside civil society. Only this improvement justifies that the state 'still receives' the culprits (in other words: does not kill the offender by capital punishment). Those who have improved 'return to society, those who are not improved within a peremptory society, are excluded as incorrigible (forever) from bourgeois society'. 'The only crime that does not require efforts of correction, and calls for absolute exclusion without further ado, is deliberate premeditated murder … But there is a reason that can persuade the state to kill the criminal; that it can only protect itself from him in this way …'[22]

Thus, Fichte represents a transition from absolute to relative theories of punishment which are also the basis for the assessment of punishment. For Fichte the capital penalty is necessary if the offender cannot improve. The penalty must go beyond a mere balancing out of the situation and can reach as far as is necessary for improvement. There is no upper limitation as long as the purpose of improvement serves as justification. Keeping this in mind, the theories of Fichte, von Liszt and Feuerbach are all connected; as is the theory of a special criminal law for enemies who are excluded from civil society. What we see in Fichte are primary ideas of special prevention and general prevention as elements of concrete sentencing, whereas the general legitimation of punishment is still retributive.[23] Fichte´s idea of an Abbüßungsvertrag also shows elements of the much later developed 'communicative blame'.[24] Both concepts state the offender has to be communicated and to accept his failure and that he will improve.

22 Fichte, *Grundlage des Naturrechts* (1922), 262, 256 ff.

23 For Fichte´s influence on sentencing see du Bois-Pedain, 'Punishment as an Inclusionary Practice' (2017).

24 Fricker, 'What's the Point of Blame?' (2016), 165–83. Traces of that idea can be found as well in the term *sozialethischer Tadel*, commonly used by the German Federal Criminal Court (BGHSt 2, 194 ff., BGHSt 11, 20 ff.)

III Consequentialist Proportionality Principles in Common Law Systems and Germany

Some writers in common law systems, including several US Supreme Court justices, have asserted that proportionality is inherently tied to retributive theories of punishment.[25] But as discussed below, there are two well-established non-retributive proportionality principles (although one of them is only labelled proportionality in foreign and international law, going by other names in Anglo-American law).

Consequentialist (or utilitarian) purposes of punishment emphasise the desirable effects (mainly, future crime reduction) which punishments have on the offender being punished or on other would-be offenders, and the costs and undesired consequences of punishments.[26] The most widely accepted of desired effects are: special (or individual, or specific) deterrence, incapacitation and rehabilitation of the offender (because he is thought likely to commit further crimes); general deterrence of other would-be violators, through fear of receiving similar punishment; and a more diffuse, long-term form of prevention (sometimes referred to as denunciation or the expressive purpose of punishment) which focuses on the norm-defining and norm-reinforcing effects that penalties have on the public's views about the relative seriousness (harmfulness, wrongness) of various crimes.[27]

From a consequentialist perspective, a penalty can be disproportionate (or excessive) in two distinct and independent ways, corresponding to the ends–benefits and alternative-means proportionality principles discussed below: (1) the costs and burdens of the sentence (or the added costs and burdens, compared to a lesser penalty) may outweigh the likely benefits (or added benefits) produced by the sentence; and (2) the sentence may be disproportionate (that is, unnecessary, and therefore excessive) when compared to other, less costly or burdensome means of achieving the same goals. Each of these consequentialist proportionality principles has ancient roots, as discussed more fully below.

25 See e.g. Lee, 'Constitutional Right' (2005); *Ewing* v. *California*, 538 US 11, 31 (2003) (Scalia, J., concurring, joined by Thomas, J., asserting that 'Proportionality – the notion that the punishment should fit the crime – is inherently a concept tied to the penological goal of retribution.'). See also *Harmelin* v. *Michigan*, 501 US 957, 989 (1991) (Scalia, J., concurring, joined by Rehnquist C.J., stating views similar to the Scalia opinion in *Ewing*).

26 See generally Frase, 'Punishment Purposes' (2005).

27 *Ibid.*; see also Greenawalt, 'Punishment' (2001), 1282, 1286–9.

1 Ends–Benefits (Cost–Benefit) Proportionality Principles

This principle has been recognised by utilitarian philosophers since the eighteenth century. Cesare Beccaria maintained that criminal penalties should be proportional to the seriousness of the offence, as measured by the social harm caused or threatened by the offence.[28] Jeremy Bentham elaborated several more specific utilitarian arguments for punishing in proportion to crime seriousness.[29] First, he argued that 'the greater an offence is, the greater reason there is to hazard a severe punishment for the chance of preventing it' – that is, greater social harm justifies greater preventive effort and expense.[30] Secondly, Bentham argued that a scale of penalties proportionate to social harm would give offenders 'a motive to stop at the lesser' crime.[31] Thirdly, he argued that 'the evil of the punishment [should not exceed] the evil of the offence'.[32] In addition to public costs, punishments impose suffering on offenders (and also often on their families), and such suffering should not be disproportionate to the seriousness of the crime(s) which the punishment hopes to prevent.

2 Alternative-Means (Necessity) Proportionality Principles

Utilitarian efficiency values require that, among equally effective means to achieve a given end, those that are less costly or burdensome should be preferred. This has sometimes been referred to as the principle of parsimony;[33] it has also been called the principle of necessity, or the requirement of narrow tailoring or least restrictive means. In German and European law, and in the Law of War, this is deemed to be a form of proportionality since, like the ends-benefit principle discussed above, it identifies excessive measures.[34] Also like ends–benefits, the alternative-

[28] Beccaria, 'Crimes and Punishments' (1992), 21–8.
[29] Bentham, *Theory of Legislation* (1882).
[30] *Ibid.*, 326.
[31] *Ibid.* See also Beccaria, 'Crimes and Punishments' (1992), 26 ('If an equal punishment be ordained for two crimes that injure society in different degrees, there is nothing to deter men from committing the greater, as often as it is attended with greater advantage.'); von Hirsch et al., *Criminal Deterrence* (1999), 41–3 (discussing the marginal deterrent benefits of penalties proportioned to harms associated with different crimes).
[32] Bentham, *Theory of Legislation* (1882), 323. See also Hart, *Punishment and Responsibility* (1968), 173 n. 20.
[33] Morris, *Future of Imprisonment* (1974), 60–1, 75, 78.
[34] See generally Sullivan and Frase, *Proportionality Principles* (2009).

means principle has been recognised since the eighteenth century. Beccaria argued that all punishments should be 'necessary; the least possible in the case given'.[35] Bentham similarly held that punishment itself is evil and should be used as sparingly as possible; in particular, a penalty should not be used 'in cases where the same end may be obtained by means more mild'.[36] In modern times, alternative-means proportionality principles have frequently been endorsed by scholars and model-code drafters.[37] Unnecessarily severe penalties and other measures have been condemned in numerous American court opinions.[38]

3 *Examples of Penalties Violating Ends–Benefits and/or Alternative-Means Principles*

A mandatory-minimum sentence provides a good example of a penalty that violates the alternative-means principle. In at least some (and perhaps many) of the cases subject to such a law, the court is forced to impose a punishment more severe than would be required to achieve all consequentialist sentencing purposes in that case (such a penalty is also likely to often be disproportionately severe in terms of ends–benefits, retributive proportionality or both of these principles).

A good example of a sentence that violates the ends–benefits principle would be the imprisonment of a low-level drug seller who will be immediately replaced on the street. The costs and burdens of such a

[35] Beccaria, 'Crimes and Punishments' (1992), 179.

[36] Bentham, *Theory of Legislation* (1882), 323. Similar means proportionality principles were endorsed in The French Declaration of the Rights of Man (1789). Art. 8 of the Declaration limited punishments to those that are 'strictly and obviously necessary'. Art. 9 specified that, to protect the presumption of innocence, 'if arrest shall be deemed indispensable, all harshness not essential to the securing of the prisoner's person shall be severely repressed by law'.

[37] See e.g. Morris, *Future of Imprisonment* (1974); Radin, 'Jurisprudence of Death' (1978), 1043–56 (discussing dignity and excessiveness in light of consequentialist theories of punishment); Singer, 'Sending Men to Prison' (1972), 72–89; Tonry, 'Parsimony' (1998), 202 ('judges should be directed to impose the least severe sentence consistent with the governing purposes at sentencing'); Zimring et al., *Punishment and Democracy* (2001), 189–91 (describing classes of excessive punishment claims); Frase, *Sentencing Principles* (1997), 94–5, noting that the original (1962) Model Penal Code, as well as all three editions of the American Bar Association's sentencing standards, explicitly or implicitly recognise the principle of parsimony. See also American Law Institute (2017), § 1.02(2)(a)(iii) cmt. F (revised Model Penal Code sentencing provisions, broadly endorsing the parsimony principle).

[38] Sullivan and Frase, *Proportionality Principles* (2009).

sentence far outweigh any likely crime-control benefits – given the offender's rapid replacement there is no incapacitation benefit, and apparently a very weak general deterrent effect (if any).

It should be noted that the two consequentialist proportionality principles operate independently – a measure can violate one of these principles but not the other. In the first example given above, a mandatory minimum penalty could violate the alternative-means proportionality principle even if its costs and burdens did not outweigh the likely crime-control benefits (if the benefits were outweighed, the penalty would violate both principles). Conversely, a long prison term given to a repetitive minor thief could violate the ends–benefits principle (because the costs and burdens of the sentence outweigh its crime-control benefits), even if the prison term has more incapacitation benefit than any shorter term would provide.

4 *Consequentialist Elements in German Sentencing Approaches*

(a) Von Liszt (Special Prevention and the Purpose of Security)

Von Liszt advocated against the criminal law science existing *communis opinio* of his time that retributivism must be the basis of punishment. In his famous *Marburger Programm*, his inaugural lecture at the University of Marburg, he demanded a reform of the criminal process towards 'special prevention'. He did not entirely object to retributivism but regarded it as an expression of an original blind and instinctive reaction to crime. According to von Liszt, as part of humanity's development an objectification of punishment has taken place. Although the compulsive element of punishment will never disappear completely, 'the impulse is being put into the service of the purpose'.[39] He further stated that, while primitive blood revenge meant the extermination of the offender, punishment gains 'measure and an objective' through objectification. He advocated for a turnaround of criminal law from a crime-oriented perspective to a criminal-oriented one.[40] He was very clear that the appropriate punishment should be oriented towards the purposes of punishment: 'The right, i.e. the just punishment is the *necessary* punishment.'[41] He drew a distinction between three types of offenders:

[39] Von Liszt, 'Zweckgedanke im Strafrecht' (1905), 145.
[40] Schwind, *Kriminologie* (2013) mn. 44.
[41] Von Liszt, 'Zweckgedanke im Strafrecht' (1905), 161.

(a) criminals capable of improvement, (b) criminals that do not require improvement because their crime resulted from a one-time episode ('occasional offenders') and (c) criminals that are not capable of improvement ('habitual' or 'incorrigible offenders'). The proportionate punishment is related to the 'type' of offender:

(i) Consequentialist Elements According to von Liszt, 'first time offenders can still be saved in a lot of cases'.[42] He therefore suggests at least one year and a maximum of five years of imprisonment with a subsequent release on parole for offenders in this category. Additionally, private organisations are supposed to provide housing and support for the released prisoners. By contrast, with regard to 'occasional offenders' systematic improvement would be pointless. Punishment should therefore 'act as a deterrent' and 'restore the authority of the broken law'.[43] For offenders of this type, von Liszt suggests imprisonment of at least six weeks and the use of financial penalties.

As for habitual offenders, according to von Liszt, there is neither hope for improvement nor does deterrence work, they 'have to be made safe' (*Unschädlichmachung*); 'the society has to protect itself against them'. Because death penalty and exile were not options to von Liszt, he suggests life imprisonment. As crimes that are typically committed 'habitually', von Liszt lists property and sex offences. Interestingly, he further suggests, very similar to the current 'three-strikes laws' in several US states, life imprisonment after the third conviction for an 'habitual crime' as defined by von Liszt.

(ii) Lack of Limitation A problem of special prevention is the lack of limitation in regard to the duration of the 'therapeutical' imprisonment. It is not possible to treat an offender only far enough to prevent him from committing in the future the crime for which he was convicted.[44] In fact, only an all-or-nothing approach seems rational. An offender-oriented criminal law therefore means dropping the sole focus on the criminal act as a limiting factor. Consequently, this can lead to endless therapy as a reaction to an offence of minimal gravity. It would furthermore be permissible for a judge to sentence an offender to indefinite imprisonment – the purpose of punishment would cease only when the criminal is

[42] *Ibid.*, 171.
[43] *Ibid.*, 172.
[44] Jakobs, *Strafrecht* (1991), s. 1, mn. 41.

fully 'recovered'. This was possible in Germany with respect to juvenile offenders according to § 19 *Jugendgerichtsgesetz* (Juvenile Court Act), which was abolished in 1990, but with a maximum duration of four years of imprisonment. Von Liszt, suggesting a maximum penalty for criminals capable of betterment, does not advocate endless therapy. But he suggests treating multiple recidivist offenders for whom imprisonment apparently has not yet worked as 'incorrigible' after a certain point.

(b) Feuerbach (Consequentialist General Prevention)

To complete the classic movements of criminal theory, one has to take a look at the theory of general prevention, mainly shaped by Feuerbach. Feuerbach developed a theory of 'psychological compulsion', stating that crimes result from certain desires and motives and that they can be outweighed by the prospects of a painful reaction to crime (punishment), thereby exercising psychological pressure on the offender not to commit the crime.[45] The weighting mechanism of potential offenders can be described as an inner battle of motives for and against the offence.[46] The motives against committing the offence have to be strengthened in order to 'succeed' and psychologically compel the person in question not to commit the offence. While the psychological compulsion is achieved through the threat of punishment (the criminal code), the purpose of the enforcement of sentences lies in the demonstration of the validity of the threat to punish. Otherwise the threat is perceived as idle.[47]

Generally, a distinction is drawn between 'positive' and 'negative' general prevention. 'Negative' general prevention means deterrence in the sense shaped by Feuerbach. Positive general prevention, by contrast, is understood as strengthening the confidence of the public in the enforceability of the legal order.[48] While negative general prevention aims to deter people that potentially consider committing crimes, positive general prevention addresses (generally) law-abiding people.[49] The approach of German sentencing law to harmonise 'special prevention' with limiting factors will be examined in the following section.

[45] Feuerbach, *Lehrbuch des Gemeinen* (1808), § 12 and §§ 13 ff.
[46] Roxin, *Strafrecht* (1997), mn. 22.
[47] Feuerbach, *Lehrbuch des Gemeinen* (1808), § 16.
[48] Roxin, *Strafrecht* (1997), mn. 25.
[49] Hörnle, *Straftheorien* (2011), 27 ff.

(c) The Approaches to Finding Adequate Sentences in Current German Jurisdiction

The German sentencing system has two tracks (*Zweispurigkeit des Strafrechts*). The first being *Kriminalstrafe* (criminal punishment), the second the measures listed in § 11 no. 8 *Strafgesetzbuch* (StGB), particularly *Maßregeln der Besserung und Sicherung* (measures for the prevention of crime and reformation of offenders). The following explains how a mixture of retributive and consequentialist elements began to dominate jurisprudence and sentencing theory in Germany

(i) Historic Development of the German Concept of Punishment

The original 1871 version of the German Penal Code (*Reichsstrafgesetzbuch*) was based on a retributive concept of punishment. However, von Liszt's 1882 *Marburger Programm* showed results: The *Reichsgericht* in 1924 accepted that the purposes of deterrence, reformation of the criminal and public security have to be considered in addition to the 'most important' purpose of retribution, thereby shaping a 'mixed theory' of punishment (*Vereinigungstheorie*).[50] In the same year, with the *Emminger Notverordnung* an exception to the mandatory prosecution principle was first introduced in § 153 *Strafprozessordnung* (StPO) for minor offences in order to disburden the judiciary system during the global economic crisis.[51] And finally in 1969, the first two reforms of the StGB fundamentally reoriented the German criminal law by implementing the necessary instruments to meet the requirements of a 'mixed' concept of punishment that respects preventive and consequentialist aspects while not abandoning retributivism completely. However, according to the Federal Supreme Court of Germany, punishment does not have the task of achieving compensation for its own sake (anymore). The systemic change was implemented by introducing a new section (today § 46) called 'principles of sentencing' that states that the guilt[52] of the offender remains *the basis* of punishment (principle of guilt – *Schuldprinzip* – see below), stipulating in the next sentence that the consequences of punishment for the future life of the offender have to

[50] RGSt 58, 106, 109.

[51] Peters, '§ 153' (2016), mn. 1.

[52] *Guilt* in this sense must not be confused with the responsibility for a crime that has to be examined in the German structure of punishability: offence – unlawfulness – responsibility.

be taken into account. This section represents a compromise – although guilt is the basis of punishment it is accepted that other purposes of punishment have to be respected as well.[53] The reform also included the abolishment of penal servitude (*Zuchthausstrafe*), a restructuring of financial penalties,[54] the preference of financial penalties over imprisonment, the extension of the possibility to suspend sentences with probation, the introduction of a warning with reserved punishment and the restructuring of measures for the prevention of crime and reformation of offenders. In 1974, the introduction of § 153a and the new formulation of § 153 StPO allowed the discontinuance of proceedings in cases where punishment does not seem necessary, thereby underlining the purpose-orientation of punishment.

(ii) Principle of Guilt What does it mean, in § 46(1) StGB, that *guilt* of the criminal is *the basis* of punishment? If punishment is justified by or conditional on individual guilt it could be assumed that the 'principle of guilt' is an expression of remaining retributive elements in the 'mixed' concept of punishment. In practice, the degree of guilt is determined by the extent of disturbance that the crime inflicted on the legal order.[55] The disturbance of the legal order consists of two elements: (a) the degree of blameworthiness represented in the *actions* of the criminal (*Handlungsunwert*) and (b) the seriousness of the *violation* that resulted from these actions (*Erfolgsunwert*).[56]

There is agreement that the 'principle of guilt' has a limiting function: where the purposes of reformation of the offender and deterrence of the public would require a particularly severe punishment, a relatively low degree of individual guilt inhibits excessive punishment.

By contrast, the doctrinal dispute of retributivism and consequentialism is reflected in the question of whether the 'principle of guilt' also influences the lower limit of punishment. Following absolute theories of punishment, it would be prohibited to choose a punishment that is not proportionate to the individual guilt of the offender because it is too mild. From the point of view of purely relative theories, however, it is recognised that punishment can be counterproductive and should

[53] Lackner, 'StGB' (2014), § 46 mn. 23.

[54] Financial penalties are now calculated by daily rates of the income of the offender.

[55] Miebach and Meier, '§ 46' (2016), mn. 29.

[56] *Ibid.*, mn. 30.

therefore in some cases be milder than the degree of individual guilt would require, or may even be dispensed with entirely.[57]

Thus, the question really is whether guilt is a category for *justifying* punishment or if it just has a *limiting function*.[58]

(iii) 'Margin Theory' – *Spielraumtheorie* – by the German Federal Criminal Court Because the courts still regard the just compensation of guilt as a constitutive function of criminal law,[59] they apply the so-called 'margin theory' (*Spielraumtheorie*) for the finding of an adequate sentence. This theory entails that the judge has to narrow down the range of sentences to a 'frame of guilt', determining a possible sentence that would *barely* be proportionate to the individual guilt as the lower limit and another that *almost* would not be proportionate on the upper end. Only then, he may fill this framework by applying consequentialist aspects such as the reformation of the offender. Although the Federal Supreme Court of Germany has accepted dropping below the limits of a guilt-proportionate punishment in exceptional cases,[60] the application of the 'margin theory' generally reflects that retribution still is a constitutive purpose of punishment.

By contrast, some writers consider that punishment may generally drop below the proportional amount of guilt if preventive purposes so require[61] and that the 'principle of guilt' is incompatible with retribution and atonement.[62] They argue that retributive elements in punishment would lead to a 'paralysis' in criminal policy and ignore the purpose-oriented efforts of the state.[63]

(iv) Theory of 'Just Deserts' – *Punktstrafetheorie* Another approach is taken by the advocates of the *Punktstrafetheorie* that was favoured in the

[57] More differentiation could be done at this point in a further article. The relation to concepts of blaming has to be analysed in more depth. The same applies to the theory of censure, as presented in current work by Tony Bottoms in relation to Fichtes's 'Abbüßungsvertrag'. As Fichtes's idea could be seen as an abstract agreement whereas the theory of 'communicative blame' requests a concrete agreement. See Fricker, 'What's the Point of Blame?' (2016), 165–83; Duff, 'Legal and Moral Responsibility' (2009), 978–86.

[58] Cf. Hörnle, *Tatproportionale Strafzumessung* (1999), 326.

[59] BVerfG 39, 1, 57.

[60] BGH MDR 1986, 331 Tatprovokation durch polizeilichen Lockspitzel.

[61] Roxin, *Strafrecht* (1997), § 3 mn. 50.

[62] Maurach and Zipf, *Strafrecht Allgemeiner Teil* (1992), § 7 III mn. 17.

[63] *Ibid.*

1962 draft of the German criminal code[64] and by the Special Committee for the Reform of Criminal Law.[65] They stipulate that there is only *one* just punishment, while accepting that it cannot be calculated *exactly*. The literature that advocates for this theory aims for a greater controllability of sentences in appellate courts as, following the 'margin theory', only sentences that lie outside of the 'frame of guilt' could be challenged.[66] The theory accepts considering preventive purposes as well and therefore allows to *moderately* undercut or exceed the just punishment for reasons of prevention.[67]

However, considering that every judge assesses crimes differently and that the 'non-reconstructable interpersonal encounter during trial'[68] plays an important role, it does not seem unlikely that one judge chooses a punishment just above the still guilt-adequate limit in the sense of the 'margin theory', while another would choose one just below the upper limit of the 'frame of guilt'. The theory therefore does not seem to be applicable in practice.

(v) Theory of 'Two Levels' – *Stellenwerttheorie* Lastly, the *Stellenwerttheorie*[69] suggests a two-step procedure. First, the guilt-adequate punishment is to be determined in the sense of a just desert *without* considering preventive aspects for upward or downward corrections. Secondly, preventive aspects can be considered for the choice of the *type* of punishment. Accordingly, if preventive considerations do not require imprisonment, a financial penalty can be imposed (cf. § 47 StGB) or the sentence of imprisonment is suspended with probation (§ 56). However, if, for example, public security requires imprisonment, these legal opportunities are not to be used. The theory is based on the assumption that the consideration of preventive aspects for the finding of adequate punishment conflicts with the fact that no purpose of punishment is given explicit priority in the StGB, and that the effectiveness of punishment with regard to prevention has not been sufficiently proven scientifically.[70] However, the Stellenwerttheorie violates clause 2 of § 46(1) StGB that states that the consequences of punishment for the future life of the

[64] BT-Drs. IV/650, 96 f.
[65] BT-Drs. V/4094.
[66] Cf. Streng, 'StGB § 46' (2017), mn. 104.
[67] Dreher, *Strafgesetzbuch* (1972), § 13 remark 3 B a.
[68] Streng, 'StGB § 46' (2017), mn. 105 with further references.
[69] *Henkel* (1969), 23 ff.
[70] Streng, 'StGB § 46' (2017), mn. 106 with further references.

offender have to be taken into account *within the sentence* and not only for the determination of the type of punishment. A theory of punishment that puts this much emphasis on retribution therefore is not compatible with German criminal law.

(d) *Ultima Ratio* (Last Resort)

The aforementioned approaches deal with a concept of guilt – with partly different interpretations. Due to its moral issues, there have been developed concepts trying just to argue legally distinguishing law and morality. Punishment and sentencing could be seen as '*ultima ratio*'. If the purpose of punishment 'within a secularised and liberal society' is to protect legal interests, it is used as a reaction appropriate to guilt, understood as a morally neutral necessity to blame (*Strafwürdigkeit*) in the sense of blameworthiness (*sozial-ethischer Tadel)* and if it is only considered justified if it is an 'effective means of prevention that is indispensable for legal protection' (*Strafbedürftigkeit*)[71] then criminal law and criminal proceedings have an *ultima-ratio* function. Accordingly, not every culpable offence entails punishment. The procedural instruments to achieve this understanding have been implemented as part of the aforementioned reforms of German criminal law: the regulations on the abatement of proceedings make it possible to avoid proceedings partially or completely.[72] Moreover, the suspension of sentences and the option of financial penalties may spare the defendant from punishment (or imprisonment). In particular, the tendency to spare first offenders with good prognosis from imprisonment has found broad support in the extremely differentiated system of legal consequences that is available today.[73] Because of this statutory framework some think that the debate on whether falling below the guilt-proportionate limit should be possible is obsolete.[74] They argue that it is not punishment itself that has to be

71 Gallas, 'Der dogmatische Teil' (1968), 1, 3.

72 Schäfer et. al., *Praxis der Strafzumessung* (2017), mn. 4.

73 BGHSt 24, 40. To some extent, however, this only applies if aspects of deterrence do not conflict with such protection of the offender. Accordingly, the abatement of proceedings as in §§ 153 and 153a StPO is only allowed if there is no public interest in the prosecution of the offender or, in the case of § 153a, it can be eliminated by means of conditions and instructions. Moreover, § 56(3) states that a sentence of imprisonment of six months is not to be suspended if the defence of the legal system requires to enforce it. These general preventive aspects are based on the idea that there are cases where the law must be enforced by punishment to prevent undermining the public's sense of justice.

74 Horn and Wolters, '§ 46 StGB' (2017), mn. 22.

proportionate to the individual guilt but the overall reaction. Being investigated for a criminal offence can act as a personal deterrent.[75]

From a common law perspective *ultima ratio* can be interpreted as a combination of the principle of necessity (alternative-means proportionality) with the retributive requirement of moral blameworthiness. These two elements correspond, respectively, to the German concepts of Strafbedürftigkeit[76] and Strafwürdigkeit, described above.

(e) Constitutional Proportionality

Another limiting principle that complements the 'principle of guilt' is constitutional proportionality (*Verhältnismäßigkeit*). It is derived directly from the rule of law laid down in *Grundgesetz*, Article 20(3). In contrast to the 'principle of guilt' it does not weigh the *occasion* of punishment (the crime) against the chosen means but the pursued *purpose*.[77] Its connecting point therefore is not the guilt of the offender but the purposes of prevention.

The history of that concept is connected with the rule of law and its interpretation by the BVerfGE. Dealing with the legitimation of punishing former GDR-agents it quotes in decision BVerfGE 92, 277:[78]

> State punishment is subject at several levels to the proportionality test required by the rule of law: at the norm level, the punishment reinforcement as such and the threatened severity of punishment, at the level of the knowledge of punishment, the allocation of the punishment according to the degree of guilt and the need for punishment. The intermediate decision on criminal prosecution must also be subjected to such a proportionality test. The suitability and necessity of criminal prosecution with regard to the attainment of the purpose of the punishment, however, results in principle from the fact that a criminal offence can only fulfil its purpose if it is also enforced. However, the examination of the third stage of constitutional proportionality, the so-called 'proportionality in the narrower sense', has its own significance. As the Senate stated in another context, the purpose of this third stage is precisely subject to the measures identified as suitable and necessary to an opposing control with regard to whether the means of prosecution and punishment used, taking into account the restrictions on fundamental rights which they entail, are still proportionate for the person concerned to the protection of legal interests

75 *Ibid.*; cf. Tomforde, *Die Zulassigkeit* (1999), 141.
76 Joerg Eisele, 'Vor § 13' (2014), 13.
77 Maurach and Zipf, *Strafrecht Allgemeiner Teil* (1992), § 7 III mn. 14.
78 BVerfGE 92, 277 ff., mn. 187 ff.

> which can thereby be achieved. This may result in the protection legitimately sought having to take a back seat under certain circumstances if the means used would lead to an unreasonable impairment of the rights of the person concerned (see BVerfGE 90, 145 (185) BVerfGE 92, 277 (326) BVerfGE 92, 277 (327)). The principle of proportionality in the narrower sense requires a balance to be struck between the public interest, the exercise of which requires intervention in fundamental rights, and the effects on the legal interests of those affected. The weighting of the conflicting interests to be linked and weighed makes it necessary to assess the interaction of the conditions and effects of the intervention rule which are significant for the respective interest. As such, however, the principle of proportionality in the narrower sense contains no substantive statements as to which effects and conditions of a state intervention are to be included in the consideration and when a means is proportionate and when it is not ... In this respect, an evaluative constitutional decision is required in each individual case. This also applies to state interventions in the area of criminal law. As far as the assessment of the proportionality of a threat of punishment or the amount of a penalty is concerned, the principle of guilt which is decisive in this respect and which demands that the consequences of a punishable offence for the seriousness of the infringement of a right and for the individual culpability are in a just relationship. In its effects limiting the punishment, it coincides with the constitutional principle of the prohibition of excessive punishment (see BVerfGE 50, 205 [215]). On the other hand, other criminal law measures must include other conditions in the assessment. This applies in particular when a certain event, such as the singular situation under state and criminal law arising in the course of reunification, which is without precedent and cannot be repeated in this way, raises the question, whether the prosecution of certain criminal offences – which is still appropriate and necessary for the enforcement of the purpose of the punishment – leads to such a strong impairment of the legal rights of those affected that this clearly outweighs the protection of legal interests achievable by the prosecution.

Compliance with the principle of constitutional proportionality is generally checked as follows:

(a) *Suitability* – the chosen means (punishment) has to be suitable for achieving the pursued (legitimate) purpose. Whether and to what extent different kinds of punishment are actually suitable for preventing further crimes is far from self-evident.
(b) *Necessity* – between several equally effective means of prevention the least harmful has to be chosen. This is reflected in the above-mentioned possibilities to abate proceedings subject to conditions and the priority of financial penalties over imprisonment.

(c) *Adequacy* – as a last step, the interests of the offender, especially the severity of the chosen punishment has to be weighed against the interests of the public, especially the necessary degree of prevention.

The relationship between constitutional proportionality and the 'principle of guilt' have remained unclarified. Some say that they are practically congruent.[79] Others want to abolish the 'principle of guilt' and rely fully on constitutional proportionality instead in order to eradicate all remaining vestiges of retributivism and also because of philosophical reservations with regard to 'guilt' as an expression of an existing free will.[80]

However, it is doubtful whether constitutional proportionality really is suitable for replacing the principle of guilt. This is because of the difficulties that derive from the application of the described elements of constitutional proportionality in the context of criminal punishment. With regard to the reformation of the offender, a lack of empirical evidence makes it difficult to say which sentence is *suitable* and *necessary* for preventing further crimes of the offender. The same applies for the purpose of deterrence – it is hard to say which degree of punishment has psychological effects on the general public. If one is to say that the *guilt-proportionate* punishment also represents the kind of punishment that is *suitable* and *necessary* for deterring the population, this would contradict the necessity of abolishing the 'principle of guilt'.[81]

On the other hand, it can be asked whether it should be unnecessary to be able to provide answers to the categories of suitability and necessity of punishment, and the principle of constitutional proportionality just demonstrates how severely we fail in that regard.[82] A consequential pursuit of this idea would lead to the application of the principle *in dubio pro libertate*, although this is hardly ever seriously demanded.[83]

However, a danger of the principle of constitutional proportionality is that the weighing of interests would allow to give priority to the interests of the public by waiving a fair punishment in particularly severe cases.[84] The principle of guilt acts as a valuable limit to overly severe punishment that would still be considered adequate according to constitutional proportionality.

[79] BVerfGE 34, 261, 267.

[80] Cf. Roxin, *Strafrecht* (1997), mn. 51.

[81] Frisch, 'Schuldgrundsatz' (2013), 251.

[82] Cf. Hassemer, 'Der Grundsatz der Verhaltnismasigkeit' (2006), 124 f.

[83] *Ibid.*, 124.

[84] Hörnle, *Tatproportionale Strafzumessung* (1999), 325.

But, if constitutional proportionality is not capable of replacing the 'principle of guilt', how useful is it in complementing it in the field of criminal punishment?

Following the 'margin theory' in sentencing requires the determination of a 'frame of guilt' before considering preventive aspects of punishment within that frame that could be subject to constitutional proportionality, the limiting function seems to be narrow. Within the frame of guilt-proportionate punishment it seems unlikely that the consideration of preventive purposes that shift the punishment further towards the upper or lower ends of the frame can be completely disproportionate. The 'principle of guilt' already sets boundaries that are generally narrower than the ones of constitutional proportionality that can only prevent an excessively low and an excessively high punishment.

However, it could be desirable to correct the principle of guilt towards the bottom if the guilt of the offender would require a certain punishment, but preventive aspects do not let punishment seem necessary. In this scenario, punishment would definitely be *unsuitable* and *unnecessary* in the sense of constitutional proportionality. At the same time, the principle of guilt acts, as just mentioned, as a corrective mechanism of constitutional proportionality towards the top. Accordingly, both principles would act as reciprocal control mechanisms, providing checks and balances in order to set or remove lower and upper limits of punishment.[85]

(f) Summary

To sum up, it can be noted that in German law the 'principle of guilt' (or a non-morally understood equivalent) at least serves as an upper limit of

[85] By contrast, for the 'second track' of the German sentencing system consisting of measures for the prevention of crime and social improvement of offenders, the principle of constitutional proportionality is of particular importance. The difference between criminal punishment and 'measures' is that the latter do not require an individual guilt of the offender and are based purely on preventive considerations. Therefore, the 'principle of guilt' is unavailable as a mediating principle. The principle of constitutional proportionality accordingly has the important function of preventing the application of measures that are disproportionately severe compared to the intended purpose. To underline the importance of constitutional proportionality, in § 62 StGB (the section preceding the regulations on 'measures') it is explicitly stated that the application of measures must not be disproportionate to 'the crimes committed by the offender and the ones that are to be expected from him in the future and the degree of danger posed by the offender for the public'.

punishment while there is debate about the question of its downward limiting function.[86] However, it is questionable to what extent it can also serve as an instrument of proportionality. While both the Punktstrafetheorie and the Stellenwerttheorie could be effective in that regard – both emphasise retributive aspects in punishment that would allow the classification of more or less severe degrees of guilt – the prevailing 'margin theory' only provides different 'frames of guilt' that can be scaled but are much vaguer. The *ultima ratio* theory in fact is an alternative but related concept to the principle of guilt (as understood in German sentencing practice) enriched with costs-and-benefits arguments. The constitutional principle of proportionality as interpreted by the German Federal Constitutional Court can be seen as a basis for a real alternative sentencing concept. But as it is primarily a balancing principle it has to be completed by criteria of retributive and consequentialist proportionality.

IV How Do Retributive and Consequentialist Proportionality Principles Differ?

The similarities and differences between the constitutive elements of retributive and consequentialist proportionality have more than theoretical importance. Any balanced and practically feasible punishment theory must accommodate all widely accepted punishment principles and goals, both retributive and non-retributive – punishment policy and practice cannot simply ignore one set of principles or the other (and, to our knowledge, no modern punishment regime ever has; all modern systems are normative hybrids of one kind or another). It is therefore necessary to find as much common ground between these conflicting principles as possible, so that their combination in a mixed or hybrid approach does as little damage to each as possible.

1 Ends–Benefits Proportionality Compared to Retributive Proportionality

Ends–benefits and retributive principles both require proportionality relative to offence severity, but the two theories measure such severity differently. Consequentialist theory punishes in proportion to the harm caused or threatened by the offence, but that theory considers not only

[86] See on the overall topic Tomforde, *Die Zulassigkeit* (1999).

the harm associated with a particular act similar to the defendant's, but also the aggregate harm caused by all such actions, and the relative difficulty of detecting and deterring such actions. As for the second retributive element of offence severity – offender culpability (intent, motive, role in the offence, etc.) – consequentialists consider culpability factors only to the extent that they are related to the likely future benefits of punishment (e.g. the dangerousness and deterrability of this offender or other potential offenders).[87] Finally, in choosing the proper sentence for a particular offender or group of similar offenders, consequentialist theory considers not only the actual crime-control or other benefits produced by sanctions, but also the costs and any undesirable consequences of the sanction. Such consequences might include the perverse incentives produced by harsh penalties (e.g. if such penalties encourage offenders to kill potential witnesses or arresting officers). Another example would be the tendency for disproportionate penalties to undermine the public's sense of the relative gravity of different crimes, and to risk public loss of respect for, and willingness to obey and cooperate with, criminal justice authorities. As the philosopher H. L. A. Hart said, '[If] the relative severity of penalties diverges sharply from this rough scale [of proportionality], there is a risk of either confusing common morality or flouting it and bringing the law into contempt.'[88]

2 The Alternative-Means Principle – Does It Have a Retributive Counterpart?

The alternative-means proportionality principle, also referred to as parsimony or the requirement of necessity or narrow-tailoring of intrusive government measures, is a central tenet of consequentialist philosophy, and one that operates in an asymmetric fashion – there is no counterpart principle of such widespread application specifying that government measures should be *no less severe* than necessary to achieve their purposes. Underlying the asymmetric parsimony principle are two more fundamental beliefs. One is the recognition that assessments of

[87] E.g. it might reasonably be assumed that offenders who cause harm deliberately (with purpose or 'specific intent') are generally more dangerous (more likely to commit future offences) than offenders who act negligently or recklessly. Offenders who act purposefully are perhaps also more likely to pay attention to, and be deterred by, a higher penalty.

[88] Hart, *Punishment and Responsibility* (1968), 25. See also American Law Institute, *Model Penal Code* (2017), Reporter's Note at 33 (addressing the concern for moral legitimacy in sentencing).

government needs can easily err in both directions – the proposed government measure can be too severe under the circumstances, or it can be too lenient. The other underlying assumption is that, as a normative matter, it is better to respond to the inherent risk of government error by choosing (through an asymmetric necessity principle) to err more often on the side of too little rather than too much, particularly where criminal penalties are concerned – we know these measures are costly and hurtful; we are much less sure what, if any, benefits they provide.

Although it might be assumed that the parsimony principle has no application to punishments justified by retributive goals, retributivists should perhaps also favour an asymmetric, parsimony-type principle – preferring to err on the side of imposing too little rather than too much punishment. As with consequentialist assessments, retributivists must recognise the inherent risks of error in making judgments of desert (even judgments of ordinal (relative) desert – offender *A* is much more blameworthy than offender *B*). Given those risks, a retributivist might further conclude that penalties exceeding desert are normatively a worse outcome than penalties less than desert. Similar premises underlie the requirement of proof beyond a reasonable doubt – it is worse to convict an innocent person (or to convict a person of a more serious crime than he or she actually committed) than to acquit a guilty person (or fail to convict for a more serious crime).[89] Likewise, the rule of strict construction of criminal statutes is asymmetric – the underlying normative assumption is that it is better to have too few convictions, and too narrow a criminal law scope, than too many convictions and too broad a scope. All of these rules probably reflect retributive as well as consequentialist concerns.

Some versions of limiting retributivism expressly endorse an asymmetric, parsimony-type principle, under which upper retributive limits on penalty severity are quite firm while lower limits are more flexible, or even non-existent.[90]

[89] Although the reasonable-doubt rule might be thought of as solely a means to ensure that innocent persons are not convicted, the rule also acts as an asymmetric limit on punishment severity. More serious crimes authorise more severe punishment. Thus, when the reasonable-doubt rule prevents conviction of a more serious crime it is effectively limiting the severity of punishment, while at the same time often allowing conviction for a less serious crime.

[90] For further discussion, see Frase, *Just Sentencing* (2013), 25–31 (citing numerous authors who have endorsed an asymmetric conception of retributive proportionality).

V How Have Common Law Systems Incorporated Proportionality Principles?

Proportionality is treated as the overarching distributive principle of sentencing in many common law jurisdictions. It has achieved this status mainly through judicial interpretation of the common law or, in some instances, of state constitutions. Few state constitutions or, for that matter, international human rights instruments expressly provide that sentences must be proportionate to offence gravity (however that may be defined). It is telling, for example, that the European Convention on Human Rights, while dealing in some detail with the rights of suspected and accused persons, mainly in Articles 5 and 6, says nothing about the values or principles that should govern the selection of sentence. Granted Article 7 gives expression to the *nulla poena sine lege* maxim by providing that a person shall not be subject to a heavier penalty than that which applied when the offence was committed, and Article 3 outlaws torture and inhuman and degrading treatment or punishment. Admittedly, Article 3 may probably be invoked to challenge a sentence that is manifestly disproportionate, having regard to the nature of the offence or the offender's personal circumstances.[91] Of course, the Convention was adopted in 1950 when sentencing was not generally viewed as a matter of great significance. This doubtless explains also why sentencing seldom features in the texts of national constitutions. By contrast, the Charter of Fundamental Rights of the European Union, which entered into force in 2009, provides (Art. 49(3)): 'The severity of penalties must not be disproportionate to the criminal offence.' At the level of domestic constitutional law, proportionality requirements have been judicially derived from express provisions outlawing cruel, unusual, inhuman or degrading treatment or punishment, or mandating trial in due course of law.

The precise legal status of proportionality within a legal system determines its capacity to control legislative efforts to introduce harsh punishments, either generally or for particular offences. If proportionality is treated as a constitutional imperative, and if the relevant constitutional order permits the judiciary to invalidate statutory measures (as is true of

[91] Emmerson et al, *Human Rights* (2012), ch. 20. In *R* v. *Qazi and Hussain* [2011] 2 Cr. App. R. (S.) 8, the English Court of Appeal said that in an extreme case sending a seriously ill or disabled person to prison could amount to a violation of Art. 3 of the Convention. However, such a case is unlikely to arise in practice: see *R* v. *Hall* [2013] 2 Cr. App. R. (S.) 68.

the United States, Canada and Ireland), mandatory and mandatory minimum sentences may be challenged on proportionality grounds. If, on the other hand, proportionality is recognised solely as a common law principle or if it is just enshrined in legislation, it may be overridden by statutes introducing mandatory measure that are likely to have a disproportionately severe impact on at least some of the offenders to whom they will apply. For example, in a landmark decision in 1979, the High Court of Australia held that proportionality is a fundamental principle of sentencing, but only in the absence of legislation to the contrary.[92] This decision undoubtedly emboldened courts in other jurisdictions to endorse proportionality as the dominant distributive principle of sentencing. Yet, in Australia itself, it remains a common law principle that may, in theory at least, be overridden by legislation. In Canada, Ireland and the United States, on the other hand, proportionality has a more secure constitutional foundation although, as we shall see, in the United States this status has been less than ineffective, at federal level at any rate, in controlling harsh mandatory penalties.

In both the United States and Canada, proportionality jurisprudence derives from similar constitutional provisions. The Eighth Amendment to the Constitution of the United States outlaws cruel and unusual punishment, while section 12 of the Canadian Charter of Rights and Freedoms states that everyone has the right not to be subject to any cruel and unusual punishment or treatment.[93] The test applied by the Supreme Courts of both jurisdictions when adjudicating upon the constitutionality of mandatory penalties is essentially the same. It must be established that the penalty is question is grossly disproportionate. Yet, the Canadian Supreme Court has invalidated relatively low mandatory penalties in circumstances where its American counterpart almost certainly would not. In *R* v. *Smith*,[94] the Canadian court struck down a provision which made the importation of narcotics punishable with at least seven years' imprisonment, irrespective of the amount involved or other

[92] *Veen* v. *The Queen (No. 1)* (1979) 143 CLR 458. In *Veen* v. *The Queen (No. 2)* (1988) 164 CLR 465, the High Court returned to the topic and treated proportionality as a limiting principle within which various purposes and values, such as deterrence and rehabilitation, may be accommodated. See Freiberg, *Fox & Freiberg's Sentencing* (2014), paras. 3.45 ff.

[93] The Canadian Criminal Code, which has the force of statute, provides (s. 718(1)) that a sentence must be proportionate to the gravity of the offence and the offender's degree of responsibility.

[94] [1987] 1 SCR 1045.

circumstances. By contrast, in *Harmelin* v. *Michigan*[95] the United States Supreme Court upheld a life sentence without the possibility of parole in the case of a person with no prior felony convictions who was convicted of possessing 650 grams of cocaine. The US court has, however, been somewhat more receptive to proportionality arguments when dealing with challenges to severe sentences, including the death penalty, for juvenile offenders.[96] Differences in legal and political culture, even between two neighbouring countries such as the United States and Canada, can propel radically different outcomes in proportionality-based challenges.

In Ireland, the proportionality principle has been derived from a set of constitutional provisions guaranteeing equality before the law, the right to trial in due course of law and the right to personal liberty.[97] Moreover, the courts have defined proportionality in quite an expansive way by holding that a sentence must be proportionate to the gravity of the offence and the personal circumstances of the offender.[98] Those circumstances must be assessed as they stand at the time of sentence, rather than when the offence was committed. Yet, if the acid test of an effective constitutionally based proportionality principle is its ability to control the use of mandatory sentences, the Irish story to-date has not been very promising. When faced with deciding if the mandatory life sentence for murder was constitutional, the Supreme Court held that the proportionality doctrine applied solely to offences governed by maximum as opposed to mandatory sentences. The court did not however give *carte blanche* to the legislature to introduce any mandatory sentences of its choosing, but it said that the constitutionality of any such sentences would be judged by reference to reasonableness rather than proportionality.[99]

By contrast, the Canadian Supreme Court has not hesitated to find certain mandatory minimum sentences to be in violation of the Charter of Rights and Freedoms which, as noted, prohibits the imposition of cruel

95 501 US 957 (1991).

96 *Graham* v. *Florida* 560 US 48 (2010); *Miller* v. *Alabama* 567 US 460 (2012); *Roper* v. *Simmons* 543 US 551 (2005).

97 *State (Healy)* v. *Donoghue* [1976] IR 325. On proportionality in Ireland, see O'Malley, *Sentencing Law and Practice* (2016), ch. 4.

98 *People (DPP)* v. *M* [1994] 3 IR 306; *People (DPP)* v. *Kelly* [2005] 2 IR 321; *Gilligan* v. *Ireland* [2013] 2 IR 745.

99 *Lynch and Whelan* v. *Minister for Justice* [2012] 1 IR 1; *Ellis* v. *Minister for Justice* [2017] IECA 237.

and unusual punishment. Admittedly, Canada has an extraordinarily high number of mandatory minimum sentences; there are currently more than seventy in the Criminal Code and the Controlled Drugs and Substances Act. The Supreme Court's decision in *Smith* struck down a mandatory minimum seven-year prison term for narcotics offences. However, almost thirty years were to elapse before it struck down any further mandatory minimum. Then, in quick succession it struck down three such sentences. In *R* v. *Nur and Charles*[100] it invalidated two mandatory minimum sentences for certain firearms offences, and in *R* v. *Lloyd*[101] the Court held that a one-year mandatory minimum sentence for possession of drugs violated s. 12 of the Charter. More recently, the Ontario Court of Appeal held that a mandatory minimum six-month sentence for possession of child pornography also violated the same Charter provision.[102] One defining and commendable feature of Canadian sentencing jurisprudence is that the courts, when faced with a proportionality-based challenge to a mandatory penalty consider not only facts of the particular case, but also whether the sentence would be grossly disproportionate in a reasonable hypothetical case with different facts. This has been a crucial factor in several cases where mandatory minimums were successfully challenged.

To an increasing extent, persons convicted of serious offences suffer consequences over and above the primary punishment – which will typically be a term of imprisonment, a fine or both. Ancillary measures such as civil penalties (especially in revenue cases), disqualification, confiscation, forfeiture and compulsory registration as a sex-offender have proliferated in recent years. Not all of these measures may be formally recognised as criminal penalties,[103] but courts in many jurisdictions, including Ireland, have been willing to accept that they can have a punitive impact and may therefore be put into the balance when

[100] [2015] 1 SCR 773. See Shanmuganathan, 'R v Nur' (2016).

[101] [2016] 1 SCR 130.

[102] *R* v. *John* (2018) ONCA 702.

[103] The United States Supreme Court, the European Court of Human Rights and the Irish High Court have all held that a sex-offender notification order is essentially a preventive measure and not, strictly speaking, a penalty: *Smith* v. *Doe*, 538 US 84 (2003); *Ibbotson* v. *United Kingdom* (1998) 27 EHRR CD 332; *Adamson* v. *United Kingdom* (1999) 28 EHRR CD 209; *Enright* v. *Ireland* [2003] 2 IR 321; *P.H.* v. *Ireland* [2006] 2 IR 540. See generally O'Malley, *Sexual Offences* (2013), ch. 27. The European Court of Human Rights was, however, willing to accept that a confiscation order was a penalty for the purpose of Art. 7 of the Convention: *Welch* v. *United Kingdom* (1995) 20 EHRR 247.

assessing a proportionate primary penalty.[104] This certainly holds true of civil penalties and sex-offender notification requirements. Other consequences of the offence (as opposed to the sentence) pose greater conceptual and policy-related difficulties. An offender may, for example, have been subject to private revenge by way of a punishment beating or may have been subject to unremitting adverse publicity which can impinge severely not only on the offender but on his or her family as well.[105] There is an argument to be made for taking these matters into account at sentencing on the basis that punishment consists of some unpleasant consequence inflicted for criminal wrongdoing. Judicially imposed punishment is, of course, the main unpleasant consequence, but it should be so tailored, the argument might run, to take account of other such consequences the offender has already endured. As against this, it may be argued that in a modern democratic system of government, committed to upholding the rule of law, the state should have a monopoly on the infliction of criminal punishment.[106] A court that takes account of, say, a punishment beating to which the offender has already been subject is, in a sense, recognising, though not necessarily legitimating, an exercise in private revenge. Be that as it may, courts are generally willing to grant some mitigation to offenders on this account. Recently, for example, the Supreme Court of Canada in *R v. Suter*[107] held that some credit should be given for violence inflicted by others on the appellant, apparently as a punishment for the conduct constituting the offence. The court said that tailoring a sentence to reflect the circumstances of both the offence and the offender may require the sentencing judge to consider collateral consequences which it defined as 'any consequence arising from the commission of an offence, the conviction for an offence or the sentence imposed for an offence, that impacts the offender'.[108] The Federal Court of Australia has also accepted that private violence inflicted on an offender for his involvement in the offence should be taken into account at sentencing,

[104] *People (DPP)* v. *Redmond* [2001] 1 IR 390 (revenue penalties); *C.C.* v. *Ireland* [2006] 4 IR 1 (sex-offender notification orders).

[105] In *People (DPP)* v. *Lyons* [2014] IECCA 27, the Irish Court of Criminal Appeal was willing to treat adverse publicity of this nature as a mitigating factor, but only to a slight degree.

[106] For a thoughtful analysis, see Thorburn, 'Proportionate Sentencing' (2012), ch. 16.

[107] 2018 SCC 34.

[108] 2018 SCC 34, paras. 46 and 47. The court was heavily influenced by arguments to this effect in Manson, *Law of Sentencing* (2001).

while stressing that this should not be interpreted as conferring any approval on the revenge attack.[109] There is Irish authority to the same effect.[110] Similar policy-related difficulties may arise when a sentencing court is urged to consider collateral consequences of an economic nature such as where the offender will lose his or her employment or pension rights as a result of the conviction or, perhaps, as a result of being sent to prison. Some would oppose granting mitigation on this account, arguing that it may favour richer offenders who are fortunate enough to have employment and pension entitlements, when many others have nothing left to lose. In practice, however, some limited mitigation is usually granted on this account.[111]

Although sentencing statutes in the United States rarely mention proportionality, and even more rarely define the criteria by which proportionality should be measured, sentencing guidelines reforms in some American states have expressly endorsed retributive proportionality ('just deserts', or 'modified just deserts').[112] Some of these systems have also expressly endorsed some version of the alternative-means proportionality (or parsimony) principle.[113] Very few systems expressly endorse ends–benefits proportionality, perhaps because cost–benefit and cost-effectiveness are such widely accepted values that it was not thought necessary to state them as goals. But the ends–benefits principle is sometimes found in statutes or constitutional provisions and case law.[114]

[109] *R* v. *Mamarika* [1982] FCA 92, 42 ALR 94.

[110] See e.g. *People (DPP)* v. *A.L.* [2014] IECA 38.

[111] For a useful discussion, see Podgor, 'White Collar Sentencing' (2007).

[112] See e.g. Minnesota Sentencing Guidelines Commission (1984), v, 1, 10–14 (endorsing proportionality of sentences to offence severity and criminal history, and adopting retribution as the primary sentencing goal).

[113] *Ibid.*, v (sanctions 'should be the least restrictive necessary to achieve the purposes of the sentence'). See generally Sullivan and Frase, *Proportionality Principles* (2009), 129–68 (discussing examples of alternative-means or parsimony principles in American and foreign sentencing and constitutional laws).

[114] See e.g. Frase, *Just Sentencing* (2013), 152, 156–7, 161 (noting that both the Kansas and the North Carolina sentencing guidelines sought to improve sentencing proportionality, and appeared to measure this relative to the public and private harms associated with each crime, rather than the standard retributive criteria of harm and offender culpability). See also *ibid.*, 162–4 (noting implicit guidelines endorsements of crime-control efficiency and effectiveness goals in Alabama, Delaware and Missouri). See generally Sullivan and Frase, *Proportionality Principles* (2009), 129–68 (discussing examples of ends–benefits proportionality principles in American and foreign sentencing and constitutional laws).

VI How Has the German System Incorporated Proportionality Principles? A Quest for Broader Theory of Proportionality in German Legal Theory?

After having demonstrated elements of proportionality in German sentencing it has become apparent that German criminal law does not recognise proportionality as a priority because it mixes retributive and consequentialist elements, thereby making punishment rather unpredictable. The following section therefore examines whether a cohesive system of proportionality can be developed on the basis of retributive and consequentialist theories.

1 *Retributive Proportionality/'Just Deserts'*

Retributivism can be regarded as the origin of proportionality. The *ius talionis* provides a simple answer to the issue of proportionality – the principle 'an eye for an eye and a tooth for a tooth' is self-explanatory. Of course, the principle cannot be applied in a modern state under the rule of law, as it would require excessive punishment such as the death penalty. It also has logical limitations as not every crime can be inflicted on the offender.[115] However, as described above, Hegel already recognised that a retributive concept could only work if it provides a punishment *proportional* or *comparable* to the offence, but not *identical* to it. In other words, a retributive concept of punishment could only work if it moves 'away from strict proportionality and into rough commensurability'.[116] However, while it is relatively easy to identify punishment that is undeserved because it is excessively low or excessively high[117] as is practised in German sentencing following the logic of the 'margin theory', the existence of *the* just punishment may be a valuable thought in legal philosophy; in practice, however, it is not possible to calculate it. Thus, irrespective of possible doctrinal reservations in regard of a retributive concept of proportionality, one would have to find a solution that can actually be applied in practice. This could be to acknowledge that, on the basis of a criminal code that provides judges with a wide discretion in regard to sentencing, it really is only possible to narrow down the commensurate punishment from both the upper and lower ends.

115 Flanders, 'Can Retributivism Be Saved?' (2014) (using the example of child abuse).
116 *Ibid.*
117 Cf. von Hirsch, *Past or Future Crimes* (1985), 43–4.

Accordingly, a retributive concept of proportionality could, like the 'margin theory', provide a scope of at least *not absolutely incommensurate* punishment. It would then be possible to scale these different ranges of punishment, thereby providing at least rough proportionality.

2 *Offence-Related Proportionality (von Hirsch/Hörnle)*

However, if this is not enough, how can the scale be made more precise? This is linked to the question of the nature of 'guilt' and the (not fully clarified) differences between retribution, atonement and the compensation of guilt. In our opinion, retribution merely plays a role for general prevention (in the sense of a communicational strengthening of the public's confidence in the legal order) while atonement is important for special prevention: one factor of the risk assessment necessary for the suspension of sentences with probation according to § 56(1) StGB is whether the offender has processed her actions.[118]

The compensation of guilt, on the other hand, recognised as a main function of criminal law by the German Federal Supreme Court,[119] provides the main source of proportionality. Guilt in this sense can be broken down to the guilt reflected in the *crime* and the personal guilt or blameworthiness of the *offender*. While, for example, the severity of a robbery can be equal between two offenders, the mental illness or extreme poverty of one of them may drastically reduce her *personal* guilt.

The crucial difference between offence-related and offender-related guilt in the context of proportionality is that the severity of a crime can be scaled much more precisely than the personal guilt of offenders that cannot be fathomed sufficiently in a trial and is generally harder to quantify. Thus, coming back to the question of making the scale of commensurable punishment more precise, this would be possible by just concentrating on the guilt reflected in the crime itself. And indeed, recently, a growing number of voices advocate for the implementation of an offence-oriented principle of proportionality – internationally and in Germany – arguing that it could provide a greater transparency, consistency and predictability in sentencing.[120] This development has internationally particularly been triggered by the different

[118] Cf. Grube, 'Strafrechtspflege Die Strafaussetzung' (2010), 762.
[119] BVerfG 39, 1, 57.
[120] Albrecht et. al., *Tatproportionalitat* (2003), 1.

'three-strikes-laws' in the United States that entail drastically increased punishment for repeat offenders.[121]

The objection that an offence-oriented concept of proportionality would necessarily have to disregard the degree of blameworthiness reflected in the personality of the offender might be countered by arguing that the consideration of personal blameworthiness could contradict the offence-related severity. Remembering the example of the mentally ill and the sane robber, one could *either* punish both commensurable with the offence *or* commensurable with their personal blameworthiness. This realisation could be regarded as an 'antinomy' of offence-related and personal guilt.

In German law, it is suggested to apply offence-oriented proportionality on the basis of the facts relevant to the guilt of the offender.[122] However, *de lege lata* it seems difficult to apply such a principle in German law. Especially clause 2 of § 46(1) StGB, stating that the consequences of punishment for the future life of the offender have to be taken into account contradicts a purely offence-related approach. Hörnle argues that sentence two of § 46(1) has to be understood as a rule-and-exception provision in the sense that divergence from the offence-oriented punishment is possible if specific instances make it necessary.[123] However, the extensive exclusion of preventive considerations is not consistent with the German system of punishment that since the 1960s has explicitly taken a preventive approach. This approach is expressed not only in § 46(1) but, for example, in §§ 47 and 56, as described in the earlier discussion of the Stellenwerttheorie.

But regardless of the compatibility of such an approach with current German law a significant increase of punishment is to be feared in some areas, for example with regard to socially integrated first offenders.[124] Furthermore, the desired limitation of the sentencing of multiple offenders would also be possible with a merely limiting retributive concept.

3 *Consequentialist Proportionality*

Can Consequentialism and proportionality go together or does the consideration of consequentialist aspects automatically lead to

[121] *Ibid.*
[122] Hörnle, *Tatproportionale Strafzumessung* (1999), 324 ff.; cf. Streng, 'StGB § 46' (2017), mn. 109 with further references.
[123] Hörnle, *Tatproportionale Strafzumessung* (1999), 330.
[124] Streng, 'StGB § 46' (2017), mn. 112.

disproportionate punishment? Consideration could be given to the idea that – similar to retributive proportionality concepts – the different consequentialist aspects of punishment are quantified and applied to a certain case by adding or subtracting the different aspects so that the result indicates the need and the extent of punishment. In practice, this might be even harder than the finding of a retributively just sentence as there is insufficient empirical evidence on the actual consequences of punishment. Moreover, even if we gain more empirical insight, a purely consequentialist approach cannot be applied because it would allow excessive punishment or 'endless therapy' in severe cases.

Traditionally the German system might be prone to consequentialist proportionality due to Fichte and von Liszt.[125] As the main adjustments against excessive punishments do not refer to retributive proportionality, German criminal politics tend to use consequentialist arguments to introduce more severe sanctions or to promote further criminalisation. The reason for that might be that the German system usually operates with single arguments of single aspects of prevention. This cannot be seen as a frame of consequentialist proportionality. Both systems seem to face problems due to consequentialist thinking. The US system justifies mass-incarceration and the three-strikes-doctrine from a consequentialist perspective,[126] but those severe policies violate the fundamental principle that no one should be punished more than they deserve. On the German side, excessive sanctions (such as for sexual offenders, or whoever is in focus at the time) are justified by general preventive arguments, losing the connection to the principle of guilt.

On the other hand, consequential arguments can also lead to the decriminalisation of certain areas, as the current discussion about turnstile jumping/fare evasion and shoplifting shows.[127] So, what the German system lacks is a permanent framework of consequentialist proportionality.

VII Can All Proportionality Principles Be Recognised in a Single Punishment Model?

1 *Retributivism and Consequentialism*

If one adopts a negative, outer-limits-setting version of retributivism, then it is quite easy to also pursue the two consequentialist

125 See above Section II.4.(c).

126 Straube and Welke, 'Coping with Systems Risk' (1998), 796 ff.; Hassemer, *Sicherheit durch Strafrecht* (2006).

127 Bundestags-Drucksache 19/1115 v. 8.3.2018.

proportionality principles; within the range of retributively permissible (not undeserved) penalties, sanctions should be no more severe than necessary to achieve all applicable consequentialist goals (alternative-means proportionality), and should also not be so severe that the costs and burdens of the penalty outweigh its crime control and other practical benefits (the ends–benefits principle). Under this approach, each of the three proportionality principles independently acts to set an upper limit on sanction severity; a severe sanction is unacceptable if it violates any of the three proportionality principles. Some American sentencing guidelines systems have adopted a version of this approach. For example, the 'modified just deserts' model applied under the Minnesota guidelines, in effect since 1980, places much stricter retributive limits on maximum-allowed sanction severity than on minimum-required severity, and expressly endorses the alternative-means principle.[128]

Under a positive, determining version of retributivism, ordinal desert defines the degree of sanction severity precisely, or within a narrow range, even if that penalty violates alternative-means proportionality (a less severe sanction would achieve practical goals just as well) and/or violates ends–benefits proportionality (the costs and burdens of the sanction outweigh its practical benefits). Under this retributive model, the two consequentialist proportionality principles could still be considered when deciding between alternative sanction types deemed to be of equal severity, or when addressing issues of cardinal proportionality – that is, when setting the top and bottom ('anchoring points') of the penalty scale, when deciding at what level of offence severity custodial penalties start to be used and, perhaps, in resolving the broader question of whether and when any form of 'hard treatment' is required to express retributive censure.

2 *Adding German Limiting Principles*

First, a solution does not have to be a proportionality principle that solely considers the guilt of an offender represented in her actions, but rather the introduction of advisory sentencing guidelines (as advisory sentencing assessment directives as mentioned above) that specify criteria of a mixed concept of punishment, thereby providing a greater predictability in sentencing.

[128] See Frase, *Sentencing Principles* (1997); Frase, *Limiting Retributivism* (2004); and Frase, *Just Sentencing* (2013).

Secondly, within a framework of proportionality, a positively understood, determining version of retributivism, ordinal desert defines the degree of sanction severity more precisely than the principle of guilt. It is more comparable and more predictable. If the penalty violates alternative-means proportionality (a less severe sanction would achieve practical goals just as well, a lack of Strafbedürftigkeit) and/or violates ends–benefits proportionality (the costs and burdens of the sanction outweigh its practical benefits), there should be a regulating mechanism. This could be the principle of constitutional proportionality. Although a retributive model, the two consequentialist proportionality principles could still be considered when deciding between alternative sanction types or how to fill in the margin of the Spielraumtheorie. On a legislative level, consequentialist arguments might be useful in addressing the two issues noted above, concerning when custodial penalties must be used, and when 'hard treatment' is required. A significant advantage of a coherent model of proportionality seems to be that it could be integrated much more easily and with less friction into the constitutional paradigm of fundamental rights protection and (constitutional) proportionality.[129] Thus, the principle can also be a frame for the parsimony principle. Constitutional proportionality as a frame for retributive proportionality on a first level and consequential proportionality on a second level could also help to decrease excessive levels of sentencing, such as capital punishment or multiple life sentences. These severe punishments distort the frame of reference within which the standards of proportionality must be set. When such excessively high penalties define the top of the sentencing range they prevent retributive proportionality from being effective as a fair control mechanism – as clearly has happened in the United States.

The central element of any legitimate right of intervention under the rule of law is proportionality. Particularly constitutional proportionality gets in trouble in a system that favours 'security' – especially when, as today, the fight for security is controlled by emotions such as fear of risk, fear of crime and the need for control rather than by experienced serenity; this increases the chances of populist criminal policy and with it the probability of delimiting preventive interests.[130]

[129] Hassemer, 'Der Grundsatz der Verhaltnismasigkeit' (2006), 124 f.; Hassemer, *Strafen im Rechtsstaat* (2000), 248 ff., 268 ff.; Hassemer, *Freiheitliches Strafrech* (2001), 165 ff., 215 ff.; Hassemer, *Symbolisches Strafrecht* (1989), 553 ff.

[130] One example is the criminal law of the United States of America with its 'habitual offender laws' (often referred to colloquially as 'three strike laws'). Cf. on this Welke,

VIII Possible Challenges on the Way to a Coherent Model of Proportionality in Sentencing

Notwithstanding the optimistic tone of the previous section, which envisioned a single punishment model incorporating all proportionality principles, it is important not to understate the major impediments – in common law systems and in Germany – to adopting such a model.

1 *The Common Law Perspective*

There are major disagreements about how proportionality principles should be defined and harmonised; no single, coherent model is possible until some degree of consensus is achieved on several key issues. Above all, there is the debate, summarised in Section I, between proponents of strict (positive, determining) retributivism, and those who favour some version of limiting (negative) retributivism. As indicated in the previous section, the resolution of this debate has major implications for the design of any single or combined proportionality model. Limiting retributivism permits other punishment goals and limitations – including consequentialist proportionality principles – to play substantial roles; positive retributivism minimises those roles. Limiting retributivism also helps to resolve several persistent objections to retributive theory, including the following: (1) the reality that penalties have unequal subjective impacts on different offenders;[131] (2) the uncertain extent to which profoundly disadvantaged offenders can fairly be said to owe a 'debt to society';[132] (3) the difficulty of finding any substantial or precise retributive basis for the near-universal application of prior-record enhancements;[133] and (4) the unclear retributive grounds for the equally widespread practice of giving 'bulk discounts' to offenders being sentenced for more than one offence.[134] Limiting retributivism may also lessen the impact of disagreements over whether and to what extent 'hard treatment' is required, in order to adequately express retributive

'Mandatory Sentencing' (2002), 207 ff.; Grasberger, 'Three Strikes' (1998), 796 ff; Hassemer, *Strafen im Rechtsstaat* (2000), 248 ff., 80; Hassemer, *Sicherheit durch Strafrecht* (2006), 130 ff.; and Hassemer, 'Der Grundsatz der Verhaltnismasigkeit' (2006), 124 f.

131 See e.g. Kolber, 'Subjective Experience' (2009), 182–236.

132 See e.g. Murphy, 'Marxism and Retribution' (1973), 217–43.

133 See generally Roberts and von Hirsch, *Previous Convictions* (2010).

134 See generally Ryberg et al., *Sentencing Multiple Crimes* (2018).

censure.[135] Finally, to achieve a single model it will be necessary, or at least easier, if retributivists can be persuaded that the consequentialist ends–benefits and alternative-means principles are, indeed, properly viewed as aspects of proportionality, and therefore worthy of inclusion in the model alongside retributive proportionality.

2 *The German Perspective*

What is wrong with a mixed and reciprocally limiting principle with retributive and consequentialist aspects? If the aim of proportionality is to make punishment more transparent and predictable, maybe this is not a matter of the underlying criteria of proportionality but of recognisability and consistent application. This aim could for example be achieved by implementing advisory sentencing guidelines that contain detailed information on the (limiting) retributive and the consequentialist and preventive aspects alongside the obligation to justify divergences from the advised range of possible punishments in the verdict. The following examines the challenges that such an approach might face.

(a) Losing Legitimacy Due to a Lack of 'Special Prevention'?

The first one is the issue of handling multiple offenders (*Intensivtäter*) that apparently are not capable of being reintegrated into society. One possible, although drastic, approach is shown by Jakobs, who shaped the term *Feindstrafrecht* ('criminal law for enemies'). He deliberates about a twofold criminal law – a liberal criminal law for citizens and an 'enemy criminal law' that purely focuses on security needs and is not bound by constitutional obligations. To some extent, this approach is congruent with the demand of von Liszt to treat multiple offenders (after the third crime of a certain category) as incorrigible.[136]

However, this would not be compatible with a proportionality concept, as such an approach requires that the same rules and criteria apply to everyone. A modern and liberal society must not differentiate between citizens and enemies; even the most dangerous offender should be accepted as a citizen who can be reintegrated into society at some point.

135 For further discussion, see Frase, *Just Sentencing* (2013), 31–2, 52–7.

136 Jakobs, 'Kriminalisierung im Vorfeld' (1985), 751, 783 ff.; Jakobs, Das 'Selbstverstandnis' (2000), 47, 51.

(b) Roll-Back into the Offender-Focused Perspective: Losing the Limits

Still, there is a danger that such an approach is subsequently realised by attaching too much weight to preventive aspects – in current criminal law, for example, by imposing preventive detention according to § 66 StGB on offenders that likely will commit severe crimes again and therefore represent a danger for the public. While it is an advantage of a mixed proportionality concept that guilt-related and preventive aspects may limit each other, the limitation of the need to preventively incarcerate dangerous offenders commensurable to their guilt (represented in their crime and their personality) can currently be bypassed by the 'second track' of German criminal law that allows certain measures (for example, preventive detention) regardless of their guilt. It should be noted in that context that, even when accepting the need to incapacitate certain dangerous offenders beyond or regardless of their blameworthiness represented in their crime, in a state under the rule of law, no offender should be regarded as incorrigible. Even if it seems likely that an offender will always continue to commit crimes after being released from prison, this cannot be regarded as certain. Accordingly, preventive detention, for example, must be accompanied by periodic – neutral – reviews of the dangerousness of the incapacitated offender. The influence of Kant, Fichte and von Liszt can be seen here.

(c) Focusing on the Public – the Offender as an Instrument of Excessive General Prevention

A coherent proportionality concept must also give consideration to the dangers of excessive general prevention that may be triggered in times of election campaigning through the introduction of 'symbolic' criminal law or 'symbolic' sentencing in cases that generated extensive media coverage. In the words of Kant, the offender must not merely be a means for the deterrence of the public. Human dignity requires that offenders are recognised as human beings; they are not mere 'objects' of state activity. This aim could be achieved by stipulating other consequentialist aspects (e.g. the consequences of punishment for the future life of the offender, aspects of special prevention) that should be considered in sentencing in criminal code and, more precisely, in advisory sentencing guidelines. The influence of Fichte, Hegel, von Liszt and Jakobs is apparent.

(d) Losing Legitimacy Due to a Lack of 'General Prevention'?

As the counterpart of possible challenges in the context of lacking special prevention, challenges might also result from aspects compromising general prevention. Particularly, a recent trend towards a 'privatisation' and 'flexibilisation' of criminal law can be observed globally as well as in Germany. This is represented by an increasing number of trials settled by the use of plea bargaining and the growing practice of internal investigations. Both examples have the potential to undermine the claim of the state to autonomously and unexceptionally prosecute crimes as an integral and original task. The opening of 'loopholes' is capable of undermining the confidence of the public towards the effective and equal prosecution of crimes. Privatisation and flexibilities of criminal law accordingly undermine the concept of proportionality that by definition aims for a greater inflexibility in sentencing and the equal consideration of the underlying criteria. Plea bargaining is a particular challenge in that regard as it allows divergence from the proportional punishment that could have been found in the normal course of a trial.

The limiting function of proportionality in regard to plea bargaining is twofold: It would, on the one hand, prevent the threat of a disproportionate punishment in order to pressure the defendant to cooperate. On the other hand, proportionality would not allow disproportionate plea discounts. Therefore, the implementation of a concept of proportionality would narrow the scope of application of plea bargaining.

IX Conclusion

In common law jurisdictions, retributive proportionality principles are widely recognised as important justifications for and limitations on punishment. The consequentialist ends–benefits and alternative-means proportionality principles are also widely recognised in common law systems,[137] although only some of these systems have expressly applied one or both principles to sentencing decisions. Sentencing guidelines systems in a few US states have adopted both retributive and alternative-means proportionality principles. Some writers have proposed a model incorporating all three proportionality principles,[138] but no common law jurisdiction has yet expressly adopted such a model.

137 See generally Sullivan and Frase, *Proportionality Principles* (2009).
138 See Frase, *Just Sentencing* (2013).

In Germany, a close analysis of the principles of guilt and special and general prevention shows that both have elements of proportionality. The principle of guilt contains ideas of retributive proportionality, whereas the preventive aspects are partly related to common law consequentialist proportionality. Although the consideration of preventive purposes tends to lead to an extension of the penalties, perhaps these can be constrained by German constitutional proportionality principles, two of which (necessity and proportionality in the narrower sense) correspond to the common law alternative-means and ends–benefits principles.

A comparison of common law systems and the German system shows that the latter is less transparent in terms of the predictability of the level of penalties; in particular, it is not exactly predictable how the retributive margin (*Spielraum*) will be filled with various prevention considerations. The lack of transparent criteria of sentencing might be compensated by more detailed catalogues or guidelines, referring more to the offence than the offender. However, in some ways such advisory sentencing assessment directives are only needed to anchor the criteria of proportionality in practice, but above all to make them transparent. There is a special need where currently no binding criteria for sentencing have been established – in the area of the termination of criminal proceedings by agreement with the public prosecutor's office (and the court) in accordance with German Code of Criminal Procedure, § 153 (Non-Prosecution of Petty Offences) and § 153a (Provisional Dispensing with Court Action; Provisional Termination of Proceedings), and in the case of some sanctions under juvenile criminal law. Again, German constitutional proportionality principles have implications for punishment and sentencing; in particular, they emphasise the need to respect interests of the offender as well as interests of the victims and the society. But since these are designed as general regulating principles, German constitutional proportionality does not (yet) offer material criteria for sentencing.

In short, German criminal law, greatly influenced by the tradition of philosophical idealism, already incorporates elements of proportionality, represented in the principle of guilt and the principle of constitutional proportionality that should be understood as reciprocally limiting. At the same time, German law does not prioritise proportionality, and the sometimes seemingly eclectic consideration of retributive and various preventive aspects in sentencing make these decisions non-transparent and unpredictable.

This comparative study has shown that similar retributive and non-retributive proportionality principles can be found in both common law systems and the German system. But in both systems, these principles need to be made more explicit and harmonised into a single coherent proportionality model.

Bibliography

Albrecht H.-J., Frisch W. and Hirsch A. von, *Tatproportionalität. Normative und empirische Aspekte einer tatproportionalen Strafzumessung*, Heidelberg, C. F. Müller (2003).

American Law Institute, *Model Penal Code: Sentencing, Proposed Final Draft*, Philadelphia, American Law Institute (2017).

Beccaria C., *An Essay on Crimes and Punishments*, Brookline Village, MA, Branden Books (1992 [1764]).

Bentham J., *Theory of legislation*, 4th edn, trans. Richard Hildreth, London, Trübner (1882 [1789]).

Du Bois-Pedain A. 'Punishment as an Inclusionary Practice: Sentencing in a Liberal Constitutional State', in Ulväng M., du Bois-Pedain, A. and Asp, P. (eds.), *Criminal Law and the Authority of the State*, London, Bloomsbury Publishing (2017).

Dreher E., *Strafgesetzbuch und Nebengesetze*, 33rd edn, Munich, C. H. Beck (1972).

Duff, A., 'Legal and Moral Responsibility', *Philosophy Compass*, 4 (2009), 978–86.

Eisele J., 'Vor § 13', in Schönke A. and Schröder H. (eds.), *Strafgesetzbuch Kommentar, 29*, Munich, C. H. Beck (2014).

Emmerson B., Ashworth A. M., Choo A. L.-T. and Summers M. (eds.), *Human Rights and Criminal Justice*, London, Sweet & Maxwell (2012).

Feuerbach P. J. A., *Lehrbuch des Gemeinen in Deutschland Gültigen Peinlichen Rechts*, 4th edn, Darmstadt, Georg Friederich Heyer (1808).

Fichte J. G., *Grundlage des Naturrechts nach Prinzipien der Wissenschaftslehre*, 2nd edn, Leipzig, Germany: von Felix Meiner (1922 [1796])

Flanders C., 'Can Retributivism Be Saved', *Brigham Young University Law Review* (2014), 309–60.

Frase R. S., 'Sentencing Principles in Theory and Practice', *Crime and Justice*, 22 (1997), 363–433.

'Limiting Retributivism', in Tonry M. (ed.), *The Future of Imprisonment*, Oxford University Press (2004).

'Punishment Purposes', *Stanford Law Review*, 58 (2005), 67–81.

Just Sentencing: Principles and Procedures for a Workable System, Oxford University Press (2013).

Freiberg A., *Fox & Freiberg's Sentencing: State and Federal Law in Victoria*, 3rd edn, Pyrmont, NSW, Australia, Thomson Reuters (2014).

Fricker M., 'What's the Point of Blame? A Paradigm Based Explanation', *Noûs*, 50 (1) (2016), 165–83.

Frisch W., 'Chuldgrundsatz und Verhältnismäßigkeitsgrundsatz', *Neue zeitschrift für strafrecht*, 33(5) (2013), 249–56.

Gallas W., 'Der dogmatische Teil des Alternativ-Entwurfs', *Zeitschrift für die gesamte Strafrechtswissenschaft*, 80(1) (1968), 1–33.

Grasberger U., 'Three Strikes and You Are Out', *Zeitschrift für die gesamte Strafrechtswissenschaft*, 110 (1998), 796.

Greenawalt K., 'Punishment', in Dressler J. (ed.), *Encyclopedia of Crime and Justice*, New York, MacMillan (2001).

Grube A., 'Strafrechtspflege Die Strafaussetzung zur Bewährung', *JURA-Juristische Ausbildung*, 32(10) (2010), 759–65.

Hart H. L. A., *Punishment and Responsibility: Essays in the Philosophy of Law*, Oxford University Press (1968).

Hassemer W., 'Symbolisches Strafrecht und Rechtsgüterschutz', *Neue Zeitschrift für Strafrecht* (1989).

Strafen im Rechtsstaat, Berlin, Berliner-Wissenschafts-Verlag (2000).

Freiheitliches Strafrecht, Berlin, Berlner-Wissenschaft-Verlag (2001).

'Der Grundsatz der Verhältnismäßigkeit als Grenze strafrechtlicher Eingriffe', in Seelman K., Wohlers W. and Hirsch A. von (eds.), *Mediating Principles*, Baden-Baden, Nomos (2006).

'Sicherheit durch Strafrecht', Eröffnungsvortrag des 30. Strafverteidigertags, Frankfurt am Main (2006).

Hassemer W. and Burkhardt B. (eds.), *Die deutsche Strafrechtswissenschaft vor der Jahrtausendwende*, Munich, C. H. Beck (2000).

Hegel G. W. F., *Grundlinien der Philosophie des Rechts*, Stuttgart, Reclam (1970 [1820]).

Henkel H., *Die "richtige" Strafe: Gedanken zur richterlichen Strafzumessung*, Tübingen, Mohr Siebeck (1969).

Hirsch A. von, *Past or Future Crimes: Deservedness and Dangerousness in the Sentencing of Criminals*, 1st edn, Rutgers, NJ, Rutgers University Press (1985).

'Proportionality in the Philosophy of Punishment', *Crime and Justice*, 16 (1992), 55–98.

Censure and Sanctions, Oxford, Clarendon Press (1993).

'Proportionate Sentences: A Desert Perspective', in Hirsch A. von and Ashworth A. (eds.), *Principled Sentencing: Readings on Theory and Policy* Oxford, Hart (1998).

Deserved Criminal Sentences: An Overview, Oxford, Hart (2017).

Hirsch A. von, Bottoms A. E., Burney E. and Wikstrom P.-O., *Criminal Deterrence and Sentence Severity: An Analysis of Recent Research*, Oxford, Hart (1999).

Hirsch A. von, Neumann U. and Seelmann K. (eds.), *Strafe – Warum?*, Baden-Baden, Nomos (2011).

Honderich T., 'Idealism, German', in Honderich E. (ed.), *The Oxford Companion to Philosophy*, 2nd edn, Oxford University Press (1995).

Horn E. and Wolters G., '§ 46 StGB', in Wolter J. (ed.), *Systematischer Kommentar zum Strafgesetzbuch*, 9th edn, Munich, C. H. Beck (2017).

Hörnle T., *Tatproportionale Strafzumessung*, Berlin, Duncker & Humblot (1999).

'Gegenwärtige Strafbegründungstheorien', in Hirsch, A. von, Neumann U. and Seelmann K. (eds.), *Strafe – Warum?*, Baden-Baden, Nomos (2011).

Straftheorien, Tübingen, Mohr Siebeck (2011).

Jakobs G., 'Kriminalisierung im Vorfeld einer Rechtsgutverletzung', *Zeitschrift für die gesamte Strafrechtswissenschaft*, 97 (1985).

Strafrecht, allgemeiner Teil: die Grundlagen und die Zurechnungslehre: Lehrbuch, 2nd edn, Berlin/New York, De Gruyter (1991).

'Das Selbstverständnis der Strafrechtswissenschaft vor den Herausforderungen der Gegenwart', in Eser A., Hassemer W. and Burkhardt B. (eds.), *Die deutsche Strafrechtswissenschaft vor der Jahrtausendwende*, Munich, C. H. Beck (2000).

Kant I., *Die Metaphysik der Sitten*, trans. Horst Ebeling, Leipzig, Reclam (1990 [1797]).

Kolber A. J. 'The Subjective Experience of Punishment Essay', *Columbia Law Review*, 109 (2009), 182–236.

Lackner K. and Kühl K., 'StGB', in Lackner K. and Kühl K. (eds.), *Strafgesetzbuch mit Erläuterungen*, 28th edn, Munich, C. H. Beck (2014).

Lee Y., 'The Constitutional Right Against Excessive Punishment', *Virginia Law Review*, 91 (2005), 677–725.

Listz, F. von, 'Der Zweckgedanke im Strafrecht', in *Strafrechtliche Aufsätze und Vorträge*, 2 vols., Berlin, J. Guttentag (1905), I.

Manson A., *The Law of Sentencing*, Toronto: Irwin Law (2001).

Maurach R. and Zipf H., *Strafrecht Allgemeiner Teil, Teilband*, 8th edn, Heidelberg, Auflage (1992), Part I.

Miebach K. and Maier S., '§ 46. Grundsätze der Strafzumessung', in Jakobs W. and Miebach K. (eds.), *Münchener Kommentar zum Strafgesetzbuch*, II: *§§ 38-79b*, Munich, C. H. Beck (2016).

Minnesota Sentencing Guidelines Commission, *The Impact of the Minnesota Sentencing Guidelines: Three Year Evaluation*, Saint Paul, MN, Minnesota Sentencing Guidelines Commission (1984).

Morris N., *The Future of Imprisonment*, University of Chicago Press (1974).

Madness and the Criminal Law, University of Chicago Press (1982).

Morris Norval and Tonry, M., *Between Prison and Probation: Intermediate Punishments in a Rational Sentencing System*, Oxford University Press (1990).

Murphy J. G., 'Marxism and Retribution', *Philosophy and Public Affairs*, 2(3) (1973), 217–43.

O'Malley T., *Sexual Offences*, 2nd edn, Dublin, Round Hall (2013).

Sentencing Law and Practice, 3rd edn, Dublin, Round Hall (2016).
Peters S., '§ 153', in Schneider H. (ed.), *Münchener Kommentar zur Strafprozessordnung*, Munich, C. H. Beck (2016).
Pinkard T., 'How Kantian Was Hegel?', *The Review of Metaphysics*, 43(4) (1990), 831–8.
Podgor E. S., 'The Challenge of White Collar Sentencing', *Journal of Criminal Law & Criminology*, 97(3) (2006), 731–60.
Radin M. J., 'Jurisprudence of Death: Evolving Standards for the Cruel and Unusual Punishments Clause', *University of Pennsylvania Law Review*, 126 (1978), 989–1064.
Roberts J. V. and Hirsch A. von (eds.), *Previous Convictions at Sentencing: Theoretical and Applied Perspectives*, Sydney, Bloomsbury Publishing (2010).
Roxin C., *Strafrecht: Allgemeiner Teil. Grundlagen, der Aufbau der Verbrechenslehre*, Munich, C. H. Beck (1997).
Ryberg J., Roberts J. V. and Keijser J. W. de (ed.), *Sentencing Multiple Crimes*. Oxford University Press (2018).
Schäfer G., Sander G. M. and Gemmeren G. van, *Praxis der Strafzumessung*, 6th edn, Munich, C. H. Beck (2017).
Schwind H.-D., *Kriminologie*, Heidelberg, Kriminalistik Verlag (2013).
Shanmuganathan J., '*R v Nur*: A Positive Step but not the Solution to the Problem of Mandatory Minimums in Canada', *The Supreme Court Law Review*, (2d) 76 (2016), 329.
Singer R. G., 'Sending Men to Prison: Constitutional Aspects of the Burden of Proof and the Doctrine of the Least Drastic Alternative as Applied to Sentencing Determinations', *Cornell Law Review*, 58(1) (1972), 51–89.
Straub, D. W. and Welke, R. J., 'Coping with Systems Risk: Security Planning Models for Management Decision Making', *Management Information Systems Quarterly*, 22 (1998), 441.
Streng, F., 'Schuld, Vergeltung, Generalprävention. Eine tiefenpsychologische Rekonstruktion strafrechtlicher Zentralbegriffe', *Zeitschrift für die gesamte Strafrechtswissenschaft*, 92 (1980), 637–81.
'Schuld ohne Freiheit? Der funktionale Schuldbegriff auf dem Prüfstand', *Zeitschrift für die Gesamte Strafrechtswissenschaft* (1980).
'StGB § 46 Grundsätze der Strafzumessung', in Kindhäuser U., Neumann U. and Paeffgen H.-U. (eds.), *Nomos Kommentar Strafgesetzbuch*, 5th edn, Germany, Nomos (2017).
Stübinger S., *Das idealisierte Strafrecht: über Freiheit und Wahrheit in der Straftheorie und Strafprozessrechtslehre*, L: *Juristische Abhandlungen*, Frankfurt, Vittorio Klostermann (2008).
Sullivan T. E. and Frase R. S., *Proportionality Principles in American Law: Controlling Excessive Government Actions*. Oxford University Press (2009).

Thorburn M., 'Proportionate Sentencing and the Rule of Law', in Zedner L. and Roberts J. V. (eds.), *Principles and Values in Criminal Law and Criminal Justice: Essays in Honour of Andrew Ashworth*, Oxford University Press (2012).

Tomforde K., *Die Zulässigkeit einer Unterschreitung der schuldangemessenen Strafe aus präventiven Gesichtspunkten*, Baden-Baden, Nomos (1999).

Tonry M., 'Parsimony and Desert in Sentencing', in Hirsch A. von and Ashworth A. (eds.), *Principled sentencing: Readings on Theory and Policy*, Oxford, Hart (1998).

Tunick M., *Hegel's Political Philosophy: Interpreting the Practice of Legal Punishment*, Princeton University Press (2014).

Weigend T., 'Kommentar zu Tatjana Hörnle, Gegenwärtige strafbegründungstheorien', in Hirsch, A. von, Neumann U. and Seelmann K. (eds.), *Strafe – Warum?*, Baden-Baden, Nomos (2011).

Welke W. A., 'Mandatory Sentencing: Ein kritischer Bericht über die Tendenzen zu absoluten Strafen im Rechtsbereich des Common Law', *Zeitschrift für Rechtspolitik*, 5 (2002), 207–14.

Zimring F. E., Hawkins G. and Kamin S., *Punishment and Democracy: Three Strikes and You're Out in California*, Oxford University Press (2003).

8

Criminal History Enhancements at Sentencing

JULIAN ROBERTS AND STEFAN HARRENDORF*

I Introduction

A defendant's prior crimes affect decision-making throughout the criminal process, from decisions taken by the police, prosecutors and investigating magistrates (bail), through to prison and parole authorities considering whether to release prisoners.[1] It is at sentencing however, that criminal history has the greatest impact on decisions and the lives of defendants. Of all the aggravating factors, a criminal record is the most commonly invoked, the most powerful and also the most controversial. In general, people with prior convictions are treated more harshly in all criminal justice systems, civil and common law.[2] This near-universal sentencing policy is variously described as a *Recidivist Sentencing Premium*, a *Prior Record Enhancement*, or *Criminal History Enhancement*; the German term is *Strafschärfung für Rückfalltäter* or, briefer, *Rückfallschärfung*. The penologist Nigel Walker referred to prior convictions as 'the most obvious example of aggravation' and Hessick and Hessick described the recidivist sentencing premium as 'one punishment issue on which everyone seems to agree'.[3] In this chapter, we argue that it is

* Julian Roberts thanks his colleagues from the Robina Criminal History Project, Faculty of Law, University of Minnesota, for many fruitful discussions on these issues. We both are grateful for the comments on earlier drafts of this chapter from Thomas Weigend and the other members of the Anglo-German Dialogue Project. The authors contributed equally to the chapter.

1 For a comprehensive analysis, see Jacobs, *Eternal Criminal Record* (2015).

2 See discussion in Roberts, *Persistent Offenders* (2008), ch. 8. The only jurisdiction of which we are aware which prohibits courts from considering prior convictions as an aggravation is Western Australia: s. 7(2) of the Sentencing Act 1995 states that 'An offence is not aggravated by the fact that – . . . (b) the offender has a previous record.'

3 Walker, *Sentencing* (1985), 44; Hessick and Hessick, 'Double Jeopardy' (2011), 45–6. The German Federal Court of Justice (*Bundesgerichtshof* (BGH)) stated that such convictions are 'one of the most important factors in sentencing' (BGH, 04.08.1971, 2 StR 13/71, Entscheidungen des Bundesgerichtshofes in Strafsachen (BGHSt) 24, 198–200 at 200; translation by S. H.).

neither as obvious nor as consensual as these quotes suggest. Other authors seem closer to the truth when they describe 'the controversial question of sentencing repeat offenders'.[4]

Despite the apparent consensus regarding the significance of prior crimes for current adjudications, Germany (and other continental jurisdictions) differ from the Anglo-American countries in the ways they use prior convictions, as well as the justifications for considering prior crimes at sentencing. Moreover, there are great differences among the common law countries: repeat offenders are treated with greater severity across the United States compared to England and Wales, Canada and other common law jurisdictions.[5] This variation across and within systems means that the role of prior crimes at sentencing is an ideal subject for greater dialogue between systems that use this factor in different ways.

The importance of prior offending is supported in several ways. First, most offenders appearing for sentencing have previous adjudications of one kind or another. As an aggravating factor, prior convictions therefore affect a large proportion of the caseload of the courts, up to 90 per cent of defendants in England and Wales.[6] Secondly, statutory sentencing provisions in many countries identify prior crimes as an important aggravating circumstance at sentencing, suggesting that legislators ascribe considerable importance to this factor (discussed later in this chapter). Thirdly, empirical research into sentencing practices demonstrates that in many jurisdictions, criminal history is the most powerful predictor of sentencing outcomes (after the seriousness of the current crime).[7] In some US jurisdictions an offender's prior crimes carry more weight at

[4] See Ashworth, *Sentencing and Criminal Justice* (2015), 205; and Hörnle, *Tatproportionale Strafzumessung* (1999), 159–64.

[5] See Frase and Hester, 'Criminal History Enhancements' (2015); and Frase and Roberts, *Paying for the Past* (2019).

[6] Estimates vary, but in England and Wales, 90% of offenders sentenced by the courts in 2013 had at least one prior conviction and approximately half had at least ten prior adjudications: Roberts and Pina-Sánchez, 'Paying for the Past' (2015), Table 9.1. In Minnesota, more than two-thirds of sentenced offenders in 2017 had at least one criminal history point: Minnesota Sentencing Guidelines Commission, *2017 Sentencing Practices* (2018), Table 10. In Anglo-American countries, first offenders therefore seem to be the exception rather than the norm in offenders appearing for sentencing. In Germany, the ratio of offenders with a prior record among those sentenced is lower, but still above 50% (exactly: 52%) in 2016; in the same year, about 23% had five or more previous convictions, see Statistisches Bundesamt, *Strafverfolgung 2016* (2017), Table 7.1.

[7] According to empirical studies conducted in Germany, prior convictions are one of the most important aggravating factors at sentencing, see Harrendorf, 'Sentencing Thresholds' (2017), 527–30.

sentencing than his current crime.[8] Fourthly, an offender's past – whether law abiding or including previous crimes – is perceived by many practitioners to be relevant to culpability and/or the offender's risk of reoffending.[9] If this is true, a criminal record may justify harsher sentencing for recidivists and/or less punitive treatment for first offenders.[10] As this chapter will demonstrate, retributive theories take conflicting positions on whether and to what extent prior crimes should affect current sentencing. Preventive justifications also vary in their approach to prior offending. Finally, intuitive theories of punishment also incorporate an offender's past as a factor: research into public views suggests that most people favour harsher treatment for recidivists and support significantly mitigated punishments for people who have led a law-abiding life up to this point. Opinion surveys of the public in all Western nations have revealed the same result. When the public are asked to identify important aggravating factors, prior convictions are the second most frequent factor, after the extent of the injury to the victim. Similarly, when required to choose a sentence for specific cases, the public favour harsher sentences for repeat offenders.[11]

This chapter compares and contrasts the use of prior convictions at sentencing in selected Anglo-American countries and Germany. The chapter focuses upon the general aggravating effect of prior crimes at sentencing rather than specific recidivist laws such as the '3 Strikes' legislation which proliferated across the United States (and elsewhere) in the 1990s. We do not discuss more limited statutory enhancements such as those which mandate enhanced custodial sentences for offenders convicted of specific offences having been previously convicted of another such serious offence.[12]

[8] See Frase and Hester, 'Criminal History Enhancements' (2015).

[9] See Roberts, *Persistent Offenders* (2008).

[10] With regard to sentencing discounts for first-time offenders, see the first sentencing text published in England over 150 years ago: 'I cannot too earnestly urge leniency in the treatment of [first-time] offenders. A first offence should always be looked upon with pity, as possibly a lapse from virtue, the result more of weakness than of wickedness': Cox, *Principles of Punishment* (1877), 133. For Germany, see e.g. BGH, 26.05.1982, 3 StR 110/82, *Neue Zeitschrift für Strafrecht* (1982), 376; Schäfer, Sander and van Gemmeren, *Praxis der Strafzumessung* (2017), mn. 647.

[11] This research is summarised in Roberts, *Persistent Offenders* (2008); see also Mitchell, 'Public Attitudes' (2017).

[12] E.g. s. 25 of the Criminal Justice Act 2007 in Ireland, discussed in O'Malley, *Sentencing Law and Practice* (2016).

As noted, enhancing sentences to reflect the offender's prior crimes carries great intuitive appeal. Our reactions to transgressions in everyday life usually become more punitive when the transgressor has previously violated a similar social norm. The first 'offence' is often treated as a momentary lapse; external pressures may be blamed, or the wronged party may exercise some tolerance. However, repetition often changes reactions, and people become more punitive when the prior and current acts are the same or similar. This response is mirrored in most sentencing regimes: first offenders are treated more leniently, and this leniency is replaced by a more severe response following repetition. Recidivist punishments also permeate non-penal regulatory schemes, the rules of professional sports[13] and are also found in religious codes,[14] offering further evidence of the appeal of the concept of record-based enhancements. However, the powerful link between informal and formal sanctions should not blind us to the need to justify prior record enhancements. Any source of aggravation at sentencing needs to be justified by the statutory purposes and principles of sentencing, and these in turn need to be founded in a sound philosophy of state punishment.

Legal punishment is imposed for a proscribed act or omission; the sentence is a judgment upon the offender for a specific act. This said, once (s)he has discharged the sentence fully, an ex-offender is entitled to regain full standing in the community, the status enjoyed prior to conviction. Yet upon reconviction, a criminal past triggers additional punishment; (s)he is not sentenced as (s)he would have been prior to the first conviction. The defendant is sentenced as a *repeat offender*. How can this additional punishment, which has a cumulative effect on sentencing over the individual's criminal career, be justified? Lesser sanctions – parking fines, some traffic violations, library fines – often follow a flat-rate approach; the magnitude of the fine tracks the seriousness of the infraction, with no regard to whether the offender has previously committed such acts.[15] Why does the severity of the criminal sanction escalate in response to the offender's prior crimes? The principal

[13] E.g. the yellow and red disciplinary cards brandished by referees in football.

[14] E.g. ancient Jewish law contains a powerful recidivist premium: 'He who was flogged and then flogged again for two transgressions, and then sinned again, is placed by the court in a cell and fed with barley bread, until his stomach bursts' (Sanhedrin, Chapter 9, Mishnah 5; 536 BCE).

[15] See e.g. the sentencing guidelines fixed for minor (non-criminal) traffic offences (*Verkehrsordnungswidrigkeiten*) in Germany in the *Bußgeldkatalog-Verordnung* (Regulation on a Catalogue of Fines).

sentencing philosophies of prevention and retribution supply answers. Additional punishment for recidivists is justified by a need to prevent further (re)offending and by the offender's enhanced blameworthiness.

Section II of this chapter examines the theoretical justifications for prior record enhancements which derive from utilitarian as well as retributive philosophies.[16] Section III discusses the complexities of criminal history as a sentencing factor. Section IV provides examples of relevant statutory provisions and enhancements in sentencing guidelines. As will be seen, although common elements emerge, there is great variability in the ways that different regimes incorporate prior crimes at sentencing. Section V explores three key issues, namely, the age and the seriousness of prior crimes, and the relationship between any prior conviction and the current crime. Section VI considers the importance of prior convictions at sentencing from a comparative perspective.

II Prior Record Enhancements and Sentencing Theories

Several US guidelines justify their prior record sentencing enhancements by reference to prevention and/or retribution.[17] The US (federal) guidelines provide an explicit justification in terms of culpability when they note that: 'A defendant with a record of prior criminal behaviour is more culpable than a first offender and thus deserving of greater punishment.'[18] Elsewhere sentencing regimes are silent with respect to the justification. In Germany, for example, § 46(2) of the *Strafgesetzbuch* (StGB) simply states that, '[w]hen sentencing the court shall weigh the circumstances in favour of and against the offender. Consideration shall in particular be given to ... the offender's prior history ...'[19] The prior

[16] Throughout this chapter, we simplify the terms 'utilitarian' and 'retributive' to distinguish two general perspectives on sentencing. By the former, we refer to sentencing in order to achieve some demonstrable social benefit. In this context, the benefit is a lower rate of (re) offending due to the enhanced punishment imposed on repeat offenders. Such a utilitarian perspective could also be labelled as 'preventive' (as in the German terms *Spezialprävention* (special prevention) and *Generalprävention* (general prevention), on which we will elaborate later in this text), since it wishes to prevent future crimes. By retributive, we refer to sentencing which reflects exclusively or primarily the crime of conviction and is therefore retrospective rather than prospective.

[17] See Roberts, 'Justifying Criminal History Enhancements' (2015), Table 1.1.

[18] US Sentencing Commission, *Guidelines Manual* (2018), para. 4A1.1.

[19] Translation by Bohlander (www.gesetze-im-internet.de/englisch_stgb/englisch_stgb.html).

history in this provision is only one among a number of different factors that shall, according to the law, particularly be considered at sentencing.

1 Preventive Sentencing Theories

All preventive sentencing perspectives seek to reduce the likelihood of future offending, both with respect to the specific offender and the larger pool of potential offenders. Objectives such as deterrence, rehabilitation and incapacitation share this concern with the future. The nature and severity of the sentence reflects the risk of future offending by the convicted person (or by others). Often, a somewhat simple rationale is followed: the higher the risk of reoffending, the harsher the punishment for the current offence. Many US guidelines endorse the deterrent purpose of a recidivist sentencing premium.[20]

(a) Types of Preventive Theories

First, it is necessary to examine differences between utilitarian sentencing theories. These theories can be categorised in respect of the targeted persons: one group aims at the current offender – attempting to prevent his or her recidivism ('special prevention'; German: Spezialprävention). Other utilitarian theories aim not at preventing crimes by the current offender, but rather at the general public ('general prevention'; German: 'Generalprävention'). A second categorisation refers to the way by which the preventive aim is to be achieved in the respective group, by 'negative' effects like deterrence or incapacitation, or by 'positive' effects such as rehabilitation, learning, trust or restoration to the community. Thus, utilitarian theories can be categorised into four groups: positive and negative special prevention, positive and negative general prevention.[21]

(b) Special Prevention

The preventive rationale seems clear, especially with respect to special prevention, the prevention of future offences that would otherwise be

[20] The US federal guidelines manual is particularly clear about this when it affirms that: 'General deterrence of criminal conduct dictates that a clear message be sent to society that repeated criminal behaviour will aggravate the need for punishment with each recurrence.' See US Sentencing Commission, *Guidelines Manual* (2018), para. 4A1.1.

[21] As to these categories in German sentencing theory, see the overviews in Roxin, *Strafrecht Allgemeiner Teil* (2006), § 3 mn. 11–32; Pawlik, *Person, Subjekt, Bürger* (2004), 21–43.

committed by the convicted person him- or herself: the heightened risk represented by a recidivist seems to justify a harsher sentence in the name of prevention. However, the strong appeal of special deterrence masks some troubling questions, some empirical, others normative or constitutional.

According to Franz von Liszt, special prevention can be achieved in three different ways:

> a) Rehabilitation of the offenders that can be rehabilitated and need to be rehabilitated;
> b) deterrence of the offenders that need not be rehabilitated;
> c) incapacitation of the offenders that cannot be rehabilitated.[22]

The question is how prior record enhancements can be legitimated vis-à-vis these offender-related preventive aims. From a *rehabilitative* perspective, a recidivist premium might be justified due to the need for a longer rehabilitation programme (e.g. a specific therapy) necessary to prepare a recidivist for a future life without crime. The rationale of *deterrence* (be it individual or general deterrence) is, more or less,[23] the rationale of the economic theory of crime.[24] According to this theory, the decisions of an offender can be predicted by the model of *homo economicus*: crime is the result of a cost–benefit analysis undertaken by the individual in which the probability and severity of punishment are the main 'cost' variables.[25] From such a perspective, it seems reasonable to increase costs by increasing the punishment for recidivists, as the previous sentence proved an insufficient deterrent. Finally, a connection between a prior record and a longer prison term may be relevant for *incapacitation*: if those with a prior record have a greater risk of recidivism than first-time offenders and this risk increases with the number of previous convictions, there might be an increased need for incapacitation of persons with a long criminal history.

22 Von Liszt, 'Zweckgedanke im Strafrecht' (1883), 36 (translation by S. H.).

23 The classical school of criminology follows these lines, see Bentham, *Principles of Morals and Legislation* (1823), 16; von Feuerbach, *Lehrbuch des peinlichen Rechts* (1832), 15–6. As to the psychological assumptions of von Feuerbach detailed Greco, *Feuerbachs Straftheorie* (2009), 87–107.

24 I.e. rational choice theory. Becker, 'Crime and Punishment' (1968), who saw his theory as an advancement of classical utilitarian ideas (see 209). For details on the economic theory of crime, its most recent developments, and future perspectives, cf. Harrendorf and Geng, 'Der rational kalkulierende Verbrecher?' (2019).

25 See Becker, 'Crime and Punishment' (1968), 177.

As a category, recidivists are more likely to reoffend than first offenders,[26] and there is a cumulative relationship: the risk of reoffending rises with the number of prior convictions; recidivists with six prior crimes are more likely to reoffend than offenders with only two priors.[27] Yet this simple association alone cannot justify the enhancement on the grounds of incapacitation.[28] The sheer number of prior convictions is insufficient proof of individual dangerousness of an offender: even among those with a long criminal record, many persons are never reconvicted again. The duration of criminal careers depends on many factors.[29] Incapacitation can, however, only be justified for persons who are sufficiently dangerous.[30] Therefore, a prognosis of the individual risk of recidivism, related to the severity of the expected offences, is necessary for any decision to incapacitate a person. Even then, we still face the problem of false positives, the volume of which increases in the case of low base-rate offending such as serious crime.[31]

Individual deterrence is even more problematic: it is necessary to establish empirically that the enhancement (more prison time, or a more severe sanction) actually reduces the likelihood of reoffending. But does it? The clear correlation between the number of prior convictions, particularly prior incarcerations, and the risk of future crime is well-documented.[32] Advocates of a robust recidivist sentencing premium take this as evidence of a causal link between past and future offending.

[26] See Frase and Roberts, *Paying for the Past* (2019) for a recent review of relevant literature.

[27] See e.g. the results of a nationwide German reconviction study: Jehle et al., *Legalbewährung* (2016), 83 (for the reference period 2010–13) and 224 (for 2004–13).

[28] Men are more likely to reoffend than women (see again Jehle et al., *Legalbewährung* (2016), 51), yet this hardly justifies a gender-based sentencing enhancement.

[29] See e.g. Sampson and Laub, *Crime in the Making* (1995); Stelly and Thomas, *Einmal Verbrecher – immer Verbrecher?* (2001); also see. Harrendorf, *Rückfälligkeit und kriminelle Karrieren* (2007).

[30] As to the German preventive detention, which is, however, according to German terminology, not a punishment, but a measure of rehabilitation and incapacitation, see German Federal Constitutional Court (*Bundesverfassungsgericht* (BVerfG)), 04.05.11 – 2 BvR 2365/09, *Entscheidungen des Bundesverfassungs-gerichts* 128, 326–409. According to the European Court of Human Rights (ECtHR), it is, however, usually a penalty: ECtHR, 07.01.2016 – 23279/14 – Bergmann/Deutschland, mn. 181.

[31] As to base rates for violent and sexual crimes, see e.g. Jehle et al., *Legalbewährung* (2016), 108–37; Harrendorf, *Rückfälligkeit und kriminelle Karrieren* (2007); regarding the problem of false positives, see, inter alia, Kinzig, *Legalbewährung gefährlicher Rückfalltäter* (2010); Alex, *Nachträgliche Sicherungsverwahrung* (2013).

[32] This finding emerges from empirical analyses of sentencing practice in many jurisdictions. For a summary and discussion, see Frase and Roberts, *Paying for the Past* (2019); also see Jehle et al., *Legalbewährung* (2016).

However, it is well known that imprisonment has desocialising and stigmatising effects.[33] This assumption is supported by findings from research which demonstrates the criminogenic effects of imprisonment.[34] It is hence equally plausible that higher reoffending rates are caused not only by the offender's prior offending but also by the previous incarceration. The remedy for reoffending (more prison time) may therefore be a cause of, as well as a response to, crime.

A wealth of empirical research has demonstrated two further important findings. First, there is no relationship between the severity of sanctions and subsequent reoffending rates: imprisonment prevents crime no more effectively than community punishments. Secondly, the length of imprisonment is not associated with lower reoffending rates: more prison time does not mean less crime. Several German studies show that different sanctions applied to similar groups of persons result in comparable reconviction rates, leading to an assumption of interchangeability of sanctions with respect to special prevention,[35] a finding which casts doubt on the assumption of deterrent effect of imprisonment. Whether a policy of progressively higher punishments for repeat offenders deters crime is a slightly different question, but the general finding of no link between severity of sanction and reoffending rates calls the recidivist premium into question.[36] Moreover, the limited research specifically addressing the deterrent effect of a recidivist premium is no more encouraging.[37] In addition, different meta-analyses examining the deterrent effect of sanctions like shock incarceration, Scared Straight or boot camps usually show a negative effect of such sanctions – namely an

[33] The prison laws of all federal states in Germany include a *Gegensteuerungsgrundsatz*, a principle which obliges the prison staff to take countermeasures against the detrimental effects of imprisonment. See e.g. § 3(4) *Berliner Strafvollzugsgesetz*. Also see, again, a classic quote by von Liszt, 'Zweckgedanke im Strafrecht' (1883), 40 (translation by S. H.): 'There is nothing more degrading and counterproductive than our short prison terms for the apprentices on the trajectory of crime. Here – if anywhere at all – society bears the lion's share of guilt under which the future career criminal will eventually collapse.'

[34] Jolliffe and Hedderman, 'Impact of Custody on Reoffending' (2015); Ministry of Justice, *Re-Offending Statistics* (2011), 16; Mews et al., *Impact on Re-Offending* (2015), 18. See also Lipsey and Cullen, 'Correctional Rehabilitation' (2007), 300–2.

[35] Meier, 'What Works?' (2010), 113–5; also Harrendorf, *Absolute und relative Bagatellen* (forthcoming).

[36] See Kazemian, 'Recidivist Sentencing Premium' (2014).

[37] Canadian researchers who compared the effects of shorter versus longer prison sentences found that longer terms of custody were associated with greater increases in recidivism, a finding which does not support the preventive rationale of prior record enhancements. See Smith, Goggin and Gendreau, *Recidivism* (2002).

increase in reconviction rates.[38] Research on the effectiveness of individual deterrence provides little support for the concept.

It is also worth examining studies on *general* deterrence: meta-analyses have shown that it is principally the perceived risk of detection and conviction that deters, while there are no or only weak effects associated with the *severity* of punishment.[39] It is likely that this will be the same for persons who have previously been convicted. The existence of previous convictions shows that the prospect of punishment was insufficient to deter.[40] Why should 'more of the same treatment' prove effective?

Comparisons of reoffending rates across jurisdictions are also instructive. Prior convictions play a more powerful role in the United States than in England and Wales, yet recidivism rates in the two countries are similar.[41] Jehle compares reconviction statistics for Germany, Austria and Switzerland and similarly concludes that 'despite strongly different sentencing practices', reconviction rates are comparable.[42] One explanation for this finding is that the factors generating reoffending (e.g. substance abuse, lack of employment, poor self-control, absence of moral guardians) are unaffected by the magnitude of a reoffending enhancement.[43] In addition, 'reoffenders' (if it is appropriate to use this term for people who simply have been convicted of more than a single crime) are generally less sensitive to future consequences, including the likely impact of a reconviction.[44] Taken together, if prior record enhancements are founded on the rationale of individual deterrence, it is unclear that they can be justified – at least when they carry as much weight as they do in some jurisdictions.[45]

38 Lipsey and Cullen, 'Correctional Rehabilitation' (2007).

39 Dölling et al., 'Is Deterrence Effective?' (2009); von Hirsch et al., *Criminal Deterrence* (1999). Becker, 'Crime and Punishment' (1968), at 178, already foresaw this and attributed it to the fact that most criminals 'are risk preferrers, at least in the relevant region of punishments'.

40 Kaspar, *Präventionsstrafrecht* (2014), 705.

41 Frase and Roberts, *Paying for the Past* (2019).

42 See Jehle, 'German Reconviction Study' (2014), 41.

43 Repeat offenders' propensity to reoffend may be unaffected by additional time in prison arising from the prior record enhancement, but there will be significant impacts on their employment prospects.

44 See Becker, 'Crime and Punishment' (1968), 178.

45 Elsewhere, Frase and Roberts identify other assumptions which should be met before an enhancement can be justified. For example, even if increments in severity do reduce risk, is it the case that they are more effective than other, non-punitive responses? And further, if they are effective, and more effective than other responses, are there any countervailing costs? Much of the racial disproportionality in prison populations in Minnesota is caused

Finally, most of the literature has focused on the preventive benefits of the recidivist premium without fully considering the unanticipated adverse consequences of this sentencing policy. For example, the use of prior records at sentencing increases the disproportionate numbers of racial minority prisoners (since racial minority defendants tend to have longer criminal histories).[46] It is well known that in the US, African-American citizens account for a disproportionate number of prison places and admissions and much of this racial disproportionality is a result of the prior record enhancements; an apparently neutral sentencing variable (criminal history) exacerbates racial disparities. The literature on the effectiveness of recidivist sentencing enhancements has also overlooked the adverse impacts of this policy on undermining other preventive approaches. Offenders with multiple priors may be incarcerated as a result of their criminal record, and this incarceration may undermine their efforts towards desistance.

But what about prior record enhancements for the purpose of rehabilitation? Imagine a therapy capable of reducing the recidivism rate by 20 percentage points, but which takes two years to be completed in a prison environment. Aside from the general effect of imprisonment alone, it is well known that rehabilitative programmes can be effective in reducing recidivism, especially if they follow the 'risk, needs and responsivity' approach.[47] This is also true for programmes provided in prison. Can this justify increasing the punishment for an offender to the time necessary to complete a therapeutic treatment? Since a prior record indicates increased risk of recidivism, the offender's risk of recidivism may be high enough to justify such a therapeutic approach focused on his or her criminogenic needs. It may also justify an increase in punishment in order to ensure that (s)he will not be released before the programme is successfully completed.

Increasing punishment for the purpose of rehabilitation should, however, be ruled out for normative reasons: notwithstanding a possible right to rehabilitation and the obligation of the state to assist,[48] from the

by prior record enhancements and such costs need to be included in any consideration of the merits of prior record enhancements: see Frase and Roberts, *Paying for the Past* (2019).

46 See Frase, 'Sentencing Enhancements' (2014), 132–3; Frase and Roberts, *Paying for the Past* (2019).

47 Lipsey and Cullen, 'Correctional Rehabilitation' (2007), 302–13.

48 In Germany, such a right to rehabilitation and a corresponding obligation of the state can be derived from the constitution, see BVerfG, 01.07.1998 – 2 BvR 441/90 and others, BVerfGE 98, 169–218, at 200.

perspective of the offender, rehabilitation is a *voluntary* act: coercive treatment of adults who are capable of making informed decisions on their own violates the individual's human dignity and/or personal autonomy.[49] Therefore, while rehabilitation is a legitimate goal, it cannot *justify* punishment, which is by nature coercive.[50] An offender should not be forced to participate in a specific therapeutic intervention and it is unethical to increase punishment simply to facilitate such participation.

Rehabilitation might constitute a mitigating factor, particularly for first-time offenders: while positive special prevention cannot justify punishment, it may justify choosing the mildest (i.e. the least desocialising and least stigmatising) sanction among those that can legally be justified.[51] The danger of social exclusion and stigma is greatest for first-time offenders, since they may be fully integrated in their community. Imprisonment severs the offender's ties with his or her family and the community more generally; this rupture often increases his or her risk of reoffending. Offenders with an extensive record, on the other hand, have already experienced some exclusion and stigma; another punishment will therefore not necessarily have the same negative effect on their social standing. Therefore, sentence reductions for first-timers can be justified with regard to positive special prevention, but not an ever-increasing sentence severity for recidivists.[52]

(c) General Prevention

In addition to the special preventive aims of sentence enhancements, there may also be general preventive aims. Might these justify prior record enhancements more easily? First there is general deterrence, which in Germany is also labelled 'negative' general prevention.[53] The assumptions of the theory are, as mentioned above,[54] derived from rational choice theory,[55] but they are also connected to classical

49 Greco, *Feuerbachs Straftheorie* (2009), 436–41; Stratenwerth, *Lehre von den Strafzwecken* (1995), 11; Roxin, *Strafrecht Allgemeiner Teil* (2006), § 3 mn. 39.

50 Greco *Feuerbachs Straftheorie* (2009), 436–7; Kaspar, *Präventionsstrafrecht* (2014), 682–4.

51 See also Kaspar, *Präventionsstrafrecht* (2014), 682–3.

52 Harrendorf, *Absolute und relative Bagatellen* (forthcoming); Frase and Roberts, *Paying for the Past* (2019), ch. 10.

53 See above at Section II.1.(a).

54 See Section II.1.(b).

55 Becker, 'Crime and Punishment' (1968); also Harrendorf and Geng, 'Der rational kalkulierende Verbrecher?' (2019).

utilitarian thought.[56] Yet, as already noted, earlier research on the deterrent effects of punishment shows that it is mainly the expected risk of detection and punishment that deters potential offenders; there is no clear evidence to support a deterrent effect of increased sentence severity.[57]

Sentence enhancements might aim at deterring others with a criminal record similar to that of the offender who is currently being punished. For this group, however, sentence severity does not seem to have a relevant deterrent effect. Apart from the results of the meta-analyses noted earlier, it can also be said that these offenders have directly experienced the effects of punishment after their first offence. It is implausible that the perception of others being sentenced in a specific (e.g. harsh) way will have an effect comparable to the direct and individual experience of being punished.[58]

In Germany, 'positive Generalprävention' is another important justification for punishment. Usually, there are three different effects associated with positive general prevention:[59]

- *Learning*: people learn through penal law and punishment which rules are most important and ought to be followed.
- *Trust*: if the penal law is enforced, this increases trust in the validity of legal rules and thus encourages compliance.
- *Restoration to the community*: punishment resolves the conflict between society and the offender and satisfies the general public. This may lead to increased willingness to comply with the law.

Some of these possible effects are close to functions that are attributed to law and punishment in Anglo-American countries as well, namely the 'expressive function of law'[60] and the 'expressive function of punishment'.[61] 'Positive' general prevention can, to some extent, also be

[56] See e.g. Bentham, *Principles of Morals and Legislation* (1823), 16: 'The value of the punishment must not be less in any case than what is sufficient to outweigh that of the profit of the offence.' Also von Feuerbach, *Lehrbuch des peinlichen Rechts* (1832), 15–6.

[57] Dölling et al., 'Is Deterrence Effective?' (2009); von Hirsch et al., *Criminal Deterrence* (1999); also see again Becker, 'Crime and Punishment' (1968), 178: 'offenders are risk preferrers, at least in the relevant region of punishments'.

[58] Kaspar, *Präventionsstrafrecht* (2014), 805–6.

[59] Roxin, *Strafrecht Allgemeiner Teil* (2006), § 3 mn. 27.

[60] Sunstein, 'Expressive Function of Law' (1996); Cooter, 'Expressive Law and Economics' (1998).

[61] Feinberg, 'Expressive Function of Punishment' (1970), 98–101; also see Dubber, 'Positive Generalprävention' (2005), 493–9.

understood to be a necessary counterpart of general deterrence – and vice versa: 'The "messages" sent by law and the legal processes contain information about the costs of lawbreaking, but they also affirm that it is wrong to disobey.'[62] The operationalisation of positive general preventive effects is, however, complex,[63] and it is not always clear that this is a utilitarian theory at all: a theory of positive general prevention necessarily relies on the expressive function of law or punishment, yet a retributive theory is also expressive.[64] For a more retributive version of positive general prevention, it would be sufficient that the *meaning* of punishment is to express the binding character of legal norms, reinstate trust and protect legal order.[65] Yet, if positive general prevention is a truly preventive theory, the damage an offender inflicts upon the legal validity of a legal norm (*Normgeltungsschaden*)[66] is an *empirical* parameter and the extent of punishment necessary to 'heal' this damage should also be empirically founded.[67] In this section, we focus on the utilitarian version of the theory of positive general prevention.

Although the effects of positive general prevention are complex,[68] results of empirical studies seem to confirm some effects. First, consider the important experiments of Fehr, Gächter and Gintis on the concept of reciprocal fairness as a precondition for norm adherence.[69] Other studies show that even sanctions which are so mild that they cannot act as a deterrent (as they would not outweigh the benefits of a deviant act) foster norm adherence.[70] Finally, Tyler was able to show that a perception of

[62] Andenaes, 'General Preventive Effects' (1966), 950.

[63] As to the problems of operationalisation, also see Baurmann, 'Theorie der Generalprävention' (1998).

[64] See, explicitly, Nozick, *Philosophical Explanations* (1981), 374–80.

[65] Based on this differentiation, Jakobs's version of the theory of positive general prevention started off as a preventive theory (in Jakobs, *Schuld und Prävention* (1976)), was modified into a retributive theory (e.g. in Jakobs, 'Funktionalismus und Prinzipiendenken'(1995)) and then modified back into a preventive theory (cf. Jakobs, *Staatliche Strafe* (2004)).

[66] Also cf. the classical 'Lehre vom intellektuellen Verbrechensschaden' (theory on intellectual damages of crime): Welcker, *Recht, Staat und Strafe* (1813), at 265–6.

[67] See Jakobs, *Staatliche Strafe* (2004), 32; Holz, *Justizgewähranspruch* (2007), 176–8.

[68] Baurmann, 'Theorie der Generalprävention' (1998).

[69] See Fehr and Gächter, 'Cooperation and Punishment' (2000); Fehr and Gintis, 'Human Motivation and Social Cooperation' (2007); detailed on these experiments Harrendorf and Geng, 'Der rational kalkulierende Verbrecher?' (2019).

[70] Feldman, 'Expressive Function of Law' (2009); Funk, 'Expressive Function of Law' (2007); Killias, 'Rechtsgefühl und Sanktionen' (1985); but also see Schumann, *Positive Generalprävention* (1989), at 35–8; detailed Harrendorf, *Absolute und relative Bagatellen* (forthcoming).

the legitimacy of a legal norm may in itself (i.e. regardless of the individual moral values) increase legal compliance.[71]

Therefore, while the empirical support for positive general prevention is weaker than for general deterrence, we can assume that positive general prevention is effective in some circumstances. Indeed, some scholars believe that prior record sentence enhancements are best justified by positive general prevention.[72]

These scholars assume that the *Normgeltungsschaden* caused by a crime is greater if it is committed by a recidivist. The demand of the public for punishment might be increased here, hence a harsher sanction might be necessary to fulfil the restorative function of sentencing for the community. There is, however, an important normative question that needs to be answered: can the increased Normgeltungsschaden in such cases actually be attributed to the criminal act, or is it something related, but not part of it?

German scholars who favour a justification of prior record enhancements via the *Normgeltungsschaden* are often also in favour of an extended definition of the criminal act when it comes to sentencing: according to this view, the sentence does not only refer to the criminal act itself, but to everything connected to the conflict society has with the offender which can influence the demand for punishment.[73] Prior record enhancements are then justified as they are seen to be necessary to resolve the conflict. Yet this approach is not feasible, as it would eradicate the difference between *Tatstrafrecht*, a criminal law punishing a person for the criminal act, and *Täterstrafrecht*, a criminal law punishing a person for their general 'criminal lifestyle'.[74] It also does not sit easily with the principle of guilt and with proportionality of sentencing: even a preventive justification of punishment should rely on culpability as a limiting factor for punishment:[75] the punishment must not exceed the blameworthiness of the offender.

There is an additional twist to this issue: scholars who endorse an expanded definition of the criminal act sometimes subscribe to a functional interpretation of guilt. According to them, guilt is externally

[71] Tyler, *Why People Obey the Law* (1990), 62.

[72] E.g. Streng, '§ 46 StGB' (2017), at mn. 66.

[73] See e.g. Streng, 'Schuld ohne Freiheit?' (1989), 310–12.

[74] See Hirsch 'Tatstrafrecht' (2002), 266.

[75] In Germany, the guilt principle is guaranteed by the constitution, see BVerfG, 30.06.2009 – 2 BvE 2/08 and others, BVerfGE 123, 267–437, at 413.

attributed by society, regardless of the mental state of the offender.[76] Such an approach, however, devalues the concept of blameworthiness and comes close to violating human dignity (since guilt is externally attributed to serve a social function and without regard to the offender as an individual).[77]

Finally, it can be questioned whether the spontaneous and emotional reaction of people when they hear of a crime by a recidivist is really relevant for sentencing: 'Criminality is an area for which awareness and knowledge is typically weak, whilst attitudes and opinions are strong.'[78] The public demand for increased punishment is often based on emotions and insufficient information (e.g. on the effects and possible aims and justifications of punishment). Hence, all one usually receives when asking the public about punishment for a certain crime is raw public opinion.[79] But if the public has something to say about punishment (which is more than plausible in a democracy), it is public *judgment* that should count – namely, an informed and considered decision based on the information available. Studies show that such an informed decision (e.g. via so-called 'deliberative polls') is significantly less punitive.[80] This is one of the most well-documented findings in the field of public opinion.[81]

2 *Retributive Perspectives*[82]

Proportionality lies at the heart of the retributive perspective: the severity of the sentence should reflect the seriousness of the crime and the offender's level of culpability – *for the offence*. At first glance, and for some scholars, even after repeated glances, this leaves little room for prior convictions. After all, prior offending cannot affect the seriousness of the current crime or the offender's culpability for this latest offence, particularly when the prior and current crimes were committed years apart. And, indeed, this position was advocated by George Fletcher and others

76 Again, see Streng, 'Schuld ohne Freiheit?' (1989).

77 Roxin, *Strafrecht Allgemeiner Teil* (2006), § 19 mn. 35.

78 Aromaa as cited in Tomášek, 'The Public and Crime' (2011), 221.

79 See Green, *When Children Kill Children* (2008), 241–69.

80 Luskin, Fishkin and Jowell, 'Considered Opinions' (2002); also see Cochran and Chamlin, 'Public Opinion' (2005); Indermaur et al., 'A Matter of Judgement' (2012); and for a review of research, Roberts and Hough *Public Attitudes* (2005).

81 See Roberts and Stalans, *Public Opinion* (2000).

82 Essays regarding the retributive perspective can be found in Roberts and von Hirsch, *Previous Convictions* (2014), and Tamburrini and Ryberg, *Recidivist Punishments* (2012).

over forty years ago.[83] Fletcher argued that an offender is fully culpable for the offence when he has no claim for diminished culpability as a result of provocation by the victim, intoxication, social adversity or other such grounds. If one or more of these mitigating circumstances are present, they may sustain a diminished culpability claim. Yet the offender cannot be considered 'hyper-culpable' as a result of prior crimes, and therefore sentence severity cannot escalate indefinitely in the way that the 'cumulative' sentencing approach implies. A glass may be only partially filled, with the wine reaching different levels, but once the brim is reached, no additional capacity exists. In Germany, this view remains a minority position, but under the influence of Anglo-American and Scandinavian concepts of sentencing proportionality (*Tatproportionalität*) it has grown stronger in recent decades.[84]

'Mainstream' German sentencing theory, in contrast, does subscribe to the concept of 'hyper-culpability', as it applies an extended definition of 'personal guilt', one which is wider than the Anglo-American notion of 'culpability'. This concept of personal guilt also encompasses the attitude of the offender at the time (s)he committed the offence, thus blameworthy motives, attitudes etc. (so-called *Gesinnungsunwerte*) are seen to increase guilt even if they are not part of the offence definition.[85] With respect to criminal record enhancements, the courts subscribe to a 'warning theory': the previous conviction is considered a warning which should raise the inhibition threshold against further offences (especially of the same kind). Hence, disregarding this inhibition – and offending – reflects increased guilt.[86] This is a very implausible assumption. Psychologically, it would be more convincing to understand previous *offences*

[83] Other theorists such as Duff also exclude the use of previous convictions: 'The mere fact that an offender is now convicted of a crime has a prior criminal record can make no justified difference to his sentence'; and 'The fact that this is the offender's twentieth burglary does not justify a harsher punishment than was imposed for the tenth burglary'; in Duff, *Punishment, Communication, and Community* (2001), 167 and 169.

[84] Hörnle, *Tatproportionale Strafzumessung* (1999), 164; von Hirsch, 'Begründung und Bestimmung tatproportionaler Strafen' (2003), 72; Schünemann, 'Akzeptanz von Normen und Sanktionen' (2003), 195.

[85] See e.g. Gallas, 'Lehre vom Verbrechen' (1955), 45–6; Jescheck and Weigend, *Lehrbuch des Strafrechts* (1996), § 39 II. 1; Schmidhäuser, *Strafrecht Allgemeiner Teil* (1975), 6/23. Dissenting: Greco, *Feuerbachs Straftheorie* (2009), 497; Hörnle, *Tatproportionale Strafzumessung* (1999), 151; Roxin, *Strafrecht Allgemeiner Teil* (2006), at § 19 Rn. 23–6.

[86] See BVerfG, 16.01.1979 – 2 BvL 4/77, BVerfGE 50, 125–41 at 136; BGH, 03.06.1997 – 1 StR 183/97, BGHSt 43, 106–9 at 108; Horstkotte, 'Reform des Strafrechts' (1970), 153; Kunz, 'Vorleben und Nachtatverhalten' (2011), 142.

(not previous *convictions*) as a marker for a lower inhibition threshold and hence for reduced guilt.[87] Somewhat paradoxically, some proponents of mainstream theory accept this, too.[88] According to this view, prior convictions usually increase guilt, but may sometimes also diminish it.

There are other reasons why prior crimes might affect an offender's level of culpability. Lee, for example, suggests that repeat offenders are guilty of a 'culpable omission', namely, of omitting to address the causes of their offending. Additional punishment is justified to reflect this culpable omission.[89] Such a position can also be found in the German literature, most prominently in the works of Köhler and Kaufmann. Kaufmann argues that reoffending violates a second duty beyond the one the penal norm includes, which is a culpable omission of 'value-oriented character development'.[90] Similarly, Köhler ascribes an increased culpability due to 'energetic and permanent reoffending' and a 'delinquent habitus'.[91] In our opinion, however, there are no convincing ways to derive such an additional duty for repeat offenders from their previous convictions. The only duty the law actually places on first time and repeat offenders alike is to refrain from offending.[92]

The approach that has had most influence on judicial practice in Anglo-American countries represents a middle ground between the cumulative and exclusionary schools. Several scholars have argued that the absence of priors should mitigate the sentence, but that once this first offender mitigation is lost, prior convictions should trigger no further enhancement. Known as the 'Progressive Loss of Mitigation', this principle finds its origins in English sentencing law.[93] Opinions differ as to why a first offender deserves mitigation. Von Hirsch argues that

87 Kaspar, *Präventionsstrafrecht* (2014), 705–6; Hörnle, *Tatproportionale Strafzumessung* (1999), 161.

88 BGH, 12.09.2006 - 4 StR 279/06, *Strafverteidiger* (2006), 689; Kunz, 'Vorleben und Nachtatverhalten' (2011), 141.

89 See Lee, 'Repeat Offenders' (2014). Von Hirsch echoes this in an older article where he observes that 'repetition after confrontation with censure also suggests a failure to make the extra effort at self-restraint': von Hirsch, 'Criminal Record Rides Again' (1991), 55. See also the recent discussion in Alexander and Ferzan, *Crime and Culpability* (2018).

90 Kaufmann, *Bindings Normentheorie* (1954), 212.

91 Köhler, *Strafrecht Allgemeiner Teil* (1997), 604.

92 Hörnle, *Tatproportionale Strafzumessung* (1999), 162.

93 E.g. Thomas noted that the 'progressive loss of credit until the offender has exhausted all the mitigating effect of good character and arrived at the point that he is exposed to the full length of the sentence appropriate to his offence'. See Thomas, *Principles of Sentencing* (1970), 197.

first offenders (and, indeed, offenders with modest records) should receive a more lenient sentence simply because to err is human; he describes this as tolerance for a lapse from a law-abiding lifestyle. Duff's theory is also consistent with the principle of the progressive loss of mitigation. Duff reasons that the mitigation extended to first offenders is appropriate because it 'makes sense of the intuitively plausible thought that, in the criminal law as in other contexts, the fact that this is the offender's first offence should be a modestly mitigating factor'.[94]

The 'tolerance for a lapse' model has been criticised.[95] First because it is unrelated to culpability – the mitigation derives not from the first offender's diminished culpability, but from some fuzzy conception of state magnanimity. This surely raises questions about its retributive significance. Secondly, scholars have questioned the logic of an iterative model which prescribes multiple, albeit diminishing degrees of mitigation.[96] Why should the state repeatedly extend mitigation to successive lapses by the offender, particularly when the offences of reconvictions are the same? Thirdly, the mitigation extends without consideration of the nature of the crime. A lapse seems plausible when the wrongfulness of the conduct is unclear, where the offence is very common, or where the crime occurred spontaneously without the offender having ample time to exercise self-restraint. But what about serious personal injury offences, or crimes that require extensive and meticulous planning? Can they reasonably be described as the product of 'a momentary lapse'?

Despite its theoretical shortcomings, the progressive loss of mitigation guides sentencers in many common law countries.[97] Even in England and Wales, where the statutory provisions regulating the use of prior convictions moved away from the progressive loss of mitigation over a decade ago, empirical research suggests that sentence severity

[94] Duff, *Punishment, Communication, and Community* (2001), 169.

[95] See e.g. Ryberg, who argues that the retributive principles that justify the use of prior convictions 'are – if not defective – theoretically under-determined'. See Ryberg, *Proportionate Punishment* (2004), 79–81.

[96] Von Hirsch and other scholars advocating this approach suggest that the first offender mitigation is not exhausted until the offender has committed up to five crimes. Mitigating the sentence on up to five successive sentencing hearings may strike many as excessive tolerance on the part of the state.

[97] And also see BGH, 26.05.1982, 3 StR 110/82, *Neue Zeitschrift für Strafrecht* (1982), 376; Schäfer, Sander and van Gemmeren, *Praxis der Strafzumessung* (2017), mn. 647 for Germany, accepting the absence of previous convictions as a mitigating factor.

rises and then levels off after a few convictions in a way that is consistent with this approach.[98]

The recidivist sentencing premium thus creates tension between competing sentencing philosophies. With respect to enhanced sentences – aggravation rather than simply mitigation for first offenders – the most convincing rationale is preventive, yet this also rests on some problematic empirical assumptions. For many repeat offenders, the offence of conviction will carry less weight: risk reduction trumps retribution. The effect can be observed for the persistent petty offender. Highly repetitive property offenders are often imprisoned to interrupt their repeat offending. When this occurs, they have been incarcerated for reasons of prior rather than present offending. US scholars refer to this as 'push in' – the offender convicted of an offence insufficiently serious to warrant imprisonment is nevertheless incarcerated for their criminal past. In Germany, persistent petty offenders are also 'pushed into prison' by virtue of their record, even where the crime involved only a few euros.[99] This is usually justified by a mixture of guilt-based ('warning theory', see above), and preventive arguments (preventive need to influence the offender by means of a prison sentence, see § 47(1) StGB),[100] all of which are questionable.

Taken together, the twin justifications of prevention and retribution offer, at best, an incomplete rationale for record-based sentencing enhancements. Mitigation for first offenders appears justified on the basis of both risk and retribution. Once the mitigation is lost, however, the grounds for progressive increases in severity – except for high risk offenders where incapacitation may be justified – remain problematic. In addition, a robust prior record enhancement would be inconsistent with the principle of proportionality, which underpins all common law sentencing regimes, and the guilt principle, which is a constitutional principle in Germany and encompasses the concept of *Schuldangemessenheit*,[101] – the

[98] See data summarised in Roberts and Pina-Sánchez, 'Previous Convictions' (2014).

[99] See e.g. Higher Regional Court (*Oberlandesgericht* (OLG)) Braunschweig, *Neue Zeitschrift für Strafrecht: Rechtsprechungs-Report* (2002), at 75 (shoplifting regarding a box of cigarettes; value: 5 Deutsche Mark; one month's imprisonment); OLG Stuttgart, *Neue Juristische Wochenschrift* (2006), 1222 (three cases of fare dodging; price per ticket: 1.65 euros; per offence one month's imprisonment); OLG Hamburg, *Neue Zeitschrift für Strafrecht: Rechtsprechungs-Report* (2004), at 72 (shoplifting regarding sweets; value: 4.44 euros; one month's imprisonment).

[100] See Harrendorf, 'Sentencing Thresholds' (2017).

[101] See e.g. BVerfG, 24.10.1996 – 2 BvR 1851/94, BVerfGE 95, 96–142 at 140.

need for an adequate relationship between the guilt and punishment. In practice, this principle is less focused on the severity of the offence alone and therefore also reflects the personality of the offender to a greater extent than the Anglo-American proportionality principle.[102] However, it also rules out any sentence enhancements which are justified only by preventive reasons.

III The Need for Guidance: The Complexity of a Criminal Record

In most jurisdictions, courts are provided with relatively little guidance regarding the consideration of a criminal record at sentencing. This paucity of detailed guidance is regrettable and reflects a failure to recognise the complexities of a criminal record. Several features set criminal history apart as an aggravating circumstance unlike any other. First, it affects most cases appearing for sentencing.[103] Secondly, it is a multidimensional[104] factor, unlike most other sentencing factors. For example, the aggravating effect of premeditation reflects the degree of planning and the amount of time and effort the offender spent planning the offence. Judicial reflection is necessary to establish the extent to which this factor should aggravate, but this determination is relatively straightforward.

Criminal history, in contrast has multiple dimensions which must be considered. These include: the age of the prior(s); the number of previous convictions; their seriousness; the relationship among the prior crimes, as well as the relationship between the previous and current offence(s); whether there has been a gap in offending (if the priors are spaced over a lengthy period); and whether there has been an escalation – or de-escalation – in the trajectory of offending seriousness, to name a few.[105] Most other aggravating factors exercise their effect uniformly across cases: remorse mitigates and premeditation aggravates, regardless of whether the offender is a young adult or in his sixties, or is convicted of burglary or buggery. The effects of prior record, however, will vary depending upon a number of characteristics relating to the offender and the offence.

102 E.g. mainstream sentencing theory in Germany also considers Gesinnungsunwerte, see text above.

103 See the figures provided in n. 6 above.

104 Wasik lists eight dimensions of a criminal record: Wasik, 'Criminal Record' (1987). See also Wasik, 'Criminal History' (2010).

105 Most of these are well established in the case law: see e.g. Thomas, *Principles of Sentencing* (1970), ch. 4.

Many aggravating factors are binomial in nature: the offender either was or was not on parole at the time of the current crime. Committing a fresh crime while still serving a sentence for a previous crime enhances the offender's level of culpability. Once the parole status is established, usually little further judicial interpretation is necessary. An offender who commits a crime while on parole will receive a higher penalty for the later offence. Criminal record is a very different proposition. The existence of prior convictions alone does not trigger an automatic enhancement; after all, these have resulted in sentences which the offender has discharged. The significance of a prior crime springs from its relationship to the current crime. For example, a prior conviction for theft should not carry aggravating force for a sentence for assault,[106] but it might for a fresh theft.

In short, without explicit direction from a statute, appellate court or sentencing guidelines individual sentencers will resort to judicial intuitions about issues relating to the relevant components of a criminal record. The prevalence, complexity and potential to affect the sentence are all powerful arguments for the provision of guidance for trial courts.

IV Representative Statutory and Guidelines Approaches to Structuring Discretion Regarding Previous Convictions

All jurisdictions adopt one of three distinct approaches to prior record enhancements: (1) formal guidelines in which prior convictions constitute a primary dimension; (2) statutory enhancement provisions; (3) appellate guidance.

1 Presumptive Sentencing Guidelines

The most visible way of structuring judicial discretion is found in the US guidelines.[107] In many states, courts apply a sentencing grid with two dimensions: the seriousness of the crime and the offender's criminal history. The architecture of a grid ensures that prior convictions exercise

[106] Unless the enhanced blameworthiness springs from the offender violating *any* law, this would appear to be an overbroad ascription of enhanced culpability; an example of punishing a defiant attitude towards legal authority.

[107] For a comprehensive survey and analysis of the role of prior convictions in the federal and state guidelines, see Frase et al., *Sourcebook* (2015); Frase and Roberts, *Paying for the Past* (2019).

a powerful impact on sentencing outcomes. In Minnesota, for example, offenders are assigned criminal history points for each prior crime which falls within a broad window of inclusion. In addition, the criminal history score reflects other components such as whether the offender was on parole, probation or bail at the time of the current offence. Once the total points have been summed, the offender is placed in one of seven criminal history categories. For offenders falling into the custodial zone of the main grid, sentence length increases by the same quantum across each criminal history category.[108]

An example illustrates: an offender convicted of a crime of seriousness level 8 with no prior convictions faces a presumptive sentence of forty-eight months. One criminal history point raises the sentence length to fifty-eight months, two criminal history points to sixty-eight months and so on. Cases falling in the highest criminal history category (six or more points) carry a presumptive sentence of 108 months. The US guidelines approach, which involves the steady accumulation of criminal history points, has been criticised, but making the components of a criminal history transparent at least promotes greater consistency of application.[109] The weakness of the US approach is the rather mechanical way in which prior crimes increase the severity of sentence, and the excessive influence of prior convictions in terms of sentence outcomes. The advantage, if it is in fact one, is that the magnitude of these enhancements is clear to all parties. It may also be argued that such a simplistic approach leads to greater consistency.

Courts in England and Wales must also follow definitive sentencing guidelines which, unlike the US grid-based approaches, are offence-specific in nature. These guidelines specify two levels of aggravating factors, and previous convictions have been placed at Step Two of the guidelines methodology, which means that they carry less weight than other factors (such as premeditation) which are located at Step One.[110] In Germany, no sentencing guidelines exist in criminal law and the ones existing for non-criminal traffic offences[111] do not include prior offences as an aggravating circumstance.

[108] Minnesota Sentencing Guidelines Commission, *Guidelines and Commentary* (2018).

[109] Parent notes that: 'The pivotal concern for the [Minnesota Sentencing] Commission was operational simplicity.' See Parent, *Structuring Criminal Sentences* (1988), 71.

[110] See Sentencing Council for England and Wales at www.sentencingcouncil.org.uk; Ashworth and Roberts, *Sentencing Guidelines* (2013).

[111] See n. 15 above

2 *Statutory Provisions Relating to Prior Convictions*

The second approach is the most common and consists of statutory directions to courts at sentencing. Most sentencing codes contain some direction to courts regarding the presence of prior convictions. This guidance is sometimes explicit, sometimes more nebulous. The guidance is usually skeletal, presumably in the expectation that appellate courts will flesh out the statutory provisions. It may also be the case that the minimal direction reflects recognition that interpreting a criminal record for the purposes of sentencing is best left to the discretion of trial courts. Without the exercise of discretion, individualisation of the sentence is greatly impaired.

England and Wales is a good example of a jurisdiction which has a statutory provision which addresses the aggravating effect of prior convictions. Section 143 of the Criminal Justice Act 2003 specifies key dimensions for courts to consider (the age and nature of the prior crime and the relationship between previous and current offences) and allows judicial discretion to ignore prior convictions if it would be unreasonable to consider them in aggravation. A provision of this kind clarifies the role of previous convictions but does not provide any guidance as to their weight in the sentencing equation.

Elsewhere, the statutory provision is vague, leaving many issues for judicial discretion to resolve. § 46 of the German StGB, which articulates the principles of sentencing, states in subsection (2):

> When sentencing the court shall weigh the circumstances in favour of and against the offender. Consideration shall in particular be given to . . . the offender's prior history . . .[112]

The prior history in this provision is, as noted above, only one among a number of different factors that should be considered at sentencing. As regards prior convictions, the law is quite vague: first, a 'prior history' in the meaning of the law includes not only prior convictions (or the absence thereof), but also other aspects of the offender's past.[113] Secondly, it is not clear that prior convictions need to be an aggravating factor, they may also serve as a source of mitigation (if the prior convictions indicate a reduced inhibition threshold). This ambivalence is indeed

[112] Translation by Bohlander (www.gesetze-im-internet.de/englisch_stgb/englisch_stgb.html).

[113] Although prior convictions are the most important factor. For details, see Eschelbach, '§ 46 StGB' (2018), mn. 107–16.

also reflected in the practice of the courts (although in the vast majority of cases German courts resort to warning theory and see prior convictions as an aggravating circumstance).[114] In addition, German courts also accept the *absence* of previous convictions as a mitigating factor.[115] The exact effect of prior convictions or their absence on sentence severity depends on a holistic assessment of the case.[116]

Section 21A(2) of the Crimes (Sentencing Procedure) Act 1999 in New South Wales is similarly brief, but refers to the criminal record only as an aggravating factor:

> The aggravating factors to be taken into account in determining the appropriate sentence for an offence are as follows:
>
> ...
>
> (d) the offender has a record of previous convictions.

Some sentencing statutes explicitly identify previous convictions as a potential aggravation, and their absence as a mitigation. For example, section 40k of the Israeli Penal Law (1977, as amended in 2012) specifies a number of circumstances which a court may consider at sentencing. These are described as 'unrelated to the ... offense' (in contrast to the English statutory provision which embeds priors within the determination of seriousness) and one of these (s. 40k (11)) is 'the offender's previous criminal convictions or lack thereof'. Legislative directions such as these examples leave much to judicial discretion to resolve. The result is likely to be a somewhat inconsistent policy with regard to enhancements for prior crimes.

Finally, a few jurisdictions provide limited guidance regarding the *quantum* of aggravation that is appropriate to reflect previous wrongdoing. The 2014 judicial guidelines in China are a good example. Section 6 of the guidelines prescribes specific ranges of aggravation expressed as a percentage of the base sentence. Thus, for repeat offenders, the base sentence should be increased by between 10 per cent and 40 per cent, with the exact percentage reflecting a number of

114 See BVerfG, 16.01.1979 – 2 BvL 4/77, BVerfGE 50, 125–41 at 136; BGH, 03.06.1997 – 1 StR 183/97, BGHSt 43, 106–9 at 108; Horstkotte, 'Reform des Strafrechts' (1970), 153; Kunz, 'Vorleben und Nachtatverhalten' (2011), 142, for an aggravating use of prior convictions. See BGH, 12.09.2006 – 4 StR 279/06, *Strafverteidiger* (2006), 689; Kunz, 'Vorleben und Nachtatverhalten' (2011), 141, for a mitigating use.

115 BGH, 26.05.1982, 3 StR 110/82, *Neue Zeitschrift für Strafrecht* (1982), 376; also see Schäfer, Sander and van Gemmeren, *Praxis der Strafzumessung* (2017), mn. 647.

116 See Schäfer, Sander and van Gemmeren, *Praxis der Strafzumessung* (2017), mn. 650–60.

dimensions including the relationship between the current and prior crime, the seriousness of the prior crime and the length of time that has passed since the previous sentence elapsed.[117] In Germany, a recent expert opinion for the 72nd *Deutscher Juristentag* in 2018 proposes a new restrictive regulation in criminal law according to which prior convictions should not aggravate the sentence by more than one-third of the punishment a first-time offender would have received under same circumstances.[118]

3 *Judicially Derived Guidance*

In a number of other countries such as Ireland,[119] there is no explicit statutory provision stipulating prior convictions as an aggravator.[120] Instead, prior convictions only constitute a judicially recognised aggravating factor. Courts of first instance in such countries rely upon guidance from the appellate level. In jurisdictions such as these it is much harder to determine the magnitude of the repeat offender premium or to uncover the various dimensions considered by a court when sentencing an offender with a lengthy criminal history. Germany in effect also belongs to this category, as the legal provision (see above, under IV.2) only vaguely refers to the consideration of the offender's prior history when deciding on the sentence length.

V Three Key Issues

As noted, a criminal record is a complex combination of different dimensions and sentencers must interpret a record to see how the prior crimes, in light of their relationship to the current offence, should affect the sentence. This creates the challenge, for courts and commissions alike, to 'read' a record with a view to determining the degree to which a sentence should be enhanced. To promote consistency of application, Sentencing Commissions in the United States usually prescribe specific counting rules for courts to apply. Three key dimensions are the age, seriousness and similarity of prior crimes. Yet there are many other aspects of a defendant's criminal past which must be considered.

117 For discussion and translation see Roberts and Pei, 'Judicial Discretion in China' (2016).
118 Kaspar, *Sentencing Guidelines* (2018).
119 See O'Malley, *Sentencing Law and Practice* (2016).
120 There is a provision relating to one specific form of offending.

Commissions and courts[121] alike must also decide whether to set a threshold for considering a prior – for example, by disregarding low seriousness crimes such as misdemeanours in the United States, by excluding crimes committed and punished when the offender was a juvenile or by ignoring older previous convictions.[122] For the sake of brevity, this chapter discusses only three principal components.

1 *Age of Prior Offences: The Long-Playing Criminal Record*

There are powerful arguments for placing temporal limits on the consideration of previous offending, for recognising significant gaps in episodes of offending and for discounting older prior crimes. The double punishment argument becomes more compelling for older convictions. Counting all priors endlessly across an offender's criminal career means that each prior offence will trigger further severity enhancements across every subsequent sentencing decision. The consequence is a snowballing effect over the duration of the individual's criminal career. In addition, both utilitarian and retributive perspectives should respect temporal limits on prior convictions, and also declining weights for crimes which are included. From a risk-based perspective, the risk associated with prior crimes declines over time as a result of changes in the offender's life. As the interval between the prior and current crime increases, the former's significance declines; this finding emerges from criminal career research.[123] Similarly, if, say, ten years have elapsed since the last conviction, the individual can reasonably claim to have regained his or her standing as a person without a criminal past.

It is unsurprising, therefore, that courts in many countries generally disregard or discount previous convictions when they are old ('stale') or separated from the latest conviction by a significant period. The US guidelines, in contrast, are much less forgiving. In many states, there is

[121] Although they are not the focus of this chapter, parole boards in Anglo-American countries or courts deciding on conditional release of prisoners in Germany must also grapple with the complexities of the prisoner's criminal history to determine what implications it may have for his or her release on parole or licence. The problems of interpreting and weighing an offender's record are therefore not restricted to the stage of sentencing.

[122] Almost all US guidelines also include custody status as a component of the criminal history score. If the offender was on bail, parole or serving a community sentence at the time of the latest crime, his criminal history score is raised. We regard custody status as a separate aggravating factor, and do not discuss it in this chapter.

[123] See Mitchell, 'Decay and Gap Policies' (2015).

no 'look-back' limit; all prior crimes count against an individual no matter how old. States that operate limits of inclusion generally include felonies occurring as long as fifteen years previously. Trends in Minnesota demonstrate the point. Over half the convictions recorded in 2014 will be counted against the offender for at least twenty years. Such lengthy windows of inclusion are hard to justify from the perspective of risk or retribution, and are further evidence of the excessive influence of prior crimes across the United States.

The US guidelines also fail to distinguish between prior crimes of very different longevities: there is no 'discounting' of older priors. In Minnesota, for example, a one-year-old prior felony carries the same weight as a fourteen-year-old felony. This indifference to the age of the prior conviction reflects a preference for a system which is easy to apply, yet it has a clear Procrustean effect. The fourteen-year-old and the one-year-old prior crimes would reflect very different levels of risk or blameworthiness yet trigger the same increase in severity. This tendency to aggregate priors which may be very different is characteristic of the point-based enhancements. Two offenders can attract the same criminal history scores with very different prior crime profiles.[124] The US approach promotes simplicity, but at a substantial cost in terms of calibrating the level of enhancement to an offender's actual level of risk or blameworthiness. The US guidelines do not provide any means by which a court may disregard (or even discount) a prior crime on the basis that it has no probative value in terms of risk or retribution.[125] In its guidance for jurisdictions across the United States, the American Law Institute's Model Penal Code project recognises the importance of temporal limits:

> § 6B.07. Use of Criminal History. (TD No. 1) (approved 2007). (3) The commission shall fix limitation periods after which offenders' prior convictions and juvenile adjudications should not be taken into account to enhance sentence.

[124] E.g. an offender with three prior crimes at the lowest levels of seriousness (1 to 2) would attract a similar criminal history score to an offender with a prior crime at a much higher level of seriousness (6 to 8). See Minnesota Sentencing Guidelines Commission, *Guidelines and Commentary* (2018), 12.

[125] E.g. courts in Minnesota may decline to impose the presumptive sentence provided in the guidelines, and sentence outside the grid. This is classified as a 'departure' sentence, and courts must first find 'identifiable, substantial, and compelling circumstances' for departing, see Minnesota Sentencing Guidelines Commission, *Guidelines and Commentary* (2018), 38. The grounds for departure upheld by the Minnesota Court of Appeals do not extend to departing because the prior conviction was too old or too different from the current crime to be considered relevant.

A second problem with the US approach is that it treats a prior conviction as an automatic sentencing enhancement, similar to others such as 'use of a weapon where this was not the subject of a separate charge'. Criminal history should not aggravate sentencing in this way. First, unlike use of a weapon, this factor will not always and uniformly justify an enhanced sentence. Many priors are of little or no relevance to the latest sentencing decision. Secondly, the conduct giving rise to the prior record enhancement has already resulted in prosecution and punishment; the use of a weapon or other such offence-related factors creates an unpunished liability for which punishment is appropriate.

Other jurisdictions have a clear advantage over the US guidelines in this respect. Statutory directions often require sentencers to consider various dimensions of a criminal record in a way that may lead to significant discounting of the prior crime, or even a total disregard. Courts in England and Wales, for example, often exercise their discretion to ignore prior convictions when they seem too old or insufficiently related to the current crime.[126] It is relatively straightforward to provide guidance on the effect of time on the weight assigned to a prior conviction. Under a points-based scheme where each prior crime results in a number of criminal history points, the number of points can be reduced to reflect the age of the prior. In more discretionary regimes, courts can be directed to discount or disregard prior crimes once they have passed a certain age.

In Germany, criminal records held at the Federal Central Register are deleted after certain periods of time without reconviction. The time limits depend on the seriousness of the offence and range from five years to fifteen years in most cases, but reach twenty years for sexual felonies (see § 46 of the Law on a Federal Central Register (*Bundeszentralregistergesetz* (BZRG)). In most cases, the time limit is additionally extended by the length of the prison sentence (§ 46(3) BZRG). Life sentences (which in practice are almost exclusively imposed for murder),[127] psychiatric hospital orders and preventive detention orders are, however, never deleted (§ 45 BZRG). There is also an 'all or nothing' rule applied. The registration of an offender is only deleted if all offences included therein have

[126] See discussion and Table 1 in Roberts and Pina-Sánchez, 'Previous Convictions' (2014).

[127] Just see Statistisches Bundesamt, *Strafverfolgung 2016* (2017), Table 6.1: Of the eighty-nine life sentences imposed in 2016 in Germany, eighty were for completed and nine for attempted murder, but none for the few other offences for which a life sentence could theoretically be imposed.

reached the time thresholds according to the above rules (§ 47(3), cl. 1 BZRG); otherwise, everything (even petty offences) will stay in the register.

Consider a person that has received a life sentence for murder. Even if released on parole, the person's criminal record will never be deleted. The life sentence will remain forever, and since the life sentence stays, all other sentences stay in as well, even a conviction for fare evasion on public transport. However, there is a special regulation for juvenile offenders, for whom all but the most serious convictions are completely discarded at the age of 24 (§ 63(1) BZRG).

For those who are registered on a regular basis, these rules set down in the BZRG ensure that even very old convictions are still visible in the record and can, in principle, be considered at sentencing. On the other hand, as soon as the register is cleared, a person is entitled by law to state that (s)he has no prior convictions (§ 51(1) BZRG). The courts have to disregard such convictions even if they receive evidence on them from other sources.[128] Apart from these legal provisions, the courts can and will of course also consider the age of convictions that are still visible in the criminal record. Usually, a reconviction shortly after the last conviction will lead to a more severe aggravation of sentence than a reconviction a long time after the last conviction.[129] Old previous convictions for offences of minor or medium severity can only be considered as an aggravator if the special circumstances of the case require the court to do so (e.g. if it can be proved that the offender has meanwhile returned to his or her former criminal lifestyle).[130]

However, a short length of time between release from prison and a reconviction is not necessarily a sign of increased dangerousness or culpability, but might also suggest problems with regard to the person's reintegration into society. The time period shortly after release is in this respect a critical phase,[131] which may explain why most people who are

[128] BGH, 25.01.2017, 1 StR 570/16, *Strafverteidiger* 2018, 219. On the few possible exceptions, cf. § 52 BZRG.

[129] See Schäfer, Sander and van Gemmeren, *Praxis der Strafzumessung* (2017), mn. 657–8; BGH, 26.11.2014, 2 StR 132/14, *Beck online*, BeckRS 2015, 01163.

[130] BGH, 16.10.1991, 5 StR 444/91, *Beck online*, BeckRS 1991, 31084024 (regarding a previous conviction for theft and fraud fifteen years ago and one for assault ten years ago).

[131] See Pruin, 'Entlassung aus dem Strafvollzug' (2015).

reconvicted after a prison sentence commit their next offence within the first months of freedom.[132]

2 *The Seriousness of Prior Convictions*

Guidance on the impact of the seriousness of the prior crimes is more challenging. As noted, many US guidelines operate a points-based criminal history enhancement regime. Each prior conviction carries criminal history points and the degree of enhancement reflects the total number of points. This approach does not always distinguish between felonies of different levels of seriousness.[133] Should they?

There is no clear answer to the question of whether the seriousness of the prior crime should affect the degree of enhancement. If risk reduction is the rationale, a very serious prior felony should carry more weight than a less serious prior crime only if the prior crime predicts the nature of any reoffending. Yet the best evidence suggests that the nature of the previous crime is an unreliable predictor of the nature of the offence of reconviction.[134] Most offenders do not specialise and the most likely subsequent crime is a non-violent offence, regardless of the nature of the previous crimes.[135] But perhaps a more severe prior offence is relevant the other way round: if the prior crime is very serious (e.g. armed robbery) and the new offence is minor (e.g. fare evasion on public transport, which is an offence in Germany), this might signal a positive development: the offender is reducing the seriousness of his or her offending, although (s)he has yet to succeed in fully refraining. This might indicate that a sentence enhancement is inappropriate. This assumption is confirmed by results from criminal career research, which show that even offenders who have decided to desist face a difficult path, as they need to change their lifestyle and habits, while lacking the necessary human and social re-integrative structures.[136] Hence, another offence might be little more than a momentary lapse on the path to desistance, and it is important that the courts have sufficient information to assess this question in each

[132] For an overview based on the nationwide German reconviction database, see Harrendorf, 'Neues zur Gefährlichkeit von Gewalttätern' (2014), 189–91.

[133] But see e.g. Minnesota Sentencing Guidelines Commission, *Guidelines and Commentary* (2018), 12, providing such a differentiation.

[134] See Roberts, 'Severity Premium' (2015).

[135] See Harrendorf, *Rückfälligkeit und kriminelle Karrieren* (2007), 318–31 for results from the German reconviction database and further references.

[136] Shapland and Bottoms, 'Young Adult Recidivists' (2011).

individual case. In any event, the individual preventive rationale would always require an individual assessment of the individual's risk of reoffending. For general prevention, the argument might be similar.

On a retributive rationale,[137] it is hard to see how the seriousness of the prior crime is a significant factor in determining the level of any enhancement. As noted, many retributivists do not see a role for prior convictions at sentencing. Those who argue the opposite do not usually discuss the nature or seriousness dimensions in relevant theoretical detail. Once again, it might, however, be argued that a decreasing level of seriousness is better than an increasing trajectory: the offender might have understood the principal message (i.e. not to commit *these specific* offences anymore). It might also be seen as a form of positive character development if someone at least manages to refrain from severe offences. From a retributive perspective, it might also be necessary to assess whether a new offence is committed because a person does not accept the legal and moral rule behind it, or merely out of personal weakness. Especially for petty offences like shoplifting, the latter is usually the case; this should justify a mild and non-increasing punishment even in cases with multiple previous convictions for such offences.[138]

3 The Similarity of Prior Convictions

Generally, the US guidelines also do not differentiate between similar and dissimilar prior felonies.[139] This is, however, also an important issue for both preventive and retributive approaches. For preventive approaches, similarity will be relevant for the prediction of future crimes, for retributive approaches, a conviction for a similar offence might carry more weight as a warning or with respect to an omission of value-oriented character development,[140] if one subscribes to these views.

VI Drawing Conclusions

Previous convictions appear to play a greater role in common law systems than in civil law systems. Support for this conclusion can be

137 We omit character-based retributivism which might include a much wider examination of the offender's character; on this construct, just see Schmidt 'Probleme in der deutschen Strafrechtsreform' (1957), 386; Herzberg, 'Setzt Schuld Vermeidenkönnen voraus?' (2012), 63.

138 See Köhler, *Strafrecht Allgemeiner Teil* (1997), 612–3.

139 Frase et al., *Sourcebook* (2015).

140 Schäfer, Sander and van Gemmeren, *Praxis der Strafzumessung* (2017), mn. 655.

found in the absence of explicit prior conviction sentencing provisions in many civil law statutes.[141] It is also supported by the limited empirical comparisons of sentencing statistics: the sentencing differential between first and repeat offenders appears greater in the United States than in European jurisdictions. Yet, even in a civil law country like Germany, previous convictions remain one of the most important aggravating factors in sentencing.[142] The German sentencing regime is however much less punitive than, for example, sentencing regimes in the United States or even England and Wales.[143] The absolute level of enhancement imposed for a prior conviction is also smaller. Still, there are some instances where a prior record has a very strong effect on sentence severity. In Germany, this effect is most pronounced for minor offences. Persons without a criminal record will often not even be formally punished for such offences, but the proceedings will be dropped due to public interest reasons. For the next offence, a person will receive a conditional disposal or a fine, but after a certain number of repetitions, reconvicted offenders will even be sent to prison for stealing a chocolate bar or for fare evasion on public transport.[144]

Previous convictions play an even greater role in common law countries. The first reason may be that recidivist sentencing statutes, in general, appear to be more frequent in Anglo-American jurisdictions, and this may reflect a greater interest in repeat offending in these countries.[145] Recidivist provisions for a range of offences including firearm offences, impaired driving, drug crimes and knife offences have proved a popular option with legislatures in most Western common law jurisdictions. Statutory sentencing regimes in common law jurisdictions highlight criminal history to a greater extent. Deterrence – at first

[141] However, such provisions are known in civil law systems as well. Germany, for example had a general aggravation rule for reconvicted offenders in § 48 StGB up to 1986, which in principle led to a minimum prison sentence of six months for the third conviction, regardless of the severity of the new offence.

[142] See Harrendorf, 'Sentencing Thresholds' (2017), 527–30 with further references.

[143] See e.g. Cavadino and Dignan, 'Penal Policy' (2006); also see Harrendorf, 'Sentencing Thresholds' (2017), regarding the custody threshold in Germany.

[144] See the references in n. 99 above; and, again, Harrendorf, 'Sentencing Thresholds' (2017).

[145] See Tonry, 'Sentencing in America' (2013). Even a jurisdiction like Canada, which has pursued a much more moderate approach to sentencing than the United States, has passed a steady stream of mandatory sentences in recent years: see Malik, 'Mandatory Minimum Sentences' (2007); and Roberts, *Mandatory Sentences* (2006).

glance[146] the most plausible justifying rationale for prior record enhancements – plays a greater role in the Anglo-American countries. All common law jurisdictions which have placed the objectives of sentencing on a statutory footing have included deterrence as one such objective.[147]

In contrast, in a number of civil law countries, deterrence assumes a lower profile as a sentencing purpose. For example, Weigend notes that 'deterrence is conspicuously absent from the general principles of sentencing under German law'.[148] This in itself does not completely exclude a sentencing premium based on grounds of general deterrence, but such a premium would only be possible within the limits of culpability – that is, it does not justify sentences that are disproportionate to the offender's guilt.[149] According to the Federal Court of Justice, such premiums are also only justified under certain circumstances:

- to deter 'copycat' crimes that would otherwise be expected, and/or
- if a certain type of offence, similar to the one the offender committed, has recently increased in a way that is dangerous to the community.[150]

Secondly, the Anglo-American countries have been particularly affected by media-driven penal populism. Populist criminal justice reforms have often targeted repeat offenders, most notoriously in the 'three strikes' statutes which originated in the United States and then proliferated around the Western nations.[151] Other countries, most prominently in Scandinavia,[152] but also others, like Slovenia,[153] and, in most respects, also Germany,[154] have more strongly withstood the temptation of penal populism.

Thirdly, risk-based sentencing instruments are far more prominent in the Anglo-Saxon jurisdictions. Courts across the United States, Canada and England and Wales routinely employ risk prediction instruments

[146] The deterrent effect of harsher punishments for recidivists is questionable; see above, at Section II.1.(b) and (c).

[147] See e.g. s. 142 of the Criminal Justice Act 2003 in England and Wales or s. 718 of the Criminal Code of Canada.

[148] Weigend, 'No News is Good News' (2016), 89.

[149] See BVerfG, 21.06.1977, 1 BvL 14/76, BVerfGE 45, 187, 260.

[150] BGH, 11.04.2013, 5 StR 113/13, *Neue Zeitschrift für Strafrecht: Rechtsprechungs-Report* (2013), 240; BGH BGH, 23.11.2010, 3 STR 393/10, *Beck online*, BeckRS 2011, 00428.

[151] See Pratt, *Penal Populism* (2007); Roberts et al., *Penal Populism* (2003).

[152] Pratt, 'Scandinavian Exceptionalism' (2008).

[153] Flander and Meško, 'Slovenian Exceptionalism' (2016).

[154] Heinz, 'Neue Straflust' (2011); Kury, Brandenstein and Obergfell-Fuchs, 'Punitiveness in Germany' (2009); more critical Klimke, Sack and Schlepper, 'Punitive Turn' (2011).

such as the Level of Service Inventory Revised (LSI-R). These scales capture a wide range of variables related to risk of reoffending, and the offender's score on the scale is then used by a sentencing court to help determine the sentence. For example, these instruments contain questions on factors related to the risk of reoffending including drug or alcohol abuse and the offender's responses to these questions result in a risk score which is then used to classify the offender as high, medium or low risk to reoffend. Courts and in some cases parole authorities then consider this risk-scale score in determining whether the offender is suitable for a community penalty, or whether (s)he can be safely released from prison on supervised parole. Because previous convictions predict subsequent reoffending, they figure prominently in risk assessment scales, and this further enhances the impact of prior crimes on sentence severity. This is especially problematic if one considers that the predictive strength of such systems still seems to be weak.[155]

As risk-based enhancements increase in strength, they come increasingly in conflict with offence-based proportionality. Sentencing regimes thus face a choice: allow sentence severity to rise indefinitely (subject only to constitutional limits) for preventive purposes, or introduce retributive limits. The challenge to sentencing regimes around the world is to ensure that prior crimes do not carry excessive weight at sentencing, thus overwhelming the offence of conviction. Offence-based proportionality is undermined when an offender's prior crimes are more important determinants of the sentence imposed. As noted, in many US schemes, prior crimes can eclipse the current offence, at least for offenders with serious criminal records. Moreover, this can occur even in states such as Minnesota which ostensibly sentence according to a principally desert-based rationale.

To conclude, prior record enhancements play a greater role at sentencing than can reasonably be justified by preventive or retributive rationales. This is particularly true in the United States, where the guidelines mandate more punitive enhancements than in other jurisdictions. One explanation for the strength, persistence and universality of prior record enhancements is that there are additional, intuitive motivations at work. Many people regard repeat offenders as less worthy of sympathy and

[155] For the COMPAS risk assessment tool, see Dressel and Farid, 'Predicting Recidivism' (2018), who showed that this programme, although including data from 137 different variables, was unable to make better predictions of recidivism than persons who had little or no criminal justice expertise.

deserving of more punishment in a way that is independent of theoretical models of desert. There is also a naïve assumption that reoffending reflects wilful recalcitrance (rather than the influence of environmental factors and lack of self-control), for which the offender is to be blamed and hence punished. Finally, there is an expectation that the offender's reaction to state censure should be desistance; when persistence is the response this triggers punitiveness. If politicians, policy-makers and judges[156] share these intuitions about offenders and offending, this may explain the enduring appeal of the recidivist sentencing premium.

Bibliography

Alex M., *Nachträgliche Sicherungsverwahrung: Ein rechtsstaatliches und kriminalpolitisches Debakel*, Bochum, Felix-Verlag (2013).

Alexander L. and Ferzan K., *Reflections on Crime and Culpability*, Cambridge University Press (2018).

Andenaes J., 'The General Preventive Effects of Punishment', *University of Pennsylvania Law Review*, 114 (1966), 949–83.

Ashworth A., *Sentencing and Criminal Justice*, 6th edn, Cambridge University Press (2015).

Ashworth A. and Roberts J. V., *Sentencing Guidelines: Exploring the English Model*, Oxford University Press (2013).

Baurmann M., 'Vorüberlegungen zu einer empirischen Theorie der Generalprävention', in Schünemann B., Hirsch A. von and Jareborg N. (eds.), *Positive Generalprävention: Kritische Analysen im deutsch-englischen Dialog*, Heidelberg, C. F. Müller (1998), 1–16.

Becker G. S., 'Crime and Punishment: An Economic Approach', *Journal of Political Economy*, 76 (1968), 169–217.

Bentham J., *An Introduction to the Principles of Morals and Legislation*, 2nd edn, 2 vols., London, W. Pickering (1823), II.

Cavadino M. and Dignan J., 'Penal Policy and Political Economy', *Criminology & Criminal Justice*, 6 (2006), 435–56.

Cochran J. K. and Chamlin M. B., 'Can Information Change Public Opinion? *Another Test of the Marshall Hypotheses*', *Journal of Criminal Justice*, 33 (2005), 573–84.

[156] Many judges certainly subscribe to some of these expectations. Walker noted that: 'The ordinary sentence regards earlier convictions and failures to respond to sentences as good reasons for sentencing more severely.' See Walker, *Aggravation, Mitigation and Mercy* (1999), 40.

Cooter R., 'Expressive Law and Economics', *Journal of Legal Studies*, 27 (1998), 585–608.

Cox E., *The Principles of Punishment: As Applied in the Administration of the Criminal Law by Judges and Magistrates*, London, Law Times Office (1877).

Dölling D., Entorf H., Hermann D. and Rupp T., 'Is Deterrence Effective? Results of a Meta-Analysis of Punishment', *European Journal on Criminal Policy and Research*, 15 (2009), 201–24.

Dressel J. and Farid H., 'The Accuracy, Fairness, and Limits of Predicting Recidivism', *Science Advances*, 4 (2018).

Dubber M. D., 'Positive Generalprävention und Rechtsgutstheorie: Zwei zentrale Errungenschaften der deutschen Strafrechtswissenschaft aus amerikanischer Sicht', *Zeitschrift für die gesamte Strafrechtswissenschaft*, 117 (2005), 485–518.

Duff R. A., *Punishment, Communication, and Community*, Oxford University Press (2001).

Eschelbach R., '§ 46 StGB', in Satzger H., Schluckebier W. and Widmaier G. (eds.), *Strafgesetzbuch: Kommentar*, 4th edn, Cologne, Heymanns (2018).

Fehr E. and Gächter S., 'Cooperation and Punishment in Public Goods Experiments', *American Economic Review*, 90 (2000), 980–94.

Fehr E. and Gintis H., 'Human Motivation and Social Cooperation: Experimental and Analytical Foundations', *Annual Review of Sociology*, 33 (2007), 43–64.

Feinberg J., 'The Expressive Function of Punishment', in Feinberg J. (ed.), *Doing and Deserving*, Princeton University Press (1970), 95–118.

Feldman Y., 'The Expressive Function of Trade Secret Law: Legality, Cost, Intrinsic Motivation, and Consensus', *Journal of Empirical Legal Studies*, 6 (2009), 177–212.

Feuerbach J. P. A. von, *Lehrbuch des gemeinen in Deutschland gültigen peinlichen Rechts*, 11th edn, Gießen, Heyer (1832).

Flander B. and Meško G., 'Penal and Prison Policy on the Sunny Side of the Alps: The Swan Song of Slovenian Exceptionalism?' *European Journal on Criminal Policy and Research*, 22 (2016), 565–91.

Frase R., 'Prior-Conviction Sentencing Enhancements: Rationales and Limits Based on Retributive and Utilitarian Proportionality Principles and Social Equality Goals', in Roberts J. V. and Hirsch A. von (eds.), *Previous Convictions at Sentencing: Theoretical and Applied Perspectives*, Oxford, Hart (2014), 117–36.

Frase R. and Hester R., 'Magnitude of Criminal History Enhancements', in Frase R., Roberts J. V., Mitchell K. and Hester R., *Sourcebook of Criminal History Enhancements*, Minneapolis, Robina Institute (2015), 19–28.

Frase R. and Roberts J. V., *Paying for the Past: Prior Record Enhancements in the US Sentencing Guidelines*, Oxford University Press (2019).

Frase R., Roberts J. V., Mitchell K. and Hester R., *Sourcebook of Criminal History Enhancements*, Minneapolis, Robina Institute (2015).

Funk P., 'Is There an Expressive Function of Law? An Empirical Analysis of Voting Laws with Symbolic Fines', *American Law and Economics Review*, 9 (2007), 135–59.

Gallas W., 'Zum gegenwärtigen Stand der Lehre vom Verbrechen', *Zeitschrift für die gesamte Strafrechtswissenschaft*, 67 (1955), 1–47.

Greco L., *Lebendiges und Totes in Feuerbachs Straftheorie*, Berlin, Duncker & Humblot (2009).

Green D., *When Children Kill Children*, Oxford University Press (2008).

Harrendorf S., *Rückfälligkeit und kriminelle Karrieren von Gewalttätern*, Universitätsverlag Göttingen (2007).

'Neues zur Gefährlichkeit von Gewalttätern: Rückfälligkeit im sechsjährigen Intervall 2004 – 2010', in Albrecht H.-J. and Jehle J.-M. (eds.), *National Reconviction Statistics and Studies in Europe*, Universitätsverlag Göttingen (2014), 183–210.

'Sentencing Thresholds in German Criminal Law and Practice: Legal and Empirical Aspects', *Criminal Law Forum*, 28 (2017), 501–39.

Absolute und relative Bagatellen: Grenzen des Strafrechts bei geringfügiger Delinquenz (forthcoming).

Harrendorf S. and Geng B., 'Der rational kalkulierende Verbrecher? Zu Entwicklung, Stand und Zukunftsperspektiven ökonomischer Kriminalitätstheorien', in Körnert J., Lege J. and Grube C. (eds.), *Recht trifft Wirtschaft*, Berlin, Duncker & Humblot (2019), 181–212.

Heinz W., 'Neue Straflust der Strafjustiz – Realität oder Mythos?' *Neue Kriminalpolitik*, 22 (2011), 14–27.

Herzberg R. D., 'Setzt strafrechtliche Schuld ein Vermeidenkönnen voraus?', *Zeitschrift für die gesamte Strafrechtswissenschaft*, 124 (2012), 12–63.

Hessick C. B. and Hessick F. A., 'Double Jeopardy as a Limit on Punishment', *Cornell Law Review*, 97 (2011), 45–86.

Hirsch A. von, 'Criminal Record Rides Again', *Criminal Justice Ethics*, 10 (1991), 2–57.

'Begründung und Bestimmung tatproportionaler Strafen', in Frisch W., Hirsch A. von and Albrecht H.-J. (eds.), *Tatproportionalität: Normative und empirische Aspekte einer tatproportionalen Strafzumessung*, Heidelberg, C. F. Müller (2003), 47–82.

Hirsch A. von, Bottoms A., Burney E. and Wikström P. O., *Criminal Deterrence and Sentence Severity*, Oxford, Hart (1999).

Hirsch H. J., 'Tatstrafrecht – ein hinreichend beachtetes Grundprinzip?', in Prittwitz C., Baurmann M., Günther K., Kuhlen L., Merkel R., Nestler C. and Schulz L. (eds.), *Festschrift für Klaus Lüderssen zum 70. Geburtstag am 2. Mai 2002*, Baden-Baden, Nomos (2002), 253–67.

Holz W., *Justizgewähranspruch des Verbrechensopfers*, Berlin, Duncker & Humblot (2007).

Hörnle T., *Tatproportionale Strafzumessung*, Berlin, Duncker & Humblot (1999).

Horstkotte H., 'Die Vorschriften des Ersten Gesetzes zur Reform des Strafrechts über den Rückfall und die Maßregeln der Sicherung und Besserung', *Juristenzeitung*, 5 (1970), 152–6.

Indermaur D., Roberts L. D., Spiranovic C., Mackenzie G. and Gelb K., 'A Matter of Judgement: The Effect of Information and Deliberation on Public Attitudes to Punishment', *Punishment & Society*, 14 (2012), 147–65

Jacobs J. B., *The Eternal Criminal Record*, Cambridge, MA, Harvard University Press (2015).

Jakobs G., *Schuld und Prävention*, Tübingen, Mohr Siebeck (1976).

'Das Strafrecht zwischen Funktionalismus und ‚alteuropäischem'Prinzipiendenken: Oder: Verabschiedung des ‚alteuropäischen Strafrechts'?', *Zeitschrift für die gesamte Strafrechtswissenschaft*, 107 (1995), 843–76.

Staatliche Strafe: Bedeutung und Zweck, Paderborn, Schöningh (2004).

Jehle J.-M., 'Approach, Structure and Outcome of the German Reconviction Study', in Albrecht H.-J. and Jehle J.-M. (eds.), *National Reconviction Statistics and Studies in Europe*, Universitätsverlag Göttingen (2014), 25–41.

Jehle J.-M., Albrecht H.-J., Hohmann-Fricke S. and Tetal C., *Legalbewährung nach strafrechtlichen Sanktionen: Eine bundesweite Rückfalluntersuchung 2010 bis 2013 und 2004 bis 2013*, Mönchengladbach, Forum Verlag Godesberg (2016).

Jescheck H.-H. and Weigend T., *Lehrbuch des Strafrechts: Allgemeiner Teil*, 5th edn, Berlin, Duncker & Humblot (1996).

Jolliffe D. and Hedderman C., 'Investigating the Impact of Custody on Reoffending Using Propensity Score Matching', *Crime and Delinquency*, 61 (2015), 1051–77.

Kaspar J., *Verhältnismäßigkeit und Grundrechtsschutz im Präventionsstrafrecht*, Baden-Baden, Nomos (2014).

Gutachten C zum 72. Deutschen Juristentag: Sentencing Guidelines versus freies tatrichterliches Ermessen – Brauchen wir ein neues Strafzumessungsrecht?, Munich, C. H. Beck (2018).

Kaufmann A., *Lebendiges und Totes in Bindings Normentheorie*, Göttingen, Otto Schwartz (1954).

Kazemian L., 'Assessing the Impact of a Recidivist Sentencing Premium on Crime and Recidivism Rates', in Roberts J. V. and Hirsch A. von (eds.), *Previous Convictions at Sentencing: Theoretical and Applied Perspectives*, Oxford, Hart (2014), 227–50.

Killias M., 'Zur Bedeutung von Rechtsgefühl und Sanktionen für die Konformität des Verhaltens gegenüber neuen Normen: Das Beispiel der Gurtanlegepflicht', in Lampe E. J. (ed.), *Das sogenannte Rechtsgefühl*, Opladen, Westdeutscher Verlag (1985), 257–72.

Kinzig J., *Legalbewährung gefährlicher Rückfalltäter*, 2nd edn, Berlin, Duncker & Humblot (2010).

Klimke D., Sack F. and Schlepper C., 'Stopping the "Punitive Turn" at the German Border', in Kury H. and Shea E. (eds.), *Punitivity: International Developments, I: Punitiveness – A Global Phenomenon?*, Bochum, Universitätsverlag Brockmeyer (2011), 289–340.

Köhler M., *Strafrecht Allgemeiner Teil*, Berlin, Springer (1997).

Kunz K. L., 'Vorleben und Nachtatverhalten als Strafzumessungstatsachen', in Frisch W. (ed.), *Grundfragen des Strafzumessungsrechts aus deutscher und japanischer Sicht*, Tübingen, Mohr Siebeck (2011), 135–50.

Kury H., Brandenstein M. and Obergfell-Fuchs J., 'Dimensions of Punitiveness in Germany', *European Journal on Criminal Policy and Research*, 15 (2009), 63–81.

Lee Y., 'Repeat Offenders and the Question of Desert', in Roberts J. V. and Hirsch A. von (eds.), *Previous Convictions at Sentencing: Theoretical and Applied Perspectives*, Oxford, Hart (2014), 49–72.

Lipsey M. W. and Cullen F. T., 'The Effectiveness of Correctional Rehabilitation: A Review of Systematic Reviews', *Annual Review of Law and Social Science*, 3 (2007), 297–320.

Liszt F. von, 'Der Zweckgedanke im Strafrecht', *Zeitschrift für die Gesamte Strafrechtswissenschaft*, 1 (1883), 1–47.

Luskin R. C., Fishkin J. S. and Jowell R., 'Considered Opinions: Deliberative Polling in Britain', *British Journal of Political Science*, 32 (2002), 455–87.

Malik A. K., 'Mandatory Minimum Sentences: Shackling Judicial Discretion for Justice or Political Expediency?', *Criminal Law Quarterly*, 53 (2007), 236–59.

Meier B. D., 'What Works? Die Ergebnisse der neueren Sanktionsforschung aus kriminologischer Sicht', *Juristenzeitung*, 3 (2010), 112–20.

Mews A., Hillier J., McHugh M. and Coxon C., *The Impact of Short Custodial Sentences, Community Orders and Suspended Sentence Orders on Re-Offending*, London, Ministry of Justice (2015).

Ministry of Justice, *Compendium of Re-Offending Statistics and Analysis*, London, Ministry of Justice (2011).

Minnesota Sentencing Guidelines Commission, *2017 Sentencing Practices, Annual Summary Statistics for Felony Offenders Sentenced in 2017*, Saint Paul, Minnesota Sentencing Guidelines Commission (2018).

Minnesota Sentencing Guidelines and Commentary, Saint Paul, Minnesota Sentencing Guidelines Commission (2018).

Mitchell K., 'Decay and Gap Policies', in Frase R., Roberts J. V., Mitchell K. and Hester R. (eds.), *Sourcebook of Criminal History Enhancements*, Minneapolis, Robina Institute (2015), 29–38.

'A Measure of Tolerance: Public Attitudes toward Sentencing Enhancements for Old and Juvenile Prior Records', *Corrections. Policy, Practice, and Research*, 3 (2017), 137–51.

Nozick R., *Philosophical Explanations*, Oxford, Clarendon Press (1981).

O'Malley T., *Sentencing Law and Practice*, Dublin, Thomson Reuters (2016).

Parent D., *Structuring Criminal Sentences: The Evolution of Minnesota's Sentencing Guidelines*, Massachusetts, Butterworths (1988).

Pawlik M., *Person, Subjekt, Bürger*, Berlin, Duncker & Humblot (2004).

Pratt J., *Penal Populism*, London, Routledge (2007).

'Scandinavian Exceptionalism in an Era of Penal Excess, Part I: The Nature and Roots of Scandinavian Exceptionalism', *British Journal of Criminology*, 48 (2008), 119–37.

Pruin I., 'Interdisziplinäre Erkenntnisse zur Entlassung aus dem Strafvollzug und ihre Bedeutung für die deutsche Reformdiskussion', in Bock S., Harrendorf S. and Ladiges M. (eds.), *Strafrecht als interdisziplinäre Wissenschaft*, Baden-Baden, Nomos (2015), 139–67.

Roberts J. V., *Mandatory Sentences of Imprisonment in Common Law Jurisdictions: Some Representative Models*, Department of Justice Canada, Research Division (2006).

Punishing Persistent Offenders: Community and Offender Perspectives on the Recidivist Sentencing Premium, Oxford University Press (2008).

'Justifying Criminal History Enhancements at Sentencing', in Frase R., Roberts J. V., Mitchell K. and Hester R. (eds.), *Sourcebook of Criminal History Enhancements*, Minneapolis, Robina Institute (2015), 11–18.

'Severity Premium for Similar Prior Offending: Patterning Rules', in Frase R., Roberts J. V., Mitchell K. and Hester R. (eds.), *Sourcebook of Criminal History Enhancements*, Minneapolis, Robina Institute (2015), 63–70.

Roberts J. V. and Hirsch A. von (eds.), *Previous Convictions at Sentencing: Theoretical and Applied Perspectives*, Oxford, Hart (2014).

Roberts J. V. and Hough M., *Understanding Public Attitudes to Criminal Justice*, Maidenhead, Open University Press (2005).

Roberts J. V. and Pei W., 'Structuring Judicial Discretion in China: Exploring the 2014 Sentencing Guidelines', *Criminal Law Forum*, 27 (2016), 3–33.

Roberts J. V. and Pina-Sánchez J., 'Previous Convictions at Sentencing: Exploring Empirical Trends in the Crown Court', *Criminal Law Review*, 8 (2014), 575–88.

'Paying for the Past: The Role of Previous Convictions at Sentencing in the Crown Court', in Roberts J. V. (ed.), *Exploring Sentencing Practice in England and Wales*, Basingstoke, Palgrave Macmillan (2015), 154–72.

Roberts J. V. and Stalans L. J., *Public Opinion, Crime, and Criminal Justice*, Boulder, Westview Press (1997).

Roberts J. V., Stalans L. J., Indermaur D. and Hough M., *Penal Populism and Public Opinion: Lessons from Five Countries*, Oxford University Press (2003).

Roxin C., *Strafrecht Allgemeiner Teil*, 4th edn, Munich, C. H. Beck (2006).

Ryberg J., *The Ethics of Proportionate Punishment: A Critical Investigation*, Dordecht, Kluwer (2004).

Sampson R. J. and Laub J. H., *Crime in the Making: Pathways and Turning Points through Life*, Harvard University Press (1995).

Schäfer G., Sander G. M. and Gemmeren G. van, *Praxis der Strafzumessung*, 6th edn, Munich, C. H. Beck (2017).

Schmidhäuser E., *Strafrecht Allgemeiner Teil: Lehrbuch*, 2nd edn, Tübingen, Mohr Siebeck (1975).

Schmidt E., 'Kriminalpolitische und strafrechtsdogmatische Probleme in der deutschen Strafrechtsreform', *Zeitschrift für die gesamte Strafrechtswissenschaft*, 69 (1957), 359–96.

Schumann K. F., *Positive Generalprävention*, Heidelberg, C. F. Müller (1989).

Schünemann B., 'Die Akzeptanz von Normen und Sanktionen aus der Perspektive der Tatproportionalität', in Frisch W., Hirsch A. von and Albrecht H.-J. (eds.), *Tatproportionalität: Normative und empirische Aspekte einer tatproportionalen Strafzumessung*, Heidelberg, C. F. Müller (2003), 185–97.

Shapland J. and Bottoms A., 'Reflections on Social Values, Offending and Desistance among Young Adult Recidivists', *Punishment & Society*, 13 (2011), 256–82.

Smith P., Goggin C. and Gendreau P., *The Effects of Prison Sentences and Intermediate Sanctions on Recidivism: General Effects and Individual Differences*, Ottowa, Solicitor General Canada (2002).

Statistisches Bundesamt, *Rechtspflege: Strafverfolgung 2016*, Wiesbaden, Statistisches Bundesamt (2017).

Stelly W. and Thomas J., *Einmal Verbrecher – immer Verbrecher?*, Wiesbaden, Westdeutscher Verlag (2001).

Stratenwerth G., *Was leistet die Lehre von den Strafzwecken?*, Berlin, De Gruyter (1995).

Streng F., 'Schuld ohne Freiheit? Der funktionale Schuldbegriff auf dem Prüfstand', *Zeitschrift für die gesamte Strafrechtswissenschaft*, 101 (1989), 273–334.

'§ 46 StGB', in Kindhäuser U., Neumann U. and Paeffgen H.-U. (eds.), *Nomos-Kommentar Strafgesetzbuch*, 5th edn, Baden-Baden, Nomos (2017).

Sunstein C. R., 'On the Expressive Function of Law', *University of Pennsylvania Law Review*, 144 (1996), 2021–53.

Tamburrini C. M. and Ryberg J. (eds.), *Recidivist Punishments: The Philosopher's View*, Lanham, Lexington Books (2012).

Thomas D. A., *Principles of Sentencing*, 2nd edn, London, Heinemann (1970).

Tomášek J., 'The Public and Crime', in Scheinost S. (ed.), *Crime from the Perspective of Criminologists*, Prague, Institute of Criminology and Social Prevention (2011), 221–32.

Tonry M., 'Sentencing in America, 1975–2025', *Crime and Justice*, 42 (2013), 141–98.

Tyler T. R., *Why People Obey the Law*, New Haven, Yale University Press (1990).

US Sentencing Commission, *US Sentencing Guidelines Manual 2018*, Washington, DC, US Sentencing Commission (2018).

Walker N., *Sentencing: Theory, Law and Practice*, London, Butterworths (1985).

Aggravation, Mitigation and Mercy in English Criminal Justice, London, Blackstone Press (1999).

Wasik M., 'Guidance, Guidelines and Criminal Record', in Wasik M. and Pease K. (eds.), *Sentencing Reform: Guidance or Guidelines?*, Manchester University Press (1987).

'Dimensions of Criminal History: Reflections on Theory and Practice', in Roberts J. V. and von Hirsch A. (eds.), *Previous Convictions at Sentencing: Theoretical and Applied Perspectives*, Oxford, Hart (2014), 161–83.

Weigend T., 'No News is Good News: Criminal Sentencing in Germany since 2000', *Crime and Justice*, 45 (2016), 83–106.

Welcker C. T., *Die letzten Gründe von Recht, Staat und Strafe: Philosophisch und nach den Gesetzen der merkwürdigsten Völker rechtshistorisch entwickelt*, Gießen, Heyer (1813).

9

Due Process

LUCIA ZEDNER* AND CARL-FRIEDRICH STUCKENBERG**

I Introduction

'Due process' is a central concept in Anglo-American criminal justice that safeguards the rights of those subject to the criminal process and guides state officials, vital to the authority of the criminal law and the legitimacy of the legal system.[1] Comparison reveals what is distinctive about Anglo-American and German conceptions of due process, and how far their development is the product of their legal history and local legal culture. As Galligan observes of dispute over 'whether the adversarial nature of the trial at common law is to be preferred to the more inquisitorial procedures of continental Europe ... the real debate in comparing the two approaches is not about which will lead to more correct outcomes, but rather what values are relevant'.[2] Comparative analysis permits a better understanding of what is distinctive in the respective systems.[3] It reveals what commonalities exist and to what extent international developments, not least the important jurisprudence on the right to a fair trial under Article 6 of the European Convention on Human Rights (ECHR),[4] foster convergence among signatory states.

* I am grateful to participants at Gordon Seminar on Criminal Law, University of Glasgow (2017) and the Anglo-German Dialogue on Current Issues in Criminal Law Seminar, Oxford (2017), in particular, Kai Ambos, Carl-Friedrich Stuckenberg and Alec Walen, and to Andrew Ashworth and Carolyn Hoyle for their insightful comments on earlier versions.

** I am indebted to Lucia Zedner and Heike Jung for helpful suggestions.

1 Dubber observes, 'The process of criminal law, as law, is shaped by what process is due to the persons that populate it'. Dubber, 'Criminal Trial' (2004), 92.

2 Galligan, *Due Process* (1997), 62–3.

3 Ramraj, 'Due Process' (2004), 495.

4 Goss, *Criminal Fair Trial Rights* (2014).

II Due Process in England and Wales

Due process is a central concept in the common law world, albeit more clearly articulated in the United States, where the constitutional guarantees of the Fifth Amendment have generated a large jurisprudence on the subject.[5] In England and Wales, due process is less well-defined[6] and, as *Ward* acknowledges, 'the terms procedural justice, procedural due process, procedural fairness, procedural rights and the "rule of law" are often used interchangeably'.[7] This chapter examines what is distinctive about due process, what role it plays in pre-trial and trial processes, and also how it relates to other analogous concepts and values.

The chapter first explores the founding reasons and historical origins of due process, the obligations it imposes and the guarantees it provides. It considers the various sources of contemporary due process values, principles and rights, most importantly, those derived from human rights conventions. It reflects critically upon recent developments in Anglo-American scholarship, especially the claim that 'procedural justice' is essential to the legitimation of state power. It then considers appeals for a more fully articulated conception of substantive due process attentive to the content of criminal law as well as procedural laws. It suggests that due process sets aspirational standards that the criminal justice system cannot always attain. So the chapter goes on to consider failings of due process, provisions for appeal against miscarriages of justice and wrongful convictions, for rectification and restitution. It concludes by considering the claim that the articulation of due process in the pre-trial and trial phases needs to be matched by a stronger elaboration of protections post-trial.

1 Due Process and the Citizen–State Relationship

Due process provides a necessary check on the exercise of state power over its citizens essential to the citizen–state relationship. It is a central tenet of political theory that the state's authority to criminalise derives partly from its duty to protect the public and provide security. This duty arises from a hypothesised social contract under which citizens cede the right to self-protection to the state in return for which it provides social

[5] Orth, *Due Process of Law* (1968).
[6] Marshall, 'Due Process in England' (1977), 69.
[7] Ward, 'Transforming "Summary Justice"' (2015), 345.

order and public protection.[8] Yet the institutions of the criminal law, policing and punishment accord immense coercive power to the state that itself threatens individual security. Police stop and search, arrest, and detention are serious intrusions on individual liberty that would constitute criminal acts of assault, theft and false imprisonment were they not performed in accordance with the rules of criminal procedure. The protections afforded by the principles and values of due process are designed to safeguard citizens against the threat that the untrammelled exercise of state coercive power might otherwise pose. Issacharoff suggests the 'due process principle can be understood in two different ways: as a guarantee creating a distinct set of rights among the citizenry, or as a constraint designed to prevent arbitrary government'.[9] Arguably, these are not in the alternative, as he suggests, rather each is a necessary complement of the other. The requirement that rules be administered through the courts in line with established legal principles provides both positive protections and negative limits that act as a powerful shield against the overreaching of state power. Yet, the scope of due process is by no means confined to these twin roles of protection and restraint: drilling down into the origins, character and values of due process reveals it to be a more complex phenomenon than that of sword and shield.

Due process underpins the very authority of the state to enact and enforce the criminal law. As one of us has argued elsewhere, 'criminal law is not only, or even primarily, a means by which to classify wrongdoing: it is also the authorisation of a particular response by the state'.[10] This authorisation is not without limits: only where officials abide by due process and uphold the right to a fair trial can state authority to promulgate and enforce the criminal law be upheld. Due process is integral to the legitimacy of the law, underlying state authority to criminalise and punish.[11] It is more central to criminal law theory than generally acknowledged in that it stipulates the manner in which criminal cases are prosecuted, it is a necessary condition of legitimate enforcement and also of the sanctions that follow.[12] Ristroph reflects, 'what is the subject of criminal law theory, if not the arc from crime to punishment'[13] and calls

[8] Hobbes, *Leviathan* (2008).
[9] Issacharoff, *Civil Procedure* (2012).
[10] Zedner, 'Arbitrary Government' (2017), 91. See also Ashworth and Redmayne, *Criminal Process* (2010), at 22.
[11] See Ristroph, 'Crime to Punishment' (2018).
[12] Dubber, 'Criminal Trial' (2004), 91–2; Duff et al., *Trial on Trial* (2007), 51.
[13] Ristroph, 'Crime to Punishment' (2018), 307.

for a more holistic account of the relationship between criminal law, process, and punishment, to which this chapter seeks to contribute.

Due process values are commonly articulated as a set of norms intrinsic to criminal procedure, not least, accordance with the rule of law, the presumption of innocence and fair trial. Some values are internal, inherent to the operation of a just criminal process, others are externally imposed by law; some values are jurisdictionally specific, others supranational.[14] Today due process is vested in positive rights elaborated in human rights conventions, incorporated into domestic law, and developed through the jurisprudence of the courts to protect citizens and non-citizens.[15] Through the articulation of and adherence to these values and rights, due process provides reassurance to the public that justice is not only done but also seen to be done. This, it is argued, contributes to perceptions of the legitimacy of the criminal process, public compliance with the criminal law (see further Section II.6 below) and to confidence in the fairness and justice of resulting outcomes.

The additional protection of due process is especially important in common law systems, where every decision by police, lawyers, magistrates and judges is mediated through the exercise of discretion.[16] In England, the ability of the police and criminal justice officials to exercise discretion is defended on the grounds that decisions must be made where rules are ambiguous and right answers elusive. In the common law world, the exercise of discretion is often regarded as an important safeguard against the unwarranted exercise of state power, rather than a feature of it. Yet, while discretion is seen as a means to mitigate rigid enforcement of otherwise potentially oppressive or unjust rules,[17] it also opens the door to the improper exercise of power by officials, to bias and racial prejudice.[18] A primary role of due process is to guide and limit official discretion, but this requires that the state itself fund the structures and procedures that enable access to justice, legal defence and redress. As a former President of the UK Supreme Court argued, 'unless a right to due process in criminal proceedings, a right to protection against abuses or excesses of the state, or a right against

[14] Ashworth and Redmayne, *Criminal Process* (2010), 26 ff.; Emmerson et al., *Human Rights* (2012).

[15] Cole, 'Basic Rights' (2007), 2541–8.

[16] Galligan, *Due Process* (1997), at 65; Hawkins, *Law as Last Resort*, 424–7.

[17] Zedner, *Criminal Justice* (2004), 129–32.

[18] Phillips and Bowling, 'Ethnicities, Racism, Crime and Criminal Justice' (2017), 190–212.

another citizen, is enforceable, it might as well not exist'.[19] It is in this complex context, in which power is exerted and must also be constrained by the self-same actors and institutions, that the profound challenges of due process should be understood.

2 *The Historical Development of Due Process*

The historical origins of due process in England lie in Magna Carta (1215), which pledged that the basic rights of citizens shall not be infringed other than through the legal process,[20] and the 1354 Liberty of Subject Act (28 Edward 3), which decreed:

> No man of what estate or condition that he be, shall be put out of land or tenement, nor taken, nor imprisoned, nor disinherited, nor put to death, without being brought in answer by due process of the law.[21]

These famous historic provisions established the requirement of procedural regularity as an essential facet of good governance and prescribed the form of investigative and trial processes that were widely acknowledged as a vital guard against abuse of sovereign power. Due process is central to the history of the common law, ensuring the pivotal role of the courts and judiciary in articulating the requirements of procedural fairness.

Due process spoke even more powerfully to those in eighteenth-century America seeking to assert procedural protections against British imperial rule. In colonial and post-independence America, constitutional protections against sovereign power were more energetically pursued than in England.[22] Due process was articulated primarily through US constitutional law:[23] the Due Process Clause incorporated in the Fifth Amendment to the Constitution was intended as 'a negative limitation on what the state may do to its citizenry'.[24] This constitutional entrenchment ensured that due process rights are much more developed in the

[19] Neuberger, 'Justice' (2013).

[20] Chapter 39 Magna Carta, translation into modern English by the British Library. See http://www.bl.uk/learning/timeline/item95692.html.

[21] See http://oll.libertyfund.org/quotes/536; See further the 1368 Observance of Due Process of Law Act (42 Edward 3), see http://www.legislation.gov.uk/aep/Edw3/42/3/section/III.

[22] Galligan asserts, 'the concept of due process of law is to modern English lawyers an American doctrine': Galligan, *Due Process* (1997), 170, 172, see also 178–9.

[23] Dubber, 'Criminal Trial' (2004).

[24] Issacharoff, *Civil Procedure* (2012), 1.

United States, where they are the subject of a richer jurisprudence than any other single family of rights.[25]

Fast-forward two centuries and a due process revolution led by the Warren Court in 1960s America galvanised the legally protected rights of defendants, by holding that the Constitution mandated publicly funded counsel for indigent defendants, clear explanation of defendants' rights and right to counsel. Packer famously identified due process as one of two models of the criminal process (the other being the consequentialist model of crime control), which recognised that the exercise of 'power is always subject to abuse' and must be checked by the 'obstacle course' of defendants' rights.[26] Although subject to sustained critique,[27] Packer's influential work placed due process squarely on the agenda of legal scholars.[28] Issacharoff observes, 'the concept of due process as a constraint on the exercise of governmental power retained its vitality', not least as a restraint 'on the penal powers of the state'.[29] Precisely what is 'due' in due process continues to be contested,[30] and as yet there has been no systematic exploration of exactly what due process requires on either side of the Atlantic.[31] Notwithstanding this lack of clarity and despite concern that the rhetoric of due process may be misused to legitimate crime control – McBarnet famously claimed, 'due process is *for* crime control'[32] – it continues to be regarded throughout the common law world as a vital restraint on the exercise of sovereign power.

3 *Due Process Values, Principles and Rights*

The criminal process differs significantly in form and approach, by jurisdiction and as between accusatorial and inquisitorial systems.[33] Some core values are nigh universal, especially where externally imposed by human rights conventions or charters of rights, yet others are

25 Nickel, 'Process Rights' (2007), 244.
26 Packer, *Criminal Sanction* (1968), 166.
27 Feeley, *Process* (1979); McBarnet, 'False Dichotomies' (1978); MacDonald, 'Criminal Justice' (2008).
28 Dubber, 'Criminal Trial' (2004), 86.
29 Issacharoff, *Civil Procedure* (2012), ch. 1 'Due Process'.
30 Hyman, 'The Little Word "Due"' (2005).
31 Dworkin offers a powerful critique of the failure to specify what due process requires in Dworkin, *A Matter of Principle* (1985), ch. 3 'Principle, Policy, Procedure'.
32 McBarnet, *Conviction* (1983), 156.
33 Damaška, *The Faces of Justice and State Authority* (1986); An insightful review of comparative scholarship is, Roberts, 'Comparative Criminal Justice' (2008).

jurisdictionally specific. The development of rights has been significantly strengthened by the enactment of successive human rights covenants and conventions, within and by which due process rights are protected. For example, Articles 6–15 of the United Nations' International Covenant on Civil and Political Rights (ICCPR) elaborates a full panoply of due process rights. Even more important in both England and Germany is the ECHR, incorporated into UK domestic law under the Human Rights Act 1998. The ECHR sets out fundamental rights of due process across several articles. The right to a fair trial under Article 6 ECHR is most important, but other significant provisions include: the right to life (Art. 2); prohibition on torture, inhuman and degrading treatment (Art. 3); right to liberty and security of person (Art. 5); requirement of non-retrospectivity (Art. 7); right to private and family life (Art. 8); and the right against discrimination (Art. 14). So well developed is the jurisprudence of the Strasbourg Court, particularly regarding Article 6, that human rights are now integral to the modern articulation of due process.[34] This section identifies the most important of these norms and rights. It goes on to discuss those that appear system specific in order to consider the implications for due process of significant divergence in its content between jurisdictions.

The core tenets of due process are those that apply at some level or in some form to all Western liberal legal systems, irrespective of differences in their articulation or approach. A founding principle, in that it underpins much of what follows, is the presumption of innocence and the corresponding burden of proof on the prosecution. This presumption can be traced back to the Roman Law rule of evidence set down in the Digest of Justinian as *ei incumbit probatio qui dicit, non qui negat* ('proof lies on him who asserts, not on him who denies').[35] The presumption of innocence accords the defendant the right to be considered innocent until proven guilty and, with some important exceptions, places the burden of proving guilt upon the accuser. Firmly established at common law in England,[36] and in Germany by Article 20(3) of the *Grundgesetz* (GG), the presumption of innocence now enjoys the formal protection of Article 6(2) ECHR. Article 6(2) stipulates, 'Everyone charged with a

[34] See Goss, *Criminal Fair Trial Rights* (2014).

[35] Digest of Justinian (22.3).

[36] Long before the Human Rights Act 1998, in *Woolmington* v. *DPP* [1935] AC 462 Viscount Sankey LC famously referred to the presumption of innocence as the 'golden thread' running through the web of English criminal law.

criminal offence shall be presumed innocent until proved guilty according to law.' This separate specification of the presumption of innocence signifies it is not simply subsumed within the general right to a fair trial,[37] but should be understood as an important precept in its own right.[38] Thus, the English Crown Prosecution Service must prove the case 'beyond all reasonable doubt' in the minds of judge or jury before a finding of guilt can be reached.

Common law lawyers think of the presumption of innocence, the requirement of proof beyond all reasonable doubt, and the accompanying privilege against self-incrimination as jewels in the crown of due process. In practice, they are subject to important limitations: some criminal offences impose reverse burdens of proof on the defence,[39] and limits to the right to silence penalise non-disclosure of evidence later relied upon by the defendant at trial.[40] The widespread practice of plea bargaining further erodes these protections by offering incentives to plead guilty before trial by way of substantial and, therefore, controversial, sentence discounts.[41] In English magistrates' courts, which hear roughly 97 per cent of all criminal cases, the rate of guilty plea is well over 90 per cent,[42] strongly suggesting that pressure to plead guilty undercuts the right of the defendant to contest the charge at trial.

The significant incentives offered defendants to plead guilty have been criticised for creating an irreconcilable conflict with the right to a fair trial,[43] a core value in the common law world long before the ECHR and whose articulation in Article 6 has been the subject of an extensive jurisprudence.[44] Article 6(1) reads:

> In the determination of his civil rights and obligations or of any criminal charge against him, everyone is entitled to a fair and public hearing within a reasonable time by an independent and impartial tribunal established by law.

37 Stumer, *Presumption of Innocence* (2010), 95–8.

38 Goss, *Criminal Fair Trial Rights* (2014), 79–86.

39 Emmerson et al., *Human Rights* (2012), ch. 15; *R* v. *Lambert* [2001] UKHL 37 held that where a reverse burden could be construed as an 'evidential' burden it did not breach Art. 6(2).

40 *R* v. *Ibrahim* [2008] EWCA Crim. 880.

41 Ashworth and Horder, *Principles of Criminal Law* (2013), 293; Darbyshire, 'Plea Bargaining' (2000).

42 Weigend notes that in 2013 only 10% of cases with a known suspect were disposed of by trial in Germany. Weigend, 'No News is Good News' (2016), 92–3.

43 Ashworth and Redmayne, *Criminal Process* (2010), 310 ff.

44 Emmerson et al., *Human Rights* (2012).

Article 6(3) sets out the minimum rights associated with the conduct of the trial, including the right to be informed of the nature and cause of the accusation, to have adequate time and facilities for preparation of a defence, to legal assistance (which is to be given freely if justice so requires), to examine witnesses, and to an interpreter if needed. Timeliness is also an important facet of the right to a fair trial, deriving from the old legal adage that 'justice delayed is justice denied'. In England, the requirement of timeliness can be traced back at least to Magna Carta (1215), clause 40, which reads, 'To no one will we sell, to no one will we refuse or delay, right or justice.'[45] Today timeliness, like many other due process values, is recognised to be a mutable concept: what constitutes a timely resolution may be contingent on the nature and complexity of the case,[46] availability of witnesses and adequacy of public resources. Although the right 'to be informed promptly . . . of the nature and cause of the accusation' is enshrined in Article 6(3)(a), the timeliness of the process and trial is not similarly protected and may stand in tension with the right under Article 6(3)(b) 'to have adequate time and facilities for the preparation of his defence'. As Ashworth and Redmayne observe, 'a problem with rights-based accounts of the criminal process is that rights may conflict with each other or with other social values'.[47] Countervailing pressures to ensure efficiency and economy in the trial process, and to reduce the burden that going to trial places on victims and witnesses, may clash with fair trial rights for defendants. This is not to dismiss the importance of these rights but rather to acknowledge conflicting interests and the complex environment in which they are realised.

Significantly, Article 6 is by far the most commonly contested of all the Convention rights. Goss records that from 1959 to 2009 more than half the judgments of the European Court of Human Rights that found a violation related to Article 6.[48] Although this has since fallen to 23 per cent, Article 6 remains the most contested Convention right.[49] Whether this attests to the court's determination to uphold the right to a fair trial, the difficulty of establishing what fairness demands, or the frequency of violations and appeals is a question beyond the scope of this chapter.

[45] See http://magnacarta.cmp.uea.ac.uk/read/magna_carta_1215/Clause_40.
[46] A complex fraud trial may take considerably longer to resolve than a simple theft.
[47] Ashworth and Redmayne, *Criminal Process* (2010), 36.
[48] Goss, *Criminal Fair Trial Rights* (2014), 1.
[49] See Council of Europe, *Facts and Figures* (2017), 7.

Nonetheless, the extensive Strasbourg jurisprudence suggests how important the right to a fair trial is for those caught up in the criminal process but also how contested it remains.

Beyond the core presumption of innocence and right to a fair trial the values of due process are even more disputed. For example, the principle of proportionality underpins human rights by requiring that any restrictions on individual liberties must be proportionate. However, the test for proportionality has been disputed in domestic and European courts. The resultant jurisprudence establishes that interference in a right must have strong justification; it must be strictly limited to what is needed to achieve the legitimate ends of public policy; and burdens on the individual must not be so severe that they outweigh the putative benefit to the community.[50] In Germany, under the *Rechtsstaat* principle, proportionality requires that the state must use the least burdensome means necessary to achieve a legitimate objective.[51] Similarly, in the UK, proportionality is held to require that there be no 'less onerous means of achieving the same aim', and there be due regard to the nature of the right involved, the seriousness of the interference with that right, and 'the nature of the justification for that interference'.[52]

Respect for dignity underpins all rights but it too is disputed. At a minimum, it should require that defendants are not subject to degrading treatment while in custody or under interrogation and that they are not subject to aggressive questioning in court.[53] Those caught up in the criminal process should be treated with respect and their rights and interests regarded.[54] A fair trial requires an opportunity for all parties to present their case, equality of arms, financial assistance to ensure adequate legal representation, a public hearing and timely resolution. Yet here again, how these principles are interpreted and applied in practice varies significantly from one jurisdiction to another. A hearing

[50] *ZZ* v. *Secretary of State for the Home Department* [2013] EUECJ C-300/11 (available at http://eur-lex.europa.eu/legal-content/EN/TXT/HTML/?uri=CELEX:62011CJ0300&from=EN); and *Pham* v. *SSHD* [2015] UKSC 19 (available at https://www.supremecourt.uk/cases/docs/uksc-2013-0150-judgment.pdf).

[51] Bohlander, *Principles of German Criminal Procedure* (2012), 22.

[52] *Pham* v. *SSHD* [2015] UKSC 19, at § 40 and § 117.

[53] Roberts, 'Theorising Procedural Tradition' (2006).

[54] The English police *Code of Ethics* requires the police to 'act with self-control and tolerance, treating members of the public with respect and courtesy' and 'remain composed and respectful, even in the face of provocation'. College of Policing, *Code of Ethics* (2014), S.2.1: 6.

may be deemed to require the right to confrontation under the principle of orality, or may be satisfied by paper proceedings.[55] The commitment to equality of arms and legal aid varies by country, over time, and according to state budgets.[56] And the openness of the hearing, the right of public attendance and press reporting may be limited by countervailing rights, not least the claimant's right to privacy or the public to security.[57] The values of consistency and certainty are also commonly regarded as important facets of due process. Ultimately, as Allan argues,

> The justice of the verdict is internally related to the justice of the procedures which produce it: it derives, not simply from the fact that the defendant committed the offence but from the fact that the charge has been proved by a rational process of argument in which the defendant was invited to engage.[58]

The idea that the right to a fair trial applies only to suspects and defendants has been challenged by those who suggest the right should be enjoyed by all participants in the trial process, not least victims and witnesses.[59] This more expansive conception of due process suggests that all parties should benefit from the protections of humane, rights-respecting procedures: a view that extends due process well beyond the rights currently articulated by human rights conventions. Although victims' rights were recognised as early as the 1980s,[60] they have yet to result in any amendment to the ECHR, which leaves victims and witnesses without the justiciable rights protections enjoyed by defendants. The reluctance to incorporate rights for victims and witnesses may derive partly from populist claims that they could be secured only at the expense of defendants' rights. Certainly, the need for a 'rebalancing' of the interests of parties is a recurrent theme in debates about criminal justice and procedural reform.[61] Yet to suggest that

55 Shipley, 'Due Process Rights' (2008), 48 ff.
56 Wilmot-Smith, 'Necessity or Ideology?' (2014).
57 Zedner, 'Criminal Justice in the Service of Security' (2016), 159–61.
58 Allan, *Constitutional Justice* (2003), 81; See also Allan, 'Procedural Fairness' (1998).
59 Roach, 'Criminal Process' (1999), 695 ff.; Hunter et al., *Integrity* (2016), 20.
60 E.g. in the Council of Europe, *The Position of the Victim the Framework of Criminal Law and Procedure* (1985) and the UN's *Declaration of Basic Principles of Justice for Victims of Crime and Abuse of Power* (1985). They are set out in national victims' codes and charters, such as the UK Victims' Code (available at www.victimsupport.org.uk/help-and-support/your-rights/victims%E2%80%99-code).
61 See e.g. Home Office, *Justice for All* (2002); Jackson, 'Justice for All – Putting Victims at the Heart of Criminal Justice?' (2003); Home Office, *Rebalancing the Criminal Justice System* (2006).

rights are somehow tradable, that to protect the rights of one party necessarily infringes on the rights and interests of the other, or that fundamental rights can be 'balanced', is deeply problematic.[62] The idea of balancing suggests an inevitable tension between competing interests in the trial process. Yet all parties have a common interest in ensuring a fair trial respectful of the rights of all, in avoiding miscarriages of justice and averting wrongful convictions.[63] Roach has expounded a persuasive account of due process and victims' rights in the Canadian context,[64] but the literature on victims' rights in England has yet to elaborate a way to protect victims' interests without infringing the due process rights of defendants.[65] An inclusive account of the criminal process respectful of the rights of all participants remains elusive.

Precisely what due process otherwise requires is far from settled and varies by jurisdiction and over time.[66] The independence and impartiality of the judiciary, for example, is a common core value, but what exactly this means and how it is to be attained differs according to the manner of judicial appointment, conditions of service, terms of tenure, freedom from political interference, the appearance and actuality of independent, disinterested adjudication and, in some parts of the world, even the physical safety of the judiciary.[67] In short, although there are common values and growing convergence on the rights underpinning the criminal process, at least in countries signatory to the ECHR, their elucidation varies over time and by jurisdiction, under the margin of appreciation allowed for domestic interpretation of Convention rights.[68]

A greater source of variation still are those due process principles and values that are system specific. Take the central goal of establishing the truth of what has occurred. In common law systems, like England, the primary means of establishing truth is the trial at which competing accounts of the case, presented by prosecution and defence, are subject

62 Ashworth and Redmayne, *Criminal* Process (2010), 41–5. Waldron, 'Security and Liberty' (2003).

63 Roach, 'Wrongful Convictions' (2010).

64 Roach, *Due Process* (1999).

65 Ashworth, 'Rights and Criminal Procedure' (2000).

66 Damaška, *The Faces of Justice and State Authority* (1986).

67 At the extreme, judicial independence may be compromised by threats to life e.g. the assassination of Judge Falcone in Sicily in 1992 by the Corleonesi mafia. See Follain, *Vendetta* (2012).

68 Ashworth and Redmayne, *Criminal Process* (2010), 21.

to cross-examination by either side. Hodgson observes, 'within the common law tradition, legal truth is seen as something which is contingent, existing not so much as an objective absolute but as the most plausible or likely account'.[69] Adversarial justice pits rival versions of the truth against each other in open court and relies on the judgement of judge or jury as to which is most persuasive. Integral to the fairness of this contest are the principles of equality of arms between parties and of orality, which upholds the accused's right to confront witnesses in court and to test and challenge evidence, whether in person or with the assistance of legal counsel. The English reliance on lay participation, both trial by jury in the Crown Court and adjudication by lay magistrates in the lower courts, is identified by Ashworth and Redmayne as a jurisdictionally specific 'external value'.[70] It is open to debate whether lay participation is better thought of as a due process value, as a politically important means of ensuring democratic accountability and citizen engagement, or rather as a largely contingent consequence of the historical development of the English criminal process.[71] Other system-specific due process values prominent in common law conceptions of due process include the principles of integrity[72] and respect for persons and principles of transparency and accountability that underlie exclusionary rules – for example, against improperly obtained evidence[73] – and that militate strongly against secrecy or resort to closed trial proceedings.[74] Of course, integrity, transparency and accountability are not the sole preserve of the common law tradition. However, the jurisdictional peculiarities of their articulation are a product of local legal culture and history.

[69] Hodgson, 'Inquisitorial and Adversarial Procedure' (2006), 225.

[70] Ashworth and Redmayne, *Criminal* Process (2010), 27.

[71] A fascinating account by a German jurist of the peculiarities of lay participation in the English criminal process is Hörnle, 'Democratic Accountability' (2006).

[72] Integrity is a fundamental and well-established concept in English criminal procedure frequently invoked by the courts to justify departure from law, exclusion of evidence, and the decision to stay legal proceedings to ensure that justice is done. Hunter et al. suggest that, 'to some extent, "integrity" might be invoked as a proxy, synonym or placeholder for other, familiar, procedural values such as "fairness", "due process", "natural justice" or "judicial legitimacy"', but they note that it also refers to the vital role of judicial discretion in 'protecting the moral integrity and legitimacy of the adjudicative process'. Hunter et al., *Integrity* (2016), 5.

[73] E.g. as a result of undercover policing or entrapment, see e.g. Redmayne, 'Exploring Entrapment' (2012).

[74] Closed trial hearings nonetheless occur. Kelman, 'Closed Trials' (2016); Zedner, 'Criminal Justice in the Service of Security' (2016), 159–61.

4 Theorising Due Process

The history of scholarly debates about due process is too extensive to permit full coverage here. Instead, this section focuses on recent Anglo-American debates about 'procedural justice' and legitimacy before going on to propose a thicker, substantive account of due process.

(a) 'Procedural Justice' and the Public Legitimation of State Power

The flourishing of Anglo-American interest in 'procedural justice' appears to signal a renewal of academic interest in due process. It is, however, open to question how much this literature has to do with procedure or justice. Arguably, 'procedural justice' is less about the justice of the legal process than public perceptions of its legitimacy, which induce them to obey the law.[75] Paradoxically, it may be that research on procedural justice diminishes the significance of due process insofar as it seeks to translate normative questions into empirical, even instrumental ones about inducing compliance. What began primarily as an empirical enquiry into 'why people obey the law' has developed into a larger claim that authority is legitimate when its audience believe decision-making to be so.[76] This perspectival definition of 'procedural justice' has prompted a body of research that examines under what conditions citizens perceive they are being treated fairly and with respect by legal officials.[77] Its central contention is that where the public deem the exercise of legal authority to be legitimate, they are more likely to comply. As an empirical account of compliance, this is relatively uncontroversial. It is more problematic to claim that 'legitimacy is to be found where there is a positive *recognition* by citizens of the power-holder's *moral right* to exercise that power'.[78] Whether or not citizens regard the exercise of state power as legitimate evidently relies upon their subjective judgement of the validity of state authority in general and of individual decisions by criminal justice officials in particular. Yet to gauge legitimacy by reference to public perception alone provides no

[75] Tyler, *Why People Obey the Law* (1990).

[76] Bottoms and Tankebe, 'Beyond Procedural Justice' (2012).

[77] Tankebe and Liebling (eds.), *Legitimacy and Criminal Justice* (2013); Bradford, 'Policing and Social Identity' (2014); Meares et al., 'Lawful or Fair?' (2016); For an overview, see Tyler et al., 'Psychology of Procedural Justice' (2014).

[78] Bottoms and Tankebe, 'Beyond Procedural Justice' (2012), 107.

independent metric by which to evaluate the justice of the procedures and decision-making. As Tyler freely acknowledges, '[a]s a psychological model, the model does not address normative issues concerning whether people ought to defer to legal authorities and generally obey the law'.[79] The procedural justice literature thus says more about what factors inform public perceptions of legitimacy than about what values ought to guide and constrain the criminal process.[80] To this extent, procedural justice appears to have less relevance for due process than its label might suggest.

In the UK, the idea that the legitimacy of the legal process depends upon external normative criteria of validity has similarly been contested by Beetham,[81] who takes the view that 'power is legitimate if it is *acknowledged as rightful* by those involved'.[82] He regards legitimacy as derived from the social belief system and opinions of the relevant public and identifies three criteria of legitimacy: conformity to legal rules, concordance between those rules and shared beliefs, and public expression of consent. However, this approach does not acknowledge that if the rules are in substance unjust, procedural conformity alone will not be productive of justice. Nor does it recognise that the 'shared beliefs' with which rules must accord may themselves be problematic. Concordance between rules and beliefs may encourage compliance, but if the rules are unfair or the public hold unjust beliefs, fit between them is hardly conducive to justice.

In these accounts of procedural justice, expressed consent is deemed to be a constituent part of the legitimation process. Yet, consent may derive from something other than recognition of the legitimacy of the law and legal process or of the moral right of the state to exercise coercive power. As Bottoms and Tankebe observe, 'there is a difficulty . . . in ascertaining whether the consent is true normative consent or something less'.[83] Consent may be less an expression of legitimation than a tactical decision to comply with state officials, whether for instrumental reasons, deference to the authority of officials or capitulation to state power. For those arrested by the police or held in detention, compliance may depend more on perceptions of what best serves their self-interest. Research by Meares

[79] Tyler, 'Procedural Justice' (2003), 285.
[80] An important exception is Bottoms and Tankebe, 'Beyond Procedural Justice' (2012).
[81] Beetham, *Legitimation of Power* (1991).
[82] *Ibid.*, 8.
[83] Bottoms and Tankebe, 'Beyond Procedural Justice' (2012), 117.

et al. suggests that, rather than being shaped by assessments of procedural fairness, public evaluations of appropriate police behaviour are 'largely shaped by . . . evaluations about the demeanor of the officers during their interactions with them'.[84] Such findings suggest that procedural justice may be less about justice than public appreciation of the civility and respect shown them by the police.

It may be that procedural justice is better understood as pursuing a different enquiry that, despite its name, has little to do with procedure or justice and more with ensuring the effectiveness of the legal system by maximising public deference and cooperation.[85] Procedural justice privileges the appearances of legitimacy and prioritises popular perception over a detached normative account of what due process *ought* substantively to entail. More is required if it is to serve as an external check on state power. If legitimacy is not merely to lie in the perception of citizens, a fully developed normative account of what due process should entail is needed.

(b) Substantive Due Process

A thicker conception of due process would engage with the substance of the laws, measures and practices that make up the criminal process. A purely formalistic conception of due process requires only adherence to principles of procedural fairness and reasonableness. At a minimum, this requires that the exercise of police power is governed by law, that procedural rules are passed by parliament, and limitations on or deprivations of liberty are formally and prospectively authorised by law.[86] However, as we have seen, formal adherence to procedural rules alone will not necessarily protect citizens against unjust or unfair laws. Substantive due process concerns itself also with the content of procedural rules,[87] to ensure that these enshrine substantive principles of justice, equality of treatment, dignity and respect for persons, and defence of individual autonomy (consistent with the autonomy of others).[88]

84 Meares et al., 'Lawful or Fair?' (2016), 300.
85 Tyler, 'Procedural Justice' (2003), 283.
86 Ramraj, 'Due Process' (2004), 496–7.
87 'Substantive' here thus goes beyond the American conception of 'substantive due process' that permits courts to protect certain fundamental rights from government interference, even if the rights are not specifically protected under the US Constitution.
88 Braithwaite and Pettit, *Not Just Deserts* (1990), 61–9.

A thicker account of substantive due process still might require, as Ramraj suggests, regard not only to the content of the due process rights but also to 'the need for coherence, consistency, and predictability in the substantive criminal law'.[89] Ramraj argues that substantive due process is the only plausible response to the indeterminacy and inconsistency of the criminal law. To test his theory, he considers claims that indeterminacy may be inherent in criminal law (following the legal realist claim that the rhetoric of legality masks the extra-legal, political reasons for criminalisation), the product of its historical development (for example, as a result of the inconsistency of case law) or the consequence of systemic factors (not least that criminal law is a mixture of common law and statutory principles).[90] He suggests that substantive due process relies upon 'the articulation of a unifying theory of criminal law'[91] and concludes that 'a normative theory of criminal fault entrenched in a constitutional doctrine of substantive due process provides the best possible response to the claim of indeterminacy of criminal doctrine'.[92] In short, ensuring procedural fairness alone does not suffice: only an account that has regard for the legitimacy of the procedures in play, and importantly also for the laws that they are called upon to uphold, will be productive of substantive due process.

Some UK scholars are likewise sceptical of purely formal or procedural accounts of due process. Allan observes, 'When the rule of law is conceived as a formal or procedural principle, there are no implicit legal limits to the scope of coercive state authority.'[93] Instead, he argues:

> the demands of due process are inextricably bound up, in practice, with the law's permissible content: the exercise of administrative discretion must respect the citizen's fundamental rights and the limits of legitimate government.[94]

Allan conceives due process not as a purely procedural device nor even as a shield against abuse of state power. Rather it is integrally linked to a defensible substantive account of the content of law. Just as the criminal law defends the domain of individual liberty against predation by private citizens, so the criminal process sets 'the proper limits of state authority'

[89] Ramraj, 'Due Process' (2004), 516.
[90] *Ibid.*, 516–23.
[91] *Ibid.*, 524.
[92] *Ibid.*
[93] Allan, 'The Rule of Law' (2016), 215.
[94] *Ibid.*, 219.

in accordance with 'a scheme of governance that, correctly interpreted, accords each individual the freedom that his human dignity demands'.[95] Tadros goes further to contend that procedure alone will not help if the substance of the law is unjust, so we need not only a right to a fair trial but a right to a fair criminal law.[96] His claim calls for closer attention to the inseparable relationship between criminal law and criminal process largely lacking from legal scholarship to-date.[97] As Roberts observes:

> [T]o the best of my knowledge, there has never been any grand conspiracy to keep Criminal Law Theory pure and uncontaminated by criminal procedure scholarship. Procedural issues have simply been ignored by the vast majority of card-carrying criminal law theorists.[98]

A substantive account of due process would rectify this oversight by recognising that the justice of the process is indivisible from the justice of the criminal law – and vice versa.[99]

5 *Evasions and Erosions of Due Process*

This chapter has sought to elaborate due process values and principles largely in the abstract, but there are obvious hazards to normative theorising divorced from the messy realities of everyday practice. To do so risks valorising idealised accounts of due process that pay insufficient regard to the limits and frailties of criminal justice institutions and processes, human apathy, prejudice and capacity for error. In practice, the criminal process rarely maintains the high standards set for it. Part of the problem is the malleability of laws: inhibitory rules designed to limit the power of criminal justice officials may encourage adaptive behaviour or even subversion, and supposedly restrictive rules may in practice be enabling.[100] Diversion, on-the-spot fines, plea bargaining, resort to summary proceedings and online trial proceedings further

95 *Ibid.*, 220.

96 Tadros, 'A Human Right to a Fair Criminal Law' (2010).

97 Though see Ristroph, 'Crime to Punishment' (2018).

98 Roberts, 'Jurisprudence of Criminal Procedure' (2011).

99 Building on the work of one of the foremost British criminal lawyers, Glanville Williams, I have defended an account of the legitimacy of the criminal law that is closely bound up with the integrity of the criminal process. See Zedner, 'Arbitrary Government' (2017), 90–3.

100 Sanders et al., *Criminal Justice* (2010), at 67–8. One of us has argued, 'Laws that purport to curb abuses of police powers also provide the authority for the exercise of that power. Rules that appear to restrict the exercise of police power, invariably allow the police to

undermine the core institutions and processes by which due process is conventionally upheld.[101] Inadequate resources and cuts to financial Legal Aid limit access to justice.[102] Competing demands and priorities undermine due process by encouraging aberrant practices like non-disclosure of evidence by the prosecution.[103] A further hazard is the side-stepping of due process occasioned by resort to civil and administrative proceedings, for example use of preventive orders at one end of the scale[104] and deferred prosecution agreements with major companies at the other.[105] Much less common in the UK, but of growing concern, is resort to closed proceedings and secret trials in cases involving terrorism and national security.[106]

More mundane but all too common are the errors and abuses that occur when criminal justice officials – subject to the influence and exigencies of their professional or 'canteen' culture,[107] political pressures and populist demands – depart from or subvert due process. Acknowledging the risk of evasion and error places a premium on setting due process norms and instituting limits and safeguards designed to protect against possible miscarriages of justice, to avert wrongful convictions[108] and to rectify those that occur. Ashworth and Redmayne recognise an 'error preference', that 'all else being equal, of the errors that criminal courts make, more will involve acquitting the guilty than convicting the innocent'.[109] The error preference is a historically important safeguard of the criminal process, most famously articulated by the eighteenth-century English jurist William Blackstone in the dictum, '[i]t is better that ten guilty persons escape than that one innocent suffer'.[110] This maxim stands behind many facets of due process and the procedural

stop, question, search, restrain, arrest and detain within the parameters set out in the rules.' Zedner, 'Arbitrary Government' (2017), 99.

101 Ward, 'Transforming "Summary Justice"' (2015); Wilmot-Smith, 'Necessity or Ideology?' (2014); Ashworth and Zedner, 'Defending the Criminal Law' (2008).

102 See e.g. www.lawsociety.org.uk/news/stories/justice-select-committee-hears-societys-evidence-on-legal-aid-cuts/; Hoyle and Sato, *Reasons to Doubt* (2018), ch. 14.

103 Hoyle and Sato, *Reasons to Doubt* (2018), ch. 14.

104 Zedner, 'Seeking Security by Eroding Rights' (2007).

105 Garrett, *Too Big to Jail* (2016).

106 Zedner, 'Criminal Justice in the Service of Security' (2016), 159–61.

107 Chan, 'Changing Police Culture' (1996); Waddington, 'Police (Canteen) Sub-Culture' (1999).

108 Roach, 'Wrongful Convictions' (2010); Hoyle, 'Victims of the State' (2016).

109 Ashworth and Redmayne, *Criminal Process* (2010), 25.

110 Blackstone, *Commentaries on the Laws of England* (1753).

hurdles it erects, including the burden of proof on the prosecution and the sufficiency of evidence test, which requires 'there is sufficient evidence to provide a realistic prospect of conviction against each suspect on each charge before proceeding to prosecution'.[111] Due process does not stop at conviction but also informs the requirement for post-trial procedures and institutions that permit review, enable appeal against wrongful convictions and rectify abuse of state power.

No process is infallible and a fuller account of due process necessitates adequate arrangements for review of possible miscarriages of justice and state-funded redress for those found to have been wrongfully convicted and punished.[112] Acknowledging the inevitability of error also requires that there be provision for training, guidance, and supervision of officials to ensure they understand the principles which bind them.[113] Anticipating error also has implications for the manner in which the pre-trial and trial processes are conducted. Contrast the duty on German judges to give reasons with the fact that the English jury is not required to give reasons for its verdict, which leaves English appeal courts with insufficient information about the grounds for conviction to judge its probity. Whereas in England it is necessary to seek leave to appeal from the Crown Court,[114] in Germany there is an automatic right to appeal the trial verdict, which gives due weight to the 'error preference' by ensuring that the verdict can be challenged.[115] The error preference would also endorse a stronger commitment to rectification, including better legal assistance and material support for those appealing their conviction or sentence, and stronger powers for independent review, redress and compensation.[116]

[111] See www.cps.gov.uk/publications/code_for_crown_prosecutors/codetest.html.

[112] E.g. the UK Criminal Cases Review Commission (www.ccrc.gov.uk/); See, Hoyle and Sato, *Reasons to Doubt* (2018).

[113] Dworkin, *A Matter of Principle* (1985), ch. 3.

[114] If leave to appeal is denied, an application can be made to the Criminal Cases Review Commission to review the conviction (or sentence). If the Commission believes there is a 'real possibility' the Court of Appeal will find the conviction to be unsafe, the Court is obliged to hear any case the Commission refers (Criminal Appeal Act 1995, s. 13(1)(a)). However, the Commission refers only a small proportion (between 1–4%) of *c*.1,400 applications each year back to the Court of Appeal. Hoyle and Sato, *Reasons to Doubt* (2018), ch. 2.

[115] Although it should be noted that the prosecution in Germany also has a right to appeal against acquittal.

[116] Hoyle, 'Victims of the State' (2016).

6 Conclusion

This chapter has considered the meanings, role and tensions within due process in the English system and observed points of difference and divergence in the German system. It has not considered the extent to which adversarial and inquisitorial conceptions of due process may be converging.[117] Even if procedural convergence is occurring, for now at least, due process retains salient and distinctive meanings, character and significance in the common law tradition that appear to have no exact equivalent in the German system.

Due process remains at the heart of the English criminal process where it plays a vital role in curtailing discretion and limiting the arbitrary exercise of power by state officials and protects the rights and interests of those subject to policing and prosecution. Due process requires that the form and structures of the criminal process conform to values of justice and fairness and to fundamental rights, and that the content of laws regulating institutions, agents and processes abide by these values. Due process is essential to the legitimacy of the criminal justice system and thus to the criminal law itself. Yet the standards it sets are not unproblematic. Dworkin asks if it follows that 'each citizen ... has a right to the most accurate procedures possible to test his guilt or innocence, no matter how expensive these procedures might be to the community as a whole'.[118] Recognising that an infallible criminal process would be inordinately expensive and likely unattainable, and that evasion and abuse inevitably occur, due process needs to be extended beyond the pre-trial and trial phrases. Practical provision for post-trial review of possible miscarriages, and for rectification and redress of injustice needs to be accompanied by a much more fully elaborated framework of due process rights and principles.

Even if due process, as currently formulated, sets an impossibly high standard that no criminal justice system can hope to attain, it still has a vital role as a normative framework for decision-making. Perfect compliance may be unobtainable, but it remains an important aspiration by which to set standards that can be calibrated to accord with the gravity of the threatened infringement of individual liberty.[119] The greater the

[117] McEwan, 'Ritual, Fairness and Truth' (2004), 51–2; Ashworth and Redmayne, *Criminal Process* (2010), 417 ff.; Shipley, 'Due Process Rights' (2008).

[118] Dworkin, *A Matter of Principle* (1985), 72.

[119] Allan, 'The Rule of Law' (2016), 214.

prospective intrusion, the greater the burden on due process to protect. Recent developments remind us that the adjustment of due process protections can go down as readily as up, particularly when threats are grave. An enduring problem is that public demands for protection against threats to collective security too easily drown out the interest of individuals to be protected against unwarranted exercise of state power.[120] The role of due process is to counter this tendency by upholding individual rights against unjustified infringement by states claiming to act in the name of public safety or national security. As MacCormick rightly observes 'no state is properly counted as a law-state unless it succeeds in erecting genuine obstacles to abuse of power'.[121] Due process is precisely such an obstacle.

III 'Due Process' in Germany

There is no single legal term in the civil law world that corresponds to the common law notion of 'due process', although today, as a result of the jurisprudence of the Strasbourg Court, the concept of 'fair trial' (*faires Verfahren, procédure équitable, giusto processo, proceso equitativo*) comes close as a collective name for the large assortment of heterogeneous requirements which are deemed desirable in the criminal procedure of a liberal, rights-respecting state.

Apart from the common body of law grown out of the ECHR, it is less clear which civil law concepts are the appropriate counterparts to 'due process'. In German law, some functional equivalents can be identified, mainly *schützende Formen*, *Justizförmigkeit*, and *faires, rechtsstaatliches Verfahren*. Despite different historical and conceptual backgrounds, the resulting normative landscape (i.e. the principles and values that govern the criminal process) appears to be fairly similar in English and German law despite the different structure of the respective procedural schemes.

1 *Historical and Conceptual Background*

The emphasis placed in German doctrine since the nineteenth century on 'Form' as a means to protect individual liberty in procedural settings is a

[120] Dworkin, 'Civil Liberties' (2003); Zedner, 'Arbitrary Government' (2017). On the political context in which erosions of due process occur, see Prime Minister Theresa May's speech after the 3 Jun. 2017 London Bridge terrorist attack, www.gov.uk/government/speeches/pm-statement-following-london-terror-attack-4–june-2017.

[121] MacCormick, *Institutions of Law* (2007), 205.

direct reaction to past misuses of coercive power, notably the lack of legal restraints of the powers of the inquisitorial judge (a). This emphasis is not a peculiarity of criminal justice but reflects the broader concept of Rechtsstaat as developed in the nineteenth century (b). These historical concepts inform the current Rechtsstaat provision of the German Basic Law (Art. 20(3), Art. 28(1) GG) which has been elaborated by the jurisprudence of the Federal Constitutional Court in light of the ECHR (c).

(a) *Schützende Formen*

From the Middle Ages to the nineteenth century, the ordinary form of criminal procedure (*processus ordinarius*) in the territories of the Holy Roman Empire was the accusatorial trial of Germanic origin. The thirteenth century saw the advent of the inquisitorial procedure, an invention of Pope Innocent III, which was soon adopted as *processus extraordinarius* by secular rulers because of its efficiency. The ordinary accusatorial procedure gradually fell into disuse without ever being completely abolished.[122]

Although ancient law is often associated with rigid rituals and formalities, this is true mainly for the final proclamation and execution of the penal judgment in the *endlicher Rechtstag*, while the (secular) inquisitorial procedure as such was surprisingly informal because there were few written rules, if any, and at that time, legislation was often poorly drafted. Therefore, many aspects were controversial in the authoritative academic literature and in effect left to the judge's discretion. If there were strict requirements (like the biblical rule[123] that proof requires the testimony of two honourable witnesses or a voluntary confession) there were often widely accepted ways to circumvent them. The main objective of the inquisitorial trial was to find the truth, save the defendant's soul and protect the people from God's wrath which was said[124] to be imminent if crimes went unpunished. Although there were always warnings to be careful in order to avoid convicting an innocent person, effective legal safeguards barely existed; this was also a minor concern because the wrongly convicted innocent would be redeemed in the next world and

[122] Schmidt, *Einführung* (1965), §§ 65 ff., 70 ff., 104 ff., 185 ff.

[123] 5 Moses 17:6; 19:15.

[124] Carpzov, *Practica Nova* (1635), qu. 101 no. 15: 'Saepe enim ob unius delictum, dum non vindicatur, Deus in universum irascitur populum.'

everything that really counted was eternal salvation. In the fifteenth century, the striving free cities became fond of other, almost completely informal procedures for getting rid of unwanted persons (*landschädliche Leute*). Accordingly, they vehemently protested against the introduction of a more stringently formalised procedure by the 1532 Criminal Ordinance of Emperor Charles V (*Constitutio Criminalis Carolina*), which had only supplementary character but was criticised for pampering wrongdoers.[125] The rise of absolutism and the police state in the seventeenth and eighteenth century was again characterised by flexible, efficient procedures. A spirit of arbitrariness prevailed and the defendant was almost completely at the mercy of the judge.

The old inquisitorial procedure was swept away first in France by the Revolution of 1789. In the German states, it became clear in the early nineteenth century that criminal procedure had to be reformed somehow and numerous publications treated the question what a new and better procedural scheme should look like, while many practitioners clung to the old 'common law' (*gemeines Recht*, Continental *ius commune*). In a famous book published in 1846, the Göttingen professor Heinrich Albert Zachariae scolded the old inquisitorial procedure for its complete lack of *schützende Formen*[126] – i.e. protections of the individual defendant in the form of statutory law against arbitrariness. Instead, he wrote, the inner logic of the inquisitorial procedure was that of a police operation which is most effective when it is not hampered by any restrictions at all so that everything which is deemed necessary or expedient can be done. The quote became famous and is still referred to today although it is gradually superseded by constitutional formulas and fair trial rhetoric.[127]

The enlarged version of schützende Formen is Justizförmigkeit, meaning the requirement to proceed only 'in due form' – namely, in well-defined lawful form: 'Das Mittel der Justizförmigkeit ist seit jeher die prozessuale Form.'[128] Until today, German courts, textbooks and commentaries insist on *Justiz-* or *Verfahrensförmigkeit* as the epitome of a legitimate criminal procedure.[129] Another famous quote still popular

125 Schmidt, 'Sinn und Notwendigkeit' (1953), 172–3.

126 Zachariae, *Gebrechen* (1846), 93, 123 ff.; Zachariae, *Handbuch* (1861), 146.

127 Hamm, 'Einsatz' (2001), 82.

128 Quoted from the classical exposition by Schmidt, *Lehrkommentar* (1964), mn. 22; see also Rieß, 'Einleitung' (1999), mn. G 20–3.

129 See BVerfGE 133, 168 (199); Roxin and Schünemann, *Strafverfahrensrecht* (2017), § 1 mn. 2–6; Kühne, *Strafprozessrecht* (2015), mn. 1; Wohlers, 'Einleitung' (2018), mn. 39–41, 191.

with defence attorneys today comes from the great jurist Rudolf von Jhering:

> Die Form ist immer noch die geschworene Feindin der Willkür, die Zwillingsschwester der Freiheit ... Formen sind ... eine Schutzmauer gegen äußere Angriffe, – sie lassen sich nur brechen, nicht biegen.[130]

The underlying idea is that all coercive state action including criminal investigation and prosecution is admissible only on the basis of and strictly in the form prescribed by law (i.e. by *parliamentary statute*). This account is in the vein of 'negative due process' because it forms part of the citizen's *status negativus*, which defends individual liberty against state power (the preservation of liberty is the positive side – these are virtually two sides of the same coin).

(b) *Justizförmigkeit* and the Nineteenth-Century *Rechtsstaat*

This leads us to the nineteenth century-concept of Rechtsstaat. Unfortunately, Rechtsstaat is one of the most ambivalent terms of German public law.[131] It is controversial whether the concept is analogous to the (no less ambiguous) common law notion of 'rule of law'.[132] Though of different origin, the legal effects of both doctrines are often quite similar. What is meant here is the political aspiration of a nomocracy, a 'government of laws, not of men' already expressed by Plato and Aristotle and revivified in the Enlightenment era – for instance in Montesquieu's *Esprit des Loix* and the French Declaration of the Rights of Man and of the Citizen of 1789 (Art. 16).[133] The idea of a state governed by law and through law reflects the classical liberal ideal and defines the modern citizen–state relationship in which fundamental (natural) rights of the individual are guarded against undue official violation by the architecture of a well-ordered state, a 'state of reason' rationally organised so as to promote liberty.[134] A central component of that liberal state is, next to the

[130] Von Jhering, *Geist* (1923), 471.

[131] See Loughlin, *Foundations* (2010), 313 n. 5.

[132] See MacCormick, 'Der Rechtsstaat' (1984), 65 ff., who sees no relevant differences; more sceptical Baratta, 'Zur Entwicklung' (1979), 6 ff.; for a deeper comparative analysis see Loughlin, *Foundations* (2010), 313–41; Morin, 'The Rule of Law' (1992); Grote, 'Rule of Law' (1999); Kirste, 'Philosophical Foundations' (2014).

[133] For references see Baratta, 'Zur Entwicklung' (1979), 1 ff.; Grote, 'Rule of Law' (1999), 270 ff.; Kirste, 'Philosophical Foundations' (2014) and the classical account by Böckenförde, 'Entstehung und Wandel' (2016), 143 ff.

[134] Loughlin, *Foundations* (2010), 317 ff.

separation of powers, the *Vorbehalt des Gesetzes* – that is, the requirement that individual rights, in particular freedom and property, can be infringed only if the legislature, ideally a democratically elected parliament, so permits. Academic writers like Robert von Mohl[135] coined the term Rechtsstaat in the early nineteenth century in contrast to the police state of the absolutist era. *Rechtsstaatlichkeit* denotes the self-restraint of the Leviathan who mistrusts itself in memory of past abuses.

The German states of the early nineteenth century were no democracies but constitutional monarchies at best, so that bourgeois political liberalism had to be content with a more moderate formal or positivist version of the Rechtsstaat, which included *Vorrang des Gesetzes* (executive and judiciary are bound to strictly obey the law), Vorbehalt des Gesetzes, *Rechtssicherheit* (legal certainty, foreseeability, non-retroactivity), *Bestimmtheit* (clarity of the law), judicial review of coercive state action, etc. Justizförmigkeit became the hallmark of the entire public law, especially of administrative law,[136] in the sense that the meticulous legal accuracy of the judicial process served as a model for the entire machinery of the state. All these restrictions aim to minimise the risks of misuse of power and arbitrariness.

As a consequence, at that time, discretion was regarded as different from and in fact opposed to the application of the law,[137] namely the permission to decide according to expediency; its natural habitat was and still is administrative law. Because a discretionary decision is not determined by law, it was considered non-legal, even illegal.[138] Accordingly, because courts were supposed to apply the law (a resonation of Montesquieu's unrealistic ideal of the judge as mere *bouche de la loi*), it seemed impossible to vest a court with discretion (e.g. to drop a case). In this context, a fierce controversy broke out in the 1860s whether a criminal prosecution should be initiated every time a suspicion becomes known (*Legalitätsprinzip*) or only when the prosecutor deems it expedient (*Opportunitätsprinzip*).[139] The latter principle was thought to lead to inequality and political or social discrimination – in fact, Prussia had abused the discretion of its newly established *Staatsanwälte* for political

135 Böckenförde, 'Entstehung und Wandel' (2016), 144 ff. with further references.

136 See e.g. Mayer, *Deutsches Verwaltungsrecht* (1895), 33.

137 Very similar to this position, Dicey, *Law of the Constitution* (1958), 202.

138 See e.g. Glaser, 'Das Princip der Strafverfolgung' (1883), 532.

139 For a detailed account see Dettmar, *Legalität und Opportunität* (2008), 69 ff.

repression.[140] It should be added that the concept of discretion has evolved in the twentieth century. Today, there is no such thing as 'free' or unrestricted discretion in German law but only 'dutiful exercise of discretion' which is subject to (limited) judicial review.[141] In the criminal justice context, justice and expediency have long been viewed as irreconcilable opposites[142] so that, unlike in administrative law, there is, at least among scholars, a general aversion to discretion[143] and arguments based on expediency, cost efficiency etc.

Justizförmigkeit and rechtsstaatliches Verfahren before 1949 were mainly formal guarantees. But since the aim of the procedural code is to establish the truth and reach a just result, it was also believed that proceedings which faithfully conform to the rules (are *prozeßordnungsgemäß*) are best qualified to achieve these aims in the individual case as well. In this sense the belief in Justizförmigkeit is also a belief in 'procedural justice' *avant la lettre.*

(c) *Rechtsstaat* as a Constitutional Principle and its Procedural Implications

The German Basic Law expressly lays down a few specific procedural guarantees, such as the independence of the judiciary (Art. 97(1)), the right to have one's case adjudicated by a judge predetermined by law (Art. 101(1), cl. 2), the right to be heard in court (*rechtliches Gehör*, Art. 103(1)), the prohibition against double jeopardy (Art. 103(3)) and an array of rights relating to arrest and other forms of deprivation of liberty (Art. 104). All other constitutional requirements regarding criminal procedure must be deduced from individual fundamental rights – which also influence procedural rules if that is necessary to give full effect to the

[140] The majority of academic writers favoured the 'legality principle' which became law in 1877 in §§ 152(2), and 170(1) of the *Reichsstrafprozeßordnung* (RStPO). However, it soon became obvious that mandatory prosecution is not feasible because of limited resources and that a selection of cases is unavoidable. The question then shifts to who should select and how. The selection criteria laid down in provisions like §§ 153 ff. StPO are fairly similar to prosecution guidelines in common law countries (like the Code for Crown Prosecutors or the United States Attorneys' Manual). The German police are still rigidly bound to investigate each and every case pursuant to § 163(1) StPO – and have long found ways not to do this, see Dölling, *Polizeiliche Ermittlungstätigkeit* (1987), 258–65.

[141] See Jung, *Straffreiheit* (1974), 58–63.

[142] E.g. Schmidt, 'Gerechtigkeit und Zweckmäßigkeit' (1947).

[143] See Erb, *Legalität und Opportunität* (1999), 52–67 with further references.

respective right[144] – or from the *Rechtsstaatsprinzip* set out in Article 20(3) GG.

The constitutional Rechtsstaat principle incorporates several strands of the pre-constitutional development. It is regarded as one of the most elementary principles of the constitution and has two aspects.[145] The first is formal (*formeller Rechtsstaat*), containing principles like legality, legal certainty, foreseeability, equal treatment, non-retroactivity (in certain cases; the older *nulla poena sine lege praevia* maxim is a special version of the general rule), reliability, protection of trust (*Vertrauensschutz*) etc., which correspond to Max Weber's notion of 'formal justice',[146] a reliance on abstract rules without regard to the outcome in the individual case. The second is a substantive one (*materieller Rechtsstaat*) which aims at 'substantive justice' (see Max Weber's 'kadi justice') – that is, the just resolution of the individual case.[147] In rare cases, these aspects clash.[148]

The Federal Constitutional Court has used the Rechtsstaatsprinzip to acknowledge a variety of unwritten constitutional guarantees like the right to remain silent,[149] the presumption of innocence,[150] and more recently 'fair trial'.[151] The combination of Article 20(3) GG with the guarantee of human dignity in Article 1(1) GG, but also with other fundamental rights like Article 2(1) GG (general freedom of action) or Article 5 GG (freedom of speech, freedom of the press), has allowed the formulation of constitutional rules that are not purely formal, thus resembling what has been called 'substantive due process' above. An example is the articulation of the so-called *Subjektstellung des Angeklagten*,[152] which means that, in order to safeguard his autonomy (human

[144] BVerfGE 86, 288, 317; 109, 133, 162; 117, 71, 105. This very important constitutional doctrine is called *Grundrechtsschutz durch Verfahren*, protection of fundamental liberties by procedure, a version of 'procedural due process' not limited to criminal law contexts. E.g. all proceedings concerning deprivation of liberty like civil commitment must guarantee a sufficient level of accuracy in fact-finding.

[145] See Gärditz, 'Art. 20: Rechtsstaatsprinzip' (2018), mn. 3–6.

[146] See Weber, *Wirtschaft und Gesellschaft* (1972), 468–513.

[147] Substantive justice (*materielle Gerechtigkeit*) has a dubious reputation because it was the declared policy of the Nazi regime to favour substantive over formal ('liberal') justice; see Gürtner, 'Der Gedanke der Gerechtigkeit' (1936), 22–3.

[148] Notably in the case of the killings at the former inner-German border which were legal according to East German law but led to convictions of GDR soldiers and political leaders after reunification, BVerfGE 95, 96.

[149] BVerfGE 20, 323, 331; 45, 187, 246; 133, 168, 201.

[150] BVerfGE 19, 342, 347; 74, 358, 371, 133, 168, 202.

[151] BVerfGE 38, 105, 111; 122, 248, 271–2; 133, 168, 200–1.

[152] BVerfGE 65, 171, 174–5; 66, 313, 318; 133, 168, 200.

dignity), the defendant must enjoy such procedural rights and privileges as to be able to actively influence the course of the proceedings (e.g. by presenting evidence etc.) instead of being a mere object of a criminal investigation like the former *inquisitus*. With regard to substantive criminal law, the Rechtsstaatsprinzip has been held to enshrine the *Schuldprinzip* (guilt principle)[153] and the proportionality of punishment (in the sense of 'just desert').[154]

Although the ECHR has only the hierarchical status of an ordinary statute, the Basic Law has to be interpreted in conformity with international treaties wherever feasible.[155] Therefore, the text of the Convention and the jurisprudence of the Strasbourg Court continue to shape the contents of German constitutional law.

The pervasive modern formula is that there is a constitutional right to a faires, rechtsstaatliches Verfahren. This formula seems to have swallowed the older schützenden Formen and Justizförmigkeit, but the old concepts are still used when informality is the main point of criticism, e.g. with respect to negotiated judgments (now § 257c StPO)[156] or the dismissal of cases after the fulfilment of imposed conditions like payment of money (§ 153a StPO).[157]

2 *Core Principles and Rules*

What exactly is required by the German Rechtsstaatsprinzip and the fair trial guarantee – in other words, which process is constitutionally 'due' – cannot be exhaustively enumerated because the Federal Constitutional Court denies that there can be a comprehensive definition and leaves the details to the legislature.[158] With regard to 'fair trial', the judges at Karlsruhe have borrowed from their Strasbourg colleagues the approach to look at the totality of the proceedings in order to (miraculously) determine whether they were fair or not.[159] The 'fair trial' aspect is treated as a supplementary guarantee which informs the interpretation

[153] BVerfGE 80, 244, 255; 95, 96, 140; 133, 168, 199.
[154] BVerfGE 45, 187, 259–60; 130, 1, 26; 133, 168, 197–8.
[155] BVerfGE 74, 358, 370; 111, 307, 317; 128, 326, 367.
[156] Stuckenberg, '§ 257c StPO' (2013), mn. 3 with further references.
[157] Stuckenberg, 'Gründe' (2016), 383–5 with further references.
[158] BVerfGE 57, 250, 276; 70, 297, 308–9.
[159] BVerfGE 133, 168, 200.

of relevant provisions and comes into play as a distinct rule only if more specific guarantees do not apply.[160]

(a) The Constitutional Duty to Prosecute and Punish . . .

With regard to criminal justice, the Rechtsstaat principle is two-sided. On the one side, it requires the establishment and operation of an effective criminal justice system (*funktionstüchtige Strafrechtspflege*),[161] because the Rechtsstaat can be realised only if crimes are investigated, prosecuted and sanctioned with just punishment.[162] This is a constitutional duty not left to the state's discretion because the protection of the citizens, the trust placed in state institutions and the principle of equal treatment require that, in principle, criminal laws are executed in each single instance. There are certain recognised exceptions for minor offences, offenses committed abroad etc. where discretion may reign.[163] Apart from these, there is even a 'constitutional prohibition' that precludes the state from withholding prosecution and punishment in individual cases or groups of cases.[164] Also, criminal justice must not be the object of negotiations so that deals, settlements and agreements in criminal matters are prohibited.[165]

(b) . . . in a Constitutional Manner

On the other side, the Rechtsstaat principle protects not only the defendant but all persons (including e.g. witnesses, alleged 'victims', private complainants) involved in a criminal procedure. The task of the criminal trial is, in the eyes of the Federal Constitutional Court, to ensure the realisation of the guilt principle, which in turn requires the search for the substantive, 'real' truth[166] in contrast to 'formal', agreed-upon truth in civil procedure. However, truth must not be sought 'at any cost' but in a way which respects all the other constitutionally protected interests like privacy. If those interests enter into conflict, usually a balance must be struck.[167]

160 For a comprehensive overview see Jahn, 'Fair Trial' (2015).
161 BVerfGE 33, 367, 383; 130, 1, 26; 133, 168, 199–200.
162 BVerfGE 57, 250, 275; 130, 1, 25–6; 133, 168, 199.
163 BVerfGE 133, 168, 225–7.
164 BVerfGE 46, 214, 223.
165 BVerfGE 133, 168, 227–8.
166 BVerfGE 57, 250, 275; 80, 367, 375; 130, 1, 26.
167 E.g. the evidentiary use of diaries is problematic, BVerfGE 80, 367. For the exclusion of evidence see BVerfGE 113, 29, 61; 125, 260, 339–40; 130, 1, 28.

(c) A Tentative Inventory

In its plentiful case law, the Federal Constitutional Court has recognised that the Rechtsstaat principle comprises, inter alia,[168] the already mentioned Subjektstellung of the defendant (in conjunction with Art. 1(1) GG). 'Equality of arms' is not required but he must have adequate possibilities to defend himself effectively, such as the right to be informed of the charges (in translation if necessary), to have access to the case file, to be represented by counsel of his choice or receive court-appointed counsel if necessary, to be assisted by a translator if needed, to present and challenge evidence, to ask questions and make statements etc.; and of course, as a prerequisite, the defendant must be competent (physically and mentally) to stand trial.

This includes the older concept of the judicial duty of care (*gerichtliche Fürsorgepflicht*) which serves to ensure that the defendant knows his rights and is able to make informed use of them; this applies in particular to the defendant who is not assisted by counsel. This further includes the expressly stated right (Art. 103(1) GG) to be heard before a decision is made (viz. the prohibition of 'surprise decisions'); the court must demonstrably take into account the defendant's statements, not only listen to him.

The presumption of innocence is an unwritten constitutional principle. Until proven guilty according to law,[169] the defendant must not be called 'guilty' nor be treated as guilty. Here, the Constitutional Court follows closely the Strasbourg precedents. Another unwritten element of the Rechtsstaatsprinzip (in conjunction with Art. 1(1) GG) is the right to remain silent (privilege against self-incrimination). This includes adequate warnings before interrogations and the prohibition to draw negative inferences from any refusal to cooperate. Formally, defendants cannot testify in Germany; if they choose to speak, this is not considered testimony but proof *sui generis*; they are also free to lie. It is controversial whether partial silence may be held against defendants.

[168] For a recent summary see BVerfGE 133, 168, 198–205.

[169] The required level of proof is the inner conviction (Ger. =*Überzeugung*, Fr. =*conviction intime*) of the judge, which is equivalent to 'proof beyond reasonable doubt'. The – persuasive and evidential – burden of proof is always on the prosecution, and the burden of proof remains on the prosecution in respect of defences (whether justification or excuse) raised by the defendant. Presumptions of guilt were always rare and most remnants have long been abolished; for an overview see Stuckenberg, *Unschuldsvermutung* (1998), 91–100.

The aforementioned duty to seek the truth encompasses the requirement that the court search for and use the 'best possible evidence' (*bestmögliches Beweismittel*).[170] Other elements of the Rechtsstaatsprinzip are the requirement of a speedy trial and compensation for undue delays, the right to a public trial (exceptions apply to protect other vital interests) and the right to independent, impartial and legally predetermined judges; this includes the corresponding right to recuse judges and expert witnesses.

Already the nineteenth-century idea of 'protecting forms' implied that the violation of these forms must have legal consequences, such as it may void the procedure wholly or in part. Hence, the RStPO in 1877 gave every defendant (and the prosecutor as well) the right to appeal (*Revision*) if he claimed to be burdened by a violation of the law. Here, an 'error preference' is the rule. It is sufficient to show the *possibility* that a proven illegality has affected the outcome so that the judgment will be set aside and a retrial will take place. Today, in principle, any deliberate violation of procedural law by police or prosecutor may amount to a *Rechtsstaatswidrigkeit*, a violation of Article 20(3) GG which must (somehow) be remedied. Exclusionary rules are a relatively recent addition to these remedies and remain problematic because the exclusion of evidence hampers the search for truth; the resulting case law has become extremely complicated. It is also conceivable that in cases of severe violations the proceedings are annulled *ex constitutione*.[171]

A general constitutional principle derived from the Rechtsstaatsprinzip as well as from the 'essence' (*Wesen*) of civil liberties is proportionality (*Verhältnismäßigkeit*). Any infringement by the state of fundamental rights is justified only if it is based on a statute and is 'proportional' in the sense that it serves a legitimate aim and is suitable and necessary to achieve that aim without being excessive. This applies to all procedural burdens like pre-trial detention, searches and seizures, observation, wire-tapping etc. While the proportionality of statutes and individual measures is subject to judicial review, the

170 Whether this implies a constitutional mandate for the inquisitorial paradigm is unclear. It may still be up to the legislator to decide which type of trial is best fit to elucidate the truth; only consensus-based procedures are constitutionally prohibited. In the 1960s, proposals were unsuccessfully made to switch to a pure accusatorial system in order to give full effect of the presumption of innocence; see Stuckenberg, *Unschuldsvermutung* (1998), 86–7 with further references.

171 Roxin and Schünemann, *Strafverfahrensrecht* (2017), § 21 mn. 20 with further references.

legislature is accorded a wide margin of appreciation as to which measures it deems useful.

Although not exhaustive, this list shows that numerous criminal procedure principles and rules have constitutional status or at least a constitutional foundation in German law. This explains the common phrase that criminal procedure law is 'applied constitutional law' and is a good indicator ('Seismograph') of the actual nature of the citizen–state relationship in a given polity.

Bibliography

Allan, T. R. S., 'Procedural Fairness and the Duty of Respect', *Oxford Journal of Legal Studies*, 18 (1998), 497–515.

Constitutional Justice: A Liberal Theory of the Rule of Law, Oxford University Press (2003).

'The Rule of Law', in Dyzenhaus D. and Thorburn M. (eds.), *Philosophical Foundations of Constitutional Law*, Oxford University Press (2016).

Ashworth A., 'Victims' Rights, Defendants' Rights and Criminal Procedure', in Crawford A. and Goodey J. (eds.), *Integrating a Victim Perspective within Criminal Justice*, Aldershot, Ashgate (2000).

Ashworth A. and Horder J., *The Principles of Criminal Law*, 7th edn, Oxford University Press (2013).

Ashworth A. and Redmayne M., *The Criminal Process*, 4th edn, Oxford University Press (2010).

Ashworth A. and Zedner L., 'Defending the Criminal Law: Reflections on the Changing Character of Crime, Procedure, and Sanctions', *Criminal Law and Philosophy*, 2 (2008), 21–51.

Baratta A., 'Zur Entwicklung des modernen Rechtsstaatsbegriffs', in Baer-Kaufert F.-W., Leistner G. and Schwaiger H. (eds.), *Liber Amicorum Bernhard C. H. Aubin*, Straßburg N.P., Engel Verlag (1979), 1–14.

Beetham D., *The Legitimation of Power*, London, Macmillan (1991).

Blackstone W., *Commentaries on the Laws of England in Four Books* (1753).

Böckenförde E.-W., 'Entstehung und Wandel des Rechtsstaatsbegriffs', in Böckenförde E.-W. (ed.), *Recht, Staat, Freiheit*, 6th edn, Frankfurt am Main, Suhrkamp (2016), 143–69.

Bohlander M., *Principles of German Criminal Procedure*, Oxford, Hart (2012).

Bottoms A. E. and Tankebe J., 'Beyond Procedural Justice: A Dialogic Approach to Legitimacy in Criminal Justice', *Journal of Criminal Law & Criminology*, 102 (2012), 119–70.

Bradford B., 'Policing and Social Identity: Procedural Justice, Inclusion and Cooperation between Police and Public', *Policing and Society*, 24 (2014), 22–43.

Braithwaite J. and Pettit P., *Not Just Deserts: A Republican Theory of Justice*, Oxford University Press (1990).

Carpzov B., *Practica Nova Imperialis Saxonica Rerum Criminalium*, Wittenberg, Haered. Zachariae Schureri Senior (1635).

Chan J., 'Changing Police Culture', *British Journal of Criminology*, 36 (1996), 109–34.

Cole D., 'Against Citizenship as a Predicate for Basic Rights', *Fordham Law*, 75 (2007), 2541–8.

College of Policing, *Code of Ethics: A Code of Practice for the Principles and Standards of Professional Behaviour for the Policing Profession in England and Wales*, London, College of Policing (2014).

Council of Europe, *The ECHR in Facts and Figures 2016*, European Court of Human Rights (2017), available at www.echr.coe.int/Documents/Facts_Figures_2016_ENG.pdf.

Damaška M., *The Faces of Justice and State Authority*, New Haven, Yale University Press (1986).

Darbyshire P., 'The Mischief of Plea Bargaining and Sentencing Rewards', *Criminal Law Review*, 79 (2000), 895–910.

Dettmar J. S., *Legalität und Opportunität im Strafprozess*, Berlin, Wissenschafts-Verlag (2008).

Dicey A. V., *Introduction to the Study of the Law of the Constitution*, 10th edn, London, Macmillan (1958).

Dölling D., *Polizeiliche Ermittlungstätigkeit und Legalitätsprinzip*, 2 vols. Wiesbaden, BKA-Forschungsreihe (1987), I.

Dubber M. D., 'The Criminal Trial and the Legitimation of Punishment', in Duff R. A. et al. (eds.), *The Trial on Trial*, 3 vols., Oxford, Hart (2004), I, 85–100.

Duff R. A. et al., *The Trial on Trial: Towards a Normative Theory of the Criminal Trial*, 3 vols., Oxford, Hart (2007), III.

Dworkin R., *A Matter of Principle*, Oxford University Press (1985).

'Terror and the Attack on Civil Liberties', *The New York Review of Books*, 50 (2003).

Emmerson B., Ashworth A. and MacDonald A., *Human Rights and Criminal Justice*, 3rd edn, London, Sweet & Maxwell (2012).

Erb V., *Legalität und Opportunität*, Berlin, Duncker & Humblot (1999).

Feeley M., *The Process is the Punishment*, New York, Russell Sage Foundation (1979).

Follain J., *Vendetta: The Mafia, Judge Falcone and the Quest for Justice*, London, Hodder & Stoughton (2012).

Galligan D. J., *Due Process and Fair Procedures: A Study of Administrative Procedures*, Oxford University Press (1997).

Gärditz K. F., 'Art. 20, 6. Teil: Rechtsstaatsprinzip', in Kahl W., Waldhof C. and Walter C. (eds.), *Bonner Kommentar zum Grundgesetz*, 25 vols., Heidelberg, C. F. Müller (2018).

Garrett B., *Too Big to Jail: How Prosecutors Compromise with Corporations*, Harvard University Press (2016).

Glaser J., 'Das Princip der Strafverfolgung', in Glaser J., *Gesammelte kleinere juristische Schriften – Teil 1: Kleine Schriften über Strafrecht und Strafproceß*, 2nd edn, Vienna, Manz (1883), 521–45.

Goss R., *Criminal Fair Trial Rights: Article 6 of the European Convention on Human Rights*, Oxford, Hart (2014).

Grote R., 'Rule of Law, Rechtsstaat and "Etat de droit"', in Starck C. (ed.), *Constitutionalism, Universalism and Democracy: A Comparative Analysis*, Baden-Baden, Nomos (1999), 269–306.

Gürtner F., 'Der Gedanke der Gerechtigkeit in der deutschen Strafrechtserneuerung', in Gürtner F. and Freisler R. (eds.), *Das neue Strafrecht*, Berlin, Decker (1936), 19–31.

Hamm R., 'Der Einsatz heimlicher Ermittlungsmethoden und der Anspruch auf ein faires Verfahren', *Strafverteidiger* (2001), 81–5.

Hawkins K., *Law as Last Resort: Prosecution Decision-Making in a Regulatory Agency*, Oxford University Press (2002), 424–7.

Hobbes T., *Leviathan*, Oxford University Press (2008 [1651]).

Hodgson J., 'Conceptions of the Trial in Inquisitorial and Adversarial Procedure', in Duff R. A. et al. (eds.), *The Trial on Trial*, 3 vols., Oxford, Hart (2006), II, 223–42.

Home Office, *Justice for All*, London, HMSO (2002).

Rebalancing the Criminal Justice System in Favour of the Law-Abiding Majority: Cutting Crime, Reducing Reoffending and Protecting the Public, London, HMSO (2006).

Hörnle T., 'Democratic Accountability and Lay Participation in Criminal Trials', in Duff R. A. et al. (eds.), *The Trial on Trial*, 3 vols., Oxford, Hart (2006), II, 135–53.

Hoyle C., 'Victims of the State: Recognising the Harms Caused by Wrongful Convictions', in Bosworth M., Hoyle C. and Zedner L. (eds.), *Changing Contours of Criminal Justice: Research, Politics and Policy*, Oxford University Press (2016).

Hoyle C. and Sato M., *Reasons to Doubt: Wrongful Convictions and the Criminal Cases Review Commission*, Oxford University Press (2018).

Hunter J. et al., *The Integrity of Criminal Process: From Theory to Practice*, Oxford, Hart (2016).

Hyman T., 'The Little Word "Due"', *Akron Law Review*, 38 (2005), 1–51.

Issacharoff S., *Civil Procedure*, St Paul-Minneapolis, Foundation Press (2012).

Jackson J., 'Justice for All – Putting Victims at the Heart of Criminal Justice?', *Journal of Law and Society*, 30 (2003), 309–26.

Jahn M., 'Fair trial als strafprozessuales Leitprinzip im Mehrebenensystem', *Zeitschrift für die gesamte Strafrechtswissenschaft*, 127 (2015), 549–615.

Jhering R. von, *Geist des römischen Rechts*, 6th edn, Breitkopf und Härtel, Leipzig (1923).

Jung H., *Straffreiheit für den Kronzeugen?*, Cologne, Heymanns (1974).

Kelman D., 'Closed Trials and Secret Allegations: An Analysis of the "Gisting" Requirement', *The Journal of Criminal Law*, 80 (2016), 264–77.

Kirste S., 'Philosophical Foundations of the Principle of the Legal State (Rechtsstaat) and the Rule of Law', in Silkenat J. R., Hickey Jr. J. E. and Barenboim P. D. (eds.), *The Legal Doctrines of the Rule of Law and the Legal State (Rechtsstaat)*, New York, Springer (2014), 29–43.

Kühne H.-H., *Strafprozessrecht*, 9th edn, Heidelberg, C. F. Müller (2015).

Loughlin M., *Foundations of Public Law*, Oxford University Press (2010).

McBarnet D., 'False Dichotomies in Criminal Justice Research', in Baldwin J. and Bottomley A. K. (eds.), *Criminal Justice: Selected Readings*, Oxford, Martin Robertson (1978), 23–34.

Conviction: Law, the State, and the Construction of Justice, London, Macmillan (1983).

McConville M., Sanders A. and Leng R., *The Case for the Prosecution: Police Suspects and the Construction of Criminality*, London, Routledge (1991).

MacCormick N., 'Der Rechtsstaat und die rule of law', *Juristen-Zeitung*, 39 (1984), 65–70.

Institutions of Law: An Essay in Legal Theory, Oxford University Press (2007).

Macdonald S., 'Constructing a Framework for Criminal Justice Research: Learning from Packer's Mistakes', *New Criminal Law Review*, 11 (2008), 257–311.

McEwan J., 'Ritual, Fairness and Truth: The Adversarial and Inquisitorial Models of Criminal Trial', in Duff R. A. et al. (eds.), *The Trial on Trial*, 3 vols., Oxford, Hart (2004), I, 51–69.

Marshall G., 'Due Process in England', in Pennock J. R. and Chapman J. W. (eds.), *Due Process*, New York University Press (1977), 69–92.

Mayer O., *Deutsches Verwaltungsrecht*, 1st edn, 2 vols. Leipzig, Duncker & Humblot (1895), I.

Meares T. L., Tyler T. R. and Gardener J., 'Lawful or Fair?: How Cops and Laypeople Perceive Good Policing', *Journal of Criminology and Criminal Law*, 105 (2016), 297–344.

Morin J.-Y., 'The Rule of Law and the *Rechtsstaat* Concept: A Comparison', in McWhinney E. (ed.), *Federalism in the Making: Contemporary Canadian and German Constitutionalism, National and Transnational*, Dordrecht, Kluwer (1992), 60–86.

Neuberger Lord D. E., 'JUSTICE – Justice in an Age of Austerity', available at www.supremecourt.uk/docs/speech-131015.pdf.

Nickel J. W., 'Due Process Rights and Terrorist Emergencies', *European Journal of Legal Studies*, 1 (2007), 243–64.

Orth J., *Due Process of Law: A Brief History*, Lawrence, University Press of Kansas (2003).

Packer H. L., *The Limits of the Criminal Sanction*, Stanford University Press (1968).

Phillips C. and Bowling B., 'Ethnicities, Racism, Crime and Criminal Justice', in Liebling A., Maruna S. and Mcara L. (eds.), *The Oxford Handbook of Criminology*, Oxford University Press (2017), 190–212.

Ramraj V. V., 'Four Models of Due Process', *International Journal of Constitutional Law*, 2 (2004), 492–524.

Redmayne M., 'Exploring Entrapment', in Zedner L. and Roberts J. V. (eds.), *Principles and Values in Criminal Law and Criminal Justice*, Oxford University Press (2012), 157–70.

Rieß P., 'Einleitung', in Rieß P. (ed.), *Löwe-Rosenberg, Die Strafprozeßordnung und das Gerichtsverfassungsgesetz, Großkommentar*, 25th edn, 8 vols., Berlin, De Gruyter (1999), I.

Ristroph A., 'The Thin Blue Line from Crime to Punishment', *Brooklyn Law School Legal Studies Research Papers*, 108 (2018), 305–34.

Roach K., *Due Process and Victims' Rights: The New Law and Politics of Criminal Justice*, University of Toronto Press (1999).

'Four Models of the Criminal Process', *The Journal of Criminal Law and Criminology*, 89 (1999), 671–716.

'Wrongful Convictions: Adversarial and Inquisitorial Themes', *North Carolina Journal of International Law and Commercial Regulation*, 35 (2010), 388–446.

Roberts P., 'Theorising Procedural Tradition: Subjects, Objects and Values in Criminal Adjudication', in Duff R. A. et al. (eds.), *The Trial on Trial*, Oxford, 3 vols., Hart (2006), II, 37–64.

'Comparative Criminal Justice Goes Global', *Oxford Journal of Legal Studies*, 28 (2008), 369–91.

'Groundwork for a Jurisprudence of Criminal Procedure', in Duff R. A. and Green S. P. (eds.), *Philosophical Foundations of Criminal Law*, Oxford University Press (2011), 380–408.

Roxin C. and Schünemann B., *Strafverfahrensrecht*, 29th edn, Munich, C. H. Beck (2017).

Sanders A., Young R. and Burton M., *Criminal Justice*, 4th edn, Oxford University Press (2010).

Schmidt E., 'Gerechtigkeit und Zweckmäßigkeit in Geschichte und Gegenwart der Strafrechtspflege', in Schmidt E., *Justitia fundamentum regnorum*, Heidelberg, Schriften der Süddeutschen Juristen-Zeitung (1947), 75–98.

'Von Sinn und Notwendigkeit wissenschaftlicher Behandlung des Strafprozeßrechts', *Zeitschrift für die gesamte Strafrechtswissenschaft*, 65 (1953), 161–77.

Lehrkommentar zur Strafprozeßordnung und zum Gerichtsverfassungsgesetz, 3 vols., 2nd edn, Göttingen, Vandenhoeck & Rupprecht (1964), I.

Einführung in die Geschichte der deutschen Strafrechtspflege, 3rd edn, Göttingen, Vandenhoeck & Rupprecht (1965).

Shipley D. E., 'Due Process Rights before EU Agencies: The Rights of Defense', *Georgia Journal of International and Comparative Law*, 37 (2008), 1–52.

Stuckenberg C.-F., *Untersuchungen zur Unschuldsvermutung*, Berlin, De Gruyter (1998).

'§ 257c StPO', in Erb V., Esser R., Franke U., Graalmann-Scheerer K., Hilger H. and Ignor A. (eds.), *Löwe-Rosenberg, Die Strafprozeßordnung und das Gerichtsverfassungsgesetz, Großkommentar*, 26th edn, 13 vols., Berlin, De Gruyter (2013), VI/II.

'Gründe für die Abschaffung des § 153a StPO', in Herzog F., Schlothauer R. and Wohlers W. (eds.), *Rechtsstaatlicher Strafprozess und Bürgerrechte, Gedächtnisschrift für Edda Weßlau*, Duncker & Humblot, Berlin (2016), 369–89.

Stumer A. C., *The Presumption of Innocence*, Oxford, Hart (2010).

Tadros V., 'A Human Right to a Fair Criminal Law', in Chalmers J. and Leverick F. (eds.), *Essays in Criminal Law in Honour of Sir Gerald Gordon*, Edinburgh University Press (2010), 103–25.

Tankebe J. and Liebling A. (eds.), *Legitimacy and Criminal Justice: An International Exploration*, Oxford University Press (2013).

Tyler T., *Why People Obey the Law*, New Haven, Yale University Press (1990).

'Procedural Justice, Legitimacy, and the Effective Rule of Law', *Crime and Justice*, 30 (2003), 283–357.

Tyler T., Jackson J. and Bradford B., 'Psychology of Procedural Justice and Cooperation', in Bruinsma G. and Weisburd D. (eds.), *Encyclopedia of Criminology and Criminal Justice*, New York, Springer (2014).

Waddington P. A. J., 'Police (Canteen) Sub-Culture: An Appreciation', *British Journal of Criminology*, 39 (1999), 287–309.

Waldron J., 'Security and Liberty: The Image of Balance', *Journal of Political Philosophy*, 11 (2003), 191–210.

Ward J., 'Transforming "Summary Justice" through Police-Led Prosecution and "Virtual Courts": Is "Procedural Due Process" Being Undermined?', *The British Journal of Criminology*, 55 (2015), 341–58.

Weber M., *Wirtschaft und Gesellschaft*, 5th edn, Mohr Siebeck, Tübingen (1972).

Weigend T., 'Why Have a Trial when You Can Have a Bargain?', in Duff R. A. et al. (eds.), *The Trial on Trial*, 3 vols., Oxford, Hart (2006), II, 207–22.

'No News Is Good News: Criminal Sentencing in Germany since 2000', in Tonry M. (ed.), *Crime and Justice*, 45 (2016), 83–106.

Wilmot-Smith F., 'Necessity or Ideology?', *The London Review of Books*, 36 (2014), 15–17.

Wohlers W., 'Einleitung', in Wolter J. (ed.), *Systematischer Kommentar zur Strafprozessordnung*, 10 vols., 5th edn, Cologne, Heymanns (2018), I.

Zachariae H. A., *Die Gebrechen und die Reform des deutschen Strafverfahrens dargestellt auf der Basis einer consequenten Entwickelung des inquisitorischen und des accusatorischen Prinzips*, Göttingen, Verlag der Dieterich'schen Buchhandlung (1846).

Handbuch des deutschen Strafprocesses, 2 vols., Göttingen, Verlag der Dieterich'schen Buchhandlung (1861), I.

Zedner L., *Criminal Justice*, Oxford University Press (2004).

'Seeking Security By Eroding Rights: The Side-Stepping of Due Process', in Goold B. and Lazarus L. (eds.), *Security and Human Rights*, Oxford, Hart (2007).

'Criminal Justice in the Service of Security', in Bosworth M., Hoyle C. and Zedner L. (eds.), *The Changing Contours of Criminal Justice*, Oxford University Press (2016).

'Security against Arbitrary Government in Criminal Justice', in du Bois-Pedain A., Ulväng M. and Asp P. (eds.), *Criminal Law and the Authority of the State*, Oxford, Hart (2017).

10

The Role of the Prosecutor

ALEXANDER HEINZE AND SHANNON FYFE*

I Introduction

The prosecutor's position within the criminal justice system cannot be overstated. Robert Jackson, former United States Attorney General, who gained worldwide reputation through his role as Chief United States Prosecutor at the International Military Tribunal in Nuremberg, remarked fully seventy-five years ago that: 'The prosecutor has more control over life, liberty, and reputation than any other person in America.'[1] Prosecutors are 'the criminal justice system's real lawmakers'[2] and 'the gatekeepers to the justice system' system', insofar as they make the crucial decisions about which individuals enter the criminal justice system and under what conditions they move through it.[3]

In this chapter, we identify and analyse these various prosecutorial roles. We begin with the common perception of US prosecutors as partisan lawyers tasked with obtaining and preserving convictions, even though prosecutors in the United States are not supposed to be mere adversaries but also have special duties to seek justice and the truth. While many scholars have accordingly condemned American prosecutors for their 'conviction mentality', comparative legal scholars have for decades held up German prosecutors for their dedication to objectivity. Yet fiscal constraints, combined with the emergence of new types of economic crimes, put pressure on the ability of the prosecution service to fulfil the ambitious fact-finding function mandated by the German

* The authors wish to thank Professor Dr Dr h.c. Kai Ambos (Georg-August University of Göttingen), Dr Antje du Bois-Pedain (University of Cambridge), Dr Matthew Dyson (University of Oxford), Professor Alec Walen (Rutgers) and the editors for their valuable comments.

1 Jackson, 'Prosecutor' (1940), 3.

2 Stuntz, 'Criminal Law' (2001), 505–6.

3 US District of Columbia Attorney General Karl Racine in: Fair and Just Prosecution (FJP), *21 Principles* (2018), 3.

Code of Criminal Procedure (StPO). Today, the StPO contains many elements that are reminiscent of an adversarial setting like that of a US (criminal) proceeding.

Accordingly, we show that, while the Anglo-American and German systems are not strict contrasts, in general the different roles of the prosecutor mirror divergent models of procedure. Going beyond the common adversarial–inquisitorial dichotomy, we employ Damaška's concepts of coordinate vs. hierarchical officialdom and reactive vs. activist states with conflict-solving vs. policy-implementing types of proceedings. The prosecutorial roles in these systems conflict with one another. Adversarial/conflict-solving lawyering aims to achieve procedural fairness, but it requires acting strategically to win, and it is the client who defines what outcome constitutes victory. Seeking the truth, however, requires choosing which substantive values to pursue. These two roles can push prosecutors in different directions. We show that for any particular choice prosecutors make in a case – such as adding a count, offering plea-bargain terms, disclosing evidence to the defendant, fighting a post-conviction innocence claim – they must decide whether they will strategically maximise their likelihood of victory (which might be defined as securing or preserving a conviction, obtaining a significant punishment, or some other outcome), or instead prioritise values like mercy and proportionality.

II The Role of the Prosecutor: Ethical Framework

The distinctive roles played by prosecutors are largely shaped by the aims of the particular criminal justice system.[4] As individual actors within an institution, they are responsible for conscientiously performing certain straightforward tasks, yet they also wield discretionary authority to make decisions about individual cases and broader institutional policies. When a prosecutor faces a situation in which he or she has discretionary power, decision-making involves the goal or a set of goals, purposes, or objectives to be achieved (or maximised or minimised).[5] Goals may be limited to the specific case or accused offender at hand, or they may take into account the larger impact of the singular case on the prosecutor's office and the entire criminal justice system. In this first section, we explore the scope of

[4] Weigend, 'A Judge by Another Name' (2012), 377 ff.

[5] Gottfredson and Gottfredson, *Criminal Justice* (1988).

prosecutorial decision-making and the role of fairness within the context of a criminal justice system's broad objectives and parameters.

1 *Justice and Fairness*

While the particular features of what constitutes justice vary between, and sometimes within, criminal justice systems, it always relates to fairness. A judicial or administrative body is tasked with serving the public, and in serving the public, a government body's most important higher-order goal is to treat every member of the public fairly. One common interpretation of the concept of fairness relies on treating 'like cases alike'. Procedural fairness can be assessed on the basis of a system's rules.[6] Rights that are guaranteed by procedures 'allow for a system of law to emerge out of a set of substantive rules and ... minimize arbitrariness'.[7] If the same established rules and procedures are applied to all defendants and suspects (or potential suspects) without bias, then a system can be said to be procedurally fair, regardless of outcomes. However, 'equal treatment involves at one extreme the impartial application of existing rules and procedures, regardless of the outcome (procedural justice), and at the other, the idea that any policies or procedures that have the effect of punishing or controlling a higher proportion of one social group than another are unjust'.[8] One might argue, then, 'that law and social policy should be adjusted so as to achieve equal outcomes'.[9] This is distributive fairness, which involves who is actually tried for crimes, out of the group of all those who could possibly be tried before the court system.[10] A criminal justice system is fair with respect to distribution if it is willing and able to try all parties who deserve to be tried. Finally, we can think about substantive fairness, which involves the protection of substantive rights, such as the right to bodily autonomy, liberty from confinement, or a trial that does not result

[6] See e.g. Franck, *Fairness* (1995); see also Fuller, *Morality* (1964); McDermott, *Fairness* (2016).

[7] May, *Global Justice* (2011), 52.

[8] Gelsthorpe and Padfield, 'Introduction' (2003), 12. See also Hollander-Blumoff, 'Fairness beyond the Adversary System' (2017), 2081–95.

[9] Gelsthorpe and Padfield, 'Introduction' (2003), 12. However, we would limit this point to mean that outcomes should be equal where inputs are equal. Proportional distributive justice treats all relevant individuals in relation to what they are due. See Aristotle, *The Nicomachean Ethics* (2009), 1130b–2b.

[10] Mégret, 'Anxieties' (2016), 211.

in a wrongful conviction.[11] A trial that results in an absurd outcome or one that is intuitively immoral would be considered substantively unfair.[12] While we should care at least somewhat about all three types of fairness, sometimes they will be at odds with one another.

It is difficult for a legal system to even attempt distributive fairness, given all of the factors that influence the selection, investigation, and outcome of cases. The public generally thinks about fairness in terms of substantive justice, in that a just result of a trial is one in which the guilty are convicted, and the innocent acquitted. Yet this results-based, substantive view of fairness can also be hard to achieve, depending on the availability and admissibility of evidence. Rawls argues that procedural fairness is essentially the same thing as justice, and that the best way to ensure that our rules are fair is to construct them based on what individuals would choose to be the rules if they did not know about their own individual interests.[13] Rawls claims that the chosen rules would (a) ensure basic liberties for all, and (b) tolerate wealth inequality only where it worked to benefit the least well-off.[14] Dworkin agrees with Rawls on the first feature, that we must ensure 'equal concern and respect' for all individuals within the legal system, and that legal systems should be focused on adhering to these sorts of principles, rather than achieving particular policy goals.[15]

In an inquisitorial/policy-implementing[16] system like Germany the criminal justice system seeks the truth, and all parties to the legal proceedings share this aim. This is especially true for the German Prosecution Service, where the employees view themselves as the 'most objective civil servants in the world'.[17] While both the Article 20(3) of the German Basic Law (*Grundgesetz*, GG) – in conjunction with Article 2(1) GG – and Article 6 of the European Convention on Human Rights (ECHR),[18] ensure the right to a fair trial and other protections for the

[11] See e.g. Alexander, 'Procedural Rights' (1998), 19.

[12] See Franck, *Fairness* (1995); see also Fuller, *Morality* (1964).

[13] See generally Rawls, *Justice* (1972); see also Rawls, *Fairness* (2001).

[14] *Ibid.*

[15] See Dworkin, *Rights* (1977).

[16] For a categorisation of procedural models see below Section III.1. and Heinze, *Procedure* (2014), 104 ff.

[17] Translation by Boyne, *Prosecution* (2014), 6. See also Fischer, 'Einleitung' (2019), mn. 203; Weigend, 'A Judge by Another Name' (2012), 381.

[18] Roxin and Schünemann, *Strafverfahrensrecht* (2017), § 11 mn. 4; Schmitt, 'Einleitung' (2019), mn. 19; Gollwitzer, 'Art. 6 MRK' (2005), mn. 65; Geppert, 'Fair-Trial-Prinzip' (1992), 597; Esser, *Strafverfahrensrecht* (2002), 401.

accused, a primary aim of the German criminal justice system is to seek the truth, or to seek the substantively fair result.[19] As we explore in the next section, the German system is also aimed, to some extent, at distributive fairness. The US criminal justice system, on the other hand, purports to be aimed at procedural fairness. The Fourteenth Amendment of the US Constitution states that no state shall 'deprive any person of life, liberty, or property, without due process of law; nor deny to any person within its jurisdiction the equal protection of the

[19] In Germany, truth in the context of criminal procedure is only a 'subgoal' of the goal 'peace under the law': see Anders, 'Verletztenorientierung' (2012), 374, 393. However, it should be stressed that the goals of criminal procedure in Germany and their relationship are highly disputed, see Dölling, 'Ziel des Strafverfahrens' (2015), 679 ff. About the divergent meanings of 'truth' in criminal procedure Weßlau, 'Debatte' (2014), 1002–5. A complete analysis of the role of truth-finding (and status afforded to the concept of 'truth' altogether) in the criminal process is outside the scope of this chapter. We succinctly note that in Germany a distinction is made between procedural truth and substantive truth, which largely corresponds with our distinction between procedural fairness and substantive fairness. As Weigend notes, '[i]f truth-finding connotes the revelation (or discovery) of an objective reality, it is the result that legitimizes the process. The judicial process is only the means to discover the hidden, "objective" reality and should be organized to optimize the chances of finding the "piece of gold".' He goes on to distinguish this substantive view of truth from procedural truth, which is 'whatever emerges from a fair and rational discourse among the parties', and 'the content of the rules that determine the process [are] more important than the outcome itself, and adherence to these rules acquires paramount importance for truth-finding'. See Weigend, 'Search for the Truth' (2011), 295, 389 (footnote omitted). Weigend cites Hodgson, 'Conceptions' (2006), 223, 225–6. For a general analysis, see Duff et al., *Trial on Trial* (2007), 61 ff. See also Safferling, *Procedure* (2012), 55. From the perspective of communication- and discourse-theory, see Rolinski, 'Unmittelbarkeit' (2013), 297, 311; Sacher, 'Absprachen im Strafverfahren' (2014), 957, 959–60. Interestingly, the German Federal Court of Justice (*Bundesgerichtshof* (BGH), translation by the BGH, available at www.bundesgerichtshof.de/EN/Home/home_node.html) has explicitly underlined the role of procedural truth in criminal procedure. See BGH, Judgment from 10 Jun. 2015 – 2 StR 97/14, in *Neue Zeitschrift für Strafrecht (NStZ)* 2016, 52, 58: '[a]cceptance and legitimacy of criminal judgments are not based on the trust in a "correctness", understood as a material truth that is discovered in the course of a criminal trial. Instead, trust in the "procedural truth" it is both necessary and sufficient. The "procedural truth" is created through a trial that complies with both the substantial and procedural law and is therefore fair' (translation by A. H.). The original quote reads: 'Akzeptanz und Legitimation strafrichterlicher Urteile werden nicht durch das Vertrauen auf "Richtigkeit"im Sinne einer im Verfahren gefundenen materiellen Wahrheit begründet. Ausreichend aber auch erforderlich ist das Vertrauen in die "prozessuale Wahrheit", die vermittelt wird durch ein rechtsrichtiges, prozessordnungsgemäßes und daher unter anderem faires Verfahren.' Despite the fascinating nature of this debate, due to space constraints, we shall not attempt to wade further into the discussion of truth here.

laws'.[20] The Fourth, Fifth, Sixth and Eighth Amendments also provide protections for accused individuals.[21] In this adversarial system, the prosecutor's role involves making the strongest case possible against a defendant, subject to the limitations imposed by due process and the supervision of the judge. Rule 3.8 of the American Bar Association (ABA) Model Rules of Professional Responsibility outlines these limitations, which include making reasonable efforts to ensure that the accused has the benefit of his or her own counsel, avoiding actions that will unfairly prejudice the public against the accused, promptly disclosing evidence to the defence when appropriate and investigating or discontinuing a case where there is evidence of a defendant's innocence.[22] Yet it remains the case that in an adversarial system like the United States, the judge is responsible for protecting the accused's due process rights, or procedural fairness, and the prosecutor is responsible for obtaining a substantively fair result within the parameters set by the judge (albeit through the adversarial process rather than a pure truth-seeking process). The same applies to the Crown Prosecution Service (CPS) in England and Wales, which searches for an '*approximation* of "the truth"', understanding 'truth *as* proof',[23] which appears to fall within the concept of 'procedural truth' rather than 'substantive truth'.[24]

2 *Prosecutorial Ethics*

The normative foundations of prosecutorial ethics consist of two main concepts: a prosecutor's general duty to seek justice,[25] and the moral theories that inform the corresponding, specific ethical obligations of the prosecutor. In both adversarial/conflict-solving and inquisitorial/policy-implementing procedural models,[26] regardless of other specific duties and areas of discretion, the prosecutor is expected to seek

20 US Const. amend. XIV.
21 US Const. amends. IX, X, XI, XIII.
22 Model R. Prof. Conduct 3.8 (ABA 2018).
23 Slapper and Kelly, *English Legal System* (2017), 394 (emphasis in the original). Cicchini argues that the truth as proof-model is now also applied by prosecutors in the United States; see Cicchini, 'Prosecutor Sophistry and the Burden of Proof' (2018), 489, 491.
24 See in more detail n. 18 above.
25 See Zacharias, 'Ethics' (1991), 45 ff.; see also Howell, 'Discretion' (2014), 306–8; Langer, 'Prosecutorial Adjudication' (2006), 236.
26 About the meaning of terms 'inquisitorial' and 'adversarial' in more detail Heinze, *Procedure* (2014), 117 ff.; and Ambos and Heinze, 'Abbreviated Procedures' (2017), 27 ff.

justice.[27] As noted earlier, while the particular features of what constitutes justice vary between, and sometimes within, criminal justice systems, it always has something to do with fairness.

The prosecutor's specific obligations for guaranteeing fair trials can be thought of in terms of deontological norms and consequentialist norms.[28] Consequentialism identifies right actions based solely on the outcomes they produce, evaluated independently of how the end-states were achieved. The right action, for consequentialists, is the action that maximises the good. The promotion of 'the good', however, requires a conception of what is good and therefore worthy of promotion. In a criminal trial, we might conceive of goodness in terms of the substantive results of the trial. A criminal trial might be considered 'good', or fair, if the person who committed a crime is convicted of said crime through the criminal trial process. A prosecutor who attempts to reach the correct substantive outcome in every case, and considers this to be the standard of what constitutes a fair trial, adopts a purely consequentialist view of her ethical obligations.

Deontology, conversely, 'takes right action to be the primary evaluative notion; it recognizes various actions as obligatory, prohibited, or permitted on the basis of their intrinsic natures and independently of the value they produce'.[29] Deontological constraints identify what actions are impermissible because they violate duties not to harm people in various ways.[30] Beyond the actions which are specifically required by duty, deontology allows for significant freedom of choice in our actions.[31]

[27] Boyne, *Prosecution* (2014), 5 ('[P]rosecutors possess an ethical obligation to pursue justice'). The fact that the search for truth in inquisitorial systems is a constitutive feature (Heinze, *Procedure* (2014), 107) does not render justice as an ethical obligation of the prosecutor less relevant. In inquisitorial systems, too, truth is a means to the end of justice, as Peters famously pointed out in his seminal work about the German criminal process (Peters, *Strafprozeß* (1985), 82: 'Das Strafverfahren kann das Ziel der Gerechtigkeit nur erreichen, wenn es die Wahrheit findet.') In the same vein Kubicek, *Justice* (2006), 37 with further references. See also Ingraham, *Structure* (1987), 13.

[28] Some have argued that virtue theory can and should inform prosecutorial ethics. See e.g. Cassidy, 'Virtue Theory' (2006), 635. We would argue that virtue ethics and its focus on the *character* of a prosecutor, rather than her decisions, does not provide clear deontic verdicts for how to act. We also assume that the duty to act with integrity is incumbent upon all participants in a criminal justice system. Therefore, we will only consider the tension between consequentialist and deontological norms here.

[29] Brink, 'Consequentialism' (2006), 381.

[30] McNaughton and Rawling, 'Deontology' (2006), 425.

[31] Kant, *Metaphysics of Morals* (2002), 4:426. Kant distinguishes between perfect duties, which admit of no exception, and imperfect duties, which must be fulfilled but not in a

In a criminal trial, deontological constraints on a prosecutor will align more with considerations of procedural fairness. A prosecutor who is focused on deontological norms will be concerned with the reasons that support the choices that are made, respect for defendants' rights, and the way trials are conducted, independent of the end-states the trials produce.

Deontological constraints are well-suited to play the primary role in shaping prosecutorial ethics and promoting fair trials. Danner has argued that prosecutorial decisions will be both actually legitimate and perceived as such if they are taken in a principled, reasoned, and impartial manner.[32] The duty to treat every individual as an end in herself and thus apply the same rules impartially, without bias or concern about outcomes, lends itself to ensuring procedural fairness. A prosecutor is constrained by 'rules which apply in an all-or-nothing, categorical manner without reference to the particular context or consequences of the prohibited or required behaviour'.[33] Deontological constraints do not permit individual rights to be violated, even if a rights violation could be 'offset by benefits that arise elsewhere' in the justice system.[34] Thus deontological constraints are crucial to the foundations of prosecutorial ethics and procedural fairness.

Concerns about the substantive outcomes of criminal trials, the overall performance or record of a prosecutor, or the social and political impacts of criminal trials likely involve more consequentialist considerations.[35] A prosecutor with an impeccable record of respect for defendants' rights, faced with the prospect of removal due to his or her failure to convict several accused persons, must consider whether he or she should treat a few defendants as means to the end of staying employed. Another prosecutor, tasked with determining which members of a large criminal enterprise should be indicted and which should receive plea deals, will necessarily take the results of his or her decisions into account – and will likely be unable to achieve a distributively fair result.

Consequentialist considerations will be inappropriate at many points in a criminal trial, because they will constitute an impermissible failure of

particular way. Perfect duties are compatible with significant freedom of choice because they tend to be formulated in the negative, while imperfect duties will somewhat constrain choices.

32 Danner, 'Discretion' (2003), 536–7.

33 Nicolson, 'Moral' (2005), 606.

34 Markovits, *Legal Ethics* (2010), 7.

35 Mégret, 'Prosecutors' (2008), 8.

procedural fairness. These sorts of considerations should be impermissible during a criminal trial phase when they are incompatible with deontological constraints. In other instances, such as during the sentencing phase, it may be appropriate to consider a defendant's particular circumstances before determining the best method and duration of punishment. In practically all domestic criminal justice systems, justice is distributed selectively according to certain, often policy-based criteria,[36] so consequentialist considerations may also be appropriate prior to the trial. It is impossible for a prosecutor to treat every *potential* defendant equally, even if it is possible to treat every *actual* defendant equally.[37] A prosecutor's conduct should always be limited by deontological constraints prohibiting bias and the use of individuals as means rather than respecting them as ends. But it is appropriate, and perhaps even obligatory in some instances, for a prosecutor to consider the potential consequences of the decisions he or she makes regarding which situations to investigate and which individuals to prosecute.

3 *Prosecutorial Misconduct*

A prosecutor's failure to abide by legal or ethical obligations is considered prosecutorial misconduct. These professional obligations are intended to locate a prosecutor between extremes, thereby compelling her to seek justice and ensure that 'guilt shall not escape nor innocence suffer'.[38] A prosecutor is required to 'refrain from improper methods calculated to produce a wrongful conviction', while also using 'every legitimate means to bring about a just one'.[39]

Specific types of prosecutorial misconduct include improper efforts to influence other parties to a trial;[40] improper statements regarding evidence that has not been presented;[41] failures to disclose evidence;[42]

36 See Jehle and Wade, *Justice Systems* (2006), 24, 60–1; see also Damaška, 'Criminal Law' (2008), 362–3, referring to the discrimination from a historical perspective; from a comparative perspective, with a view to mandatory prosecution or prosecutorial discretion (principle of opportunity), see Kuczyńska, *Accusation Model* (2015), 94–106.

37 In a similar vein, Armenian, 'Selectivity' (2016), 646.

38 *Berger* v. *United States*, 295 US. 78, 88 (1935).

39 *Ibid.*

40 Alschuler, 'Misconduct' (1971), 629, 633.

41 *Ibid.*

42 *Ibid.* See also Section III.2.(c) below with n. 168.

and making abusive, insulting, inflammatory or prejudicial statements.[43] Each of these forms of misconduct is unprofessional, and this is one reason why prosecutors may face legal, professional or social sanctions for engaging in these behaviours. But the most damning impact of prosecutorial misconduct is on individual cases, where defendants might be wrongfully convicted or wrongfully acquitted on the basis of biased or improper statements. The corresponding concern is the impact of unfairly influenced individual cases on the overall actual and perceived legitimacy of legal institutions, and on the profession of lawyers in general.

Not all instances of unprofessionalism on the part of a prosecutor rise to the level of prosecutorial misconduct, and not every instance of prosecutorial misconduct rises to the level of appellate courts sanctioning prosecutors or overturning convictions. In the 'ardor of advocacy, and in the excitement of trial, even the most experienced counsel are occasionally carried away by' the temptation to make abusive, insulting, inflammatory or prejudicial statements during the trial.[44] But it can be argued that in any legal system, regardless of the prosecutor's specific role, rhetoric should not be necessary to obtain the most rational verdicts in criminal cases.[45] A view of the adversarial system as one in which a certain kind of rhetorical strategy with rhetorical flourish is desirable, if not necessary to obtain rational verdicts, looks like it will do little to discourage certain kinds of prosecutorial misconduct (or at least unprofessionalism). There is something to the thought that 'if a judgment of criminal conviction should not rest upon emotionalism, we should encourage the prosecutor not to argue in emotional terms. If the basis for a criminal conviction should be a detailed sifting of the evidence, we should encourage the prosecutor to present arguments that will promote a careful sifting of the evidence.'[46]

Some prosecutorial misconduct, even egregious misconduct, will not be remedied or sanctioned if it occurs behind closed doors. Decisions related to case selection, plea bargaining, and charging are rarely transparent and rarely reviewable.[47] Many decisions made by prosecutors are never revealed to the public, and even defendants and their attorneys are

[43] Alschuler, 'Misconduct' (1971), 629, 633; Soubise and Woolley, 'Prosecutors and Justice' (2018), 587, 593.

[44] Alschuler, 'Misconduct' (1971), 635, citing *Dunlop* v. *United States*, 165 US. 486, 498 (1897).

[45] Alschuler, 'Misconduct' (1971), 629, 637.

[46] *Ibid.*, 637.

[47] See American Civil Liberties Union (ACLU), 'Unlocking the Black Box' (2019).

not entitled to discover how certain decisions were made behind the scenes.[48] Even when these behaviours are specifically forbidden by codes of conduct, they do not seem to serve as a deterrent,[49] because the opportunities for discovering the misbehaviour are so limited. And as Duff argues, '[d]iscretion is most troubling not only when it is un- or under-constrained, but when it is unaccountable'.[50]

III The Role of the Prosecutor: Normative Framework

We now turn to our analysis of the role of the prosecutor in selected European jurisdictions and in both the United States and the UK. First, we adopt Damaška's distinction between conflict-solving and policy-implementing models as the most useful normative framework, due to the fact that it reveals the dual and ambiguous roles of the prosecutor. We go on to analyse the role of the prosecutor, from an institutional perspective, and draw some preliminary conclusions. Finally, we explore the decision-making role played by prosecutors and analyse the normative underpinnings of prosecutorial discretion in various jurisdictions, in terms of the opportunity principle and the legality principle. The final subsection considers a crucial site of discretion within jurisdictions that prioritise the legality principle: penal orders.

1 The Conceptualisation of the Normative Framework: Beyond the Adversarial/Inquisitorial Divide

A conceptualisation of a normative framework should never be made in a vacuum, but instead it should be premised on a taxonomy. Going beyond the inquisitorial/adversarial or common law/civil law models, and other models such as crime control, due process model and offensive model,[51] we employ Damaška's concepts of coordinate vs. hierarchical officialdom and a reactive vs. an activist state with conflict-solving vs. policy-implementing types of proceedings.

According to Damaška, hierarchical structures of authority are characterised by the professionalisation of officials, a strict hierarchical ordering and technical standards for decision-making, reflecting a

48 See Davis, *Arbitrary Justice* (2007), ch. 7; see also Kreag, 'Disclosing Misconduct' (2019).
49 Caldwell, 'Prosecutor' (2013).
50 Duff, 'Discretion' (2017).
51 A detailed analysis of these models can be found in Heinze, *Procedure* (2014), 104 ff.

'logical legalism'[52] that values logical consistency more highly than individual justice.[53] 'Coordinate officialdom' is marked by lay people performing official duties, who belong to a 'single echelon of authority',[54] with a similar application to judicial authorities.[55] Damaška's second pair of procedural models refers to the notions of the state: the 'reactive state' and the 'activist state'. The task of the reactive state is limited to 'providing a supporting framework within which its citizens pursue their chosen goals'.[56] Proceedings in a reactive state are 'conflict solving',[57] which have the character of contests between two formally coequal disputants before a state official as the neutral decision-maker.[58] By contrast, in an activist state, state interests prevail over individual interests.[59] Proceedings in an activist state are not conflict-solving but 'policy implementing' – that is, the justice system is considered to be an instrument for implementing policies.[60] Thus, the adjudicator dominates the proceedings, and those proceedings have the character of an inquest.[61]

What conclusions can be drawn about the role of the prosecutor based on the existence of a conflict-solving or policy-implementing form of procedure? In a conflict-solving procedure, the proceedings are characterised by partisan interests.[62] Applied to criminal procedure, a pure conflict-solving model locates the conflict between the representatives of the victim and the alleged perpetrator, respectively.[63] As Damaška points out, 'as soon as the prosecutor is equipped with power to disregard the interests of the victim for the sake of broader concerns, the premises of adversarial arrangement are weakened: the proceedings no longer involve a clash of two partial (partisan) interests, but rather a clash between the aggregate interest of the state and the partisan interest of an individual'.[64] Of course, this does not mean that a prosecutor who

[52] Damaška, *Face of Justice* (1986), 23.
[53] *Ibid.*, 18–23.
[54] *Ibid.*, 16.
[55] *Ibid.*, 57.
[56] *Ibid.*, 73.
[57] *Ibid.*, 97.
[58] *Ibid.*, 73–80, 97–147.
[59] *Ibid.*, 87.
[60] *Ibid.*, 82, 84.
[14] *Ibid.*
[62] *Ibid.*, 103.
[63] *Ibid.*
[64] *Ibid.*

does not represent the victim – but the public at large[65] – precludes a conflict-solving form of procedure and necessitates a policy-implementing form of procedure. Rather, the conflict-solving form of procedure is retained if 'the interests of the state are treated by analogy as private interests, and the legal process cannot legitimately be used to promote the politics and values of government'.[66]

2 *Institutional Comparisons*

Despite some similarities, there are important differences between prosecutorial regimes in the United States, the UK and Germany.[67]

(a) The Prosecutor in the United States from an Institutional Perspective

In the United States, prosecution offices are organised at both the state and federal level. US attorneys – the federal prosecutors – belong to the executive branch and are part of the Department of Justice, headed by the Attorney General.[68] They are each appointed by the President, with the consent of the Senate, for a term of four years.[69] The fact that US attorneys are appointed by the President makes them 'probably more politically responsive'[70] than their elected district attorney counterparts in most state systems. In their respective districts, US attorneys prosecute federal crimes such as drug trafficking, organised crime, political corruption, tax evasion, fraud and bank robbery.[71] Even though they must act within the guidelines promulgated by the Department of Justice,[72] US attorneys retain considerable autonomy in practice.[73] There is no

65 A critical and more differentiated approach to the notion that the prosecutor represents the public or 'the people' provides Simonson, '"The People" in Criminal Procedure' (2019), 250 ff.

66 *Ibid.*, 104.

67 For a recent comparative study on the institutional differences and similarities between US, French and Canadian prosecutors, see Soubise and Woolley, 'Prosecutors and Justice' (2018), 587, 590–1.

68 Gilliéron, *Public Prosecutors* (2014), 65; Barkow, 'Prosecutorial Administration' (2013), 276 ff.

69 28 USC § 541.

70 Sklansky, 'Prosecutors' (2018), 451–9.

71 Title 18 of the USC.

72 See e.g. USAM.

73 Gilliéron, *Public Prosecutors* (2014), 66; Boerner, 'Prosecution in Washington State' (2012), 167.

national police force in the United States. Instead, police are organised on a state and local level, and thus they do not play a significant role in determining how a federal prosecution proceeds.[74]

At the state level, the prosecution system in the United States is decentralised.[75] Each smaller political unit (city or county) has its own prosecutor's office, a hierarchical agency organised under its own auspices.[76] The head of a district attorney's office is the district attorney, or chief prosecutor, who does not report to any state-wide hierarchy.[77] The district attorney is responsible for the internal organisation of the office.[78] He or she also establishes – with wide discretion – certain prosecution policies.[79] Complaints about acts and decisions made by assistant district attorneys are handled internally: they may be directed to the district attorney, who will often initiate a review of the incident.[80]

District attorneys are either elected or appointed.[81] The United States is the only nation which elects prosecutors.[82] Beginning in the mid-nineteenth century, US states began changing their constitutions to allow the public to elect prosecutors, rather than having them appointed by governors or other state officials.[83] Many US states prefer local political control[84] over judicial and bureaucratic supervision, as is the preference in other jurisdictions.[85] Thus, prosecutors in the United States are ultimately accountable to the public. These 'democratic impulses'[86] arguably caused the advocates of elected prosecutors to overlook the potential for prosecutors to be affected by 'untoward political influences'.[87] Yet states

[74] Gilliéron, *Public Prosecutors* (2014), 73.
[75] *Ibid.*, 69.
[76] Gramckow, 'Prosecutor' (2008), 390; Gilliéron, *Public Prosecutors* (2014), 69.
[77] Gilliéron, *Public Prosecutors* (2014), 70–1.
[78] There are no rules or regulations for this matter, see *ibid.*, 70.
[79] Gramckow, 'Prosecutor' (2008), 392–3; Gilliéron, *Public Prosecutors* (2014), 70–1.
[80] Gramckow, 'Prosecutor' (2008), 396; See American Bar Association, *Standards* (2008); see also Gilliéron, *Public Prosecutors* (2014), 70.
[81] See Damaška, 'Structures of Authority' (1975), 480, 512; see also Tonry, 'Penal Policies' (2007), 35.
[82] See Damaška, 'Structures of Authority' (1975), 480, 512; see also Tonry, 'Penal Policies' (2007), 35; Lippke, 'Criminal Prosecutors: Experts or Elected Officials?' (2014), 163 ff. As of May 2019, there are roughly 2,400 elected prosecutors across the United States, see American Civil Liberties Union (ACLU), 'Unlocking the Black Box' (2019), 2.
[83] Scalia, *State Constitutions* (1999), 6–9.
[84] Ellis, 'Elected Prosecutor' (2012), 1528–58.
[85] Pizzi, 'Prosecutorial discretion' (1993), 1325–73; Sklansky, 'Prosecutors' (2018), 451, 459.
[86] Ellis, 'Elected Prosecutor' (2012), 1528–32.
[87] Stone, 'Law Improvement' (1924), 633, 636.

joining the United States after the mid-nineteenth century based their state constitutions on the constitutions of existing states, including the election of prosecutors,[88] and only Connecticut, Delaware, New Jersey and Rhode Island have retained appointed prosecutors.[89]

Police departments and prosecutors' offices are independent from each other; the police are not accountable to the prosecutor.[90] It is the police who control both the investigation and arrest aspects of a criminal prosecution.[91] This means that decisions about which crimes are investigated and who is arrested rest entirely under the police's discretion.[92] A case only receives the attention of a prosecutor once the investigation phase is complete.[93] He or she may sometimes receive a case only after the charges have been filed, depending on state jurisdiction.[94] It is generally not possible for private citizens to initiate criminal prosecutions.[95] However, many states provide exceptions to this rule. In Pennsylvania, for instance, a private citizen may issue a private complaint and submit it 'to an attorney for the Commonwealth, who shall approve or disapprove it without unreasonable delay'.[96] In several states, the prosecutors' offices accept – and even solicit – contributions from the private sector for a variety of purposes, including financing certain prosecutions.[97]

[88] See e.g. Utter and Spitzer, *Washington State Constitution* (2002).

[89] Jacoby, 'American Prosecutor' (1997), 12, 25, 28.

[90] One exception is the state of New Jersey (Gramckow, 'Prosecutor' (2008), 417). See generally Gilliéron, *Public Prosecutors* (2014), 74.

[91] Gilliéron, *Public Prosecutors* (2014), 74.

[92] Harris, 'Interaction' (2011), 54–5; McDonald et al., 'Relations' (1982), 46; Weigend, *Anklagepflicht* (1978), 111–13.

[93] Gilliéron, *Public Prosecutors* (2014), 74.

[94] *Ibid.*, adding, however: 'There are also jurisdictions in which the prosecutor must first give his permission, if a felony is to be charged by the police, whereas for misdemeanors, prior consultation with the prosecutor is usually not required.'

[95] *Linda R.S.* v. *Richard D.*, 410 US 614 (1973) ('in American jurisprudence . . . a private citizen lacks a judicially cognizable interest in the prosecution or nonprosecution of another'); *Smith* v. *Kreiger*, 389 Fed. Appx. 789 (10th Cir. 2010), ruling that the private citizen 'has no right to initiate a criminal prosecution in the name of the United States under the Ninth or Tenth Amendments, or otherwise'. See also Cardenas, 'Prosecutorial Process' (1986), 374: 'Courts generally grant the public prosecutor the exclusive power to initiate criminal proceedings.'

[96] Rule 506 of the Pennsylvania Rules of Criminal Procedure, available at www.pacode.com/secure/data/234/chapter5/s506.html. For a comprehensive list of states that allow for a limited private complaint, see Welty, 'Private Citizens Initiating Criminal Charges' (2015).

[97] Kennedy, 'Private Financing' (1996), 665 ff.

In the US systems, the prosecutor – although created under French, English and Dutch influence[98] – enjoys full discretion over whether or not to prosecute,[99] whether to accept or decline a case and, on occasion, whether an individual should be arrested in the first place.[100] The prosecutor decides whether and how to engage in plea negotiations.[101] US prosecutors also determine all aspects of pre-trial and trial strategy; and very often, 'they essentially decide the punishment that will be imposed upon conviction'.[102] In many cases, there is neither an external nor an internal review.[103] As Luna and Wade summarise: 'For all intents and purposes, he makes the law, enforces it against particular individuals, and adjudicates their guilt and resulting sentences.'[104] In that sense, the role of US prosecutors – as is the case in Germany – includes elements both of law enforcement and adjudication.[105] The result of such broad discretion is that US district attorneys can establish policies 'that best respond to the needs of their jurisdictions and their budgets'.[106] This has been both welcomed and criticised.[107] It has been welcomed because it makes the prosecutor more flexible, especially by following a policy of not prosecuting certain misdemeanour violations, or having a policy of pursuing certain crimes leniently. A prosecutor can also implement a strategy of community-oriented prosecution,[108] attempting to facilitate

98 Albonetti, 'Discretion' (1987), 291; Romero, 'Profit-Driven Prosecution' (2017), 161, 169.

99 Safferling, *Criminal Procedure* (2001), 175; Cummings, 'Ethical Prosecutor' (2010), 2139, 2146; Davis, *Arbitrary Justice* (2007), 19 ff.; Luna and Wade, 'Prosecutors' (2010), 1413–15.

100 Luna and Wade, 'Prosecutors' (2010), 1413–15.

101 *Ibid.*

102 *Ibid.*

103 *Ibid.*

104 *Ibid.*

105 Sklansky, 'Prosecutorial Power' (2016), 473, 504.

106 Gilliéron, *Public Prosecutors* (2014), 70–1. See also Romero, 'Profit-Driven Prosecution' (2017), 161–212.

107 For a novel and instructive analysis of the impact wide prosecutorial discretion has on the 'stress' level of a prosecutor, see Na et al., 'Job-Related Stress among Prosecutors' (2018), 329–53. The authors conclude that the wide discretion 'can affect not merely the general well-being of individual prosecutors themselves, but also either directly or indirectly influence the lives of the accused, the victims, their families, or even the general public' (at 330).

108 See e.g. Goldkamp et al., *Community Prosecution* (2003); Gilliéron, *Public Prosecutors* (2014), 70–1. Crit. Simonson, '"The People" in Criminal Procedure' (2019), 253 ff., 271.

greater responsiveness to neighbourhood concerns.[109] Prosecutors' broad discretion in the establishment of policies raises concerns, however, considering that most district attorneys are elected. It may create incentives for prosecutors to adopt 'tough-on-crime' policies[110] in order either to reflect the will of their community, or to ensure their re-election. Yet in recent years, there have been several examples of prosecutors being elected on a platform of criminal justice reform, ushering in a new wave of criminal justice reform coming from within the prosecutors' own offices.[111]

(b) The Prosecutor in England and Wales from an Institutional Perspective

In England and Wales, the role of the Prosecution Service has evolved significantly since 1985 when the Prosecution of Offences Act (POA) 1985 established the Crown Prosecution Service (CPS),[112] which started operating in 1986.[113] While it was (practically)[114] the police who had the task to prosecute prior to 1985, that task passed over to the CPS, and the charging decision remained in the hands of the police,[115] before it transferred the case to the CPS, which then decided whether or not there was sufficient evidence and 'public interest' required a prosecution.[116] Since 1 April 2005, the decision-making process has been simplified by the Criminal Justice Act 2003. The police no longer have the power to charge (except in very minor cases),[117] and the CPS now lays all charges and acts 'as an advisory capacity to the police. Practically, this means that

109 Thompson, 'Prosecute' (2002), 321–72; Sklansky, 'Prosecutors' (2018), 451, 461.

110 See e.g. Rapping, 'American Prosecutor' (2012); Davis, *Arbitrary Justice* (2007); Bellin, 'Prosecutors' (2019), 208; Lynch, *Criminal Justice* (1998), 2117, 2136–7; Barkow, *Prosecutors* (2009), 869, 880.

111 E.g. avowed reformers of the criminal justice system have been elected as prosecutors in Baltimore, Philadelphia, Brooklyn, Mississppi and Louisiana, to name a few. See Sklansky, 'Political Landscape' (2017), 647; see also Sklansky, 'Democracy' (2017).

112 POA 1985, Chapter 23, available at www.legislation.gov.uk/ukpga/1985/23. See also Elliott and Quinn, *English Legal System* (2016), 432.

113 Elliott and Quinn, *English Legal System* (2016), 432.

114 Prosecutions were officially brought by private citizens, see Elliott and Quinn, *English Legal System* (2016), 432.

115 Slapper and Kelly, *English Legal System* (2017), 391. As an alternative to charging, the police could caution the person instead, without charging her or him, see Brants and Field, *Criminal Justice* (1995), 127, 130–1.

116 Fionda, *Public Prosecutors* (1995), 26.

117 Smart, *Criminal Justice* (2006), 69. The police may charge: '(i) any Summary Only offence (including criminal damage where the value of the loss or damage is less than

a CPS representative is located in most police stations to speed up the charging process.'[118] The CPS is headed by the Director of Public Prosecutions (DPP), who reports to the Attorney General.[119] It has fourteen regional teams for local prosecution,[120] each of which is headed by a Chief Crown Prosecutor.[121]

The CPS has the discretion to prosecute or to discontinue cases.[122] A two-stage test is applied: an evidential sufficiency test and a public interest test. The Prosecution 'must be satisfied that there is sufficient evidence to provide a realistic prospect of conviction against each suspect on each charge'.[123] The test of a 'realistic prospect of conviction' is an objective one – namely, 'that an objective, impartial and reasonable jury or bench of magistrates or judge hearing a case alone, properly directed and acting in accordance with the law, is more likely than not to convict the defendant of the charge alleged. This is a different test from the one that the criminal courts themselves must apply. A court may only convict if it is sure that the defendant is guilty' (ss. 4.6 and 4.7 of the Code for Crown Prosecutors). Furthermore, in relation to the public interest test, 'prosecutors must go on to consider whether a prosecution is required in the public interest'[124] – the *fons et origo* of that test is a statement of Lord Shawcross in a House of Commons debate in 1951: 'It has never been the rule in this country – I hope it never will be – that suspected criminal offences must automatically be the subject of prosecution.' He added that

£5000) irrespective of plea; (ii) any offence of retail theft (shoplifting) or attempted retail theft irrespective of plea provided it is suitable for sentence in the magistrates' court; and (iii) any either way offence anticipated as a guilty plea and suitable for sentence in a magistrates' court'; see Guidance to Police Officers and Crown Prosecutors Issued by the Director of Public Prosecutions under s. 37A of the Police and Criminal Evidence Act 1984 (revised arrangements), para. 15 with qualifications, available at www.cps.gov.uk/legal-guidance/charging-directors-guidance-2013-fifth-edition-may-2013-revised-arrangements.

118 Smart, *Criminal Justice* (2006), 68.

119 Elliott and Quinn, *English Legal System* (2016), 432.

120 CPS, *Annual Report and Accounts 2017–2018 (for the period April 2017 – March 2018)*, 4, available at www.cps.gov.uk/sites/default/files/documents/publications/CPS-Annual-Report-2017-18.pdf.

121 *Ibid.*

122 Marsh, *Criminal Justice* (2004), 166–7; Davies, Croall and Tyrer, *Criminal Justice* (2005), 188; Spencer, 'Introduction' (2002), 142, 161; see also – and importantly – the Code for Crown Prosecutors. There are many non-CPS prosecuting authorities in England and Wales that deal mainly, although not exclusively, with less serious and regulatory offences, see Lewis, 'Prosecution' (2006), 151–2.

123 s. 4.5 of the Code for Crown Prosecutors.

124 *Ibid.*, s. 4.11

there should be a prosecution 'wherever it appears that the offence or the circumstances of its commission is or are of such a character that a prosecution in respect thereof is required in the public interest'.[125] The more serious the offence or the offender's record of criminal behaviour, the more likely it is that a prosecution will be required in the public interest.[126] The nearly unlimited power of US prosecutors is not mirrored in the English and Welsh context.[127] Moreover, in 2013, a Victims' Right to Review Scheme was introduced.[128] This scheme 'makes it easier for victims to seek a review of a CPS decision not to bring charges or to terminate all proceedings'.[129] The establishment of the Scheme was prompted by the judgment in *R* v. *Christopher Killick*, where the Court of Appeal concluded that victims have a right to seek a review in certain circumstances,[130] referring to Article 10 of Directive 2012/29/EU of the European Parliament and the Council of 25 October 2012 establishing minimum standards on the rights, support and protection of victims of crime, and replacing Council Framework Decision 2001/220/JHA.[131] Prior to the introduction of the Scheme, the victim could only make a complaint about the level of service received from the CPS, or seek judicial review of the CPS's decision.

Furthermore, prosecutions can still be 'instituted and conducted other than by the Service', pursuant to section 6 of the Prosecution of Offences Act 1985.[132] The term 'otherwise than by the Service' may include a private individual, but also a variety of other public bodies such as certain charitable bodies to protect animals and other vulnerable groups,[133] local authorities and the Financial Services Authority. They act as private

[125] House of Commons Debates, Volume 483, 29 Jan. 1951.

[126] s. 4.12 of the Code for Crown Prosecutors.

[127] Langbein, 'Prosecutorial Discretion' (1974), 439–41.

[128] CPS, Victims' Right to Review Scheme, Last updated: Jul. 2016, available at www.cps.gov.uk/legal-guidance/victims-right-review-scheme.

[129] *Ibid.*

[130] [2012] 1 Cr. App. R. 10, at 132.

[131] 'This Directive does not address the conditions of the residence of victims of crime in the territory of the Member States. Member States should take the necessary measures to ensure that the rights set out in this Directive are not made conditional on the victim's residence status in their territory or on the victim's citizenship or nationality. Reporting a crime and participating in criminal proceedings do not create any rights regarding the residence status of the victim', see *ibid.*

[132] Large numbers of private prosecutions are launched by commercial organisations, Elliott and Quinn, *English Legal System* (2016), 437.

[133] *R (Virgin Media Ltd)* v. *Zinga* [2014] EWCA Crim. 52, [15].

individuals and sometimes under specific statutory powers.[134] The residual right to bring a private prosecution has been described as being 'of questionable value, and can be exercised in a way damaging to the public interest'.[135] The major limitation to private prosecutions[136] is that the DPP has power to take over the conduct of the proceedings at any time[137] and in practice, this power is mostly used as a precursor to discontinuing the case.[138] The benefit of the private prosecutor is that these cases are often quicker and cheaper than civil claims, especially as there is a straightforward method for obtaining costs upon a conviction,[139] and compensation orders are also available. In one case in 2014,[140] Virgin Media Ltd successfully prosecuted one Mr Zinga for selling devices which evaded paying for subscription television services. As a result, the defendant was imprisoned for eight years.[141] The case is a perfect example of how far private prosecutions can go: the Court of Appeal confirmed that a private prosecutor was entitled to bring confiscation proceedings under the Proceeds of Crime Act 2002 even if it had no financial or personal interest in the outcome, and that it was appropriate for a private prosecutor to procure assistance from the police in return for a 'donation' to police funds.[142] The decision certainly leaves an aftertaste, provoking critique such as the (admittedly polemic) question asked by Leonard Leigh: 'Where is this

[134] *R* v. *Rollins* [2010] UKSC 39, [7]–[31]; now the Prudential Regulation Authority and the Financial Conduct Authority.

[135] *Jones* v. *Whalley* [2006] UKHL 41, [16], holding that it would be an abuse of process to bring a private prosecution after a defendant had accepted a caution: the victims should instead have challenged the lawfulness of the caution.

[136] See especially The Law Commission, *Consents to Prosecution Report*, LC255, 20 Oct. 1998, paras. 2.14–2.20, available at www.lawcom.gov.uk/project/consents-to-prosecution/.

[137] s. 6(2) POA.

[138] See now *R (Gujra)* v. *CPS* [2012] UKSC 52, [2013] 1 AC 484 on the CPS's extensive policy, such as requiring a 'reasonable prospect of success'; previously *DPP ex parte Duckenfield* [2000] 1 WLR 55.

[139] Practice Direction (Costs in Criminal Proceedings) 2015 [2015] EWCA Crim. 1568 consolidated with Amendment No. 1 [2016] EWCA Crim. 98, para. 2.6.1., available at https://www.judiciary.uk/wp-content/uploads/2016/04/pd-costs-in-crim-cases-2015-consolidated-with-amendment-no1.pdf.

[140] *R (Virgin Media Ltd)* v. *Zinga* [2014] EWCA Crim. 52; see also Leigh 'Private Prosecutors' (2014), 439.

[141] Virgin's estimated loss from the fraud had been £380 million.

[142] *R (Virgin Media Ltd)* v. *Zinga* [2014] EWCA Crim. 52.

process of creeping privatisation of criminal justice (the illegitimate child of financial stringency) to stop?'[143]

(c) The Prosecutor in Germany from an Institutional Perspective and Comparative Remarks

Germany's prosecution offices are assigned to the state-level Ministries of Justice and belong to the executive branch.[144] Thus, German prosecutors do not enjoy the constitutional protections judges do (see especially Art. 97 of the Basic Law that guarantees judicial independence). Quite the contrary, German prosecutors are civil servants and bound by instructions.[145] The German Constitutional Court has declared: 'Police forces and public prosecutors do not enjoy independence and cannot be expected – with regard to their investigatory powers and duties – to show the same strict neutrality as judges do.'[146]

The lowest-level prosecutors are the public prosecutors (*Staatsanwälte*). Their departmental leaders are the senior public prosecutors (*Oberstaatsanwälte*). Senior public prosecutors are supervised by the chief office prosecutor who serves as the director of a prosecution office (*Leitender Oberstaatsanwalt*). The chief office prosecutor reports to the highest prosecuting officer at the state level – the General Public Prosecutor (*Generalstaatsanwalt*).[147] The head of the prosecution service is the Minister of Justice.[148] While he or she is a political appointee appointed by the state's Minister-President and subject to pressure from other cabinet ministers as well as from their political party, prosecutors are career civil servants, protected from arbitrary dismissal after they

[143] Leigh 'Private Prosecutors' (2014), 444.

[144] Krey, *Criminal Procedure* (2009), 70.

[145] Krey, *Criminal Procedure* (2009), 70.

[146] German Constitutional Court, Judgment of 20 Feb. 2001, 2 BvR 1444/00, reported in *Neue Zeitschrift für Strafrecht* (2001), 382: 'Polizei und StA genießen aber keine Unabhängigkeit, und von ihnen kann – im Hinblick auf ihre Aufgabe, beim Verdacht von Straftaten den Sachverhalt zu erforschen (§§ 160 Absatz 1, 160 Absatz 2, 163 Abs. 1 StPO) – auch nicht, wie vom Richter, strikte Neutralität erwartet werden.' (Translation by A. H.). Similarly, the Court of Justice of the EU (Grand Chamber) recently held German prosecutor's offices 'are exposed to the risk of being subject, directly or indirectly, to directions or instructions in a specific case from the executive, such as a Minister for Justice' and therefore do not count as 'issuing judicial authority' within the meaning of Article 6(1) of Framework Decision 2002/584, see EU Court of Justice, Judgment of 27 May 2019 in Joined Cases C-508/18 and C-82/19 PPU, para. 90. Crit. Ambos, 'Case Comment' (2019), 732 ff.

[147] About the structure in detail see Boyne, *Prosecution* (2014), 35–6.

[148] Beining, 'Die Weisung an den Staatsanwalt' (2015), 547.

complete a period of probationary service.[149] An exception to that rule exists in four states, where the General Public Prosecutor is a political appointee, serving in collaboration with the Minister of Justice.[150] German law assigns the prosecution service auxiliary police officers (*Ermittlungspersonen/Hilfsbeamte der Staatsanwaltschaft*, § 152 of the Law on Judicial Organisation, *Gerichtsverfassungsgesetz* (GVG)) with special powers and a closer relationship to the prosecution.[151]

Prosecutors are required by statute to implement the orders of their superiors. Moreover, because political responsibility for the prosecution service is vested in the Ministry of Justice, the Minister may issue general rules and regulations that seek to guide prosecutorial decision-making.[152] As Boyne describes: 'In his or her capacity as a member of the federal state's governing party, the Minister possesses an external right of instruction (*externes Weisungsrecht*) – a general right to instruct the General Public Prosecutor in broad terms regarding how cases should be handled.'[153] However, prosecutors are protected from hierarchical interference by the legality principle (see below), which demonstrates an 'affinity' for the judicial branch.[154] Thus, the Minister may not instruct a prosecutor to file charges against an innocent person nor dismiss charges that are supported by a sufficient factual basis. Nevertheless, there is of course a practice of issuing informal instructions to prosecutors.[155] As Boyne summarises: 'The fact that the Minister of Justice is a political figure charged with following their party's mandate, on paper, poses an existential threat to prosecutorial objectivity.'[156] Even if we ignore concerns about improper influence in individual cases, it is readily apparent that the policies developed at the top of the prosecutorial chain of command influence the delivery of justice on the front lines.

In Germany, pursuant to § 153 StPO, the Prosecution can terminate the proceedings when the offence is considered minor and when there is

149 Boyne, *Prosecution* (2014), 98.
150 Boyne, *Prosecution* (2014), 100.
151 Jehle and Wade, *Justice Systems* (2006), 227; Juy-Birmann, 'German System' (2002), 300.
152 Boyne, *Prosecution* (2014), 36.
153 *Ibid.*
154 See Begründung zum Gesetzesentwurf der Bundesregierung, Bundestagsdrucksache, a print of draft laws, major and minor interpellations, opinions and memorials of the German Bundestag that is distributed amongst the members of the Bundestag, Bundesrat and the governmental departments ('BT-Drs') 16/12310, 17; Fischer, 'Absprache-Regelung' (2009), 181. In more detail below Section III.3.(b). About the 'affinity' for the judicial branch, see Volk and Engländer, *Grundkurs StPO* (2018), mn. 13.
155 Boyne, *Prosecution* (2014), 37.
156 *Ibid.*, 98–9.

no 'public interest' in launching a prosecution. However, with the exception of the most trivial cases, the prosecutor needs judicial approval to discontinue the investigation. Moreover, the principle of legality (*Legalitätsprinzip*) compels the Prosecution to investigate, prosecute and indict any offence for which sufficient evidence exists (§§ 160(1), 152(2) StPO). Control over whether to continue or discontinue a prosecution is exercised by an investigating magistrate in some countries,[157] while in other systems this prerogative lies with a pre-trial judge[158] and sometimes with the trial judge in a pre-trial hearing or pre-trial review.[159]

Interestingly, the German legal system allows a victim to first lodge a complaint with the prosecutor's superior against a decision of that prosecutor and ultimately appeal to a judge to compel the prosecution to file an indictment (*Klageerzwingungsverfahren* (§§ 172 ff. StPO)).[160] This is a conflict-solving element, since the victim – as the original party vis-à-vis the offender – has an instrument to start the conflict himself or herself.[161] In the Netherlands, the 'person directly involved' can lodge an appeal with the court against the prosecutor's decision not to prosecute.[162] The 'person directly involved' has a twofold meaning, referring to both the victim (the natural person) and the legal person promoting an interest that would be directly affected by the decision not to prosecute.[163] Moreover, some legal systems incorporate private prosecutions into their procedural rules[164] – an instrument that mirrors the conflict-solving ideal to a great extent. This means that the aggrieved party may either prosecute minor offences without the mandatory participation of the public prosecutor[165] or participate as a kind of auxiliary (second) prosecutor with full procedural rights.[166] As

157 E.g. in France, see Guinchard and Buisson, *Procédure Pénal* (2008), 206; Thaman, *Procedure* (2002), 21 ff.

158 E.g. as is the case in the United States, see Kamisar et al., *Criminal Procedure* (2008), 13 ff.; for South Africa and Italy (*guidice dell'udienza preliminare*) see Thaman, 'Rechtsvergelijking' (2007), 1, 4, with fn. 20.

159 In Germany, Roxin and Schünemann, *Strafverfahrensrecht* (2017), § 42; in Poland, see Grajewski, *Przebieg procesu karnego* (2008), 162 ff.

160 Roxin and Schünemann, *Strafverfahrensrecht* (2017), § 41; Volk and Engländer, *Grundkurs StPO* (2018), 114. For the Spanish *acusación particular* see Cancio, 'Erledigung von Strafverfahren' (2018), 478.

161 Cf. Damaška, *Face of Justice* (1986), 103.

162 Groenhuijsen and Simmelink, 'Criminal Procedure' (2008), 462.

163 E.g. an animal protection society who appeals against non-prosecution of a case of cruelty to animals, see Groenhuijsen and Simmelink, 'Criminal Procedure' (2008), 462.

164 Regarding Poland, see Grzegorczyk and Tylman, *Polskie Postępowanie Karne* (2007), 702.

165 E.g. in Roxin and Schünemann, *Strafverfahrensrecht* (2017), § 63.

166 E.g. in Poland, Germany, Spain; see Thaman, 'Rechtsvergelijking' (2007), 4.

previously described, in England this system was criticised as being 'of questionable value'.[167] This assessment could have been made by a lawyer originating from a legal system that favours policy-implementing elements of procedure. The same view is taken in Scotland where, while it is in theory possible for the victim to compel prosecution through private prosecution, this right has only been granted twice in the last century.[168]

A US prosecutor is under no legal duty to seek out exonerating evidence, in contrast with a German prosecutor.[169] In Germany, a prosecutor is under a duty to investigate both incriminating and exonerating evidence, as set out in § 160(2) StPO. The reason for this approach is the belief that state organs must seek the entire truth and behave in accordance with the rule of law.[170] This objective truth-seeking is a typical hierarchical feature.[171] A party in a contest model will carry out investigations to his or her own benefit, but may not collect evidence that diminishes his or her chances of winning a case. This was the reason why England and Wales introduced the CPS: before the introduction of the CPS, the police were both investigators and prosecutors. Several reports indicated that the function of an objective investigation for crime control conflicted with the interest of the prosecution as a party to the proceedings.[172] Moreover, it has been said that the 'anxiety to convict those whom the police believed were guilty' could lead to the abuse of the rights of the arrested person by the police.[173] Thus, in England, which in many respects leans towards the conflict-solving ideal,

167 See n. 135 above.

168 Sheehan et al., *Criminal Procedure* (2003), §§ 82, 84, 119.

169 In more detail Heinze, *Procedure* (2014), 263 with fn. 1223. There is, however, an obligation for US prosecutors to disclose exculpatory evidence if it is found in the course of their investigation, see Heinze, *Procedure* (2014), 322 ff. Unfortunately, we cannot go into the important issue of disclosure and discovery as it pertains to the role of the prosecutor. In fact, broad discovery is one of the greatest demands to prosecutors, voiced, inter alia, by the FJP, *21 Principles* (2018), 17–18. For more details, see Heinze, *Procedure* (2014). Recently: Jones, '*Brady* Disclosure Duty' (2018), 87; Crump, '*Brady* v. *Maryland*, Attorney Discipline, and Materiality' (2016), 515.

170 Schmitt, '§ 160' (2019), mn. 14; Safferling, *Criminal Procedure* (2001), 74.

171 Damaška, *Face of Justice* (1986), 160 ff.

172 See generally The Royal Commission on Criminal Procedure, *Prosecution* (1981), analysing the powers and duties of the police in relation to the responsibility to detect criminals in the course of interrogating suspected persons, to decide whether or not to prosecute persons suspected of criminal offences and to conduct themselves prosecutions for the less serious offences.

173 Davies et al., *Criminal Justice* (2005), 187–8.

the separation of the (investigating) police and the prosecuting agency is in line with the conflict-solving ideal.

3 *Prosecutorial Decision-Making*

(a) Official Decision-Making

When an individual is operating as an official, he or she may not rely on personal preferences as reasons for making a particular decision. Accordingly, the relevant goals cannot be (or at least cannot be limited to) those of the individual decision-maker. An official cannot make choices in his or her official capacity simply in order to remain in post, to obtain a raise, or garner public praise. The relevant considerations must be those of the institution. Discretionary powers are, in fact, 'conferred in order to serve and achieve certain ends and goals, and no matter how difficult they may be to discern, or no matter how vaguely they may be stated, officials must seek them out and direct their actions towards them in ways that are rational'.[174]

The main goals of a for-profit organisation, regardless of other discrete aims like scientific progress or bettering society, are economic. Governmental institutions must make decisions that take economic analysis into account, but their ultimate goals are not to make a profit. These entities may be aimed at the promulgation of regulations for an administrative agency, the completion of a tribunal's task, resulting in either acquittal or punishment for a criminal court, the imposition of damages or no damages for a civil court, or other kinds of outcomes for an administrative court. For all criminal justice systems, the broad goal of 'seeking justice'[175] is often propounded, but more particular understandings of what it means to seek justice could involve conflicting goals of, inter alia, deterrence, rehabilitation, retribution and community reconciliation. An official is required 'to find ways, if possible, of reconciling the apparent conflicts and, to the extent that this is impractical, to assign weights to the conflicting goals'.[176] Yet this process will still rely on some higher-order commitment to justice.

Maintaining the organisation itself should also be a primary goal of most governmental institutions, in that the public is better served by a well-functioning institution. Accordingly, a government institution

174 Galligan, *Discretionary Powers* (1990), 5.
175 See Zacharias, 'Ethics' (1991), 45 ff.
176 Gifford, 'Decisions' (1972), 9.

should take the goal of institutional legitimacy into account when making decisions, including both perceptions of legitimacy and normative legitimacy. It may be that an institution has succeeded in maintaining very high standards of procedural fairness, and that this is one way to understand the institution as achieving its goal of justice. However, if the institution is perceived as being substantively or distributively unjust, despite its normative legitimacy, the institution may suffer based on the perception of illegitimacy. Accordingly, there may be some situations in which an institution will be required to prioritise the goal of the continued existence of the institution, and will need to make decisions to improve public perceptions of justice. However, when discretion is given to individuals within an institution, like prosecutors, they may or may not be concerned about maintaining the legitimacy of the institution. Even if they are, prosecutors may only be concerned about maintaining their *own* legitimacy as an individual participant in the enterprise, and this goal may conflict with a longer-term concern for the overall legitimacy of the criminal justice system.

(b) Opportunity Principle vs. Legality Principle

The overburdening of our criminal justice systems has led to the introduction of 'consensual' forms in criminal procedure, where agreements are reached which obviate the need for a criminal trial.[177] In this respect, the principle of procedural economy has taken centre stage.[178] These measures include not only the charging process but also 'penal orders' (see below) and 'plea bargaining',[179] and they require the agreement of the accused. Apart from the divergent translations in different legal systems, this so-called 'negotiated justice' broadly[180] describes the 'negotiation and social interactions involved in the routine production of justice'.[181] Negotiated justice is found at all stages of criminal procedure: during the police investigation, at the prosecutorial decision to charge or not to charge (and of course post-charge) and during trial.

177 See Damaška, 'Criminal Procedure' (2001), 485; Frase and Weigend, 'Criminal Justice' (1995), 345. For more details, see Chapter 11 in this volume.

178 Thaman, 'Plea-Bargaining' (2007), 1.

179 For a detailed analysis see Ambos and Heinze, 'Abbreviated Procedures' (2017), 51 ff.

180 Others prefer a narrower interpretation, describing negotiated justice as 'a diarchic process of regulation which "consists in two persons or their representatives themselves seeking a solution to their conflict"': see Tulkens, 'Negotiated Justice' (2002), 641, fn. 4, taking recourse to (and translating) Faget, *Médiation* (1997), 12–3.

181 Carrabine et al., *Criminology* (2014), 333.

For the purposes of this chapter, we only refer to negotiated justice during the latter two stages; the police stage, albeit of great practical importance, is not the subject of our analysis. We also disregard the concept of discretion within the disclosure process and post-trial discretion.[182]

In addition to the search for truth,[183] prosecutorial discretion is influenced by the principles of legality (mandatory prosecution, *legalité de poursuites*) and opportunity (prosecutorial discretion, *opportunité des poursuites*).[184] These 'principles' need to be distinguished from the previously-mentioned policies and previously-discussed ethical obligations of prosecutors in decision-making. In the context of procedural discretion, they 'refer to fundamental, normative premises about prosecutorial decision-making that ideally underlie both prosecutorial policies and ad hoc decision making'.[185] Thus, some legal systems rest on the idea of 'legality' or 'compulsory/mandatory prosecution', whereby the relevant official agencies are expected to act on a formal standard when dealing with all breaches of criminal law which come to their knowledge.[186] In some countries, like Italy, the principle of legality (*principio di legalità*) is primarily related to the substantive (material) criminal law, and thus prohibits the punishment of a crime that was not explicitly punishable at the time it was committed.[187]

The (procedural) principle of legality is either subject to important exceptions or qualified by prosecutorial discretion.[188] Thus, most countries operate in practice on both legality and opportunity, tending either, in normative terms, more to the former (France,[189]

[182] See in detail Heinze, *Procedure* (2014), 322 ff.
[183] See above Sections I. and II.1.
[184] See in detail Ambos and Heinze, 'Abbreviated Procedures' (2017), 27, 32 ff.
[185] Green and Zacharias, 'Neutrality' (2004), 837, 843–4.
[186] See generally Kuczyńska, *Accusation Model* (2015), 94–106; Harding and Dingwall, *Diversion* (1998), 1. About the application of the principles of mandatory prosecution and discretion on the level of International Criminal Justice see Ambos, 'Justice System' (2016), 30; Kuczyńska, *Accusation Model* (2015), 106–11.
[187] Mantovani, *Diritto Penale* (2017), 3; however, there are procedural forms of the principle of legality in Italy, namely 'the principle of the legitimate judge' and the 'principle of legality'. On the distinction between legality in substantive and procedural law, see also Caianiello, 'Disclosure' (2010), 98.
[188] Harding and Dingwall, *Diversion* (1998), 1.
[189] The legality principle is included in the Constitution (Arts. 34 and 37), although criminal proceedings are mainly governed by the opportunity principle (Art. 40 Code de Procedure Penale). See further Mathias, *Procureurs* (1999); Beale, 'Prosecutorial Discretion' (2015), 27, 42 ('France does not recognise the principle of mandatory prosecution').

Germany,[190] Italy,[191] Spain,[192] Poland[193]) or to the latter (Belgium,[194] England,[195] Japan,[196] the Netherlands,[197] Norway[198] and the United States[199]). China is an example of one of the few legal systems where prosecutors have no discretion whatsoever as to the disposition of a case on the grounds of public interest considerations.[200]

Both the opportunity principle and the legality principle have advantages and disadvantages. The opportunity principle 'allows prosecutors to target resources for serious offences; it is effective against organised crime by facilitating charge-bargaining and opens up opportunities for diversionary[[201]] disposal of offenders'.[202] On the other hand, there is a danger of 'inappropriate government interference' and the risk of 'corrupt decision-making'.[203] While the legality principle does not share these disadvantages, when considered with the principle of full clarification of the facts, the legality principle can be seen as a luxury. In an overloaded criminal justice system it can result in 'a backlog of cases, which can impair the right to a fair and speedy trial'[204] and effectively impede alternative procedures that may expedite trial proceedings.[205] Consequently, it is said that criminal proceedings 'run more speedily in

[190] Here the principle of legality has even a constitutional status, see n. 153 above.

[191] Art. 112 of the Italian Constitution. Cf. Di Federico, 'Independence' (1998), 371–87; Panzavolta, 'Reforms' (2005), 591; Ruggeri, 'Discretion' (2015), 59–60, 65 ff.

[192] The legality principle is included in Art. 124 of the Constitution as well as in the Spanish Ley de Enjuiciamiento Criminal (LECrim, Art. 198); Bachmaier, 'Principle of Legality' (2015), 89–94.

[193] Kuczyńska, *Accusation Model* (2015), 103–6.

[194] Reydams, 'Jurisdiction' (2000), 183–216.

[195] Fionda, *Prosecutor* (2003), 14–64.

[196] Since its first Code of Criminal Procedure in 1880, the Japanese criminal justice system has been governed by the opportunity principle; cf. § 248 of the Japanese Code of Criminal Procedure ('JCCP'); see Taguchi, 'Strafprozessrecht' (2008), 72.

[197] Some even say that the criminal justice system of the Netherlands is 'the least adversarial of the trial systems'; see Pizzi, *Trials* (1999), 94.

[198] *Ibid.*, 102.

[199] *Ibid.*, 104.

[200] Mou, 'Discretionary Power' (2015), 119.

[201] For a detailed analysis of 'diversion' see Ambos and Heinze, 'Abbreviated Procedures' (2017), 27, 77 ff. Furthermore, 'Make Diversion the Rule' is also a recent demand for prosecutors by the FJP. See FJP, *21 Principles* (2018), 4.

[202] Vogler and Huber, *Criminal Procedure* (2008), 25; see also Kuczyńska, *Accusation Model* (2015), 94.

[203] Kuczyńska, *Accusation Model* (2015), 94.

[204] *Ibid.*

[205] Fezer, 'Inquisitionsprozess' (2010), 177.

England than they do in continental Europe'.[206] Notwithstanding this criticism, legality sometimes possesses an almost sacred status, as it does in Germany, since it is intimately related to the search for material truth.[207] The 'pure' German doctrine would perhaps even accept the 'collapse' of the criminal justice system before renouncing this principle,[208] ignoring the fact that other continental systems are likewise overloaded.[209] On the other hand, it is said that common law countries are forced to deal with a much higher risk of miscarriages of justice and substantive unfairness, especially wrongful convictions.[210] Some even say that the adversarial system in general, with its discretionary decision-making,[211] lends itself to wrongful convictions 'either by injecting error because of its inherent features' or by being 'inefficient in weeding out errors that arise during the investigation of crimes'.[212] Or, even worse: '[M]any false convictions result from the nature of the current adversarial system', whereby a divergence of 'enhanced accuracy' designed by the doctrine on the one hand and the reality on the other hand is significant.[213]

Of course, an abstract (alleged) nexus between wrongful convictions statistics and a particular procedural model should be treated with caution, since it risks oversimplification. Thus, Zalman's remark, 'A guilty defendant has a better chance of acquittal in a common law

206 Spencer, 'Introduction' (2002), 33.

207 Cf. Mittermaier, *Beweise* (1834), 48; Fezer, 'Inquisitionsprozess' (2010), 177.

208 The point is made Fezer, 'Inquisitionsprozess' (2010), 182.

209 Spencer, 'Introduction' (2002), 33.

210 *Ibid.* A statistical overview of the wrongful convictions in the United States in 2014 is provided in Jordan et al., 'Wrongful Conviction' (2016), 365–6. See also Slobogin, 'Lessons from Inquisitorialism' (2014), 709; Deiters, 'Abgekürzte Strafverfahren' (2018), 494. For an overview of the literature on wrongful convictions in the United States, see Nejdl and Pettitt, 'Wrongful Convictions' (2017), 401–19. Crit. on that literature and disputing the 'conventional wisdom' of high rates of wrongful convictions, Cassell, 'Wrongful Conviction Rate' (2018), 815 ff.; Thomas III, 'Innocents' (2018), 866 ff.

211 Damaška, *Face of Justice* (1986), 4.

212 See Zalman, 'Wrongful Conviction' (2008), 74. See also Yoffe, 'Innocence is Irrelevant' (2017).

213 Givelber, 'Acquittals' (1997), 1360; Innocence Commission for Virginia, *Vision for Justice* (2005), xvi identified eight factors found to 'underlie' the wrongful convictions that preceded eleven exonerations: mistaken eyewitness identification, suggestive identification procedures, police tunnel vision, antiquated forensic testing, inadequate assistance of defence counsel, failure to disclose exculpatory evidence, high pressure interrogation with vulnerable suspects and inconsistent or suspicious statements by the defendant.

court whereas an innocent would fare better in a continental court',[214] does not mean that innocent people are not convicted in Continental courts. Instead it demonstrates that the procedural model has an influence on the attitude of the legal system's protagonists – regardless of certain procedural rules. For instance, when Italy introduced adversarial elements into its procedural code in 1988, both judges and prosecutors retained the style of legal thought that was known to a hierarchical and policy-implementing setting. The result was, as Elisabetta Grande describes it:

> that the transplant ended up being little more than an acoustic imitation, in which the mixture of the new 'adversarial' elements with the old non-adversarial ones produced effects diametrically opposed to those expected: the defendant in the Italian legal system is today less protected against abuses of power than he was prior to the introduction of common law adversarial elements.[215]

(c) Abbreviated Criminal Proceedings and the Paramount Role of the Prosecutor

At the end of the nineteenth century, a well-equipped judiciary, at least in Germany, experienced no problems handling the cases entering the system.[216] Nowadays, however, it is generally acknowledged that justice works slowly, as there are 'simply too many offences, too many offenders, and too few resources to deal with them all'.[217] Similarly, the number of cases in US lower criminal courts have increased substantially, 'overwhelming prosecutors, defenders, and judges',[218] due to policies like over-policing.[219] As a consequence, populations increasingly lose confidence in the criminal justice system and its operators. One response has been the introduction of measures and methods to lower trial costs and expedite criminal trials.[220] A common theme of these expedited trials is the leading role of public prosecutors in such proceedings. As Gilliéron notes, 'prosecutors in both the US and Europe have gradually slipped

[214] Zalman, 'Wrongful Conviction' (2008), 79.
[215] Grande, 'Italian Criminal Justice' (2000), 232, footnote omitted.
[216] Fezer, 'Inquisitionsprozess' (2010), 178.
[217] Goldstein, 'Guilty Pleas' (1997), 169.
[218] Howell, *Discretion* (2014), 290.
[219] *Ibid.*
[220] As suggested by Jehle, 'Public Prosecution' (2006), 6. A current debate in Germany revolves around the reform of abbreviated proceedings, initiated through the so-called 'Alternativ-Entwurf Abgekürzte Strafverfahren im Rechtsstaat' [Alternative Draft for Abbreviated Criminal Trials within the confines of the Rule of Law, translation A. H.] in Bommer et al., 'Alternativ-Entwurf' (2019), 1–128; Schmoller, 'Einvernehmliche Verurteilung' (2019), 270–81.

into the role of decision-makers'.[221] In fact, prosecutors in some instances may act as the sole adjudicator of the criminal case.[222]

The discretion afforded to US prosecutors throughout the criminal justice process has already been discussed, as has the influence of the opportunity principle within US criminal procedure and how it provides numerous opportunities for prosecutorial decision-making. The increasing need for curtailed criminal proceedings, however, has expanded the decision-making role of prosecutors to jurisdictions governed by the legality principle. Three ways of curtailing proceedings through a dominating role of the prosecutor deserve special attention: the charging decision, plea bargaining and the penal order. Since charging and plea bargaining are dealt with elsewhere in this volume by Jenia Turner and Thomas Weigend (see Chapter 11), the focus shall be – *exempli gratia* – on the practically relevant concept of penal orders.

There is a manifest similarity between what is known in the United States as the guilty plea and in Germany as the penal order.[223] According to a general and prefatory definition, a penal order can be seen as a 'written proposal by the state to a defendant stipulating the crime committed and the penalty to be levied if the defendant does not object'.[224] In countries like Germany,[225] France[226] and Italy[227] the penal order may be used in cases sanctioned by fines, which practically applies to misdemeanours (such as traffic or shoplifting offences) in most cases.[228] Furthermore, the penal order may also be used in cases of imprisonment of up to six months in Italy,[229] up to one year in Germany,[230] up to five years in Luxembourg,[231] up to six years in the Netherlands[232] and up to ten years in Poland.[233]

221 Gilliéron, *Public Prosecutors* (2014), 322.
222 *Ibid.* See also Langer, 'Prosecutorial Adjudication' (2006), 248 ff.
223 Langbein, 'Prosecutorial Discretion' (1974), 439, 456. See in detail Ambos and Heinze, 'Abbreviated Procedures' (2017), 27, 49 ff.
224 Felstiner, 'Plea Contracts' (1979), 309.
225 Roxin and Schünemann, *Strafverfahrensrecht* (2017), § 68 mn. 1; Deiters, 'Abgekürzte Strafverfahren' (2018), 492, 505.
226 Bouloc and Matsopoulou, *Droit pénal* (2016), 515 ff.; Beale, 'Prosecutorial Disrection' (2015), 27, 42.
227 See Corso, 'Italy' (2000), 254.
228 Jehle, 'Fehlurteile' (2013), 220, 224.
229 See Corso, 'Italy' (2000), 254; the judge can reduce the sentence to half the minimum laid down by statute.
230 Roxin and Schünemann, *Strafverfahrensrecht* (2017), § 68 mn. 1.
231 Spielmann and Spielmann, 'Luxembourg' (2000), 276.
232 Vriend, *Avoiding a Full Criminal Trial* (2016), 53–4.
233 Waltoś, *Proces Karny* (2008), 300.

In Germany, the prosecutor may submit an application for a penal order at any time, even after the beginning of trial (§ 408a StPO). Generally speaking, this penal order will inform the defendant that he or she will receive a specified sentence for a specified crime unless he or she objects within two weeks,[234] in which case the matter will proceed to a normal trial before the appropriate court by a single professional judge.[235] The judge must issue the penal order if he or she has no substantial objections.[236] In practice, this means that judges grant virtually all applications for a penal order as a matter of course.[237] The requirement of the defendant's consent entails the possibility of bargaining between the defence and the prosecution over the specific fine to be imposed.[238]

Penal orders reflect even more prosecutorial power in France,[239] where the *juge de police* delivers a judgment without giving any reasons, without a hearing, and even without the presence of a defence lawyer.[240] Nearly the same procedural rules apply in Italy, where a penal order (*decreto penale*), regarded as a conviction, is issued upon request of the prosecutor, in the absence of the accused and without a trial.[241] Last but not least, a prosecutor's request for a penal order, without any hearing or debate, can also be made in Luxembourg (*ordonnance penale*).[242]

Needless to say, a penal order may not always be the appropriate answer to a crime. In France, inter alia, the public prosecutor may choose ordinary proceedings instead of a penal order for three reasons: first, if the facts present certain difficulties which can only be resolved in a hearing; secondly, if a fine is not regarded as sufficient punishment in a particular case;[243] and thirdly, if a case is referred to the *juge de police* by

[234] See Alschuler, 'Right to Trial' (1983), 956–7; Dannecker and Roberts, 'Criminal Procedure' (1996), 445–6.

[235] §§ 407, 409 StPO; Combs, 'Plea Bargaining' (2003), 41.

[236] Cf. §§ 408(3), 408a(2) StPO: *keine Bedenken*.

[237] Dubber, 'Plea Bargains' (1997), 559.

[238] Dubber, 'Plea Bargains' (1997), 559–60: 'In penal order bargains, the prosecutor may offer to initiate a penal order proceeding instead of filing the case in the single judge court, thereby limiting the defendant's maximum exposure to a suspended one year prison sentence.'

[239] The penal order procedure in France has existed since 3 Jan. 1972.

[240] Pradel, 'France' (2000), 130.

[241] Corso, 'Italy' (2000), 254.

[242] *Ibid.*, 276.

[243] Pradel, 'France' (2000), 130.

the public prosecutor's department, and he or she refuses to deal with the case by penal order, instead taking the view that a more severe sentence should be imposed.[244] Further, once the decision for a penal order is made, the accused is by no means bound to that decision, but instead can apply for a review of the order (*opposition*).[245] If he or she does so in France, his or her case will be publicly heard by the *juge de police* in an ordinary proceeding.[246] The accused can also oppose the penal order in Germany,[247] Italy (*opposizione*)[248] and Luxembourg.[249] He or she then risks, of course, a costly trial, potentially resulting in a more severe penalty in court.[250] In 2017, the German prosecution services applied for a penal order in 575,869 cases, and in 141,946 cases these orders were opposed.[251] That is roughly 25 per cent – a rather high number that indicates that the risks of going to trial are not so considerable in Germany to conclude that defendants are regularly pressured into plea bargaining. In Germany, a penal order might also be inappropriate whenever a full trial seems necessary for a full discovery of the facts or to further special or general prevention.[252] Both requirements are reflective of the role of the prosecutor who both aims at obtaining the truth and – a more consequentialist role – special and general prevention.[253]

244 *Ibid.*, 131.

245 Regarding France, within a month of notification of the order, *ibid.*, 131.

246 *Ibid.*, 131.

247 See above n. 224 ff. and main text.

248 But only if filed within fifteen days; he may also ask for summary, immediate trial (*patteggiamento*) or, if possible, financial settlement; see Corso, 'Italy' (2000), 254; Ruggeri, 'Discretion' (2015), 59, 71.

249 Van den Wyngaert, *Criminal Procedure* (2000), 276.

250 Frase and Weigend, 'German Criminal Justice' (1995), 345.

251 Statistisches Bundesamt, *Rechtspflege Strafgerichte*, Fachserie 10, Reihe 2.3, 2018, 15, 23, available at www.destatis.de/DE/Publikationen/Thematisch/Rechtspflege/GerichtePersonal/Strafgerichte21002 30177004.pdf?__blob=publicationFile.

252 No. 175(3), cl. 1 of the Guidelines for Criminal and Summary Proceedings (*Richtlinien für das Strafverfahren und das Bußgeldverfahren* (RiStBV)): 'Im Übrigen soll von dem Antrag auf Erlass eines Strafbefehls nur abgesehen werden, wenn die vollständige Aufklärung aller für die Rechtsfolgenbestimmung wesentlichen Umstände oder Gründe der Spezial- oder Generalprävention die Durchführung einer Hauptverhandlung geboten erscheinen lassen.' See generally Preuß, 'Strafbefehlsverfahren' (2017), 178.

253 For an explanation of the terms 'special prevention' and 'general prevention' see Ambos, *Treatise I* (2013), 68 ff. About the (alleged) tension between a search for truth according to § 244(2) StPO and the German form of a plea agreement (*Verständigung* § 257c StPO) see Gössel, 'Wahrheitsermittlung' (2015), 737–45.

IV Conclusion

Upon identifying the multiple roles of the prosecutor, we conclude that prosecutorial work is influenced by two role-related factors: role duality and role ambiguity.

As to the former, the prosecutor is expected to fulfil dual roles, and these are often in conflict. In sum, the duality unfolds as follows, exemplified by the prosecutor in the United States and Germany:

- *The prosecutor as the seeker of procedural or substantive justice*: in the United States, the criminal justice system is aimed at ensuring procedural justice, yet the prosecutor is also expected to seek substantive justice within the framework of procedural due process constraints. In Germany, the prosecutor is tasked with seeking the truth, or a substantively fair result.
- *The prosecutor as part of the executive branch or the judiciary*: in Germany, the prosecution service is a judicial organ of the executive branch. In the United States, at the federal level, prosecutors also belong to the executive branch. They are part of the Department of Justice. At the state level, however, district attorneys have a unique position compared to other jurisdictions: even though they belong to the executive branch, they are completely independent, and usually only responsible to their voters (and their ethical obligations).[254]
- *The prosecutor is led by the principle of mandatory prosecution or opportunity*: while a US prosecutor enjoys considerable discretion as to whether to prosecute, the German prosecutor is subject to the principle of legality. However, this domination is increasingly weakened by the opportunity principle in the face of an overloaded criminal justice system. This also has an impact on the prosecutor's role as a policy-implementer or conflict-solver. While in Germany the prosecutor is tasked with implementing the policy of the executive branch, the same might be true in the US system, considering that prosecutors are part of the executive branch. However, this role changes once we consider the concept of community-oriented prosecution.[255] Under this scheme, prosecutors are not just case processors and policy implementers, but instead they approach their role with the objective that 'the problems they attempt to solve should be the ones that matter to the communities that they serve'.[256]

[254] See also Gilliéron, *Public Prosecutors* (2014), 314.
[255] See n. 108 above.
[256] Thompson, 'Prosecute' (2002), 321–72. Sklansky, 'Prosecutors' (2018), 451, 461.

- *The prosecutor as impartial minister of justice and forceful advocate of the victim*: in conflict-solving procedures, the proceedings are characterised by partisan interests. In a pure conflict-solving (criminal) procedure, this conflict takes place between the representative of the victim and the alleged perpetrator. Strictly speaking, in a pure conflict-solving role, the prosecutor functions as the representative of the victim and mainly advocates for his or her interests. This, needless to say, is an ideal that is far from prosecutorial reality. In the United States, victims have no legal remedies to compel the prosecutor to initiate proceedings, and prosecutors have the unreviewable power to reject cases.[257] The German legal system, however, allows the victim to first lodge a complaint to the prosecutor's superior against a decision of that prosecutor and ultimately appeal to a judge to compel the prosecution to file an indictment (*Klageerzwingungsverfahren*). This is a conflict-solving element, since the victim – as the original party vis-à-vis the offender – has an instrument to start the conflict himself or herself. In England and Wales, until 1985, prosecutions were officially brought by private citizens. Prosecutions can still be 'instituted and conducted otherwise than by the Service [CPS]', pursuant to section 6 of the POA 1985.
- *Prosecutors as officers of the court with judicial functions and leaders of law enforcement*: to cope with the caseloads, both the German and the US system provide public prosecutors with an almost judicial role within abbreviated criminal proceedings. At the same time, German law assigns the prosecution service auxiliary police officers with special powers and a closer relationship with the prosecution. In the United States, however, the police are not accountable to the prosecutor.
- *A centralised and decentralised prosecution service*: both Germany and the United States are federal states and thus have a system of public prosecution that is decentralised. Within each state, each district has its own prosecutor's office with its own organisation.
- *The prosecutor as elected or appointed official*: in Germany, upon the proposal of the Minister of Justice and with the consent of the legislative chamber, the federal prosecutor general and federal prosecutors are appointed by the President of Germany. State prosecutors are appointed by the State Minister of Justice. US district attorneys, by contrast, are usually elected. Only US attorneys are appointed by the

[257] Gilliéron, *Public Prosecutors* (2014), 329.

President of the United States with the advice and consent of the Senate for a four-year term. In both instances, prosecutors are part of the executive branch, which consists of elected officials who are accountable to the public. The difference between the two jurisdictions is the nature of the accountability mechanism: while in the US citizens directly elect the district attorney, in Germany citizens vote for the party that nominates the government official who eventually appoints the prosecutors.

As noted above, prosecutorial work is influenced by two role-related factors: role duality and role ambiguity. We have provided examples of role duality. However, these dichotomies do not always unfold as cogently as we might want them to in order to perfectly assign prosecutorial roles to the conflict-solving or policy-implementing ideals. In fact, quite the opposite: more often than not, prosecutorial roles that seem clear cut prima facie are, upon closer consideration, blurred. The distinction between prosecutors as elected officials, directly accountable to the public, and appointed officials, indirectly accountable to the public, reveal the limitations of a role duality analysis.

We borrow from Sklansky and refer to this departure from clear role duality as 'role ambiguity'. This ambiguity is not an accident, but rather seems to be a tool for permitting a prosecutor to select and characterise his or her own roles. In other words: to increase prosecutorial discretion and – eventually – power, the roles of the prosecutor are left largely undefined. According to Sklansky, this has had the effect of, inter alia, allowing the criminal justice system 'to soften the edges of its purported commitments and to redirect its resources quickly and informally'.[258] At the same time, role ambiguity reduces transparency and accountability, and increases the opportunity for illegal prosecutorial acts of the prosecutor, such as non-disclosure of exculpatory evidence[259] and arbitrary prosecution.[260] This role ambiguity can be clarified if prosecutors have a means to identify and interpret rules, and Damaška's conflict-solving and policy-implementing models supply such a blueprint.

[258] Sklansky, 'Prosecutors' (2018), 451, 461; Sklansky, 'Prosecutorial Power' (2016), 473–520. See also Levine, 'Prosecutorial Discretion' (2006), 691–750; Parrillo, *Salary Revolution* (2013).

[259] In detail Heinze, *Procedure* (2014), 322 ff.

[260] Sklansky, 'Prosecutors' (2018), 451, 461.

Bibliography

Albonetti C. A., 'Prosecutorial Discretion', *Law and Society Review*, 21 (1987), 291–314.

Alexander L., 'Are Procedural Rights Derivative Substantive Rights?', *Law and Philosophy*, 17 (1998), 19–42.

Alschuler A. W., 'Courtroom Misconduct by Prosecutors and Trial Judges', *Texas Law Review*, 50 (1972), 629–735.

'Implementing the Criminal Defendant's Right to Trial', *University of Chicago Law Review*, 50 (1983), 931–1050.

Ambos K., *Treatise on International Criminal Law, I: Foundations and General Part*, Oxford University Press (2013).

'The International Criminal Justice System and Prosecutorial Selection Policy', in Ackerman B., Ambos K. and Sikirić H. (eds.), *Visions of Justice – Liber Amicorum Mirjan Damaška*, Berlin, Duncker & Humblot (2016), 23–55.

Ambos K., 'Case comment on EU Court of Justice, Judgment of 27 May 2019 in Joined Cases C-508/18 and C-82/19 PPU', *Juristenzeitung* (2019), 732–5.

Ambos K. and Heinze A., 'Abbreviated Procedures in Comparative Criminal Procedure', in Bergsmo M. (ed.), *Abbreviated Criminal Procedures for Core International Crimes*, Brussels, Torkel Opsahl Academic EPublisher (2017), 27–100.

American Bar Association, *Standards for Criminal Justice relating to Prosecutorial Investigations*, 3rd edn, Washington, DC, American Bar Association (2008).

American Civil Liberties Union, *Unlocking the Black Box – How the Prosecutorial Transparency Act Will Empower Communities and Help End Mass Incarceration* (2019), available at www.aclu.org/report/unlocking-black-box.

Anders R. P., 'Straftheoretische Anmerkungen zur Verletztenorientierung im Strafverfahren', *Zeitschrift für die gesamte Strafrechtswissenschaft*, 124 (2012), 374–410.

Aristotle, *The Nicomachean Ethics*, trans. Ross D. and Brown L., Oxford University Press (2009).

Armenian A. V., 'Selectivity in International Criminal Law', *International Criminal Law Review*, 16 (2016), 642–72.

Bachmaier L., 'The Principle of Legality, Discretionary Justice and Plea Agreements: The Practice in Spain', in Caianiello M. and Hodgson J. (eds.), *Discretionary Criminal Justice in a Comparative Context*, Durham, Carolina Academic Press (2015), 89–114.

Barkow R. E., 'Institutional Design and the Policing of Prosecutors: Lessons from Administrative Law', *Stanford Law Review*, 61 (2009), 869–921.

'Prosecutorial Administration: Prosecutor Bias and the Department of Justice', *Virginia Law Review*, 99 (2013), 271–342.

Beale S. S., 'Prosecutorial Discretion in Three Systems', in Caianiello M. and Hodgson J. (eds.), *Discretionary Criminal Justice in a Comparative Context*, Durham, Carolina Academic Press (2015), 27–58.

Bellin J., 'The Power of Prosecutors', *New York University Law Review*, 94 (2019), 171–212.

Boerner D., 'Prosecution in Washington State', in Tonry M. (ed.), *Prosecutors and Politics: A Comparative Perspective*, Chicago, Illinois, The University of Chicago Press (2012), 167–210.

Bommer F., Deiters M., Eser A., Frister H., Gleß S., Jahn M., Jung H., Meier B.-D., Rengier R., Roxin C., Schmoller K., Schöch H., Stuckenberg C.-F., Verrel T., and Weigend T. 'Alternativ-Entwurf Abgekürzte Strafverfahren im Rechtsstaat (AE-ASR)', *Goltdammer's Archiv für Strafrecht* 166 (2019), 1–128.

Bouloc B. and Matsopoulou H., *Droit pénal général et procédure pénal*, 20th edn, Paris, Sirey (2016).

Boyne S. M., *The German Prosecution Service*, Berlin, Springer (2014).

Brants C., Field S. and Jörg N., 'Discretion and Accountability in Prosecution: A Comparative Perspective on Keeping Crime out of Court', in Harding C., Fennell P. W. H., Jörg N. and Swart B. (eds.), *Criminal Justice in Europe: A Comparative Study*, Oxford, Clarendon Press (1995), 127–48.

Brink D. O., 'Some Forms and Limits of Consequentialism', in Copp D. (ed.), *The Oxford Handbook of Ethical Theory*, Oxford University Press (2006), 380–423.

Caianiello M., 'Disclosure before the ICC', *International Criminal Law Review*, 10 (2010), 23–42.

Caldwell H. M., 'The Prosecutor Prince: Misconduct, Accountability, and a Modest Proposal', Catholic University Law Review, 63 (2013), 51–101.

Cancio Meliá, M., 'Erledigung von Strafverfahren ohne Hauptverhandlung: erste Schritte in Spanien', *Zeitschrift für die gesamte Strafrechtswissenschaft*, 130 (2018), 476–90.

Cardenas, J., 'The Crime Victim in the Prosecutorial Process', *Harvard Journal of Law & Public Policy*, 9 (1986), 357–98.

Carrabine E., Cox P., Lee M., Plummer K. and South N., *Criminology: A Sociological Introduction*, 3rd edn, London, Routledge (2014).

Cassell P. G., 'Overstating America's Wrongful Conviction Rate?', *Arizona Law Review*, 60 (2018), 815–63.

Cassidy R. M., 'Character and Context: What Virtue Theory Can Teach Us about a Prosecutor's Ethical Duty to Seek Justice', *Notre Dame Law Review*, 82 (2006), 635–98.

Cicchini, M., 'Spin Doctors: Prosecutor Sophistry and the Burden of Proof', *University of Cincinnati Law Review*, 87 (2018), 489–521.

Combs N. A., 'Copping a Plea to Genocide: The Plea Bargaining of International Crimes', *University of Pennsylvania Law Review*, 51 (2003), 1–157.

Corso P., 'Italy', in Wyngaert C. van den (ed.), *Criminal Procedure Systems in the European Community*, 2nd edn, London, Butterworths (2000), 223–60.

Crump D., '*Brady* v. *Maryland*, Attorney Discipline, and Materiality', *Hofstra Law Review*, 45 (2016), 515–36.

Cummings L. P., 'Can an Ethical Person Be an Ethical Prosecutor?', *Cardozo Law Review*, 31 (2010), 2139–59.

Damaška M. R., 'Structures of Authority and Comparative Criminal Procedure', *Yale Law Journal*, 84 (1975), 480–544.

The Faces of Justice and State Authority, New Haven and London, Yale University Press (1986).

'Models of Criminal Procedure', *Zbornik Pravnog Fakulleta u Zagrebu*, 51 (2001), 477–516.

'What Is the Point of International Criminal Law?', *Chicago Kent Law Review*, 83 (2008), 329–65.

Dannecker G. and Roberts J., 'The Law of Criminal Procedure', in Ebke W. F. and Finkin M. W. (eds.), *An Introduction to German Law*, The Hague, Kluwer Law Internation (1996), 413–48.

Danner A. M., 'Enhancing the Legitimacy and Accountability of Prosecutorial Discretion at the International Criminal Court', *The American Journal of International Law*, 97 (2003), 510–52.

Davies M., Croall H. and Tyrer J., *Criminal Justice*, 3rd edn, London, Pearson Education Limited (2005).

Davis A. J., *Arbitrary Justice: The Power of the American Prosecutor*, Oxford University Press (2007).

Deiters M., 'Abgekürzte Strafverfahren', *Zeitschrift für die gesamte Strafrechtswissenschaft*, 130 (2018), 491–512.

Delmas-Marty M. and Spencer J. R. (eds.), *European Criminal Process*, Cambridge University Press (2002).

Dölling D., 'Über das Ziel des Strafverfahrens', in Fahl C., Müller E., Satzger H. and Swoboda S. (eds.), *Festschrift für Werner Beulke zum 70 Geburtstag*, Heidelberg, C. F. Müller (2015), 679–87.

Dubber M. D., 'American Plea Bargains, German Lay Judges, and the Crisis of Criminal Procedure', *Stanford Law Review*, 49 (1997), 547–72.

Duff R. A., Farmer L., Marshall S. and Tadros V., *The Trial on Trial, III: Towards a Normative Theory of the Criminal Trial*, Oxford, Hart (2007).

'Discretion and Accountability in Democratic Criminal Law', in Langer M. and Sklansky D. A. (eds.), *Prosecutors and Democracy: A Cross-national Study*, Cambridge University Press (2017), 1–8.

Dworkin R., *Taking Rights Seriously*, Cambridge, MA, Harvard University Press (1977).

Elliott C. and Quinn F., *English Legal System*, 17th edn, London, Pearson (2016).

Ellis M. J., 'The Origins of the Elected Prosecutor', *Yale Law Journal*, 121 (2012), 1528–69.

Esser R., *Auf dem Weg zu einem europäischen Strafverfahrensrecht*, Berlin, De Gruyter (2002).

Faget J., *La médiation: Essai de politique pénale*, Toulouse, Erès (1997).

Fair and Just Prosecution, *21 Principles for the 21st Century Prosecutor* (2018), available at www.brennancenter.org/sites/default/files/publications/FJP_21Principles_FINAL.pdf.

Federico G. di, 'Prosecutorial Independence and the Democratic Requirement of Accountability in Italy', *British Journal of Criminology*, 38 (1998) 371–87.

Felstiner W. L. F., 'Plea Contracts in West Germany', *Law and Society Review*, 13 (1979), 309–25.

Fezer G., 'Inquisitionsprozess ohne Ende? Zur Struktur des *neuen* Verständigungsgesetzes', *Neue Zeitschrift für Strafrecht*, 30 (2010), 177–85.

Fionda J., *Public Prosecutors and Discretion: A Comparative Story*, Oxford, Clarendon Press (1995).

Fischer T., 'Absprache-Regelung: Problemlösung oder Problem?', *Strafverteidiger Forum*, 5 (2009), 177–88.

'Einleitung', in *Karlsruher Kommentar zur Strafprozessordnung*, 8th edn, Munich, C. H. Beck (2019).

Franck T. M., *Fairness in International Law and Institutions*, Oxford University Press (1995).

Frase R. S. and Weigend T., 'German Criminal Justice as a Guide to American Law Reform: Similar Problems, Better Solutions?', *Boston College International and Comparative Law Review*, 18 (1995), 317–60.

Fuller L. L., *The Morality of Law*, New Haven, Yale University Press (1964).

Galligan D. J., *Discretionary Powers: A Legal Study of Official Discretion*, Oxford University Press (1990).

Gelsthorpe L. and Padfield N., 'Introduction', in Gelsthorpe L. and Padfield N. (eds.), *Exercising Discretion: Decision-Making in the Criminal Justice System and Beyond*, New York, Willian Publishing (2003), 1–28.

Geppert K., 'Zum "fair-trial-Prinzip" nach Art. 6 Abs. 1 Satz 1 der Europäischen Menschenrechtskonvention', *Juristische Ausbildung* (1992), 597–604.

Gifford D. J., 'Decisions, Decisional Referents, and Administrative Justice', *Law and Contemporary Problems*, 37 (1972), 3–48.

Gilliéron G., *Public Prosecutors in the United States and Europe*, Berlin, Springer (2014).

Givelber D., 'Meaningless Acquittals, Meaningful Convictions', *Rutgers Law Review*, 49 (1997), 1317–97.

Goldkamp J. S., Irons-Guynn, C. and Weiland D., *Community Prosecution Strategies*, US Department of Justice (2003), available at www.ncjrs.gov/pdffiles1/bja/195062.pdf.

Goldstein A. S., 'Converging Criminal Justice Systems: Guilty Pleas and the Public Interest', *Israel Law Review*, 31 (1997), 169–82.

Gollwitzer W., 'Art. 6 MRK: Internationaler Pakt über bürgerliche und politische Rechte vom 19. Dezember 1966', in Gollwitzer W. (ed.), *Menschenrechte im Strafverfahren: MRK und IPBPR*, Berlin, De Gruyter (2005), 37–60.

Gössel K. H., 'Wahrheitsermittlung', in Fahl C., Müller E., Satzger H. and Swoboda S. (eds.), *Festschrift für Werner Beulke zum 70. Geburtstag*, Heidelberg, C. F. Müller (2015), 737–45.

Gottfredson M. R. and Gottfredson D. M., *Decision Making in Criminal Justice: Toward the Rational Exercise of Discretion*, Berlin, Springer Science & Business Media (1988).

Grajewski J., *Przebieg procesu karnego*, 4th edn, Munich, C. H. Beck (2008).

Gramckow H., 'Prosecutor organization and operations in the United States', in Open Society Institute Sofia (ed.), *Promoting Prosecutorial Accountability, Independence and Effectiveness – Comparative Research*, Sofia, Open Society Institute Sofia (2008), 385–429.

Green B. A. and Zacharias F. C., 'Prosecutorial Neutrality', *Wisconsin Law Review* (2004), 837–904.

Groenhuijsen M. and Simmelink J. B., 'Criminal Procedure in the Netherlands', in Vogler R. and Huber B. (eds.), *Criminal Procedure in Europe*, Berlin, Duncker & Humblot (2008), 377–481.

Grzegorczyk T. and Tylman J., *Polskie Postępowanie Karne*, 6th edn, New York, Lexis Nexis (2007).

Guinchard S. and Buisson J., *Procédure pénal*, 4th edn. New York, Lexis Nexis (2008).

Harding C. and Dingwall G., *Diversion in the Criminal Process*, London, Sweet and Maxwell (1998).

Harris D. A., 'The Interaction and Relationship between Prosecutors and Police Officers in the US, and How this Affects Police Reform Efforts', in Luna E. and Wade M. (eds.), *The Prosecutor in Transnational Perspective*, Oxford University Press (2011), 54–66.

Heinze A., *International Criminal Procedure and Disclosure*, Berlin, Duncker & Humblot (2014).

Hodgson J., 'Conceptions of the Trial in Inquisitorial and Adversarial Procedure', in Duff R. A., Farmer L., Marshall S. and Tadros V., *The Trial on Trial, II: Judgment and Calling to Account*, Oxford, Hart (2006), 223–43.

Hollander-Blumoff, R., 'Fairness Beyond the Adversary System', *Fordham Law Review*, 85 (2017), 2081–95.

Howell K. B., 'Prosecutorial Discretion and the Duty to Seek Justice in an Overburdened Criminal Justice System', *Georgetown Journal of Legal Ethics*, 27 (2014), 286–334.

Hungerford-Welch P., *Criminal Procedure and Sentencing*, 7th edn, London, Routledge-Cavendish (2009).

Ingraham B. L., *The Structure of Criminal Procedure*, New York, Greenwood Press (1987).

Innocence Commission for Virginia, *A Vision for Justice: Report and Recommendations Regarding Wrongful Convictions in the Commonwealth of Virginia*, Arlington, Innocence Commission for Virginia (2005).

Jackson R. H., 'The Federal Prosecutor', *American Journal of Criminal Law and Criminology*, 31 (1940), 3–6.

Jacoby J. E., 'The American Prosecutor: From Appointive to Elective Status', *Prosecutor*, 31 (1997), 33–8.

Jehle J.-M., 'The Function of Public Prosecution within the Criminal Justice System', in Jehle J.-M. and Wade M. (eds.), *Coping with Overloaded Criminal Justice Systems: The Rise of Prosecutorial Power across Europe*, Berlin, Springer (2006), 3–25.

'Was und wie häufig sind Fehlurteile?', *Forensische Psychiatrie, Psychologie, Kriminologie*, 7 (2013), 220–9.

Jones C. E., 'Here Comes the Judge: A Model for Judicial Oversight and Regulation of the Brady Disclosure Duty', *Hofstra Law Review*, 46 (2018), 87–138.

Jordan G., Kaplan A. B., Beety V. and Findley K. A., 'Contemporary Perspectives on Wrongful Conviction: An Introduction to the 2016 Innocence Network Conference, San Antonio, Texas', *Hofstra Law Review*, 45 (2016), 365–71.

Juy-Birmann R., 'The German System', in Delmas-Marty M. and Spencer J. R. (eds.), *European Criminal Procedures*, Cambridge University Press (2002), 292–347.

Kamisar Y., LaFave W. R., Israel J. H., King N. J., Kerr O. S. and Primus E. B. (eds.), *Basic Criminal Procedure: Cases, Comments and Questions*, 12th edn, Eagan, Thomson West (2008).

Kant I., *Groundwork for the Metaphysics of Morals*, ed. and trans. Wood A. W., New Haven, Yale University Press (2002).

Kennedy J. E., 'Private Financing of Criminal Prosecutions and the Differing Protections of Liberty and Equality in the Criminal Justice System, *Hastings Constitutional Law Quarterly*, 24 (1996), 665–707.

Kreag J., 'Disclosing Prosecutorial Misconduct', *Vanderbilt Law Review*, 72 (2019), 297–352.

Krey V., *German Criminal Procedure*, Stuttgart, Kohlhammer (2009).

Kubicek T. L., *Adversarial Justice: America's Court System on Trial*, New York, Algora (2006).

Kuczyńska H., *The Accusation Model before the International Criminal Court*, Berlin, Springer (2015).

Langbein J. H., 'Controlling Prosecutorial Discretion in Germany', *University of Chicago Law Review*, 41 (1974), 439–67.

Langer M., 'Rethinking Plea Bargaining: The Practice and Reform of Prosecutorial Adjudication in American Criminal Procedure', *American Journal of Criminal Law*, 33 (2006), 223–99.

Levine K. L., 'The Intimacy Discount: Prosecutorial Discretion, Privacy, and Equality in the Statutory Rape Caseload', *Emory Law Journal*, 55 (2006), 691–750.

Lewis C., 'The Prosecution Service Function within the English Criminal Justice System', in Jehle J.-M. and Wade M. (eds.), *Coping with Overloaded Criminal Justice Systems*, Berlin, Springer (2006), 151–84.

Lippke R., 'Criminal Prosecutors: Experts or Elected Officials?', in Ryberg J. and Roberts J. (eds.), *Popular Punishment: On the Normative Significance of Public Opinion for Penal Theory*, Oxford University Press (2012), 163–82.

Luna E. and Wade M., 'Prosecutors as Judges', *Washington and Lee Law Review*, 67 (2010), 1413–532.

Lynch G. E., 'Our Administrative System of Criminal Justice', *Fordham Law Review*, 66 (1998), 2117–51.

McDermott Y., *Fairness in International Trials*, Oxford University Press (2016).

McDonald W. F., Rossman H. H. and Cramer J. A., *Police–Prosecutor Relations in the United States - Executive Summary*, Washington, National Institute of Justice, Georgetown University Law Center (1982).

McNaughton D. and Rawling P., 'Deontology', in Copp D. (ed.), *The Oxford Handbook of Ethical Theory*, Oxford University Press (2006), 424–58.

Mantovani F., *Diritto Penale, Parte Generale*, 10th edn, Milanofiori Assago, Wolters Kluwer (2017).

Markovits D., *A Modern Legal Ethics: Adversary Advocacy in a Democratic Age*, Princeton, NJ, Princeton University Press (2010).

Marmor A., *Interpretation and Legal Theory*, 2nd edn, Oxford, Hart (2005).

Marsh I., *Criminal Justice*, Abingdon, London, Routledge (2004).

Mathias E., *Les Procureurs du droit: de l'impartialité du ministère public en France et en Allemagne*, Paris, CNRS Éditions (1999).

May L., *Global Justice and Due Process*, Cambridge University Press (2011).

Mégret F., 'International Prosecutors: Accountability and Ethics', Leuven Centre for Global Governance Studies Working Paper No. 18 (2008).

'The Anxieties of International Criminal Justice', *Leiden Journal of International Law*, 29 (2016), 197–221.

Mittermaier C. J. A., *Die Lehre vom Beweise im deutschen Strafprozesse*, Darmstadt, Johann Wilhelm Heyer's Verlagshandlung (1834).

Mou Y., 'Beyond Legitimate Grounds: External Influences and the Discretionary Power Not to Prosecute in the People's Republic of China', in Caianiello M. and Hodgson J. (eds.), *Discretionary Criminal Justice in a Comparative Context*, Durham, Carolina Academic Press (2015), 115–40.

Na C., Choo T. and Klingfuss J. A., 'The Causes and Consequences of Job-Related Stress among Prosecutors', *American Journal of Criminal Justice*, 43 (2018), 329–53.

Nejdl C. S. and Pettitt K., 'Wrongful Convictions and Their Causes', *Northern Illinois University Law Review*, 37 (2017), 401–19

Nicolson D., 'Making Lawyers Moral? Ethical Codes and Moral Character', *Legal Studies*, 25 (2005), 601–26.

Panzavolta M., 'Reforms and Counter-Reforms in the Italian Struggle for an Accusatorial Criminal Law System', *North Carolina Journal of International Law and Commercial Regulation*, 30 (2005), 577–624.

Parrillo N. R., *Against the Profit Motive: The Salary Revolution in American Government, 1780–1940*, New Haven, Yale University Press (2013).

Peters K., *Strafprozeß*, Heidelberg, C. F. Müller (1985).

Pizzi W. T., 'Understanding Prosecutorial Discretion in the United States', *Ohio State Law Journal*, 54 (1993), 1325–73.

Trials without Truth, New York University Press (1999).

Pradel J., 'France', in Wyngaert C. van den (ed.), *Criminal Procedure Systems in the European Community*, 2nd edn, London, Butterworths (2000), 105–36.

Preuß T., 'Das Strafbefehlsverfahren', *Zeitschrift für das juristische Studium* (2017), 176–87.

Rapping J. A., 'Who's Guarding the Henhouse? How the American Prosecutor Came to Devour Those He Is Sworn to Protect', *Washburn Law Journal*, 51 (2012), 513–69.

Rawls J., *A Theory of Justice*, Oxford University Press (1972).

Justice as Fairness: A Restatement, Cambridge, MA, Harvard University Press (2001).

Reydams L., 'Universal Criminal Jurisdiction: The Belgian State of Affairs', *Criminal Law Forum*, 11 (2000), 183–216.

Rolinski K., 'Der Grundsatz der Unmittelbarkeit: Garant der Wahrheitsfindung?', in Esser R., Günther H.-L., Jäger C., Mylonopoulos C. and Öztürk B. (eds.), *Festschrift für Hans-Heiner Kühne*, Heidelberg, C. F. Müller (2013), 297–316.

Romero, M., 'Profit-Driven Prosecution and the Competitive Bidding Process', *Journal of Criminal Law and Criminology*, 107 (2017), 161–212.

Roxin C. and Schünemann B., *Strafverfahrensrecht*, 29th edn, Munich, C. H. Beck (2017).

Ruggeri S., 'Investigative and Prosecutorial Discretion in Criminal Matters: The Contribution of the Italian Experience', in Caianiello M. and Hodgson J. (eds.), *Discretionary Criminal Justice in a Comparative Context*, Durham, Carolina Academic Press (2015), 59–88.

Sacher M., 'Diskurstheorie als Legitimation für die Absprachen im Strafverfahren?', in Hefendehl R., Hörnle T. and Greco L. (eds.), *Festschrift für Bernd Schünemann zum 70. Geburtstag*, Berlin, De Gruyter (2014), 957–68.

Safferling C., *Towards an International Criminal Procedure*, Oxford University Press (2001).

International Criminal Procedure, Oxford University Press (2012).

Scalia L. J., *America's Jeffersonian Experiment: Remaking State Constitutions, 1820–1850*, Northern Illinois University Press (1999).

Schmitt B., 'Einleitung', in Meyer-Goßner L. and Schmitt B. (eds.), *Kommentar zur Strafprozessordnung*, 62nd edn, Munich, C. H. Beck (2019).

'§ 160', in Meyer-Goßner L. and Schmitt B. (eds.), *Kommentar zur Strafprozessordnung*, 62nd edn, Munich, C. H. Beck (2019).

Sheehan A. V. et al., *Criminal Procedure*, 2nd edn, Edinburgh, Lexis Nexis (2003).

Simonson J., 'The Place of "The People" in Criminal Procedure', *Columbia Law Review*, 119 (2019), 249–307.

Sklansky D. A., 'The Nature and Function of Prosecutorial Power', *Journal of Criminal Law and Criminology*, 106 (2016), 473–520.

'The Changing Political Landscape for Prosecutors', *Ohio State Journal of Criminal Law*, 14 (2017), 647–74.

'Unpacking the Relationship between Prosecutors and Democracy in the United States', in Langer M. and Sklansky D. A. (eds.), *Prosecutors and Democracy: A Cross-National Study*, Cambridge University Press (2017), 250–75.

'The Problems with Prosecutors', *Annual Review of Criminology*, 1 (2018), 451–69.

Slapper G. and Kelly D., *The English Legal System*, 18th edn, London, New York, Routledge (2017).

Slobogin S., 'Lessons from Inquisitorialism', *Southern California Law Review*, 87 (2014), 699–731.

Smart U., *Criminal Justice*, London, Sage Publications (2006).

Soubise L. and Woolley A., 'Prosecutors and Justice', *Fordham International Law Journal*, 42 (2018), 587–626.

Spencer J. R., 'Introduction', in Delmas-Marty M. and Spencer J. R. (eds.), *European Criminal Process*, Cambridge University Press (2002), 1–80.

Spielmann A. and Spielmann D., 'Luxembourg', in Wyngaert C. van den (ed.), *Criminal Procedure Systems in the European Community*, 2nd edn, London, Butterworths (2000), 261–78.

Stone H. F., 'Progress in Law Improvement in the United States', *American Bar Association Journal*, 10 (1924), 633–37.

Stuntz W. J., 'The Pathological Politics of Criminal Law', *Michigan Law Review*, 100 (2001), 505–600.

Swart B., 'Damaška and the Faces of International Criminal Justice', *Journal of International Criminal Justice*, 6 (2008), 87–114.

Taguchi M., 'Der Prozessgegenstand im japanischen Strafprozessrecht', *Zeitschrift für Internationale Strafrechtsdogmatik*, 2 (2008), 70–5.

Thaman S. C., *Comparative Criminal Procedure*, Cheltenham, Edward Elgar Publishing (2002).

'Plea-Bargaining, Negotiating Confessions and Consensual Resolution of Criminal Cases', *Electronic Journal of Comparative Law*, 11 (2007), 1–54.

'Nederlandse Vereniging voor Rechtsvergelijking', *Electronic Journal of Comparative Law*, 11 (2007), 1–54.

The Royal Commission on Criminal Procedure, *The Investigation and Prosecution of Criminal Offences in England and Wales*, London, Her Majesty's Stationary Office (1981).

Thomas G. C. III, 'Where Have All the Innocents Gone?', *Arizona Law Review*, 60 (2018), 865–90.

Thompson A. C., 'It Takes a Community to Prosecute', *Notre Dame Law Review*, 77 (2002), 321–71.

Tonry M., 'Determinants of Penal Policies', *Crime & Justice*, 36 (2007), 1–48.

Tuinstra T., *Defence Counsel in International Criminal Law*, Berlin, Springer (2009).

Tulkens F., 'Negotiated Justice', in Delmas-Marty M. and Spencer J. R. (eds.), *European Criminal Procedures*, Cambridge University Press (2002), 641–87.

Utter R. F. and Spitzer H., *The Washington State Constitution: A Reference Guide*, Oxford University Press (2002).

Vogler R. and Huber B. (eds.), *Criminal Procedure in Europe*, Berlin, Duncker & Humblot (2008).

Volk K. and Engländer A., *Grundkurs StPO*, 9th edn, Munich, C. H. Beck (2018).

Vriend K., *Avoiding a Full Criminal Trial*, The Hague, Asser, Springer (2016).

Waltoś S., *Proces Karny* [Penal Proceedings], 9th edn, Warsaw, Lexis Nexis (2008).

Weigend T., *Anklagepflicht und Ermessen. Die Stellung der Staatsanwalts zwischen Legalitäts- und Opportunitätsprinzip nach deutschem und amerikanischem Recht*, Baden-Baden, Nomos (1978).

'Should We Search for the Truth, and Who Should Do it?', *North Carolina Journal of International Law and Commercial Regulation*, 36 (2011), 389–416.

'A Judge by Another Name? Comparative Perspectives on the Role of the Public Prosecutor', in Luna E. and Wade M. (eds.), *The Prosecutor in Transnational Perspective*, Oxford University Press (2012), 377–391.

Welty J., 'Private Citizens Initiating Criminal Charges', *North Carolina Criminal Law*, 9 April 2015, available at https://nccriminallaw.sog.unc.edu/private-citizens-initiating-criminal-charges/.

Weßlau E., 'Wahrheit und Legenden: die Debatte über den adversatorischen Strafprozess', in Hefendehl R., Hörnle T. and Greco L. (eds.), *Festschrift für Bernd Schünemann zum 70 Geburtstag*, Berlin, De Gruyter (2014), 995–1018.

Yoffe, E., 'Innocence Is Irrelevant', *The Atlantic*, September 2017, available at www.theatlantic.com/magazine/archive/2017/09/innocence-is-irrelevant/534171/.

Zacharias F. C., 'Structuring the Ethics of Prosecutorial Trial Practice: Can Prosecutors Do Justice?', *Vanderbilt Law Review*, 44 (1991), 45–114;

Zalman M., 'The Adversary System and Wrongful Conviction', in Huff C. R. and Killias M. (eds.), *Wrongful Conviction: International Perspectives on Miscarriages of Justice*, Philadelphia, Temple University Press (2008), 71–91.

11

Negotiated Case Dispositions in Germany, England and the United States

JENIA I. TURNER AND THOMAS WEIGEND*

I Introduction

In the United States, the Supreme Court recently acknowledged that 'criminal justice today is for the most part a system of pleas, not a system of trials'.[1] More than 95 per cent of convictions in the federal and state systems are the product of negotiated guilty pleas.[2] In England and Wales, that number is about 90 per cent.[3]

The practice of bargaining instead of holding criminal trials, which has grown deep roots in England and the United States, is now sprouting up across the globe. Over the last three decades, it has spread to a broad range of jurisdictions, from Argentina, France and China to Australia, Nigeria and Germany.[4] A recent study of ninety jurisdictions around the world found that sixty-six of them used some type of 'trial waiver'

* This chapter is based in part on the authors' earlier work on plea bargaining, especially Weigend and Turner, 'Constitutionality of Negotiated Criminal Judgments' (2014), 81, and Turner, 'Plea Bargaining' (2017), 73.

1 *Lafler* v. *Cooper*, 566 US 156, 170 (2012).

2 Bureau of Justice Statistics, *Federal Justice Statistics 2012* (2015), Table 4.2 (97% of federal convictions disposed of via guilty plea). For state statistics, see Bureau of Justice Statistics, *State Court Sentencing of Convicted Felons* (2007), Table 4.1 (95% of state convictions obtained through a guilty plea); National Center for State Courts, Court Statistics Project Data Viewer, www.ncsc.org/Sitecore/Content/Microsites/PopUp/Home/CSP/CSP_Criminal showing that for most states, jury trials amounted to only about 1–2% of criminal dispositions).

3 Fair Trials, 'Disappearing Trial' (2017), 32. In 2017, defendants entered a guilty plea in 67% of cases sent to trial (the percentage of guilty pleas is lower at least in part because the percentage is calculated from all cases sent to trial, rather than just from convictions). Ministry of Justice, *Criminal Court Statistics Quarterly, England and Wales, January to March 2018* (annual 2017), 11.

4 Fair Trials, 'Disappearing Trial' (2017), 20–1. Even international criminal courts, dealing with the gravest crimes against humanity, have relied on plea bargaining to dispose of cases. Turner, 'Plea Bargaining and International Criminal Justice' (2017), 219.

procedures in criminal cases[5] – namely, procedures 'not prohibited by law under which criminal defendants agree to accept guilt and/or cooperate with the investigative authority in exchange for some benefit from the state, most commonly in the form of reduced charges and/or lower sentences'.[6] Such practices – known as plea bargains in Anglo-American systems, or simply agreements (*Verständigung*) in Germany – are favoured because they shorten or entirely eliminate the trial, thus expediting the proceedings and helping courts and prosecutors resolve cases more efficiently.

Even as bargaining in criminal cases spreads across the globe, questions about its fairness, accuracy, and legitimacy linger. Instances of innocent people admitting guilt in exchange for a lenient sentence cause spectators to question whether the efficiency that bargaining produces is worth the costs. This chapter examines the operation and regulation of bargaining practices in criminal cases in Germany, England and Wales, and the United States. It concludes with an evaluation of bargaining and some tentative thoughts on alternatives to bargaining and avenues for regulating bargaining.

II Scope and Regulation of Bargaining Procedures in the United States, England and Germany

We concentrate our discussion in this chapter on explicit exchanges of concessions in criminal cases. This includes express agreements by defendants to tender a guilty plea or admission of guilt or to provide information to the prosecution about other cases in exchange for benefits such as a sentence or charge reduction, favourable probation or detention conditions, or reduced collateral consequences. Such exchanges can easily be observed and regulated. By contrast, *implicit* exchanges that have long occurred in many legal systems, such as the practice of rewarding confessions and expressions of remorse with reduced sentences, are more difficult to detect and subject to different considerations. We therefore focus our attention in this chapter on express, rather than implied, agreements to waive full-blown trial procedures. And because the purpose of this volume is to promote an Anglo-German dialogue on criminal justice, we concentrate on bargaining procedures in Germany,

[5] Fair Trials, 'Disappearing Trial' (2017), 4.
[6] *Ibid.*, 2.

England and Wales ('England'), and the United States, with only occasional references to other legal systems.

There are certain notable similarities in the way bargaining proceeds and is regulated in the three systems we examine. In all three, the defendant may either plead guilty (as in England and the United States) or admit guilt (as in Germany) in exchange for sentencing concessions. Likewise, the defendant may cooperate with the prosecution and provide information about other cases in exchange for a reduced sentence. In all three systems, the court has a responsibility to ensure that a guilty plea or admission of guilt is valid – that it is, at a minimum, voluntary, knowing, and factually based.[7] While the precise mechanisms and standards differ in the United States, England and Germany, the end result is the same – a guilty plea or admission of guilt that significantly shortens the criminal process.

1 *Adversarial Influences on Bargaining: United States and England*

While the broad outline of agreements is similar in the three systems, differences persist and reflect contrasting goals and structures of the underlying criminal procedure frameworks in these countries. England and the United States are adversarial systems in which the parties dominate evidence gathering and presentation and the prosecutor has broad discretion to bring or dismiss charges. Accordingly, plea bargaining in these two systems typically occurs between the parties, with the court stepping in only after an agreement has been reached. The role of judges is generally limited to examining whether the guilty plea is voluntary, informed and based on the facts. A more active involvement by judges is generally seen as inconsistent with the adversarial tradition and the separation of powers between the prosecution and the court. It is also considered as potentially coercive, given the judge's ultimate say over the punishment of the defendant. Finally, as a practical matter, the lack of an evidentiary file also constrains the ability of judges to evaluate fully the evidence presented by the parties.

These concerns notwithstanding, a few US jurisdictions permit judges to participate in plea negotiations. Such participation is allowed in an

[7] For the United States, see *Brady* v. *US*, 397 US 742 (1970); Fed. R. Crim. P. 11. For England, see Ashworth and Redmayne, *Criminal Process* (2010), 291. In Germany, § 257c(1), cl. 2 of the Code of Criminal Procedure (*Strafprozessordnung*, StPO) provides that the trial court remains responsible for collecting all evidence necessary for the judgment.

effort to provide predictability about the sentence and a more impartial and timely review of the bargain's fairness and accuracy.[8] In England, negotiations occur between the prosecution and the defence, and judges are generally not involved. But since 2005, English judges have been permitted, upon request by the defence, to give the parties an indication of the maximum sentence to be expected in the event of a guilty plea.[9] Sentence indications provide some predictability and encourage defendants to plead guilty. But they also raise the concern that defendants might feel pressured by the judge's pronouncement; accordingly, the parties and the court must follow special procedures to neutralise any such effect. For example, judges must not give sentence indications on their own initiative, but only when requested by the defendant; when asked to give such an indication, they must ensure that they do so on the record, with both sides represented, and in the presence of the defendant.[10] For similar reasons, in the United States, some jurisdictions that permit judicial participation in plea negotiations require that, if the negotiations fall apart, the judge involved in the negotiations recuse herself and a different judge preside over the trial.[11]

In addition to limiting judicial involvement, the adversarial tradition emphasises the autonomy of the defendant to decide on legal representation. In the bargaining context, this means that the defendant may waive his right to counsel as part of a plea bargain.[12] Particularly in misdemeanour cases, where resources limit the availability of counsel, defendants in both England and the United States often enter guilty pleas without legal advice.[13]

Because the adversarial system largely focuses on the dispute between the parties, rather than on the public interest in criminal adjudication, it also does not impose weighty requirements on the parties or the court to document and publicise the content of the negotiations. In a number of state systems in the United States, plea agreements are not required to be

[8] King and Wright, 'Invisible Revolution' (2016), 325; Turner, 'Judicial Participation' (2006), 199.

[9] See *R* v. *Goodyear* [2005] EWCA Crim. 888 (permitting advance sentence indications in Crown Court cases).

[10] See *ibid.*; Crown Prosecution Service Legal Guidance, Sentencing: Overview, available at www.cps.gov.uk/legal-guidance/sentencing-overview.

[11] E.g. *State* v. *D'Antonio*, 877 A.2d 696 (Conn. 2005).

[12] *Iowa* v. *Tovar*, 541 US 77 (2004).

[13] Fair Trials, 'Disappearing Trial' (2017), 52 (discussing England); Boruchowitz, Brink and Dimino, *Minor Crimes, Massive Waste* (2009), 14–17.

in writing.[14] In England, only the sentencing discount given in exchange for a guilty plea is supposed to be placed on the record.[15]

Consistent with the modern focus on public prosecutions in common law jurisdictions, victims in England and the United States have a limited voice in plea bargaining. While victims are supposed to be informed and, in some cases, consulted about plea bargains, they have no veto power over the final agreement between the defence and the prosecutor.[16]

Jurors in the United States and England are never involved in the bargaining process. In the vast majority of cases, bargaining occurs in advance of trial. Even when it does occur in the midst of trial, its purpose is to bypass, rather than involve the jury. Should the pre-trial negotiations fall apart and the case proceed to trial, jurors are also not told about the occurrence or outcome of plea negotiations, lest this prejudice their verdict.[17]

Both in the United States and England, the parties are able to bargain not only about the sentence, but also about the charges (though as we discuss later, charge bargaining is somewhat more constrained in England than in the United States). The availability of charge bargaining reflects the commitment of the English and US criminal procedure systems to broad prosecutorial discretion. In these systems, the prosecutor conclusively determines the scope of the trial and possible judgment, and the trial court's judgment must not go beyond the demands of the prosecutor. The prosecutor's charges hence define the maximum of the harm that the defendant may suffer if convicted.

Broad prosecutorial discretion opens the door for negotiations between the prosecution and the defence about the scope and nature of the charges. In cases where the defendant has notice of an investigation against him, a defence lawyer may approach the prosecutor before the

[14] Mirza, 'Plea Bargaining Process' (2015), 506 ('Only a small minority of states, however, currently requires plea agreements to be in writing and signed by both parties.').

[15] Fair Trials, 'Disappearing Trial' (2017), 56.

[16] For the United States, see LaFave et al., *Criminal Procedure* (2015), § 21.3(f). For England, see Attorney General's Guidelines on the Acceptance of Pleas and the Prosecutor's Role in the Sentencing Exercise (2009), available at www.gov.uk/guidance/the-acceptance-of-pleas-and-the-prosecutors-role-in-the-sentencing-exercise. Under English law, victims have the right to challenge a prosecutor's decision to dismiss filed charges. Brown, 'Judicial Power to Regulate Plea Bargaining' (2016), 1258 (noting that under English law, victims have the right to challenge a prosecutor's decision to dismiss filed charges).

[17] See Thomas, 'What Happened to the American Jury?' (2017), 28 (noting current practice, but arguing in favour of informing juries of failed plea bargains).

filing of an indictment and try to persuade her to bring charges of lesser seriousness in exchange for the defendant's cooperation and/or guilty plea. Because the prosecutor may reduce the original charges later in the process, either before or during the trial, the defence has another opportunity for negotiations, typically offering a change of plea to 'guilty' to a sufficiently reduced charge.

While the United States and England share the above-mentioned features of plea bargaining as a reflection of their adversarial tradition, important differences remain between the two systems. In some ways, the English process is less regulated than the process in the United States. For example, there is no formal plea hearing at which the judge is supposed to evaluate the validity of a guilty plea.[18] On the other hand, as we discuss below,[19] English courts have taken certain measures to constrain bargaining – requiring that guilty pleas not be equivocal, imposing a cap on sentence discounts and permitting judges to review certain charge bargains – that US courts and legislatures have been reluctant to take, but that can help improve the fairness and accuracy of the process.

(a) Bargaining in the United States

The first feature of plea bargaining that distinguishes the US system is the wide extent to which prosecutors can induce guilty pleas through offers to reduce or drop charges. This occurs for two principal reasons. First, US courts have interpreted separation of powers to preclude judicial review of prosecutorial charging decisions.[20] And secondly, most US jurisdictions rely on mandatory minimums and sentencing guidelines, which means that prosecutorial decisions about charges have profound effects on sentencing. As a result, prosecutors have significant leverage to induce guilty pleas by offering favourable charging concessions to defendants.[21]

The US system also gives defendants broad autonomy to waive constitutional and statutory rights, meaning that few subjects are off limits in plea bargaining. US defendants may waive their rights to appeal the sentence, to attack the judgment collaterally on grounds of ineffective assistance of counsel, to file a civil action on related matters (such as

[18] Fair Trials, 'Disappearing Trial' (2017), 54.

[19] See Section II.1.(b).

[20] See e.g. *Inmates of Attica Corr. Facility* v. *Rockefeller*, 477 F2d 375, 379–81 (2nd Cir. 1973); *United States* v. *Giannattasio*, 979 F2d 98, 100 (7th Cir. 1992).

[21] See e.g. Wright and Engen, 'The Effects of Depth' (2006), 1977.

police misconduct), or to receive potentially exculpatory evidence from the prosecution.[22] In addition, as part of so-called 'wired pleas', prosecutors may condition a plea bargain in the defendant's case to the disposition of a case against a relative of the defendant.[23]

Because baseline sentences in the United States are very high, and plea discounts are not capped, prosecutors can offer charge and sentence bargains that produce significant – and potentially coercive – plea discounts. One study found that, even after excluding any effects of charge and fact bargaining, 'federal defendants convicted at trial receive sentences that are sixty-four percent longer than similar defendants who plead guilty'.[24] Another study, focusing on drug cases in federal court, found that average federal drug sentences in cases that went to trial were three times harsher than average sentences in cases that were resolved by a plea.[25] Finally, research examining sentencing practices at the state level found that the penalty for going to trial (rather than pleading guilty) ranged from a 13 to 461 per cent increase in sentence length.[26] In capital cases, defendants may be offered a bargain that would take the possibility of the death penalty off the table.[27] Despite the risk of sizeable plea discounts coercing innocent defendants to plead guilty, courts have refused to hold such discounts unconstitutional.

US courts have also not been particularly demanding in their review of the evidence supporting a guilty plea. Judges rarely go beyond reviewing the indictment and then confirming that the facts alleged comport with the defendant's brief statement at the plea colloquy.[28] Given this rather perfunctory factual inquiry, parties remain free to

[22] See Klein et al., 'Waiving the Criminal Justice System' (2015), 73.

[23] See e.g. *United States* v. *Pollard*, 959 F2d 1011, 1021–2 (DC Cir. 1992); *State* v. *Bey*, 17 P3d 322 (Kan. 2001).

[24] Kim, 'Underestimating the Trial Penalty' (2015), 1202.

[25] Human Rights Watch, *An Offer You Can't Refuse* (2013), 102.

[26] King et al., 'When Process Affects Punishment' (2005), 973–5, 992 (studying sentencing practices in five states and finding trial penalties ranging from 13 to 461%); see also McCoy, 'Plea Bargaining as Coercion' (2005), 90 (finding an average trial penalty of 44.5 months in state felony cases).

[27] *Brady* v. *United States*, 397 US 742 (1970).

[28] Turner, 'Judicial Participation' (2006), 212–23; Johnson and Gilbert, *The U.S. Sentencing Guidelines* (1997), 10 (reporting that 25% of judges stated that they have never '"go[ne] behind" a plea agreement and rule[d] against a prosecutor's recommendation that tends to lower a sentence by either stipulating facts or recommending the application, or nonapplication, of specific offense characteristics' and that of the 75% who do 'go behind plea agreements', only about 8% do so 'very frequently').

engage in fact bargaining and frequently do so.[29] Judges are also permitted to accept guilty pleas even when defendants profess their innocence, as long as a sufficient factual basis independently supports the conviction.[30]

Finally, the standard for an informed guilty plea is not particularly demanding in US law. Judges do have to confirm that the defendant understands the essential elements of the crime to which he is pleading guilty.[31] They must also tell the defendant about the direct consequences of a guilty plea[32] and about the rights that the defendant is waiving by pleading guilty. But a guilty plea may be informed even when the prosecution fails to disclose evidence favourable to the defence.[33] Likewise, judges need only give minimal notice of the meaning of the right to counsel before defendants waive that right at a plea hearing.[34]

(b) Bargaining in England and Wales

While plea bargaining occurred for a long time in England surreptitiously and without regulation, courts have now imposed some important constraints on the practice. For example, the scope and effect of charge bargaining in England is somewhat more limited than in the United States. To begin, English judges have broader sentencing discretion than many of their US counterparts. English sentencing guidelines do

29 Turner, 'Judicial Participation' (2006), 212–23.

30 *North Carolina* v. *Alford*, 400 US 25, 38 (1970) (equivocal guilty pleas are acceptable when there is strong factual evidence supporting guilt). But cf. US Department of Justice, US Attorneys' Manual § 9–16.015, at www.justice.gov/usam/usam-9%9616000%96pleas-federal-rule-criminal-procedure-11#9%16.015 (instructing federal prosecutors not to consent to *Alford* pleas 'except in the most unusual of circumstances' and only after supervisory approval). For a German assessment of the *Alford* case, see Ransiek, 'Zur Urteilsabsprache im Strafprozess' (2008).

31 *Henderson* v. *Morgan*, 426 US 637, 652–3 (1976).

32 E.g. *United States* v. *Rivera-Maldonado*, 560 F3d 16, 22 (1st Cir. 2009); *Jamison* v. *Klem*, 544 F3d 266, 276–7 (3rd Cir. 2008); LaFave et al., *Criminal Procedure* (2015), § 21.4(d) n. 116.

33 *Ruiz* v. *United States*, 536 US 622, 623 (2002) (holding that a guilty plea may be informed even when the prosecution has failed to disclose evidence that serves to impeach the credibility of prosecution witnesses).

34 *Iowa* v. *Tovar*, 541 US 77, 80 (2004) (holding that the court must inform the defendant 'of the nature of the charges against him, of his right to be counseled regarding his plea, and of the range of allowable punishments attendant upon the entry of a guilty plea' but does not need to '(1) advise the defendant that "waiving the assistance of counsel in deciding whether to plead guilty [entails] the risk that a viable defense will be overlooked"; and (2) "admonis[h]" the defendant "that by waiving his right to an attorney he will lose the opportunity to obtain an independent opinion on whether, under the facts and applicable law, it is wise to plead guilty"').

constrain judicial sentencing, but they are still more flexible than grid-based guidelines used in more than a dozen states and at the federal level in the United States.[35] The remaining judicial discretion over sentencing blunts the effect of charging concessions by the prosecutor.

In addition, unlike US law, English law permits some judicial scrutiny of charging decisions, holding prosecutors to policies promulgated by the Crown Prosecution Service (CPS). Specifically, judicial review of a decision not to prosecute may be granted where the CPS arrived at the decision not to prosecute:

> (i) because of some unlawful policy . . . or
> (ii) because the Director of Public Prosecutions failed to act in accordance with her own settled policy as set out in the Code; or
> (iii) because the decision was perverse. It was a decision at which no reasonable prosecutor could have arrived.[36]

In this context, it is important to note that section 10.2 of the Code for Crown Prosecutors admonishes prosecutors not to agree to charge reductions just 'because it is convenient' and to make sure that the court can still pass a sentence 'that matches the seriousness of offending'. In

[35] See Frase, 'State Sentencing Guidelines' (2005), 1201 (noting that eighteen states and the federal system use sentencing guidelines and that the 'two-dimensional grid of offense severity by criminal history or offender risk score' is standard). For an in-depth comparison of the Minnesota (grid-based) and English sentencing guidelines, see Roberts, 'Sentencing Guidelines' (2013), 24 (draft manuscript on file with authors) ('[English] courts have considerable discretion *within* the guideline ranges, as well as the ability to impose a sentence outside the guideline range, if following the guideline would be contrary to the interests of justice.'), 25 ('[I]t seems reasonable to conclude that judges in England have greater freedom than their counterparts in Minnesota.').

[36] *R* v. *DPP, ex p C* [1995] 1 Cr. App. R. 136. In another case, the court elaborated that a decision not to prosecute may be judicially reviewed:

> (i) If it could be demonstrated on an objective appraisal of the case that a serious point or serious points supporting a prosecution had not been considered, that would give a ground for ordering reconsideration of the decision.
> (ii) If it could be demonstrated that in a significant area a conclusion about what the evidence was to support a prosecution was irrational, that would provide a ground for ordering reconsideration.
> (iii) The points had to be such to make it seriously arguable that the decision would otherwise be different, but the decision was one for the prosecutor and not for the court.
> (iv) Where an inquest jury had found unlawful killing, the reasons why a prosecution should not follow needed to be clearly expressed. *R (on the application of Dennis)* v. *DPP*, [2006] EWHC 3211 (Admin), [2007] All ER (D) 43.

theory, therefore, a charge bargain may be judicially reviewed by an English court if it was entered purely on convenience grounds, though the motivation of the prosecutor would be difficult to prove in practice.[37]

English law on validity of guilty pleas is also in some ways more demanding than US law. Unlike in the United States, guilty pleas must be unequivocal, meaning that the defendant may not plead guilty and at the same time assert his innocence or advance a legal defence to the charges. The court must try to resolve any ambiguity in the guilty plea, and 'if the plea remains ambiguous, the court must reject it and hear evidence before convicting or acquitting'.[38] If the court erroneously accepts an ambiguous guilty plea, the accused can appeal against conviction, notwithstanding the general rule that plea-based convictions may not be appealed.[39]

As in the United States, courts must ensure that a guilty plea rests on a solid factual basis. If the parties disagree about sentence-related facts, the court may hold a hearing (a so-called *Newton* hearing) to resolve the disagreement.[40] It appears that courts occasionally use such hearings when they detect and disagree with a fact bargain reached by the parties.[41] How often judges assume control in such circumstances, however, remains to be tested empirically.

Although both English and US law require that guilty pleas be voluntary, English law has imposed some limits on the plea discount, which reduces the risk that an innocent defendant might be coerced into pleading guilty. The Sentencing Council has issued guidelines to judges that presumptively set plea discounts to a maximum of one-third of the custodial term when a guilty plea is entered at the earliest reasonable opportunity and less if entered later.[42] The Council has stated that the recommended reduction should be given 'unless the court is satisfied that it would be contrary to the interests of justice to do so'.[43] A 2015 empirical study found

37 See Brown, 'Judicial Power to Regulate Plea Bargaining' (2016), 1259–60.

38 Hooper and Ormerod, *Blackstone's Criminal Practice 2012* (2011), 1892.

39 Hooper and Ormerod, *Blackstone's Criminal Practice 2012* (2011), 1892. On the other hand, a defence lawyer is not legally or ethically obliged to refuse to assist a defendant who claims he is innocent, but wishes to enter a guilty plea for tactical reasons, '[p]rovided that such a defendant and his lawyers do not repeat his protestations of innocence to the court': Horne, 'Plea Bargains' (2016), 6.

40 Newton (1982) 4 Cr. App. R. (S) 388; Ashworth and Redmayne, *Criminal Process* (2010), 291.

41 Ashworth and Redmayne, *Criminal Process* (2010), 300.

42 Sentencing Council, *Reduction in Sentence for a Guilty Plea* (2017), 5.

43 *Ibid.*, 4.

that English courts do in fact follow the guidelines and that 'almost all cases where a plea was entered attracted reductions of one-third or less'.[44]

While the fixed sentencing discount is an important step in reducing coerciveness in plea negotiations, it does not eliminate all pressure on defendants. The discount may still be coercive where it results in a reduction from a custodial to a non-custodial sentence,[45] which appears to occur frequently.[46] As Jill Peay and Elaine Player argue, the reduction to a non-custodial sentence poses special risks for defendants with vulnerabilities, particularly when it is combined with the pressure imposed by the guidelines to enter a guilty plea at the earliest reasonable opportunity.[47] In addition, judges have some flexibility in determining the sentencing range that applies to the offence and in assessing the relevant aggravating and mitigating factors that influence the final sentence;[48] this flexibility allows judges to effectively provide a larger than one-third discount in certain cases, providing a more significant inducement for defendants to plead guilty.[49] Most significantly, charge bargaining, which occurs frequently in England, can further expand the final plea discount that a defendant receives, thus placing additional pressure to plead guilty.[50] Finally, as some commentators have observed, courts have

[44] Roberts and Bradford, 'Sentence Reductions' (2015), 187.

[45] Sentencing Council, *Reduction in Sentence for a Guilty Plea* (2017), 6.

[46] See Ashworth and Redmayne, *Criminal Process* (2010), 293 (noting that the guidelines allow such a reduction where the offense 'is already close to the custody threshold'). In 2007, 67% of convicted indictable offenders who pleaded not guilty received a prison sentence, whereas only 55% of those who pleaded guilty were punished by imprisonment. Ashworth and Redmayne, *Criminal Process* (2010), 302.

[47] Peay and Player, 'Pleading Guilty' (2018), 929.

[48] See Roberts, 'Sentencing Guidelines' (2013), 13 ('More serious offences carry a much wider range of sentence within which a court may impose a sentence and remain compliant with the guidelines ... In the event that the court imposes a sentence outside the overall range – in the interests of justice – it must give reasons for its decision. The provisions in the Coroners and Justice Act 2009 focus a court's attention on the relevance of the guidelines, yet permit considerable judicial discretion to impose a fit sentence'), 22 ('There is therefore a high degree of flexibility – courts are able to move around within the guidelines and are not restricted to a particular category-level range; as well, they may escape the guidelines altogether by means of the "interests of justice" test.').

[49] In a survey of defence representatives, the Sentencing Council heard from some of them that some judges know what their desired end point sentence is and assess the relevant sentencing range and aggravating or mitigating factors based on that predetermined sentence. Sentencing Council, *Research to Support the Development of a Guideline for Reduction in Sentence for a Guilty Plea* (2017), 13.

[50] See Ashworth and Redmayne, *Criminal Process* (2010), 297–9. General sentencing statistics (which do not take into account previous convictions or mitigating factors

not gone far enough in regulating the coercive effects of certain bargains, such as bargains that implicate the disposition of the case against a relative.[51] More generally, courts have focused primarily on procedural propriety in assessing coercion in plea bargaining and have shied away from considering how systemic incentives (such as overly generous charge bargains) and the personal circumstances of a defendant might influence the voluntariness of a guilty plea.[52]

2 *Inquisitorial Influences on Bargaining: Germany*

(a) Principles Limiting Bargaining

Germany's inquisitorial tradition constrains bargaining more strictly than is the case in England and the United States. The concept of resolving the outcome of a criminal case through a consensual agreement between the parties and the court remains in tension with key German constitutional and procedural principles.

Under the inquisitorial principle that is basic to German criminal procedure, judges have a duty to investigate the substantive truth.[53] They have at their disposal the tools to investigate regardless of any offers of evidence or motions of the parties. Judges receive, along with the prosecutor's written accusation, the file of the investigation containing all evidence gathered by the police and the prosecution. At trial, the presiding judge calls and questions witnesses, summons experts, examines real evidence and organises the reading of documents.[54] Since the verdict must have a firm basis in the facts established by the court through its own fact-finding at the trial,[55] the German system does not accept the

and should therefore be treated with caution) indicate that indictable offenders who pleaded guilty were sentenced on average to twenty-four months of imprisonment, whereas the same class of offenders who pleaded not guilty were sentenced to an average of forty-two months of imprisonment, suggesting that the average plea discount is roughly 45%.

51 Horne, 'Plea Bargains' (2016), 10 (discussing *R* v. *Herbert*, 94 Cr. App. R. 230, 235, which held that a guilty plea motivated by prosecutor's assurance that a defendant's wife would not be charged was not improper as long as the original decision to charge the defendant's wife had not been motivated by a desire to influence the defendant's plea).

52 Horne, 'Plea Bargains' (2016), 9; see also Peay and Player, 'Pleading Guilty' (2018).

53 § 244(2) German Code of Criminal Procedure (StPO).

54 Documents can be read out aloud in court or can be assigned to judges and parties for 'at home' reading: § 249 StPO.

55 § 261 StPO requires the court to base its conclusion exclusively on the evidence taken at the trial.

idea that a formal declaration of guilt by the defendant could be a sufficient basis for the court's verdict.[56] Even a full confession made by the defendant in open court does not necessarily relieve the court of the duty to 'discover the truth'.[57] Nor can the parties' stipulations of fact bind the court; the judge remains obliged to find out what really happened.

Another central tenet of the German legal system is the principle of culpability (*Schuldprinzip*), according to which the punishment of the defendant must be proportionate to his blameworthiness. The Schuldprinzip, which has been accorded constitutional status,[58] implies that an offender's sentence may not depart from its purpose to provide just punishment commensurate with culpability. Sentences therefore must not be reduced below the level that would reflect the defendant's blameworthiness, even if that were done in order to expedite proceedings and reduce caseload pressure.[59] Conversely, courts are prohibited from increasing the sentence of a defendant who rejects a 'deal' and insists on a full trial. According to the Federal Constitutional Court, the culpability principle also has procedural implications: it obliges the trial court to find the facts necessary to establish the level of the defendant's guilt.[60]

Another tenet of German criminal procedure that affects bargaining is the principle of mandatory prosecution, which demands that prosecutors file charges whenever sufficient evidence for conviction is likely to exist.[61] This principle applies, in effect, only to serious offences with a mandatory minimum sentence of one year's imprisonment – for example, murder, robbery, rape, and arson. Prosecutors are thus precluded from dropping felony charges, even as a result of an agreement with the defence. This limitation also stands in the way of most deals with 'crown witnesses': the principle of mandatory prosecution prohibits prosecutors from dropping provable serious charges against suspects in

[56] Federal Court of Justice, Judgment of 28 Aug. 1997, 43 *Entscheidungen des Bundesgerichtshofes in Strafsachen* (BGHSt), 195 at 208. See Brodowski, 'Verfassungsrechtliche Legitimation' (2012), 765–6, 774 (explaining the difference between American and German attitudes toward plea bargaining by the fact that US law relies on other mechanisms than judicial truth-finding for protecting the innocent).

[57] Weigend, 'Decay of the Inquisitorial Ideal' (2008), 44.

[58] Federal Constitutional Court, Judgment of 19 Mar. 2013, 133 *Entscheidungen des Bundesverfassungsgerichts* (BVerfGE) 168 at 197–8. The culpability principle is rooted in the guarantee of human dignity and personal liberty and the principle of the rule of law (Art. 1(1), Art. 2(1), Art. 20(3) *Grundgesetz* (GG)).

[59] 133 BVerfGE 168 at 198.

[60] *Ibid.*, at 199.

[61] § 170(1) StPO.

exchange for their testimony against others. German law seeks instead to accommodate the interest in obtaining insiders' testimony through sentencing law: if an offender provides information on a serious offence connected with his own and thereby facilitates the successful investigation of that offence, the court may reduce his sentence, or may even refrain from imposing a sentence which would have been three years imprisonment or less.[62]

(b) Instances of Bargaining

Most cases in the German system of criminal justice concern less serious offences, to which the principle of mandatory prosecution does not apply. In such cases, prosecutors may dismiss charges, either for lack of a sufficient public interest in prosecution,[63] or in exchange for the suspect making a payment to the state treasury or to a charitable organisation.[64] The latter disposition does not require the suspect to plead guilty or even to admit his responsibility for the crime; it is therefore quite attractive especially for white-collar suspects. Although the statute construes the offer of such a *quid pro quo* as a unilateral decision of the prosecutor, the conditions of the bargain, especially the amount to be paid, are in practice often the subject of prior negotiations between the prosecutor's office and the defence lawyer.[65]

Similar negotiations sometimes occur in connection with a penal order (i.e., a criminal judgment drafted by the prosecutor and signed by a judge without a trial).[66] A penal order becomes a valid judgment unless the defendant files an appeal within two weeks after receiving it.[67] It is thus in effect an offer by the prosecutor (ratified, often without close examination, by the judge) to the defendant to accept, without a trial, a fine or a

[62] § 46b(1) German Penal Code (StGB).

[63] § 153 StPO.

[64] § 153a StPO. For critical assessments of the constitutionality of this statutory option see Stuckenberg, 'Abschaffung des § 153a StPO' (2016), 369; Weigend, 'Verfahrenseinstellung nach § 153a StPO' (2016), 413.

[65] The statute does not provide for a maximum of payments. In one famous case, Formula 1 car-racing organiser Bernie Ecclestone paid US$100 million in exchange for having bribery charges dismissed. See Kudlich, 'Ecclestone, Verständigungsgesetz und die Folgen' (2015), 10.

[66] § 407 StPO.

[67] § 410 StPO. If the defendant files an appeal, the case automatically goes to trial. The defendant may however withdraw the appeal, with the consent of the prosecutor, even during the trial (§ 411(3) StPO).

suspended prison sentence of up to one year. As with conditional dismissal, this seemingly unilateral disposition opens up the possibility for the defence to bargain with the prosecutor about the severity of the sanction; if an informal agreement as to the amount of the fine is reached, the prosecutor's office can be fairly certain that the defendant will not appeal against the penal order.

(c) Sentence Bargaining at the Trial Stage

Despite the serious constitutional obstacles noted above, sentence bargaining has gradually infiltrated the German system of criminal justice. Starting in the 1970s, practitioners secretly negotiated the exchange of lenient sentences for confessions, which had the potential of significantly shortening trials. In 1997, the Federal Court of Justice grudgingly accepted the practice, within certain limits,[68] and in 2009, the legislature expressly authorised and regulated it.[69] Four years later, the Constitutional Court upheld the legislation, setting additional constitutional guidelines within which bargaining is to proceed.[70] The current framework reflects these efforts by the courts and the legislature to reduce the conflict between bargaining practice and Germany's procedural principles.[71]

Reflecting the central role of judges in directing criminal proceedings, German law places the decision to engage in bargaining with the court. Article 257c(1) of the Criminal Procedure Code (StPO) provides that the court may in suitable cases come to an agreement with the parties about the further proceedings and the outcome of the case.[72] Judges are thus expected to be – and in fact are – actively engaged in negotiations about the sentence. Since Article 257c(1), clause 2 StPO explicitly refers to the inquisitorial principle, which obliges the court to independently search for the truth, judges may not simply rely on the facts presented by the parties, including the defendant's confession, but must independently

[68] Federal Court of Justice, Judgment of 28 Aug. 1997, 43 BGHSt 195.

[69] Deutscher Bundestag, Drucksache 16/12310 (18 Mar. 2009), available at http://dip21.bundestag.de/dip21/btd/16/123/1612310.pdf.

[70] 133 BVerfGE 168.

[71] For criticism of the legislation and case law on bargaining in Germany, see e.g. Schünemann, 'Urteilsabsprachen' (2013), 1107, and Stuckenberg, 'Entscheidungsbesprechung' (2013), 212.

[72] This legal arrangement does not rule out an initiative of the defence lawyer, who may approach the presiding judge requesting an 'offer'.

assemble a sufficient factual basis for the judgment.[73] Unlike their counterparts in Anglo-American systems, German judges will have received and read the investigative file before the start of any negotiations and thus have available at least a provisional overview of the relevant facts of the case.

German law strictly limits the subject matter of possible bargains. According to § 257c(2) StPO, the verdict is not subject to negotiation; a bargain may concern only the sentence, procedural measures,[74] and the procedural conduct of the persons taking part in the trial. In most cases, the defendant's main bargaining chip is an admission of guilt.[75] In exchange, the defendant expects a sentence that is lower than would be imposed after a full contested trial. Even if the defendant is willing to admit guilt, a trial must be held, but in many cases the court's taking of evidence will be limited to hearing the defendant's confession, possibly complemented by a few questions posed by the judge or the prosecutor. Importantly, victims will often not be called as witnesses if the defendant's confession paints a sufficiently clear picture of the offence.[76]

The 'procedural conduct' clause of § 257c(2) StPO covers a defendant's waiver of his right to request the court to take additional evidence.[77] Some other procedural rights may, on the other hand, not be subject to waiver.[78] For example, defendants are precluded from bargaining away

[73] For an assessment that negotiations actually broaden the factual basis of the judgment (because they induce the defendant to make a confession), see von Frankenberg, *Konfliktlösungsprozesse* (2013), 241–6.

[74] It is not clear what such 'measures' might be, because the trial court is obliged to take all evidence that is necessary to establish the truth (§ 244(2) StPO, expressly declared to be applicable in bargaining cases in § 257c(1), cl. 2 StPO) and can therefore not 'waive' the taking of relevant evidence. Cf. Meyer-Goßner and Schmitt, *Strafprozessordnung* (2018), § 257c n. 13.

[75] As a consequence, there will be no bargaining if the defendant has already made an admissible confession in the course of the pre-trial investigation.

[76] According to an empirical study, judges as well as prosecutors cited their interest in sparing witnesses and victims the necessity to appear in court as the most powerful motive for entering into negotiations with the defence. Altenhain et al., *Praxis der Absprachen* (2013), 47, 49.

[77] See Kudlich, *Münchener Kommentar zur StPO* (2016), § 257c n. 104; Moldenhauer and Wenske, '§ 257c' (2013), n. 22. The waiver of the defendant's right to ask for additional evidence is difficult to square with the trial court's duty to discover the truth (see Federal Constitutional Court, 133 BVerfGE 168 at 230: trial court must not bargain away its obligation to seek the truth), and it is questionable to link such a waiver to a mitigation of punishment; cf. Meyer-Goßner and Schmitt, *Strafprozessordnung* (2018), § 257c nn. 14–15.

[78] Cf. Slobogin, 'Plea Bargaining' (2016), 1505.

their right to effective counsel, since counsel must be present and support the defendant whenever the crime is serious or the defendant is personally unable to conduct his defence.[79] Discovery waivers cannot occur in practice because defence counsel receives full access to the prosecutor's file before negotiations even begin.[80] Likewise, if the court calls a witness at the trial, it cannot be part of the bargain that the defendant waives his right to question that witness. Nor may a defendant waive in advance his right to appeal against the judgment; in fact, § 302(1), clause 2 StPO precludes any waiver of appeal[81] against a negotiated judgment, because the defendant should have the opportunity to consider whether the court kept its side of the bargain when sentencing him.

The restriction of bargaining to the sentence means that charge bargaining – so frequent in the United States – is impermissible in Germany.[82] Charge bargaining would also be ineffective since the German prosecutor's choice of charge (i.e. the legal provision cited as reflecting the accused person's conduct) does not bind the trial court. The prosecutor's formal accusation conclusively defines the conduct subject to trial as to its time and place; its legal assessment by the prosecutor is only preliminary and may be overridden by the court, even to the defendant's detriment (if proper notice has been given during trial).[83] This characteristic is a feature of the inquisitorial system: the criminal

79 § 140 StPO; see also Turner, *Plea Bargaining across Borders* (2019), 109.

80 See § 147 (1) and (6) StPO (access to file must be granted as soon as prosecutorial investigation has been terminated).

81 However, most courts permit the defendant to withdraw an appeal after he has filed it; see Federal Court of Justice, Judgment of 14 Apr. 2010, 1 StR 64/10, 2010 Strafverteidiger 436; Court of Appeals Köln, Judgment of 12 Jun. 2017, 2 Ws 368/17, 2018 Strafverteidiger 803; but see, *contra*, Court of Appeal München, Judgment of 28 Aug. 2013, 4 StRR 174/13. According to Jahn and Kudlich, *Münchener Kommentar StPO* (2016), § 257c n. 105, it is therefore permissible for the defendant to promise to *withdraw* an appeal.

82 Practitioners report, however, that 'fact bargaining' does exist, for example, with respect to aggravating factors that are being withheld from the court; see Heger and Pest, 'Verständigungen im Strafverfahren' (2014), 459–60; see also Altenhain et al., *Praxis der Absprachen* (2013), 86–7 (14% of judges, but 54% of defence lawyers indicated that negotiations had led to 'downgrading' an intentional offence to a negligent one; 19% of judges and 69% of defence lawyers reported instances of 'ignoring' aggravating factors). But such practices clearly violate the law.

83 The trial court decides in a special proceeding whether to accept the prosecutor's formal accusation (§§ 199–211 StPO). If the court orders a trial to be opened, it may deviate from the legal assessment that the prosecutor had given to the facts of the case (§ 207(2) no. 3 StPO). The court may also change the legal assessment during the trial. If the court finds, in the course of the trial, that the original legal charges do not adequately reflect the facts as they appear from the evidence taken at the trial, the court informs the defendant

process is not about proving the prosecutor's charges but about finding the truth.

Like English and US law, German law prohibits coerced admissions of guilt.[84] But unlike US law, which focuses almost exclusively on physical coercion, German courts seek to regulate the size of negotiated sentence discounts in an effort to prevent an innocent defendant from being lured into admitting guilt by an 'offer he can't refuse'. The German Constitutional Court has thus invalidated a negotiated sentence reduction of over 50 per cent (from a four-year *custodial* sentence to a two-year *probated* sentence), out of concern that it unduly pressured the defendant into confessing.[85] More broadly, German courts have held that even a bargained sentence must remain proportionate to the defendant's blameworthiness.[86] Empirical studies show that this case law has had an effect and, in practice, the reduction for admitting guilt tends to be no higher than one-third of the expected trial sentence.[87]

German law related to bargaining also emphasises the importance of transparency, publicity and a full documentation of negotiated proceedings.[88] Courts must indicate the maximum and minimum limits of the sentence they would impose as part of the bargain, and the presiding judge must publicly announce for the trial record the content and outcome of any negotiations about the sentence before or during trial. Courts must even document the absence of any such discussions to ensure that no secret informal deals are taking place.[89] Finally, judges must warn the defendant about the possibility that their sentence may deviate from the agreement if new factual or legal circumstances arise.[90]

that he may be convicted of an offence different from the original charges (§ 265 StPO). The defendant may then ask for an adjournment in order to adjust his defence.

84 § 136(1) StPO.

85 Federal Constitutional Court, 133 BVerfGE 168 at 240.

86 *Ibid.*, 229–30.

87 See Altenhain et al., *Absprachen in Wirtschaftsstrafverfahren* (2007), 130–1 (presiding judges in white-collar crime courts indicated discount of 25–33% of 'normal' sentence for bargained confession); Altenhain et al., *Praxis der Absprachen* (2013), 116 (76% of judges indicated that they would grant a discount between 25% and 33% for a bargained confession).

88 Federal Constitutional Court, 133 BVerfGE 168 at 206–7. For a critical assessment of this tendency see Duttge, 'Urteilsabsprachen als Signum' (2014), 884–6.

89 §§ 243(4), 273(1a) StPO.

90 § 257c(5) StPO. If the court rejects a deal previously agreed upon, any confession the defendant had made pursuant to the deal becomes inadmissible as evidence (§ 257c(4), cl. 3 StPO).

Unlike English and US law in most states, German law permits victims in certain cases[91] to take part in the proceedings as 'supplementary prosecutors' (*Nebenkläger*), and this right extends to negotiations as well as contested trials. In negotiated proceedings, Nebenkläger must be heard and be given an opportunity to express their views about the proposed bargain.[92] In contrast to the public prosecutor, however, a Nebenkläger has no right to veto a proposed judgment accepted by the prosecution and the defence.[93] The victim's role in negotiated proceedings is thus quite limited.[94]

3 *The European Court of Human Rights and Bargaining*

Because both Germany and England are parties to the European Convention on Human Rights (ECHR), their law is guided by the Convention's provisions, as interpreted by the European Court of Human Rights (ECtHR). As forms of bargaining have expanded across Europe (the ECtHR found in a survey of 2014 that twenty-seven out of thirty of its Member States had some variant of plea bargaining procedures in place[95]) the European Court was faced with the question whether and under what conditions plea bargaining is compatible with the right to a fair hearing as guaranteed by Article 6(1) ECHR. The Court does not see any principled objection to abbreviated proceedings based on the defendant's consent: the procedural rights afforded by Article 6 ECHR can be validly waived, either expressly or tacitly, if the waiver is 'established in an unequivocal manner and [is] attended by minimum safeguards commensurate with its importance. In addition, waiver must not run counter to any important public interest.'[96] The Court emphasised

[91] The right to act as a Nebenkläger extends mainly to victims of serious offences against the person, e.g. attempted murder, sexual offences, intentional bodily injury and human trafficking (see § 395 StPO).

[92] Nebenkläger is a participant at the trial (*Verfahrensbeteiligte*) and hence has the same procedural rights as the other participants, i.e. the prosecutor, the defendant and the defence lawyer (see § 257c(1) StPO).

[93] See § 257c(3), cl. 4 StPO: 'An agreement becomes valid if the defendant and the prosecution declare their consent with the court's proposition.'

[94] For an empirical study of the participation of lawyers representing victims see Niemz, *Urteilsabsprachen und Opferinteressen* (2011).

[95] *Natsvlishvili* v. *Georgia*, ECtHR, No. 9043/05, Judgment of 29 Apr. 2014, paras. 62–75.

[96] *Scoppola* v. *Italy* (no. 2), ECtHR, No. 10249/03, Judgment of 17 Sept. 2009, § 135; see also *Natsvlishvili* v. *Georgia*, ECtHR, No. 9043/05, Judgment of 29 Apr. 2014, § 91; *Navalnyy and Ofitserov* v. *Russia*, ECtHR, No. 46632/13, Judgment of 23 Feb. 2016, § 100; *Leuska and others* v. *Estonia*, ECtHR, No. 64734/11, Judgment of 7 Nov. 2017, § 74.

that any waiver of the right to trial must be made by the defendant 'in full awareness of the facts of the case and the legal consequences and in a genuinely voluntary manner', and that 'the content of the bargain and the fairness of the manner in which it had been reached between the parties [must] be subjected to sufficient judicial review'.[97] Sufficient judicial review is more likely to be found where the court has enquired 'whether the accusations … [are] well founded and supported by prima facie evidence'[98] and where it can reject or alter any agreement between the parties 'depending upon its own assessment of the fairness of the terms contained in it and the process by which it had been entered into'.[99]

In the *Natsvlishvili* judgment of 2014, the European Court clearly endorsed the practice of plea bargaining: 'There cannot be anything improper in the process of charge or sentence bargaining in itself.'[100] The Court's guidelines confirm the need to regulate bargaining in order to ensure that it complies with the principle of fair trial and the presumption of innocence. Yet the minimal rules established by the Court do little to make certain that the defendant's consent is truly voluntary and uncoerced, and they more or less ignore the fact that most defendants are not in a position to match the legal and financial means of the prosecution and are in the end subjected to the court's sentencing authority.[101] In any event, ECtHR case law does not add any safeguards to the domestic systems of England and Germany.

III Evaluating Bargaining Procedures

Efficiency is the main reason that courts and legislatures around the world have given for adopting bargaining procedures. Bargaining expedites case dispositions and allows courts and prosecutors to resolve more cases with limited resources.[102] In countries with significant backlogs of

97 *Natsvlishvili* v. *Georgia*, ECtHR, No. 9043/05, Judgment of 29 Apr. 2014, § 92. A written record of the bargain should exist to enable judicial review 'in a clear and incontrovertible manner': § 94.

98 The Court does not consider it relevant whether the defendant admits guilt to the charges or simply agrees to the sentence. One dissenting judge argued that the Court should require a stronger factual basis in the absence of a guilty plea; *ibid.*, Partly Dissenting Opinion of Judge Gyulumyan, § 7.

99 *Ibid.*, § 95.

100 *Ibid.*, § 90.

101 For similar criticism, see Bachmaier, 'European Court of Human Rights on Negotiated Justice' (2018), 236.

102 See e.g. Ashworth and Redmayne, *Criminal Process* (2010), 308.

cases and excessive delays, plea bargaining has been recommended as a means of ensuring compliance with defendants' rights to a trial within a reasonable period of time.[103] Some advocates of bargaining take the efficiency argument a step further. They argue that bargaining helps allocate resources more sensibly – away from trials of clear-cut cases and toward more valuable programmes, such as probation and parole services.[104]

Another stated advantage of bargaining is that it helps the prosecution to obtain cooperation in complex cases. Informants are often indispensable to uncovering the operation of organised crime, for example, and plea discounts can be critical to obtaining their cooperation.[105] In this respect, bargaining can be said to help uncover the truth in criminal cases. The European Court of Human Rights emphasised this aspect of plea bargaining in *Natsvlishvili* v. *Georgia*, noting that plea bargaining 'if applied correctly, [can be] a successful tool in combating corruption and organised crime'.[106]

Plea bargaining has also been defended for sparing reluctant and vulnerable witnesses the ordeal of testifying and for providing victims with closure more quickly than trials do.[107] Some courts and commentators have also stated that guilty pleas can facilitate the rehabilitation of defendants by encouraging them to accept responsibility and by leading to the swifter imposition of punishment.[108]

A number of authors have, however, disputed the extent to which bargaining in fact produces these benefits. For example, some victims have criticised the sentencing reduction that their assailants have received as a result of plea bargaining and have stated they would have preferred to testify rather than seeing the perpetrators receive a significant plea discount.[109] The argument in favour of using plea bargaining to obtain cooperation in complex crimes has been met with the counterpoint that cooperation agreements allow participants in serious criminal

[103] Fair Trials, 'Disappearing Trial' (2017), 36.
[104] White, 'A Proposal for Reform' (1971), 440–1 (quoting Enker, 'Perspectives on Plea Bargaining' (1967), 112); Fair Trials, 'Disappearing Trial' (2017), 36.
[105] See e.g. Natapoff, *Snitching* (2009), 31; Richman, 'Cooperating Defendants' (1996), 293.
[106] *Natsvlishvili* v. *Georgia*, ECtHR, No. 9043/05, Judgment of 29 Apr. 2014, para. 90.
[107] Wilkinson, 'In Defense of American Criminal Justice' (2014), 1142; Ashworth and Redmayne, *Criminal Process* (2010), 309.
[108] E.g. *Brady* v. *United States*, 397 US 742, 753 (1970); Wilkinson, 'American Criminal Justice' (2014), 1142.
[109] Ashworth and Redmayne, *Criminal Process* (2010), 309.

enterprises to evade full responsibility and receive unduly lenient sentences. Similarly, some have questioned whether the financial benefits of guilty pleas outweigh the additional costs of imprisonment resulting from the higher number of convictions.[110] As guilty pleas free up prosecutorial resources, these resources are likely to be used to process less serious cases that might otherwise have been dropped by prosecutors.

More fundamentally, commentators have expressed concern that the costs of bargaining in many cases outweigh its benefits. Perhaps the most significant criticism of bargaining is that excessive sentencing and charging discounts may pressure innocent defendants into waiving their right to a trial.[111] In the United States, data reported by the National Registry of Exonerations (NRE) in January 2017 showed that roughly 18 per cent of recorded exonerations (343 out of 1,956) concerned the product of guilty pleas.[112] The NRE identified large plea discounts as a key factor driving false guilty pleas.[113] Other analyses of exonerations have similarly found that innocent defendants plead guilty to avoid the risk of harsher punishment after trial.[114] In England, research suggests that a significant percentage of guilty pleaders 'claim innocence' or are 'possibly innocent of one or more charges'.[115] In Germany, more than half of the defence attorneys surveyed in a 2012 study believed that at least one of their clients had falsely admitted guilt in exchange for a lenient sentence.[116]

Empirical studies from the United States suggest that innocent defendants are at the greatest risk of pleading guilty in four situations. First, false

[110] Fair Trials, 'Disappearing Trial' (2017), 37; Brown, 'Perverse Effects of Efficiency' (2014), 183.

[111] See e.g. Langer, 'Rethinking Plea Bargaining' (2006), 224–8; McCoy, 'Plea Bargaining as Coercion' (2005), 87–90.

[112] National Registry of Exonerations, *Exoneration Detail List* (2017); for a discussion of some of the reasons why exoneration data might underrepresent the prevalence of false guilty pleas, see Dervan and Edkins, 'The Innocent Defendant's Dilemma' (2013), 21–2.

[113] National Registry of Exonerations, *Innocents Who Plead Guilty* (2015); see also Blume and Helm, 'The Unexonerated' (2014), 180.

[114] Covey, 'Police Misconduct' (2013), 1173 (examining the mass exonerations in the Rampart case in California and the Tulia case in Texas and finding that, in those two cases involving police misconduct, innocent defendants pleaded guilty at a rate of 77%).

[115] Ashworth and Redmayne, *Criminal Process* (2010), 310; see also Peay and Player, 'Pleading Guilty' (2018), 938 (noting that 26.7% of those who applied for review of their conviction by the Criminal Case Review Commission over the previous three years had entered a guilty plea); Rauxloh, *Plea Bargaining in National and International Law* (2012), 54 (discussing a study suggesting that as many as 26% of guilty pleaders stood a good or fairly good chance of being acquitted at trial).

[116] Altenhain et al., *Die Praxis der Absprachen* (2013), 134.

guilty pleas can occur when there is a significant differential between the negotiated sentence and the sentence expected upon conviction after trial.[117] This risk is particularly serious when steep discounts are combined with harsh baseline sentences.[118] Of the three systems examined here, the risk is greatest in the United States, given its very severe baseline sentences and lack of regulation of plea discounts. In England and Germany, baseline sentences tend to be lower than those in the United States, particularly for recidivists,[119] and sentencing guidelines or courts limit plea discounts to about one-third of the expected post-trial sentence.[120] However, in Germany the trial judges who conduct the bargaining also have authority to pass sentence upon the defendant. This fact gives their sentencing 'offer' a special coercive flavour: a defendant who insists on a trial knows that at sentencing he will be faced with judges who may well resent his 'recalcitrance' and will hence not be disposed toward leniency.[121]

[117] Wright, 'Trial Distortion' (2005), 84–6, 116–7, 147–8; Dervan and Edkins, 'Innocent Defendant's Dilemma' (2013), 36 (in an experiment involving college students accused of cheating, finding that 'well over half of the innocent study participants . . . were willing to falsely admit guilt in return for a reduced punishment').

[118] See e.g. Ross, 'Entrenched Position' (2006), 718.

[119] For data showing that sentences imposed for similar crimes were more severe in the United States than in England, see Tonry and Farrington, 'Punishment and Crime' (2005), 32. In Germany, imprisonment for life (with the possibility of parole after fifteen years) is available only for genocide and intentional homicide; for all other offences, the statutory maximum punishment is fifteen years imprisonment (§§ 38, 57a Penal Code). Moreover, very few persons convicted in German criminal courts actually serve a prison sentence. In 2016, German courts convicted 501,765 persons of a non-traffic criminal offence. Only 6.2% of them received a prison sentence that was not suspended (see Statistisches Bundesamt, *Rechtspflege Strafverfolgung 2016* (2017), 160). Even assuming that some of those whose sentences were suspended failed on probation and eventually had to serve a prison sentence, the overall imprisonment rate is below 10%. For a comparison with the US system, see Kleinfeld, 'Two Cultures of Punishment' (2016), 933.

[120] Sentencing Council, *Reduction in Sentence for a Guilty Plea* (2017), 5. In an empirical study of German courts, 59% of judges said that they told defendants that there would be a 25% sentence differential between a negotiated judgment and sentencing after a full trial, and 24% offered a 33% decrease for a confession. Prosecutors and defence lawyers thought that the indicated sentence differential was closer to 33% in the majority of the cases. Altenhain et al., *Praxis der Absprachen* (2013), 130–1.

[121] In a study conducted in 2012, German trial judges indicated that 71% of those defendants who had initially remained silent or had denied guilt made a confession after the judge told them the possible sentence increase after a full trial; Altenhain et al., *Praxis der Absprachen* (2013), 132.

Secondly, a plea bargain can be coercive when the prosecutor's plea offer is a prison sentence, while capital punishment is a possibility after trial. Because the death penalty has been abolished in England and Germany, this risk only exists in the United States (in the federal system and the thirty US states that retain the death penalty). A recent study of capital charging and sentencing decisions in the state of Georgia in the period between 1993 and 2000 found 'strong evidence that the threat of the death penalty ha[d] a robust causal effect on the likelihood of a plea agreement'.[122] While the study did not reach any conclusions about the effects of the death-penalty threat on *innocent* defendants, other studies have documented cases in which innocents have pleaded guilty to avoid the death penalty.[123] As the NRE noted, '[e]xcluding drug cases, most guilty-plea exonerations are for homicide or sexual assault, two categories that account for 70% of all known exonerations'.[124] Among the homicide exonerees who had pleaded guilty, '[i]t appears that the great majority [pleaded guilty] to avoid the risk of execution. All but 2 were prosecuted in death penalty states, and 70% had falsely confessed (31/44).'[125]

The risk of a coercive plea bargain also arises when the plea offer is to probation or another non-custodial alternative, while the expected sentence post-trial entails imprisonment. This is a risk that exists in all three systems studied here. In the United States, mock experiments have revealed that subjects feel extreme pressure to plead guilty when the choice is between prison and probation.[126] Likewise, commentators have argued that the choice between a custodial and a non-custodial sentence in England and Germany is a powerful – and potentially coercive – influence on defendants in deciding whether to admit guilt.[127]

[122] Thaxton, 'Leveraging Death' (2013), 475.

[123] Gross et al., 'Exonerations in the United States' (2005), 544–6; National Registry of Exonerations, *Innocents Who Plead Guilty* (2015).

[124] National Registry of Exonerations, *Innocents Who Plead Guilty* (2015), 2.

[125] *Ibid.*, 3; see also Blume and Helm, 'The Unexonerated' (2014), 180 (identifying the threat of the death penalty as a factor in pushing innocent defendants to plead guilty).

[126] A 1984 mock bargaining experiment involving college students found that in certain circumstances, particularly when conviction was seen as highly likely and probation was offered upon a guilty plea, 'innocent' study subjects would accept a plea bargain 'in order to cut their losses'; Bordens, 'Likelihood of Conviction' (1984), 71.

[127] For England, see Ashworth and Redmayne, *Criminal Process* (2010), 293, 302; Peay and Player, 'Pleading Guilty' (2018), 937. For Germany, see Altenhain et al., *Praxis der Absprachen* (2013), 118 (indicating that negotiations often turn on suspension of a prison sentence).

Fourthly, a risk of coercion arises when the defendant is detained before trial on misdemeanour charges, and a guilty plea is offered that results in immediate release from detention for time served. Because a plea bargain in this scenario allows the defendant to return to his family and his job, it places an enormous pressure even on innocent defendants to accept it.[128] A recent US empirical study found that misdemeanour defendants who are detained 'plead guilty at a 25% higher rate than similarly situated' defendants who are released pending trial.[129] The authors concluded that '[m]isdemeano[u]r pretrial detention … seems especially likely to induce guilty pleas, including wrongful ones'.[130]

Certain structural features may exacerbate the pressure on defendants to plead guilty. For example, in a number of US jurisdictions, defence attorneys are paid per case rather than per hour and therefore have an incentive to encourage plea bargains even when they are not in the best interest of the client. In legal aid systems, caseload pressure may have a similar effect on lawyers to resolve many of their cases quickly – that is, through plea bargaining. Likewise, overburdened prosecutors may not have an adequate incentive to ensure that plea bargains accurately reflect the facts of the case, as long as the bargain saves them resources and ensures a conviction.

In England and the United States, bargains may not only be coercive but also uninformed. In these two systems, plea bargains in less serious cases are often negotiated without the presence of counsel.[131] Although defendants voluntarily waive the right to counsel, the decision to do so occurs under the pressure to resolve the matter quickly in order to receive the most favourable bargain, such as immediate release from pre-trial detention and sentencing to 'time served'. But the absence of counsel means that the defendant may not fully comprehend the law and evidence in the case and may forfeit valid defences. The defendant is also not likely to be fully aware of the collateral consequences accompanying a criminal conviction. The absence of legal advice under the circumstances

128 After reviewing real cases of exonerees who had pleaded guilty, John Blume and Rebecca Helm identified a similar set of factors contributing to false guilty pleas. See Blume and Helm, 'The Unexonerated' (2014).

129 Heaton et al., 'Downstream Consequences' (2017), 711.

130 *Ibid.*, 711.

131 Fair Trials, 'Disappearing Trial' (2017), 52; Boruchowitz, Brink and Dimino, *Minor Crimes, Massive Waste* (2009), 14–17; Brook et al., 'Comparative Look at Plea Bargaining' (2016), 1173.

increases the risk that the bargain is unfair and does not accurately reflect the facts of the case.[132]

Defendants in England and the United States also frequently lack access to material evidence in their cases before they must decide whether to accept a plea offer. In both systems, there are significant pressures on defendants to plead early in the process, when only limited evidence has been disclosed.[133] These features sharply increase the risk that a plea bargain will not accurately reflect the facts. In theory, judicial review could help remedy the lack of access to the evidence by the defendant before a bargain is reached. But because judges review the factual basis of a bargain only briefly, without access to an investigative file, and only after the parties have reached a bargain, judicial review is not sufficient to redress inadequate pre-plea disclosure of evidence. Consequently, even if defendants are guilty of *some* offence, inadequate disclosure, limited adversarial testing, perfunctory judicial oversight and sizeable plea discounts can lead defendants to plead guilty to crimes that are more serious than those they actually committed.[134]

In England and the United States, bargaining also lacks important procedural protections – such as publicity and judicial review at the trial and appellate level – that accompany ordinary trials. The parties negotiate the disposition in private, typically without the participation of a

[132] Fair Trials, 'Disappearing Trial' (2017), 52; Boruchowitz, Brink and Dimino, *Minor Crimes, Massive Waste* (2009), 14–20; Brook et al., 'Comparative Look at Plea Bargaining' (2016), 1173.

[133] For England, see UK Human Rights Blog, *Early Guilty Pleas: Justice for Whom*? (2016), available at https://ukhumanrightsblog.com/2016/02/15/early-guilty-pleas-justice-for-whom/; Brook et al., 'Comparative Look at Plea Bargaining' (2016), 1197. The guidelines in England do provide that the full sentencing discount would still be available to defendants who delay pleading in order to receive adequate disclosure and legal advice. Sentencing Council, *Reduction in Sentence for a Guilty Plea* (2017). Research suggests that at least in some cases, judges apply the exception to account for late disclosure. But as commentators have pointed out, defendants often nonetheless feel pressure to plead early, whether out of concern that the court will not grant the full discount under this exception or because of inadequate legal advice. See e.g. Peay and Player, 'Pleading Guilty' (2018), 935 (noting that 'the exception justified by the need for further disclosure may be infrequently applied in an arguably chaotic system geared to efficiency' and that 'where disclosure of unused [and therefore possibly favourable to the defence] material routinely occurs at a very late stage, vulnerable defendants may end up understanding neither the elements of the offence charged nor the relevance of the exculpatory material').

[134] Turner, 'Plea Bargaining' (2017). In Germany, by contrast, formal plea bargaining takes place only after both the defence lawyer and the trial court have seen the prosecution file containing all relevant evidence.

neutral third party or direct input from victims. Plea bargains, particularly in misdemeanour cases, are frequently entered orally, and their terms may not be formally recorded.[135] The lack of an adequate record and transparency hinders accountability for flaws in the process or the outcome. It also taints the process in the eyes of the public and victims.[136] In the German system, by contrast, any agreement reached by the court and the parties before trial must be announced at the public trial and be placed on the record.[137] The defendant also has the right to file an appeal against the eventual judgment even if the sentence imposed by the court lies within the limits previously announced by the court and accepted by the parties.[138]

To the extent that bargaining allows the parties to create individualised dispositions outside the public gaze and with minimal judicial review, it also increases the risk of unequal treatment of similarly situated defendants. The concessions negotiated as part of a bargain may vary based on arbitrary factors such as race, gender, age, wealth, the relationship between defence counsel and the prosecutor, or the workload of the lawyers working on the case.[139] For example, in the United States, a recent study found that white defendants are over 25 per cent more likely than black defendants to obtain a charge reduction; the disparity is especially pronounced in misdemeanour cases, where 'white defendants were 45.1% more likely than black defendants to see their top charge dropped or reduced'.[140] In England, disparities are found in the rates of guilty pleas among white and black defendants, which also affects the ultimate sentences.[141]

When transparency and procedural safeguards are lacking, bargaining can also exacerbate problems of corruption in the legal system. As the

135 In England, only the sentencing discount given in exchange for a guilty plea is supposed to be placed on the record. Fair Trials, 'Disappearing Trial' (2017), 56.

136 Bibas, 'Plea Bargaining' (2004), 2547; O'Hear, 'Plea Bargaining and Procedural Justice' (2008), 444–6.

137 See § 243(4) StPO.

138 See Meyer-Goßner and Schmitt, *Strafprozessordnung* (2018), § 302 notes 26c, 26d.

139 See Alschuler, 'Trial Judge's Role in Plea Bargaining' (1976), 1125–6; Berdejó, 'Criminalizing Race' (2018), 1187; Bibas, 'Plea Bargaining' (2004), 2468; Kutateladze et al., 'Opening Pandora's Box' (2016), 420; Spohn and Fornango, 'US Attorneys and Substantial Assistance Departures' (2009), 835–6.

140 Berdejó, 'Criminalizing Race' (2018), 1215; see also Metcalfe and Chiricos, 'Race, Plea, and Charge Reduction' (2018), 223 (finding that 'pleading guilty increases the probability of a charge reduction by 50.1% for blacks, as opposed to 55.8% for whites').

141 Lammy Review, *Final Report* (2017), 5, 25–9.

dissenting judge in *Natsvlishvili* v. *Georgia* observed, the Council of Europe had urged Georgian authorities in 2006 to review that country's plea bargaining system, which in its then-present form 'on the one hand allow[ed] some alleged offenders to use the proceeds of their crimes to buy their way out of prison and, on the other, risk[ed] being applied arbitrarily, abusively and even for political reasons'.[142] For a struggling criminal justice system, it is difficult to prevent existing problems, such as political favouritism and discrimination, from spilling over into plea negotiations.[143]

To properly evaluate bargaining, however, it is not enough to highlight its costs and benefits and weigh them against one another; we must also consider how bargaining's features compare to those of full-blown criminal trials. In fact, trials can also lead to wrongful convictions and unequal treatment of defendants. But as the previous discussion suggests, there is good reason to believe that the risks of false convictions and unjust sentences are higher in systems that rely on largely unregulated bargaining that lacks meaningful judicial control.

IV Regulating Bargaining and Alternatives to Bargaining

Scholars have long debated whether legal systems would be better off if bargaining were entirely abolished. At this point, complete abolition is not practically viable in any of the three systems we have examined. Even if it were, we are not convinced it would be desirable, if the only alternative is the full-blown trial as currently practiced in those systems. For one, affording every defendant a complete trial with a (potentially adversarial) presentation of all relevant evidence would create burdens on personal and material resources that hardly any state would be willing to bear. Secondly, there are many simple, clear-cut cases in which conviction and sentencing do not require the taking of (much) evidence, especially when the defendant was caught in the act, confessed to the crime or does not contest his guilt. For such cases, simplified forms of adjudication should be available, albeit with the possibility of switching to a full trial if serious doubts as to guilt arise. Such arrangements should fit into the structure of each jurisdiction's procedural system. They could be variants of the guilty plea procedure typical of common law

[142] *Natsvlishvili* v. *Georgia*, ECtHR, No. 9043/05, Judgment of 29 Apr. 2014, Partly Dissenting Opinion of Judge Gyulumyan, para. 1.

[143] Alkon, 'Plea Bargaining as a Legal Transplant' (2010), 365–8, 372–3.

jurisdictions, or they could be abbreviated 'inquisitorial' trials. Such alternatives to present procedural arrangements should be designed in a way that avoids the problems described in Section III.

A thorough study of these alternatives is beyond the scope of this chapter, but we sketch out a few possibilities. One promising option for promoting efficiency while preserving procedural fairness would be to encourage better screening of cases by prosecutors.[144] An early and careful assessment of each case by sufficiently trained prosecutors would end the clogging of the system by cases that would not hold up at trial or do not merit sanctioning – cases that today are prime candidates for plea bargaining later in the process. A system of intensive screening appears to exist in Japan, and it reduces the need for negotiations with the defence at a later stage.[145] In Germany, prosecutors also tend to closely examine cases sent to them by the police, ultimately prosecuting only about one-fifth of the cases in which the police identified a suspect.[146] One should, however, make sure that prosecutorial discretion to dismiss cases is subject to control, lest the interests of victims in having their offenders tried and convicted be disregarded. In Germany, victims may appeal against the dismissal of their cases for lack of sufficient evidence,[147] though such appeals are rarely successful.[148]

In most inquisitorial systems, the law provides for written procedures that lead to the conviction of defendants without a trial.[149] In Germany,

144 Ronald Wright and Marc Miller have argued that strict prosecutorial screening is a viable alternative to plea bargaining. Wright and Miller, 'The Screening/Bargaining Tradeoff' (2002), 117.

145 Luna and Wade, *Prosecutor in Transnational Perspective* (2012), 102, 112–4; Johnson, *Japanese Way of Justice* (2002), 56, 106–7.

146 In 2017, German prosecutors filed an indictment or an application for a penal order in 19.6% of all cases with a known suspect. They dismissed 27.7% of the cases for lack of sufficient evidence, and another 29.5% for lack of a public interest in prosecution; 22% of the cases were disposed of in some other way (e.g., treated as an administrative infraction or joined with another case). See Statistisches Bundesamt, *Staatsanwaltschaften 2017* (2018), 30.

147 See § 172 StPO. The Federal Constitutional Court decided in 2014 that victims of certain serious crimes against the person have a constitutional claim for an effective prosecution of the offender; Federal Constitutional Court, Judgment of 13 Nov. 2014, 2 BvR 1568/12, *Neue Juristische Wochenschrift* (2015), 3500.

148 Zöller, '§ 172' (2019), n. 1.

149 See e.g. Art. 524–528–2 French Code de procédure pénale (*ordonnance pénale*); Art. 459–464 Italian Codice di procedura penale (*decreto penale*). For a review of abbreviated procedures in inquisitorial systems, see Ambos and Heinze, 'Abbreviated Procedures in Comparative Criminal Procedure' (2017).

the prosecutor may initiate a penal order proceeding to resolve less serious cases without a hearing. As has been described above, penal orders are drafted by the prosecutor and issued by a judge. Judges may impose fines and suspended prison sentences of up to one year in this proceeding.[150] The penal order thus makes it possible for the prosecution and the court to dispose of uncontested cases quickly, while preserving the defendant's ability to request a trial if he wishes to contest the charges.

While even more efficient than bargains, penal orders also raise concerns about fairness and accuracy. Judicial control over the orders drafted by prosecutors may be less than thorough in many routine cases. Moreover, since the defendant is not asked for his consent before the penal order issues and has only two weeks to file an appeal and thus prevent the penal order from becoming a definitive judgement, the defendant may overlook the document or not realise in time that he needs to take action if he wishes to object to the verdict or sentence.[151] Research on penal orders in Switzerland has indeed found that 'penal order proceedings were more vulnerable to error compared to ordinary proceedings' and suggests that the convenience of the procedure may induce factually innocent defendants to accept responsibility.[152] Further study of the operation of penal orders is therefore needed before suggesting the introduction of this mechanism to other jurisdictions.

For common law jurisdictions, a viable alternative to bargaining might be short bench trials with less complex procedures. In such a trial, both parties could present their evidence briefly, without having to adhere to complex rules of evidence, and the judge would then pronounce the verdict and the sentence. A study of bench trials from the 1980s suggests that they could offer a fair, yet sufficiently expeditious and cost-effective alternative to plea bargaining.[153] Of course, holding a bench trial in the US system presupposes the defendant's waiver of his constitutional right to a jury, and such waiver will be forthcoming only if the defendant can expect a similar or better outcome from a bench trial than from a jury trial.

150 A suspended prison sentence may be imposed only if the defendant is represented by counsel (§ 407(2) StPO).

151 For criticism of the penal order proceeding, see Arbeitskreis, 'Abgekürzte Strafverfahren' (2019).

152 Gillieron, 'Abbreviated Trial Procedures' (2019).

153 Schulhofer, 'Is Plea Bargaining Inevitable?' (1984), 1037.

Even if some of these possible alternatives are adopted, criminal justice systems are likely to retain a certain amount of bargaining. The task then is to reform bargaining so that it produces fair and just results. We highlight a few key safeguards that courts and legislatures can adopt to reduce the risk of coercive, uninformed, unfair and inaccurate bargains.

First, to minimise coercion, criminal justice systems can limit the charging and sentencing discounts that may be negotiated. As the Sentencing Council has done in England, sentence discounts can be fixed to no more than about a third of the expected post-trial sentence. Indeed, studying the English experience, some scholars have maintained that an even lower discount cap may be needed. Ashworth and Redmayne have suggested that if a discount is to be retained, the incentive should be 'no more than a 10 percent reduction'.[154] Others have argued that a reduction from a custodial to a non-custodial sentence should never hinge solely on a guilty plea or the timing of the guilty plea.[155] Such suggestions appear sensible with regard to maintaining the defendant's freedom of choice, but they may go too far in that they make bargaining unattractive for defendants, potentially leading to a sharp increase in trials. Alternatively, courts can police discounts through proportionality review, as is done in Germany, to ensure that they are not too coercive and are not out of proportion with the defendant's blameworthiness.

In systems that give prosecutors broad charging discretion, such as England and the United States, more must be done to ensure that prosecutors do not circumvent any sentence discount limits through their charging decisions. Courts should have the authority to scrutinise charges and modify them when they appear to be excessive. Excising overlapping criminal statutes – a stated goal of reformers in the United States and England – would also help constrain prosecutorial discretion to evade plea-discount limits through charge bargains. In the United States, reducing sentencing severity and restoring judicial discretion over sentencing could also help ensure that plea discounts remain reasonable.

Another useful measure would be to provide broad pre-plea discovery to the defence and to ensure that defence lawyers have the time and resources to review the evidence. Full discovery is available in Germany, but is lacking in many cases in England and the United States. Only if the defence is granted access to relevant information gathered by the prosecution can bargained pleas be regarded as voluntary and intelligent.

[154] Ashworth and Redmayne, *Criminal Process* (2010), 317.

[155] Peay and Player, 'Pleading Guilty' (2018), 955.

Where negotiations are conducted between the parties, judicial oversight of plea bargains should be strengthened, whether during the negotiations or after the fact. While all three systems formally require that an admission of guilt have a factual basis, judicial review of this basis is underdeveloped in England and the United States. German law requires that judges independently verify the facts on which a conviction is to be based, but even here practice frequently contents itself with accepting the defendant's own declaration of guilt. An empirical study conducted in 2012 (before the German Constitutional Court specifically emphasised the obligation of judges to independently review the facts) found that over a quarter of the judges admitted to only rarely or occasionally verifying the facts on which the admission of guilt was based.[156] There still seems to exist a tension between the court's legal obligations and caseload pressures. In the United States and England, a growing emphasis on metrics of judicial performance – namely, how many cases a judge has resolved how quickly – is increasing the risk that judges may dispense with an in-depth review of the facts for the sake of efficient case processing.

Another practical concern in the United States and England is that even when the judge is inclined to engage in independent review, she has no source of evidence apart from the parties' submissions. If the parties have reached an agreement, they are unlikely to present facts that are inconsistent with those underlying the agreement lest the deal be disrupted. To alleviate this concern about 'fact bargaining', some or all of the discovery material exchanged between the parties could also be made available to the judge (which would be akin to the 'investigative file' system in Germany).[157] Alternatively, it has been suggested that a type of pre-plea report, similar to the pre-sentence report that is currently prepared by probation officers before sentencing in federal cases, be made available to judges before they accept a guilty plea.[158] Solutions along these lines can help ensure that plea bargains in England and the United States are fair to all concerned and accurately reflect the facts of the case.

[156] Altenhain et al., *Die Praxis der Absprachen* (2013), 99 (these findings were based on the judge's own admissions, while prosecutors and defence attorneys reported that an even lower percentage of judges verified the facts of the bargain).

[157] Turner, 'Judicial Participation' (2006), 562.

[158] Alschuler, 'Trial Judge's Role in Plea Bargaining' (1976), 1146; Turner, 'Judicial Participation' (2006), 562.

Finally, criminal justice systems must require greater transparency and documentation of the negotiations. A few US jurisdictions already require that plea bargains be put in writing and on the record.[159] In England, the law requires that the sentence discount in exchange for a guilty plea be stated clearly on the record.[160] As discussed earlier, Germany has the most demanding recording requirements of the three systems examined and demands that the substance as well as the outcome of the negotiations be placed on the record.

However, the German system also has its flaws. The most serious problem occurs if negotiations fail. This may happen if, for example, the prosecutor vetoes a deal achieved by the judge and the defence lawyer, or if the trial court subsequently reneges on an agreement because circumstances or the perspective of the judges on the deal have changed.[161] If that happens, the case must go to a full trial. However, the trial court will be composed of the same judges who were previously involved in the negotiations with the defence, and the defendant may already have made a confession in open court as part of the agreement. The Code of Criminal Procedure provides that the confession must not be used as evidence in this case,[162] but it is not clear whether evidence derived from the information provided by the defendant may be admitted. In any event, the judges will find it difficult to erase a detailed confession from their minds and to mentally return to the *status quo ante* and the presumption that the defendant is innocent. In order to relieve this serious problem, it would be preferable that the trial be held by a judge or chamber different from those who had taken part in plea negotiations, as is done in some US jurisdiction permitting judicial involvement in plea bargaining.

V Conclusion

Negotiated criminal justice is here to stay. Although the phenomenon has adopted different shapes and forms, its basic structure (the exchange of leniency in sentencing for the defendant's procedural cooperation) can be found in almost all legal systems of both the adversarial and the inquisitorial universe. Since plea bargaining accommodates the professional

159 Mirza, 'Plea Bargaining Process' (2015), 506.
160 Fair Trials, 'Disappearing Trial' (2017), 56.
161 See § 257c(4), cl. 1 StPO.
162 § 257c(4) cl. 3 StPO.

interests of the lawyers and judges involved, any effort to eradicate it is bound to fail. What we should strive for, then, is to limit the realm of negotiated justice to those types of cases where it is appropriate, that is, non-serious, essentially uncontested cases. For this type of case, legal systems should provide procedural arrangements that ensure that defendants' admissions of guilt are voluntary and intelligent. In working toward that goal, each system can learn from the best practices – and the faults – of any other system.

Bibliography

Alkon C., 'Plea Bargaining as a Legal Transplant: A Good Idea for Troubled Criminal Justice Systems?', *Transnational Law and Contemporary Problems*, 19 (2010), 355–418.

Alschuler A. W., 'The Trial Judge's Role in Plea Bargaining (pt. 1)', *Columbia Law Review*, 76 (1976), 1059–154.

Altenhain K., Hagemeier I., Haimerl M. and Stammen K.-H., *Die Praxis der Absprachen in Wirtschaftsstrafverfahren*, Baden-Baden, Nomos (2007).

Altenhain K., Dietmeier F. and May M., *Die Praxis der Absprachen im Strafverfahren*, Baden-Baden, Nomos (2013).

Ambos K. and Heinze A., 'Abbreviated Procedures in Comparative Criminal Procedure: A Structural Approach with a View to International Criminal Procedure', in Bergsmo M. (ed.), *Abbreviated Criminal Procedures for Core International Crimes*, Brussels, Torkel Opsahl (2017), 27–102.

Arbeitskreis deutscher, österreichischer und schweizerischer Strafrechtslehrer, 'Alternativ-Entwurf Abgekürzte Strafverfahren im Rechtsstaat (AE-ASR)', *Goltdammer's Archiv*, 166 (2019), 1–128.

Ashworth A. and Redmayne M., *The Criminal Process*, 4th edn, Oxford University Press (2010).

Attorney General's Guidelines on the Acceptance of Pleas and the Prosecutor's Role in the Sentencing Exercise (2009), available at www.gov.uk/guidance/the-acceptance-of-pleas-and-the-prosecutors-role-in-the-sentencing-exercise.

Bachmaier L., 'The European Court of Human Rights on Negotiated Justice and Coercion', *European Journal on Crime, Criminal Law and Criminal Justice*, 26 (2018), 236–59.

Berdejó C., 'Criminalizing Race: Racial Disparities in Plea-Bargaining', *Boston College Law Review*, 59 (2018), 1187–249.

Bibas S., 'Plea Bargaining Outside the Shadow of Trial', *Harvard Law Review*, 117 (2004), 2464–547.

Blume J. H. and Helm R. K., 'The Unexonerated: Factually Innocent Defendants Who Plead Guilty', *Cornell Law Review*, 100 (2014), 157–92.

Bordens K. S., 'The Effects of Likelihood of Conviction, Threatened Punishment, and Assumed Role on Mock Plea Bargaining Decisions', *Basic and Applied Social Psychology*, 5 (1984), 59–74.

Boruchowitz R. C., Brink M. N. and Dimino M., *Minor Crimes, Massive Waste: The Terrible Toll of America's Broken Misdemeanor Courts*, Washington, DC, National Association of Criminal Defense Lawyers (2009).

Brodowski D., 'Die verfassungsrechtliche Legitimation des US-amerikanischen "plea bargaining"', *Zeitschrift für die gesamte Strafrechtswissenschaft*, 124 (2012), 733–77.

Brook C. A., Fiannaca B., Harvey D., Marcus P., McEwan J. and Pomerance R., 'A Comparative Look at Plea Bargaining in Australia, Canada, England, New Zealand, and the United States', *William and Mary Law Review*, 57 (2016), 1147–224.

Brown D. K., 'The Perverse Effects of Efficiency in Criminal Process', *Virginia Law Review*, 100 (2014), 183–223

'Judicial Power to Regulate Plea Bargaining', 57 *William and Mary Law Review*, 57 (2016), 1225–76.

Bureau of Justice Statistics, *State Court Sentencing of Convicted Felons, 2004 – Statistical Tables*, Washington, DC, Bureau of Justice Statistics (2007).

Federal Justice Statistics, 2012 – Statistical Tables, Washington, DC, Bureau of Justice Statistics (2015).

Covey R., 'Police Misconduct as a Cause of Wrongful Convictions', *Washington University Law Review*, 90 (2013), 1133–89.

Dervan L. E. and Edkins V. A., 'The Innocent Defendant's Dilemma: An Innovative Empirical Study of Plea Bargaining's Innocence Problem', *Journal of Criminal Law and Criminology*, 103 (2013), 1–48.

Duttge G., 'Die Urteilsabsprachen als Signum einer rechtlichen Steuerungskrise', in Hefendehl R., Hörnle T. and Greco L. (eds.), *Streitbare Strafrechtswissenschaft. Festschrift für Bernd Schünemann*, Munich, C. H. Beck (2014), 875–89.

Enker A., 'Perspectives on Plea Bargaining', in President's Commission on Law Enforcement and Administration of Justice (ed.), *Task Force Report: The Courts*, Washington, DC, National Criminal Justice Reference Service (1967).

Fair Trials, 'The Disappearing Trial' (2017), available at www.fairtrials.org/wp-content/uploads/2017/12/Report-The-Disappearing-Trial.pdf.

Frase R., 'State Sentencing Guideline: Diversity, Consensus, and Unresolved Policy Issues', *Columbia Law Review*, 105 (2005), 1190–232.

Frankenberg K. von, *Grundlagen konsensualer Konfliktlösungsprozesse*, Berlin, Wissenschaftlicher Verlag (2013).

Gercke B., Julius K.-P., Temming D. and Zöller M. A., *Strafprozessordnung. Heidelberger Kommentar*, 6th edn, Heidelberg, C. F. Müller (2019).

Gillieron G., 'Comparing Plea Bargaining and Abbreviated Trial Procedures', in Brown D. K., Turner J. I. and Weißer B. (eds.), *Oxford Handbook of Criminal Process*, Oxford University Press (2019).

Gross S. R., Jacoby K., Matheson D. J. and Montgomery N., 'Exonerations in the United States 1989 through 2003', *Journal of Criminal Law and Criminology*, 95 (2005), 523–60.

Heaton P., Mayson S. G. and Stevenson M., 'The Downstream Consequences of Misdemeanor Pretrial Detention', *Stanford Law Review*, 69 (2017), 711–94.

Heger M. and Pest R., Verständigungen im Strafverfahren nach dem Urteil des Bundesverfassungsgerichts, *Zeitschrift für die gesamte Strafrechtswissenschaft*, 126 (2014), 446–86.

Hooper, Lord Justice and Ormerod D. (eds.), *Blackstone's Criminal Practice* 2012, Oxford University Press (2011).

Horne J., *Plea Bargains, Guilty Pleas and the Consequences for Appeal in England and Wales*, Warwick School of Law Research Paper No. 2013/10 (2013).

Human Rights Watch, *An Offer You Can't Refuse: How U.S. Federal Prosecutors Force Drug Defendants to Plead Guilty*, New York, Human Rights Watch (2013).

Johnson D. T., *The Japanese Way of Justice*, Oxford University Press (2002).

Johnson M. T. and Gilbert S. A., *The U.S. Sentencing Guidelines – Results of the Federal Judicial Center's 1996 Survey*, Federal Judicial Center (1997), available at www.fjc.gov/sites/default/files/2012/gssurvey.pdf.

Kim A. C., 'Underestimating the Trial Penalty: An Empirical Analysis of the Federal Trial Penalty and Critique of the Abrams Study', *Mississippi Law Journal*, 84 (2015), 1195–256.

King N. J., Soulé D. A., Steen S. and Weidner R. R., 'When Process Affects Punishment: Differences in Sentences after Guilty Plea, Bench Trial, and Jury Trial in Five Guidelines States', *Columbia Law Review*, 105 (2005), 959–1009.

King N. J. and Wright R. F., 'The Invisible Revolution in Plea Bargaining: Managerial Judging and Judicial Participation in Negotiations', *Texas Law Review*, 95 (2016), 325–97.

Klein S. R., Remis A. S. and Elm D. L., 'Waiving the Criminal Justice System: An Empirical and Constitutional Analysis', *American Criminal Law Review*, 52 (2015), 73–130.

Kleinfeld J., 'Two Cultures of Punishment', *Stanford Law Review*, 68 (2016), 933–1036.

Kudlich H., 'Ecclestone, Verständigungsgesetz und die Folgen', *Zeitschrift für Rechtspolitik* (2015), 1–15.

(ed.), *Münchener Kommentar zur Strafprozessordnung*, 3 vols., Munich, C. H. Beck (2016), II.

Kutateladze B. L., Andiloro N. R. and Johnson B. D., 'Opening Pandora's Box: How Does Defendant Race Influence Plea Bargaining?', *Justice Quarterly*, 33 (2016), 398–426.

LaFave W. R., Israel J. H., King N. J. and Kerr O. S., *Criminal Procedure*, 4th edn, Eagan, Thomson Reuters (2015).

Lammy D., *The Lammy Review: Final Report*, London (2017).

Langer M., 'Rethinking Plea Bargaining: The Practice and Reform of Prosecutorial Adjudication in American Criminal Procedure', *American Journal of Criminal Law*, 33 (2006), 223–99.

Luna E. and Wade M. (eds.), *The Prosecutor in Transnational Perspective*, Oxford University Press (2012).

McCoy C., 'Plea Bargaining as Coercion: The Trial Penalty and Plea Bargaining Reform', *Criminal Law Quarterly*, 50 (2005), 67–107.

Metcalfe C. and Chiricos T., 'Race, Plea, and Charge Reduction: An Assessment of Racial Disparities in the Plea Process', *Justice Quarterly*, 35 (2018), 223–53.

Meyer-Goßner L. and Schmitt B., *Strafprozessordnung mit GVG und Nebengesetzen (Beck'sche Kurzkommentare)*, 61st edn, Munich, C. H. Beck (2018).

Ministry of Justice, *Criminal Court Statistics Quarterly, England and Wales, January to March 2018 (Annual 2017)* (2018), available at https://assets.publishing.service.gov.uk/government/uploads/system/uploads/attachment_data/file/720026/ccsq-bulletin-jan-mar-2018.pdf.

Mirza S., 'Formalizing the Plea Bargaining Process after Lafler and Frye', *Seton Hall Legislative Journal*, 39 (2015), 487–514.

Moldenhauer G. and Wenske M., '§ 257c', in Hannich R. (ed.), *Karlsruher Kommentar zur Strafprozessordnung*, 7th edn, Munich, C. H. Beck (2013).

Natapoff A., *Snitching: Criminal Informants and the Erosion of American Justice*, New York University Press (2009).

National Registry of Exonerations, *Exoneration Detail List*, available at www.law.umich.edu/special/exoneration/Pages/detaillist.aspx.

Innocents Who Plead Guilty (24 November 2015), available at www.law.umich.edu/special/exoneration/Documents/NRE.Guilty.Plea.Article1.pdf.

Niemz S., *Urteilsabsprachen und Opferinteressen – in Verfahren mit Nebenklagebeteiligung*, Baden-Baden, Nomos (2011).

O'Hear M. M., 'Plea Bargaining and Procedural Justice', *Georgia Law Review*, 42 (2008), 407–69.

Peay J. and Player E., 'Pleading Guilty: Why Vulnerability Matters', *Modern Law Review*, 81 (2018), 929–57.

Ransiek A., 'Zur Urteilsabsprache im Strafprozess: Ein amerikanischer Fall', *Zeitschrift für internationale Strafrechtsdogmatik*, 3 (2008), 116–22.

Rauxloh R., *Plea Bargaining in National and International Law*, Abingdon, Taylor & Francis (2012).

Richman D. C., 'Cooperating Defendants: The Costs and Benefits of Purchasing Information from Scoundrels', *Federal Sentencing Reporter*, 8 (1996), 292–5.

Roberts J. V., 'Sentencing Guidelines in England and Wales: Recent Developments and Emerging Issues', *Law and Contemporary Problems*, 76 (2013), 1–25.

Roberts J. V. and Bradford B., 'Sentence Reductions for a Guilty Plea in England and Wales: Exploring New Empirical Trends', *Journal of Empirical Legal Studies*, 12 (2015), 187–210.

Ross J. E., 'The Entrenched Position of Plea Bargaining in United States Legal Practice', *American Journal of Comparative Law*, 54 (2006), 717–32.

Schulhofer S. J., 'Is Plea Bargaining Inevitable?', *Harvard Law Review*, 97 (1984), 1037–107.

Schünemann B., 'Die Urteilsabsprachen im Strafprozess – ewige Wiederkunft des Gleichen?', in Zöller M. A., Hilger H., Roxin C. and Küper W. (eds.), *Gesamte Strafrechtswissenschaft in internationaler Dimension. Festschrift für Jürgen Wolter*, Berlin, Duncker & Humblot (2013), 1107–29.

Sentencing Council, *Research to Support the Development of a Guideline for Reduction in Sentence for a Guilty Plea*, London (2017), available at www.sentencingcouncil.org.uk/wp-content/uploads/Guilty-plea-research-report_final.pdf.

Slobogin C., 'Plea Bargaining and the Substantive and Procedural Goals of Criminal Justice: From Retribution and Adversarialism to Preventive Justice and Hybrid-Inquisitorialism', *William and Mary Law Review*, 57 (2016), 1505–47.

Spohn C. and Fornango R., 'U.S. Attorneys and Substantial Assistance Departures: Testing for Interprosecutor Disparity', *Criminology*, 47 (2009), 813–46.

Statistisches Bundesamt, *Fachserie 10 Reihe 3: Rechtspflege Strafverfolgung 2016* (2017), available at www.destatis.de/DE/Publikationen/Thematisch/Rechtspflege/GerichtePersonal/Staatsanwaltschaften2100260167004.pdf?__blob=publicationFile.

Fachserie 10, Reihe 2.6: Rechtspflege Staatsanwaltschaften 2017 (2018), available at www.destatis.de/DE/Publikationen/Thematisch/Rechtspflege/GerichtePersonal/Staatsanwaltschaften2100260177004.pdf?__blob=publicationFile.

Stuckenberg C.-F., 'Entscheidungsbesprechung: BVerfG, Urt. v. 19.3.2013', *Zeitschrift für internationale Strafrechtsdogmatik*, 8 (2013), 212–19.

'Gründe für die Abschaffung des § 153a StPO', in Herzog F., Schlothauer R. and Wohlers W. (eds.), *Rechtsstaatlicher Strafprozess und Bürgerrechte. Gedächtnisschrift für Edda Weßlau*, Berlin, Duncker & Humblot (2016), 369–89.

Thaxton S., 'Leveraging Death', *Journal of Criminal Law and Criminology*, 103 (2013), 475–552.

Thomas S. A., 'What Happened to the American Jury? Proposals for Revamping Plea Bargaining and Summary Judgment', *Litigation*, 43 (2017), 25–30.

Tonry M. and Farrington D. P., 'Punishment and Crime across Space and Time', *Crime & Justice*, 33 (2005), 1–39.

Turner J. I., 'Judicial Participation in Plea Negotiations: A Comparative View', *American Journal of Comparative Law*, 54 (2006), 199–267.

Plea Bargaining across Borders, New York, Aspen Publishers (2009).

'Prosecutors and Bargaining in Weak Cases: A Comparative View', in Luna E. and Wade M. (eds.), *The Prosecutor in Transnational Perspective*, Oxford University Press (2012).

'Plea Bargaining', in Luna E. (ed.), *Reforming Criminal Justice*, 4 vols., Phoenix, Arizona State University (2017), III, 73–99.

'Plea Bargaining and International Criminal Justice', *University of the Pacific Law Review*, 48 (2017), 219–47.

Weigend T., 'The Decay of the Inquisitorial Ideal: Plea Bargaining Invades German Criminal Procedure', in Jackson J., Langer M. and Tillers P. (eds.), *Crime, Procedure and Evidence in a Comparative and International Context. Essays in Honour of Professor Mirjan Damaška*, Oxford University Press (2008), 39–64.

'Verfahrenseinstellung nach § 153a StPO: praktikabel, aber nicht legitim', in Herzog F., Schlothauer R. and Wohlers W. (eds.), *Rechtsstaatlicher Strafprozess und Bürgerrechte. Gedächtnisschrift für Edda Weßlau*, Berlin, Duncker & Humblot (2016), 413–25.

Weigend T. and Turner J. I., 'The Constitutionality of Negotiated Criminal Judgments in Germany', *German Law Journal*, 15 (2014), 81–105.

White W. S., 'Proposal for Reform of the Plea Bargaining Process', 119 *University of Pennsylvania Law Review*, 119 (1971), 439–65.

Wilkinson III J. S., 'In Defense of American Criminal Justice', *Vanderbilt Law Review*, 67 (2014), 1099–172.

Wright R. F., 'Trial Distortion and the End of Innocence in Federal Criminal Justice', *University of Pennsylvania Law Review*, 154 (2005), 79–156.

Wright R. F. and Engen R. L., 'The Effects of Depth and Distance in a Criminal Code on Charging, Sentencing, and Prosecutor Power', *North Carolina Law Review*, 84 (2006), 1935–82.

Wright R. F. and Miller M., 'The Screening/Bargaining Tradeoff', *Stanford Law Review*, 55 (2002), 29–118.

Zöller M. A., '§ 172', in Gercke B., Julius K.-P., Temming D. and Zöller M. A., *Strafprozessordnung. Heidelberger Kommentar*, 6th edn, Heidelberg, C. F. Müller (2019).

12

Exclusion or Non-Use of Illegally Gathered Evidence in the Criminal Process: Focus on Common Law and German Approaches

STEPHEN C. THAMAN AND DOMINIK BRODOWSKI

I Introduction

What consequences should state wrongdoing in the course of gathering evidence in a criminal investigation have on its admissibility in the criminal trial or usability as a foundation for the criminal judgment? Answering these questions sheds much light on the core features of criminal justice and its theoretical as well as constitutional underpinnings. In this chapter, we will compare the approach to exclusion or non-use of evidence taken in the predominantly English-speaking world of the common law with that taken in Germany. Under the common heading 'exclusionary rules' or 'exclusion of evidence' we will address both the common law perspective of excluding evidence *ex ante* (i.e. by declaring it inadmissible) and the German perspective of taking evidence first, but not using ('excluding') it for the evaluation of the merits of the case (*Beweisverwertungsverbote*).[1] After laying out the theoretical framework, we focus on the development of balancing tests and the factors which may and may not be taken into account, and come to some comparative conclusions. We will, however, need to omit a discussion of specific grounds for excluding evidence as well as some other important issues: (1) whether judges and juries, who are aware of excluded evidence, actually are able to ignore this knowledge in passing judgment;[2] (2) the extent to which exclusions actually lead to dismissals or acquittals, or whether they are mainly used by the defence to obtain a mitigated sentence.

[1] See generally Ambos, *International Criminal Law III* (2016), 513–14.
[2] Just see Koriath, *Beweisverbote* (1994), 48.

II The Rule or the Exception? On the Use of Evidence in the Criminal Trial

1 Does the Inclusion/Use or the Exclusion/Non-Use of Evidence Require Justification?

Why may a court take evidence in the course of a criminal trial, and why may it evaluate evidence and come to a conclusion – generally speaking: a conviction or an acquittal – based on the evidence? This question, which may sound alien to the Anglo-American audience, has actually been addressed recently by the German Federal Constitutional Court in a landmark decision in December 2011.[3] It builds upon a German constitutional understanding that any non-trivial state activity encroaching on the rights of citizens requires a clear statutory legal basis,[4] and that this includes any collection or use of personal information, including its use in a criminal trial.[5] Therefore, it is a constitutional requirement in Germany that criminal courts operate on a solid legal basis when they take evidence, evaluate evidence, and rule on the basis of the evidence. Based on such an understanding,[6] the burden is on the state and the courts to justify the inclusion, admissibility or use of evidence.

Reality hardly could be more different. In its landmark decision, the German Federal Constitutional Court held that the procedural provision which allows for the 'free evaluation of evidence by the court' (§ 261 *Strafprozessordnung* (StPO)[7]) is a sufficient legal basis to evaluate both

[3] German Federal Constitutional Court (*Bundesverfassungsgericht* (BVerfG)), Decision of 7 Dec. 2011 – 2 BvR 2500/09 = BVerfGE 130, 1, 115 ff., in particular 120.

[4] See German Federal Constitutional Court, Judgment of 12 Apr. 2005 – 2 BvR 581/01 = BVerfGE 112, 304, 315 for the area of criminal procedure, and generally German Federal Constitutional Court, Judgment of 21 Dec. 1977 – 1 BvL 1/75, 1 BvR 147/75 = BVerfGE 47, 46, 78–9; Robbers, *Introduction* (2017), 42 (*Gesetzesvorbehalt*), 50 (*Vorbehalt des Gesetzes*); Tiedemann, *Rechtsstaat* (2014), 178–9.

[5] See German Federal Constitutional Court, Decision of 7 Dec. 2011 – 2 BvR 2500/09 = BVerfGE 130, 1, 137, and fundamentally German Federal Constitutional Court, Judgment of 15 Dec. 1983 – 1 BvR 209, 269, 362, 420, 440, 484/83 18 = BVerfGE 65, 1, 42–3; von dem Bussche and Voigt, *Data Protection* (2017), 2: The judgment introduced the 'right to informational self-determination' as a fundamental right derived from Art. 2(1) in conjunction Art. 1(1) of the German Constitution (GG).

[6] On the scholarly views building upon this view – in particular by Amelung, *Informationsbeherrschungsrechte* (1990), 66 ff.; Jahn, *Gutachten* (2008), 66 ff. – see below at Section III.2.(b).

[7] German Code on Criminal Procedure. An unofficial English translation provided for by the German Ministry for Justice and Consumer Protection is available at www.gesetze-im-internet.de/englisch_stpo/index.html. For consistency with other English-language

lawfully acquired evidence and – subject to a balancing test – also unlawfully acquired evidence. Such a broad understanding reverses, in the end, the burden of justification toward the non-use or exclusion of evidence. And under this heading of 'exclusion' instead of 'inclusion' of evidence our topic has mostly been discussed in Germany, but also in common law countries.

2 *Exclusion of Evidence as a Limitation on Law Enforcement and the Search for the Truth*

Addressing the question from a different angle, this reality is hardly surprising. Excluding or not using evidence runs – at least in typical settings – contrary to the traditional and central aims of criminal justice, be it law enforcement (the common law perspective), be it conflict resolution on a sound factual basis, or be it to determine the 'material truth' and therefore the guilt of the defendant (the traditional perspective held in post-inquisitorial systems like Germany). To some extent, this relates to what *Herbert Packer* called the 'crime control' approach to criminal justice, as opposed to the 'due process' approach.[8]

German post-inquisitorial jurisprudence, by and large, still pays tribute to the 'principle of material truth' – namely, that all evidence that is relevant to prove the truth or untruth of the charges should be available and usable by courts, and that executive investigative and prosecutorial organs, and indeed, even the courts, have a duty to ascertain the 'material'[9] truth. Originally, German scholars considered that the principle of material truth, in combination with the 'free evaluation of evidence' by independent judges, would exclude arbitrary misuse of criminal justice by the executive branch of government, and thereby help to guarantee individual liberties.[10] Building upon these historical roots and the protection they provide, the German Federal Constitutional Court has

publications on German criminal procedure, we will mostly use the same terminology as is used in this translation.

8 Packer, 'The Courts' (1966), 238, 239.

9 In contrast to a procedurally determined, consensus-orientated or even a negotiated truth. See further Jahn, *Gutachten C, 67. DJT* (2008), 24; Neumann, *Wahrheit im Recht* (2004), 14 ff.; Weigend, 'Law and Truth' (2003), 157 ff.

10 Just see Küper, *Richteridee* (1967), passim; Landau, 'Reichsjustizgesetze' (1977), 161 ff.; Schubert, *Gerichtsverfassung* (1981), 4 ff., 118; Öztürk and Wörner, 'Fernwirkendes Beweisverbot' (2014), 109, 129 ff.; see additionally Ambos, *Beweisverwertungsverbote* (2010), 49.

deduced the requirement to determine the material truth from the *Schuldprinzip* (principle of individual guilt), which it holds to be part of Germany's constitutional identity[11] and to be rooted in the protections of human dignity (Art. 1(1) GG[12]) and the rule of law (Art. 20(3) GG).[13] By its double roots, however, the Court and some scholars have postulated that the Schuldprinzip not only serves as a protection against too harsh punishment, but that it is also a constitutional command prohibiting too lenient punishment.[14] On this double-edged background, the German Federal Constitutional Court *and* the German Federal Court of Justice consistently stress the importance of a thorough investigation of the 'material truth' and of an evaluation of the evidence by the trial court (§ 244(2) StPO),[15] even if the defendant confesses to the acts for the commission of which she has been charged.[16] Following from this constitutional reasoning (and leaving aside the possibility that rules limiting evidence-taking or the use of evidence may also increase the chances to determine the material truth),[17] any such rule can possibly undermine the fundamental *Schuldprinzip* and therefore needs to be construed as narrowly as possible, and may only be a rare exception.[18] In this vein,

[11] German Federal Constitutional Court, Decision of 15 Dec. 2015 – 2 BvR 2735/14 = BVerfGE 140, 317 paras. 51 ff.; Reinbacher and Wendel, 'European Arrest Warrant II' (2016), 702–13.

[12] German Basic Law, the functional equivalent to Germany's constitution. An unofficial English translation provided for by the German Ministry for Justice and Consumer Protection is available at www.gesetze-im-internet.de/englisch_gg/index.html.

[13] See German Federal Constitutional Court, Decision of 15 Dec. 2015 – 2 BvR 2735/14 = BVerfGE 140, 318 paras. 54–5; German Federal Constitutional Court, Judgment of 19 Mar. 2013 – 2 BvR 2628, 2883/10, 2155/11 = BVerfGE 133, 168, 197. See further Vogel, 'Core Legal Concepts' (2018), 39, 43–4.

[14] Most prominently, this view was expressed by Herbert Landau, a former judge at the German Federal Constitutional Court, in Landau, 'Absprachen' (2014), 425, 428, comparing 'guilt' with a barrel which has not only a bottom but also a top – and punishment may neither exceed the top nor fall short of the bottom of this barrel.

[15] See German Federal Constitutional Court, Judgment of 19 Mar. 2013 – 2 BvR 2628, 2883/10, 2155/11 = BVerfGE 133, 168 (headnote 1, paras. 119, 225 ff.); German Federal Constitutional Court, Decision of 15 Dec. 2015 – 2 BvR 2735/14 (= BVerfGE 140, 318 para. 57); German Federal Court of Justice, joint senate in criminal matters, Decision of 3 Mar. 2005 – GSSt 1/04 = BGHSt 50, 40, 63; German Federal Court of Justice, joint senate in criminal matters, Decision of 23 Apr. 2007 = BGHSt 51, 29, 310; German Federal Court of Justice, Judgment of 20 Dec. 2012 – 3 StR 117/12 = BGHSt 58, 84, 96, para. 31.

[16] See, in particular, German Federal Constitutional Court, Judgment of 19 Mar. 2013 – 2 BvR 2628, 2883/10, 2155/11 = BVerfGE 133, 168, 231.

[17] Jahn, *Gutachten* (2008), 25; Greco, 'Warum gerade Beweisverbote?' (2018), 485, 504.

[18] Just see German Federal Constitutional Court, Decision of 27 Nov. 1973 – BvL 12/72 and 3/73 = BVerfGE 36, 174, 187; German Federal Constitutional Court, Decision of 7

the increasing recognition of rules limiting the taking or using of evidence has led courts to qualify the search for truth *only* with the *caveat* of 'not at any cost'.[19]

Despite the lack of a recognised truth-finding principle in the jurisprudence of common law countries, the rules of evidence have traditionally operated in a similar fashion: any relevant evidence was admissible to prove the truth of the charges, even if gathered in violation of the law. Even following the introduction of exclusionary rules in the United States and other countries, the 'search for truth' is still invoked by courts to limit the reach of court-sanctioned exclusionary rules.[20] In stating that the exclusionary rule's 'costly toll upon truth-seeking and law enforcement objectives presents a high obstacle for those urging [its] application',[21] the US Supreme Court (USSC) clearly expressed the link between exclusionary rules and the functioning of law enforcement.

3 *Evolution of Exclusionary Rules in the Common Law*

Based on such an understanding, in Common Law countries, police lawlessness did not, generally, affect the admission of evidence. In England and Wales, the courts did not worry about the methods used to acquire evidence if it was relevant and material.[22]

The United States, on the other hand, though sharing the common law heritage, had its Bill of Rights of 1791, the purpose of which was to restrict the new federal government from passing any laws which would impact on the freedoms of the citizens of the thirteen states which made up the new union. But nearly all criminal cases in the United States were handled in the state courts, governed by state laws and constitutions. Until the end of the Civil War in 1865, African-American slaves were granted little protection under the laws of the states or the federal

Dec. 1982 – BvR 900/82 = BVerfGE 62, 338, 346; German Federal Court of Justice, Judgment of 18 Apr. 2007 – 5 StR 546/06 = BGHSt 51, 285, 290 para. 20; Peters, *Gutachten* (1966), 93–4; Rogall, 'Gegenwärtiger Stand' (1979), 1, 8; Arzt, 'Strengbeweis' (1974), 223, 235; Bockemühl, *Private Ermittlungen* (1996), 89–90.

19 The groundwork for this famous – and most heavily cited (Koriath, *Beweisverbote* (1994), 82) – quote from a 1960 German Federal Court of Justice Judgment of 14 Jun. 1960 – 1 StR 683/59 = BGHSt 14, 358, 365 was actually laid in Beling's *Beweisverbote* treatise.

20 Thus, in *United States* v. *Leon*, 468 US 897, 907 (1984), the USSC said: 'an unbending application of the exclusionary sanction to enforce ideals of governmental rectitude would impede unacceptably the truth-finding functions of judge and jury'.

21 *Herring* v. *United States*, 555 US 135, 141 (2009).

22 Hooper and Ormerod, *Blackstone's Criminal Practice* (2003), 2374, para. F2.12.

government. The enactment of the Fourteenth Amendment to the US Constitution in 1865, however, granted anyone, including the freed slaves, 'due process of law' in relation to the states. Yet it was only in the 1930s that the USSC began to overturn, as 'violations of due process',[23] state criminal convictions based on torture and the use of other coercive tactics which undermine the freedom of will of the accused.

Already in 1914, the USSC adopted an exclusionary rule which prevented the use of evidence seized by federal officials in violation of the Fourth Amendment.[24] The problems this rule addressed, and the need for 'policing the police', were made abundantly clear:

> The tendency of those who execute the criminal laws of the country to obtain conviction by means of unlawful seizures and enforced confessions, the latter often obtained after subjecting accused persons to unwarranted practices destructive of rights secured by the Federal Constitution, should find no sanction in the judgments of the courts which are charged at all times with the support of the Constitution and to which people of all conditions have a right to appeal for the maintenance of such fundamental rights.[25]

But the USSC only became a true constitutional court for the entire country when, influenced by the civil rights movement in the 1950s and 1960s, it decided that the Fourth, Fifth[26] and Sixth Amendments[27] to the US Constitution were binding on the states, thus enabling it to change racist practices in many, mainly Southern, states which deprived African-American citizens of the protection of the law in criminal cases.

Thus, the development in the United States, with its historic Bill of Rights, signalled a completely different approach to the use of illegally gathered evidence from that taken by other common law countries.

[23] The most notorious of the dozens of cases decided in this area prior to the incorporation of the Fifth Amendment in 1964, was *Brown* v. *Mississippi*, 297 US 278 (1936), which involved the torture of black suspects in a murder case and their hurried sentence to death three days later in a kangaroo jury court.

[24] The Fourth Amendment of the US Constitution reads: 'The right of the people to be secure in their persons, houses, papers and effects against unreasonable searches and seizures shall not be violated, and no Warrants shall issue but upon probable cause, supported by Oath or affirmation, and particularly describing the place to be searched and the persons or things to be seized.'

[25] *Weeks* v. *United States*, 232 US 383, 392 (1914).

[26] The Fifth Amendment of the US Constitution provides, inter alia, that: 'No person . . . shall be compelled in any criminal case to be a witness against himself . . .'

[27] The Sixth Amendment provides, inter alia, 'In all criminal prosecutions, the accused shall have the Assistance of Counsel for his defense.'

But we should not think that exclusionary rules are American inventions based in the forward-thinking wisdom of the USSC during the years when Earl Warren was Chief Justice.[28] Inquisitorial systems on the European Continent had a developed system of exclusion or prohibitions on the use of evidence at a time when common law courts never questioned the provenance of evidence brought to it. Continental European codes of criminal procedure prescribed rather strict rules for the gathering of evidence and the performance of other acts during the preliminary criminal investigation and nullified the validity of these acts if they were performed in violation of the rules. So-called 'nullities' could and did lead to exclusion of evidence. The legalistic approach of early inquisitorial codes mirrored the pedantic nature of the formal rules of evidence which informed the judgment in criminal trials in pre-nineteenth-century Europe.[29] In fact, one of the most influential treatises on exclusionary rules was written in Germany even before the USSC's decision in *Weeks*, and represents perhaps the first scholarly fashioning of a balancing test for the introduction of illegally gathered evidence.[30] It has also influenced the approach of the German courts up to this day.

4 Systematisation of Exclusionary Rules

Exclusionary rules come in a variety of forms.[31] While some of the fine distinctions drawn might be of lesser relevance than it seems, they may provide some background on why similar questions are addressed under different 'headings' in different criminal justice system.

(a) Obtaining or Using Evidence

A first important theoretical distinction drawn in the German criminal justice system is between rules forbidding the obtaining or taking of

[28] From 1953 to 1969. We will discuss some of these influential decisions later.

[29] On how inquisitorial Europe developed 'extrinsic' exclusionary rules relating to 'values unrelated to the pursuit of truth' at a time when the Common law only knew 'intrinsic' rules relating to the probative value of evidence; Damaška, *Evidence Law Adrift* (2013), 12–17.

[30] Beling, *Beweisverbote* (1903), 13.

[31] On the differentiations in Germany, just see the recent overviews by Ambos, *Beweisverwertungsverbote* (2010), 21 ff. and Jahn, *Gutachten* (2008), 26 ff. as well as Foster and Sule, *German Legal Systems* (2010), 400–1; Frase and Weigend, 'German Criminal Justice' (1995), 317, 334 ff.

evidence (*Beweiserhebungsverbote*), and rules prohibiting the use of evidence by the court in its assessment of the defendant's guilt, namely Beweisverwertungsverbote. The former category may further be split up: some rules exclude certain topics (*Beweisthemenverbote*), such as surveilling telecommunications relating to the core area of private life (*Kernbereich privater Lebensgestaltung*, e.g. § 100d(1) StPO). Other rules exclude certain means (*Beweismittelverbote*), such as taking witness statements from those who have made use of their right to refuse testimony (§§ 52 ff. StPO). Yet other rules forbid certain methods of taking evidence (*Beweismethodenverbote*), such as – most prominently – torture (§ 136a StPO).[32]

The distinction between prohibited topics, means and methods is mostly of systematic relevance. Distinguishing the stage of gathering evidence from that of its use, however, is of great practical importance[33] because not all evidence obtained in a perfectly legal manner may later be used as evidence. For instance, some autonomous prohibitions of the use of evidence (*selbständige Beweisverwertungsverbote*), typically derived from the constitution, are applicable regardless of the legality of the acquisition of the evidence.[34] Moreover, the distinction between taking and using evidence prepares the ground for a fundamental rule to be found in German jurisprudence, and increasingly also in the US: not every error or violation in the obtaining of evidence leads to its exclusion.[35] If the reason for excluding or non-use of evidence is based on illegalities in the gathering of evidence, and not on its intrinsic nature, the exclusion or non-use – in the German terminology – 'depends' on the illegality (*unselbständige Beweisverwertungsverbote*). In this chapter, we will focus on such dependent exclusionary rules.

[32] See Ambos, *Beweisverwertungsverbote* (2010), 21; Peters, *Gutachten* (1966), 94; critically Jahn, *Gutachten* (2008), 28.

[33] Most far-reaching is a theory coined by Jäger, *Beweisverwertung* (2003), 137–8, who considers to separate these two stages to a very broad extent.

[34] See Ambos, *Beweisverwertungsverbote* (2010), 23.

[35] See German Federal Constitutional Court, Decision of 20 Sept. 2018 – 2 BvR 708/18 – para. 40; German Federal Constitutional Court, Decision of 16 Feb. 2006 – 2 BvR 2085/05 = BVerfG *NStZ* 2006, 46, 47; German Federal Constitutional Court, Decision of 2 Jul. 2009 – 2 BvR 2225/08 = NJW 2009, 3225; German Federal Court of Justice, Judgment of 13 Jan. 2011 – 3 StR 332/10 = BGHSt 56, 127, para. 13; Ambos, *Beweisverwertungsverbote* (2010), 22; Beulke and Swoboda, *Strafprozessrecht* (2018), para. 457; Jäger, *Beweisverwertung* (2003), 135; Jahn, *Gutachten* (2008), 36.

(b) Long-Term or Limited Effect

An important distinction relates to whether the exclusion of evidence only applies in the case at hand, or whether (and to what extent) it also affects other cases. Exclusionary rules may affect whether the (same) evidence may be used in other proceedings against the same or other defendants. For example, § 477(2) sentence 2 StPO states that, generally speaking, evidence taken by a wiretap operation may be used also in other criminal proceedings, but only if the other case also relates to a crime which is of sufficient seriousness for the issuance of a wiretap order.[36] Secondly, exclusionary rules may relate to the question of whether a new investigation may be launched at all. And thirdly, exclusionary rules need to address whether further evidence taken on the basis of excluded evidence needs to be excluded as well ('fruit of the poisonous tree' – *Fernwirkung*).[37] The terminology on these and related questions – such as the effects a possible exclusion of evidence at the trial stage would have on pre-trial detention (*Frühwirkung*) – is blurred at best.[38] It is only a broad approximation that whenever the term *Verwertung* is used in the German Code on Criminal Procedure it relates to the use as evidence, and when the broader term *Verwendung* is used it relates also to use as a basis for further investigative measures.[39]

(c) Written or Unwritten Rules

In the German criminal justice system, another important distinction relates to the legal source of rules prohibiting the use of evidence. Only a few specific rules can be found in the German Code of Criminal Procedure;[40] most rules on the exclusion of evidence follow from jurisprudence.[41] In a similar vein, most rules in the United States relating to the exclusion of evidence come from the case law of the higher courts. On the contrary, in England and Wales, as well as in some other European countries, exclusionary rules have been created by the legislature as exceptions to the general rule of admissibility of relevant evidence.

36 On the details, see Brodowski, *Überwachungsmaßnahmen* (2016), 201 ff.

37 See Öztürk and Wörner, 'Fernwirkendes Beweisverbot' (2014), 109 ff. with a comparison of US, Turkish and German rules.

38 Allgayer and Klein, 'Zufallserkenntnisse' (2010), 130–1; Singelnstein, 'Strafprozessuale Verwendungs-regelungen' (2008), 854, 870.

39 Ambos, *Beweisverwertungsverbote* (2010), 23–4.

40 An overview of written exclusionary rules is provided *ibid.*, 25 ff.

41 An overview of unwritten exclusionary rules is provided *ibid.*, 51 ff.

(d) Balancing Test or Strict Exclusion

Most exclusionary rules imply a kind of balancing of interests, primarily, the interest in ascertaining the truth in a particular criminal case and, indirectly, society's interest in criminal enforcement, against the respect for the rights of criminal defendants and, indirectly, of the entire civilian population, which have been declared to be so important to the legal order that they have been enshrined in human rights conventions and national constitutions. Such a balancing may be conducted in an abstract way by the legislature, or may be left to the courts.

Exclusionary rules, whether found in constitutions, codes or case law, can be formulated in absolute terms, strictly requiring the exclusion of any evidence gathered in violation of 'the law'[42] or of certain constitutional or fundamental rights,[43] or can be formulated so as to allow judges discretion in deciding whether to admit or exclude illegally gathered evidence. An example of the former is § 136a(3) sentence 2 StPO, barring the use of evidence obtained through prohibited methods of examination (such as 'physical interference, administration of drugs, torment, deception or hypnosis'), an example of the latter is Article 24(2) of the Canadian Charter of Rights and Freedoms, which provides:

> [W]here ... a court finds that evidence was obtained in a manner that infringed or denied any of the rights or freedoms guaranteed by this Charter, the evidence shall be excluded if it is established that, having regard to all the circumstances, the admission of it in the proceedings would bring the administration of justice into disrepute.[44]

5 *Conclusion*

Should the use of evidence which was obtained illegally be the norm or the exception? The jury is still out on this subject, and it may well result

[42] The Russian Constitution and CCP require exclusion of any evidence gathered in violation of federal law or the constitution. Thaman, 'Balancing Truth against Human Rights' (2013), 403, 415.

[43] Art. 32(6) Const.-Portugal provides that 'Any evidence obtained by torture, force, violation of the physical or moral integrity of the individual, wrongful interference in private life, the home, correspondence, or telecommunications are of no effect.' Spanish law provides: 'Evidence obtained, directly or indirectly in violation of fundamental rights and liberties is without effect.' § 11.1 Ley Orgánica del Poder Judicial, Ley Orgánica 6 (1 Jul. 1985), available at http://noticias.juridicas.com/base_datos/Admin/lo6–1985.html.

[44] Canadian Charter of Rights and Freedoms, Enacted by the Canada Act 1982 [U.K.] c.11; proclaimed in force 17 Apr. 1982, available at www.efc.ca/pages/law/charter/charter.text.html.

in a hung jury. In light of the multitude of reasons which may lead to the illegality of gathering evidence – from minor violations of statutory law or case law up to most severe violations of international human rights standards – and also in light of the multitude of legal effects which need to be differentiated, the conflicting interests – and starting points – more often than not will require a balancing. Therefore, it is all but surprising that statutory exclusionary rules found in the United Kingdom, and those developed from case law and theory in Germany, but also in common law countries such as New Zealand and Australia allow the court to balance several factors before making the ultimate decision on use.[45] But in light of the aforementioned complexity of the question, and especially in light of the starting point that any use of evidence requires a legal basis, one should not be as quick as German courts which sometimes state that the exclusion of illegally gathered evidence is an exception requiring specific justification.[46]

III Balancing of Factors in Deciding on Admissibility or Exclusion of Evidence

In this section, we will discuss in particular the judicial balancing tests found in Germany and compare it with the US approach, which began as a categorical exclusionary rule and gradually has been massaged into a kind of balancing test in many respects.

1 *Balancing Tests Relating to the Exclusion of Evidence: The Common Law Perspective*

(a) Preliminary Remarks

The most critical question in this balancing is: what kinds of official law violations are serious enough to trigger non-use of the evidence resulting therefrom? This value judgement is sometimes made at the level of international law, as with the prohibition of torture, sometimes in

45 See Section III. below.

46 But see German Federal Constitutional Court, Decision of 20 May 2011 – 2 BvR 2072/10 = BVerfGK 18, 444, 448; German Federal Constitutional Court, Decision of 20 May 2011 – 2 BvR 2072/10 – para. 13; German Federal Court of Justice, Judgment of 3 May 2018 – 3 StR 390/17 – para. 24; German Federal Court of Justice, Decision of 20 May 2015 – 4 StR 555/14 = NJW 2015, 2594, para. 17; German Federal Court of Justice, Judgment of 20 Dec. 2012 – 3 StR 117/12 = BGHSt 58, 84, para. 31; BGHSt 54, 69, para. 47; and also Ambos, *Beweisverwertungsverbote* (2010), 23–4.

constitutions and codes, and sometimes by the courts. The prevailing view is that the violations must be 'serious', or of 'fundamental rights' – namely, of constitutional rights. But even the decision to limit exclusion to constitutional violations requires courts to decide whether the violation was of constitutional magnitude.

But even if a constitutional violation has been identified, which could trigger exclusion or 'non-use' of evidence, judges must again decide whether the evidence the prosecution seeks to use derives inexorably from the constitutional violation. For even if one agrees that a constitutional violation has been committed and the evidence sought to be admitted derives therefrom, some jurisdictions still require the judge to engage in a balancing of other important interests before deciding on admissibility.

If further balancing is required, courts may or must take into account some or all of the following seven criteria in deciding whether or not to admit the evidence: (1) the seriousness of the constitutional violation (including whether it was intentional, reckless, negligent, etc.); (2) the gravity of the crime which is before the court; (3) the character of the evidence subject to exclusion (its credibility, importance for proving guilt, whether it constitutes the *corpus delicti* of the crime or is 'mere evidence', etc.); (4) the public impact of the decision (i.e. whether it will cause alarm in the community); (5) whether exclusion is needed to deter future violations of the law by police or other officials; (6) whether the decision will bring the court into disrepute; and (7) whether use of the evidence would violate the defendant's right to a fair trial. The last and nowadays predominant balancing factor, whether use of illegally evidence would violate the defendant's right to a fair trial, tends to be a factor-intensive test on its own, which includes many of the other six factors.

(b) Balancing under a 'Fair Trial' Model

In England and Wales, section 78 of the Police and Criminal Evidence Act 1984 (PACE) provides:

> (1) In any proceedings the court may refuse to allow evidence on which the prosecution proposes to rely to be given if it appears to the court that, having regard to all the circumstances, including the circumstances in which the evidence was obtained, the admission of the evidence would have such an adverse effect on the fairness of the proceedings that the court ought not to admit it.

> (2) nothing in this section shall prejudice any rule of law requiring a court to exclude evidence.[47]

The discretion given the judge by section 78 PACE has been described in the literature as 'broad and unstructured' due to the plethora of factors which may be weighed in addition to the legality of the police actions: the seriousness of the offence, good faith of the officers, type of evidence and its reliability, existence of corroborative evidence, type of illegality and type of right infringed.[48]

The rule in England and Wales is not explicitly limited to violations of a constitutional magnitude, yet the judge, in assessing the factor relating to the gravity of the breach, will often be focusing on violations of fundamental rights. Still, this test is flexible enough to include a plethora of factors. In a sense, each judge can give her own stamp on what is a 'fair trial' with so many factors in the balance.[49]

This approach is also in line with the European Convention on Human Rights (ECHR) and the European Court of Human Rights (ECtHR) jurisprudence, as the ECHR contains no express exclusionary rules and the ECtHR traditionally defers to domestic exclusionary practices. In *Schenk* v. *Switzerland*, a case involving an unlawful recording of a telephone conversation, the ECtHR stated: 'While Article 6 of the Convention guarantees the right to a fair trial, it does not lay down any rules on the admissibility of evidence as such, which is therefore primarily a matter for regulation under national law.'[50] This doctrine was followed in a number of cases against the United Kingdom, dealing mostly with illegal wiretaps or secret tape-recordings. In *Allan* v. *United Kingdom*, the court cited *Schenk* in holding:

> It is not the role of the Court to determine, as a matter of principle, whether particular types of evidence – for example, unlawfully obtained evidence – may be admissible or, indeed, whether the applicant was guilty or not. The question which must be answered is whether the proceedings as a whole, including the way in which the evidence was obtained, were fair. This involves an examination of the 'unlawfulness' in question and,

[47] Police and Criminal Evidence Act 1984.

[48] Ormerod, 'ECHR' (2003), 61, 64.

[49] According to Ashworth, 'if courts are allowed simply to pick and choose the guiding principle(s) in the circumstances of any individual case, there is unlikely to be a consistent approach and a danger of the question of admissibility being left to the "whim of the particular court"'. Ashworth, 'Excluding Evidence' (1977), 723, 732, discussed in Duff, 'Admissibility' (2004), 152, 159.

[50] *Schenk* v. *Switzerland*, 13 EHRR 242, 265–6 (1988), para. 46.

where violation of another Convention right is concerned, the nature of the violation found.[51]

In our opinion, the ECtHR basically adopted or at least accepted the 'fair trial' test set out in section 78 PACE, and has been developing it since. In 1950, the Scottish High Court developed a test which balanced: '(a) the interest of the citizen to be protected from illegal or irregular invasions of his liberties by the authorities, and (b) the interest of the State to secure that evidence bearing upon the commission of crime and necessary to enable justice to be done.' It thus held that evidence shall not be withheld from courts of law 'on any merely formal or technical ground'.[52] Although the approach of the Scottish High Court has been described as 'conspicuously malleable', commentators seem to think that the courts take into account the typical factors used in other balancing tests, such as the seriousness of the violation, the 'good faith' of the officers and whether they were acting under emergency circumstances, the seriousness of the criminal offence, and the 'fairness' to the accused. While the Scottish courts have struggled for decades in applying this test, the High Court, in 2006, simply equated the Scottish test with that articulated by the ECtHR in interpreting the Article 6 fair trial right.[53]

(c) Was the Violation of Constitutional Magnitude?

The great decisions of the USSC in the era of Earl Warren all provided in a fairly categorical manner for exclusion of any evidence gathered in violation of three important constitutional rights: the protection against unreasonable searches, guaranteed by the Fourth Amendment of the US Constitution;[54] the right to counsel, guaranteed by the Sixth Amendment;[55] and the privilege against self-incrimination, or right to silence, guaranteed by the Fifth Amendment.[56] § 38.23 CCP-Texas (US) provides: '(a) No evidence obtained by an officer or other person in violation of any provisions of the Constitution or laws of the State of Texas,

[51] *Allan* v. *United Kingdom*, 36 EHRR 12, 144, 156 (2003), para. 42. The courts in England and Wales have by and large accepted that the test used by the ECtHR is the same as that used under s. 78 PACE, discussed above.

[52] *Lawrie* v. *Muir*, 1950 SLT 37, at 39–40, 1950 JC 19, at 26. See in general, Stark and Leverick, 'Scotland' (2013), 70–83.

[53] *HM Advocate* v. *Higgins*, 2006 SLT 946, 950, SC, 9.

[54] *Mapp* v. *Ohio*, 367 US 643 (1961).

[55] *Massiah* v. *United States*, 377 US 201 (1964).

[56] *Miranda* v. *Arizona*, 384 US 436 (1966).

or of the Constitution or laws of the United States of America, shall be admitted in evidence against the accused on the trial of any criminal case.'[57]

Despite the apparent categorical nature of exclusionary rules in the United States, courts still engage in a kind of balancing to determine what infringements of procedural rules actually rise to the level of a constitutional violation, or will make the discovery of evidence actually a consequence of the constitutional violation.

(d) Was the Violation Serious or Forgivable? – On 'Policing the Police'

The first, and perhaps most important attempt at balancing constitutional rights against other considerations undertaken by the USSC, was in *United States* v. *Leon*,[58] which introduced the 'good faith' exception to the theretofore categorical exclusionary rule for Fourth Amendment violations. Whereas in *Mapp*, the USSC had based the necessity for the exclusionary rule in deterrence of police lawlessness and in preserving judicial integrity, the *Leon* court collapsed the two tests and simply stated that they were the same: if exclusion would not deter lawless police conduct, then the integrity of the courts would not be violated by admitting and using unconstitutionally acquired evidence to prove guilt.[59] The so-called 'cost–benefit' analysis of the court was similar to the rationale of German jurisprudence when it balanced the gravity of the violation against the duty to determine truth in the criminal trial. The *Leon* court pronounced truth-finding, a classically inquisitorial value, to be a cardinal value of US criminal procedure.[60] *Leon* excluded the 'good faith' exception in cases of intentional or reckless violations, where the allegations of probable cause were clearly inadequate, thus preventing a 'sneaky' police officer from presenting a clearly inadequate affidavit of probable cause to a judge who merely rubber-stamps search warrants.[61]

[57] Cf. § 136.4320 Or. Rev. Stats, which limits exclusion of evidence to situations when required by the constitutions of Oregon or the United States.

[58] *United States* v. *Leon*, 468 US 897, 921 (1984).

[59] *Ibid.*, 918.

[60] *Ibid.*, 907.

[61] For a case recognising 'good faith' despite a rubber-stamping judge, see *McCommon* v. *Mississippi*, 474 US 984, 985–7 (1985) (Brennan, dissenting). See also *United States* v. *Breckenridge*, 782 F2d 1317, 1321 (5th Cir. 1986), where it was held that 'good faith' could still be applied when the judge did not even read the affidavit.

The USSC has also extended the 'good faith' exception to cases where the search warrant itself contained erroneous or inadequate descriptions of the things to be seized or the places to be searched,[62] to searches based on unconstitutional statutes,[63] and illegal detentions based on erroneous court records.[64] Finally, the court has recently lowered the bar to allow admission of evidence which was gathered when the police officer was guilty of 'isolated negligence' in believing there was probable cause, and has stated that exclusion will always be its 'last resort'.[65]

The Irish courts traditionally distinguished between evidence gathered in violation of the law, where the judge had much discretion to weigh various factors before deciding whether to admit or exclude the evidence, and constitutional violations. Up until 1965, a judge could still refuse to exclude evidence gathered in violation of constitutional rights in the case of 'extraordinary excusing circumstances'.[66] But in 1990, the Irish High Court recognised a categorical exclusionary rule in cases where police clearly violate the constitutional rights of citizens, rejecting the 'good faith' doctrine of *Leon*. According to Judge Finlay: '[t]he detection of crime and the conviction of guilty persons, no matter how important they may be in relation to the ordering of society, cannot, however, in my view, outweigh the unambiguously expressed constitutional obligation as far as practicable to defend and vindicate the personal rights of the citizen'.[67]

Many courts which 'balance' constitutional violations against other interests or values, including the 'seriousness' of the constitutional violation, have specifically provided that a non-intentional or 'good faith' violation would weigh in favour of using the evidence. For instance, the Australian High Court has fashioned a general balancing test to determine the excludability of illegally seized evidence, which emphasises consideration of whether there was bad faith on the part of the police, the importance of the evidence, the seriousness of the offence and the ease with which the law might have been complied with.[68] The Scottish

62 *Massachusetts* v. *Shepard*, 468 US 981, 988–90 (1984), decided on the same day as *Leon*.
63 *Illinois* v. *Krull*, 480 US 340, 349–50 (1987).
64 *Arizona* v. *Evans*, 514 US 1, 14–5 (1995).
65 *Herring* v. *United States*, 555 US 135, 144–7 (2009).
66 See *People (A.G.)* v. *O'Brien* [1965] IR 142, 160–1.
67 *People (D.P.P.)* v. *Kenny* [1990] 2 IR 110, 134; [1990] ILRM 569, 579. For a discussion of the development from the *O'Brien* case to *Kenny*, see Cras and Daly, 'Ireland' (2013), at 35–45.
68 *Bunning* v. *Cross* (1978) 141 CLR 54 (Austl.), cited in Bradley, 'Mapp Goes Abroad' (2001), 375, 380.

courts also occasionally refer to whether there was bad faith on the part of the police in deciding whether to exclude.[69]

In 2002 the New Zealand Court of Appeal adopted a multi-factor 'fairness' test which gives the trial judge broad discretion based on a list of criteria including the 'seriousness of the offense' and the 'importance of the evidence' and replaced a stricter prima facie test, in place since 1992, which recognised a rebuttable presumption that illegally seized evidence was inadmissible.[70] The reason for exclusion, both according to the overruled prima facie test and the new 'fairness' test, is the 'vindication of the right that has been breached'[71] and not, as with the US Fourth Amendment exclusionary rule, the deterrence of the police.[72]

Originally, Canadian courts developed two separate tests to determine whether exclusion was appropriate under Article 24(2). Under the first test, exclusion would result, regardless of the seriousness of the violation, if it had as a consequence that a suspect-defendant was 'conscripted' to produce evidence against himself, such as through a confession or by extracting bodily fluids etc., and this was, more or less categorically, considered to affect the fairness of the trial. The second test focused exclusively on the seriousness of the violation such that a failure to exclude would bring the administration of justice into disrepute. Important factors here would be the intentionality of the violation and whether police acted in 'good faith', but not whether there might have been a hypothetical clean path to the evidence (i.e. inevitable discovery).[73] The Canadian courts have now moved to a more simple balancing test which weighs three factors: (1) the severity of the violation; (2) whether the admission of the evidence would bring the administration of justice into disrepute from the perspective of society's interest in respect for Charter

[69] *See Edgley* v. *Barbour*, 1994 SCCR 789, 792, cited in Duff, 'Admissibility' (2004), 152, 165.

[70] *R* v. *Shaheed* [2002] 2 NZLR 377, CA; cited in Mahoney, 'Abolition' (2003), 607; Optican and Sankoff, 'The New Exclusionary Rule' (2003), 1, 45.

[71] Mahoney, 'Abolition' (2003), 607, 610.

[72] On the development of the deterrent rationale of the US Fourth Amendment exclusionary rule, see n. 58 ff.

[73] Roach, 'Canada' (2007), 57, 71–2. German courts have also broadly interpreted the notion of 'hypothetical clean path' in applying the exception of 'inevitable discovery' (on the link between these exceptions, see Öztürk and Wörner, 'Fernwirkendes Beweisverbot' (2014), 109, 138–9. For the seminal US decision recognising the 'inevitable discovery' exception to the doctrine of the 'fruit of the poisonous tree' see *Nix* v. *Williams*, 467 US 431, 443–6 (1984).

rights; and (3) the effect of admitting the evidence on the public interest in having the case adjudicated on its merits.[74]

(e) Balancing the Quality or Importance of the Evidence

Coerced or otherwise involuntary confessions were traditionally excluded in the United States due to their lack of credibility, rather than on constitutional grounds.[75] Even potentially probative evidence may be excluded if the judge decides that its prejudicial nature outweighs its probative value.[76] This line of reasoning has continued on the international level, such as with the International Criminal Tribunals for the Former Yugoslavia (ICTY) and Rwanda (ICTR) and the International Criminal Court (ICC). Rule 95 of the ICTY Rules of Procedure and Evidence provides: 'No evidence shall be admissible if obtained by methods which cast substantial doubt on its reliability or if its admission is antithetical to, and would seriously damage, the integrity of the proceedings.'[77] Identical language was incorporated into section 69(7) of the Rome Statute for the International Criminal Court.[78]

As a general rule, courts have a hard time excluding physical evidence, even when they recognise it is the fruit of a serious constitutional violation. For instance, even if a confession is suppressed as being the product of 'oppression', per section 76(2) PACE (England and Wales), section 76(4)–(6) PACE provides that this 'shall not' have any influence on the admissibility in evidence of 'any facts' discovered by utilising the suppressed confession.[79] Thus, even if a dwelling search is found in gross violation of a warrant requirement, courts will often let the object found in as evidence just due to its probative value.[80] This unwillingness to

[74] *See R* v. *Grant*, 2009 SC 32; *R* v. *Harrison*, 2009 SC 34.

[75] *Hopt* v. *Territory of Utah*, 110 US 574, 585 (1884).

[76] Fed. Rule of Evidence 403, § 352 Cal. Evidence Code.

[77] United Nations, IT/32/Rev.40, 12 Jul. 2007.

[78] The Rome Statute of the International Criminal Court. 17 Jul. 1998. UN GAOR, 53d Sess, UN Doc.A/CONF. 183/9 (1998). For details on the (in)admissibility of evidence and exclusionary rules, see Ambos, *International Criminal Law III* (2016), 46 ff., especially 513–20.

[79] s. 76(5) PACE provides, albeit, that the jury shall not be told that the 'facts' were derived from the statements of the defendant. Alleging that there are no English cases upholding the suppression of physical evidence, Duff, 'Admissibility' (2004), 152.

[80] See the English case of *R* v. *Sanghera* [2001] 1 Cr. App. R. 20, 299, 305–6, in which police searched a robbery suspect's home without a warrant or consent and the loot was allowed into evidence due to its unimpeachable probative value and the 'good faith' of the officers, who believed the suspect would have consented. See Choo, 'England and Wales' (2013), 331, 335.

suppress physical evidence is justified by some courts in employing their balancing tests, by asserting that the admission of physical evidence can never violate the right to a fair trial because it is not really the 'fruit' of the violation, nor dependent thereon, having existed before the violation occurred.

(f) The Gravity of the Crime Which Is Being Prosecuted

Balancing tests often consider the seriousness of the crime allegedly committed by the defendant. Beling, in his treatise on evidentiary prohibitions, is clearly more generous when it comes to admissibility of evidence of capital crimes, than less serious ones: 'the interest in the solving of high treason or a murder is infinitely greater than the interest in investigating and punishing a cyclist who drives on the wrong side of the road, or a sassy young man who gives his desire for singing too long a rein during nighttime hours'.[81]

Andrew Ashworth has, in our view correctly, asserted that the seriousness of the charges facing the defendant should never go into the balancing process, because the more serious the charge, the more detrimental will be the introduction of the evidence to the defendant, presuming that the punishment will be commensurately more severe.[82]

(g) Preserving the Integrity of the Courts

Duff correctly notes that, if exclusionary rules are to have any meaning they must be 'extrinsic', and not anchored in the 'intrinsic' emphasis on probative value/credibility. The notion of 'judicial integrity' is such an 'extrinsic' justification for exclusion, yet scholars differ as to its theoretical underpinnings. Duff points to: (1) the 'disciplinary' model adopted by the United States which focuses on deterrence of unconstitutional police conduct; (2) the 'vindicatory' model, which focuses on protecting citizens' constitutional rights and would tend to automatic exclusion once a significant violation has been ascertained;[83] and (3) the 'moral legitimacy' approach, which is more aimed at proportionality balancing

[81] Beling, *Beweisverbote* (1903), 35.

[82] Ashworth, 'Excluding Evidence' (1977), 723, 732, as discussed in Duff, 'Admissibility' (2004), 152, 159.

[83] The New Zealand courts have rejected the deterrent rationale and focus exclusively on 'vindication of the right' that has been breached., though they still balance. Mahoney, 'Abolition' (2003), 607, 610.

of the seriousness of the constitutional violation and the harm to the public if a dangerous criminal were to go free.[84] For the *Mapp* court, of course, the 'imperative of judicial integrity' was vindicatory, and meant that 'the criminal goes free, if he must, but it is the law that sets him free. Nothing can destroy a government more quickly than its failure to observe its own laws, or worse, its disregard of the charter of its own existence.'[85] The court in *Leon*, of course, abandoned this high ground by equating judicial integrity with an exclusively disciplinary rationale,[86] while at the same time Canada elevated judicial integrity to constitutional status in Article 24(2) of its Charter.

It is thus evident that even an insistence that the courts not launder dirty evidence may in the end lead to a vague balancing test where constitutional violations can be weighed out of the picture.

(h) The Public Impact of the Admissibility Decision

But what is the 'public interest'? This could mean that the public would be appalled if evidence resulting from torture or pervasive warrantless wiretapping were used in the courts.[87] The Australian High Court has also mandated exclusion when 'the public interest in maintaining the integrity of the courts and in ensuring the observance of the law and minimum standards of propriety by those entrusted with powers of law enforcement' requires it.[88]

In *Leon*, the USSC proclaimed: 'The substantial social costs exacted by the exclusionary rule for the vindication of Fourth Amendment rights have long been a source of concern. Our cases have consistently recognised that unbending application of the exclusionary sanction to enforce ideals of governmental rectitude would impede unacceptably the truth-finding functions of judge and jury.' The court continued: 'particularly when law enforcement officers have acted in objective good faith or their transgressions have been minor, the magnitude of the benefit conferred on such guilty defendants offends basic concepts of the criminal justice

[84] Duff, 'Admissibility' (2004), 152, 160–74.
[85] *Mapp* v. *Ohio*, 367 US 643, 659 (1961).
[86] The *Leon* court simply proclaims that if exclusion is not justified by its deterrent effect on *police* misconduct, not misconduct or errors of judges, then judicial integrity is not compromised. *United States* v. *Leon*, 486 US 897, 916 (1984).
[87] See Duff, 'Admissibility' (2004), 152, 155, for examples.
[88] *Ridgeway* v. *The Queen* (1995) 184 CLR 19, 38, cited in Bradley, 'Mapp Goes Abroad' (2001), 375, 380.

system'.[89] Thus, the USSC posits a 'public interest' in 'having juries receive all probative evidence of a crime'.[90] More recently, the court bemoaned the exclusionary rule's 'costly toll upon truth-seeking', which consists in 'letting guilty and possibly dangerous defendants go free'.[91] The same logic is used in confession cases where the court weighs the benefits of exclusion in terms of deterring future *Miranda* violations against the exclusion of reliable evidence.[92]

With the US disciplinary, cost–benefit approach, it appears that intrinsic emphasis on probative evidence is pushing back the vindicatory interest in protecting constitutional rights and that there is a danger of a return to old common law presumptions of admissibility of relevant evidence, or its old inquisitorial counterpart which prioritised truth over rights.

2 *Balancing Tests Relating to the Non-Use of Evidence: The German Perspective*

(a) Introduction

From the German perspective, there is still no consensus on what rationale the (judicial) balancing test should be built, and therefore no clear consensus on which factors may play a role – and to what extent – within the balancing test. This makes the task of the coalition government formed in 2018 more difficult, which, according to the coalition agreement, has set out to introduce draft legislation on (generic) rules on the (non-)use and exclusion of evidence in criminal proceedings.[93] It can, however, build upon several recent studies and draft rules published on this matter.[94]

89 *United States* v. *Leon*, 468 US 897, 907–8, 921 (1984).

90 *Murray* v. *United States*, 487 US 533, 537 (1988).

91 *Herring* v. *United States*, 555 US 135, 141 (2009).

92 *Michigan* v. *Tucker*, 417 US 433, 450–1 (1974). This case dealt not with a statement of often questionable reliability, but the testimony of a witness discovered through a *Miranda*-defective interrogation.

93 Available at www.bundesregierung.de/resource/blob/975226/847984/5b8bc23590d4cb2892b31c987ad672b7/2018-03-14-koalitionsvertrag-data.pdf?download=1, 123, lines 5779–80.

94 See, in particular, the treatises by Ambos, *Beweisverwertungsverbote* (2010); Jahn, *Gutachten* (2008); Jäger, *Beweisverwertung* (2003); an extensive study by the German Association of Judges, available at www.bmjv.de/SharedDocs/Downloads/DE/Service/StudienUntersuchungenFachbuecher/Gutachten_Beweisverbote_Strafverfahren.pdf;jsessionid=ED5D36A3C28C0B8FF0F8A93FA278628B.2_cid289?__blob=publicationFile&v=1 and a draft

(b) Justifying the Inclusion of Evidence

Several scholars focus on the need to justify the use of evidence, in particular of evidence which was gathered illegally. A theory first coined by Amelung focuses on data protection and the (in Germany: constitutional) right of each person to primarily decide themselves on how their data may be used (*Informationsbeherrschungsanspruch*), at least unless there is a clear and constitutional legal basis to operate with data against the will of the data subject.[95] According to this view, any illegal obtaining of evidence includes an illegal obtaining of information or personal data. As a remedy and to avoid a perpetuation of the illegality,[96] the prosecution and the court may not utilise that tainted information. However, it is already questionable whether evidence and personal data indeed are sufficiently equivalent.[97] The constitutional rights to data protection – which refers to the data subject – may belong to persons other than the accused, and the constitutional or procedural laws which were violated when gathering evidence may relate to issues other than data protection and should therefore not be reduced to that matter.[98]

Another theory, prominently presented by Jahn, considers the procedural norm requiring the court to thoroughly investigate the 'material truth' (§ 244(2) StPO) to be the proper legal basis for introducing and using evidence in court (*Beweisbefugnislehre*).[99] That legal basis is, however, limited by constitutional law including the principle of proportionality. Evidence may be introduced only in order to determine the factual basis for deciding the case (legitimate aim), if it is fit for this purpose (*Geeignetheit*), if there are no less intrusive means available (*Erforderlichkeit*) and its use is adequate (*Angemessenheit*).[100] Secondly, when determining the adequacy, the affected constitutional rights must be

bill by the German Federal Bar Association (Gesetzentwurf der Bundesrechtsanwaltskammer für die Einführung einer Zustimmungslösung als Alternative zu der von der Rechtsprechung entwickelten Widerspruchslösung bei zu Gunsten des Angeklagten bestehenden Beweisverwertungsverboten), Opinion No. 17 of 24 Apr. 2012, available at www.brak.de/zur-rechtspolitik/stellungnahmen-pdf/stellungnahmen-deutschland/2012/april/stellungnahme-der-brak-2012-17.pdf.

95 Amelung, *Informationsbeherrschungsrechte* (1990); Amelung, 'Grundlagen' (2001), 1259; see also Singelnstein, 'Unselbstständige Beweisverwertungsverbote' (2009), 643, 645 ff.; Störmer, *Dogmatische Grundlagen* (1992), 223 ff.

96 Cf. the summary of this theory by Ambos, *Beweisverwertungsverbote* (2010), 46–7.

97 Jahn, *Gutachten* (2008), 66.

98 *Ibid.*, 65–6; see also Jäger, *Beweisverwertung* (2003), 100–4, 140–1.

99 Jahn, *Gutachten* (2008), 66 ff.

100 *Ibid.*, 71.

taken into account, and only that evidence may be included and used which is essential for protecting legitimate public interests.[101] This forbids the inclusion of evidence if this would violate or perpetuate the violation of human dignity (Art. 1(1) GG), and forbids the inclusion of evidence (at least) if it would violate the 'essence' of a constitutional right (Art. 19(2) GG).[102] While some criticise this approach as being too narrow,[103] it offers a clear constitutional structure and systematisation of the problem.

(c) Justifying the Non-Use of Evidence

Jurisprudence and most scholars, however, take a different perspective and require a specific justification for the non-use ('exclusion') of evidence.[104] In particular, the German Federal Court of Justice, supported by the German Federal Constitutional Court,[105] has developed a multi-step balancing process to be used by the trial court. The first step of this process focuses on the type of law enforcement violation:

> The decision as to whether or not there will be a prohibition on use is made on the basis of a comprehensive balancing ... The weight of the procedural violation as well as the importance for the legally protected sphere of the affected party must be considered and placed in the balance as well as the consideration that the truth may not be investigated at any price ... On the other hand, one must consider that prohibitions on use impede the possibilities of determining the truth ... and that the State according to the case law of the Constitutional Court must constitutionally guarantee an administration of justice which is capable of functioning without which justice cannot be realized ... If the procedural provision which has been violated, does not, or not primarily, serve to protect the defendant, then a prohibition on use will be unlikely; On the other hand, a prohibition on use is appropriate when the violated procedural provision is designed to secure the foundations of the procedural position of the accused or defendant in a criminal prosecution.[106]

[101] *Ibid.*

[102] *Ibid.*, 72.

[103] Rogall, 'Beweiserhebungs- und Beweisverwertungsverbote' (2008), 818, 825; see also Ambos, *Beweisverwertungsverbote* (2010), 48–9.

[104] See n. 46 above.

[105] See, in general, German Federal Constitutional Court, Decision of 7 Dec. 2011 – 2 BvR 2500/09 = BVerfGE 130, 1.

[106] German Federal Court of Justice, Decision of 27 Feb. 1992 – 5 StR 190/91 = BGHSt 38, 214, 218–22. English translation in Thaman, *Comparative Criminal Procedure* (2008), 111.

This modern, multi-factor balancing test incorporates elements of two further theories: one theory asked, mostly from the perspective of the procedural rules on appeal (*Revision*), whether the 'legally protected sphere' of the defendant has been affected by the violation, or merely the sphere of third parties.[107] Another theory focused on the *ratio legis* of the provision which was breached,[108] though that – by itself – seems to be inconclusive due to the ambiguity of this criterion.[109]

Last but not least, Rogall[110] and others[111] have extended this balancing test by pointing out that the exclusion or non-use of evidence is one, but not necessarily the most apt, reaction to an illegal gathering of evidence. According to them, whether this response is the right answer depends more on systemic aspects than on the individual situation of the accused.

In the end, however, most balancing tests lack a clear structure, a clear dividing line on what aspects may be included in the balancing – and what weight to assign to them – and a clear normative basis, though that is sometimes sought in the constitutional protection of a fair trial.[112] While such tests can lead to fair and just results, their outcome is difficult to predict.[113]

(d) Relevant Factors

In applying the multi-factor balancing test, jurisprudence relies on – at least – the following factors:[114]

- the gravity of *objective* and *subjective misconduct*, such as the clear lack of a (sufficient) legal basis for the specific act of gathering evidence; a wilful, widespread and/or arbitrary misuse of state powers or a wilful, widespread and arbitrary circumvention of a requirement of *ex ante* judicial authorisation, especially if that requirement is prescribed in the constitution; the German Federal Court of Justice repeatedly applies a

[107] German Federal Court of Justice, Decision of 21 Jan. 1958 – GSSt 4/57 = BGHSt (GrS) 11, 213, 214 ff.

[108] See Fezer, *Strafprozessrecht* (1995), 220.

[109] See Ambos, *Beweisverwertungsverbote* (2010), 43; Jahn, *Gutachten* (2008), 56 ff.

[110] Originally Rogall, 'Gegenwärtiger Stand' (1979), 1, 31–5; later modified, such as in Rogall, 'Folgen' (1996), 944, 947–8; and Rogall, 'Zur Lehre' 523, 546.

[111] See Wolter, 'Beweisverbote und Umgehungsverbote' (2000), 963, 985–6, and most recently Greco, 'Warum gerade Beweisverbote?' (2018), 485, 512 ff.

[112] German Federal Court of Justice, Judgment of 20 Dec. 2012 – 3 StR 117/12 = BGHSt 58, 84, para. 33; Ambos, *Beweisverwertungsverbote* (2010), 50.

[113] See further Jahn, *Gutachten* (2008), 60 ff.

[114] See *ibid.*, 46–7 with extensive references to jurisprudence.

test according to which the exclusion or non-use of evidence may in particular be warranted 'in cases of grave, willful or objectively arbitrary violations of the law, where protections offered by the constitution were ignored in a purposeful or systematic manner'[115]

- the *ratio legis* of the protected norm, including whether the 'legally protected sphere' of the defendant has been affected
- the *quality of the evidence* in light of the misconduct; the existence of *supporting evidence*; and a *hypothetical clean path* doctrine[116] (i.e. whether the evidence could have been gathered legally)
- the *gravity* of the crime being prosecuted, in particular based on the guilt of the defendant and the expected punishment[117]
- *systemic effects* on society's trust in criminal justice *and* in the lawfulness of state actions.

Let us take a closer look at three of these factors.

Regarding the gravity of objective misconduct and its reference to violations of the constitution, it is important to remember that not all constitutional norms were created equal. Instead, there seems to be growing consensus that there are different levels of constitutional protections, be it the German focus on 'human dignity' (Art. 1(1)1 GG), be it those constitutional elements forming the national constitutional identity (the EU perspective), or be it a more formalistic differentiation of core constitutional norms.[118]

115 Most recently in German Federal Court of Justice, Judgment of 20 Dec. 2012 – 3 StR 117/12 = BGHSt 58, 84, para. 33 (own translation).

116 But see Ambos, *Beweisverwertungsverbote* (2010), 50–1.

117 Thus, even if the court finds that the violation is important enough to give rise to a prohibition on use – German courts, for instance, view the use of diary entries to prove guilt as a grave violation of the right to develop one's personality – the court must still weigh the seriousness of the crime charged before deciding whether to exclude. 'If the accusation is less weighty, then the personality interest of the author of the writings will often prevail. In cases of probable cause that a serious attack on life, other important legal interests or the state or other serious attacks on the legal order have been committed, then the protection of the private life-sphere must give way. The balancing must be undertaken while taking into consideration the interest in criminal prosecution in light of the importance of the constitutional right, whereby the alleged wrongful act, to the extent it can be judged, must also be considered.' German Federal Court of Justice, Judgment of 27 Feb. 1964 – 4 StR 519/63 = BGHSt 19, 325, 331. English translation in Thaman, *Comparative Criminal Procedure* (2008), 113. Thus, the German Federal Court of Justice allowed use of a diary in a brutal rape-murder case, but not in a perjury case.

118 See generally German Federal Constitutional Court, Decision of 15 Dec. 2015 – 2 BvR 2735/14, especially para. 43; European Court of Justice, Opinion of the Advocate General Bot of 18 Jul. 2017 – C-42/17 (*M.A.S. and M.B.*), paras. 181 ff.

On the question of the gravity of subjective misconduct, German courts somewhat surprisingly focus on the individual perspective of the law enforcement official who broke the law when gathering evidence, and not on the objective wrongdoing by a state agent, although it is the state, not the individual officer that prosecutes the presumed criminal. If the rationale of exclusionary rules in Germany were disciplinary – that is, to sanction the police or prosecution for its wrongdoing – subjective wrongdoing would be an eminently valid criterion. If the rationale were to mitigate the infringement of the defendant's rights, that infringement would have to be undone or mitigated regardless of whether the suspect's right was infringed intentionally. If the rationale is, however, a mixed bag to balance all sorts of legitimate aspects, the line between valid and invalid factors becomes much more difficult to draw.

Since Beling,[119] the gravity of the crime being prosecuted has been a major factor. While the public interest in a successful prosecution of a crime may indeed depend on its gravity, it also raises serious doubts: first, when focusing on the time when the evidence is introduced, the accused enjoys the presumption of innocence: we cannot justify the introduction of evidence based on the gravity of the offence as that has not yet been proven in court. Secondly, such an approach disregards material limits such as categories or lists of offences which the legislature has determined suitable for certain investigation measures, as such limits are easily surpassed if the present case is grave enough. Thirdly, it opens the door to the idea that the end – a severe enough punishment – can 'justify' the means, namely gravely illegal conduct in gathering evidence.

(e) Obligation to Object or Requirement of Consent?

Since 1992, the German Federal Court of Justice has required in ever more situations that the defence raises an objection against the inclusion of arguably illegal evidence. If no timely objection has been made, the accused is barred from raising the issue that the evidence should have been excluded in appeals proceedings (*Widerspruchslösung*).[120] This objection needs to be raised in the trial court – right after the tainted evidence has been introduced – by defence counsel or, if no counsel is

[119] See Section III.1.(f) above.

[120] German Federal Court of Justice, Judgment of 27 Feb. 1992 – 5 StR 190/91 = BGHSt 38, 214, 225 f.; German Federal Court of Justice, Judgment of 7 Mar. 2006 – 1 StR 316/05 = BGHSt 51, 1, para. 8; most recently German Federal Court of Justice, Judgment of 9 May 2018 – 5 StR 17/18 = NJW 2018, 2279, 2280.

present, by the defendant him- or herself, after instruction by the court.[121] As a justification, the German Federal Court of Justice points out that there is a presumption that the investigation was conducted in a legal manner.[122] Furthermore, it refers to the court's duty to gather inculpating as well as exculpating evidence; therefore, the inclusion of evidence may also be to the advantage of the accused.[123] Moreover, the Federal Court of Justice considers the trial court to be in a better position than the appeal court for determining the validity of the objection.[124]

However, the defendant and – partly – defence counsel at the trial stage are frequently overwhelmed by the need to make this decision, and cannot reliably predict the consequences of the decision for the further course of the trial.[125] Therefore, a different viewpoint taken in German legal literature requires that the inclusion of inadmissible evidence should require the defendant's affirmative, voluntary and clear consent (*Zustimmungslösung*), since consent by lack of objection is often a mere fiction.[126]

3 (Dis-)Similarities and Lessons to Be Learned

Similar but not identical multi-factor balancing tests have evolved in the United States and the German criminal justice systems for the solution of a similar but not identical fundamental dilemma: a struggle between law

121 For more details and case law, see Jahn, *Gutachten* (2008), 109–10; Ambos, *Beweisverwertungsverbote* (2010), 53.

122 See German Federal Court of Justice, Judgment of 7 Mar. 2006 – 1 StR 316/05 = BGHSt 51, 1, para. 8.

123 See German Federal Court of Justice, Judgment of 7 Mar. 2006 – 1 StR 316/05 = BGHSt 51, 1, para. 8.

124 German Federal Court of Justice, Judgment of 9 May 2018 – 5 StR 17/18 = NJW 2018, 2279, 2280; on this aspect, see Beining, 'Widerspruchslösung' (2018), 413, 416.

125 Just see Jahn, *Gutachten* (2008), 111; Jahn, 'Strafverfolgung' (2011), 117, 124; Leipold, 'Erklärungsrecht' (2011), 302–3.

126 Jahn, *Gutachten* (2008), 111–12; Gleß, '§ 136' (2007), paras. 83–5; Jahn, 'Strafverfolgung' (2011), 117, 124; Kühne, *Strafprozessrecht* (2015), para. 908.4; Leipold, 'Erklärungsrecht' (2001), 302–3; Beulke and Swoboda, *Strafprozessrecht* (2018), 342, para. 460a; Lesch, 'Unterlassene Belehrung' (1995), 157, 162. See further a draft bill by the German Federal Bar Association (Gesetzentwurf der Bundesrechtsanwalts-kammer für die Einführung einer Zustimmungslösung als Alternative zu der von der Rechtsprechung entwickelten Widerspruchslösung bei zu Gunsten des Angeklagten bestehenden Beweisverwertungsverboten), Opinion No. 17 of 24 Apr. 2012, available at www.brak.de/zur-rechtspolitik/stellungnahmen-pdf/stellungnahmen-deutschland/2012/april/stellungnahme-der-brak-2012-17.pdf.

enforcement and the quest to determine the guilt of the defendant on the one hand, and honouring the rights of everyone (including the defendant) and requiring the lawfulness of state actions on the other hand. In both systems, the objective and subjective gravity of the misconduct in gathering the evidence is taken into account, as well as – though only explicitly in Germany – the gravity of the crime being prosecuted. Both criminal justice systems also pay – at least some – regard to systemic effects, be it the (German) question whether there is systematic, wilful and arbitrary disregard of procedural provisions and on how the exclusion decision affects society's trust in the criminal justice system, or the (US) interest in preserving the integrity of the courts and in the public impact on the admissibility decision.[127]

Some differences can be seen, however, with regard to the quality of the evidence. Presumably out of fear of police misconduct and police tampering with evidence, the US criminal justice system pays far more attention to this topic, while the German system generally trusts the police to act in good faith – and relies on different means of 'policing the police' than exclusionary rules, such as disciplinary proceedings. Yet, the German system may be more willing to include illegally gathered evidence if it is supported by other evidence.[128] Beyond the predominant rationale that the existence of other evidence lessens the effect of the inclusion of the tainted evidence, it provides also some safeguard on the reliability of the evidence.

Generally speaking, both Germany and the United States recognise hypothetical events. The US doctrine of 'inevitable discovery' allows admission of illegally gathered evidence if it would have been found in any event in a legal manner, through an independent search party or some other obligatory legal procedure.[129] In Germany, the doctrine of a 'hypothetical clean path' may even be applied more broadly. The most striking difference may (still) relate to cases where the police or prosecutor searches without a judicial search warrant. Some German courts hold the evidence to be admissible, reasoning that a judge would have issued a search warrant based on the evidence known to the police.[130] So far,

[127] See further Öztürk and Wörner, 'Fernwirkendes Beweisverbot' (2014), 109, 137 ff.

[128] While recent jurisprudence mentions the criterion whether other evidence is available (just see German Federal Court of Justice, Judgment of 3 May 2018 – 3 StR 390/17, para. 25), it does not seem to have become decisive so far.

[129] *Nix* v. *Williams*, 467 US 431, 443–6 (1984); see already n. 73 above.

[130] See German Federal Constitutional Court, Decision of 20 Sept. 2018 – 2 BvR 708/18, para. 40; German Federal Court of Justice, Decision of 7 Feb. 2016 – 2 StR 25/15 = *NStZ*

courts in the United States have by a great majority rejected this rationale as being tantamount to discarding the Fourth Amendment warrant requirement,[131] but some recent case law has accepted this rationale.[132]

The US criminal justice system relies on the notion that the exclusion of evidence can 'police the police', and considers the judge as an arbiter between conflicting interests, who also has a duty to assess the legality of police actions.[133] In contrast, German courts and scholars tend to point out that other modes of reacting to police wrongdoing exist, such as disciplinary proceedings or even criminal prosecutions against individual officers.[134] Both systems, however, pay attention to the gravity of subjective misconduct of the individual law enforcement officials. In both systems, mere 'individual', 'minor' violations, especially of 'technicalities', are factors arguing in favour of the inclusion of evidence. But why are Germans so quick to accept wrongdoing on the part of the state?[135] State adherence to the laws – and not the subjective gravity of the law enforcement official's misconduct – seems to be decisive for the question of whether a defendant considers the proceedings to be fair; and some empirical evidence has emerged that the preventive effects of criminal justice are stronger if the defendant considers the criminal proceeding to be fair.[136]

Concerning the requirement that the defendant and/or defence counsel needs to object to the inclusion of tainted evidence, the German courts' argument that the introduction of evidence by the court and/or the prosecution may also be to the advantage of the accused is clearly only applicable in a post-inquisitorial but not in an adversarial criminal justice system. Based on the adversarial criminal justice system model, it is not surprising that in the United States, defence counsel must also move to exclude arguably tainted evidence to preserve the issue on appeal. However, with adversarial elements more deeply rooted, the US

2016, 551, 552–3. But see also German Federal Court of Justice, Judgment of 18 Apr. 2007 – 5 StR 546/06 = BGHSt 51, 285, 295–6, para. 29.

131 *United States* v. *Echegoyen*, 799 F2d 1271, 1279–80 (9th Cir. 1986).

132 *United States* v. *Christy*, 739 F3d 534, 541–3 (10th Cir. 2014).

133 See Öztürk and Wörner, 'Fernwirkendes Beweisverbot' (2014), 109, 135–6.

134 See Greco, 'Warum gerade Beweisverbote?' (2018), 485, 507 ff.

135 It is attributable to the state, as the law enforcement officials act or fail to act in their official capacity.

136 Augustyn, 'Irrelevance' (2015), 388. On procedural justice and the 'acceptance' of decisions by defendants, see generally Tyler, 'Fairness'(1988), 103; Tyler, 'Effective Rule of Law' (2003), 283; Paternoster et al., 'Fair Procedures' (1997), 163; Jung, 'Formalisierungskonzept' (2010), 73, 79–80; Gaede, *Fairness als Teilhabe* (2007), 365.

system pays more attention to the quality of defence, and defendants may appeal on the ground of ineffective assistance of counsel in violation of the Sixth Amendment right to counsel if he or she neglegted to move to exclude inadmissible evidence.[137] In contrast, improper defence is hardly ever a valid ground for overturning a conviction in Germany, and some German lawyers fail to object to the inclusion of tainted evidence.

IV Towards a Moral and Legal High Ground in Criminal Justice

First, our analysis has shown that in relation to the exclusion of tainted evidence a common theme is predominant in both the US and the German justice system: the quest for truth – be it from the perspective of law enforcement, be it from the perspective of handing out 'just' punishment (or acquittals). Yet when trial judges are considered to be investigators of the truth of the charges – as they are in Germany – they may fall prey to intentionally, instinctively or implicitly giving too much priority to the principle of 'material' truth in exercising their Herculean balancing act and neglect their role as guarantors of freedom. Yet, US judges may also not be immune from meandering away from their role as impartial arbiter. Therefore, to the extent that judicial balancing and discretion are allowed in deciding admissibility of illegally gathered evidence, this task should – whenever possible – be carried out by a neutral judge of the investigation, or liberty judge, and not the trial judge.[138]

Secondly, we fear that balancing tests – especially when they focus on the 'end justify the means' aspect of the gravity of the offence – tend to expand state powers beyond what is prescribed by the law, and, to a lesser, though more binding, extent, by the constitutions. What is more, balancing tests used today tend to down-play the use of 'loopholes', the breaking of the law 'by the good guys' (law enforcement), and violations of (partly constitutional) rights enjoyed by the defendant and third parties. When the state punishes a criminal, it should – also in light of the preventive effects of criminal justice[139] – strive to serve as a prime

[137] See *Kimmelman* v. *Morrison*, 477 US 365, 368–75 (1986).

[138] In Germany, independent judicial review of special investigation methods (§ 101(7) StPO) has no legal effect on the inclusion or exclusion of evidence in a (later) criminal trial, and runs therefore contrary to this goal.

[139] See n. 136 above.

example of adhering to the law, even if it is 'complicated', even if it relates only to 'technicalities' and even against involuntary but negligent breaches.

Thirdly, one should be aware that, if a defendant cannot be convicted by evidence obtained in a legal manner, a dismissal or acquittal does not violate fundamental human rights, not even those of the victim of the (alleged) crime. Victims have, at most, a right to demand that the state makes use of its legal (and legally and constitutionally limited) powers to investigate and adjudicate a crime. And one should never forget that the victim of an act of violence remains a victim, independent of whether the defendant is convicted.

Fourthly, mainly in the United States, exclusionary rules are justified based on their deterrent effect of 'policing the police'. In Germany, the prevailing view is that police misconduct is sufficiently – and more aptly – addressed by other means, such as by disciplinary proceedings and by criminal prosecution of law enforcement officials. Indeed, one can doubt whether the exclusion of evidence is really the best vindication for police wrongdoing, especially if the individual officer has no personal interest in a conviction. Yet the situation is more blurred, especially when law enforcement officials consider themselves to be on a 'mission' in a 'war on crime'. They should never forget – and many police officers in the United States and Germany do never forget – that they are only on the side of the law as long as they adhere to the law. Moreover, there is more need for – empirical – studies on how police misconduct can effectively be reduced in both criminal justice systems.

Fifthly, mistakes do happen. They happen to each of us, and they happen to law enforcement officials as well. They may be more severe and actually constitute criminal offences, or they may be minor. In any case, we should not only look for 'mitigating circumstances' and for counterbalancing in relation to state wrongdoing when trying to include tainted evidence. Instead, criminal justice should not only be about trying to understand why police broke the law, but also be about trying to understand why a criminal broke the law, and aim at reconciliation. The more criminal justice asks the defendant to 'accept' state wrongdoing in a criminal trial against him or her, the more criminal justice should also ask under what reasonable, fair and just conditions society should come to terms with the wrongdoing of the criminal.

Bibliography

Allgayer P. and Klein O., 'Verwendung und Verwertung von Zufallserkenntnissen', *Zeitschrift für Wirtschafts- und Steuerstrafrecht* (2010), 130–3.

Ambos K., *Beweisverwertungsverbote*, Berlin, Duncker & Humblot (2010).

Treatise on International Criminal Law, III: International Criminal Procedure, Oxford University Press (2016).

Amelung K., *Informationsbeherrschungsrechte im Strafprozeß: Dogmatische Grundlagen individualrechtlicher Beweisverbote*, Berlin, Duncker & Humblot (1990).

'Zum Streit über die Grundlagen der Lehre von den Beweisverwertungsverboten', in Schünemann B. and Achenbach H. (eds.), *Festschrift für Claus Roxin zum 70. Geburtstag am 15. Mai 2001*, Berlin, De Gruyter (2001), 1259–81.

Arzt G., 'Zum Verhältnis von Strengbeweis und freier Beweiswürdigung', in Baumann J. and Tiedemann K. (eds.), *Einheit und Vielfalt des Strafrechts: Festschrift für Karl Peters zum 70. Geburtstag*, Tübingen, J. C. B. Mohr Paul Siebeck (1974), 223–35.

Ashworth A., 'Excluding Evidence as Protecting Rights', *Criminal Law Review* (1977), 723–32.

Augustyn M., 'The Irrelevance of Procedural Justice in the Pathways to Crime', *Law and Human Behavior*, 39 (2015), 388–401.

Beining S., 'Neues zur Widerspruchslösung; Zugleich Anmerkung zu BGH Urt. vom 09.05.18', *Höchstrichterliche Rechtsprechung zum Strafrecht* (2018), 413–18.

Beling E., *Die Beweisverbote als Grenzen der Wahrheitserforschung im Strafprozess*, Breslau, Schletter (1903).

Beulke W. and Swoboda S. (eds.), *Strafprozessrecht*, 14th edn, Heidelberg, C. F. Müller (2018).

Bockemühl J., *Private Ermittlungen im Strafprozess; Ein Beitrag zu der Lehre zu den Beweisverboten*, Baden-Baden, Nomos (1996).

Bradley C. M., 'Mapp Goes Abroad', *Case Western Reserve Law Review*, 52 (2001), 375–80.

Brodowski D., *Verdeckte technische Überwachungsmaßnahmen im Polizei- und Strafverfahrensrecht*, Tübingen, Mohr Siebeck (2016).

Bussche A. von dem and Voigt P. (eds.), *German Law Accessible: Data Protection in Germany*, 2nd edn, Munich, C. H. Beck (2017).

Choo A. L.-T., 'England and Wales: Fair Trial Analysis and the Presumed Admissibility of Physical Evidence', in Thaman S. C. (ed.), *Exclusionary Rules in Comparative Law*, Dordrecht, Springer (2013), 331–54.

Cras A. and Daly Y. M., 'Ireland: A Move to Categorical Exclusion?', in Thaman S. C. (ed.), *Exclusionary Rules in Comparative Law*, Dordrecht, Springer (2013), 33–68.

Damaška M., *Evidence Law Adrift*, Yale University Press (2013).

Duff P., 'Admissibility of Improperly Obtained Physical Evidence in the Scottish Criminal Trial: The Search for Principle', *Edinburgh Law Review*, 8 (2004), 152–76.

Fezer G., *Strafprozessrecht*, 2nd edn, Munich, C. H. Beck (1995).

Foster N. and Sule S. (eds.), *German Legal Systems and Laws*, 4th edn, Oxford University Press (2010).

Frase R. and Weigend J., 'German Criminal Justice as a Guide to American Law Reform: Similar Problems, Better Solutions?', *Boston College International and Comparative Law Review*, 18 (1995), 317–60.

Gaede K., *Fairness als Teilhabe – Das Recht auf konkrete und wirksame Teilhabe durch Verteidigung gemäß Art. 6 EMRK*, Berlin, Duncker & Humblot (2007).

Gleß S., '§ 136', in Erb V., Esser R., Franke U., Graalmann-Scheerer K., Hilger H. and Ignor A. (eds.), *Löwe-Rosenberg, Die Strafprozessordnung und das Gerichtsverfassungsgesetz, Großkommentar, IV: §§ 112–136*, 26th edn, Berlin, De Gruyter (2007).

Greco L., 'Warum gerade Beweisverbot? Ketzerische Bemerkungen zur Figur des Beweisverbots', in Stein U., Greco L., Jäger C. and Wolter J. (eds.), *Systematik in Strafrechtswissenschaft und Gesetzgebung, Festschrift für Klaus Rogall zum 70. Geburtstag am 10. August 2018*, Berlin, Duncker & Humblot (2018), 485–515.

Hooper A. and Ormerod D., *Blackstone's Criminal Practice*, Oxford University Press (2003).

Jäger C., *Beweisverwertung und Beweisverwertungsverbote im Strafprozess*, Munich, C. H. Beck (2003).

Jahn M., *Beweiserhebung und Beweisverwertungsverbote im Spannungsfeld zwischen den Garantien des Rechtsstaates und der effektiven Bekämpfung von Kriminalität und Terrorismus, Gutachten C, 67. Deutscher Juristentag*, Munich, C. H. Beck (2008).

'Strafverfolgung um jeden Preis? Die Verwertbarkeit rechtswidrig erlangter Beweismittel', *Strafverteidiger-Forum* (2011), 117–28.

Jung H., 'Zum sozialpsychologischen Gehalt des Formalisierungskonzepts', in Herzog F. and Neumann U. (eds.), *Festschrift für Winfried Hassemer*, Heidelberg, C. F. Müller Verlag (2010), 73–83.

Koriath H., *Über Beweisverbote im Strafprozess*, Frankfurt, Peter Lang (1994).

Kühne H., *Strafprozessrecht: Eine systematische Darstellung des deutschen und europäischen Strafverfahrensrechts*, 9th edn, Heidelberg, C. F. Müller (2015).

Küper W., *Die Richteridee der Strafprozessordnung und ihre geschichtlichen Grundlagen*, Berlin, De Gruyter (1967).

Landau P., 'Die Reichsjustizgesetze von 1879 und die deutsche Rechtseinheit', in Bundesministerium der Justiz (ed.), *Vom Reichsjustizamt zum Bundesministerium der Justiz*, Cologne, Bundesanzeiger Verlag (1977).

'Das Urteil des zweiten Senats des BVerfG zu den Absprachen im Strafprozess vom 19. März 2013', *Neue Zeitschrift für Strafrecht*, 8 (2014), 425–31.

Leipold K., 'Form und Umfang des Erklärungsrechts nach § 257 StPO und seine Auswirkungen auf die Widerspruchslösung des Bundesgerichtshofes', *Strafverteidiger-Forum* (2001), 300–3.

Lesch H., 'Der Beschuldigte im Strafverfahren – über den Begriff und die Konsequenzen der unterlassenen Belehrung', *Juristische Arbeitsblätter* (1995), 157–66.

Mahoney R., 'Abolition of New Zealand's Prima Facie, Exclusionary Rule', *Criminal Law Review* (September 2003), 607–17.

Neumann U., *Die Wahrheit im Recht: Zu Problematik und Legitimität einer fragwürdigen Denkform*, Baden-Baden, Nomos (2004).

Optican S and Sankoff P, 'The New Exclusionary Rule: A Preliminary Assessment of R v Shaheed', *New Zealand Law Review* (2003), 1–45.

Ormerod D, 'ECHR and the Exclusion of Evidence: Trial Remedies for Article 8 Breaches?', *Criminal Law Review* (2003), 61–80.

Öztürk B. and Wörner L., 'Das fernwirkende Beweisverbot im türkischen und im deutschen Strafverfahrensrecht – Zu den Auswirkungen der fruit of the poisonous tree Doktrin im kontinentaleuropäisch geprägten Strafverfahren', in Gropp W., Öztürk B., Sözüer A. and Wörner L. (eds.), *Die Entwicklung von Rechtssystemen in ihrer gesellschaftlichen Verankerung*, Baden-Baden, Nomos (2014).

Packer, H., 'The Courts, the Police, and the Rest of Us', *Journal of Criminal Law, Criminology & Police Science*, 57 (1966), 238–43.

Paternoster R, Bachman R, Brame R and Sherman L, 'Do fair Procedures matter? The Effect of Procedural Justice on Spouse Assault', *Law & Society Review*, 31 (1997), 163–204.

Peters K., *Beweisverbote im deutschen Strafverfahren, Gutachten A, 46. Deutscher Juristentag*, Munich, C. H. Beck (1966).

Reinbacher T. and Wendel M., 'The Bundesverfassungsgericht's European Arrest Warrant II Decision', *Maastricht Journal of European and Comparative Law*, 23 (2016), 702–13.

Roach K., 'Canada', in Bradley C. M. (ed.), *Criminal Procedure: A Worldwide Study*, 2nd edn, Durham, Carolina Academic Press (2007), 57–90.

Robbers G., *An Introduction to German Law*, 6th edn, Baden-Baden, Nomos (2017).

Rogall K., 'Gegenwärtiger Stand und Entwicklungstendenzen der Lehre von den strafprozessualen Beweisverboten', *Zeitschrift für die gesamte Strafrechtswissenschaft* (1979), 1–44.

'Über die Folgen der rechtswidrigen Beschaffung des Zeugenbeweises im Strafprozeß', *Juristenzeitung* (1996), 944–55.

'Zur Lehre von den Beweisverboten', in Samson E., Dencker F., Frisch P., Frister H. and Reiß W. (eds.), *Festschrift für Gerald Grünwald zum siebzigsten Geburtstag*, Baden-Baden, Nomos (1999), 523–49.

'Beweiserhebungs- und Beweisverwertungsverbote im Spannungsfeld zwischen den Garantien des Rechtsstaates und der effektiven Bekämpfung von Kriminalität und Terrorismus', *Juristenzeitung* (2008), 818–30.

Schubert W., *Die deutsche Gerichtsverfassung 1869–1877: Entstehung und Quellen*, Frankfurt/Main, Klostermann (1981).

Singelnstein T., 'Strafprozessuale Verwendungsregelungen zwischen Zweckbindungsgrundsatz und Verwertungsverboten', *Zeitschrift für die gesamte Strafrechtswissenschaft*, 120 (2008), 854–94.

'Unselbstständige Verwertungsverbote und informationelle Selbstbestimmung', in Müller H. E. and Sander G. (eds.), *Festschrift für Ulrich Eisenberg zum 70. Geburtstag*, Munich, C. H. Beck (2009), 643–57.

Stark F. and Leverick F., 'Scotland: A Plea for Consistency', in Thaman S. C. (ed.), *Exclusionary Rules in Comparative Law*, Dordrecht, Springer (2013), 69–91.

Störmer R., *Dogmatische Grundlagen der Verwertungsverbote: Eine Untersuchung über die Strukturen strafprozessualer Verwertungsverbote unter dem Einfluß der Verfassung und der Grundsätze des öffentlichen Rechts*, Marburg, Elwert Verlag (1992).

Thaman S. C., *Comparative Criminal Procedure: A Casebook Approach*, 2nd edn, Durham, Carolina Academic Press (2008).

'Balancing Truth against Human Rights: A Theory of Modern Exclusionary Rules', in Thaman S. C. (ed.), *Exclusionary Rules in Comparative Law*, Dordrecht, Springer (2013), 403–15.

Tiedemann P., 'The Rechtsstaat-Principle in Germany: The Development from the Beginning until Now', in Silkenat J. R., Hickey J. E. and Barenboim P. (eds.), *The Legal Doctrines of the Rule of Law and the Legal State (Rechtsstaat)*, Cham, Springer (2014), 171–92.

Tyler T. R., 'What Is Procedural Justice? Criteria Used by Citizens to Assess the Fairness of Legal Procedures', *Law & Society Review*, 22 (1988), 103–34.

'Procedural Justice, Legitimacy, and the Effective Rule of Law', *Crime and Justice*, 30 (2003), 283–357.

Vogel B., 'The Core Legal Concepts and Principles Defining Criminal Law in Germany', in Dyson M. and Vogel B. (eds.), *The Limits of Criminal Law: Anglo-German Concepts and Principles*, Cambridge, Intersentia (2018), 39–70.

Weigend T., 'Law and Truth – Is the Criminal Process about Truth?: A German Perspective', *Harvard Journal of Law & Public Policy*, 26 (2003), 157–74.

Wolter J., 'Beweisverbote und Umgehungsverbote zwischen Wahrheitserforschung und Ausforschung', in Canaris C., Heldrich A., Hopt K., Roxin C., Schmidt K. and Widmaier G. (eds.), *50 Jahre Bundesgerichtshof, Festgabe aus der Wissenschaft*, 4 vols., Munich, C. H. Beck (2000), IV, 965–1009.

INDEX